CASS SERIES ON SOVIET (RUSSIAN) MILI'

THE SOVIET STRATEGIC OFFENSIVE IN MANCHURIA, 1945

CASS SERIES ON SOVIET (RUSSIAN) MILITARY EXPERIENCE

Series Editor: David M. Glantz

ISSN: 1462–0944

This series focuses on Soviet military experiences in specific campaigns or operations.

1. David M. Glantz, *From the Don to the Dnepr, Soviet Offensive Operations, December 1942 to August 1943* (ISBN 0 7146 3401 8 cloth, 0 7146 4064 6 paper)
2. David M. Glantz, *The Initial Period of War on the Eastern Front: 22 June–August 1941* (ISBN 0 7146 3375 5 cloth, 0 7146 4298 3 paper)
3. Carl van Dyke, *The Soviet Invasion of Finland, 1939–40* (ISBN 0 7146 4653 5 cloth, 0 7146 4314 9 paper)
4. Leonid Grenkevich, *The Soviet Partisan Movement 1941–1944*, edited and with a Foreword by David M. Glantz (ISBN 0 7146 4874 4 cloth, 0 7146 4428 5 paper)
5. Tony Le Tissier, *Race for the Reichstag: The 1945 Battle for Berlin* (ISBN 0 7146 4929 5 cloth, 0 7146 4489 7 paper)
6. Robert Seely, *Russo-Chechen Conflict, 1800–2000: A Deadly Embrace* (ISBN 0 7146 4992 9 cloth, 0 7146 8060 5 paper)

CASS SERIES ON THE SOVIET (RUSSIAN) STUDY OF WAR

Series Editor: David M. Glantz

ISSN: 1462–0960

This series examines what Soviet military theorists and commanders learned from the study of their own military operations.

1. Harold S. Orenstein, translator and editor, *Soviet Documents on the Use of War Experience*, Volume I, *The Initial Period of War 1941*, with an Introduction by David M. Glantz (ISBN 0 7146 3392 5 cloth)
2. Harold S. Orenstein, translator and editor, *Soviet Documents on the Use of War Experience*, Volume II, *The Winter Campaign 1941–1942*, with an Introduction by David M. Glantz (ISBN 0 7146 3393 3 cloth)
3. Joseph G. Welsh, translator, *Red Armor Combat Orders: Combat Regulations for Tank and Mechanized Forces 1944*, edited and with an Introduction by Richard N. Armstrong (ISBN 0 7146 3401 8 cloth)
4. Harold S. Orenstein, translator and editor, *Soviet Documents on the Use of War Experience*, Volume III, *Military Operations 1941 and 1942*, with an Introduction by David M. Glantz (ISBN 0 7146 3402 6 cloth)
5. William A. Burhans, translator, *The Nature of the Operations of Modern Armies* by V.K. Triandafillov, edited by Jacob W. Kipp, with an Introduction by James J. Schneider (ISBN 0 7146 4501 X cloth, 0 7146 4118 9 paper)
6. Harold S. Orenstein, translator, *The Evolution of Soviet Operational Art, 1927–1991: The Documentary Basis*, Volume I, *Operational Art, 1927–1964*, with an Introduction by David M. Glantz (ISBN 0 7146 4547 8 cloth, 0 7146 4228 2 paper)
7. Harold S. Orenstein, translator, *The Evolution of Soviet Operational Art, 1927–1991: The Documentary Basis*, Volume II, *Operational Art, 1965–1991*, with an Introduction by David M. Glantz (ISBN 0 7146 4548 6 cloth, 0 7146 4229 0 paper)
8. Richard N. Armstrong and Joseph G. Welsh, *Winter Warfare: Red Army Orders and Experiences* (ISBN 0 7146 4699 7 cloth, 0 7146 4237 1 paper)
9. Lester W. Grau, *The Bear Went Over the Mountain: Soviet Combat Tactics in Afghanistan* (ISBN 0 7146 4874 4 cloth, 0 7146 4413 7 paper)
10. David M. Glantz and Harold S. Orenstein, editor and translator, *The Battle for Kursk 1943: The Soviet General Staff Study* (ISBN 0 7146 4933 3 cloth, 0 7146 4493 5 paper)
11. Niklas Zetterling and Anders Frankson, *Kursk 1943: A Statistical Analysis* (ISBN 0 7146 5052 8 cloth, 0 7146 8103 2 paper)
12. David M. Glantz and Harold S. Orenstein, editor and translator, *Belorussia 1944: The Soviet General Staff Study* (ISBN 0 7146 5102 8 cloth)
13. David M. Glantz and Harold S. Orenstein, editor and translator, *The Battle for L'vov, July 1944: The Soviet General Staff Study* (ISBN 0 7146 5201 6 cloth)
14. Alexander O. Chubaryan and Harold Shukman, editors, *Stalin and the Soviet–Finnish War, 1939–40* (ISBN 0 7146 5203 2 cloth)

THE SOVIET STRATEGIC OFFENSIVE IN MANCHURIA, 1945:

'AUGUST STORM'

DAVID M. GLANTZ

FRANK CASS
LONDON • PORTLAND, OR

First published in 2003 in Great Britain by
FRANK CASS PUBLISHERS
2 Park Square, Milton Park,
Abingdon, Oxon, OX14 4RN

and in the United States of America by
FRANK CASS PUBLISHERS
270 Madison Ave,
New York NY 10016

Transferred to Digital Printing 2006

Website: www.frankcass.com

British Library Cataloguing in Publication Data

Glantz, David M.
The Soviet strategic offensive in Manchuria, 1945: 'August Storm'. – (Cass series on Soviet (Russian) military experience)
1. Union of Soviet Socialist Republics. Armiia – Drills and tactics
2. World War, 1939–1945 – Campaigns – China – Manchuria
3. World War, 1939–1945 – Russian (Federation) 4. Strategy
I. Title
940.5′425

ISBN10: 0–7146–5279–2 (hbk)
ISBN10: 0–415–40861–X (pbk)
ISBN13: 978–0–7146–5279–5 (hbk)
ISBN13: 978–0–415–40861–5 (pbk)
ISSN 1462–0944

Library of Congress Cataloging-in-Publication Data

Glantz, David M.
The Soviet strategic offensive in Manchuria, 1945: August storm/David M. Glantz.
p. cm. – (Cass series on Soviet (Russian) military experience; 7)
Includes bibliographical references and index.
ISBN 0-7146-5279-2 (cloth)
1. World War, 1939–1945 – Campaigns – China – Manchuria. 2. World War, 1939–1945 – Soviet Union. 3. Manchuria (China) – History – 1931–1945. 4. Soviet Union – History, Military. I. Title: August storm. II. Title. III. Series

D767.3.G58 2000
940.54′25–dc21

2002074078

Typeset in 10.5/12 Ehrhardt MT by Cambridge Photosetting Services

Cover illustration: An artist's impression of the Japanese surrender to the Soviet forces in August 1945.

Contents

PART III: ANALYSIS AND CONCLUSIONS

APPENDICES

Illustrations

25. Marshal A. M. Vasilevsky, Commander, Far East Command; Marshal R. Ia. Malinovsky, Commander, Trans-Baikal Front; and Marshal K. A. Meretskov, Commander, 1st Far Eastern Front
26. Marshal A. M. Vasilevsky, Commander, Far East Command; Lieutenant General S. P. Ivanov, Chief of Staff, Far East Command; and Colonel General I. I. Liudnikov, Commander, 39th Army
27. Army General I. I. Maslennikov, Deputy Commander, Far East Command, Marshal of Aviation A. A. Novikov, Commander, Red Army Air Forces; Marshal A. M. Vasilevsky, Commander, Far East Command; and Lieutenant General S. P. Ivanov, Chief of Staff, Far East Command
28. The Pacific Fleet's Military Council: Vice Admiral A. S. Frolov, Chief of Staff, Pacific Fleet; Admiral I. S. Iumashev, Commander, Pacific Fleet; and Lieutenant General of the Coastal Service S. E. Zakharov

GROUP 3: Trans-Baikal Front

29. Colonel General I. A. Pliev, Commander, Soviet–Mongolian Cavalry-Mechanized Group
30. Lieutenant General A. I. Danilov, Commander, 17th Army
31. Colonel General A. G. Kravchenko, Commander, 6th Guards Tank Army (center), accompanied by Marshal of Aviation S. A. Khudiakov, Commander, 8th Air Army (left), and Colonel General M. D. Solomatin, Commander, Far East Command's Armored and Mechanized Forces (right)
32. Colonel General I. I. Liudnikov, Commander, 39th Army
33. Lieutenant General A. A. Luchinsky, Commander, 36th Army
34. Colonel General I. M. Managarov, Commander, 53d Army
35. The 6th Guards Tank Army's reconnaissance units
36. The 6th Guards Tank Army approaching the Grand Khingan Mountains
37. Tank units at a rest halt
38. Lieutenant General M. P. Kovalev, Deputy Commander, Trans-Baikal Front (center), observes the forward movement of 6th Guards Tank Army
39. The 6th Guards Tank Army's tanks crossing the Grand Khingan Mountains
40. The 6th Guards Tank Army's 20th Tank Brigade enters the central Manchurian plain
41. The 6th Guards Tank Army's 5th Guards Tank Corps advances on Lupei
42. Tanks of the 9th Guards Mechanized Corps' 46th Guards Tank Brigade conduct a river crossing

Maps

Figures, Tables and Charts

FIGURES

TABLES

CHARTS

Preface

This critical examination of the Manchurian strategic offensive of August 1945, the Red Army's final and most ambitious strategic offensive operation during the Second World War, challenges two inaccurate but enduring judgments Western historians have made regarding the Red Army's performance during the war. The first is that the Red Army prevailed over the German *Wehrmacht*, the twentieth century's most formidable fighting machine, solely because of geographical and climatic factors and sheer numerical superiority, a view that relegates Red Army military accomplishments to utter oblivion. The second is that the Red Army's contributions to Allied victory over Japan were minimal and insignificant, rendering Soviet military operations in the Asian theater irrelevant and unworthy of meaningful study.

As this study indicates, these judgments reflect a distinct German bias on the war that has colored the history and analysis of operations on the German Eastern Front in particular and the entire war in general for more than a generation and are patently false. Nevertheless, they persist, and in so doing perpetuate a woefully inaccurate view of the war, the Red Army's performance in it, and the Soviet Union's overall contributions to Allied victory. In turn, this inaccurate view continues to warp contemporary attitudes and serves as a barrier to closer United States–Russian relations at a time when the national interests of both countries are sharply convergent.

The first biased judgment of the Soviet–German War is derived largely from the *Wehrmacht's* spectacular performance during Operations Barbarossa and *Blau* [Blue] in the summer and fall of 1941 and 1942, when the *Wehrmacht* skillfully employed Blitzkrieg tactics to rout poorly trained and inadequately led Red Army forces, inflict immense casualties on the army, and conquer vast swaths of Soviet territory. Exploiting the element of surprise, German panzer and panzer grenadier (motorized) troops, supported by the ubiquitous *Stuka* dive-bombers, repeatedly overcame desperate but crudely fashioned Red Army defenses to capture vast areas of Soviet territory and the imagination of the world.

Just as Erwin Rommel's performance against the British in North Africa made him a legend, the postwar writings of Heinz Guderian, W. F. von

Mellenthin, Hermann Balck, Erich von Manstein, and others who achieved victory in the East on the wings of Blitzkrieg created a myth of *Wehrmacht* invincibility that somehow outlived the ultimate German defeat.

In reality, however, the brilliant operational and tactical successes the Germans achieved in 1941 and 1942 blinded them to strategic realities they were unable to understand. Having fashioned a war machine ideally suited to achieving victory within the limited confines of western Europe, the Germans unleashed their armed forces in the east, a theater they did not understand against an opponent they woefully underestimated and misunderstood. Therefore, the imposing string of *Wehrmacht's* victories abruptly ceased in the summer of 1943 and was followed by a nearly unbroken series of increasingly spectacular defeats in 1944 and 1945 that culminated in the destruction of Hitler's Third Reich. Despite occasional tactical successes, after the summer of 1943, the *Wehrmacht* suffered continuous and ever more costly strategic defeats that sapped its strength and tore the Axis coalition apart.

Ironically, the spectacular feats of the victorious German conquerors of 1941 and 1942 still dominate Western historical literature and color Western perceptions regarding the *Wehrmacht's* performance in the Soviet–German war as a whole. At least in part, this is because, unlike their victorious predecessors of 1941 and 1942, the desperate German defenders of 1944 and 1945, such as Ferdinand Schoener and Gotthard Heinrici, who presided over the *Wehrmacht's* ultimate defeat, wrote no memoirs, since few Germans considered their experiences either memorable or glorious. Their impressions, along with those of countless field grade officers who experienced the defeats in 1944 and 1945, are all but lost.

Finally, this unbalanced and inaccurate perception of the war on the German Eastern Front masks the larger truth that Germany and its *Wehrmacht* lost the war and did so primarily in the east against what so many historians portray as a brutally inept Soviet regime and its 'artless' Red Army.

The second biased judgment, that the Red Army made no major contribution to the Allied victory over Japan, has been reinforced by Western historians' general neglect of warfare in the Pacific theater during the Second World War. Together with the prevalent German bias on the war, this neglect has utterly concealed the Red Army's most ambitious military operation in the Second World War, its massive and spectacularly successful strategic offensive in Manchuria during August 1945.

On the other hand, Russian historians and military analysts have long considered the Red Army's offensive in Manchuria, an offensive conducted with surgical precision with almost predestined results, to be a postgraduate exercise by the Red Army and a logical byproduct of their extensive war experience in the West. Even though most military planners, US and Russian alike, realized that the Japanese Empire and its army were in a seriously weakened state by the summer of 1945, few actually believed that Japan would surrender China, Manchuria, or its Home Islands without a fight. In fact, given the dramatic manner in which Germany capitulated in April and May 1945, these planners were convinced that the Japanese would replicate Germany's *Götterdämmerung* on an even larger scale.

The human costs the United States expected to pay for reducing fortress Japan were indeed staggering to contemplate. The case of Okinawa stood as stark evidence of this grim prospect, where as late as April through June 1945, about 117,000 fanatically resisting Japanese troops inflicted more than 49,000 casualties, including 12,500 dead on attacking American forces. With more than 2.3 million Japanese soldiers defending the Home Islands and a million more in Manchuria, Allied planners prepared for the worst in the expectation of a prolonged and complicated campaign to reduce the remaining Japanese strongholds.

Because they appreciated the capabilities of the Japanese High Command, the vaunted Kwantung Army in Manchuria, and the individual Japanese soldier, Soviet military planners prepared an offensive plan that was as innovative as any prepared during the entire war. The superbly executed plan produced complete victory in only two weeks of combat.

Even though Soviet planners clearly overestimated Japanese military capabilities in Manchuria, the tenacious Japanese soldier lived up to Soviet expectations. The Japanese soldier proved his reputation as a brave, self-sacrificing samurai who, though poorly employed, inflicted 32,000 casualties on the Red Army and won its grudging respect. Had Japanese planners and commanders been bolder and Soviet planners less audacious, the price of the Red Army's victory could well have been significantly higher.

Its vast scope, magnitude, complexity, timing, and unprecedented success have made the Red Army's Manchurian strategic offensive a continuing topic of study for Soviet and Russian military theorists and historians, who perceive it as a textbook case of how to begin war and quickly bring it to a successful conclusion. In short, they study the Manchurian offensive because it was an impressive and decisive campaign.

More recently, Western study of 'August Storm' provided inspiration, concrete guidance, and a virtual model for its namesake Operation 'Desert Storm', the US-led coalition that crushed the Iraqi Army in 1991.[1]

Western neglect of Red Army operations in the Second World War, in general, and in Manchuria, in particular, testifies not only to our apathy toward history and the past in general, but also to our particular blindness to Soviet and Russian military experiences. That blindness, born of the biases we bring to the study of the Second World War, is a dangerous phenomenon that inhibits full understanding of and future cooperation with the Russian Federation.

NOTE

1. US military planners in the Gulf War initially intended to name the offensive phase of the war against Iraq 'Desert Sword' to match the defensive phase 'Desert Shield'. However, planning cells sent to the Gulf from Fort Leavenworth's School of Advance Military Studies, which had studied the Soviet Manchurian offensive in detail, developed an offensive operational plan that replicated the Soviet offensive, and named it 'Desert Storm'.

Abbreviations

SOVIET FORCES

A	army
AEB	assault engineer-sapper brigade
BGBn	border guards battalion
Cav-Mech GP	cavalry-mechanized group
CD	cavalry division
FD	forward detachment
FFR	field fortified region
FR	fortified region
Gds	guards
GKO	*Gosudarstvennoi komitet oborony* (State Defense Committee)
GRU	*Glavnoe razvedyvatel'noe upravlenie* (Main Intelligence Directorate)
HSPR	heavy self-propelled artillery regiment
MB	mechanized brigade
MC	mechanized corps
MNRA	Mongolian People's Red Army
MnRR	mountain rifle regiment
MRD	motorized rifle division
NKO	*Narodnyi komissariat oborony* (People's Commissariat of Defence)
NKPS	*Narodnyi komissariat put' soobshchenii* (People's Commissariat of Communications Routes)
NKVD	*Nordnyi Komissariat Vnutrennykh Del* (People's Commissariat of Internal Affairs)
PGB	*Primorskaia gruppa voisk* (Coastal Group of Forces)
RBA	Red Banner Army
RBn	rifle battalion
RC	rifle corps
RD	rifle division

RAG	regimental artillery group
TA	tank army
TB	tank brigade
TC	tank corps
TD	tank division
TO&Es	tables of organization and equipment or establishments
TVD	*teatr voennykh deistvii* (theaters of military operations)
UR	*ukreplennyi raion* (fortified regions)

JAPANESE FORCES

BGU	border guards unit
IB	independent mixed brigade
ID	infantry division
IR	infantry regiment
IBn	infantry battalion

Symbols

SOVIET

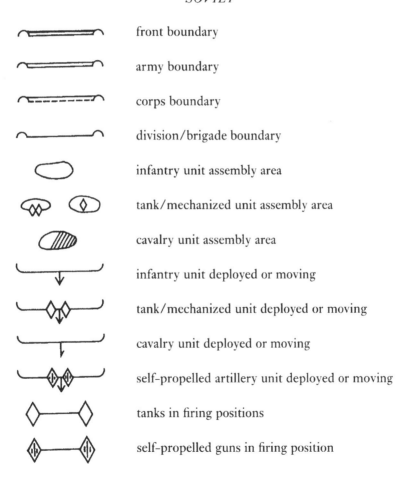

front boundary

army boundary

corps boundary

division/brigade boundary

infantry unit assembly area

tank/mechanized unit assembly area

cavalry unit assembly area

infantry unit deployed or moving

tank/mechanized unit deployed or moving

cavalry unit deployed or moving

self-propelled artillery unit deployed or moving

tanks in firing positions

self-propelled guns in firing position

JAPANESE

field fortifications, defensive positions

fortified region, permanent

section position

squad position

platoon position

company position

battalion position

regiment position

brigade position

division position

-- XX -- division boundary

-- XXXX -- army boundary

-- XXXXX -- area army boundary

-- XXXXXX -- Kwantung Army boundary

Introduction

Shortly after midnight on 9 August 1945, assault parties of Red Army troops crossed the Soviet–Manchurian frontier and attacked Japanese defensive positions around the periphery of Manchukuo, Japanese occupied Manchuria. These assault groups, which represented the vanguard of a force of more than 1.5 million soldiers, advanced along multiple axes across a front of more than 2,730 miles (4,394 kilometers), traversing virtually every type of terrain from the arid deserts of Inner Mongolia to the forested shores of the Sea of Japan. Thus began one of the most significant military campaigns of the Second World War.

For the Soviet Union, its Manchurian offensive marked the culmination of four years of bitter and costly military struggle with Germany in the west and a similar period of worried attentiveness to Japanese intentions in the east. The Red Army had absorbed the German *Wehrmacht's* potent attacks in 1941, 1942, and 1943 and responded with its own massive offensives in 1943, 1944, and 1945, which finally crushed Germany's vaunted military machine. While the Soviets waged a war of survival with the Germans, precious Red Army forces remained in the Far East on guard against a possible Japanese attack in support of its Axis partner.

By 1945, the combination of Soviet victories in the west and Japanese defeats in the Pacific diminished the potential for any Japanese offensive in the Soviet Far East. At the same time, as Allied victory over Germany loomed, Franklin D. Roosevelt, the United States President, and his military advisers, urged Stalin to join the war against Japan to complete the destruction of the Axis powers.[1]

Moved by his Allies' appeals for assistance against Japan and wishing to cement the Soviet Union's postwar position in the Far East, Stalin and his *Stavka* (Headquarters of the Supreme High Command) began planning a final campaign to defeat Japanese forces in the Far East and wrest Manchuria, northern Korea, southern Sakhalin Island, the Kuril Islands, and possibly at least the northern portion of Hokkaido Island from Japan.

The enormity of the task of conquering the vast expanse of Manchuria before a Japanese surrender rivaled the challenges of earlier military operations.

The main area of Red Army operations in Europe was located more than 6,200 miles (10,000 kilometers) distant from Manchuria. Soviet planners and logisticians had to move forces, weaponry, and other military equipment earmarked for employment in Manchuria along a fragile transportation network, the Trans-Siberian railroad, the carrying capacity of which was extremely limited. Along the eastern segment of that network, Japanese forces, particularly artillery and aviation, threatened the viability of the railroad line.

Soviet estimates of force requirements necessary to undertake such an extensive campaign were correspondingly large. Thus, the anticipated campaign involved extensive planning and careful preparations stretching over a five-month period from April through August 1945. The dramatic results of the campaign bore witness to the success of the planning and the thoroughness of preparations. Within only nine days, Red Army forces penetrated from 310 to 590 miles (500–950 kilometers) deep into Manchuria, captured every major population center, and forced the Japanese Kwantung Army and its Manchukuoan and Inner Mongolian auxiliaries to surrender. Thus, despite severe terrain obstacles and significant Japanese resistance, Red Army forces achieved their territorial objectives and accomplished their assigned missions within an extremely limited period of time.

The successes the Red Army achieved in the Manchurian offensive validated the experiences its forces had amassed in the war against Nazi Germany. The Red Army applied the advanced tactical and operational techniques it had learned in the brutal school of war in the west and displayed the requisite degree of audacious leadership Soviet commanders had laboriously developed during the campaigns in the west. The Manchurian campaign represented and still represents the highest stage of military art the Red Army reached during its operations during the Second World War. Then and now, serious students of contemporary warfare can learn significant lessons from their study of this unique campaign.

Entitled *The Soviet Strategic Offensive in Manchuria, August 1945: 'August Storm'*, this book provides general information on the campaign by concentrating on Red Army ground force and amphibious operations. It covers the strategic context of the campaign and details the strategic and operational techniques employed by *fronts*, armies, tank armies, and corps and divisions of various types, and the tactics employed by brigades, regiments, and lower echelon units and subunits. It also includes significant information regarding initial strategic and operational planning by *fronts* and armies, redeployment and regrouping of forces to and within the Far East and Mongolia, and Red Army organization for combat at every command level. While doing so, it analyzes the Red Army force structure and published operational and tactical doctrine governing the employment of these forces in 1945, highlighting tactical innovations and emphasizing adjustments made to the force structure that contributed to Soviet victory. The book concludes with an extensive assessment of the usefulness of these tactical and structural innovations and their implications for the future.

The companion volume on Red Army operations in the Far East in August 1945, *Soviet Operational and Tactical Combat in Manchuria, August 1945: 'August Storm'*, presents a broad mosaic of the diverse types of operations the campaign encompassed by describing in detail the conduct of operations in ten specific sectors.

This volume is based primarily on Soviet primary and secondary sources, including after-action assessments by the Red Army General and Main Naval Staffs, supplemented with Japanese materials prepared on the basis of interviews with Japanese officers who participated in the defense of Manchuria. Russian-language secondary source literature on the Manchurian campaign is extensive, and coverage has intensified in recent years. Many of the participants in the campaign have written memoirs or shorter commentaries on the role they or their forces played in the operation. These include Marshal of the Soviet Union A. M. Vasilevsky, the commander of the Far Eastern Command, *front* commanders and chiefs of staff, army commanders, and service commanders. In addition, military historians have written numerous books or articles on various aspects of the operations or the operation as a whole, many in the Soviet Army's official journal, *Voenno-istoricheskii zhurnal* [Military-historical Journal], which has published tens of such articles.

Japanese source materials on the Manchurian campaign are in shorter supply, in large part because the Soviets captured the records of the Kwantung Army during the campaign The Japanese monograph series on operations in Manchuria, published by the US Army in the early 1950s, provides a sketchy account of the operation reconstructed from the memories of Japanese officers who served in Manchuria. Unfortunately, few of these monographs detail the fighting in the regions where the heaviest combat occurred. Those few existing Japanese memoirs are of only limited value.

In contrast to Japanese sources, Soviet sources are generally fairly complete and accurate in much of their operational detail. While they candidly discuss operational and tactical difficulties, as is the case with other works in this genre, they sometimes exaggerate the scale of individual victories or denigrate the impact of local defeats. Frequently, these Soviets sources also simply gloss over unpleasant events. This study compares Soviet accounts with accounts contained in the Japanese monographs and other Japanese studies, notes where details do and do not match, and highlights some differences regarding interpretation and emphasis.

Dr Edward J. Drea of the Combat Studies Institute, Fort Leavenworth, KS deserves special thanks for the assistance he provided in translating Japanese source materials. Throughout this study, all Japanese personal names appear in the Japanese manner with surname preceding given name.

NOTE

1. Herbert Feis, *The Atomic Bomb and the End of World War II* (Princeton, NJ: Princeton University Press, 1966); Charles L. Mee, Jr, *Meeting at Potsdam* (New York: M. Evans, 1975); and P. N. Pospelov, ed., *Istoriia Velikoi Otechestvennoi voiny Sovetskogo Soiuza 1941–45 v shesti tomakh,* T. 5 [A history of the Great Patriotic War of the Soviet Union 1941–45 in six volumes, Vol. 5.] (Moscow: Voenizdat, 1963), 530–42. The Allies had urged Soviet participation in the war against Japan since the Teheran conference of 1943.

Part I:

Before the Offensive

1

Preparations for the Manchurian Strategic Offensive

BACKGROUND

Despite negotiating a non-aggression pact with Nazi Germany in August 1939, during the perilous days after the beginning of the Second World War in September, Stalin and the Red Army General Staff realized that Germany still posed a considerable military threat to the Soviet Union. Therefore, from September 1939 to the outbreak of the Soviet–German War in June 1941, the Soviet political leadership and General Staff formulated a military policy and strategy that sought to defend the Soviet Union against the frightening prospect of a war on two fronts. This defensive strategy accorded priority, first and foremost to the west, and secondarily to the east. In the west, the Soviets exploited their agreement with Germany for a partition of eastern Europe by subsequently occupying and annexing the Baltic States and Belorussia. The policy also promoted Stalin to wage war against Finland after Soviet threats had failed to intimidate that small nation.

Soviet defensive concerns assumed even greater urgency after the spring of 1940 when German forces seized Denmark, Norway, the Low Countries, and France, and drove British forces from the continent. Subsequent Soviet war planning reflected this urgency. In July 1940 the General Staff prepared a new strategic plan, drafted by Major General A. M. Vasilevsky, Deputy Chief of the General Staff's Operations Division and approved by B. M. Shaposhnikov, the Chief of the Red Army General Staff.[1] Like previous plans, this plan postulated an attack by Germany supported by Italy, Finland, Rumania, and possibly Hungary against the western Soviet Union and by Japan in the Soviet Far East. The General Staff assessed a total threat of 270 infantry division, 11,750 tanks, 22,000 guns, and 16,400 aircraft, the bulk of which would be directed against the most critical western theater. Soviet strategic deployment in accordance with this plan required the formation of three wartime *fronts* in the western theater: the northwestern and western protecting the main strategic axis and the southwestern protecting the region south of the Pripiat Marshes.

The General Staff planned to employ the Far Eastern Front and Trans-Baikal Military District, whose forces manned the boundaries of Japanese-occupied Manchuria, to deal with the Japanese threat to the Far East. The Far Eastern Front, whose original name was the Red Banner Far Eastern Front, had been organized in late June 1938 from the Special Red Banner Far Eastern Army. Initially, the *front* consisted of the 1st and 2d Red Banner Armies and the Khabarovsk Group of Forces. After the battle with the Japanese at Lake Khasan in late summer 1938, the General Staff disestablished the *front*, only to form it again in July 1940 on the base of the Chita Front Group of Forces with its subordinate 1st and 2d Separate Red Banner and 15th Armies and Northern Army Group. The *Stavka* added the 25th and 35th Armies to the *front* in July 1941.[2]

The Trans-Baikal Military District had been formed in May 1935 on the base of the Special Red Banner Far Eastern Army's Trans-Baikal Group of Forces. When war began in 1941, it included the territory of Irkutsk and Chita *oblasts* [regions] and Buriat-Mongolian and Iakutsk ASSRs, and its headquarters was at Chita. From June 1941 the military district consisted of the 16th and 17th Armies, and after July 1941, the 36th Army. Soon after the outbreak of war, the *Stavka* transferred the 16th Army to its reserve and then westward to the Smolensk region to reinforce the Western Front. The Trans-Baikal Military District then mobilized fresh forces to defend its borders with Manchuria. In September 1941 the *Stavka* reorganized the military district into the Trans-Baikal Front consisting of the 17th and 36th Armies, and after August 1942, the 12th Air Army.[3]

Diplomatic measures supplemented the Soviet's new military strategy. As an adjunct to war planning, the Soviet government sought to defuse the threat in the east by signing a non-aggression pact with Japan, which would in turn allow the Soviet State to pay principal attention to its western borders and the German threat. Since it was angry over the German–Soviet non-aggression pact of 1939, which it viewed as a violation of its Anti-Comintern Pact with Germany, in April 1941 the Japanese signed a pact of neutrality with the Soviet Union.[4]

Reassured by its non-aggression pact with Japan but distressed over Germany's evident mobilization, the Soviet Union began a strategic regrouping of forces from the Far East in the spring of 1941. In the second half of April, the People's Commissariat of Defense [*Narodnyi komissariat oborony* – NKO] decided to reinforce its forces in the West at the expense of forces stationed in the Far East and Trans-Baikal regions. By 22 June 1941, it had dispatched the field headquarters of the 16th Army, two rifle and one mechanized corps, and two airborne brigades westward. This force, which included two rifle and two tank divisions, one motorized division and two separate regiments with a total strength of more than 57,000 men, 670 guns and mortars, and 1,070 light tanks, later participated in the Western and Southwestern Fronts' defensive operations during the tragic initial months of war.[5]

SOVIET WARTIME STRATEGY *VIS-À-VIS* JAPAN

The Soviet–Japanese neutrality pact benefited the Soviet Union immensely after June 1941 by partially mitigating against the adverse effects of the German Operation Barbarossa and permitting the Soviet Union to devote its energies to meeting and defeating the German threat. Despite the pact's existence, however, the fragility of the earlier German–Soviet non-aggression pact and its violation by Germany prompted Stalin to suspect that the same fate might befall his pact with Japan. Consequently, while the Soviet Union shifted its strategic attention westward, nagging concerns over Japanese actions forced the *Stavka* (Headquarters of the Supreme High Command), which directed the Soviet war effort after late June 1941, to maintain strong defenses in the Far East. After December 1941, however, Japanese involvement in a Pacific war with the United States largely negated Soviet concerns over its eastern flank.

From 22 June 1941 through mid-1944, Stalin and his *Stavka* applied to the conduct of the war strategic concepts that had been fundamental tenets of Soviet military strategy during the 1920s and 1930s. In particular, the Soviet Union accorded the highest priority to, first, the conduct of strategic defense in the west to halt the German invasion and, second, the conduct of strategic offensive operations to defeat Nazi Germany. Whether or not Japan entered the war, the Soviet Union's survival depended on successful defense and, ultimately, counteroffensive action in the west. All Soviet strategic measures served that essential end. Virtually from the first day of the war, Stalin and his military advisers shifted vital military resources westward from the Far East. All subsequent Soviet strategists agree that 'The forces of the Far Eastern Military District made a worthy contribution to the overall matter of victory in the great Patriotic War.'[6]

In June 1941 Stalin ordered the Far Eastern Front and Trans-Baikal Military District to erect firm defenses along the Manchurian and Korean border and on 29 June begin transferring westward the bulk of their well-trained and battle-tested divisions.

To defend their territories once their best forces had departed, commanders in the East relied heavily on 14 fortified regions (12 in the Far Eastern Front and two in the Trans-Baikal Military District), some of which had been created as early as 1932, but the bulk of which were formed between 1938 and August 1941. Fortified regions [*ukreplennyi raion* – UR] consisted of from eight to 12 machine gun-artillery and antitank battalions positioned in increasingly well-fortified defensive positions. Although they were dispersed along the entire Soviet–Manchurian border, most of these fortified regions were concentrated in eastern Manchuria, 'since it was in this area that the Soviets expected the main body of the Japanese Army to attack' should hostilities break out.[7] Japanese sources recognized their defensive nature, noting, 'There is no room to doubt the initially defensive nature of the URs.'[8]

Behind this fortified defensive shield, the Soviets maintained a skeletal force structure in the Far East made up of rifle divisions, cavalry divisions, and a minimal number of mixed formations. After 22 June 1941, the vast majority of other forces moved westward to play a vital role in the war in the west, even though the *Stavka* still had reason to be concerned about its eastern flank.[9] The force the *Stavka* allocated for wartime defense in the Far East was based on the assumption that it was possible to conduct a two-front war successfully if sufficient forces could be mustered to defend the Far East. The *Stavka* assumed 'that Japan could allocate up to 50 divisions, 1,200 tanks, and 3,000 aircraft against the Soviet Union'. Therefore, 'it was necessary to have 33–34 divisions and a specific quantity of forces and ships in the Pacific Fleet to guarantee fully a stable situation and for defense of the Far Eastern borders'.[10]

The wartime deployment of Red Army forces from the Far East to the west began in early July 1941 and accelerated thereafter. From July through November, the *Stavka* recalled 13 rifle, tank, and motorized divisions from the Far East, divisions that subsequently played a significant role in halting German forces on the approaches to Moscow and in launching the Red Army's ensuing Moscow counteroffensive.[11] A second wave of Far Eastern divisions, sent westward in 1942, contributed to Red Army success at Stalingrad in November 1942. This included two rifle divisions between 5 December 1941 and 30 April 1942 and ten rifle divisions and four rifle brigades with a total of 150,000 men and more than 1,600 guns and mortars between 1 May and 19 November 1942.[12]

Later still, in the winter of 1942–43, the NKO transferred one rifle division, three cavalry divisions, six howitzer artillery brigades, and three mortar regiments totaling 35,000 men, 557 guns and mortars, and 32 light tanks westward to reinforce the post-Stalingrad offensive.[13] The transfers decreased sharply as Red Army combat fortunes soared in the summer of 1943. From March to May 1943, the NKO shipped eight newly formed howitzer artillery brigades with 9,000 men and 230 guns back to the west, and in 1944 an airborne brigade and four howitzer artillery regiments.[14]

In total, from 1941 to 1945, the *Stavka* redeployed 39 divisions, 21 brigades, and ten regiments totaling 402,000 men, 5,000 guns and mortars, and more than 3,300 tanks from the Far East to the western theater. In addition, it also sent as many as 150,000 personnel replacements.[15] Deprived of these forces, by December 1941 Red Army strength in the Far East had dwindled to 32 divisions or divisional equivalents, barely enough to defend in accordance with the General Staff's calculations.

Throughout the period from June 1941 through January 1944, Red Army forces in the Far East remained on the strategic defense, although the army's strength in the region slowly crept up from 32 to 48 divisional equivalents.[16] By mid-1944, when it became apparent that victory in the west was only a matter of time, Soviet strategic planners began entertaining thoughts of an offensive in the Far East and adjusted their Far Eastern strategic posture accordingly.

TRANSITION FROM DEFENSE TO OFFENSE, 1941–44

The *Stavka* began strengthening its strategic posture in the Far East in earnest during the summer of 1943 in the expectation that offensive operations would be required in the future. In August it formed the Coastal Group of Forces (the 1st and 25th Armies and the 9th Air Army) from the existing Far Eastern Front. This group, initially under 25th Army control, took over the 'deployment of forces and responsibility for the separate coastal strategic axis protecting the approaches from the Far East into eastern Manchuria'.[17] Ultimately, it provided the basis for the formation of the 1st Far Eastern Front in 1945.

Throughout the summer of 1943, the General Staff transferred personnel between theaters to improve its expertise on Far Eastern matters. The General Staff brought Major General N. A. Lomov from his previous position as Deputy Chief of Staff of the Far Eastern Front to the Operational Directorate of the General Staff, where he began serving as deputy to Lieutenant General S. M. Shtemenko, the directorate's chief. Lomov brought with him extensive experience in the Far East. At the same time, the *Stavka* replaced Lomov with Major General F. I. Shevchenko from the General Staff to strengthen its representation in the Far East.[18]

At the meeting of the 'Big Three' Allied leaders (Stalin, Roosevelt, and Churchill) at Teheran in November 1943, in response to Anglo-American requests for assistance in the war against Japan, Stalin announced that, in principle, the Soviet government would agree to join the war once Germany had been defeated. Following Soviet victories in the West in 1943 and 1944, the Red Army General Staff began preliminary planning for military operations in the Far East. In the summer of 1944, for example, Stalin designated Marshal of the Soviet Union A. M. Vasilevsky, the Chief of the General Staff, as future Far Eastern Theater commander.[19]

Throughout 1944 the *Stavka* and General Staff beefed up their force in the Far East by dispatching to that region from the west 11 rifle divisions, together with the command group of a mechanized corps, a mechanized brigade, and several artillery regiments, thus raising the strength of their forces in the Far East to about 59 division equivalents by December 1944 and 47 divisions and 31 separate brigades by May 1945. During the same period, the Red Army's personnel strength in the Far East rose to 1,185,000 troops, supported by 20,695 guns and mortars, 2,338 tanks and self-propelled guns, and 4,314 combat aircraft (see Tables 1 and 2).[20]

TABLE 1: ORGANIZATIONAL STRENGTH OF SOVIET FORCES IN THE FAR EAST, 1941–45

	Date						
Forces	*22.6.41*	*1.12.41*	*1.7.42*	*19.11.42*	*1.7.43*	*1.1.44*	*9.5.45*
Divisions:							
Rifle	23	24	29	20	20	31	45
Cavalry	1	2	3	3	3	2	2
Tank	8	4	2	2	2	2	2
Aviation	13	23	10	24	27	29	29
PVO (antiaircraft defense)	–	–	–	–	–	–	6
Brigades:							
Rifle	3	11	20	31	30	26	6
Tank	1	7	20	22	25	26	27
Aviation	4	4	4	3	4	–	–
PVO	1	–	–	–	1	4	4
Fortified regions	13	15	15	15	15	18	19
Total divisional equivalents*	32	39	49.5	46	45.5	55	59.5

*Divisional equivalents count one rifle and cavalry as one division and two brigades and fortified regions as one division.

Source: Istorii Vtoroi Mirovoi voiny 1939–1945, T. 11 [History of the Second World War, 1939–1945, Vol. 11] (Moscow: Voenizdat, 1980), 183.

Planning for the transition from defense to offense continued to accelerate. In late September 1944, Stalin tasked the General Staff's Operations Directorate, headed by Shtemenko, with drafting estimates for concentrating and logistically supporting forces necessary to conduct offensive operations against Japanese forces in Manchuria. Preliminary estimates, based on assessments made by the General Staff's Main Intelligence Directorate [*Glavnoe razvedyvatel'noe upravlenie – GRU*] of Japanese strength in the theater and the enemy's overall strategic situation, were ready by late October. They assessed Japanese ground strength at over 680,000 men, including 443,000 in the Kwantung Army, 1,215 tanks, 6,700 guns, and 1,900 aircraft in Manchuria and Korea. According to these estimates, another 100,000 troops were deployed on southern Sakhalin Island and the Kuril Islands. Additional

TABLE 2: PERSONNEL AND WEAPONS STRENGTH OF SOVIET FORCES IN THE FAR EAST, 1941–45

Date	*Personnel*	*Guns and mortars*	*Tanks and SP guns*	*Combat aircraft*	*Combat ships*
22.6.41	703,714	10,080*	3,188**	4,140	94***
1.12.41	1,343,307	8,777	2,124	3,193	96
1.7.42	1,446,012	11,759	2,589	3,178	107
19.11.42	1,296,822	12,728	2,526	3,357	98
1.7.43	1,156,961	13,843	2,367	3,949	101
1.1.44	1,162,991	16,827	2,069	4,006	102
9.5.45	1,185,058	20,695	2,338	4,314	93

*Does not include 50 mm mortars.
**All tanks shown are light types and the only self-propelled guns included 132 in May 1945.
***Includes special classes of combat ships only and not transport ships.
Source: Istorii Vtoroi Mirovoi voiny 1939–1945, T. 11 [History of the Second World War 1939–1945, Vol. 11] (Moscow: Voenizdat, 1980), 184.

forces in northern China were also available to bolster the Kwantung Army. The Soviets also noted Japanese efforts to improve their defenses in Manchuria by the construction of 17 fortified regions consisting of substantial permanent fortifications.[21]

The General Staff assumed that a major Soviet offensive in Manchuria aimed at destroying the Kwantung Army would also break Japanese power in China and Korea and hasten the end of the war. Set within the context of Soviet strategic objectives, these assessments of overall Japanese strength established the basic norms that Soviet planners would employ to determine the scale and other parameters of the strategic redeployment the Red Army would have to conduct to create a correlation of forces requisite for the achievement of victory in the Far Eastern theater of military operations.[22]

During the fall of 1944, the General Staff focused its attention on logistical problems, since, in the final analysis, logistics would determine the size of the force that it could commit against the Kwantung Army. To improve its logistical posture, the Soviet government initiated preliminary discussions with representatives of the United States and Great Britain regarding additional Lend-Lease aid to support Soviet preparations for hostilities against Japan. Logistical support for specific Red Army operations in Manchuria figured prominently in these conversations.

The most important of these discussions took place in Moscow during October 1944 when Stalin and his military planners met with Winston Churchill, the British Prime Minister, his Foreign Minister, Anthony Eden, and US observers, including Ambassador Averill Harriman and General John Deane, head of the US Military Mission. At a high-level session on 15 October, Harriman and Deane presented a series of questions to the Soviet leadership:

1. How long after the war with Germany ends will the Russians declare war on Japan?
2. How much time is necessary for the Russians to begin active offensive operations?
3. To what degree can the Trans-Siberian railroad be used for the accumulation of strategic ground and air forces?[23]

The next day Stalin and A. I. Antonov, the chief of the General Staff answered:

> The Soviet Union has 30 divisions and 19 rifle brigades stationed in the Far East against 24 Japanese divisions and 42 brigades located in Manchuria and Korea. To secure the necessary superiority in forces and equipment and be in a state to commence offensive operations, we need to transfer about another 30 divisions to the Far East for which we need to run no fewer than 1,000 military trains along the Trans-Siberian railroad. The daily load capacity of this railroad is about 36 trains, of which 26 can be allocated for military aims. In such circumstances the transfer of 30 divisions will take 2.5–3 months. Thereafter we can open offensive operations in the event that the western Allied powers prevent the enemy, who possesses more favorable communications, from bringing up reinforcements to Manchuria and Korea from other regions. Not considering the Japanese to be a sufficiently strong enemy, we suggest that we will complete our military operations within two months after the declaration of war ... The Soviet Union can strike a blow several months after the destruction of Germany.[24]

At the same time, Stalin and Antonov emphasized that the Trans-Siberian railroad lacked the load capacity to transport to the Far East supplies necessary to sustain successful military operations by so large a force. Therefore, 'the Soviet leadership insisted it was necessary to supply our Far Eastern armies from the United States via Petropavlovsk on Kamchatka and Vladivostok'.[25]

At the conference's third session, which took place on 17 October, the General Staff presented the Allied representatives with a detailed list of supplies necessary for Soviet forces to conduct successful operations in the Far East. It stated that, since the forces required a two-month reserve of food and other types of supplies, about 860,410 tons of dry goods and 206,000 tons of liquids (primarily fuel) were necessary to support the planned force, which would consist of 'more than 1.5 million men, 500 aircraft, 3,000 tanks, and 75,000 vehicles'.[26] The General Staff requested that the Western Allies provide all of the necessary supplies by the end of June 1945 and that they be considered to be outside the parameters of present Lend-Lease agreements. During the same session, Stalin agreed to commence operations against Japanese forces in Manchuria approximately three months after the capitulation of Germany.

The 'Big Three' heads of state and their representatives met once again four months later at Yalta in the Crimea. During the sessions, which met from 7 to 12 February, they formalized agreement on matters negotiated in Moscow during the previous October. Specifically, on 11 February, Roosevelt and Stalin signed an agreement announcing the Soviet Union's intent to enter the war against Japan. Thereafter, the General Staff began preparing detailed operational plans for the campaign, and other state organs began making decisions regarding the transport of troops and supplies to the Far East. The General Staff and NKO Directorates responsible for planning military operations in Manchuria assumed that 'The military-political aims could be achieved in a short period only if three powerful offensive groupings and considerable superiority over the enemy in troops and equipment existed in the Far Eastern theater.'[27]

From the Japanese perspective, in late 1943 and 1944, the military situation took a sharp turn for the worse. Consequently, for the first time in the war, in June 1944 Japanese military planners began preparing plans for a future defense of Manchuria. A postwar Japanese assessment noted that, during wartime, the Soviet Far Eastern defensive structure of fortified regions gradually took on a more ominous offensive tone:

> There is no room to doubt the initially defensive nature of the URs. The character of the URs changed, however, when the Soviets were able to step up war preparations and reinforce the border areas. With the adoption of an offensive operational policy, the Soviets' reliance upon the URs as defensive installations decreased. The URs began to be considered as springboards for offensive action in Manchuria. Proof of this can be found in the construction of the Dauriya positions in front of the Borzya positions in the Trans-Baikal in 1939, and also in the fact that, when the unit in charge of defending the UR in the vicinity of Poltavka was pulled back in 1940, it was reorganized into the 105th Infantry Division, apparently for future use in offensive operations in this vicinity.[28]

Although these concerns surfaced in retrospect, in 1944 and 1945, the Japanese High Command clearly appreciated the maturing Soviet offensive capability. They did not, however, anticipate the scope of these preparations or the timing of what was about to occur.

PLANNING THE STRATEGIC REGROUPING OF RED ARMY FORCES TO MANCHURIA

The Soviet Union began actively preparing for war against Japan in February and March 1945, shortly after Stalin reiterated his promise to do so to his 'Big Three' partners at the February conference in the Crimea.

During March the General Staff approved plans for deploying forces and *matériel* to the Far East, and several weeks later, on 19 March the State Defense Committee [*Gosudarstvennoi komitet oborony* – GKO] decided to reinforce its air defenses in the Far East and Trans-Baikal region. Shortly thereafter, Soviet state organs issued a steady stream of orders improving its military posture in the region. On 19 March the *Stavka* created its third strategic grouping in the region by removing the Coastal Group of Forces from Far Eastern Front control and subordinated it directly to its control, and on 26 March the *Stavka* issued new orders to the Far Eastern Front and Coastal Group of Force concerning the concealment and protection of its force deployments.[29]

Given the decisive role armored forces would obviously play in the upcoming campaign, in March 1945 the *Stavka* also began upgrading the equipment in Red Army tank forces already in the Far East, which were still equipped only with older model light T-26 and BT (fast-moving) tanks. To improve the capability of these forces, the *Stavka* equipped one battalion of each tank brigade and one regiment of the 61st and 111th Tank Divisions with T-34 tanks as the first installment of 670 T-34 tanks it planned to dispatch to the Far East.[30] The limited carrying capacity of the Trans-Siberian railroad prevented the dispatch of enough tanks to the Far Eastern theater to equip the Red Army's entire armored force in the region. Therefore, the United States agreed to ship the several hundreds of tanks required to make up the difference via Vladivostok.

The most serious logistical problems Soviet military planners faced in 1945 were the inadequate carrying capacity of the rail network to the Far East, the poor condition of the railroad, and the lack of qualified personnel and equipment to repair the vital line. The GKO began resolving the problem on 13 April when it issued instructions, 'Concerning Measures to Improve the Operations of Far Eastern (Krasnoiarsk, Eastern-Siberian, Trans-Baikal, Amur, Far Eastern, and Coastal) Railroads.'[31] Among other measures, the People's Commissariat of Communications [*Narodnyi komissariat put' soobshchenii* – NKPS] increased the carrying capacity of some rail sectors from 12 to 38 trains per day and the number of locomotives available along rail lines in the Far East from 2,708 on 1 May 1945 to 2,947 on 1 July and 3,107 on 1 September, in part by providing 800 locomotives from its reserve.[32]

Also in April the Communications Commissariat began dispatching railroad forces to the Far East, first, elements of three railroad exploitation regiments and three exploitation squads from Poland and Rumania numbering over 14,000 men, and augmenting them with 8,000 conscripts who had been called to limited service due to poor health. Soon after, two railroad brigades and several specialized formations began to perform repair work on the railroad lines.[33]

In May the GKO and NKPS dispatched the 6th, 7th, 8th, and 9th Railroad

Brigades to the Trans-Baikal region from the west to construct and maintain another more secure railroad line from Irkutsk to Sliudianka, a 191-mile (307-kilometer) rail sector connecting the Eastern Siberian and Trans-Baikal railroads.[34] In addition, these forces significantly improved the Trans-Baikal Front's vital single-track railroad line from Karymskaia in Siberia through Borzia to Chiobalsan (Baian-Tumen') in Mongolia, increasing its capacity from seven to ten trains per day.[35]

During the same period, the NKPS transferred its 3d Railroad Brigade from Czechoslovakia to the 1st Far Eastern Front to work on the Coastal Railroad and the 25th Railroad Brigade to the 2d Far Eastern Front to improve the condition of the Amur and Far Eastern Railroads, increasing the capacity of these railroads from 25 to 30 trains per day.[36]

While the railroads serving the Far East and Trans-Baikal regions were being improved and repaired, road administrations were carrying out similar measures to improve the road network in the region to support internal force movements and the forward deployment of forces. By 9 August, road construction and repair forces built or repaired 2,610 miles (4,200 kilometers) of roads in the Far East, including 1,416 miles (2,279 kilometers) in the Trans-Baikal Front, 938 miles (1,509 kilometers) in the 1st Far Eastern Front, and 301 miles (485 kilometers) in the 2d Far Eastern Front.[37]

To help provide necessary political context for its military operations in Manchuria, on 5 April 1945 the Soviet government renounced its neutrality pact with Japan.[38] During the same period, while operations in the west were entering their final phase, the *Stavka* dispatched its first warning orders regarding impending military action against Japan to the headquarters of the Far Eastern Front and Coastal Group of Forces. Also in March, Stalin centralized all operational planning for the Manchurian offensive under the *Stavka's* direction. Soviet forces were to conduct the offensive according to a common *Stavka* plan, which included 'a complex of diplomatic, military-technical, and strategic measures on an all-governmental scale'.[39]

Also during April, the State Defense Committee [GKO], the People's Commissariat of Defense [NKO], and the Red Army General Staff began the arduous process of assembling sufficient forces in the Far Eastern theater of military operations with which to conduct the offensive. First, these organs stockpiled equipment in the Far East and reequipped and reorganized forces already located in that region. Later, primarily in May and June, they began shifting men, *matériel*, and equipment to the Far East, in general, transferring combat units and their equipment separately.[40] All the while, the United States geared up its efforts to send requisite equipment and supplies to the Far East through the ports of Petropavlovsk and Vladivostok.

On the basis of the General Staff's assessments of Japanese strength in the Far East, the Manchurian operation turned out to be slightly larger than the offensive operation the Red Army had conducted against German Army

Group Center in Belorussia in June 1944. Using the Belorussian experience as a guide, to guarantee success in the Manchurian operation the General Staff believed it had to increase its military strength in the Far East to a total of more than 1.5 million soldiers, more than double their June 1941 strength and almost 50 per cent higher than the strength on 1 January 1945.

Several stark realities differentiated the Manchurian offensive from its Belorussian predecessor, delayed its preparation, increased its importance, and magnified the importance of deception and surprise in its preparation and conduct. As Shtemenko later recalled:

> Our efforts to achieve surprise were much hindered by the fact that the Japanese had for long been convinced of the inevitability of war with the Soviet Union. Strategic surprise seemed altogether impossible. Nevertheless, in considering this problem, we reflected more than once on the first days of the war we were still fighting. Our country had also expected war and prepared for it, but the German attack had come as a surprise. So there was no need to abandon the idea prematurely.[41]

The first reality the General Staff had to address was the fact that the immense size of the theater of military operations and its staggering distance from European Russia required it to move almost 700,000 men and vast amounts of weapons, equipment, and other military supplies over 5,590 miles (9,000 kilometers) along the tenuous umbilical of the Trans-Siberian railroad from the European theater to the Far East. To achieve surprise, this movement had to be kept as secret as possible. Second, the General Staff was confronted with severe time constraints. Japanese reinforcement of Manchuria, the United States' employment of the atomic bomb against Japan on the eve of the offensive, and possible ensuing Japanese collapse before the Soviet Union was in a position to avail itself of the spoils of victory, made it imperative that the offensive achieve its goals in a matter of days, rather than weeks or months. In short, Manchuria had to be secured within 30 days and the main entrances into central Manchuria within one week, as much for political as for military reasons.

From virtually every perspective, successful strategic deception would be a large factor determining Soviet success or failure. In this instance, and for the first time, the Soviet Union would have to employ strategic deception to achieve surprise in an initial period of war. This required political finesse to dull Japanese apprehensions over possible Soviet military intentions and creation and orchestration of a deception plan outside the confines of ongoing combat. Hence, the *Stavka* could not rely on the 'noise of war' to conceal their offensive preparations. Ultimately, however, although the Japanese well understood the Soviet intention to attack, they were totally deceived regarding the timing, scale, location, and form of the offensive.[42]

THE STRATEGIC REGROUPING OF FORCES TO THE FAR EAST

Movement associated with the strategic regrouping of Red Army forces to the Far East took place from May through July of 1945, and forces were still arriving in the Far Eastern Theater when the campaign commenced in early August. The regrouping process involved massive troop and material movements to the Far East and Trans-Baikal regions from the west and within and between the *fronts* designated to conduct the offensive (see Map 1).

By 9 August 1945, the total number of railroad cars employed in this movement reached 222,331, including 127,126 railroad cars dispatched from central regions of the Soviet Union. Of this total, 75,345 cars carried reinforcements and material for the Trans-Baikal Front, 31,100 for the 1st Far Eastern Front, and 17,916 for the 2d Far Eastern Front, and a total of 81,538 cars were used to transport military formations and units.[43]

Overall, the forces regrouped during the summer of 1945 included:

- two *front* [army group] headquarters, including a reserve *front* headquarters formed from the former Karelian Front from the *Stavka* reserve and the headquarters of the 2d Ukrainian Front;
- four army headquarters, including the 5th, 39th, and 53d Combined-arms armies and the 6th Guards Tank Army;
- 15 rifle, artillery, tank, and mechanized corps headquarters;
- 36 rifle, artillery, and antiaircraft artillery divisions;
- 53 brigades of various types;
- two fortified regions; and
- additional air, air defense, and naval units.

Although the GKO reached its final decision regarding the transfer of a massive number of military formations to the Far East on 3 June 1945, the actual movement of these forces had begun many month before, even before the war in Europe ended. For example, in April it ordered the headquarters of its former Karelian Front, then in *Stavka* reserve, to move to the Far East, where it became the headquarters of the Coastal Group of Forces. On 9 May the GKO transferred two field-fortified regions to the area, also from its reserve. By month's end, it had completed the first wave of transfers by regrouping the 5th Army headquarters, the headquarters of three rifle corps, and four rifle divisions to the east.[44]

All told, the GKO extracted sizeable forces from four *fronts* that had already completed their operations in the west (the 3d Belorussian, 2d Ukrainian, Leningrad, and 1st Belorussian Fronts) as its principal source of reinforcements for the new Far East Command. The most important source

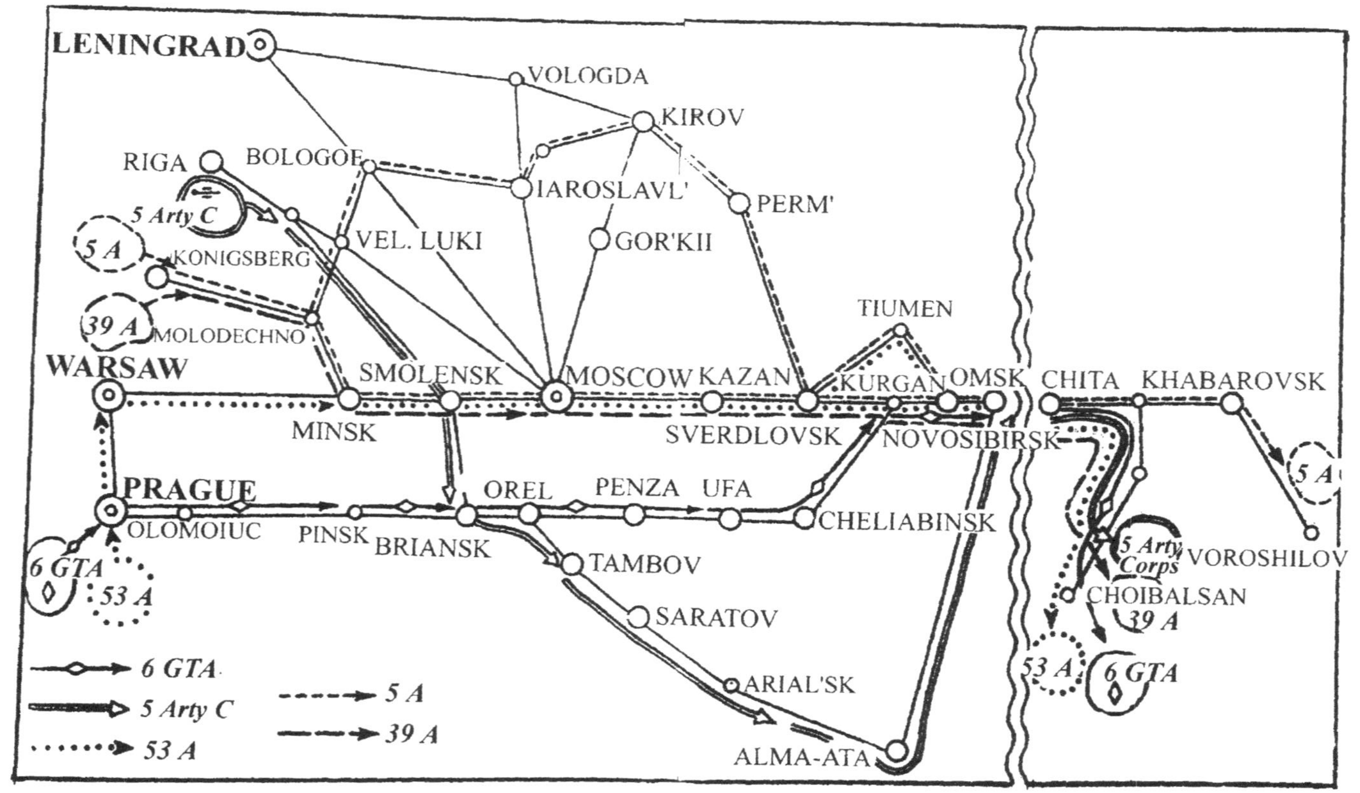

Map 1. Regrouping Routes of Soviet Forces to the Far East

was the 3d Belorussian Front, which had just completed operations to destroy German forces defending the Konigsberg region. The forces taken from this *front* included the headquarters of the 5th and 39th Armies, six rifle corps headquarters, 18 rifle and two antiaircraft artillery divisions, and eight artillery and two guards-mortar brigades, comprising 60 per cent of the *front's* overall strength.[45]

In addition, the GKO deployed eastward from the 2d Ukrainian Front its headquarters and those of the 53d and 6th Guards Tank Armies, six tank, mechanized, and rifle corps headquarters, ten rifle and antiaircraft artillery divisions, and 15 brigades of various types, and, from the Leningrad Front, the headquarters of an artillery penetration and mechanized corps, six divisions, and 17 brigades. Finally, the 1st Belorussian Front provided three guards-mortar brigades, the Moscow Military District, two tank brigades, and the *Stavka* reserve, a *front* headquarters, three brigades, and two fortified regions.[46]

The headquarters staff of Vasilevsky's new Far East Command arrived in Chita on 5 July 1945. Vasilevsky's immediate staff included Army General I. I. Maslennikov, deputy commander, Lieutenant General I. V. Shikin, political deputy, and Colonel General S. P. Ivanov, chief of staff. The command element numbered 30 generals and 190 officers, all of whom had held responsible positions in the General Staff and central directorates and other organs of the NKO. All of the leading figures traveled to the region under false names (Vasilevsky was called Colonel General Vasil'ev). In essence, with its subordinate headquarters and chiefs of services, this assemblage formed a secret Main Command of Soviet Forces in the Far East.[47]

Vasilevsky's staff included 12 generals and 66 officers made up of groups of officers from the General Staff's Main Operations, Intelligence, Operational Rear, 8th (Cipher), and Topographical Directorates, a communications group of four generals and ten officers led by Colonel General N. D. Psurtsev, and a Naval Section formed in July 1945 with one admiral and 13 officers. In addition, the command staff included:

- an Air Force group of six generals and 29 officers headed by Chief Marshal of Aviation A. A. Novikov;
- an artillery group of five officers under Marshal of Artillery N. M. Chistiakov;
- a tank group of eight officers led by Colonel General M. D. Solomatin, the chief of staff, Red Army Armored and Mechanized Forces;
- an engineer group of five officers under Colonel General K. S. Nazarov, the chief of engineer forces;
- a group of chemical forces headed by Major General A. S. Kubasov;
- a rear services group of 12 generals and 74 officers under the command of Colonel General V. I. Vinogradov, which included subgroups from the

principal staff rear service departments and directorates, the road, automotive, construction, quartermaster, medical, veterinary, fuel supply, trophy (captured material), and other directorates.[48]

Eventually, all of these staff groups manned corresponding staffs, directorates, and departments subordinate to the Far East Command. In addition, the Red Army's Main Political Directorate formed a Political Directorate in the Far East Command consisting of six generals and 59 officers. When fully manned, the Far East Command consisted of 525 men, including 45 generals, 300 officers, 130 non-commissioned officers and soldiers, and 50 non-military workers. Finally, in June 1945 the People's Commissar of the Navy, Fleet Admiral N. G. Kuznetsov, arrived in the Far East with a group of admirals and officers and formed a Naval Department in the Far East Command and the 1st and 2d Far Eastern Fronts.[49]

Beginning in the spring of 1945, the *Stavka* replaced the command cadre and senior staff officers in the major strategic force groupings in the Far East and Trans-Baikal regions and at every level down to brigade with more experienced officers. For example, the staffs of the former Karelian and 2d Ukrainian Fronts replaced those of the 1st Far Eastern and Trans-Baikal Fronts, which were designated to operate along the most important strategic axes. In addition, the Main Cadres Directorate replaced with more experienced officers 20 senior command and political cadre in combined-arms and air armies and 40 commanders of corps, divisions, and tank brigades. When this process was complete, the Far East Command included 60 generals and admirals and more than 10,000 officers, including 3,000 who had fought successfully on the Soviet–German front.[50]

As far as the actual movement of forces was concerned, the first headquarters to deploy eastward was Meretskov's Reserve Front headquarters, which moved from the Iaroslavl' region to the region west of Vladivostok between 1 and 13 April 1945. Following the established pattern, Meretskov used the false name Colonel General Maksimov, and his chief political officer (Member of the Military Council) and chief of staff also used false ranks and names. Shortly after its arrival and redesignation as the Coastal Group of Forces (*Primorskaia gruppa voisk* – PGB), on 20 April Meretskov's group came under direct *Stavka* control with the mission of defending the coastal region of the Far East and improving his forces' offensive capabilities. At the time, the Coastal Group consisted of the 35th, 1st Red Banner, 25th Combined-arms, and 9th Air Armies.

In late April, the *Stavka* formed the Chuguevka group within the Coastal Group of Forces to protect the group's rear and the southeastern coast of the Sea of Japan. It did so by dispatching to the Far East an operational group of two fortified regions from the White Sea Military District, which was experienced in coastal defense. The 150th and 162d Fortified Regions completed the bulk of their movement by 10 May, before the massive process of regrouping major forces from the west began. They completed their movement over a distance of 199–217 miles (320–350) kilometers through exceedingly difficult terrain to their assigned positions by road and track between 21 May and 17 July.[51]

The massive movement of forces eastward from European Russia began with the dispatch of Army General N. I. Krylov's 5th Army from East Prussia. The army began its movement preparations in accordance with a 19 April *Stavka* directive and began loading its three rifle corps (the 45th, 65th, and 72d) and nine rifle divisions (the 63d, 97th, 144th, 157th, 159th, 184th, 215th, 277th, and 371st, which averaged 6,400 men each) into railroad cars at Konigsberg, Insterberg, and Tilsit on 22 April. While 110 railroad trains were transporting the army eastward, on 26 April Krylov and his senior staff flew to Moscow to receive specific movement instructions.

Ultimately, the army's final elements were loaded on 10 May, a process requiring 19 rather than the planned 15 days. The army's first series of trains, which carried its operational group, arrived at Muchnaia Station, located 62 miles (100 kilometers) north of Voroshilovgrad, on 21 May, and the remainder of the army closed into Muchnaia, Shmakovka, and Manzovka Stations by 10 June, a total period of 50 days.[52]

After their arrival in the Far East, from 2 May through 11 June, the 5th Army's forces moved into their concentration areas around Lunza, Muchnaia, and Arkhangelovka, where they began regrouping, replenishing, and training. Commanders' meeting and reports highlighted a variety of problems, including soldier fatigue, lack of training, shortages of mid-level and junior officers, shortages of food and fuel, and a large number of soldiers 50 years of age or older. The corps commanders reported that between ten and 15 days were required to bring their forces to full combat readiness.[53] Krylov responded by emphasizing the importance of the army's mission and the necessity of completing training and combat preparations rapidly and effectively, noting he intended to bring all of the army's divisions up to a strength of 7,000 men as soon as possible.[54]

In addition to the 5th Army, 70 combat formations and units deployed eastward to support the Coastal Group of Forces on the following schedule:

April and May 1945:

- the 60th Antiaircraft Artillery Division from Czechoslovakia;
- the 15th Guards Antitank (Tank Destroyer) Artillery Brigade (with the 5th Army) from East Prussia; and
- six separate artillery regiments and 19 separate self-propelled artillery battalions (SU-76) from East Prussia to support rifle divisions.

July and August 1945:

- the 126th Mountain Rifle Corps (with three brigades) from L'vov;
- the 33d and 48th Antiaircraft Artillery Divisions RGK (Reserve of the *Stavka*) from East Prussia;
- five separate artillery and mortar brigades, four separate engineer brigades, one signal brigade, and nine separate self-propelled artillery regiments to support the rifle corps.[55]

The *Stavka* regrouped the fewest number of formations and units from the west to reinforce and support the Far Eastern Front. The 30 formations and units moved east included the 73d Antiaircraft Artillery Division RGK, two separate antitank artillery brigades, one separate antiaircraft artillery brigade, one separate engineer brigade, two signal brigades, six separate artillery and mortar regiments, and 12 separate self-propelled artillery battalions (SU-76).

The greatest proportion of forces regrouped to the east went to the Trans-Baikal Front for employment along its intended main offensive axis. The largest formations were the 39th Army with three rifle corps and nine rifle divisions from East Prussia, the 53d Army with three rifle corps and nine rifle divisions from Czechoslovakia, and the 6th Guards Tank Army with one tank and two mechanized corps, also from Czechoslovakia.

Colonel General I. I. Liudnikov's 39th Army, which had recently finished destroying German forces on the Zemland peninsula, reverted from 3d Belorussian Front to *Stavka* control, concentrated in the Insterberg region on 1 May, and began loading on railroad cars at nine stations in East Prussia on 12 May. Its three rifle corps (the 5th Guards, 94th, and 113th), nine rifle divisions (the 17th, 19th, and 91st Guards, and the 124th, 192d, 221st, 262d, 338th, and 358th Rifle Divisions), and supporting formations and units (the 139th Army Gun Artillery Regiment, 555th Mortar Regiment, 610th Antitank Artillery Brigade, 32d Engineer-Sapper Brigade, and others) loaded on 110 railroad trains in 28 days and completed its departure from East Prussia on 9 July. After a 56-day trip, the 39th Army completed its movement on 4 July and concentrated in the Choibalsan region of Mongolia.[56] While the rail movement was under way, on 22 June the 39th Army's forces began moving forward into new concentration areas around Tamsag-Bulag, 155–208 miles (250–335 kilometers) southeast of Choibalsan, and completed its deployment on 16 July after a grueling 25-day march along one desert route.

Since Liudnikov's army had suffered heavy losses in the fighting for Konigsberg and the Zemland peninsula, it was woefully under strength and required considerable reinforcement. The General Staff satisfied that need by dispatching 2,000 officers and 33,000 non-commissioned officers and enlisted men in ten more trains, together with massive amounts of weapons and equipment.[57] About 80 per cent of the personnel replacements were from the 1927 year group (17 and 18 years old) primarily from Chkalov, Stavropol', Stalingrad, and Novosibiirsk *oblasti'* [regions], and Kazakhstan, and only a few had any military experience. Worse still, medical exams indicated that 15 per cent of the youth were ill, 30 per cent were in poor physical shape, and only 55 per cent were in good physical condition at a time when 84 per cent of the *front's* total manpower satisfied required physical standards.[58]

With reinforcement of the Far East well under way, in June 1945 the GKO and *Stavka* began regrouping forces from Czechoslovakia to the Trans-Baikal region. The former 2d Ukrainian Front headquarters, which had just deployed to the region to become the Trans-Baikal Front, supervised the concentration and deployment of these forces and their preparations for forthcoming operations. On 1 July the 53d and 6th Guards Army began loading for rail transport to the Trans-Baikal region.

Colonel General I. M. Managarov's 53d Army, led by an operational group consisting of the army, corps, and division headquarters, loaded at Vlashim, Beneshov, Cherchany, Stranchina. Rzhichany, and Brno Station in Czechoslovakia on 1 June. The army's three rifle corps (the 18th Guards, 49th, and 57th), nine rifle divisions (the 1st Guards Airborne, 6th, 52d, 109th, and 110th Guards Rifle, and the 203d, 227th, 243d, and 317th Rifle), and supporting formations and units completed their loading at the same stations by 20 June.[59] The 120 trains transporting the army reached the Choibalsan region in Mongolia between 30 June and 26 July. After a brief rest in the Choibalsan region, the army's forces deployed forward on foot by road to the Matat-Somona region near the Mongolian–Manchurian border, where it began preparing for future offensive operations. The entire regrouping traversed 5,623 miles (9,050 kilometers), mostly by rail, in a period of 30 to 40 days.

After being alerted for movement to the Far East, Colonel General A. G. Kravchenko's 6th Guards Tank Army loaded for transport east in the Prague region between 1 and 15 July. The 92 trains carrying the army's three mobile corps (the 5th Guards Tank and 9th Guards and 7th Mechanized Corps) and supporting forces (the 208th Self-propelled Artillery Brigade, 15th Antitank Artillery Brigade, 4th Guards Motorcycle Regiment, and 57th Guards-Mortar Regiment) traveled along a single rail route and reached the Choibalsan region between 9 and 23 July. The 5,592-mile (9,000-kilometer) redeployment took a total of 23 days.[60]

After a short rest in Choibalsan, Kravchenko's tank army deployed forward 186 miles (300 kilometers) by road and desert track to its concentration region around Tamsag-Bulag. The 5th Guards Tank and 7th Mechanized Corps brought with them from Czechoslovakia 208 and 285 tanks respectively, but the 9th Guards Mechanized Corps, which had brought no tanks with it during its redeployment, was issued Lend-Lease Sherman tanks shortly after its arrival.[61] Soon after it reached Choibalsan, the army also received 15,000 personnel replacements and was reinforced by the 36th and 57th Motorized Rifle Divisions, which were already subordinate to the Trans-Baikal Front.

Once the Trans-Baikal Front's major combat forces regrouped eastward, the *front's* command elements quickly followed. Ten trains left Bratislava, Czechoslovakia from 7 through 16 June, carrying Marshal of the Soviet Union R. Ia. Malinovsky, the former commander of the 2d Ukrainian Front, who traveled under the false name Colonel General Morozov, and his principal staff officers. His party included Generals A. N. Tevhenkov, *front* commissar, M. V. Zakharov, chief of staff, N. O. Pavlovsky, chief of the Operations Directorate, N. S. Fomin, chief of artillery, A. V. Kurkin, chief of armored and mechanized Forces, A. D. Tsirlin, chief of engineer forces, A. I. Leonov, chief of communications, V. I. Vostrukhov, chief of the rear, and I. A. Pliev, the former commander of the 1st Guards Cavalry-Mechanized Group. The trains carrying the new *front's* command group reached Chita, its designated command post, between 6 and 21 July.[62]

The Trans-Baikal Front's most important supporting forces regrouped according to plan and reached the Choibalsan region between 14 and 31 July. These forces included:

- the 208th Self-propelled Artillery Brigade on 14–15 July from Czechoslovakia (loaded on 14–15 June);
- the 231st Self-propelled Artillery Brigade on 14–15 July from Osipovichi, Belorussia (loaded on 14–15 June);
- the 201st Separate Tank Brigade on 6 August from the Moscow Military District Tank Center (loaded on 10 July); and
- the 3d Guards Mechanized Corps on 16–26 August from Siauliai, Lithuania (loaded on 25–31 July).[63]

While the Trans-Baikal Front's combined-arms and tank formations were regrouping, the GKO and *Stavka* dispatched trains carrying its vital artillery, engineer, and other supporting forces eastward from the Baltic region, East Prussia, Poland, and Czechoslovakia. These included the 5th Artillery Penetration Corps, consisting of the 3d and 6th Guards Artillery Penetration Divisions (with 13 artillery and mortar brigades), four antiaircraft artillery divisions, five separate antitank artillery brigades, five separate artillery and mortar brigades, and eight engineer brigades. These formations traversed a distance of up to 11,600 kilometers during an average period of 30–35 days and reached the Choibalsan region between 2 and 28 July.[64]

The regrouping of such massive amounts of artillery to the east drastically increased the Trans-Baikal Front's firepower relative to the Far Eastern Front (see Table 3).

TABLE 3: RELATIVE ARTILLERY FIREPOWER OF RED ARMY FRONTS IN THE FAR EAST, 1 JANUARY 1945.

	Fronts		
Artillery Forces	*Trans-Baikal*	*Far Eastern*	*Total*
Separate artillery regiments (howitzer, gun, antitank)	15	53	68
Separate mortar regiment	4	13	17
Separate guards-mortar regiments	1	1	2
Separate antiaircraft artillery regiments	5	7	12
Separate antiaircraft artillery battalions	9	16	25

Source: N. V. Eronin, *Strategicheskaia peregruppirovka Sovetskikh vooruzhennykh sil (pri podgotovka Dal'nevostochnoi kampanii 1945 goda)* [The strategic regrouping of the Soviet armed forces (during the preparations for the Far Eastern campaign of 1945)] (Moscow: Voroshilov General Staff Academy, 1980), 59.

When the Coastal Group of Forces was formed as an independent entity in April 1945, the problem of providing it with artillery support was resolved between April and July by forming 27 artillery and mortar brigades around the nucleus of its existing 27 artillery and ten mortar regiments, primarily by transfers from the west. By July the Coastal Group consisted of three antitank, seven gun, two howitzer, two high-power howitzer, seven corps, and six mortar brigades.

On the other hand, virtually all of the Trans-Baikal Front's artillery had to be transported from the west (see Table 4).

Overall, the GKO regrouped nine artillery divisions, 13 separate artillery brigades, five separate guards-mortar brigades, 38 separate artillery and mortar regiments, 22 of which were guards-mortar regiments, and 14 separate battalions to the east. The bulk of these reinforcements went to the Trans-Baikal Front. So great was the quantity of forces flowing to Malinovsky's *front* and so restricted the carrying capacity of the railroad lines that many formations had to detrain between Chita and Karymskaia and complete the 124–249 miles (200–400 kilometers) to their concentration areas on foot.

The dual requirements to prepare the theater of operations for a full-fledged strategic offensive and the forces to operate in diverse, difficult, and often roadless terrain necessitated the creation of a massive engineer support structure in all operating *fronts*. First and foremost this meant transferring large numbers of engineers and engineer forces from the west. As a first step, in early 1945 the two *fronts* and Coastal Group of Forces formed new brigades and regiments from a nucleus of 20 separate engineer battalions and other small engineer and sapper subunits already in the theater. From these forces the Trans-Baikal Front formed the 67th Motorized Engineer Brigade and the 68th Engineer-Sapper Brigade, the Far Eastern Front, the 47th Motorized Engineer Brigade, the 10th Pontoon-Bridge Brigade, and the 3d Pontoon-Bridge Regiment, and the Coastal Group, the 27th Engineer-Sapper

TABLE 4: ARTILLERY ASSIGNED TO TRANS-BAIKAL AND FAR EASTERN FRONTS AND COASTAL GROUP OF FORCES, 1 AUGUST 1945

Artillery Forces	*Fronts*			
	Trans-Baikal	*Far Eastern*	*Coastal Group*	*Total*
Artillery corps headquarters	1	–	–	1
Artillery divisions	2*	–	–	2
Antiaircraft artillery divisions RVGK	4	1	2	7
Separate antitank artillery brigades	5	2	–	7
Separate army gun artillery brigades	2	–	1	3
Separate high-power howitzer artillery brigades	–	–	2	2
Separate light artillery brigades	1	–	–	1
Separate guards-mortar brigades	2	–	3	5
Separate antitank artillery regiments	2	–	1	3
Separate gun artillery regiments	1	–	1	2
Separate mortar regiments	2	–	1	3
Separate guards-mortar regiments	11	3	8	22
Separate antiaircraft artillery regiments	2	–	1	3
Separate special-power artillery battalions	–	–	2	2
Separate antiaircraft artillery battalions	5	3	4	12

*Includes the 3d Guards Artillery Penetration Division (the 8th Guards Howitzer Artillery, 22d Guards Gun Artillery, and 99th Heavy Howitzer Artillery, the 43d Mortar and 50th Heavy Mortar, and the 14th Guards-Mortar Brigades) and the 6th Guards Artillery Penetration Division (the 29th Guards Light Artillery, 69th Light Artillery, 87th Heavy Howitzer Artillery, and 134th Howitzer Artillery, the 4th Mortar, and the 10th Guards-Mortar Brigades).

Source: N. V. Eronin, *Strategicheskaia peregruppirovka Sovetskikh vooruzhennykh sil (pri podgotovka Dal'nevostochnoi kampanii 1945 goda)* [The strategic regrouping of the Soviet armed forces (during the preparations for the Far Eastern campaign of 1945)] (Moscow: Voroshilov General Staff Academy, 1980), 60.

Brigade, the 46th Motorized Engineer Brigade, the 11th Pontoon-Bridge Brigade, and the 6th Pontoon-Bridge Regiment.

However, even these forces fell far short of meeting requirements. Therefore, at the GKO and *Stavka's* direction, the General Staff's Engineer Directorate dispatched a large quantity of fresh engineer forces to the East (see Table 5).

The regrouping of so many engineer forces to the east lowered the percentage of those who had experience operating in the unique conditions of the Manchurian theater. By August, for example, the engineer force in the newly formed 2d Far Eastern Front consisted primarily of experienced local units with the exception of the 21st Motorized Assault Engineer-Sapper Brigade, which arrived in the region in June. Toward the other end of the spectrum, 50 per cent of the 1st Far Eastern Front's engineer force was made

TABLE 5: ENGINEER FORCES DISPATCHED TO THE EAST, SUMMER 1945

Engineer Forces	*Fronts*			
	Trans-Baikal	*Far Eastern*	*Coastal Group*	*Total*
Assault engineer-sapper, motorized engineer, and engineer-sapper brigades	7	1	4	12
Pontoon-bridge brigades	1	–	–	1
Separate pontoon-bridge regiment	1	–	–	1
Separate pontoon-bridge battalion	–	–	4	4
Separate maskirovka companies	2	–	1	3
Separate hydro-technical companies	7	–	2	9

Source: N. V. Eronin, *Strategicheskaia peregruppirovka Sovetskikh vooruzhennykh sil (pri podgotovka Dal'nevostochnoi kampanii 1945 goda)* [The strategic regrouping of the Soviet armed forces (during the preparations for the Far Eastern campaign of 1945)] (Moscow: Voroshilov General Staff Academy, 1980), 20.

up of local units, and the other 50 per cent arrived from the west in April and May. Fortunately, most of these regrouped engineers arrived early enough to permit them to train extensively and become quite familiar with the region. At the other extreme, the bulk of the Trans-Baikal Front's engineers regrouped from the west.[65]

While the personnel manning level in engineer forces reached 85–90 per cent fill and organic equipment was generally adequate to sustain operations, some shortages were evident. For example, the hydro-technical companies lacked their equipment and could not be used in their specialty. More serious was the deficit of vehicles in the motorized engineer units, which required up to 50 per cent replacement vehicles, and, in some cases, severely reduced the unit's maneuverability and mobility. Finally, shortages in bridging equipment also inhibited operations in some regions. In general, however, official assessments noted that, despite their experience in the Far Eastern theater, the engineer forces transferred from the west performed their missions well, although they lagged behind the 'easterners' in several respects, particularly regarding 'water discipline' in desert operations.[66]

The vast extent of the theater of operations made effective signal communications immensely important. As was the case in other realms, in January 1945 in-theater signal forces were wholly inadequate to support a major offensive. On hand signal forces consisted of a total of 15 separate battalions and 37 separate companies of various types. To establish internal communications between the *fronts*, fleet, and main command and external communications with the *Stavka* and the General Staff, the GKO formed the 5th Signal Brigade in theater and during the summer dispatched substantial signal forces from the west. These included the 2d and 8th RGK Signal Brigades, the 9th, 13th, and 16th NKVD Signal Brigades, the 252d Separate

Aviation Signal Regiment, 33 separate signal battalions, and 46 separate signal companies, including ten VNOS (early aircraft detection and warning) companies.[67] The vast majority of these units supported the Trans-Baikal Front, where local communications were virtually non-existent.

A summary of the overall scale of the regrouping effort in terms of the number of ground force formations and units regrouped within and to the region in shown by Table 6.

TABLE 6: FORCES REGROUPED WITHIN AND TO THE TRANS-BAIKAL AND FAR EAST REGIONS, 1945

Forces	*Fronts*			
	Trans-Baikal	*2d Far Eastern*	*1st Far Eastern*	*Total*
Front headquarters	1	–	1	2
Combined-arms army headquarters	2	–	1	3
Rifle corps headquarters	6	–	4	10
Artillery corps headquarters	1	–	–	1
Tank armies	1*	–	–	1
Separate mechanized corps	1**	–	–	1
Rifle Divisions	18	–	9	27
Artillery divisions	2***	–	–	2
Antiaircraft artillery divisions	4	1	3	8
Fortified regions	–	–	2	2
Separate rifle and machine gun-artillery brigades	2	–	3	5
Separate tank brigades	1	–	–	1
Separate self-propelled artillery brigades	2	–	–	2
Separate artillery brigades	6	3	4	13
Separate mortar brigades	3	–	3	6
Engineer brigades	8	1	4	13
Signal brigades	2	2	1	5
Separate self-propelled artillery regiments	–	–	9	9
Separate artillery and mortar regiments	13	6	17	36
Separate self-propelled artillery battalions	30	12	19	61
Separate artillery battalions	–	–	11	11
Separate antiaircraft artillery battalions	9	8	6	23
Separate signal battalions	14	10	9	33
Other units and subunits	150	101	127	378

* Includes 1 tank and 2 mechanized corps with a total of 5 tank and 6 mechanized brigades and 1 motorized rifle brigade.
** Includes 1 tank and 3 mechanized brigades.
*** Includes 12 artillery and mortar brigades.
Source: N. V. Eronin, *Strategicheskaia peregruppirovka Sovetskikh vooruzhennykh sil (pri podgotovka Dal'nevostochnoi kampanii 1945 goda)* [The strategic regrouping of the Soviet armed forces (during the preparations for the Far Eastern campaign of 1945)] (Moscow: Voroshilov General Staff Academy, 1980), 63–64.

The quantities of forces, weapons, and equipment regrouped from the west during the summer of 1945 are shown in Table 7.

TABLE 7: FORCES AND EQUIPMENT REGROUPED TO FAR EAST, SUMMER 1945

Forces and Equipment	*May*	*June*	*July*	*1–8 August*	*Total*
Personnel	33,456	152,408	206,042	11,449	403,355
Rifles and carbines	13,343	79,295	83,334	4,644	180,616
Machine pistols	4,041	37,802	38,061	3,073	82,977
Submachine guns and machine guns	1,177	5,800	3,482	164	10,623
Guns and mortars	504	2,624	3,723	286	7,137
Tanks and self-propelled guns	156	564	1,229	170	2,119
Cargo vehicles	1,059	4,475	10,424	1,416	17,374
Tractors and locomotives	77	477	895	33	1,482
Horses	4,983	18,533	12,764	–	36,280

Source: Istoriia Vtoroi Mirovoi voiny 1939–1945, T. 11 [History of the Second World War 1939–1945, Vol. 11] (Moscow: Voenizdat, 1980), 193.

A total of 63 per cent of the forces regrouped during the summer did so by rail. Table 8 shows the intensity of this rail movement to and within the Far Eastern Theater.

TABLE 8: INTENSITY OF OPERATIONAL REGROUPING BY RAIL

Type of Regrouping	*Quantity by Month*							
	May		*June*		*July*		*Total*	
	Trains	*Rail cars*	*Trains*	*Rail cars*	*Trains*	*Rail cars*	*Trains*	*Rail cars*
GKO-planned operational trains	33	1,143	226	13,514	466	25,460	725	40,117
Front-planned operational trains	95	2,510	180	6,900	141	5,020	416	14,430
Total	128	3,658	406	20,414	607	30,480	1,141	54,547

Source: N. V. Eronin, *Strategicheskaia peregruppirovka Sovetskikh vooruzhennykh sil (pri podgotovka Dal'nevostochnoi kampanii 1945 goda)* [The strategic regrouping of the Soviet armed forces (during the preparations for the Far Eastern campaign of 1945)] (Moscow: Voroshilov General Staff Academy, 1980), 65.

Similarly, the GKO had to regroup substantial numbers of air force formations and units to the Far Eastern theater to support the planned offensive operation. Tables 9–11 indicate the scope and magnitude of this regrouping effort.

TABLE 9: AIR FORCES IN FAR EAST, JANUARY 1945

Force	*No. of of aircraft*	*Bomber aviation divisions*	*Assault aviation divisions*	*Fighter aviation divisions*	*Total*
12th Air Army	730	30th and 247th	248th and 316th	245th and 246th	6
10th Air Army	1,000	83d	96th and 253d	29th, 254th, and 296th	6
9th Air Army	770	33d	251st and 252d	32d, 249th, and 250th	6
Total	2,500	4	6	8	18
Pacific Fleet Air Force	1,000	2	1	1	4

Source: N. V. Eronin, *Strategicheskaia peregruppirovka Sovetskikh vooruzhennykh sil (pri podgotovka Dal'nevostochnoi kampanii 1945 goda)* [The strategic regrouping of the Soviet armed forces (during the preparations for the Far Eastern campaign of 1945)] (Moscow: Voroshilov General Staff Academy, 1980), 67.

TABLE 10: GENERAL COMPOSITION OF FAR EAST COMMAND AIR ARMIES, 9 AUGUST 1945

Force	*Bomber aviation divisions*	*Assault aviation divisions*	*Fighter aviation divisions*	*Mixed aviation divisions*	*Transport aviation divisions*	*Total*
12th Air Army, Trans-Baikal Front	6	2	3	–	2	13
10th Air Army, 2d Far Eastern Front	1	2	3	2	–	8
9th Air Army, 1st Far Eastern Front	3	2	3	–	–	8
Total	10	6	9	2	2	29

Source: N. V. Eronin, *Strategicheskaia peregruppirovka Sovetskikh vooruzhennykh sil (pri podgotovka Dal'nevostochnoi kampanii 1945 goda)* [The strategic regrouping of the Soviet armed forces (during the preparations for the Far Eastern campaign of 1945)] (Moscow: Voroshilov General Staff Academy, 1980), 68.

The GKO resolved the problem of reinforcing the 9th Air Army, which it assigned to the Coastal Group of Forces in April 1945, by allocating to it forces from the 19th Long-range Bomber Aviation Corps (the 34th and 55th Long-range Bomber Aviation Divisions), which had been formed in the Komsomol'-on-the-Amur region in late 1944. It also reinforced the Far Eastern Front's 10th Air Army with the 128th and 255th Mixed Aviation Divisions, which it allocated to support the *front's* forces deployed on northern Sakhalin Island and in Kamchatka, and the 15th and 16th Mixed Aviation Divisions to support the *front* as a whole.

As was the case with its ground forces, the Trans-Baikal Front obtained

TABLE 11: SPECIFIC COMPOSITION OF AIR FORCES IN MANCHURIAN THEATER, 9 AUGUST 1945

Forces	*12th Air Army*	*10th Air Army*	*9th Air Army*	*Fleet Air Force*	*Total*
Aviation divisions	13	8	8	6	35
Fighter	3	3	3	1	10
Assault	2	2	2	1	7
Bomber	6	1	3	1	11
Mine-Torpedo	–	–	–	1	1
Mixed	–	2	–	2	4
Transport	2	–	–	–	2
Aircraft	1,365	1,269	1,158	1,126	5,058
Fighter	581	779	536	554	2,450
Assault	115	178	168	177	638
Bomber	404	130	258	426	1,218
Torpedo	–	–	–	–	–
Reconnaissance	40	47	61	109	257
Correction (artillery)	–	39	34	–	73
Communications	46	72	86	–	204
Transport	179	24	15	–	218

Source: N. V. Eronin, *Strategicheskaia peregruppirovka Sovetskikh vooruzhennykh sil (pri podgotovka Dal'nevostochnoi kampanii 1945 goda)* [The strategic regrouping of the Soviet armed forces (during the preparations for the Far Eastern campaign of 1945)] (Moscow: Voroshilov General Staff Academy, 1980), 72.

most of its air assets from the west, which made up 38 per cent of all forces dispatched to the East. These included:

- the 6th Bomber Aviation Corps, consisting of the 113th and 179th Bomber Aviation Divisions and the 368th Separate Fighter Aviation Regiment;
- the 7th Bomber Aviation Corps, consisting of the 326th and 334th Bomber Aviation Divisions;
- the 21st Guards and 54th Transport and 190th Fighter Aviation Divisions;
- the 117th Separate Corrective Reconnaissance Aviation Regiment and the 4th, 25th, and 207th Guards Separate Signal Aviation Regiments; and
- the 365th, 424th, 563d, and 572d Separate Aviation Squadrons.[68]

At the same time, the GKO, *Stavka*, and Far East commands created an extensive new network of bases in the Far East and Trans-Baikal regions to accommodate the immense number of aircraft.[69] By 9 August construction forces had built six new airfields for the 9th Air Army, four for the 10th Air Army, and 43 for the 12th Air Army, in addition to hundreds of main and auxiliary command posts, protected covers for aircraft, and other air facilities. Table 12 shows the bases available to these forces on 9 August and the relative distance of these bases from the front lines

TABLE 12: AIR BASES IN FAR EASTERN THEATER AND DISTANCE FROM FRONT LINES

		Distance from the front lines (km)			
Air Army	*Total airfields*	*Up to 25*	*25–50*	*50–75*	*Over 75*
9th	110	–	–	–	–
10th	170	23	–	53	94
12th	96	56	9	24	7

Source: N. V. Eronin, *Strategicheskaia peregruppirovka Sovetskikh vooruzhennykh sil (pri podgotovka Dal'nevostochnoi kampanii 1945 goda)* [The strategic regrouping of the Soviet armed forces (during the preparations for the Far Eastern campaign of 1945)] (Moscow: Voroshilov General Staff Academy, 1980), 76.

THE REGROUPING OF LOGISTICAL FORCES, WEAPONRY, EQUIPMENT, AND SUPPLIES TO THE FAR EAST

The GKO and *Stavka* supported their expanded force structure in the Far East logistically by deploying an impressive numbers of specialized facilities, units, equipment, and supplies to the region. This massive logistical effort included medical, armored repair and reconstruction, and road construction and maintenance forces and weaponry, equipment, and supplies of every type. While many of these units and supplies flowed eastward from the European theater and the central Soviet Union, many also arrived from the United States, as supplemental Lend-Lease materials shipped on non-US flag-ships to the port of Vladivostok.

In early March 1945, Antonov, the chief of the General Staff, examined and approved a report prepared by the Main Medical Directorate concerning medical support for Red Army forces in the Far Eastern theater, which recommended the transfer of 348 different medical support units and facilities to the Far East and the filling out of units and facilities already in the Trans-Baikal and Amur Districts. Owing to the heavy traffic along the rail network, however, many of these medical forces arrived late. For example, by 9 August the 2d Far Eastern Front fielded only 30 per cent of its planned medical support.[70]

Table 13 shows the number of medical units and facilities organic and regrouped to the Far Eastern theater by the time the Manchurian campaign began.

In a theater as vast as the Far East, aviation should have played a significant role in the evacuation of wounded and sick soldiers. However, the medical service lacked the requisite numbers of aircraft to perform this function adequately. For example, by 9 August the Trans-Baikal Front had only one medical aviation regiment and two medical aviation squadrons, for a total of

TABLE 13: MEDICAL INSTALLATIONS AND FACILITIES ORGANIC AND DEPLOYED TO FAR EASTERN THEATER, BY 9 AUGUST 1945

Type	*Organic*	*Arrived*	*Total*	*Total in each* front		
				Trans-Baikal	*1st Far Eastern*	*2d Far Eastern*
Total facilities and units, including:	316	425	741	376	250	115
Field hospitals and	88	111	199	93	83	23
bed capacity				36,800	28,300	6,500
Evac. hospitals and	69	144	213	114	68	31
bed capacity				38,400	34,200	16,300
Field evacuation points	11	8	19	7	6	5
Separate medical companies	2	8	10	2	4	4
Separate auto-medical companies	11	5	16	7	5	4
Separate cavalry medical companies	–	13	13	5	4	4
Separate auto-medical platoons	5	5	10	4	2	4
Anti-epidemic facilities	33	30	63	40	14	9
Disinfectant trains	9	–	9	2	5	2
Disinfectant detachments and points	26	50	76	54	11	11
Military-medical teams	17	30	47	17	28	2
Laboratories	11	6	17	8	5	4
Transfusion stations	2	2	4	2	1	1
Veterinary hospitals	15	3	18	9	6	3
Medical warehouses	17	10	27	12	8	7

Source: N. V. Eronin, *Strategicheskaia peregruppirovka Sovetskikh vooruzhennykh sil (pri podgotovka Dal'nevostochnoi kampanii 1945 goda)* [The strategic regrouping of the Soviet armed forces (during the preparations for the Far Eastern campaign of 1945)] (Moscow: Voroshilov General Staff Academy, 1980), 80.

56 aircraft. At the same time, the 1st Far Eastern Front had one medical aviation regiment with 32 aircraft and the 2d Far Eastern Front four aviation squadrons with 48 aircraft. Nor was the situation with doctors any better. The 2d Far Eastern Front had only 46 per cent of its required doctors, and doctors could not be mobilized from the local community. Therefore, the bulk of replacement doctors came from more than 150 disbanded military hospitals in the European theater.[71]

Most medical support was provided to arriving troops either at medical control points along the railroad, at unloading stations, or in the force concentration areas. The dispatch and receipt of reinforcements made up for most of the shortages in medical support. By 9 August, each operating army had up to 12 mobile field hospitals, two to four military hospitals for the lightly wounded, two for infectious deceases, and one to two sorting-evacuation hospitals, and the 1st and 2d Far Eastern Fronts had a variety of railroad medical clinics. In addition, the three *fronts* fielded tens of mobile field and evacuation hospitals and a considerable number of fixed or temporary medical trains.

Given the large number of armored and mechanized formations taking part in the Manchurian campaign, it was necessary to reinforce the three *fronts* with a great number of tank repair and reconstruction units and facilities. Table 14 shows the quantity of the supporting forces which the GKO and *Stavka* planned to field in the Far East Command.

TABLE 14: ARMOR REPAIR AND EVACUATION ORGANIZATIONS AND FACILITIES PLANNED FOR DEPLOYMENT TO FAR EAST

Organizations and Facilities	Fronts			
	Trans-Baikal	*2d Far Eastern*	*1st Far Eastern*	*Total*
PTARZ – Mobile tank-assembly repair factories	2	1	1	4
PTRZ – Mobile tank repair factories	1	1	1	3
OTRB – Separate tank repair battalions	8	1	4	13
PTRB – Mobile tank repair battalions	9	4	8	21
BTRB – Armored repair bases	1	–	–	1
BTRTsP – Mobile armored repair centers	–	–	1	1
BTRZ – Stationary armored repair factories	1	1	1	3
OPKS – Separate mobile collection stations	1	1	1	3
SPAM – Damaged vehicle collection points	7	2	3	12
ETR – Evacuation transport companies	9	2	5	16
EtrB – Evacuation transport battalions	2	–	1	3
EvB – Evacuation battalions	1	1	1	3
PSRP – Field collection distribution points	1	1	1	3
BTRETs – Armored repair and evacuation centers	1	–	1	2
Warehouses	3	2	2	7

Source: N. V. Eronin, *Strategicheskaia peregruppirovka Sovetskikh vooruzhennykh sil (pri podgotovka Dal'nevostochnoi kampanii 1945 goda)* [The strategic regrouping of the Soviet armed forces (during the preparations for the Far Eastern campaign of 1945)] (Moscow: Voroshilov General Staff Academy, 1980), 81.

Of the 94 armor repair and reconstruction units and facilities the GKO and *Stavka* planned to field in the Far East, only 26 were organic to the theater in April 1945 (see Table 15).

The remaining 68 repair and evacuation units had to be regrouped from the European theater and the central Soviet Union. However, only 57 managed to reach the region by 9 August (see Table 16 for their distribution).

By 25 August another eight units had arrived, including 2 PTRZ, 2 SPAM, 1 PTRB, 2 EvB, and 1 PSRP, but the remainder failed to reach the theater before the campaign ended. Those repair and reconstruction units already

TABLE 15: ARMOR REPAIR AND EVACUATION ORGANIZATIONS AND FACILITIES IN FAR EAST, APRIL 1945

Organizations and Facilities	*Trans-Baikal*	*Far Eastern*	*Coastal Group*	*Total*
OTRB – Separate tank repair battalions	–	–	1	1
PTRB – Mobile tank repair battalions	2	3	4	9
BTRB – Armored repair bases	1	–	–	1
BTRP – Armored repair regiments	–	–	1	1
BTRZ – Stationary armored repair factories	1	1	1	3
ETR – Evacuation transport companies	1	–	–	1
ORVB – Separate repair and reconstruction battalions	–	–	1	1
RVR – Repair and reconstruction companies	2	–	–	2
Warehouses	3	2	2	7

Source: N. V. Eronin, *Strategicheskaia peregruppirovka Sovetskikh vooruzhennykh sil (pri podgotovka Dal'nevostochnoi kampanii 1945 goda)* [The strategic regrouping of the Soviet armed forces (during the preparations for the Far Eastern campaign of 1945)] (Moscow: Voroshilov General Staff Academy, 1980), 82.

TABLE 16: ARMOR REPAIR AND EVACUATION ORGANIZATIONS AND FACILITIES IN FAR EAST, 9 AUGUST 1945

Organizations and Facilities	*Trans-Baikal*	*2d Far Eastern*	*1st Far Eastern*	*Total*
PTARZ – Mobile tank-assembly repair factories	1	1	1	3
PTRZ – Mobile tank repair factories	–	–	1	1
OTRB – Separate tank repair battalions	4	1	2	7
PTRB – Mobile tank repair battalions	7	1	3	11
OPKS – Separate mobile collection stations	1	1	1	3
SPAM – Damaged vehicle collection points	7	2	2	11
ETR – Evacuation transport companies	7	1	5	13
EtrB – Evacuation transport battalions	2	–	1	3
EvB – Evacuation battalions	–	–	1	1
PSRP – Field collection distribution points	1	–	1	2
BTRETs – Armored repair and evacuation centers	1	–	1	2

Source: N. V. Eronin, *Strategicheskaia peregruppirovka Sovetskikh vooruzhennykh sil (pri podgotovka Dal'nevostochnoi kampanii 1945 goda)* [The strategic regrouping of the Soviet armed forces (during the preparations for the Far Eastern campaign of 1945)] (Moscow: Voroshilov General Staff Academy, 1980), 82.

in theater when the campaign was being planned required considerable training to be able to service the newer model tanks, since until that point the tank park in the Far East consisted only of older model light tanks. While many of the deploying units had the necessary field experience, their original personnel required training in the repair of older model tanks, and their replacements needed training for operations in field conditions.

One of the most challenging tasks associated with planning the Manchurian offensive was the necessity of 'preparing' the theater of military operations, in particular, building a road network that could support such large-scale military operations. In April 1945 the road network in the Far East and Trans-Baikal region was woefully underdeveloped. At this time, there were only 1,415 miles (2,278 kilometers) of military-automobile roads in the Trans-Baikal Front's sector, 938 miles (1,509 kilometers) in the 1st Far Eastern Front's sector, and 298 miles (485 kilometers) in the 2d Far Eastern Front's sector. The military-automotive roads [*voenno-automobil'nye doregy* – VAD] in the 35th Army's sector encompassed slightly more than 93 miles (150 kilometers) of road, in the 25th Army's sector, 349 miles (568 kilometers) of roadway, and in the 39th and 6th Guards Tank Armies' sector, only about 217 miles (350 kilometers) of suitable roads.[72]

Nor were the road construction and maintenance forces in the region able to erect or maintain a more suitable road network (see Table 17).

TABLE 17: ROAD CONSTRUCTION UNITS IN FAR EAST, APRIL 1945

Types of Units	Fronts			
	Trans-Baikal	*Far Eastern*	*Coastal Group*	*Total*
VAD – Military-automotive roads	1	–	–	1
Separate road exploitation regiments	1	–	–	1
Separate road exploitation battalions	1	2	2	5
Separate road construction battalions	–	1	–	1
Separate bridge construction battalions	–	–	–	–
Total units	3	3	2	8

Source: N. V. Eronin, *Strategicheskaia peregruppirovka Sovetskikh vooruzhennykh sil (pri podgotovka Dal'nevostochnoi kampanii 1945 goda)* [The strategic regrouping of the Soviet armed forces (during the preparations for the Far Eastern campaign of 1945)] (Moscow: Voroshilov General Staff Academy, 1980), 84.

Although the *fronts* and armies in the Far East fielded a large number of road construction battalions, they were ill equipped to enlarge the network in such difficult terrain. Consequently, the GKO and *Stavka* regrouped significant numbers of road construction and maintenance forces from the West (see Table 18).

The deployment and concentration of so large a force within the theater also required a significant number of trucks and other prime movers that were not available in early 1945. These too were regrouped into the region from the West and central portions of the country (see Tables 19 and 20).

TABLE 18: ROAD CONSTRUCTION UNITS REGROUPED TO FAR EAST, MAY–JULY 1945

Types of Units	Fronts			
	Trans-Baikal	*2d Far Eastern*	*1st Far Eastern*	*Total*
VAD – Military-automobile roads	2	1	1	4
Separate road exploitation battalions	6	1	5	12
Separate road construction battalions	9	7	10	26
Separate bridge construction battalions	3	2	5	10
Total units	20	11	21	52

Source: N. V. Eronin, *Strategicheskaia peregruppirovka Sovetskikh vooruzhennykh sil (pri podgotovka Dal'nevostochnoi kampanii 1945 goda)* [The strategic regrouping of the Soviet armed forces (during the preparations for the Far Eastern campaign of 1945)] (Moscow: Voroshilov General Staff Academy, 1980), 84.

TABLE 19: TRANSPORT UNITS IN FAR EAST, APRIL 1945

Types of Units	Fronts			
	Trans-Baikal	*Far Eastern*	*Coastal Group*	*Total*
Automobile brigade headquarters	–	–	–	–
Separate automobile regiment	–	1	–	1
Separate auto-transport battalions	3	6	6	15
Separate automobile tanker-truck battalions	–	–	–	–
Separate animal drawn transport companies	1	–	–	1
Total units	4	7	6	17

Source: N. V. Eronin, *Strategicheskaia peregruppirovka Sovetskikh vooruzhennykh sil (pri podgotovka Dal'nevostochnoi kampanii 1945 goda)* [The strategic regrouping of the Soviet armed forces (during the preparations for the Far Eastern campaign of 1945)] (Moscow: Voroshilov General Staff Academy, 1980), 85.

TABLE 20: TRANSPORT UNITS REGROUPED TO FAR EAST, MAY-JULY 1945

Types of Units	Fronts		
	Trans-Baikal	*1st Far Eastern*	*Total*
Automobile brigade headquarters	2	1	3
Separate automobile regiment	8	5	13
Separate auto-transport battalions	11	2	13
Separate automobile tanker-truck battalions	3	3	6
Separate animal drawn transport companies	5	–	5
Total units	29	11	40

Source: N. V. Eronin, *Strategicheskaia peregruppirovka Sovetskikh vooruzhennykh sil (pri podgotovka Dal'nevostochnoi kampanii 1945 goda)* [The strategic regrouping of the Soviet armed forces (during the preparations for the Far Eastern campaign of 1945)] (Moscow: Voroshilov General Staff Academy, 1980), 86.

Thanks to this effort, by 9 August 1945, the Far Eastern Command was able to field more than 100,000 trucks and numerous tractors subdivided as follows:

Trans-Baikal Front	–	49,053 trucks
1st Far Eastern Front	–	37,119 trucks
Air armies	–	3,000–4,000 trucks each
PVO army	–	800 trucks
6th Guards Tank Army	–	7,000 trucks

In addition, the United States shipped several thousand trucks through the port of Vladivostok to augment the vehicles being shipped from the west. These were above and beyond the quantities already agreed upon under the auspices of Lend Lease. This required thousands of men to be mobilized to drive and service the vehicles.

All of these regroupings necessitated the shipment of thousands of tons of supplies to the theater, both from the west and from the United States via Vladivostok, and the construction of a vast network of warehouses to store and distribute these supplies. To support such a massive effort, the GKO and *Stavka* deployed or constructed about 400 warehouses, including 96 for fuel and lubricants, 66 for artillery pieces and ammunition, and 41 for aviation support. Of this number, 70 arrived from the European theater or central region of the country.[73]

Military supplies to support the Far East Command came from two sources: internally collected reserve stocks, and shipments from the west during the preparatory stage of the operation. Existing in-theater stocks ranged from a four-month supply in the 1st Far Eastern Front to a year's supply in Kamchatka and on Sakhalin Island. Since weaponry had routinely been shipped to the West during the war, inadequate stocks existed in the Far East. However, from December 1944 through April 1945, 4,640 mortars, about 2,200 guns of various caliber, more than 410 million rounds of rifle ammunition, and about 3.2 million artillery were shipped to the Far East.

Modern tanks, in particular, were in short supply in the region. Most of the existing tank arsenal consisted of light T-26 and BT tanks, which had been in service for between seven and 12 years. Since armored and mechanized forces would play a significant role in the upcoming offensive, in March 1945 the *Stavka* decided to accelerate the shipment of tanks to the east. These shipments included 1,400 tanks from the Ural tank factories, 500 each for the Trans-Baikal and 1st Far Eastern Fronts and 400 for the 2d Far Eastern Front.

This permitted the formation of one battalion of T-34 medium tanks in each of the tank brigades in the Far East and the equipping of one regiment each in the 61st and 111th Tank Divisions with T-34 tanks. In June and July, the 6th Guards Tank Army picked up 400 T-34 tanks from the Ural tank factories during its regrouping to the Trans-Baikal region. Thus, by late July, the forces in the Far East had received about 1,800 new T-34 tanks. In addition, between April and July, the *Stavka* dispatched 1,400 self-propelled guns to the Far East, including about 200 ISU-152s, 260 SU-100s, and 940 SU-76s.[74]

The overall supply effort involved massive shipments of all sorts of supplies to the Far Eastern theater. These shipments totaled 45,596 loaded railroad cars, including 9,438 in May, 13,462 in June, 16,892 in July, and 6,804 in the first nine days of August. In June, the transport authorities allocated eight trains per day to carry the cargo, including two for fuel and lubricants, three for shipment from various commissariats, and three for other equipment. By volume, 13 per cent was allocated for ammunition, 51 per cent for fuel and lubricants, and 19 per cent for foodstuffs and animal feed. As of 30 May, 320 supply trains were concentrated at the railhead at Mariinsk Station, meaning that it would take 40 days to move the trains to the east (at a rate of eight per day).

The movement of Lend-Lease cargoes earmarked for the Far East took place between 1 and 20 June. The Chief of the Soviet Army Rear Services ordered 24,000 tons of Lend-Lease stocks to be moved from Vladivostok to *front* warehouses. This included 15,000 tons of animal fat, 8,000 tons of meat products, and 1,000 tons of milk products. In addition, Lend-Lease fuel, equipment, vehicles, and weapons, in particular about 500 Sherman tanks for the 6th Guards Tank Army, were transferred from the ports of Vladivostok and Nakhodka.[75]

Despite these strenuous efforts to supply the forces in the Far East with necessary materials and supplies, Soviet critiques identified many problems and shortages. These included bottlenecks in the movement of artillery supplies and slower than planned fuel resupply because of 'poorly trained *front* rear service personnel and organs'. The Irkutsk–Chita–Karymskaia sector proved to be the greatest transport bottleneck as well as the limited lines and routes into Mongolia.[76] Table 21 summarises the total quantity of supplies on hand in the three operating *fronts* on 9 August 1945.

Overall, the GKO, *Stavka*, and General Staff planned and conducted the regrouping of up to 500,000 troops, two *front*, four army, and 17 corps headquarters, 125 divisions and brigades, 500 separate combat units, 700 rear service units and facilities, 3,340 tanks and self-propelled guns, more than 12,000 guns and mortars, and 1,400 combat aircraft to the Far East, which nearly doubled the combat strength of the theater of military operations. The redeployment process had the cumulative effect of increasing the strength of Soviet forces in the Far East from one million men organized into 47 divisions (41 rifle, two cavalry, two motorized rifle, and two tank) and 31 separate brigades (four rifle, three motorized rifle, and 24 tank) on 1 May 1945 to more than 1.5 million men in four tank and mechanized corps,

TABLE 21: RESERVES OF SUPPLIES IN FAR EASTERN COMMAND'S *FRONTS*, 9 AUGUST 1945

Types of Supplies	Fronts		
	Trans-Baikal	*2d Far Eastern*	*1st Far Eastern*
Fuel and lubricants:			
Refills	4.8	1.8	1.8
Weight per refill	8,100 tons	3,250 tons	7,800 tons
Total weight	38,880 tons	5,850 tons	14,040 tons
Ammunition:			
Combat loads	4.0	3.4	4.0
Weight per combat load	20,000 tons	7,020 tons	22,980 tons
Total weight	80,000 tons	23,868 tons	95,920 tons
Food and forage:			
Flour	14 days of supply	76 days of supply	36 days of supply
Groats	19 days of supply	46 days of supply	27 days of supply
Meat	36 days of supply	73 days of supply	54 days of supply
Sugar	72 days of supply	237 days of supply	66 days of supply
Fat and oils	68 days of supply	314 days of supply	90 days of supply
Vegetables	6 days of supply	25 days of supply	7 days of supply
Weight of one day of supply	1,273 tons	553 tons	903 tons

Source: N. V. Eronin, *Strategicheskaia peregruppirovka Sovetskikh vooruzhennykh sil (pri podgotovka Dal'nevostochnoi kampanii 1945 goda)* [The strategic regrouping of the Soviet armed forces (during the preparations for the Far Eastern campaign of 1945)] (Moscow: Voroshilov General Staff Academy, 1980), 93.

80 divisions and 37 separate brigades on 9 August 1945.[77] Tables 22 and 23 show the dynamics of the time-phased build-up of Soviet military forces in the Far East.

TABLE 22: COMBAT COMPOSITION OF SOVIET GROUND AND AIR FORCES IN FAR EAST, 1941–45

Type of Force	*Date*						
	22.6.41	*11.1.42*	*1.1.43*	*1.1.44*	*1.1.45*	*9.8.45*	*Regrouped 1.1.45–9.8.45*
Combined-arms army headquarters	7	7	7	8	8	11	3
Tank army headquarters	–	–	–	–	–	1	1
Air armies	–	–	4	4	3	3	–
PVO (air defense) armies	–	–	–	–	–	3	3
Rifle corps headquarters	6	4	7	10	10	19	9[(a)]
Tank and mechanized corps	1	–	–	–	1	4	3[(b)]
Artillery corps	–	–	–	–	–	1	1

Aviation corps	–	–	–	–	2	4	2
PVO corps	–	–	–	–	–	3	3
Rifle, motorized rifle, and cavalry divisions	24	26	23	32	45	78	33[c]
Tank and mechanized divisions	8	4	2	2	2	2	–
Artillery divisions	–	–	–	–	–	2	2[d]
Antiaircraft artillery divisions (RGK)	–	–	–	–	–	7	7
Antiaircraft artillery divisions (PVO)	–	–	–	–	–	8	8
Aviation divisions	6	23	20	23	23	31	8
Fortified regions	13	14	15	18	19	21	2
Separate rifle, motorized rifle, airborne, and machine gun–artillery brigades	4	5	29	26	5	7	2
Separate tank, mechanized, and motorized rifle, and self-propelled artillery brigades	1	6	21	24	27	30	3
Separate artillery and mortar brigades	–	–	2	–	–	46	46
Separate engineer brigades	–	–	3	3	5	20	15
Separate signal brigades	–	–	–	–	–	5	5
Separate railroad and technical brigades	2	2	2	2	2	11	9
Separate automobile brigades	–	–	–	–	–	3	3

[a]The 136th Mountain Rifle Corps (the 31st, 32d, and 72d Mountain Rifle Brigades) arrived on 16 August 1945.
[b]The 3d Guards Mechanized Corps (the 7th, 8th, and 9th Guards Tank and 35th Guards Mechanized Brigades and 43d Guards Tank Regiment) arrived on 25 August 1945.
[c]Includes the 5th, 6th, 7th, and 8th Mongolian Cavalry Divisions.
[d]Each artillery division contains six artillery and mortar brigades.
Source: N. V. Eronin, *Strategicheskaia peregruppirovka Sovetskikh vooruzhennykh sil (pri podgotovka Dal'nevostochnoi kampanii 1945 goda)* [The strategic regrouping of the Soviet armed forces (during the preparations for the Far Eastern campaign of 1945)] (Moscow: Voroshilov General Staff Academy, 1980), 127.

The volume of rail traffic involved in the massive regrouping effort best illustrates the complexity and magnitude of the redeployment. Overall, the Soviets employed 136,000 railroad cars to complete the movement, which extended from distances of 5,592–7,456 miles (9,000–12,000 kilometers). In June and July 1945, 22 to 30 trains were traveling along the Trans-Siberian railroad each day.[78] The redeploying forces also made extensive use of local roads to reach their final deployment areas. For example, the Trans-Baikal Front deployed from the main line of the Trans-Siberian railroad to Choibalsan, Mongolia, a distance of some 310–373 miles (500–600 kilometers), by both rail and road. Extensive redeployment also took place among units

TABLE 23: PERSONNEL AND WEAPONS STRENGTH OF SOVIET GROUND AND AIR FORCES IN FAR EAST, 1941–45

Category	*Date*						
	22.6.41	*11.1.42*	*1.1.43*	*1.1.44*	*1.1.45*	*9.8.45*	*Regrouped 1.1.45–9.8.45*
Personnel	650,700	1,206,300	1,131,700	1,033,900	1,010,400	1,577,700	567,300
In combat units	431,600	773,000	771,400	699,100	686,300	1,059,000	372,700
In rear service units	219,100	434,900	360,300	334,800	324,100	518,700	194,600
Tanks	5,571	2,361	2,518	2,066	2,197	3,704	1,507
Self-propelled guns	—	—	—	—	8	1,852	1,844
Guns		6,067	6,396	7,980	8,848	16,325	7,477
100 mm and greater		1,974	2,077	1,751	1,847	3,449	1,602
45–76 mm		3,182	3,197	4,955	5,477	8,674[a]	3,197
Antiaircraft		911	1,122	1,280	1,524	4,202[b]	2,678
Mortars		1,801	5,203	6,784	8,040	11,630	3,590
MRLs (M-8 and M-13)	—	—	48	48	48	1,171	1,123
Combat aircraft	3,021	2,271	2,482	3,135	2,503	3,889	1,386
Vehicles		65,380	55,011	43,935	45,010	83,143	38,133

[a]Includes 3,707 45–57 mm antitank guns.
[b]About 50 per cent of the antiaircraft guns belonged to PVO.
Source: N. V. Eronin, *Strategicheskaia peregruppirovka Sovetskikh vooruzhennykh sil (pri podgotovka Dal'nevostochnoi kampanii 1945 goda)* [The strategic regrouping of the Soviet armed forces (during the preparations for the Far Eastern campaign of 1945)] (Moscow: Voroshilov General Staff Academy, 1980), 128.

already located within the Far East and Trans-Baikal regions. From May to June 1945, for example, 30 divisions moved to new locations, a shift involving about one million men.[79]

Of the total number of railroad cars used to conduct the regrouping, 63 per cent transported operational forces and 37 per cent logistical materials. Operational trains were allocated as shown by Table 24.

TABLE 24: NATURE AND DESTINATION OF OPERATIONAL TRAINS

Total operational trains, 1,692

By origin
- Formations and units from the *Stavka* reserve and military districts, 588 trains (34.7 per cent)
- Formations and units from *fronts* in the west, 1,104 trains (65.3 per cent)

By type
- Rifle forces, 502 trains (29.7 per cent)
- Armored forces, 250 trains (14.8 per cent)
- Artillery forces, 261 trains (15.4 per cent)
- Engineer and other forces, 579 trains (40.1 per cent)

By destination
- Trans-Baikal Front, 827 trains (48.5 per cent)
- 1st Far Eastern Front, 629 trains (37.2 per cent)
- 2d Far Eastern Front, 236 trains (14.3 per cent)

Combat formations and units by destination (638 trains)
- Trans-Baikal Front, 265 trains (41.5 per cent)
- 1st Far Eastern Front, 227 trains (35.5 per cent)
- 2d Far Eastern Front, 146 trains (23 per cent)

By time (month)
- June 1945, 387 (23 per cent)
- July 1945, 676 (40 per cent)
- August 1945, 304 (18 per cent)

Source: N. V. Eronin, *Strategicheskaia peregruppirovka Sovetskikh vooruzhennykh sil (pri podgotovka Dal'nevostochnoi kampanii 1945 goda)* [The strategic regrouping of the Soviet armed forces (during the preparations for the Far Eastern campaign of 1945)] (Moscow: Voroshilov General Staff Academy, 1980), 98.

In general, the forces the GKO transferred from European Russia to the Far East and Trans-Baikal region provided a leavening of necessary combat experience and effective command and control for the newly created Far East Command. When selecting forces for transfer to the Far East, the *Stavka* and GKO consciously chose forces whose past combat experience ideally suited them to operate in the specific terrain in their newly assigned sector.

For example, the 39th Army, which had conducted operations in the heavily fortified Konigsberg region of East Prussia, was assigned the mission to overcome Japanese defenses in the Halung-Arshaan Fortified Region of western Manchuria. The 5th Army, which had also participated in the reduction of Konigsberg, was to penetrate the heavily fortified Japanese defensive zone in eastern Manchuria. Likewise, the 6th Guards Tank Army, which had fought its way through the Carpathian Mountains in 1944, was to advance across the forbidding terrain of the Grand Khingan Mountains in western Manchuria along with the 53d Army, which had also fought in the Carpathian Mountains.

Stalin and the *Stavka* also hand picked new commanders to organize and lead Red Army forces in the campaign. Once again, experience and performance were the primary criteria used in this selection process. Two *front* commanders, Marshals of the Soviet Union R. Ia. Malinovsky and K. A. Meretskov, two *front* chiefs of staff, Lieutenants General M. V. Zakharov and A. N. Krutikov, and four army commanders, Lieutenants General A. P. Beloborodov, I. M. Chistiakov, N. D. Zakhvataev, and A. A. Luchinsky, received postings to the Far East. Colonel General I. A. Pliev received command of the joint Soviet–Mongolian Cavalry-Mechanized Group.[80]

Most of these commanders either had previous experience fighting in the Far East or were associated with major headquarters that moved eastward. In June 1945 Stalin appointed his most trusted *Stavka* member, Marshal of the Soviet Union A. M. Vasilevsky, as *Stavka* coordinator of overall operations in the Far East and Trans-Baikal regions. Vasilevsky's major qualification for the position was his excellent prior service as representative of the *Stavka* in the west, where he had coordinated many successful operations, including the Stalingrad counteroffensive, the Battle of Kursk, and the Belorussian and East Prussian offensives.

Soon, however, it became apparent that the scope of operations in Manchuria was too great for a mere coordinator to handle. Consequently, on 30 June 1945, Stalin formed the Far East Command, officially termed the Main Command of Soviet Forces in the Far East [*Glavnoe komandovanie Sovetskikh voisk na Dal'nem Vostoke*], under Vasilevsky's command, backed by a full staff.[81] In effect the Far East Command was a full-fledged theater of military operations [*teatr voennykh deistvii – TVD*] headquarters, the first of its kind formed by the *Stavka* during the Second World War.[82]

To ensure the secrecy of the regrouping process and their intention to conduct an offensive, the *Stavka* employed deception extensively, including such measures as natural and artificial cover, concealment, and camouflage, to mask the massive movement of men and *matériel* eastward into the Far East and Trans-Baikal regions. Forces also relied heavily on night movements and simulated movements of forces away from the immediate border regions to deceive the Japanese as to the grand scale of redeployment. While the use of assembly areas remote from the border masked Soviet attack intentions, ultimately it also required forces to advance a considerable distance to occupy their jumping-off positions for the attack. All the while, most high-ranking commanders assigned to the theater command arrived using assumed names and wearing the rank of junior officers.[83]

Although the sheer size of Soviet troop and equipment movements into the Far East and Trans-Baikal regions made them impossible to mask completely, the deceptive measures employed managed to obscure the scale of those redeployments and caused the Japanese to underestimate the Soviet's offensive capabilities. In August most Japanese commanders believed that the Red Army would not be able to launch an offensive until the fall of 1945 or the spring of 1946. Few saw August as even a remote possibility. With the bulk of force deployments to the Far East complete by 25 July, the Soviet Far Eastern Command had only to set the date to begin offensive operations.

NOTES

1. M. V. Zakharov, *General'nyi shtab v predvoennye gody* [The General Staff in the prewar years] (Moscow: Voenizdat, 1989), 213–14.
2. M. M. Kozlov, ed., *Velikaia Otechestvennaia voina 1941–1945: Entsiklopediia* [The Great Patriotic War 1941–1945: An encyclopedia] (Moscow: 'Sovetskaia entsiklopediia', 1985), 229. Hereafter cited as *VOV*.
3. *VOV*, 274.
4. For the circumstances surrounding the negotiation of this pact, see G. V. Efimov, A. M. Dubinsky, *Mezhdunarodnye otnosheniia na Dal'nem Vostoke,* T. 2, *1917–1945 gg.* [Foreign relations in the Far East, Vol. 2, 1917–1945] (Moscow: 'Mysl',' 1973), 173–6.
5. *Istorii Vtoroi Mirovoi voiny 1939–1945*, T. 11 [History of the Second World War 1939–1945, Vol. 11] (Moscow: Voenizdat, 1980), 184–5. Hereafter cited at *IVMV*.
6. *Krasnoznamennyi dal'nevostochnyi* [The Red Banner Far Eastern] (Moscow: Voenizdat, 1985), 134.
7. 'Study of Strategical and Tactical Peculiarities of Far Eastern Russia and Soviet Far East Forces', in *Japanese Special Studies in Manchuria*, Vol. XIII (Washington, DC: Department of the Army, Office of the Chief of Military History, 1955), 95. This is a 1953 study prepared by the Military History Section, Headquarters, Army Forces Far East, on the basis of interviews with Japanese officers of the Kwantung Army.
8. Ibid., 108.
9. These Soviet concerns are detailed in *Krasnoznamennyi dal'nevostochnyi*, 136–8. This account catalogues the many border incidents and diplomatic maneuvering undergirding Soviet suspicions.
10. N. V. Eronin, *Strategicheskaia peregruppirovka Sovetskikh vooruzhennykh sil (pri podgotovka Dal'nevostochnoi kampanii 1945 goda)* [The strategic regrouping of the Soviet armed forces (during the preparations for the Far Eastern campaign of 1945)] (Moscow: Voroshilov General Staff Academy, 1980), 10. Classified secret.
11. These redeployments included the 65th, 93d, and 114th Rifle, the 82d Motorized Rifle and the 57th Tank Divisions from the Trans-Baikal Military District and the

21st, 26th, 32d, 78th, and 92d Rifle, the 69th Motorized, and the 58th and 60th Tank Divisions from the 1st Far Eastern Front. See David M. Glantz, *Red Army Ground Forces in June 1941* (Carlisle, PA: author, 1997). This brought the total of forces transferred from the Far East to 122,000 men, more than 2,000 guns and mortars, 2,209 light tanks, 12,000 vehicles, and 1,500 tractors. See *IVMV*, 11: 185.

12. *IVMV*, 11: 185.
13. Ibid.
14. Ibid., 186.
15. Ibid.
16. *Krasnoznamennyi dal'nevostochnyi*, 136–52.
17. Ibid., 190.
18. S. M. Shtemenko, *General'nyi shtab v gody voiny, T. 1* [The General Staff in the war years, Vol. 1] (Moscow: Voenizdat, 1981), 399.
19. A. M. Vasilevsky, *Delo vsei zhizni* [Life's work] (Moscow: Politizdat, 1953), 496.
20. *Krasnoznamennyi dal'nevostochnyi*, 190. The exact breakdown of Soviet forces in the Far East in May 1945 was 41 rifle, two cavalry, two motorized rifle, and two tanks divisions and four rifle, three motorized rifle, and 24 tank brigades. See Eronin, *Strategicheskaia peregruppirovka*, 10.
21. A. A. Grechko, *Osvoboditel'naia missiia Sovetskikh vooruzhennykh sil vo Vtoroi Mirovoi voine* [The liberation mission of the Soviet armed forces during the Second World War] (Moscow: Voenizdat, 1974), 414–15. For an expanded examination of Soviet logistical preparations for the campaign, see Jacob W. Kipp, *The Soviet Far Eastern Build-up and the Manchurian Campaign, February–August 1945: Lessons and Implications* (Fort Leavenworth, KS: Soviet Military Studies Office, 1988).
22. L. N. Vnotchenko, *Pobeda na dal'nem vostoke: Voenno-istoricheskii ocherk o baevykh deistviiakh Sovetskikh voisk v auguste–sentiabre 1945 g* [Victory in the Far East: A military-historical survey about the operations of Soviet forces in August–September 1945] (Moscow: Voenizdat, 1971), 16–17.
23. Eronin, *Strategicheskaia peregruppirovka*, 11, quoting the transcript of the conference.
24. Ibid.
25. Ibid.
26. Ibid., 11–12.
27. *IVMV*, 11: 187.
28. 'Study of Strategical and Tactical Peculiarities', 108–9.
29. *IVMV*, 11: 187.
30. Ibid. For more details on railroad reconstruction, see I. Kovalev, *Transport v Velikoi Otechestvennoi voine 1941–1945 gg.* [Transport in the Great Patriotic War 1941–1945] (Moscow: Nauka, 1981).
31. *IVMV*, 11: 188.
32. Ibid., 189.
33. Ibid.
34. Eronin, *Strategicheskaia peregruppirovka*, 24.
35. *IVMV*, 11: 190.
36. Ibid.
37. Ibid., 191.
38. For Soviet justification of the renunciation, see *Krasnoznamennyi dal'nevostochnyi*, 190.
39. Ibid.
40. *IVMV*, 11: 187–8. For example, the Soviets dispatched new T-34 tanks eastward to re-equip one battalion of each tank brigade and one regiment of each of the two

tank divisions in the Far East. They stockpiled additional tanks to outfit a tank army destined for transfer from the western theater of operations. The United States shipped Lend-Lease equipment (vehicles and tanks) to the Port of Vladivostok.

41. S. M. Shtemenko, *The Soviet General Staff at War, 1914–1945* (Moscow: Progress Publishers, 1974), 413. Hereafter cited as *The Soviet General Staff.*
42. For more detail on deceptive measures the Soviets employed when preparing their Manchurian offensive, see David M. Glantz, *Soviet Military Deception in the Second World War* (London: Frank Cass, 1989), 544–55.
43. *IVMV*, 11: 189.
44. Ibid., 191.
45. Ibid., 192.
46. Ibid.
47. Eronin, *Strategicheskaia peregruppirovka*, 46.
48. Ibid., 46–7.
49. Ibid., 47.
50. Ibid., 48.
51. Ibid., 49.
52. Ibid., 50–1.
53. Ibid., 51.
54. Ibid., 52–3.
55. Ibid, 53.
56. Ibid., 54.
57. Ibid., 55. The weapons included 21,000 rifles, 12,000 submachine guns, 1,100 light, 500 medium, and 160 heavy machine guns, 1,500 antitank rifles, 230 mortars, and 478 guns.
58. Ibid.
59. Ibid., 57. The supporting forces included the 25th Separate Tank Regiment, 152d Separate Gun Artillery Brigade, 1316th Antitank (Tank Destroyer) Artillery Regiment, 461st and 53 Guards-Mortar Regiments, 54th Engineer Brigade (with the 522d, 523d, 524th, 526th, 527th Separate Sapper Battalions), and other smaller units.
60. Ibid., 57–8.
61. See Dmitriy Loza, *Commanding the Red Army's Sherman Tanks*, trans. and ed. James F. Gebhardt (Lincoln, NE: University of Nebraska Press, 1996), 111–14. Soviet sources are generally silent about the fact that the corps was armed with over 200 Sherman tanks.
62. Eronin, *Strategicheskaia peregruppirovka*, 58.
63. Ibid.
64. Ibid., 59.
65. Ibid., 62.
66. Ibid., 63.
67. Ibid.
68. Ibid., 68.
69. Ibid., 69–72, provides greater detail regarding the movement of air forces into the Far East and Trans-Baikal regions.
70. Ibid., 79.
71. Ibid., 80.
72. Ibid., 84.
73. Ibid., 86.
74. Ibid., 88. For more details on the movement of tank and artillery to the Far East see pp. 100–2.
75. Ibid., 89.

76. Ibid. See also 90–3 for details on the supply effort on a time-phased basis measured in train loads and tons of cargo.
77. Ibid., 98, and *Istoriia Velikoi Otechestvennoi voiny Sovetskogo Soiuza 1941–1945*, T. 5 [A history of the Great Patriotic War of the Soviet Union, 1941–1945, Vol. 5] (Moscow: Voenizdat, 1963), 5: 551. Hereafter cited as *IVOVSS*.
78. M. V. Zakharov *et al.*, eds, *Finale* [The Finale] (Moscow: Progress Publishers, 1972), 71; see also *IVMV*, 11: 189.
79. Zakharov, *Finale*, 72–3. See also I. V. Kovalev, *Transport v Velikoi Otechestvennoi voine (1941–1945 gg)* [Transport in the Great Patriotic War, 1941–1945] (Moscow: 'Nauka', 1981), 384–402.
80. Shtemenko, *The Soviet General Staff*, 327–8. See also Shtemenko, 'Iz istorii razgroma kvantunskoi armii' [From the history of the rout of the Kwantung Army], *Voenno-istoricheskii zhurnal* [Military-historical Journal], No. 3 (April 1967), 57–8. Hereafter cited as *VIZh* with number and page.
81. *IVMV*, 11: 193–4. See the full text of Vasilevsky's assignment order in 'Stavki VGK: Dokumenty i materially, 1944–1945' [The *Stavka VGK*: Documents and Materials, 1941–1945] in *Russkii arkhiv: Velikaia Otechestvennaia*, T. 16 (5–4) [The Russian Archives: The Great Patriotic [War], Vol. 16 (5–4)], 248–9.
82. The Soviets had unsuccessfully experimented with a theater command structure in the summer of 1941 when German forces thrust into the Soviet Union. Called Main Commands of Strategic Directions, the *Stavka* abolished the last of these unwieldy headquarters in late 1942.
83. Shtemenko, *The Soviet General Staff*, 341–2. See also K. A. Meretskov, *Serving the People* (Moscow: Progress Publishers, 1971), 337–8 and I. M. Chistiakov, *Sluzhim otchizne* [In the service of the Fatherland] (Moscow: Voenizdat, 1975), 271–3.

2

The Theater of Military Operations

The Far Eastern theater of military operations (Manchuria) encompasses a huge area of more than 579,150 square miles (1.5 million square kilometers) and is characterized by wildly differing geographical and climatic conditions.[1] Manchuria, whose circumference extends a total of 3,188 miles (5,130 kilometers), is bounded on the south by Korea, the Liaotung Gulf, and China, on the east and north by the Russian Federation's (then the Soviet Union's) Far Eastern province and Siberia, and on the west by Outer Mongolia and Inner Mongolia. Ultimately, the Trans-Baikal Front deployed in a 1,429-mile (2,300-kilometer) operational sector in the west, the 2d Far Eastern Front in a 1,324-mile (2,130-kilometer) sector in the north, and the 1st Far Eastern Front in a 435-mile (700-kilometer) sector in the east.

By virtue of its geographic location, rich natural resources, and large population, Manchuria is an area of considerable strategic value. Its fertile central regions are both industrially and agriculturally important, and its vital geographical location gives to it a dominant position *vis-à-vis* China and the Soviet Union's Far Eastern region. For these reasons, the major powers of the region, China, Russia, and Japan, have long sought to dominate or occupy the region.

Because of its large size and its geographical and climatic diversity, Manchuria can best be described as a series of concentric circles, each characterized by distinctly differing terrain (see Maps 2–8). The inner circle contains the heartland of Manchuria, the large central valley containing the cities of Harbin, Changchun, and Mukden. Around this valley runs a large circle of mountains of various size and ruggedness, which protect the central valley from the west, north, east, and southeast. To the south, this circle opens onto the Liaotung Gulf. Beyond this circle of mountains is a peripheral area abutting Mongolia, Siberia, and the Soviet Far East.

The central valley of Manchuria, which contains the basins of the Liao, Sungari, Nen, Hsiliao Choerh, and other rivers, extends 621 miles (1,000 kilometers) from north to south and 249–311 miles (400–500 kilometers)

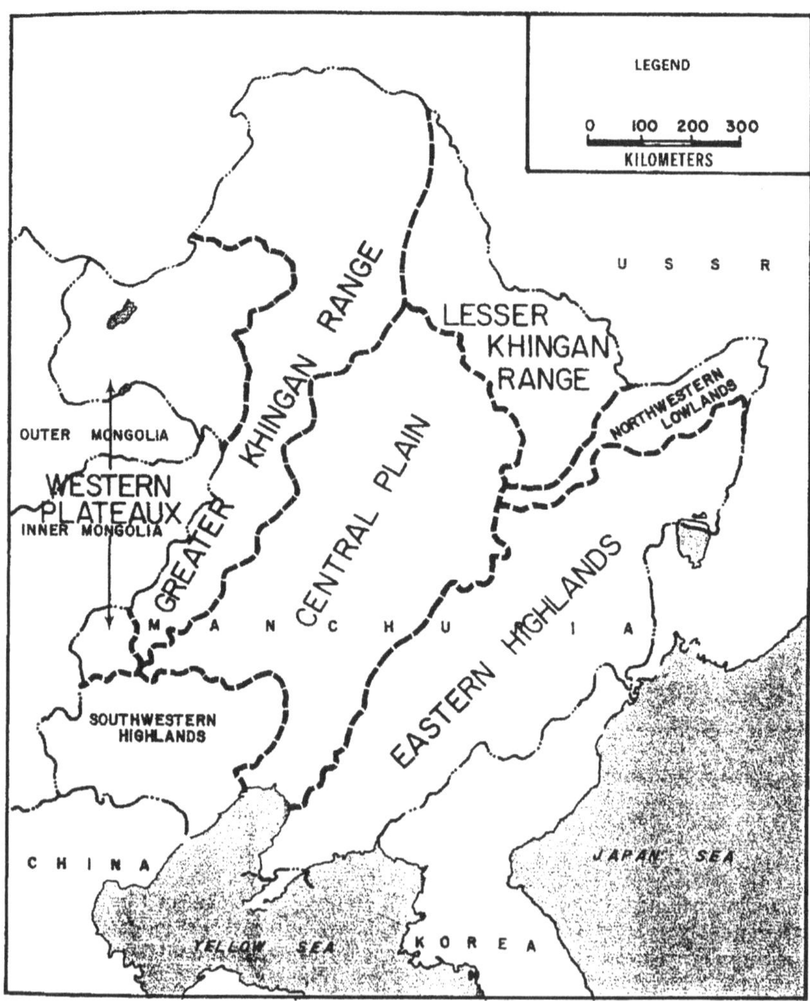

Map 2. Regions and General Terrain in Manchuria

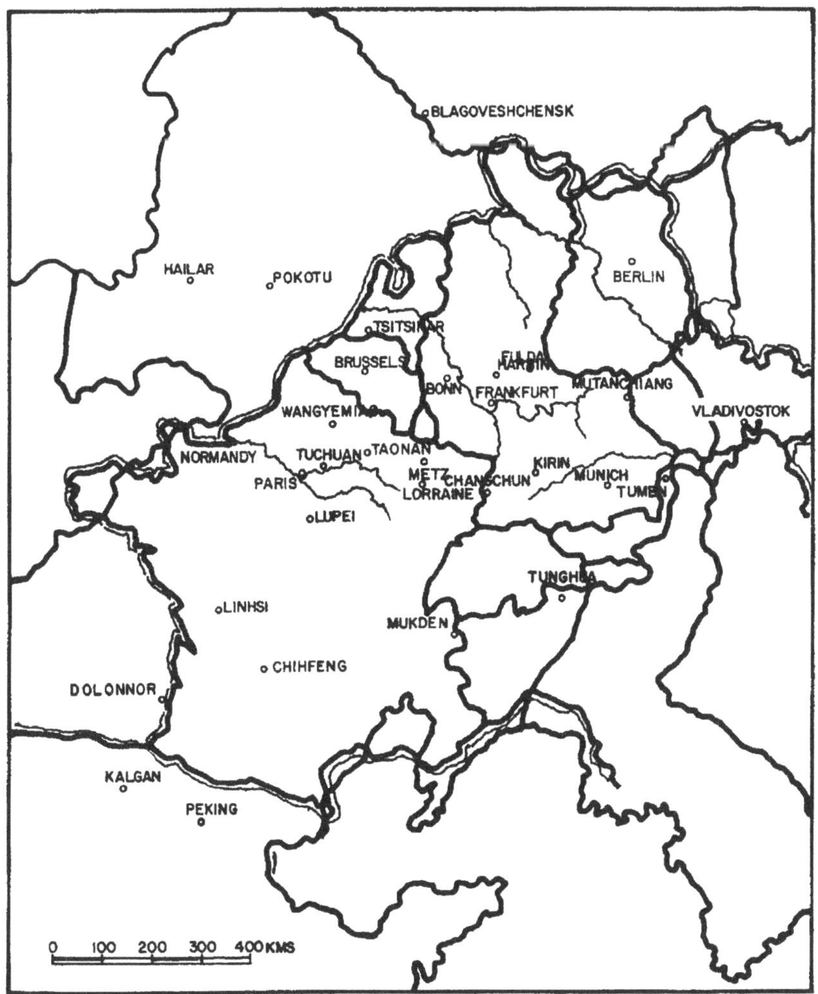

Map 3. Comparison of the Size of Manchuria and Western Europe

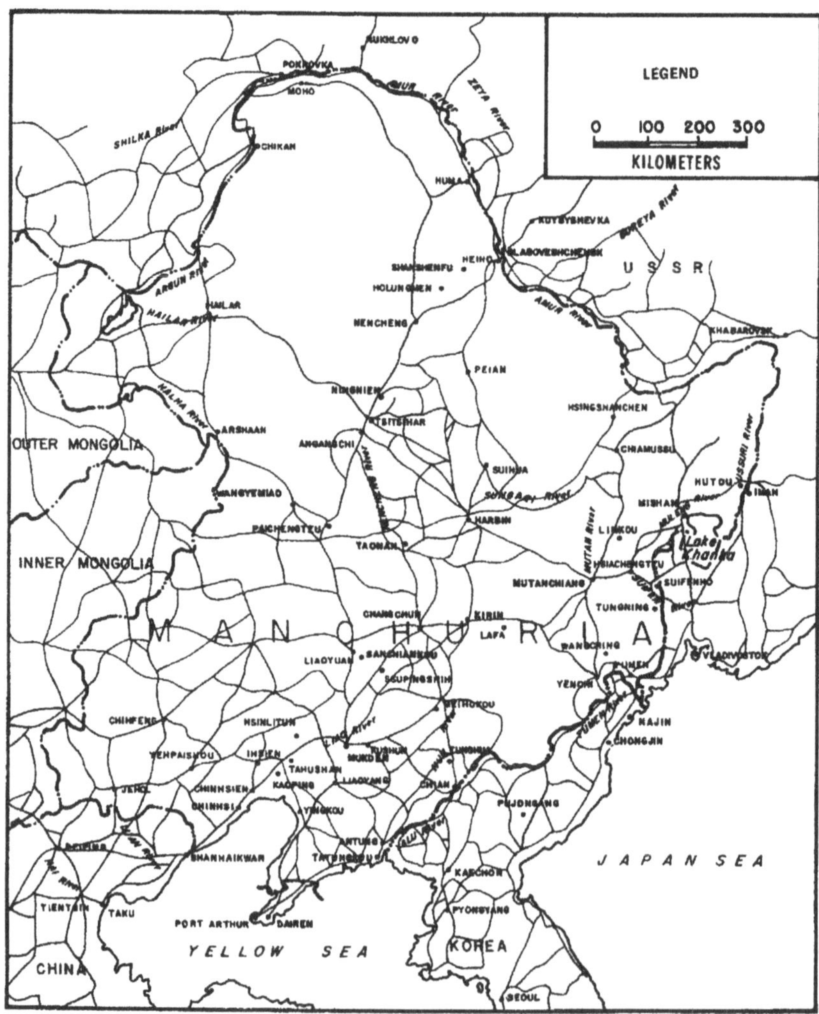

Map 4. Road Network in Manchuria, 1945

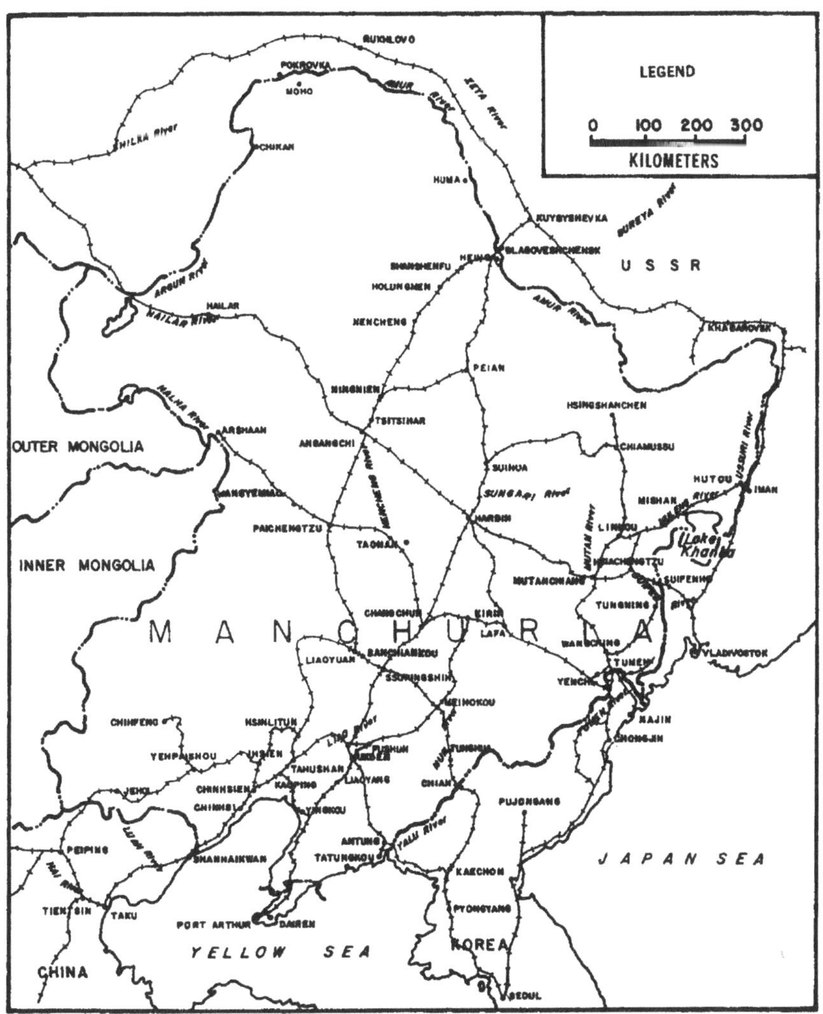

Map 5. Rail Network in Manchuria, 1945

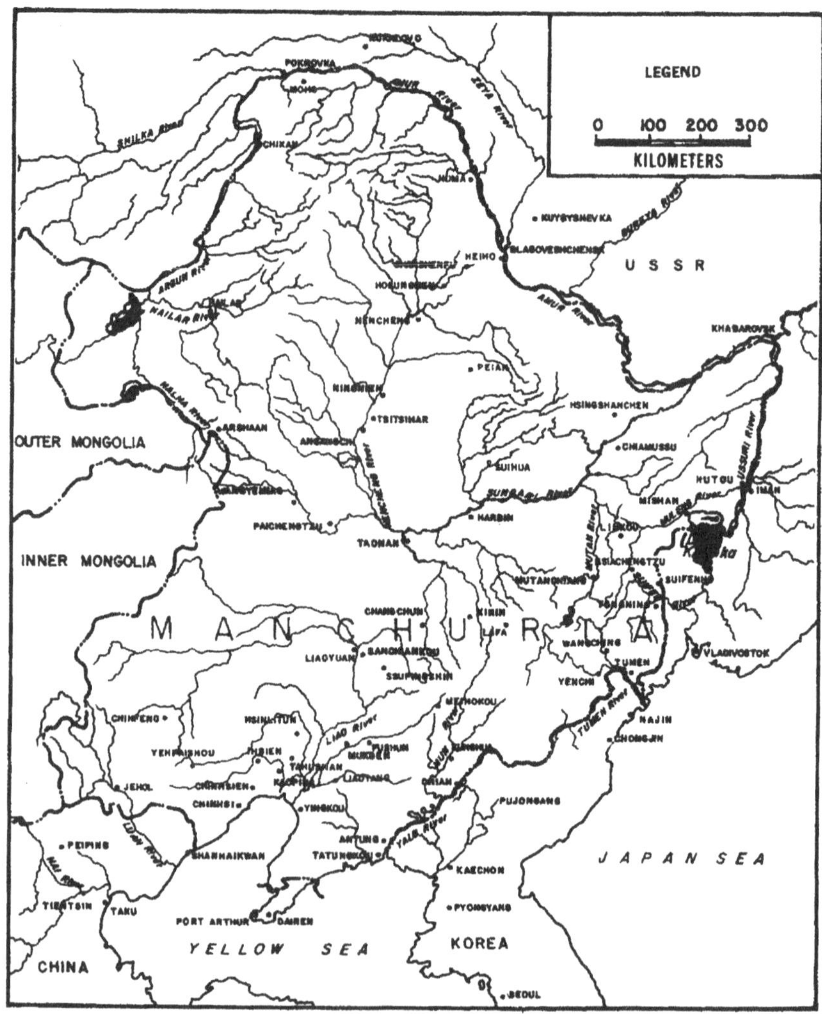

Map 6. Waterways in Manchuria

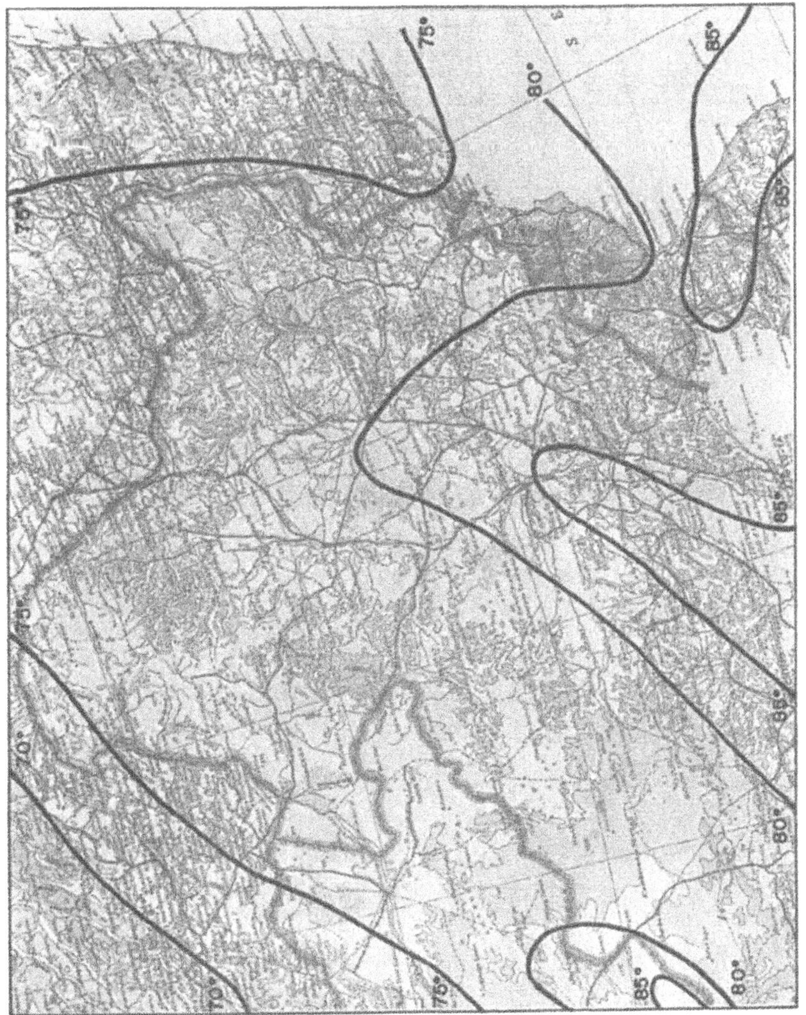

Map 7. Temperature Ranges in Manchuria, August

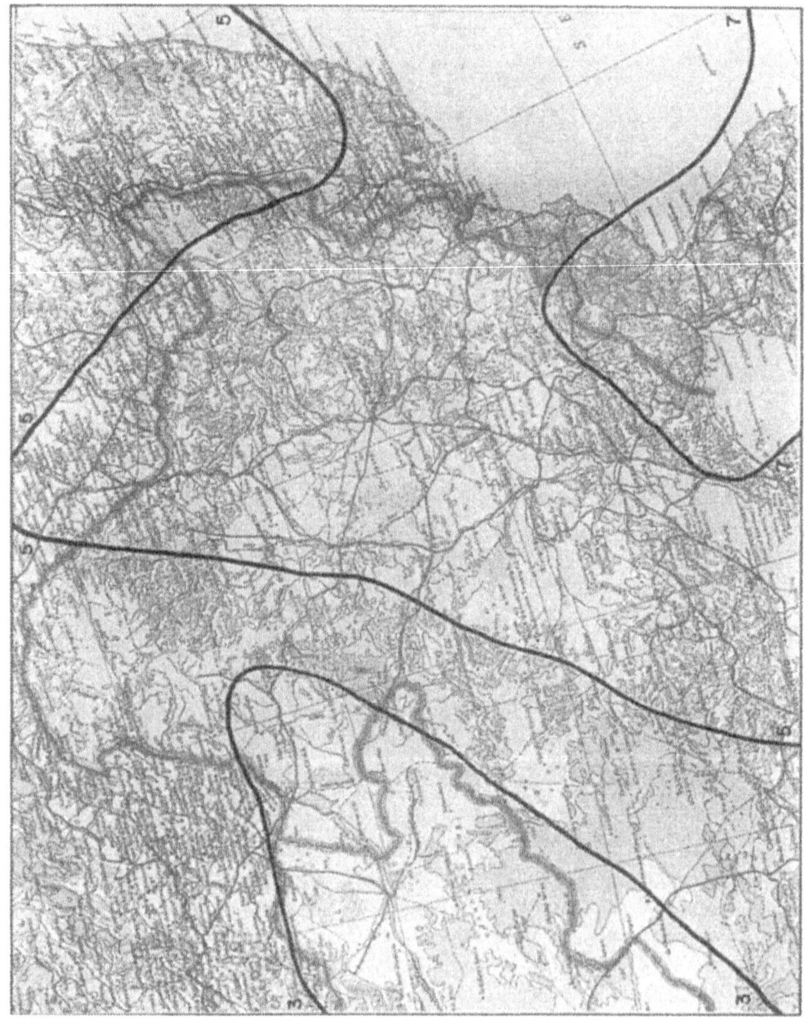

Map 8. Rainfall in Manchuria

from east to west. In 1945 a well-developed road and rail network traversed the region, connecting the major industrial cities of Mukden, Changchun, Harbin, and Tsitsihar. Terrain in the central valley is generally flat, and cultivated areas predominate.

West of the central valley is the rugged Grand Khingan mountain range. Running roughly north to south, this range extends from the Amur River region of northern Manchuria southward to a junction with the mountains of northern China. These mountains, which vary in height from 5,904 feet (1,800 meters) in the north, to 4,920 feet (1,500 meters) in the central region, and finally to 6,232 feet (1,900 meters) in the south, rise less steeply from the west than from the east. The arid deserts and plains on the plateau west of the Grand Khingans average 3,280–3,936 feet (1,000–1,200 meters) in elevation, thus the mountains rise from 984 to 2,952 feet (300 to 900 meters) above the plateau floor. The central plain east of the Grand Khingans averages from 1,640 to 2,296 feet (500 to 700 meters) above sea level, thus the mountains loom at even greater heights.

The Grand Khingan Mountain range, which consists of a belt of dissected mountains and sharp ridges punctuated by broad but swampy valleys, varies in width from 311 miles (500 kilometers) in the north to 50 miles (80 kilometers) in the south. The mountains are heavily forested in the north, but these forests decrease in density to the south, finally giving way to brush and scrub grass. Of several passes and narrow valleys that traverse the Grand Khingans, in 1945 the two most important passes contained the railroad lines from Yakoshih to Pokotu and from Halung-Arshaan to Solun. Barely trafficable dirt roads paralleled these rail lines, and, elsewhere, numerous pack and cart trails traversed the mountain range. During the rainy season (July, August, and September), virtually all of these roads became almost impassable.

Bounding the northern portion of the central valley of Manchuria, the Lesser Khingan Mountain range extends from northwest to southeast for a distance of 373 miles (600 kilometers), varying in average width from 62 to 186 miles (100 to 300 kilometers). These mountains, which consist of a series of heavily wooded rounded hills, conical summits, and open valleys, range in elevation from 2,296 to 4,264 feet (700 to 1,300 meters). In 1945, the main passages through the mountains contained the rail lines from Tsitsihar and Harbin to Aihun on the Amur River.

East of the central valley are the Eastern Highlands, which extend for 932 miles (1,500 kilometers) from the Liaotung Peninsula in the south to the junction of the Amur and Ussuri rivers. These highlands, at places almost 217 miles (350 kilometers) wide, separate the Central Lowlands from the Soviet Far Eastern provinces. In the south, the Tunghua Mountains average 1,640–4,264 feet (500–1,300) meters in elevation. Farther to the north near Mutanchiang, elevations run from 2,952–4,920 feet (900 to 1,500 meters), while south of the Sungari River, elevations average 2,296 to 3,280 feet (700–1,000 meters).

In 1945, rail lines and roads traversed the Eastern Highlands from Changchun via Kirin to Tumen; from Harbin via Mutanchiang to Ussurysk; and from Harbin via Mutanchiang and Mishan to Iman on the Ussuri River. Less important military railroad lines ran from Tungning to Wangching and parallel to the Soviet border from Liaoheishan to Suiyang.

Heavy forests cover the southern portion of the Eastern Manchurian Highlands, and dense thickets of small trees and brush cover the central and northern portions. The valley of the Sungari River, which flows northeast from Harbin to Chiamussu, separates the Eastern Highlands and Lesser Khingan Mountains. Prior to 1945 the Japanese built several military roads through the Eastern Highlands to provide communications between adjacent units and rear installations.

Beyond the circle of mountains encasing the central valley are regions on the periphery of Manchuria. In the west the deserts of Inner Mongolia extend from the Grand Khingan Mountains to the Outer Mongolian border, and the Barga Plateau stretches from the northern reaches of the Grand Khingans to Mongolia and the Argun River border between Manchuria and Siberia. Northeast and east of the Eastern Highlands are marshy lowlands along the Ussuri River and at the junction of the Ussuri, Amur, and Sungari rivers.

The arid deserts of Inner Mongolia (the Dalai Plateau, an eastern extension of the Gobi Desert) extend westward from the Grand Khingan Mountains into Mongolia. The distance from the mountains to the Mongolian border varies from 124 miles (200 kilometers) in the north to 249 miles (400 kilometers) in the Linhsi area in the south. This high plateau region, which averages 3,280–3,936 feet (1,000–1,200 meters) in elevation, contains numerous sand dunes, many small hills 328–492 feet (100–150 meters) high, frequent dry streambeds, and occasional saline lakes. Obviously, since the region is essentially desert waste, water is in scarce supply.

Farther to the north, the Barga Plateau stretches west of the Grand Khingans from the Yakoshih area to the Argun River and the Soviet–Outer Mongolia border. The plateau, which is characterized by extensive sand dunes and numerous shallow depressions, punctuated by wide rocky mesas, averages 1,968–2,624 feet (600–800 meters) in elevation, with isolated hills rising an additional 656 feet (200 meters). The Hailar River meanders from east to west across the plateau, and two large saline lakes, the Dali Nuur and the Buyr Nuur, are located in the west. Numerous small tracks, but no hard-surfaced roads, traversed the Dalai Plateau in 1945. Running from Manchouli in northwest Manchuria to the Grand Khingans' mountain passes at Yakoshih, the historic single-track Chinese Eastern Railroad bisected the Barga Plateau. A third-class road paralleled the railroad, and other similar roads radiated from north and south of Hailar.

In northeastern Manchuria, an immense flat and marshy lowland averaging 98–328 feet (30–100 meters) in elevation covers the region where the

Amur, Ussuri, and Sungari rivers converge. The Sungari River cuts through the region from southwest to northeast. This flat and undulating region contains the Sungari River valley proper, which is 21.5 miles (35 kilometers) wide, and occasional hills. The lowland extends across the Amur River into Siberia. The entire region is swampy, covered with marsh grass and other water vegetation, and usually flooded during the months of July and August. At the time of the 1945 campaign, overland routes consisted of third and fourth-rate (dirt) roads and trails, the most important of which extended from the Amur River at Lopei and Tungchiang along both banks of the Sungari to the city of Chiamussu.

The climatic characteristics of various regions in Manchuria differ as much as the region's geographical features. In general, the climate in the more temperate coastal region clashes sharply with more extreme temperature and rainfall ranges found in the interior. In the interior winter brings extremely low temperatures, which decrease even more west of the Grand Khingan Mountains. Generally, the interior also lacks significant rainfall during the winter. Summer brings the heaviest rains to most of Manchuria. The monsoon drift of moist warm maritime air from the southeast crosses central Manchuria, bringing with it widespread low overcasts and heavy rains. Most of the year's precipitation occurs during July and August.

While rainfall is heaviest in the east, rain occurs as far west as the Grand Khingan Mountains and the Barga Plateau during the summer. The highest temperatures occur throughout Manchuria during July and August, with the severest temperatures recorded in the desert regions of the west. Spring and fall are transitional periods with limited rainfall and moderate temperatures. From a military standpoint, the fall (from September through November) is the best season during which to conduct military operations, since during this period the heavy rains stop, temperatures moderate, and high winds and dust storms subside.

Militarily, the key to Manchuria is the central valley region. With its high population densities, its agricultural and industrial value, and its strategic position, control of the valley means control of Manchuria as a whole. Thus, defense of the central valley is a critical issue for any would-be occupying power. As is the case in similar regions elsewhere, in order to control the central valley, an occupying force must deny enemy access to the area by establishing adequate defenses in mountainous regions surrounding the central valley and by controlling potential axes of advance.

Feasible military axes of advance into Manchuria in 1945 were at a distinct premium (see Map 9). At first glance, period maps of Manchuria seemed to indicate that the major rail lines through the mountain barriers into and out of Manchuria were the best avenues of advance into the central valley. However, closer examination of these routes indicated that all of them were extremely restrictive and difficult to traverse.

For example, although the Chinese Eastern Railroad, which ran from Manchouli across the Barga Plateau and hence across the Grand Khingans from Yakoshih to Pokotu, did offer limited space for a military advance, the roads parallel to the rail line were of poor quality and prone to deterioration in bad weather. The branch rail line from the Halung-Arshaan region near the Mongolian border to Solun, Wangyemaio, and Taonan suffered from the same restrictions. Even though a military force could cross the Grand Khingans farther south through a number of narrow passes, any force crossing these passes first had to traverse hundreds of miles of trackless desert waste. While the actual height and slopes of the Grand Khingans do not prohibit military operations by mechanized forces, the absence of good roads, shortage of water, and rough terrain inhibited rapid movement.

Two potential axes of advance traverse the Lesser Khingan Mountains in northeastern Manchuria. The first, extending south and southwest from Sunwu, requires crossing hilly, wooded terrain on poor roads. The second, along the Sungari River by way of Chiamussu, involves mastering swamp-lands and is also traversed by poor roads. The Sungari River itself, however, offers an excellent arena for an amphibious advance.

Eastern Manchuria offers a wide variety of axes of advance, but none of these is particularly suitable for effective military operations. The better of these axes follow the rail lines, rivers, or major roads in the region. In the northern sector of this region, the Iman–Hutou–Mishan axis is limited by marshlands, which are virtually inundated during the rainy period of July and August. In eastern Manchuria south of Lake Khanka, the roads that pass through Suifenho and Tungning offer restricted movement of forces through barely adequate corridors of advance across hilly and brushy terrain. The roads themselves lack hard surfaces and turn to gluey mud during the rainy season. In the southeast a force could advance along the Tumen River by way of Hungchun, Tumen, Yenchi, or Tunhoa, but, as in other areas, water obstacles, bottlenecks, and poor roads are likely to limit any rapid advance.

Compounding the Red Army's problems, the Japanese constructed formidable fortified zones, separate forts and associated fortifications, and extensive belts of obstacles along all of these potential axes of advance (at Halung-Arshaan, Hailar, Yakoshih, Sunwu, along the Sungari River, and in eastern Manchuria), to block the passage of military forces. These obstacles were often concrete and steel pillboxes, bunkers, and other fortifications supplemented by extensive field fortifications extending across the axes of advance. The Japanese also fortified in depth those major passes through the Grand Khingan Mountains containing major rail lines or roads but neglected to fortify mountain passes that lacked major roads. Significantly, the Japanese also failed to fortify or even defend in strength other areas they considered unsuitable as potential attack axes, such as those lacking roads or made up predominantly of swampy terrain.

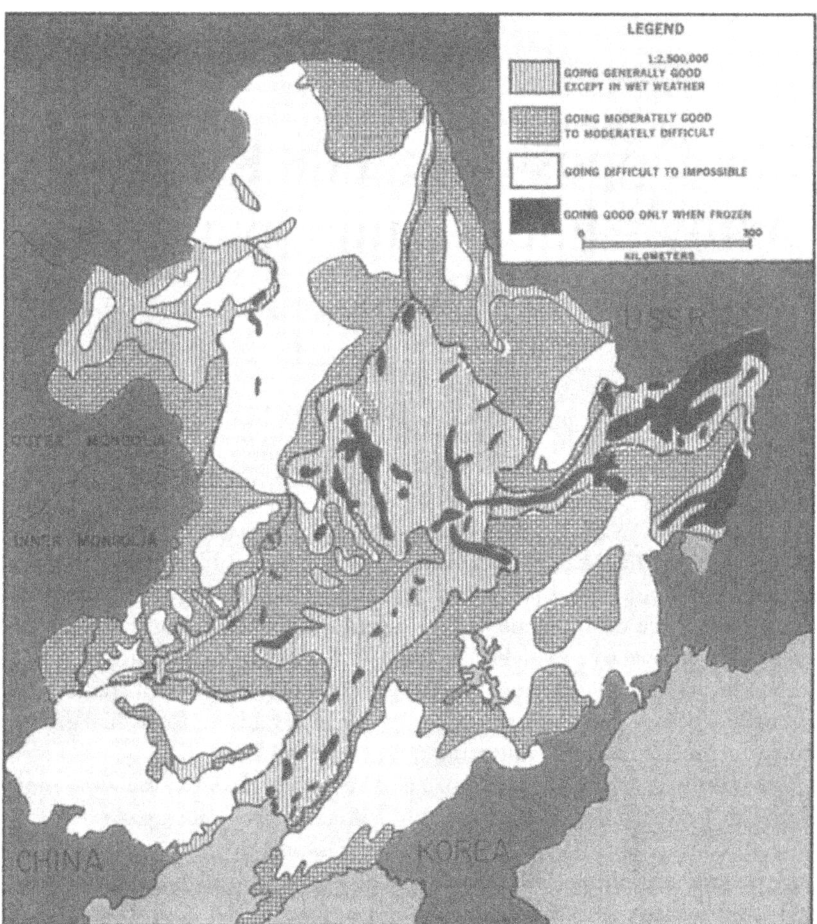

Map 9. Trafficability and Axes of Advance into Manchuria

In view of the paucity of good advance axes through the barrier-mountains surrounding central Manchuria, any military force wishing to penetrate into the region would have to rely on its imagination and resourcefulness by either overcoming terrain obstacles or mastering techniques for conducting operations in remote regions.

NOTE

1. Information in this chapter is taken from *Organization of a Combat Command for Operations in Manchuria* (Fort Knox, KY: The Armor School, US Army, May 1952), 12–77, Classified confidential but re-graded unclassified on 12 April 1974; Vnotchenko, *Pobeda*, 29–38; and Eronin, *Strategicheskaia peregruppirovka*, 18–20.

3

The Opposition: The Kwantung Army's Forces and Operational Plans

GENERAL

Opposing the Red Army's Far East Command (High Command of Soviet Forces in the Far East) were the Japanese Kwantung Army and its Manchukuoan and Inner Mongolian auxiliaries. The Kwantung Army was a venerable force whose name had, for years, evoked respect and fear on the part of its prospective foes. Formed in 1919 to defend Kwantung territory (the Liaotung peninsula) but responsible for the defense of all of Manchuria after the Japanese seized the region in 1931, the Kwantung Army had grown into a formidable force of one million men by 1941.

Most military authorities, in Japan and abroad, considered the Kwantung Army to be the most prestigious and powerful force the Japanese Army fielded. Throughout the 1930s, the army's principal mission was to support and sustain the puppet Manchukuoan government and provide security from and perhaps offensive capability against the Soviet Union should the need arise. During the later years of that decade, Red Army forces in the region experienced numerous border incidents with the Kwantung Army. The most significant confrontations occurred at Lake Khasan along the Korean border in 1938 and at Khalkhin-Gol (Nomonhan) along the Mongolian border in the summer of 1939. During the former, the Japanese fought a small Soviet force to a virtual draw, but during the latter, the 1st Army Group commanded by G. K. Zhukov annihilated two Japanese divisions that had audaciously violated the Mongolian border.[1]

After Hitler began his invasion of the Soviet Union in June 1941 (in Operation Barbarossa), the Kwantung Army figured heavily in Soviet political calculations and military planning, even though the Soviet Union signed a pact of neutrality with Japan in April 1941. While contending with the serious threat that the German *Wehrmacht* posed to the Soviet Union's very survival, Stalin and the *Stavka* had to keep a wary eye on Germany's Axis partner, Japan, lest the Kwantung Army violate the neutrality pact by undertaking offensive operations against the Soviet Far East. The dangers associated with conducting a two-front war loomed particularly large in the fall of 1941 when German forces reached the outskirts of Moscow. In desperation, however, Stalin ordered many of his best divisions in the Far East to race westward to defend his capital city, although never as many as Westerners and the Germans have assumed.

Concerns over a possible two-front war and the potential loss of its Far Eastern territories impelled the Soviet Union to retain a major force of between 32 and 59 divisions (including two tank and two motorized rifle) in the Far East and the Trans-Baikal areas throughout the war years.[2] Those forces could have been put to valuable use helping counter the German threat in the west. Fortunately for the Soviet Union, Japan's preoccupation with events in China and the Pacific accorded the Soviets a measure of security that increased as the war progressed. Nevertheless, the Kwantung Army remained a major Soviet concern right up to the hour of the Red Army's offensive in August 1945.

During war in the Pacific theater and China, the Kwantung Army eroded in strength and quality as the requirements of other theaters drew off its assets.[3] Many experienced units were siphoned off and replaced by units formed from draft levies, reservists, and cannibalized smaller units. Soviet estimates of Japanese strength in the Far East vary according to source. According to formerly classified accounts, the Kwantung Army's forces (including the Seventeenth Area Army in southern Korea) consisted of 31 infantry divisions, nine mixed infantry brigades, two tank brigades, and one special purpose (destruction-suicide [*kamikaze*]) brigade formed into three area armies (army groups), one separate combined army, two air armies, and the Sungarian Naval Flotilla.[4] The Soviets assert that this force numbered 1,040,000 men, supported by 1,155 tanks, 8,620 guns and mortars, 1,800 combat aircraft, and 25 combat ships (see Appendices 1–3 and Map 10).[5]

In addition to the Japanese forces in Manchuria and northern Korea, the Soviets also include the Manchukuoan and Inner Mongolian armies and Japanese forces on southern Sakhalin and the Kuril Islands in their total count of opposing forces in the Far East. This included the 170,000 troops of the Army of Manchukuo, which were organized into eight infantry and seven cavalry divisions and 14 infantry and cavalry brigades, and the roughly 44,000 men of the Inner Mongolian Army, which were formed into five or six cavalry divisions and brigades and auxiliaries, and three infantry divisions and one infantry brigade on southern Sakhalin Island and on the Kuril Islands subordinate to the Japanese Imperial High Command's Fifth Area Army.

Therefore, the strength of the entire Japanese and allied force in the Far East facing the Red Army totaled 47 divisions and 27 brigades manned by 1,420,000 troops and supported by 1,215 tanks, 10,000 guns and mortars,

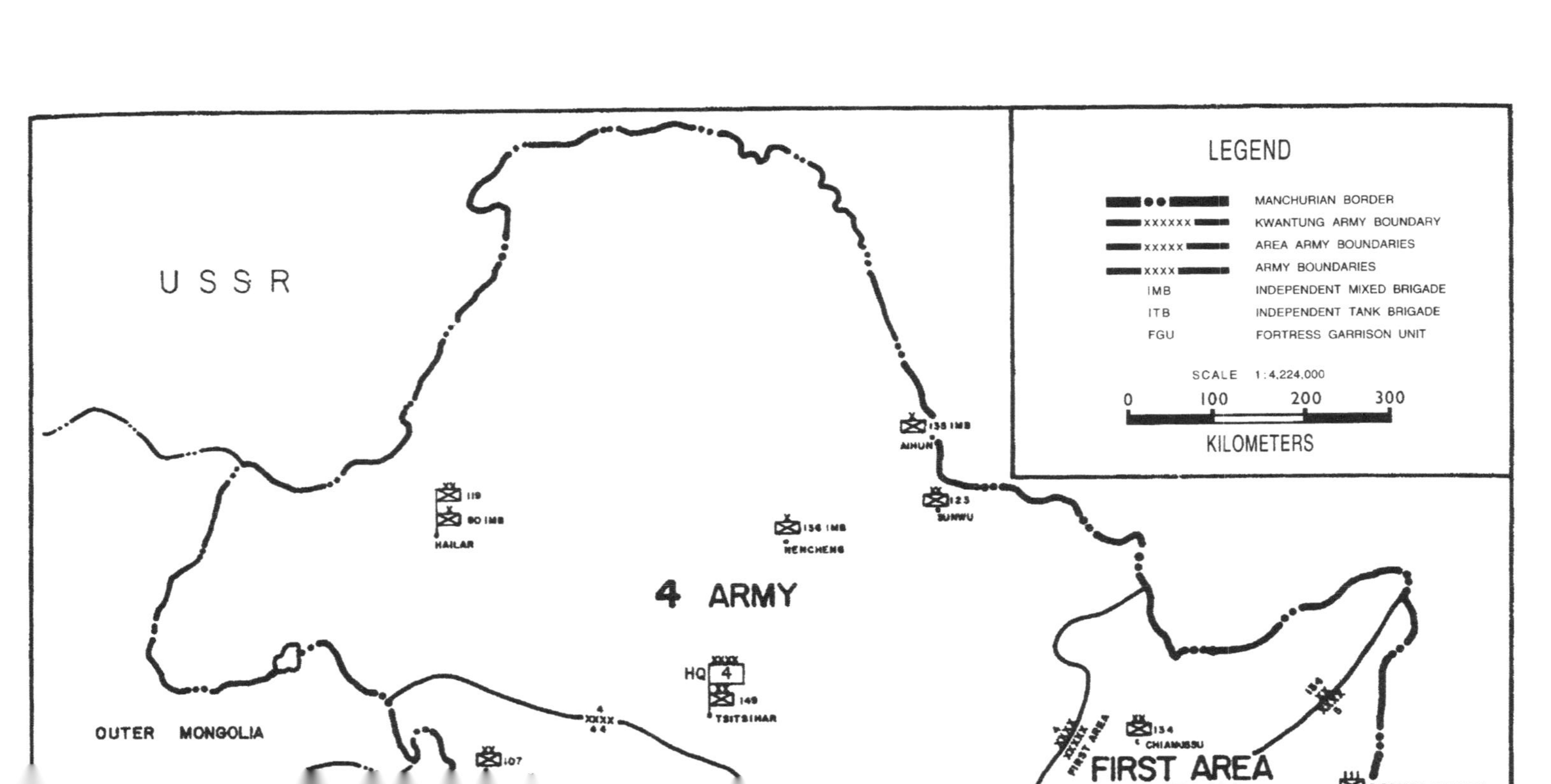

LEGEND
MANCHURIAN BORDER
KWANTUNG ARMY BOUNDARY
AREA ARMY BOUNDARIES
ARMY BOUNDARIES
IMB INDEPENDENT MIXED BRIGADE
ITB INDEPENDENT TANK BRIGADE
FGU FORTRESS GARRISON UNIT
SCALE 1:4,224,000
0 100 200 300
KILOMETERS
USSR
OUTER MONGOLIA
4 ARMY
FIRST AREA
HQ 4
119
80 IMB
HAILAR
136 IMB
NENCHENG
135 IMB
AIHUN
123
SUNWU
149
TSITSIHAR
107
134
CHIAMUSSU
15 BORDER GARRISON

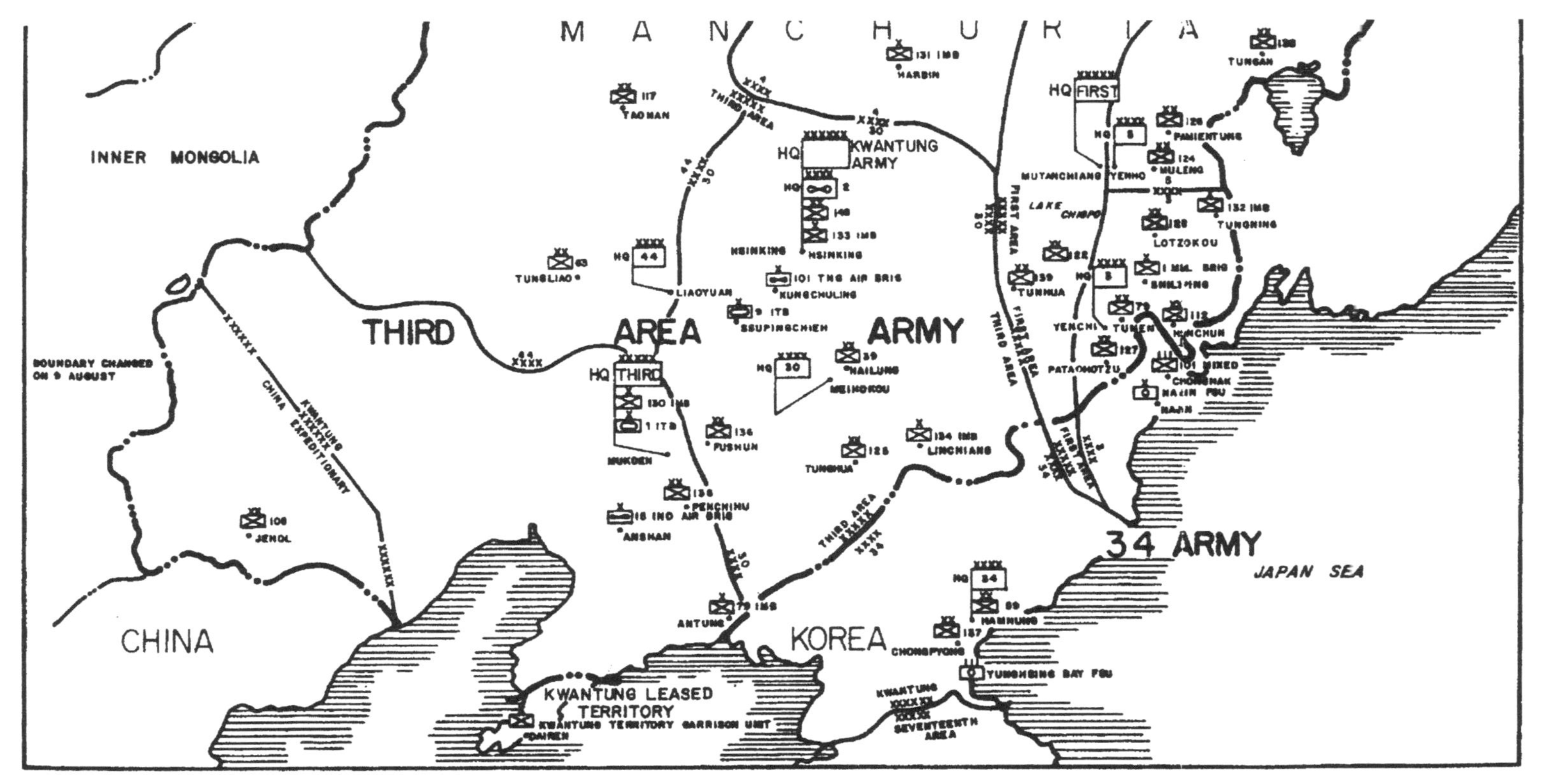

Map 10. Kwantung Army Dispositions, Early August 1945

1,907 combat aircraft, and 25 ships. Of this total, roughly one million of the soldiers were Japanese.[6]

Japanese sources, however, provide a strikingly different calculation. Discounting their forces in southern Korea, southern Sakhalin Island, and the Kuril Islands, Japanese sources place the number of Japanese troops in Manchuria at 713,724 men and the overall total of forces in the theater at roughly one million men.[7] Thus, while Soviet sources claim that the correlation between Soviet and Japanese forces in the theater (including Manchukuoan and Inner Mongolian auxiliaries) was only 1.2 to 1 in manpower, 4.8 to 1 in tanks and artillery, and 2 to 1 in aviation, the Japanese count indicates a Soviet superiority in Manchuria proper of 2.2 to 1 in manpower, greater than 5 to 1 in artillery, and an absolute superiority in tanks and aircraft (see Table 25).

TABLE 25: ASSESSMENT OF COMPOSITION OF FORCES FACING RED ARMY FAR EAST COMMAND

Japanese Forces	*993,000 men*
Kwantung Army (Manchuria) and northern Korea	713,000 men
2 area armies	
2 separate armies	
24 divisions	
9 infantry brigades	
2 tank brigades	
Southern Korea	190,000
1 area army	
7 infantry divisions	
2 infantry brigades	
Southern Sakhalin and the Kuril Islands	90,000
3 infantry divisions	
1 infantry brigade	
Allied Forces	*214,000*
Manchukuoan Army	170,000
8 infantry divisions	
7 cavalry divisions	
14 infantry and cavalry brigades	
Inner Mongolian Army	44,000
5–6 cavalry divisions and brigades	
Total Forces	*1,217,000*

Sources: 'Kampaniia sovetskikh vooruzhennikh sil na dal'nem vostoke v 1945g (facti i tsifry)' [The campaign of the Soviet armed forces in the Far East in 1945: Facts and figures], *Voenno-istoncheskii zhurnal* [Military-historical Journal], No. 8 (August 1965); L. N. Vnotchenko, *Pobeda na dal'nem vostoke* [Victory in the Far East] (Moscow: Voenizdat, 1971); and 'Record of Operations Against Soviet Russia on Northern and Western Fronts of Manchuria and in Northern Korea (August 1945)', *Japanese Monograph No. 155* (Tokyo: Military History Section, US Army Forces, Far East, 1954), Table 1.

ORDER OF BATTLE

In early August 1945, the Japanese Kwantung Army, under the command of General Yamada Otozo, consisted of the First and Third Area Armies (army groups), the 4th and 34th Separate Armies, and the 2d and 5th Air Armies, supported by the Sungari Naval Flotilla (see Charts 1 and 2). The most powerful of Yamada's area armies was the First Area Army, commanded by General Kita Seiichi. Headquartered in Mutanchiang, Kita's force consisted of the 3d and 5th Armies, each made up of three infantry divisions, and four separate infantry divisions and one independent mixed brigade. The First Area Army was responsible for the defense of eastern Manchuria and numbered 222,157 men (see Map 11).[8]

The 3d Army, commanded by Lieutenant General Murakami Keisaku, was responsible for defending the southern portion of the First Area Army's sector. Headquartered at Yenchi, Murakami's army was made up of the 79th Infantry Division with headquarters at Tumen, the 112th Infantry Division at Hungchun, the 127th Infantry Division at Pataiohotzu, deeper into the depths of Manchuria, and the Nagin Fortified Zone. Murakami's army numbered 62,940 men.[9]

The 5th Army, commanded by Lieutenant General Shimizu Noritsune, was headquartered at Yehho and was responsible for defending the northern portion of the First Area Army's sector, including the fortified zones and towns at Hutou, Tungan, Linkou, Pamientung, and Muleng. The 5th Army consisted of the 124th Infantry Division with headquarters at Muleng, the 126th Infantry Division at Pamientung, the 135th Infantry Division at Tungan, and the 15th Border Guards Unit stationed at Hutou. Shimizu's army numbered 75,771 men.

Directly subordinate to Kita's First Area Army were the 122d Infantry Division with its headquarters at Lake Chingpo, the 128th Infantry Division at Lotzokou, the 134th Infantry Division at Chiamussu, the 139th Infantry Division at Tunhua (Tunghua), the 132d Independent Mixed Brigade at Tungning, and a variety of area army supporting forces.

The forces of Kita's First Area Army manned three defensive lines that extended well into the depths of Manchuria. The first defensive line, which was occupied by border guard forces, included fortified regions directly adjacent to the border. To the rear, the bulk of the area army's forces defended a second line extending north and south along the eastern tributaries of the Mutanchiang River east of Mutanchiang. The third line was located along the Mutanchiang River. While the fortified zones along the border contained substantial heavily fortified permanent defensive structures and installations, the second and third lines consisted predominantly of lighter field fortifications and trenches. In the depths, the Japanese erected strong-point defenses at or around the towns of Mutanchiang, Yenchi, and Hungchun.

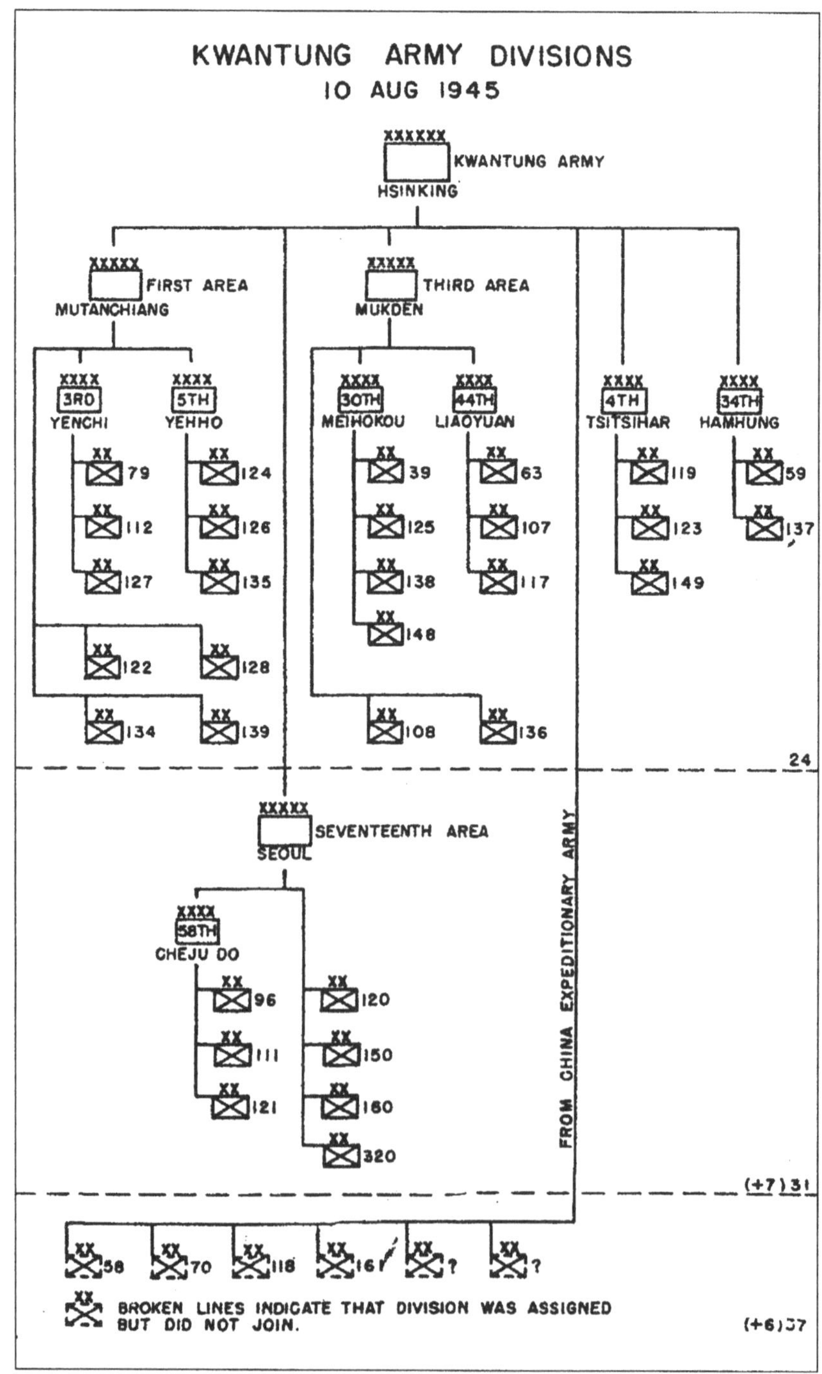

Chart 1: Organization of Kwantung Army, 10 August 1945 (divisions only) (Japanese View)

List of Commanders in Kwantung Army
(31 July 1945)

Kwantung Army, General Otozo Yamada

Fourth Army, Lt Gen Mikio Uemura
119th Division, Lt Gen Kiyonobu Shiozawa
123d Division, Lt Gen Teijiro Kitazawa
149th Division, Lt Gen Toichi Sasaki

Thirty-fourth Army, Lt Gen Senichi Kushibuchi
59th Division, Lt Gen Shigeru Fujita
137th Division, Lt Gen Yoshisuke Akiyama

First Area Army, General Seiichi Kita
122d Division, Lt Gen Tadashi Akashika
134th Division, Lt Gen Jin Izeki
139th Division, Lt Gen Kyoji Tominaga

Third Army, Lt Gen Keisaku Murakami
79th Division, Lt Gen Teisho Ota
112th Division, Lt Gen Jikizo Nakamura
127th Division, Lt Gen Ryutaro Koga
128th Division, Lt Gen Yoshishige Mizuhara

Fifth Army, Lt Gen Noritsune Shimizu
124th Division, Lt Gen Masatake Shiina
126th Division, Lt Gen Kazuhiko Nomizo
135th Division, Lt Gen Yoichi Hitomi

Third Area Army, General Jun Ushiroku
108th Division, Lt Gen Torajiro Iwai
136th Division, Lt Gen Toru Nakayama

Thirtieth Army, Lt Gen Shojiro Iida
39th Division, Lt Gen Shinnosuke Sasa
125th Division, Lt Gen Tatsuo Imari
138th Division, Lt Gen Tsutomu Yamamoto
148th Division, Lt Gen Motohiro Suemitsu

Forty-fourth Army, Lt Gen Yoshio Hongo
63d Division, Lt Gen Kenichi Kishikawa
107th Division, Lt Gen Koichi Abe
117th Division, Lt Gen Hiraku Suzuki

Seventeenth Area Army,* Lt Gen Yoshio Kozuki
120th Division, Lt Gen Shinichi Yanagawa
150th Division, Lt Gen Giichiro Mishima
160th Division, Lt Gen Masao Yamawaki
320th Division, Lt Gen Kinzaburo Yasumi

Fifty-eighth Army, Lt Gen Sahiju Nagatsu
96th Division, Lt Gen Mamoru Iinuma
111th Division, Lt Gen Tamio Iwasaki
121st Division, Lt Gen Yoshito Masai

* Assigned to Kwantung Army on 10 August 1945

Chart 2: Kwantung Army Commanders, 31 July 1945 (to division level)

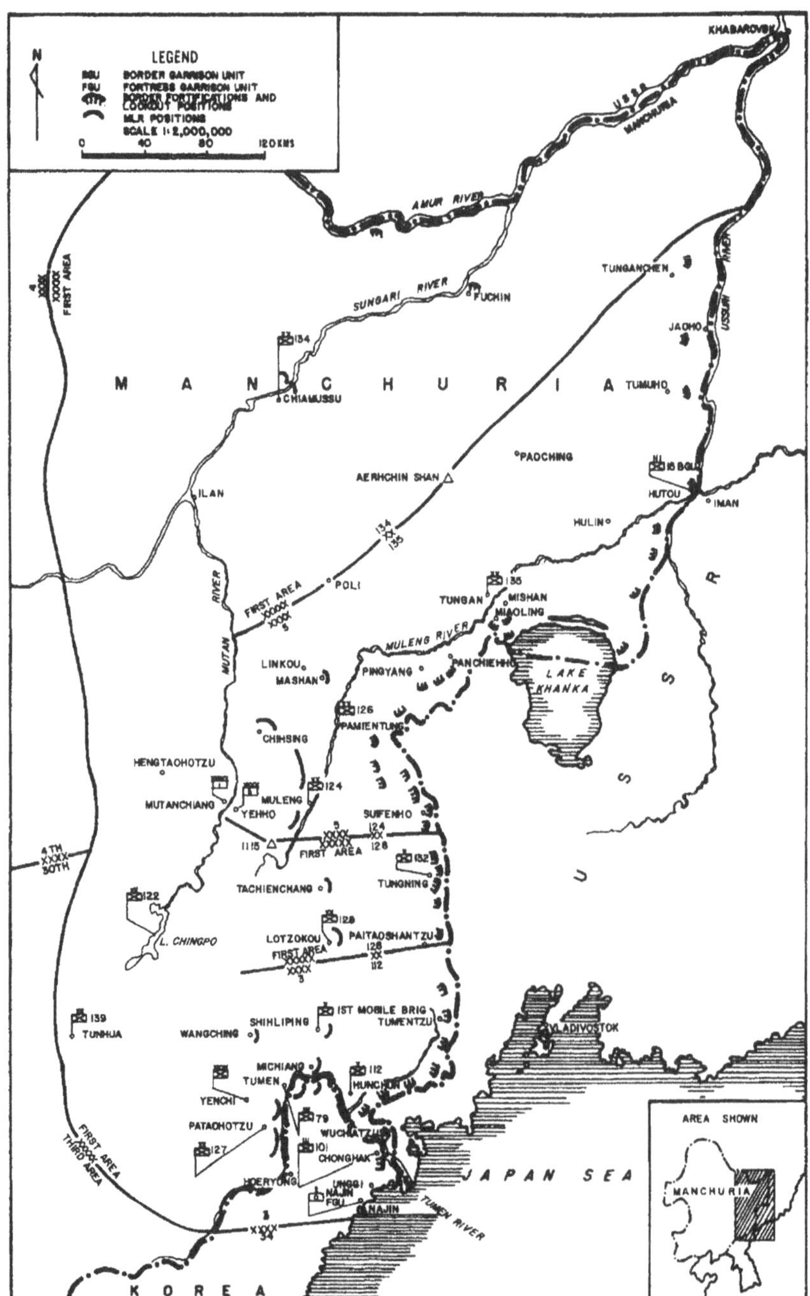

Map 11. Japanese First Area Army Dispositions, 8 August 1945 (Japanese View)

The Third Area Army, commanded by General Ushiroku Jun, was responsible for defending central and western Manchuria from the Amur River to the Liaotung Peninsula. Ushiroku's area army consisted of the 30th Army with first three and later four infantry divisions, one independent mixed brigade, and one tank brigade, and the 44th Army with three infantry divisions, one independent mixed brigade, and one tank brigade. In addition, the Third Area Army directly controlled one infantry division and two independent mixed brigades. Ushiroku's Third Area Army numbered 180,971 men (see Maps 12 and 13 and Chart 3).[10]

The 30th Army, commanded by Lieutenant General Iida Shojiro and headquartered at Meihokou, was responsible for the defense of south-central Manchuria, including Changchun (Hsingking) and Kirin, vital railroad centers in the central valley, and the Tunghua Fortified Zone north of the Korean border. Iida's army consisted of the 39th Infantry Division with headquarters at Hailung, the 125th Infantry Division at Tunghua, the 138th Infantry Division at Fushun, the 148th Infantry Division at Changchun, and the 134th Independent Mixed Brigade at Linchiang.

Shortly after the Soviet attack began, late on 9 August, the Kwantung Army assumed control of the 125th Infantry Division and 134th Independent Mixed Brigade. On 15 August the Kwantung Army assigned the 30th Army control of the 9th Tank Brigade from the 44th Army and the 133d Independent Mixed Brigade from the 34th Army. By this time, the 30th Army had transferred control of its 138th and 148th Infantry Divisions to the 44th Army and had assumed control of the 44th Army's 107th and 117th Infantry Divisions. In essence, Iida's army took over responsibility for the defense of western Manchuria. By 15 August Iida's army, which was also reinforced shortly after the Soviet attack by the 125th Infantry Division at Tunghua, numbered 69,403 men.[11]

Lieutenant General Hongo Yoshio's 44th Army, with its headquarters at Liaoyuan, was responsible for defending west-central Manchuria, including the key fortified zones at Halung-Arshaan and Wuchakou along the railroad into western Manchuria (see Maps 14 and 15). Hongo's army was made up of the 63d Infantry Division at Tungliao, the 107th Infantry Division at Wuchakou and the Halung-Arshaan fortified zone, the 117th Infantry Division at Taonan, and the 130th Independent Mixed Brigade and 9th Tank Brigade at Ssupingchieh. On 15 August the 44th Army transferred the 107th and 117th Infantry Divisions with their defensive sector in western Manchuria to the 30th Army and assumed control over the 108th and 136th Infantry Divisions, the 130th Independent Mixed Brigade, and the 1st Tank Brigade from the Third Area Army. By this time the 44th Army's overall strength was 69,090 men.

Initially, Ushiroku's Third Area Army directly controlled the 108th Infantry Division at Jehol, the 136th Infantry Division at Penchihu, the 79th

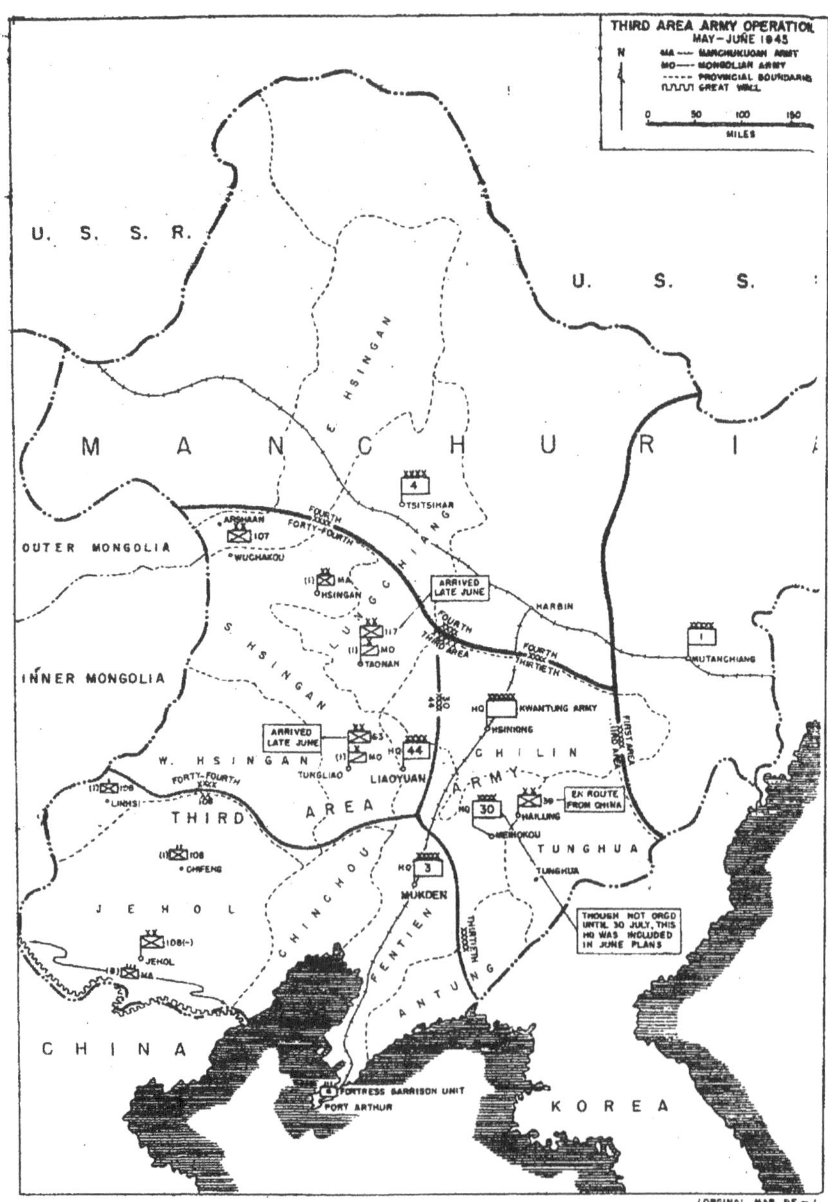

Map 12. Japanese Third Area Army Operations, May–June 1945 (Japanese View)

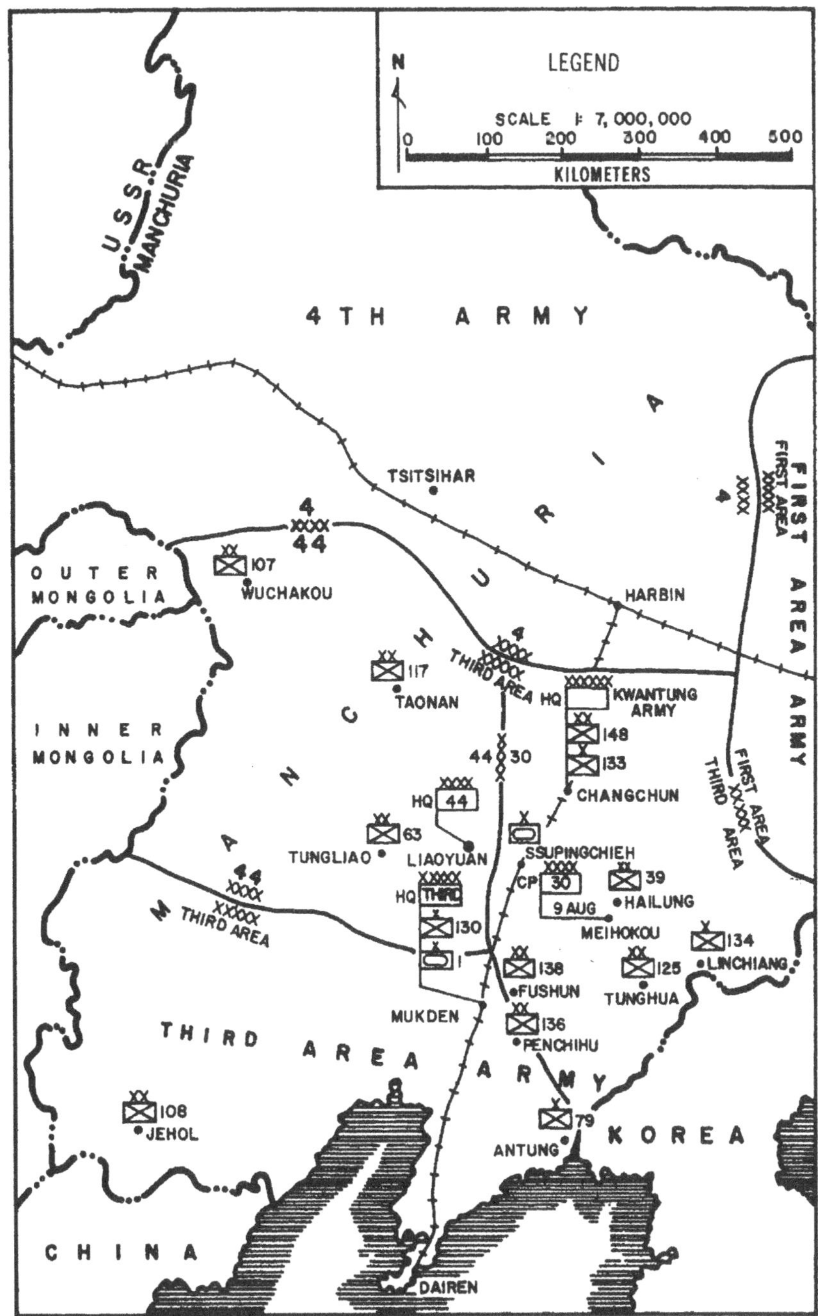

Map 13. Japanese Third Area Army Dispositions, 8 August 1945 (Japanese View)

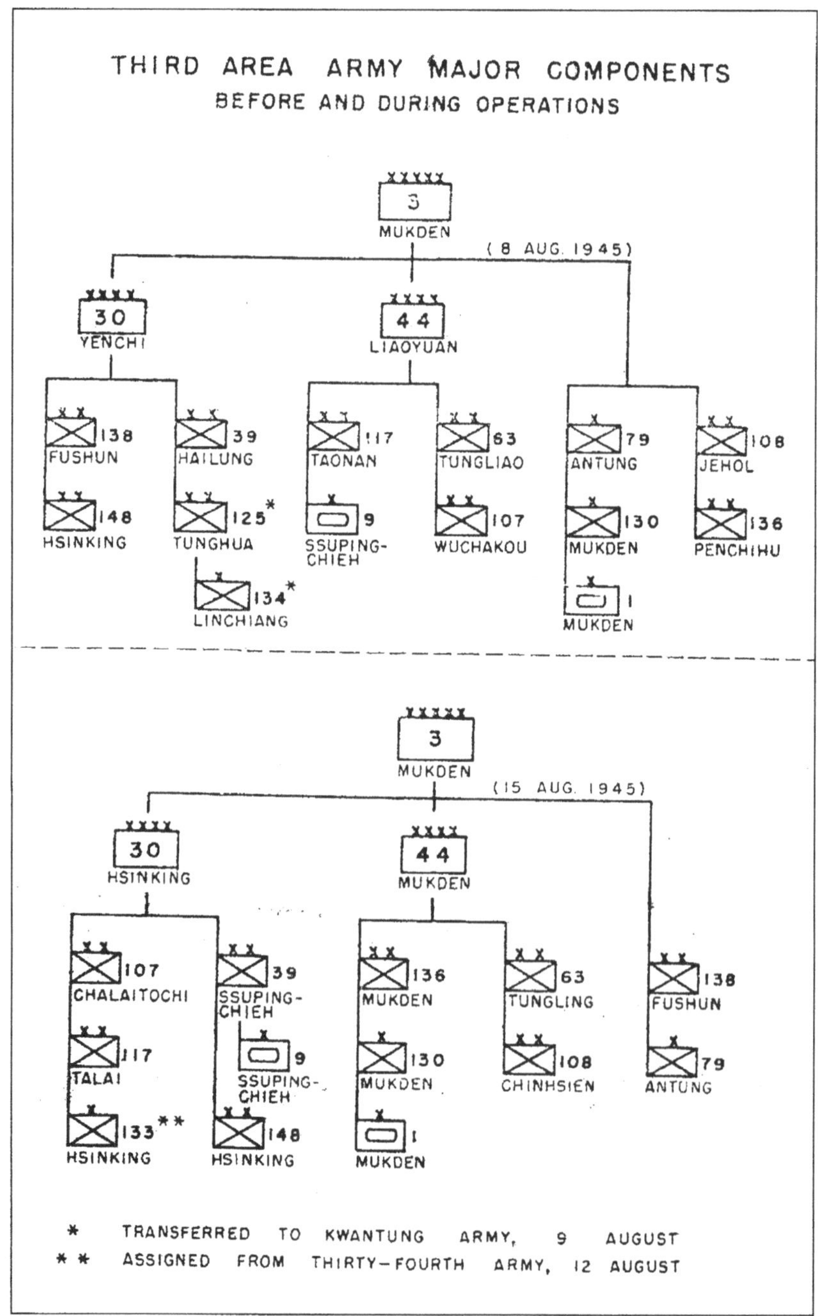

Chart 3: Japanese Third Area Army Major Components, 9–15 August 1945 (Japanese View)

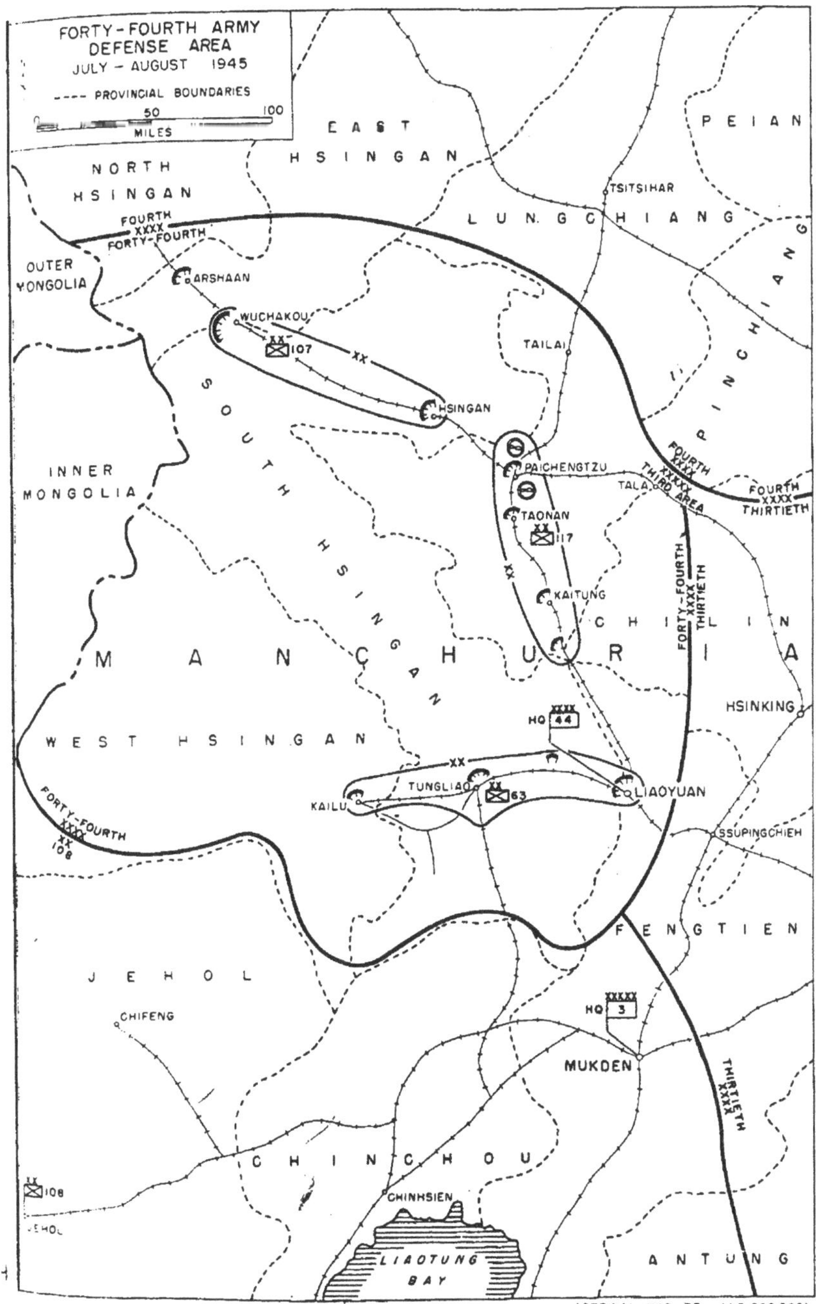

Map 14. Japanese 44th Army Defense Area, July–August 1945 (Japanese View)

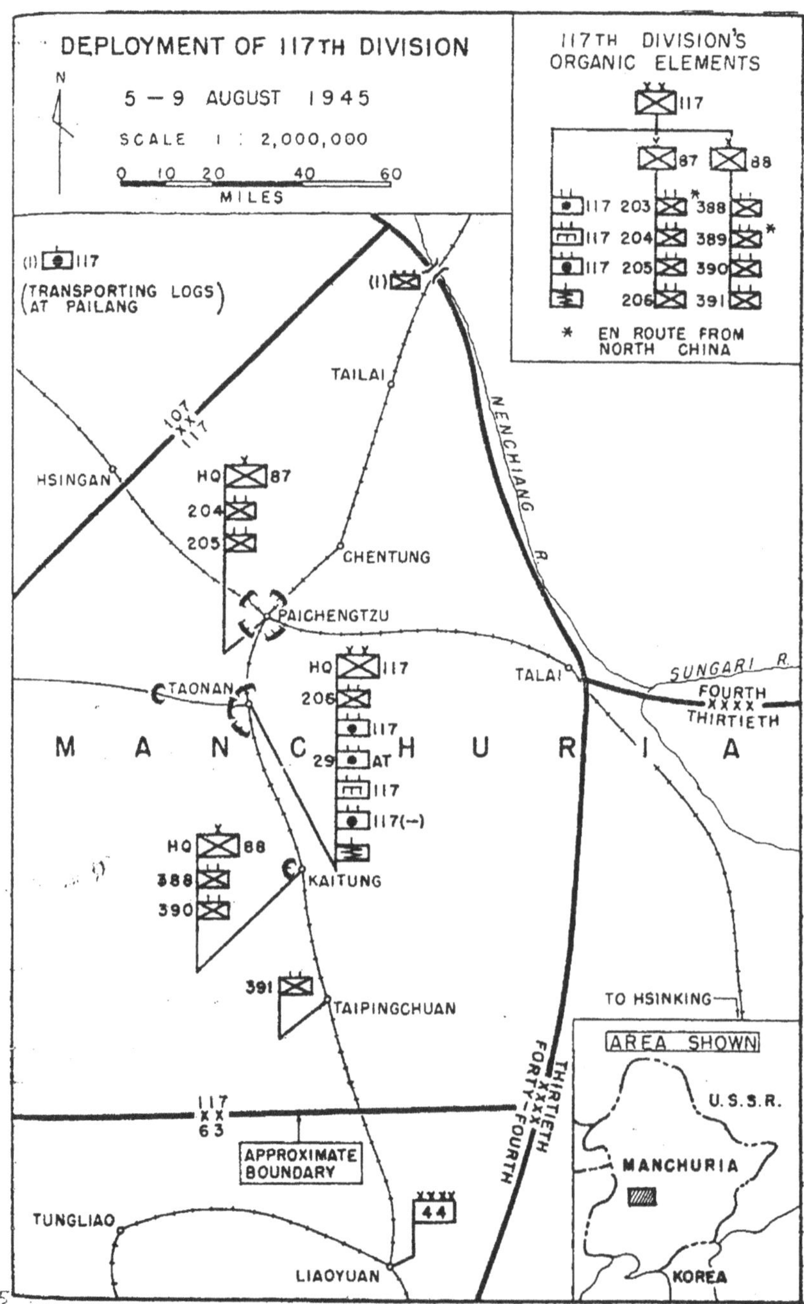

Map 15. Redeployment of the 117th Infantry Division, 5–9 August 1945 (Japanese View)

Independent Mixed Brigade at Antung, the 130th Independent Mixed Brigade at Mukden, the 134th Independent Mixed Brigade at Linchiang, and the 1st Tank Brigade at Mukden. However, on 15 August it transferred the 108th and 136th Infantry Divisions, the 130th Independent Mixed Brigade, and the 1st Tank Brigade to the 44th Army together with responsibility for the defense of western Manchuria.

The 4th Separate Army, commanded by Lieutenant General Uemura Mikio and headquartered at Tsitsihar, was responsible for the defense of north-central and northwestern Manchuria, in particular, the vital western terminus of the Chinese Eastern Railroad at Manchouli, the railroad center of Harbin, the Hailar Fortified Zone, the vital passes through the Grand Khingan Mountains from Yakoshih to Pokotu, and the Amur River crossings near Sunwu. Uemura's army consisted of three infantry divisions and four independent mixed brigades and numbered 96,464 men (see Map 16).[12]

The 4th Army's 119th Infantry Division and the 80th Independent Mixed Brigade were stationed at Hailar; the 123d Infantry Division and 136th Mixed Independent Brigade at Sunwu and nearby Aihun, the 149th Infantry Division at Tsitsihar, the 131st Independent Mixed Brigade at Harbin, and the 136th Independent Mixed Brigade at Nencheng. Finally, the 125th Infantry Division, which defended the Tunghua Fortified Zone, was directly subordinate to Kwantung Army headquarters until transferred to 30th Army control after the Soviet attack.

Shortly after the outbreak of hostilities, on 10 August the Imperial High Command subordinated Lieutenant General Kushibuchi's 34th Army and Lieutenant General Kozuki Yoshio's Seventeenth Area Army to the direct control of the Kwantung Army (see Maps 17–19). Prior to this date, the 34th Army had been responsible for the defense of northern Korea and the Seventeenth Area Army southern Korea. With its headquarters in Hamhung, Kushibuchi's 34th Army consisted of the 59th Infantry Division at Hamhung, the 137th Infantry Division at Chongpyong, and the 134th Independent Mixed Brigade in Linchiang (which had already been reassigned to the 30th Army the day before), for an overall strength of 50,104 men.[13]

Kozuki's Seventeenth Area Army, stationed in southern Korea, consisted of seven infantry divisions and two independent mixed brigades. Three of these divisions (the 96th, 111th, and 121st) were directly subordinate to Lieutenant General Nagatsu Sahiju's 58th Army and four (the 120th, 150th, 160th, and 320th) were under direct area army control. The area army's approximate strength was 200,000 men.

The Sungari Military Flotilla, which supported the Kwantung Army, consisted of 25 ships organized into naval detachments and three naval infantry (marine) regiments equipped with about 110 assault boats of various types. The 2d and 5th Air Armies provided the Kwantung Army with air support. They numbered approximately 2,000 aircraft, including 600 bombers, 1,200

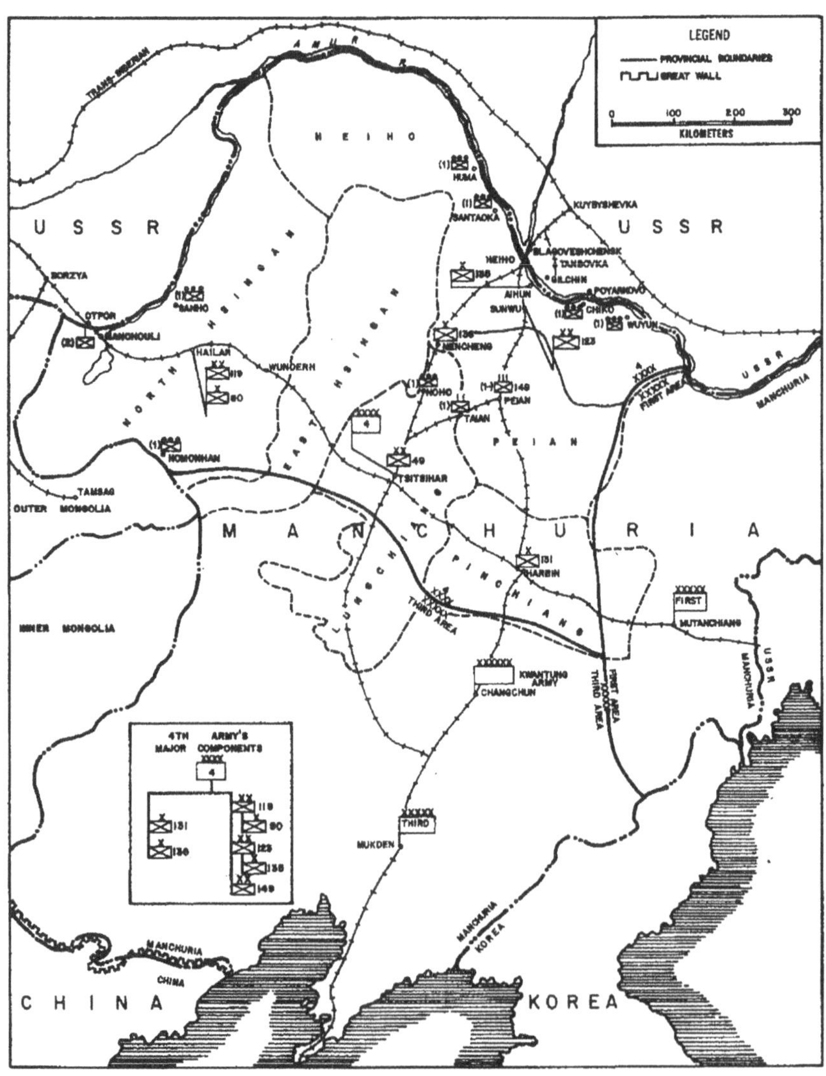

Map 16. Japanese 4th Separate Army's Dispositions, 8 August 1945 (Japanese View)

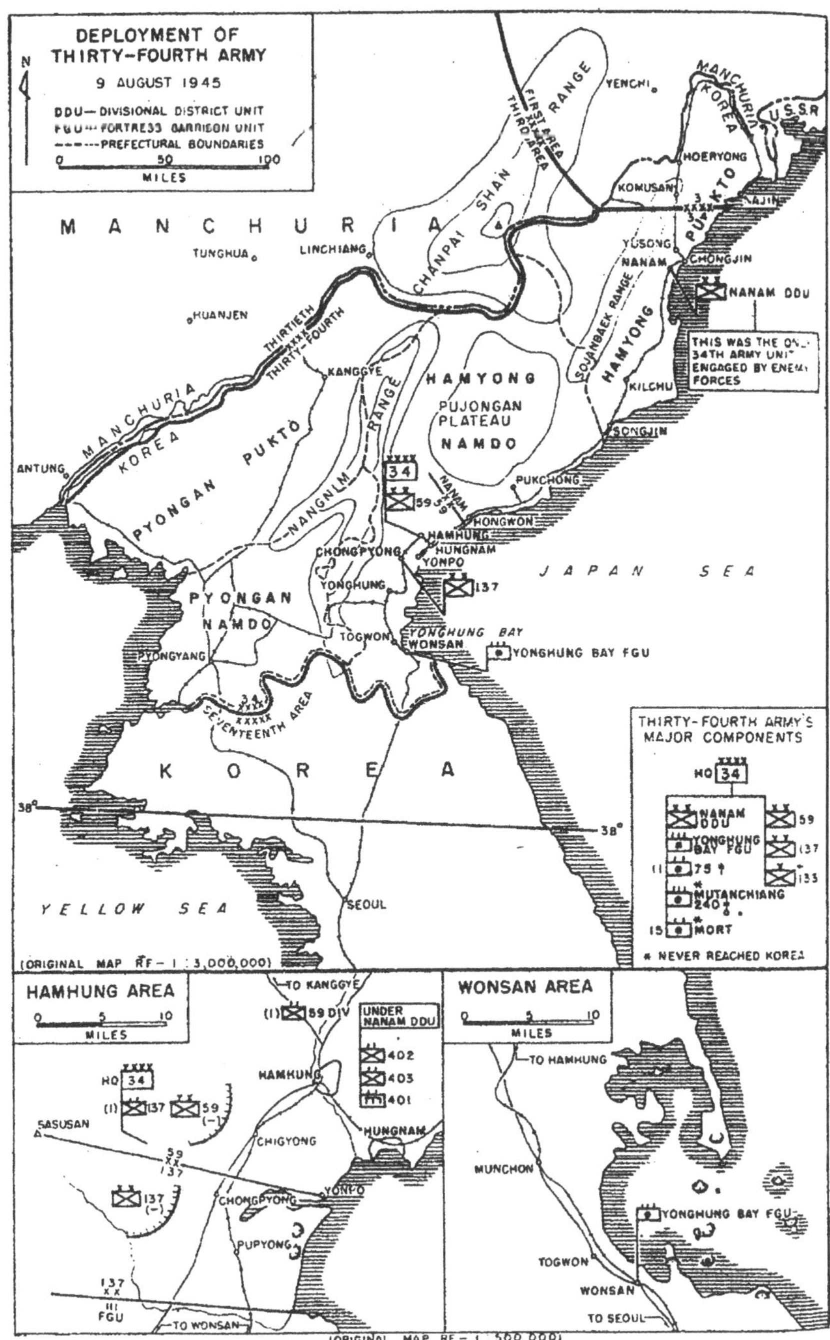

Map 17. Japanese 34th Army's Dispositions, 8 August 1945 (Japanese View)

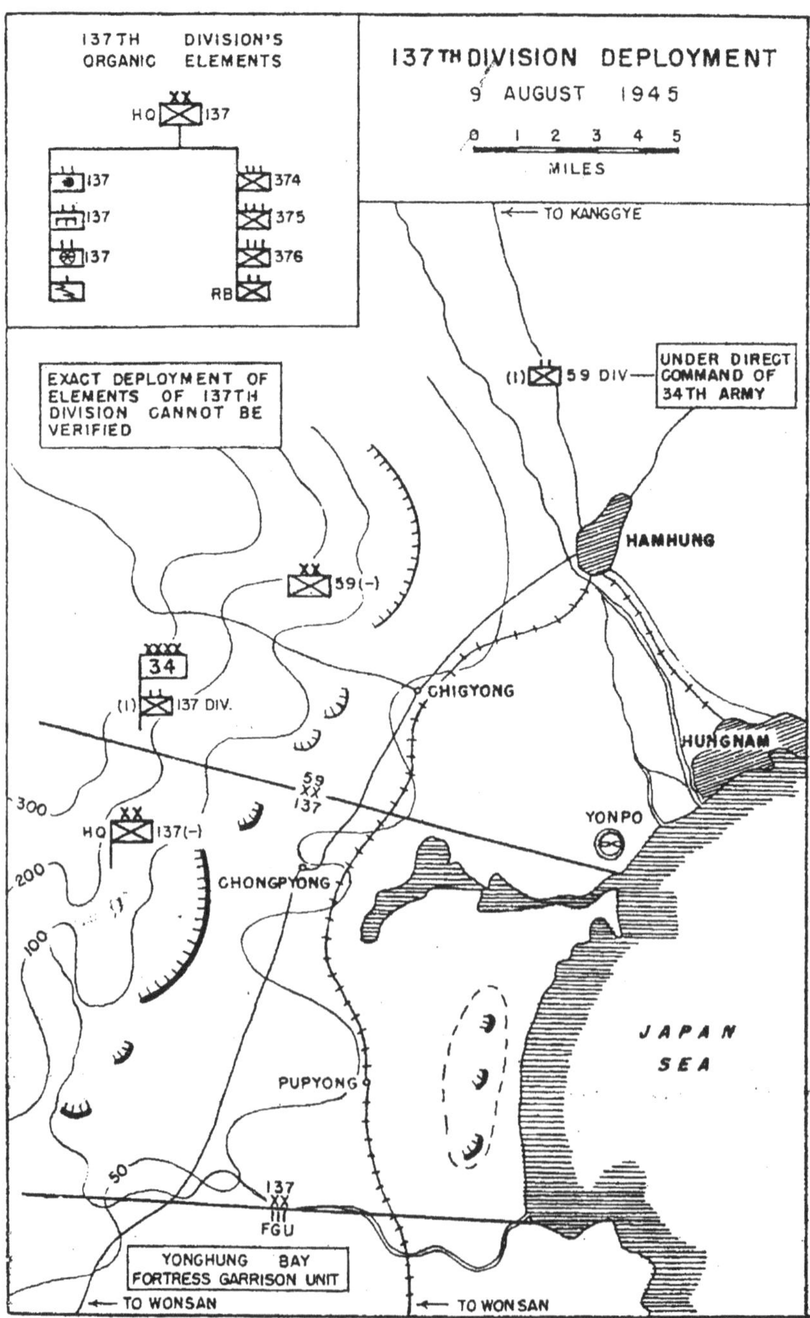

Map 18. Japanese 137th Infantry Division Dispositions, 8 August 1945 (Japanese View)

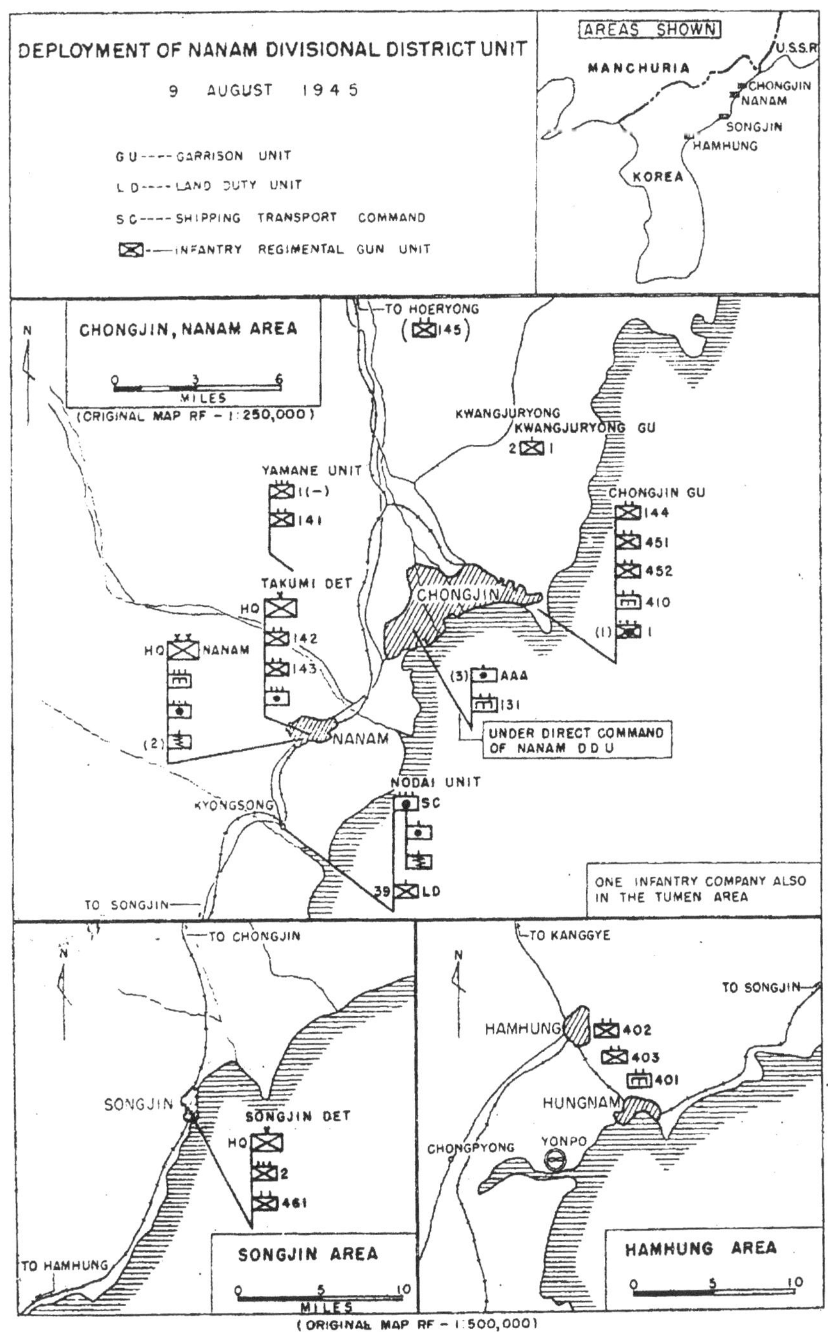

Map 19. Nanam Divisional District Units, 8 August 1945 (Japanese View)

fighters, 100 reconnaissance aircraft, and 1,000 transport and support aircraft. Many of these aircraft, however, were older types and obsolescent.[14]

In addition to the Kwantung Army, Japanese forces defending in the Far East included the Fifth Area Army, which was responsible for defending the northern Japanese island of Hokkaido, the southern portion of Sakhalin Island, and the Kuril Islands. Commanded by Lieutenant General Higuchi Kiichiro, the Fifth Area Army consisted of five infantry divisions, two independent mixed brigades, and a separate infantry and separate tank regiment. These consisted of the 88th Infantry Division with roughly 19,000 men stationed on southern Sakhalin, whose 5,400 man 125th Infantry Regiment defended the Koton Fortified Region blocking the Soviet advance down the center of the island. The 91st Infantry Division's 73d and 74th Infantry Brigades, the 129th Mixed Infantry Brigade, the 41st Separate Mixed Infantry and 11th Tank Regiments defended the northern portion of the Kuril Islands and the 89th Infantry Division the southern portion with a force totaling roughly 80,000 men and 77 tanks. The 7th and 42d Infantry Divisions and the 101st Independent Mixed Brigade were stationed on Hokkaido with another 115,000 men.

The Japanese defended the northernmost of the Kuril Islands, Shumshu (Shumshir), with 8,500 men and 60 tanks of the 91st Infantry Division's 73d Infantry Brigade, the 31st Antiaircraft Regiment, a fortress artillery regiment, and two battalions of the 11th Tank Regiment. The 91st Infantry Division's 74th Infantry Brigade, the 18th and 19th Mortar Battalions, and one battalion of the 11th Tank Regiment (17 tanks) defended nearby Paramoshiri (Paramushir) Island with a force of roughly 12,000 men. Finally, the 41st Separate Infantry Regiment defended Matau Island, the 129th Separate Infantry Brigade manned defenses on Urup Island, and the 89th Infantry Division defended Etorofu (Iturup), Kunashiri (Kunashir), and the lesser Kuril islands. The Fifth Area Army provided air and naval support for its forces from nine airfields, six of which were on Shumshu and Paramoshiri Islands, and naval bases at Kataoka and Kasivabara.[15]

FORCE STRUCTURE

Largely because of its extensive combat experience in conducting large-scale mechanized operations, in August 1945 the Red Army's force structure was far more intricate, well developed, and combat capable than that of the Japanese forces. The basic building block of the Japanese force structure was the infantry division. Organizationally, Japanese infantry divisions were stronger in manpower than Soviet rifle divisions. Even in their reduced 1945 state, most Japanese divisions still out manned their Soviet equivalents. In weaponry, however, Japanese infantry divisions were far weaker than their

Soviet counterparts, and few Japanese divisions actually possessed all the weapons they were authorized.

Two types of infantry divisions existed in the Japanese force structure. The normal and more numerous type of division was triangular in structure and configured to conduct tactical operations (see Chart 4). Although each of these divisions originally numbered 20,000 men, by 1945 their strength ranged from 12,000 to 16,000 men, some with as many as 18,000 men and others as few as 9,000 men.[16] The average strength of those Japanese divisions that actually engaged in active combat was 15,361 men (the 79th, 107th, 112th, 119th, 123d, 124th, 126th, 128th, 134th, and 135th Infantry Divisions). By 1945 the Japanese triangular division (see Table 26) consisted of three infantry regiments of three battalions each, a raiding (*kamikaze*) battalion, an artillery regiment with three battalions (36 guns total), an engineer regiment, a transport regiment, a signal company, and support units.[17]

The second type of Japanese division was the square division, essentially a light infantry division originally organized to perform garrison duty in China (see Chart 5). The square division (see Table 26) consisted of two infantry brigades, each with four infantry battalions, an engineer battalion, a signal company, and support units.[18] Because it was designed for garrison duty only, the division lacked the artillery and antitank support necessary to perform combat missions. Thus, if these divisions were to fight, higher commands had to attach artillery and antitank units to them before they could perform significant field service.

TABLE 26: TO&E (ESTABLISHMENT) OF JAPANESE INFANTRY DIVISIONS, AUGUST 1945

Type	*Triangular*	*Square*
Average personnel strength	13,500	13,500
Organization	3 infantry regiments 3 infantry battalions 1 artillery regiment 2 artillery battalions 1 antitank battalion (16 × 37 mm guns) 1 engineer regiment 1 raiding battalion 1 transport regiment 1 signal company	2 infantry brigades 4 infantry battalions 1 engineer battalion 1 signal company

Source: 'Record of Operations Against Soviet Russia On Northern and Western Fronts of Manchuria and in Northern Korea', *Japanese Monograph No. 155* (August 1945) (Tokyo: Military History Section, US Army Forces Far East, 1954), charts 1, 2.

The Kwantung Army's 63d and 117th Infantry Divisions were square divisions, but all of the remaining divisions were triangular. The triangular

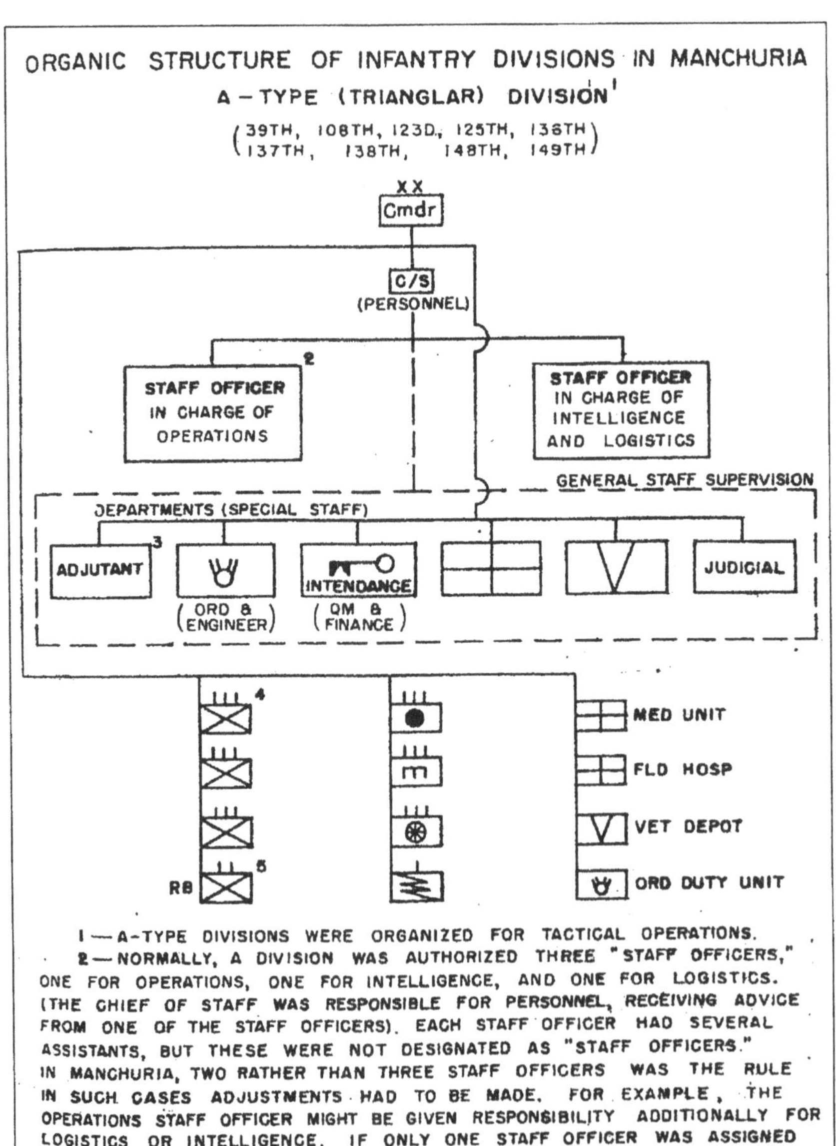

1 — A-TYPE DIVISIONS WERE ORGANIZED FOR TACTICAL OPERATIONS.

2 — NORMALLY, A DIVISION WAS AUTHORIZED THREE "STAFF OFFICERS," ONE FOR OPERATIONS, ONE FOR INTELLIGENCE, AND ONE FOR LOGISTICS. (THE CHIEF OF STAFF WAS RESPONSIBLE FOR PERSONNEL, RECEIVING ADVICE FROM ONE OF THE STAFF OFFICERS). EACH STAFF OFFICER HAD SEVERAL ASSISTANTS, BUT THESE WERE NOT DESIGNATED AS "STAFF OFFICERS." IN MANCHURIA, TWO RATHER THAN THREE STAFF OFFICERS WAS THE RULE IN SUCH CASES ADJUSTMENTS HAD TO BE MADE. FOR EXAMPLE, THE OPERATIONS STAFF OFFICER MIGHT BE GIVEN RESPONSIBILITY ADDITIONALLY FOR LOGISTICS OR INTELLIGENCE. IF ONLY ONE STAFF OFFICER WAS ASSIGNED TO A DIVISION, HE WAS RESPONSIBLE FOR ALL GENERAL STAFF FUNCTIONS.

3 — NORMALLY, A DIVISION HAD TWO ADJUTANTS. THE SENIOR WAS IN CHARGE OF PERSONNEL AND ADMINISTRATION; THE JUNIOR WAS AN AIDE-DE-CAMP TO THE DIVISION COMMANDER.

4 — NORMALLY, THE THREE INFANTRY REGIMENTS WERE UNDER THE CONTROL OF AN INFANTRY GROUP COMMANDER.

5 — RAIDING BATTALION ASSIGNED TO ALL BUT THE 39TH DIVISION.

Chart 4: Structure of the Japanese Triangular Division (Japanese View)

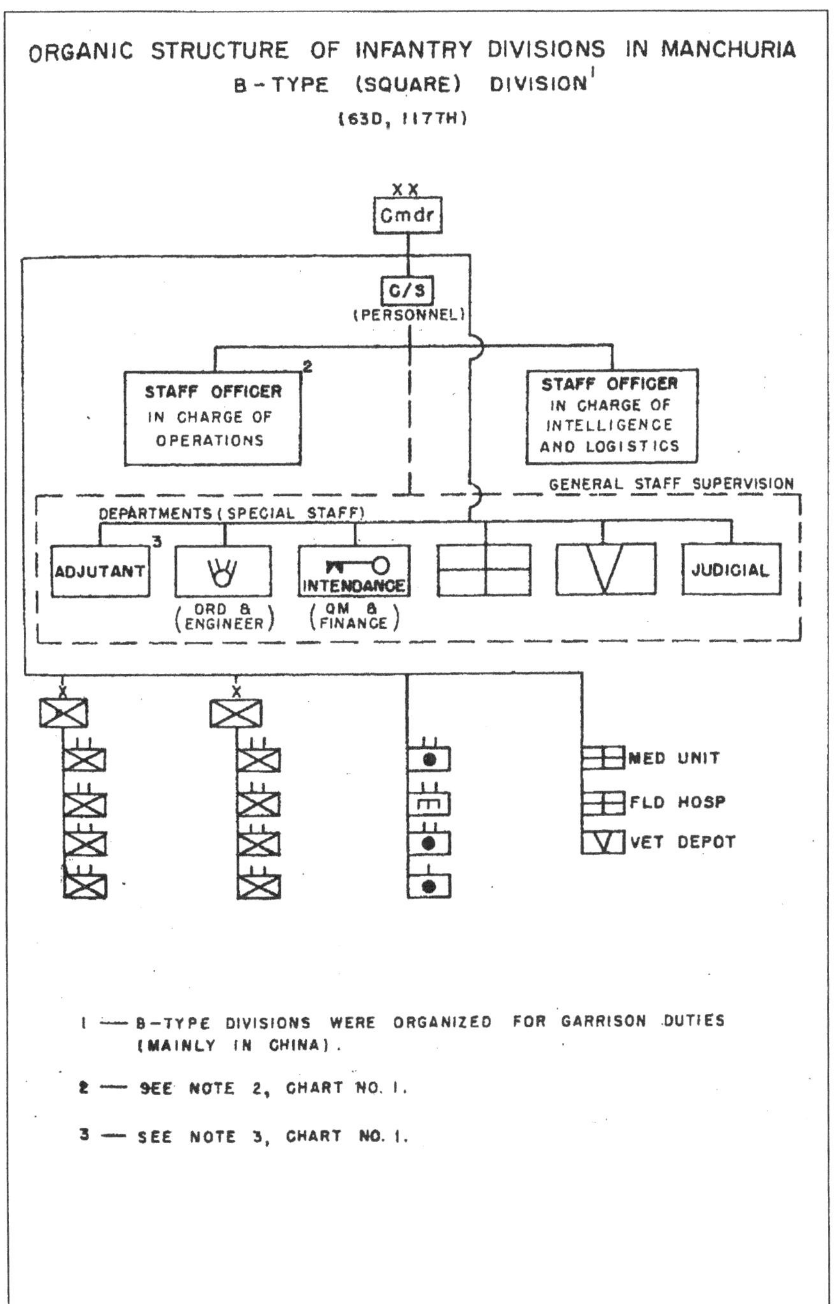

Chart 5: Structure of the Japanese Square Division (Japanese View)

infantry divisions were armed with rifles, machine guns, mortars, and artillery pieces but had no submachine guns, antitank rifles, or rocket artillery. A single battalion of 16 37 mm antitank guns provided the division's only antitank capability, but these antiquated guns proved woefully ineffective against modern medium and heavy tanks. Therefore, the divisions had to employ their raiding battalions to destroy enemy tanks.

The Japanese independent mixed brigade was a small division or, more properly termed, a demi-division. It normally consisted of five infantry battalions with limited separate support and supply units with an average strength of 5,300 men.[19] Above divisional level, the Kwantung Army also suffered from a serious deficiency of weaponry, particularly tanks, self-propelled guns, and heavy engineer equipment. Japanese tanks were armed with only 57 mm guns and machine guns and had not developed self-propelled guns. In addition to being outgunned, Japanese tanks lacked sufficient armor and were vulnerable to rapid destruction by any Soviet tank or antitank gun.

Even though the Kwantung Army maintained an imposing strength on paper of almost one million men, its forces lacked adequate training, in particular in modern mechanized warfare, and lacked combat experience. The Japanese Imperial High Command had transferred most of Kwantung Army's veteran divisions from Manchuria before the summer of 1945. Most of the remaining divisions were either newly formed from reservists or from cannibalized smaller units or recently transferred from duty in China. Of its 31 infantry divisions, only six (the 119th, 107th, 108th, 117th, 63d, and 39th) had been formed before January 1945.[20] All of the army's units were inadequately trained, and equipment, *matériel*, and ammunition shortages plagued the Kwantung Army at every level. The Japanese considered none of the Kwantung Army divisions combat ready, and they assessed some divisions as being only 15 per cent combat ready.[21]

OPERATIONAL PLANNING

The difficulties the Japanese High Command experienced in maintaining the strength and readiness posture of its force structure had a significant impact on its strategic and operational planning. As the Kwantung Army weakened, its strategic planning shifted inexorably from an offensive to a defensive focus. Prior to June 1944, the army maintained plans for a potential offensive into the Soviet Far East, concentrating primarily on an advance toward Vladivostok in the coastal region. In June 1944, however, the army abandoned plans for any offensive operations and instead began developing rudimentary defense plans. By September 1944 it was contemplating a 'realistic' defense, meaning a defense of all of its Manchurian territory.

In early 1945, however, the army's obvious weakness prompted it to shift to a new strategy calling for a defense-in-depth, which involved a planned withdrawal and delaying action along successive lines deep into Manchuria. Total Japanese acquiescence to a new strategy of delay followed by defense became apparent in May 1945 when the Kwantung Army headquarters drafted new plans calling for the conduct of 'Fabian' tactics. The army distributed these new plans to its area armies in June 1945.[22]

The defensive plan the Kwantung Army promulgated in May and June 1944 required Japanese forces to conduct a brief but stubborn delaying action along the borders. Subsequently, they were to defend a series of successive positions, culminating in the final defense of a redoubt stronghold constructed in the Tunghua region (see Map 20). In accordance with this plan, together with border guards detachments, the forward elements of infantry divisions and brigades assigned to the First Area Army's 3d and 5th Armies were to conduct a delaying action along Manchuria's eastern border. They were to do so by employing platoon- to battalion-size elements to defend the heavily fortified zones along the border.

At the same time, the forward divisions' and brigades' main forces were to occupy positions in prepared defensive lines located 25–43 miles (40–70 kilometers) to the rear, in the vicinity of the towns and villages of Fangcheng, Chihsing, Tachienchang, Lotzokou, and Tumen. The plan specifically directed the main force divisions and brigades to conduct a fighting withdrawal to new defensive lines and positions at Tunghua and Antu without becoming decisively engaged (see Map 21).

The 1945 defense plan ordered the Third Area Army, deployed in western Manchuria, to employ company- and battalion-size detachments to delay any Red Army advance through the fortified zone extending southward from Handagai to Wuchakou in the passes through the Grand Khingan Mountains. Simultaneously, main force divisions were to avoid becoming engaged in decisive combat and withdraw eastward also through a series of successive defensive positions. The first defensive line stretched from Changchun southward along the railroad line to Mukden, and the final position extended from Huanjen through Hsinpin to Chinchuan in the redoubt area around Tunghua.

Finally, the 4th Separate Army was to delay stubbornly in fortifications along the border in northwest Manchuria and then along the rail line through the Grand Khingan Mountains. After withdrawing to new defenses stretching from Pokotu through Nencheng to Peian, ultimately the 4th Army was to withdraw to Tsitsihar and Harbin to join the main Kwantung Army forces (see Maps 22 and 23).

These defense plans required roughly one-third of the Kwantung Army's forces to deploy into positions in the border region and the remaining two-thirds to concentrate in the operational depth to form and man the series of intermediate defensive lines. The army command hoped that the rough

Map 20. Kwantung Army Defense Plan (Japanese View)

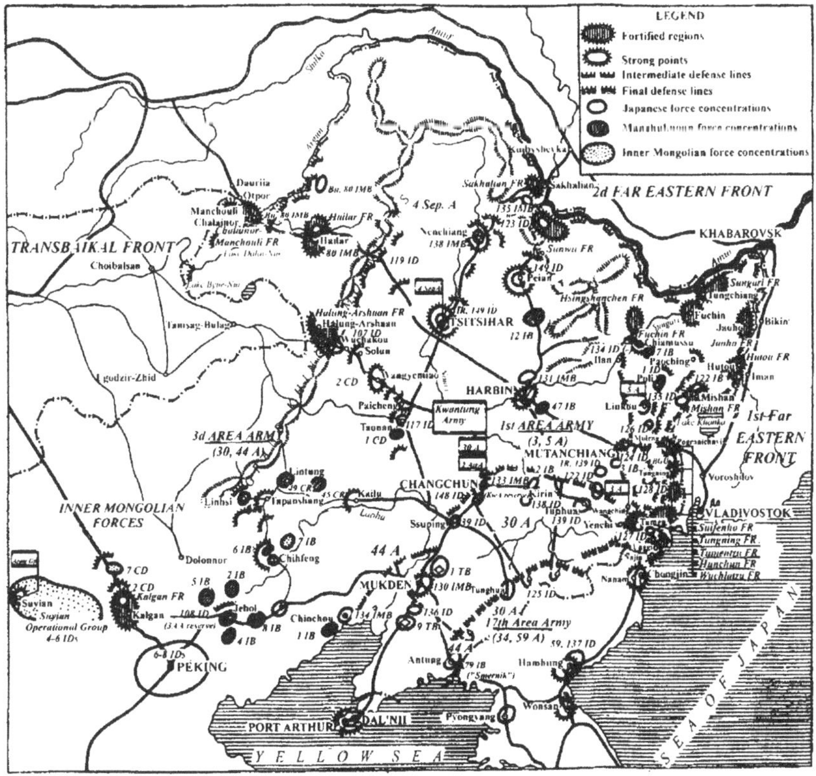

Map 21. Soviet Perceptions of Kwantung Army Dispositions and Defenses

Map 22. Japanese First Area Army Defense Plan (Japanese View)

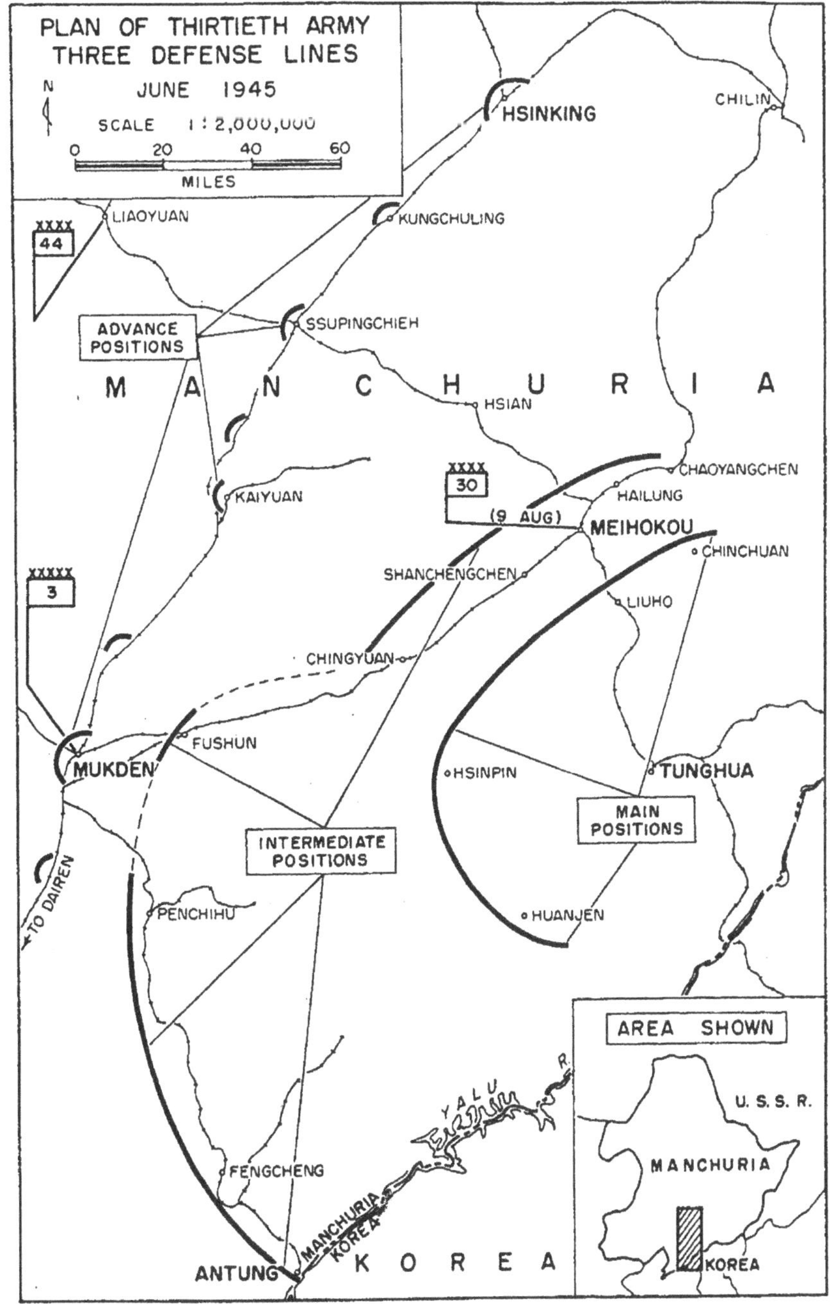

Map 23. Japanese 30th Army Defense Plan (Japanese View)

terrain, long distances, and determined opposition would take a toll on Red Army forces by eroding their strength to the point of exhaustion by the time they reached the redoubt area. If this was the case, the Kwantung Army could halt the Soviet advance and perhaps even counterattack.

However, the Kwantung Army faced two formidable problems after it had formulated its plans, which would spell disaster if they could not be resolved. First, for the defense to be effective, as soon as possible, but certainly before the end of the summer, the army had to effect the necessary regrouping of forces to man the projected defenses. Second, the army had to complete the ambitious fortifications program, which it had neglected to accomplish while the army's mission had been offensive in nature. Sadly for the Kwantung Army, both the redeployment and the fortification programs were still incomplete when the Red Army offensive began.

NOTES

1. For details on the Khalkhin-Gol conflict, see Edward J. Drea, *Nomonhan: Japanese–Soviet Tactical Combat, 1939, Leavenworth Paper No. 2* (Fort Leavenworth, KS: Combat Studies Institute, US Army Command and General Staff College, 1981).
2. *IVMV*, 11: 183
3. See *Japanese Monograph No. 138* (Tokyo: Military History Section, US Army Forces Far East, 1953), App. 6, I–xvi for details. Hereafter cited as *JM 138*.
4. These strength figures for the Kwantung Army include the Seventeenth Area Army of seven infantry divisions and two independent mixed brigades, which was based in Korea and subordinated to the Kwantung Army on 9 August 1945.
5. See Eronin, *Strategicheskaia peregruppirovka*, 12. See also *IVMV*, 11: 182, Vnotchenko, *Pobeda*, 43–5, and 'Japanese Preparations for Operations in Manchuria, January 1943–August 1945', *JM 138*, App. 6, I–xvi for different calculations.
6. See Eronin, *Strategicheskaia peregruppirovka*, 12. 'Kampaniia sovetskikh vooruzhennikh sil na dal'nem vostoke v 1945g (facti i tsifry)' [The campaign of the Soviet armed forces in the Far East in 1945: Facts and figures], *VIZh*, No. 8, August 1945, lists Japanese (and their auxiliary) strength as follows:

Kwantung Army (including Korea)	1,040,000
Manchukuoan Army	170,000
Inner Mongolian Army	44,000
Suyan Army Group	66,000
South Sakhalin forces	20,000
Kurils forces	80,000
Total	1,420,000

The more recent Soviet sources, such as Vnotchenko, *Pobeda*, scales down estimates of Japanese strength. Vnotchenko credits Japan and its partners with fielding slightly more than 1,200,000 men in the Far East (including southern Sakhalin and the Kuril Islands). Subtracting Manchukuoan and Inner Mongolian forces and Japanese forces in southern Korea, southern Sakhalin, and the Kurils would leave the Kwantung Army a strength of about 700,000 men, a figure that agrees with the Japanese monograph totals. Confusion over these figures results largely from Soviet inclusion in the Japanese strength figures of more than 100,000 paramilitary personnel, including reservists, farmer militiamen, and even civilians who threw in their lot with Japanese forces after war began.

The Soviet figure for Japanese armor strength is far higher than the Japanese figure. Even Soviet sources claim that only 369 tanks were captured and that few were destroyed in combat. In addition, most Japanese tanks and aircraft were too antiquated and under-gunned to be of any use in combat.

7. 'Records of Operations Against Soviet Russia on Northern and Western Fronts of Manchuria and in Northern Korea (August 1945)', *Japanese Monograph No. 155* (Tokyo: Military History Section, US Army Forces Far East, 1954), 266–7, Table 1, lists Japanese Army strength in Manchuria and northern Korea as 713,724 men. Hereafter cited as *JM 155*. An earlier Japanese source, Saburo Hayashi and Alvin Coox, *Kogun: The Japanese Army in the Pacific War* (Quantico, VA: The Marine Corps Association, 1959), cites Japanese strength as follows:

Manchuria (including North Korea)	780,000
South Korea	260,000
Total	1,040,000

8. *JM 155*, Table 1, 266.
9. Ibid.
10. Ibid., 266–7.
11. Ibid., 267.
12. Ibid., 267.
13. Ibid., 279.
14. *IVMV*, 11: 182.
15. V. Akshinsky, *Kuril'skii desant* [The Kuril amphibious landing] (Petropavlovsk-Kamchatka: Dal'nevostochnoe knizhnoe izdatel'stvo, 1984), 12.
16. Ibid., 166–7. See also Vnotchenko, *Pobeda*, 46.
17. *JM 155*, chart 1.
18. Ibid., chart 2.
19. Ibid., 266–7; Vnotchenko, *Pobeda*, 46.
20. *JM 138*.
21. Ibid., 161, provides the Japanese High Command's assessment of divisional readiness (see Appendix A).
22. Ibid., 90–110, 141–51; cf. Vnotchenko, *Pobeda*, 39–43.

4

Soviet Organization for Combat and Force Structure

ORGANIZATION FOR COMBAT

The *Stavka* organized Red Army forces in the Far East and Trans-Baikal regions into a unified command because it had to. The diversity and complexity of the terrain in Manchuria, the vastness of the theater of military operations, and the necessity for a well-coordinated and precisely timed operation made such unity of command imperative. The resulting Far East Command, under the command of Marshal of the Soviet Union A. M. Vasilevsky, was a true theater command structure unique to 1945. When fully formed, the command was far more formal in terms of its composition and more precise in its functions than earlier Soviet experiments with command and control of forces in a military theater.

Earlier *Stavka* experiments with theater command structures had involved the formation and employment of Main Commands of (Strategic) Directions [*Glavnye komandovaniia napravlenii*] in 1941 and 1942 and the use of *Stavka* representatives to plan and control operations by groups of *fronts* from 1942 through 1945. The five Main Direction Commands had proved unwieldy and ineffective, due largely to varying degrees of incompetence on the part of Direction commanders, the absence of an effective headquarters or support structure, the excessive span of control, and the general inexperience of Red Army troops and their commanders.

Although the *Stavka* coordinators planned and controlled multi-*front* operations far more effectively, the position was an *ad hoc* one, and they had limited power and a negligible staff. Marshals A. M. Vasilevsky, G. K. Zhukov, and many others had served effectively as *Stavka* representatives on numerous occasions, but they and others had also failed on occasion, partly due to the nature of the position.

By contrast, as the commander of the new Far East Command, Vasilevsky had the opportunity and authority to plan, coordinate, and execute the operation in full and had a complete staff to carry out his orders and support the operations. In brief, the Far East Command had responsibility for all land, sea, and air operations conducted in the Far East and Trans-Baikal regions (see Appendix 4 and Map 24). When fully assembled, Vasilevsky's Far East Command consisted of three experienced *front* headquarters: the Trans-Baikal, 1st Far Eastern, and 2d Far Eastern Fronts (see Tables 27–30).

Commanded by Marshal of the Soviet Union R. Ia. Malinovsky, the Trans-Baikal Front consisted of the 6th Guards Tank Army, the 53d, 39th, 17th, and 36th Armies, a Soviet–Mongolian Cavalry-Mechanized Group, the 12th Air Army, the Trans-Baikal PVO (Air Defense) Army, and a small reserve. The *front* comprised 654,040 troops organized into 30 rifle divisions, five cavalry divisions, two tank divisions, 10 tank brigades, eight mechanized, motorized rifle, or motorized armored brigades, and numerous supporting tank, artillery, engineer, and logistical units and subunits. It made up 41.4 per cent of the total strength of the Far East Command and was assigned an operational front of about 1,430 miles (2,300 kilometers).[1]

The 1st Far Eastern Front, commanded by Marshal of the Soviet Union K. A. Meretskov, consisted of the 1st Red Banner, 5th, 25th, and 35th Armies, the 10th Separate Mechanized Corps, the Chuguevka Operational Group, the 9th Air Army, the Coastal PVO Army, and a reserve. The *front* numbered 586,589 men organized into 31 rifle divisions, one cavalry division, 12 tank brigades, two mechanized brigades, and a wide variety of support units. Operating on a frontage of only 435 miles (700 kilometers), the *front* made up 37.2 per cent of the Far East Command's overall strength.[2]

The combat records of the Far East Command's commander and his subordinate *front* commanders were all indicative of their vast experience.

Vasilevsky, Aleksandr Mikhailovich (1895–1977), commander, Far East Command

1915 – Joined the Russian Army: Alekseev Military School; junior officer, company and battalion commander, 103d Infantry Division's Novokhopersk Regiment with service during the First World War.

1918 – Joined the Red Army; assistant platoon commander, company commander, and detachment commander during the Civil War.

1919 (October) – Battalion commander; commander, 2d Tula Rifle Division's 5th Rifle Regiment; regimental commander, 48th Rifle Division; and regimental commander, 11th Petrograd Rifle Division during the Soviet–Polish War.

1920 – Assistant regimental commander, 48th Rifle Division; chief of staff, divisional school; and regimental commander, 48th Rifle Division.

1931 – Training Administration, RKKA (Workers' and Peasants' Red Army).

1934 – Training Department, Volga Military District.

1936 – General Staff officer, RKKA.

1936 – Attended General Staff Academy.

Map 24. Soviet Far East Command Dispositions, 8 August 1945

TABLE 27: SOVIET FAR EAST COMMAND COMPOSITION

	Total Strength	*Trans-Baikal Front*	*1st Far Eastern Front*	*2d Far Eastern Front*
Personnel				
Combat	1,058,982	416,000	404,056	238,926
Rear Service	518,743	238,040	182,533	98,170
Total	1,577,725	654,040	586,589	337,096
	100 per cent	41.4 per cent	37.2 per cent	21.4 per cent
Weapons				
Guns/mortars	27,086	9,668	11,430	5,988
Multiple rocket launchers	1,171	583	516	72
Tanks/SP guns[(a)]	5,556	2,416	1,860	1,280
Aircraft	3,721	1,324	1,137	1,260
Vehicles	85,819	49,053	4,850	31,916
Frontage	5,130 km	2,300 km	700 km	2,130 km

Organizations:[(b)]	Total	Combined-Arms	Air	Tank	Cavalry-Mech.	Rifle	Cavalry	Mot. Rifle Mech.	Arty	AA, PVO	Engineer
Fronts	3	3									
Armies	18	11	3	1						3	
Groups	1				1						
Corps	24			1		19		3	1		
Divisions	89			2		72	6		2	7	
Brigades	113			30		4		12	47		20
Regiments	98			5		5[(c)]			72	16	
Fortified regions	21										

[(a)] Includes a total of 3,704 tanks and 1,852 SP guns in the Far East Command. [(b)] See Appendix 2 for force designations.

[(c)] Includes one motorcycle regiment.

Sources: 'Kampaniia sovetskikh vooruzhennikh sil na dal'nem vostoke v 1945g (facti i tsifry)' [The campaign of the Soviet armed forces in the Far East in 1945: Facts and figures], *Voenno-istoricheskii zhurnal* [Military-historical journal], No. 8 (August 1965), 67; M. V. Zakharov, ed., *Final: istoriko-memuarny ocherk o razgrome imperialisticheskoi iapony v 1945 godu* [Finale: A historical memoir-survey about the rout of imperialistic Japan in 1945] (Moscow: Izdatel'stvo 'Nauka', 1969), 398–402.

TABLE 28: TRANS-BAIKAL FRONT COMPOSITION

	Total	*17th Army*	*39th Army*	*6th Guards Tank Army*	*Cav.-Mech. Group*	*36th Army*	*53d Army*
Personnel:							
Combat	416,000						
Rear Service	238,000						
Total	654,040						
	41.4 per cent of the Far East Command						
Weapons:							
Guns/mortars	9,668	830	2,708	1,150	610		
Multiple rocket launchers	538	24					
Tanks/SP guns[a]	2,416	137	502	1,019	403		
Aircraft	1,324						
Vehicles	49,053						
Frontage:	2,300 km						

Organizations:[a]	Total	Combined-Arms	Air	Tank	Cavalry-Mech.	Rifle	Cavalry	Mot. Rifle Mech.	Arty	AA, PVO	Engineer
Armies	7	4	1	1						1	
Groups	1				1						
Corps	12			1		8		2	1		
Divisions	43			2		30[b]	5		2	4	
Brigades	42			10[c]				10	12		10
Regiments	34			3[d]					24	7	
Fortified regions	2										

[a] See Appendix 2 for force identifications. [b] Includes two motorized rifle divisions. [c] Includes one armored brigade. [d] Includes motorcycle regiments. This table includes only verifiable data.

Sources: 'Kampaniia sovetskikh vooruzhennikh sil na dal'nem vostoke v 1945g. (facti i tsifry)' [The campaign of the Soviet armed forces in the Far East in 1945: Facts and figures], *Voenno-istoricheskii zhurnal* [Military-historical Journal], No. 8 (August 1965), 67; M. V. Zakharov, ed., *Final: istoriko-memuarny ocherk o razgrome imperialisticheskoi iapony v 1945 godu* [Finale: A historical memoir-survey about the rout of imperialistic Japan in 1945] (Moscow: Izdatel'stvo 'Nauka', 1969), 398–9.

TABLE 29: 1ST FAR EASTERN FRONT COMPOSITION

	Total	*1st Red Banner Army*	*5th Army*	*25th Army*	*35th Army*
Personnel:					
Combat	404,056				
Rear Service	182,533				
Total	586,589				
	37.2 per cent of the Far East Command				
Weapons:					
Guns/Mortars	11,430		2,945	1,669	955
Multiple rocket launchers	516		432		
Tanks/SP guns	1,860	402	692	121	205
Aircraft	1,137				
Vehicles	4,850				
Frontage:	700 km				

Organizations:[a]	Total	Combined-Arms	Air	Tank	Cavalry-Mech.	Rifle	Cavalry	Mot. Rifle Mech.	Arty	AA, PVO	Engineer
Armies	6	4	1							1	
Groups	1										
Corps	10					9		1			
Divisions	34					31	1			2	
Brigades	54			12				2	33		7
Regiments	29			2[b]					23	4	
Fortified regions	14										

[a] See Appendix 2 for force designations. [b] Includes motorcycle regiment. This table includes only verifiable data.

Sources: 'Kampaniia sovetskikh vooruzhennikh sil na dal'nem vostoke v 1945g. (facti i tsifry)' [The campaign of the Soviet armed forces in the Far East in 1945: Facts and figures], *Voenno-istoricheskii zhurnal* [Military-historical Journal], No. 8 (August 1965), 67; M. V. Zakharov, ed., *Final: istoriko-memuarny ocherk o razgrome imperialisticheskoi iapony v 1945 godu* [Finale: A historical memoir-survey about the rout of imperialistic Japan in 1945] (Moscow: Izdatel'stvo 'Nauka', 1969), 401.

TABLE 30: 2D FAR EASTERN FRONT COMPOSITION

	Total	*2d Red Banner Army*	*15th Army*	*16th Army*	*5th Sep. Rifle Corps*
Personnel:					
Combat	238,926				
Rear Service	98,170				
Total	337,096				
	21.4 per cent of the Far East Command				
Weapons:					
Guns/Mortars	5,988	1,270	1,433		
Multiple rocket launchers	72				
Tanks/SP guns	1,280	240	164		
Aircraft	1,260				
Vehicles	31,916				
Frontage:	2,130 km				

Organizations:[a]	Total	Combined-Arms	Air	Tank	Cavalry-Mech.	Rifle	Cavalry	Mot. Rifle Mech.	Arty	AA, PVO	Engineer
Armies	5	3	1							1	
Groups	0										
Corps	2					2					
Divisions	12					11				1	
Brigades	17			8		4			2		3
Regiments	35					5			25	5	
Fortified regions	14										

[a] See Appendix 2 for force designations. This table includes only verifiable data.

Sources: 'Kampaniia sovetskikh vooruzhennikh sil na dal'nem vostoke v 1945g. (facti i tsifry)' [The campaign of the Soviet armed forces in the Far East in 1945: Facts and figures], *Voenno-istoricheskii zhurnal* [Military-historical Journal], No. 8 (August 1965), 67; M. V. Zakharov, ed., *Final: istoriko-memuarny ocherk o razgrome imperialisticheskoi iapony v 1945 godu* [Finale: A historical memoir-survey about the rout of imperialistic Japan in 1945] (Moscow: Izdatel'stvo 'Nauka', 1969), 400.

1940 (May) – Assistant chief, Operations Division, General Staff.
1941 (August) – Assistant chief of General Staff; chief, Operations Division, General Staff.
1941 (August) – Chief of staff, Northwestern Front.
1942 – (May) Chief of General Staff.
1942 – (October) Assistant Peoples' Commissar of Defense, USSR; representative of the *Stavka* during the Stalingrad, Ostrogozhsk-Rossosh', Kursk, Donbas, Krivoi-Rog, Nikopol', and Belorussian operations.
1945 (February) – Commander, 3d Belorussian Front (the East Prussia operation).
1945 (June) – Supreme commander, Soviet Far East Command.
1946 – Chief of the General Staff and Deputy Minister of Defense.
1948 (November) – First Deputy Minister of the Armed Forces of the USSR.
1949 (March) – Minister of the Armed Forces of the USSR.
1953 – First Deputy Minister of Defense.
1956 – Deputy Minister of Defense for Military Science.
1959 (January) – General inspector, General Inspectors' Group, Ministry of Defense.

Malinovsky, Rodion Iakovlevich (1898–1967), commander, Trans-Baikal Front
1916 – Joined the Russian Army with service in Russia and France.
1918 – Joined the Red Army; service with the 27th Rifle Division on the eastern front during the Civil War.
1920 – Commander, machine gun platoon and machine gun command; assistant battalion commander and battalion commander during the Civil War.
1930 – Attended the Frunze Academy.
1930 – Chief of staff, cavalry regiment, 10th Cavalry Division; staff officer, North Caucasus and Belorussian Military Districts; chief of staff, 3d Cavalry Corps.
1937 – Service in Spain during the Spanish Civil War.
1939 – Instructor, Frunze Academy.
1941 (March) – Commander, 48th Rifle Corps during the border battles.
1941 (August) – Commander, 6th Army.
1941 (December) – Commander, Southern Front.
1942 (August) – Commander, 66th Army during the Stalingrad defense.
1942 (October) – Commander, Voronezh Front during the Stalingrad counter offensive.
1943 (February) – Commander, Southern Front during the Donbas operation.
1943 (March – Commander, Southwestern Front (October 1943 renamed the 3d Ukrainian Front), participated in the Donbas, Right Bank of Ukraine, and Odessa operations.
1944 (March) – Commander, 2d Ukrainian Front during the Lassy-Kishinev, Debrecen, Budapest, Balaton, and Vienna operations.

1945 (July) – Commander, Trans-Baikal Front.
1945–47 – Commander, Trans-Baikal–Amur Military District.
1947 – Commander of Soviet Forces in the Far East.
1953 – Commander of the Far East Military District.
1956 (March) – First Deputy Minister of Defense and commander of the Ground Forces.
1957 (October) – Minister of Defense.

Meretskov, Kirill Afanas'evich (1897–1968). Commander, 1st Far Eastern Front
1918 – Joined the Red Army.
1919 – Detachment commander, brigade chief of staff, and division chief of staff during the Civil War.
1921 – Attended RKKA Military Academy.
1922 – Chief of staff, 1st Tomsk Siberian Cavalry Division; assistant chief of staff, 15th Rifle Corps; and chief of staff, 9th Don Rifle Division.
1924 – Chief, Mobilization Department, Moscow Military District; and assistant chief of staff, Moscow Military District.
1930 – Commander, 14th Rifle Division.
1931 – Chief of staff, Moscow and Belorussian Military Districts.
1935 – Chief of staff, Special Red Banner Far Eastern Army.
1936 – Service in Spain during the Spanish Civil War.
1937 – Deputy chief of the General Staff.
1938 (September) – Commander, Volga and Leningrad Military Districts; and commander 7th Army during the Finnish War.
1940 (August) – Chief of the General Staff.
1941 (January) – Deputy, People's Commissar of Defense.
1941 (June) – Arrested by the NVKD imprisoned, but released.
1941 (July) – Representative of the *Stavka* to the Northwestern and Karelian Fronts.
1941 (September) – Commander, 7th Separate Army.
1941 (November) – Commander, 4th Army during the Tikhvin operation.
1941 (December) – Commander, Volkhov Front during the Leningrad–Liuban' operation.
1942 (May) – Commander, 33d Army.
1942 (June) – Commander, Volkhov Front during operations around Leningrad.
1944 (February) – Commander, Karelian Front during the Vyborg–Petrozavodsk operation.
1945 (April) – Commander, Maritime Army in the Far East.
1945 (August) – Commander, 1st Far Eastern Front.
1945 – Commander, Maritime, Moscow, White Sea, and Northern Military Districts; chief of the Vystrel' [Infantry] Course.
1955 – Deputy Minister of Defense for Higher Military Schools.

1964 (April) – General Inspectors Group, Central Inspectorate, Ministry of Defense.

Purkaev, Maksim Alekseevich (1894–1953), Commander 2d Far Eastern Front

1916 – Joined the Russian Army; attended Warrant Officers School.
1917 – Member of regimental soldiers committee (28th Rifle Division).
1918 (July) – Joined the Red Army; commander, rifle company and battalion, 215th Rifle Regiment, 24th Samara Iron Rifle Division during the Civil War (Eastern Front).
1919 (August) – Commander, 215th Rifle Regiment, 24th Samara Iron Rifle Division.
1921 (August) – Commander, rifle regiment, 33d Rifle Division.
1923 – Attended Vystrel' Course.
1923 – Commander, 99th Rifle Regiment, 33d Rifle Division.
1927 (June) – Chief of staff, 33d Rifle Division.
1930 – Chief of the organizational mobilization department, Moscow Military District; deputy chief of staff, Moscow Military District.
1936 – Attended Frunze Academy.
1936 – Commander, motorized rifle division.
1938 (April) – Chief of staff, Belorussian Special Military District (invasion of Poland).
1939 – Military attaché to Germany (Berlin).
1940 (February) – Chief of staff, Belorussian Military District.
1940 (June) – Chief of staff, Kiev Special Military District and Southwestern Front (Border battles).
1941 (July) – Member, Special Commission to raise forces in the Volga Military District.
1941 (July) – Commander, 63d (3d Shock) Army (Battle of Moscow and Toropets offensive).
1942 – Commander, Kalinin Front (Operations 'Mars' and Velikie Luki offensive).
1943 (April) – Commander, Far Eastern and 2d Far Eastern Fronts (Manchurian offensive).
1945 – Commander, Far Eastern Military District.
1947 – Chief of staff and 1st deputy commander, Far Eastern Forces.
1952 (July) – Chief, Directorate of Higher Military Schools, Ministry of Defense.

The 2d Far Eastern Front, under the command of Army General M. A. Purkaev, consisted of the 15th, 16th, and 2d Red Banner Armies, the 5th Separate Rifle Corps, the Kamchatka Defensive Region, the 10th Air Army, the Amur PVO Army, and a reserve. The *front's* 337,096 men were deployed along an extended frontage of 1,324 miles (2,130 kilometers).[3] The smallest of the Far East Command's three *fronts*, Purkaev's force made up 21.4 per cent of Vasilevsky's total force.

The overall force with which Vasilevsky could conduct operations against Japanese forces in the Far East totaled 1,577,725 troops. This included 1,058,982 soldiers assigned to combat forces, 21,384 of which were serving in the Mongolian Peoples' Red Army (MNRA), and 518,743 soldiers serving in rear service units and installations. This force included three mechanized corps, one tank corps, 70 rifle division, two motorized rifle divisions, six cavalry divisions (including four Mongolian), two tank divisions, 24 separate tank brigades, two separate self-propelled artillery brigades, two separate mechanized brigades (including one Mongolian), two separate machine gun-artillery brigades, one separate motorized rifle brigade, five separate sapper brigades, and 21 fortified regions. The *front's* weaponry totaled 3,704 tanks, 1,852 self-propelled guns, 26,137 guns and mortars, and 3,446 aircraft. Finally, the Pacific Fleet and Red Banner Amur Flotilla totaled more than 500 military ships, and 1,549 aircraft manned by about 178,000 personnel.[4]

THE DYNAMICS OF SOVIET FORCE STRUCTURING

Given the challenging and varied terrain conditions that characterized the Far Eastern theater of military operations, the Soviets carefully tailored all of their forces from *front* down to battalion level so that they could better accomplish their assigned missions. This tailoring process reflected not only the strength and dispositions of Japanese forces but also the terrain across which the force was to operate and the desired pace (speed) of the operation. The parent headquarters assigned each subordinate force the quantity of armor, artillery, antitank, air defense, and engineer support it required to fulfill its specific mission. For example, since the 1st Far Eastern Front was assigned the task of penetrating the heavily fortified Japanese defensive zone along the eastern Manchurian border, to provide it with the requisite firepower, the Far East Command assigned to Meretskov's *front* extremely large quantities of heavy artillery.

Likewise, the Far East command assigned the Trans-Baikal Front extensive vehicular and motorized rifle support to enable it to conduct a rapid and balanced combined arms advance across the broad expanse of desert in Inner Mongolia and the formidable Grand Khingan Mountains in western Manchuria. In general, *front* commanders provided significantly more artillery to those armies designated to operate against strong enemy fortified zones than to armies operating on more open axes of advance. Similarly, the *fronts* assigned extensive engineer support to forces operating over the most difficult terrain. While *front* commanders employed forward detachments at every level to lead the advance and preempt Japanese defenses before they formed, at the tactical level tailored rifle divisions and tank and mechanized corps, as well as rifle regiments and rifle battalions, formed tailored forward detachments or special assault groups to provide the firepower and mobility necessary to overcome defenses and conduct high-speed operations.

The employment of imaginative tailoring of forces at every level to accommodate terrain conditions and specific force missions prompted significant modifications to normal force TO & Es (tables of organization and equipment or establishments). While this tailoring process often reflected practices developed earlier in the war, many of these force adjustments proved so constructive that the Soviet Army institutionalized them during the immediate postwar years. More detailed investigation of the Soviet force structuring process prior to, during, and after the Manchurian campaign illustrates the dynamic nature of Red Army and Soviet force structuring.

The evolution of the Red Army's force structure during the Second World War is the story of an army adjusting to the hard realities of war. After the Red Army barely weathered the beating it suffered at the hands of the German *Wehrmacht* in 1941, it scaled back the complexity of its force structure to create units that its inexperienced commanders could more effectively command and control. As the tide of war shifted in the Soviets' favor during late 1942 and 1943, the Red Army grew in size and complexity to match the increasing experience of its commanders and operate more effectively against the more experienced *Wehrmacht*.

Although massive in size, the Red Army of 1941 was a complex, ponderous, cumbersome, and largely ineffective force. Infantry forces (termed by the Soviet 'rifle'), organized in regiments, divisions, corps, and full armies, provided the backbone of the Red Army force structure. Theoretically, the large rifle armies consisted of as many as three or four rifle corps totaling from 12 to 15 rifle divisions, reinforced by mechanized, cavalry, tank, and artillery formations (corps), units (regiments or brigades), and sub-units (battalions or squadrons).[5]

Supplementing the rifle forces and providing the Red Army with its mobile offensive punch were mechanized corps, each of which had a paper strength of more than 1,000 tanks, and separate cavalry corps.[6] In addition, the Red Army force structure included an imposing array of separate tank brigades and battalions, separate antitank brigades, artillery regiments, and airborne corps and brigades. This force was so large and cumbersome that it was difficult to command and control, it required quantities of equipment and supplies not available in 1941, and it required first-rate leadership that was also generally absent when the war began.

Launched by surprise and characterized by audacious maneuver to great depths, the German invasion of 1941 utterly shattered the Red Army's force structure and left the Soviet military leadership with no choice but to retrench. Heavy and truly catastrophic manpower and materials losses at the hands of the *Wehrmacht* and the Red Army command cadre's inability to control large units effectively forced the Peoples' Commissariat of Defense (NKO) to truncate and simplify its military forces of every type and at every level. It drastically scaled down the size of its rifle armies, abolished the rifle corps link between division and army, and severely decreased the manpower and weaponry of its rifle divisions.

At the same time, the NKO abolished the large but ineffective mechanized corps, which had already been partly destroyed by the Germans, and replaced them with tank brigades and battalions designated to provide a base minimum of armor support to infantry units. The NKO also replaced the army's rifle divisions, many of which the Germans had also destroyed, with smaller but more easily formed and controlled rifle brigades. Finally, it disbanded the large but incomplete antitank brigades and other supporting forces, pooling antitank and other weaponry in battalions and regiments under the control of its reserve, and parceled these precious supporting forces out to armies and *fronts* as required.

Fortunately for the Red Army and Soviet state, the retrenchment and reorganization program worked, and Red Army forces survived the harsh winter of 1941–42. Throughout 1942 the NKO slowly rebuilt the Red Army's force structure by increasing the number and strength of rifle forces and forming new offensively oriented tank and mechanized forces. Beginning in early 1942, the NKO gradually reintroduced rifle corps headquarters into its rifle armies. In April 1942 it fielded the first of its reorganized tank corps, followed in September 1942 by new mechanized corps of various types. From May through June 1942, it formed new tank armies of *ad hoc* composition (tank and cavalry corps and rifle divisions) in time to help absorb the shock of the German summer offensive of 1942 and to participate in the hour of victory at Stalingrad.

In January 1943 the NKO completed the reconstruction of its basic armored force by forming new tank armies organized on a unified TO&E (establishment). The complexity and strength of Red Army field forces grew throughout 1944 and into 1945. The quantity, strength, and complexity of Red Army tank corps, mechanized corps, and tank armies increased markedly. The rifle corps links appeared in virtually every army, the number and firepower of rifle divisions grew inexorably, and rifle brigades dwindled in number as the Soviets replaced them with more numerous and powerful streamlined rifle divisions.

Over time, the NKO created a host of units of every type including artillery brigades, divisions, and corps; tank destroyer regiments and brigades; anti-aircraft regiments and divisions; engineer sapper units from battalion to army size; guards-mortar (multiple rocket launcher) regiments, brigades, and divisions; self-propelled artillery battalions, regiments, and brigades; and antiaircraft divisions and regiments to provide necessary combat support.

Soviet forces slowly developed a capability – so lamentably absent in the first two years of the war – to implement fully Soviet operational and tactical concepts prevalent since the early 1930s but forgotten on the eve of war. Slowly, and at great cost, the older tenets of 'Deep Battle' and 'Deep Operations' finally reemerged on the field of battle during late 1942 and 1943. The increasing ability of Red Army commanders to realize these concepts and the harsh but effective education of Red Army forces in the art of mobile warfare inevitably generated greater sophistication in the force structure, which became manifest throughout 1944 and 1945.

By war's end in May 1945, the Red Army force structure had fully matured. Bloodied by its heavy wartime losses, by this time the Red Army relied on firepower, maneuver, and mobile weaponry to compensate for its shortage of manpower. The Soviet military leadership combined their new operational and tactical techniques with a carefully articulated force structure designed to carry them out to achieve even more spectacular success on the field of battle. Nowhere was this process more apparent than in Manchuria, where the Soviet military leadership effected final adjustments to the Red Army force structure and its combat employment before reforming its forces in the postwar years.

In August 1945 the basic force building block subordinate to the *front* was the combined-arms army, the lineal descendent of the wartime rifle army. The typical combined-arms army of 1945 (see Table 31) consisted of three rifle corps headquarters controlling a total of seven to 12 rifle divisions, one or two gun-artillery brigades, one tank destroyer brigade, one antiaircraft division, one mortar regiment, one signal regiment, one engineer-sapper

TABLE 31: ORGANIZATIONAL STRUCTURE OF A SOVIET COMBINED-ARMS ARMY, 1945

Subordinate Units	*Weapons*	*Personnel*
3 rifle corps	320–460 tanks	80,000–100,000
7–12 rifle divisions	100–200 SP guns	
1–2 artillery brigades	1,900–2,500 guns/mortars	
1 antitank (tank destroyer) artillery brigade		
1 antiaircraft division		
1 mortar regiment		
1 signal regiment		
1 engineer-sapper brigade		
2–3 tank brigades or regiments		
1 tank or mechanized corps		

Sources: P. A. Kurochkin, ed., *Obshchevoiskovaia armiia v nastuplenii* [The combined-arms army in the offensive] (Moscow: Voenizdat, 1966), 192, and *Sovetskaia voennaia entsiklopediia* [Soviet military encyclopedia] (Moscow: Voenizdat, 1978), Vol. 1:256.

TABLE 32: SOVIET COMBINED-ARMS ARMIES IN MANCHURIA AND TERRAIN CONDITIONS IN OPERATIONAL SECTORS

Army	*Terrain*	*Forces*	*Weapons*
35th	Swampy marshy with low fortified hills	3 rifle divisions 2 tank brigades 4 artillery brigades 1 antiaircraft regiment 1 guards-mortar regiment	205 tanks and SP guns 955 guns and mortars
15th	Marshy flooded plain with major rivers	3 rifle divisions 3 tank brigades 6 artillery regiments 2 mortar regiments 1 antitank brigade 2 antitank regiments 1 antiaircraft division 1 antiaircraft regiment 2 guards-mortar regiments	164 tanks and SP guns 1,433 guns and mortars
2d Red Banner	Rolling, heavily fortified hills and mountains	3 rifle divisions 3 tank brigades 5 artillery regiments 2 mortar regiments 1 antitank regiment 1 antiaircraft regiment 1 guards-mortar regiment	240 tanks and SP guns 1,270 guns and mortars
5th	Heavily fortified zone with rolling forest and brush-covered hills	4 rifle corps 12 rifle divisions 5 tank brigades 5 self-propelled artillery regiments 12 self-propelled artillery battalions 15 artillery brigades	692 tanks and SP guns 2,945 guns and mortars 432 multiple rocket launchers

39th	Fortified zone in arid mountains	3 rifle corps 9 rifle divisions 1 tank division 2 tank brigades 3 self-propelled artillery regiments 2 artillery divisions 14 artillery brigades	455 tanks and SP guns 2,586 guns and mortars
1st Red Banner	Mountainous, heavily fortified taiga	2 rifle corps 6 rifle divisions 3 tank brigades 3 self-propelled artillery regiments 6 self-propelled artillery battalions 1 heavy tank and SP gun regiment 5 artillery brigades	410 tanks and SP guns 1,413 guns and mortars

Sources: L. N. Vnotchenko, *Pobeda na dal'nem vostoke* [Victory in the Far East] (Moscow: Voenizdat, 1971), 88, 92, 94, 97; N. I. Krylov, N. I. Alekseev, and I. G. Dragan, *Navstrechu pobede: Boevoi put 5-i armii, oktabr 1941g–avgust 1945g.* [Toward victory: The combat path of the 5th Army, October 1941–August 1945] (Moscow: 1970), 462–27; M. Sidorov, 'Boevoe primenenie artillerii' [The combat use of artillery], *Voenno-istoricheskii zhurnal* [Military-historical Journal], No. 9 (September 1975), 14; and V. Ezhakov, 'Boevoe primenenie tankov v gorno-taezhnoi mestnosti po opytu 1-go dal'nevostochnogo fronta' [The combat use of tanks in mountainous-taiga regions based on the experience of the 1st Far Eastern Front], *Voenno-istoricheskii zhurnal* [Military-historical Journal], No. 1 (January 1974).

brigade, one to three tank brigades or regiments, and one tank or mechanized corps. The *front* usually augmented the combined-arms army with a variety of combat and combat service support units and subunits. So organized, combined-arms armies varied in strength from 80,000 to 100,000 soldiers, supported by 320 to 460 tanks, 1,900 to 2,500 guns and mortars, and 100 to 200 self-propelled guns.[7]

As had been the case since summer 1943, the experience of Red Army forces in Manchuria demonstrated the increased Soviet penchant for tailoring the size of their armies to suit the concrete conditions each army faced. In Manchuria, the Far East Command deployed its largest and strongest armies opposite the heavily fortified regions in eastern and western Manchuria sectors or in the *fronts'* main attack sectors and provided these armies with massive quantities of supporting firepower. At the other end of the spectrum, the command employed smaller armies tailored to suit local terrain conditions along secondary or supporting attack axes. Table 32 shows the composition of Soviet armies in Manchuria and the conditions that dictated how they were tailored.

The practice of tailoring an army's composition to suit the terrain and enemy defenses characterized the maturity and flexibility of Soviet force structure development produced by over four years of intense warfare in the west. Furthermore, the NKO retained many of the improvements it had introduced in Manchuria when it restructured the Soviet Army in 1946. For example, it incorporated the heavy tank and self-propelled gun regiment, the tank destroyer brigade, and the antiaircraft division, which it had attached to its armies in Manchuria, into the structure of the Soviet Army's new combined-arms army after war's end.[8]

In 1945 the structure of the rifle corps subordinate to a combined-arms army was less well defined than that of the army. Prior to 1945 the typical Soviet rifle corps (see Table 33) consisted of three rifle divisions, one artillery brigade with two artillery regiments, one self-propelled artillery regiment, one guards-mortar regiment, and antiaircraft, sapper (engineer), and signal battalions for a total strength of 300–400 guns and 450–500 mortars.[9]

The tank or mechanized corps, which served as the army's mobile group, and separate infantry support tank brigades and regiments provided the rifle corps with armored support. In Manchuria rifle corps were assigned either to a combined-arms army or to separate entities subordinate directly to the *front*. The Soviets flexibly structured each corps to satisfy the conditions prevalent in its assigned operational sector. Rifle corps consisted of two to five rifle divisions (most often three) reinforced by one to two tank brigades, two self-propelled artillery regiments, and from two to four self-propelled artillery battalions, and most corps had additional tank and artillery reinforcements. Table 34 shows the composition of representative rifle corps and the characteristics of their areas of operations.

TABLE 33: ORGANIZATIONAL STRUCTURE OF A SOVIET RIFLE CORPS, 1945

Subordinate Units	*Weapons*
3 rifle divisions	300–400 guns
1 artillery brigade	450–500 mortars
2 artillery regiments	
1 SP gun regiment	
1 guards-mortar regiment	
1 antiaircraft battalion	
1 sapper battalion	
1 signal battalion	

Source: Sovetskaia voennaia entsiklopediia [Soviet military encyclopedia] (Moscow: Voenizdat, 1979), 7:571.

TABLE 34: SOVIET RIFLE CORPS IN MANCHURIA AND TERRAIN CONDITIONS IN OPERATIONAL SECTORS

Corps	*72d Rifle Corps, 5th Army*	*5th Separate Rifle Corps*	*39th Rifle Corps, 25th Army*
Terrain	Heavily fortified, rolling wooded and brush-covered hills	Fortified low hills with sparse vegetation	Heavily fortified, heavily wooded mountains with limited road net
Forces	3 rifle divisions 2 tank brigades 2 heavy SP regiments 8 artillery brigades (2 high-power) 4 artillery regiments 3 artillery battalions (2 high-power) 2 mortar brigades 2 guards-mortar brigades 2 guards-mortar regiments 1 engineer sapper brigade	2 rifle divisions 1 tank brigade 2 SP battalions 1 antitank brigade 1 antiaircraft regiment 2 antiaircraft battalions	5 rifle divisions 1 tank brigade 4 SP battalions
Weapons	Undetermined	Undetermined	121 tanks/SP guns 1,669 guns/mortars

Note: Most rifle corps had three rifle divisions, one–two tank brigades, two self-propelled gun regiments, and heavier than usual artillery.
Sources: L. N. Vnotchenko, *Pobeda na dal'nem vostoke* [Victory in the Far East] (Moscow: Voenizdat, 1971), 94, 109–10, 125, and N. I. Krylov, N. I. Alekseev, and I. G. Dragan, *Navstrechu pobede: Boevoi put 5i armii, oktiabr 1941g–avgust 1945g.* [Toward victory: The combat path of the 5th Army, October 1941–August 1945] (Moscow: 'Nauka', 1970), 436–7.

Early during the postwar years, the NKO formalized their earlier *ad hoc* practice of attaching tanks and antitank weapons to the rifle corps by formally incorporating a mechanized division and an antitank regiment into each rifle corps' structure.[10]

The rifle division was the basic tactical combat formation in the Red Army. Its structure too underwent significant modification during the Manchurian operation. Validated in combat, the NKO later incorporated these modifications into the rifle division organizational structure at war's end. According to the June 1945 TO&E, the rifle division (see Table 35) consisted of three rifle regiments, each with a battery of four 76-mm guns; an artillery brigade of three regiments of guns, howitzers, and mortars; single self-propelled artillery, antitank, sapper, signal, and training battalions; and a reconnaissance company. The division's personnel strength was 11,780 men, and it was equipped with 16 self-propelled guns, 52 field artillery pieces, 136 mortars, 12 antiaircraft guns, and 66 antitank guns.[11]

TABLE 35: ORGANIZATIONAL STRUCTURE OF A SOVIET RIFLE DIVISION, 1945

Subordinate Units	*Weapons*	*Personnel*
3 rifle regiments	16 SP guns	11,780 troops
4 rifle battalions	52 guns (field)	
1 artillery battery (4 × 76 mm)	136 mortars	
1 artillery brigade*	12 AA guns	
1 gun artillery regiment (20 × 76 mm)	66 AT guns	
1 howitzer artillery regiment (20 × 122 mm)		
1 mortar regiment (20 × 160 mm)		
1 SP gun battalion (16 × SU-76 SP)		
1 antiaircraft battalion		
1 antitank battalion (57 mm, 76 mm)		
1 sapper battalion		
1 signal battalion		
1 reconnaissance company		
1 training battalion		

*Most rifle divisions had only one organic artillery regiment.
Sources: A. I. Radzievsky, ed., *Taktika v boevykh primerakh (diviziia)* [Tactics by combat example (the division)] (Moscow: Voenizdat, 1976), scheme 1, and P. A. Kurochkin, ed., *Obshchevoiskovaia armiia v nastuplenii* [The combined arms army in the offensive] (Moscow: Voenizdat, 1966), 204.

Because of the delay in implementing the June 1945 organization, most rifle divisions in Manchuria still had one artillery regiment in accordance with the older June 1943 TO&E instead of the artillery brigade. However, the Far East Command and army commanders routinely modified the structures of divisions by attaching to them a diverse array of supporting units to accommodate the situation and specific terrain conditions. Table 36 shows the composition of selected rifle divisions.

The attachment of tank brigades or regiments to rifle divisions was a normal Soviet practice throughout the entire campaign in all regions of the Far Eastern theater of military operations. After war's end the NKO

TABLE 36: SOVIET RIFLE DIVISIONS IN MANCHURIA AND TERRAIN CONDITIONS IN OPERATIONAL SECTORS

Division	*300th Rifle Division, 1st Red Banner Army*	*363d Rifle Division, 35th Army*	*Main attack divisions, 1st Red Banner and 5th Army*
Terrain	Lightly defended, heavily wooded mountains without roads	Swampy region punctuated by low, lightly fortified hills	Heavily fortified, rolling areas flanked by heavily wooded, brush covered mountains
Forces	3 rifle regiments 1 artillery regiment 1 SP battalion (13 × SU-76) 1 antitank battalion 1 signal battalion 1 sapper battalion 1 training battalion	3 rifle regiments 1 artillery regiment 1 SP battalion (13 × SU-76) 1 antitank battalion 1 signal battalion 1 sapper battalion 1 training battalion	3 rifle regiments 1 artillery regiment 1 SP battalion (13 × SU-76) 1 antitank battalion 1 signal battalion 1 sapper battalion 1 training battalion
	Attached: 1 howitzer regiment 1 heavy artillery regiment (6 × 150mm) 1 heavy artillery regiment (8 × 240mm, 2 × 150mm) 1 howitzer artillery battalion (3 × 300mm) 1 tank company 1 sapper battalion 1 tank brigade (10 August)	**Attached**: 1 tank brigade 1 mortar brigade 1 antitank regiment 1 guards-mortar regiment	**Attached**: 1 tank brigade 1 heavy SP regiment
Weapons	Undetermined	Undetermined	65 tanks 34 × SU-76 SP guns

Sources: A. A. Strokov, ed., *Istoriia voennogo iskusstva* [A history of military art] (Moscow: Voenizdat, 1966), 507; M. Zakharov, 'Nekotorye voprosy voennogo iskusstva v Sovetsko-iaponskoi voina 1945 goda' [Some questions concerning military art in the Soviet–Japanese War of 1945], *Voenno-istoricheskii zhurnal* [Military-historical Journal], No. 9 (September 1969), 20; S. Pechenenko, '363-ia strelkovaia diviziia v boiakh na Mishan'skom napravlenii' [The 363d Rifle Division in combat along the Mishan axis], *Voenno-istoricheskii zhurnal* [Military-historical Journal], No. 7 (July 1975), 39; and V. Timofeev, '300-ia strelkovaia diviziia v boiakh na Mudan'tsianskom napravlenii' [The 300th Rifle Division in combat along the Mutanchiang axis], *Voenno-istoricheskii zhurnal* [Military-historical Journal], No. 8 (August 1978), 50.

formalized this *ad hoc* practice by including additional artillery, tanks, and self-propelled guns in newly reorganized rifle divisions. The reformed divisional structure the NKO issued in 1946 incorporated a complete two-regiment artillery brigade and a medium tank and self-propelled gun regiment with 52 tanks and 16 self-propelled guns into the standard rifle division.[12]

The tank armies and separate tank and mechanized corps provided the Red Army with most of its mobile offensive punch in 1945. By 1945 the normal tank army consisted of two tank corps; one mechanized corps; a motorcycle regiment; a light artillery brigade; two mortar regiments; two antiaircraft regiments; a light self-propelled artillery brigade; a guards-mortar regiment; a motorized engineer brigade; and signal, transport, and logistical units and subunits (see Table 37). So configured, the tank army's 21 tank and 15 motorized rifle battalions totaled 808 tanks and self-propelled guns.[13] However, because most tank armies in 1944 and 1945 operated without a mechanized corps, their strength was lower and their ratio of tank to motorized rifle battalions was higher than the normal organizational structure required.

TABLE 37: ORGANIZATIONAL STRUCTURE OF A SOVIET TANK ARMY, 1945

Subordinate Units	*Weapons*
2 tank corps	620 tanks
1 mechanized corps	188 SP guns
1 motorcycle regiment	
1 light artillery brigade	
2 regiments (76 mm guns)	
1 regiment (100 mm guns)	
2 mortar regiments	
2 antiaircraft regiments	
1 light SP brigade	
1 guards-mortar regiment	
1 motorized engineer brigade	
1 signal regiment	
1 aviation communications regiment	
1 transport regiment	
2 repair and reconstruction battalions	

Sources: I. Anan'ev, 'Sozdanie tankovykh armii i sovershenstvovanie ikh organizatsionnoi struktury' [The creation of tank armies and the perfection of their organizational structure], *Voenno istoricheskii zhurnal* [Military-historical Journal], No. 10 (October 1972), 38–47, and *Sovetskaia voennaia entsiklopediia* [Soviet military encyclopedia] (Moscow: Voenizdat, 1979), 660–1.

The Trans-Baikal Front's 6th Guards Tank Army differed in structure significantly from the tank armies the Red Army employed in the West and the normal tank army's organizational structure. This was so because the NKO and Far East Command army's exploited experiences learned in previous operations and adjusted the army's structure to suit the terrain over which it was to operate. In short, they shifted the balance between tank and motorized rifle forces within the army from tank-heavy to motorized rifle-heavy by augmenting the army with additional motorized rifle forces.

When reconfigured, the 6th Guards Tank Army consisted of two mechanized corps, one tank corps, two motorized rifle divisions (a remnant of the 1941 mechanized corps), two self-propelled artillery brigades, two light artillery brigades, a motorcycle regiment, and other normal support units. This reconfiguration provided the 6th Guards Tank Army with 25 tank and 44 motorized rifle battalions totaling 1,019 tanks and self-propelled guns.[14] With its larger number of motorized rifle battalions, this structure resembled the Soviet Army's 1946 mechanized army more than it did the Red Army's 1945 standard tank army.

The 1946 mechanized army would consist of 28 tank battalions and 30 motorized rifle battalions with a strength of about 1,000 tanks and self-propelled guns.[15] Thus, the balance of tank and motorized forces in the tank army that the Soviets developed in Manchuria persisted into the postwar years in the makeup of the mechanized army. The postwar mechanized armies, which were formed in 1946, were the lineal descendent of the wartime tank armies, and the mechanized armies' tank and mechanized divisions descendents of the wartime tank and mechanized corps.

Despite the changes in the tank army's structure, the structure of its tank corps and separate tank corps did not significantly change (see Table 38). The tank corps' basic tactical units were three tank brigades and one motorized rifle brigade, with a total strength of 270 tanks and self-propelled guns and 11,788 men.[16]

TABLE 38: ORGANIZATIONAL STRUCTURE OF A SOVIET TANK CORPS, 1945

Subordinate Units	*Weapons*	*Personnel*
3 tank brigades	288 tanks	11,788
1 motorized rifle brigade	42 SP guns	
1 SP regiment (SU-76)		
1 SP regiment (SU-100)		
1 mortar regiment		
1 antiaircraft regiment		
1 light artillery regiment		
1 heavy tank regiment		
1 guards-mortar battalion		
1 motorcycle battalion		
1 transport company		

Sources: A.I. Radzievsky, ed., *Taktika v boevykh primerakh (diviziia)* [Tactics by combat example (the division)] (Moscow: Voenizdat, 1976), scheme 3, and P. A. Kurochkin, ed., *Obshchevoiskovaia armiia v nastuplenii* [The combined-arms army in the offensive] (Moscow: Voenizdat, 1966), 208.

Nor did the structure of the separate mechanized corps that operated in Manchuria vary significantly from mechanized corps that operated in the European theater of military operations. The 1945 mechanized corps consisted of three mechanized brigades, one tank brigade, three self-propelled artillery regiments, and a variety of supporting units and subunits (see Table 39). Its strength was 16,314 men and 246 tanks and self-propelled guns.[17] For example, the 10th Mechanized Corps, which operated as the mobile group [*podvizhnaia gruppa*] of the 1st Far Eastern Front, comprised two mechanized brigades (one fewer than normal), one tank brigade, and normal supporting units and subunits. Its only attachments were a single motorcycle regiment for use in long-distance reconnaissance and an antitank (tank destroyer) regiment. So configured, the 10th Mechanized Corps numbered 249 tanks and self-propelled guns.[18]

TABLE 39: ORGANIZATIONAL STRUCTURE OF A SOVIET MECHANIZED CORPS, 1945

Subordinate Units	*Weapons*	*Personnel*
3 mechanized brigades	183 tanks	16,314
1 tank brigade	63 SP guns	
13 SP regiments (light, medium, and heavy)		
1 mortar regiment		
1 antiaircraft regiment		
1 guards-mortar battalion		
1 motorcycle battalion		
1 signal battalion		
1 sapper battalion		
1 medical battalion		
1 transport company		
1 repair and reconstruction company		

Source: A. I. Radzievsky, ed., *Taktika v boevykh primerakh (diviziia)* [Tactics by combat example (the division)] (Moscow: Voenizdat, 1976), scheme 2.

Tactical level tank forces also experienced significant structural changes during and as a result of the Manchuria campaign that endured into the post-war years. As had been the case in previous operations, tank brigades organic to tank and mechanized corps and separate tank brigades were designed to provide direct armor support to rifle forces and to lead the advance as a forward detachment while on the offensive. The tank brigade consisted of three tank battalions, each with two tank companies, a motorized rifle battalion, antitank and antiaircraft companies, and only weak support (see Table 40). The tank brigade's strength totaled 65 tanks.[19]

Prior to its offensive, the Far East Command routinely reinforced the tank brigades that were to lead its advance with a self-propelled artillery regiment or battalion, a guards-mortar battalion, a light artillery regiment or battalion, and a sapper company or platoon. The reinforcements enabled the tank brigade to assist in the penetration of heavily defended positions and sustain flexible operations while operating independently during the pursuit phase of the operation.

TABLE 40: ORGANIZATIONAL STRUCTURE OF A SOVIET TANK BRIGADE, 1945

Subordinate Units	*Weapons*	*Personnel*
3 medium tank battalions	65 tanks	1,354
1 motorized rifle battalion		
1 antiaircraft machine gun company		
1 antitank company		
1 medical sanitary platoon		

Source: P. A. Kurochkin, ed., *Obshchevoiskovaia armiia v nastuplenii* [The combined-arms army in the offensive] (Moscow: Voenizdat, 1966), 206.

After war's end, the NKO abolished the separate tank brigades and in 1946 converted the tank brigades assigned to tank and mechanized corps into tank regiments that were subordinate to the newly formed tank and mechanized divisions. These reorganized tank regiments consisted of three tank battalions, one motorized rifle battalion, one self-propelled gun battalion, and minimal supporting subunits.[20] Thus, even at the tactical level, the NKO retained the structural changes it introduced in Manchuria in the Soviet Army's 1946 force structure.

By the end of the war in Europe, the Red Army's force structure also included an impressive host of specialized tank and artillery units designed to provide armor and fire support essential to the conduct of effective and sustained offensive operations. The armored force included separate tank units for infantry support and a wide array of lightly armored but extremely mobile self-propelled guns for use in smashing heavy enemy defenses, defeating enemy tanks, and protecting the advance of Red Army armor, particularly in the exploitation phase of any operation.

Specifically, separate medium tank regiments (with 39 T-34 medium and T-70 light tanks each), separate heavy tank regiments (with 21 JS-2 heavy tanks each), light self-propelled artillery brigades (SU-76), medium self-propelled artillery brigades (SU-100), and heavy self-propelled artillery brigades (SU-152) provided fire support for rifle divisions, rifle, tank, and mechanized corps, and tank armies' corps.[21]

While need was the primary criterion for assignment of additional armor and armored artillery, by 1945 virtually every large Red Army force was supported by these tank and self-propelled gun units. This support proved so useful that, in 1946, the NKO incorporated tank and self-propelled gun units throughout the Soviet Army's entire reformed force structure. By 1951 each Soviet Army rifle corps included a heavy tank and self-propelled gun regiment, each rifle division a medium tank and self-propelled gun regiment, and each tank and mechanized division a heavy tank and self-propelled gun regiment.[22]

In addition to its tank and self-propelled artillery forces, the Red Army included a staggering amount of artillery in 1945. It had developed an

TABLE 41: BASIC ORGANIZATIONAL STRUCTURE OF RED ARMY ARTILLERY FORCES, 1945

Major Units	*Subordinate Units*	*Weapons*
Artillery penetration (breakthrough) corps	2 artillery penetration (breakthrough) divisions 1 guards-mortar division	728–800 guns and mortars 864 multiple rocket launcher ramps
Artillery penetration (breakthrough) division	1 light artillery brigade (48 × 76 mm) 2 regiments 1 howitzer artillery brigade (84 × 122 mm) 3 regiments 1 heavy gun artillery brigade (36 × 152 mm) 2 regiments 1 heavy howitzer brigade (32 × 152 mm) 4 battalions 1 high-power howitzer brigade (24 × 203 mm) 4 battalions 1 mortar brigade (108 × 120 mm) 3 regiments 1 heavy mortar brigade (36 × 160 mm) 4 battalions 1 guards-mortar brigade (36 × BM 31) 3 battalions	364–400 guns/ mortars/rockets
Antitank artillery (tank destroyer) brigade	3 antitank regiments 1 self-propelled gun regiment (SU-76) 1 self-propelled gun regiment (SU-85)	72 AT guns (57 mm, 100 mm)
Antiaircraft artillery division	1 medium antiaircraft artillery regiment (16 × 85 mm) 3 light antiaircraft artillery regiments (16 × 37 mm each)	64 AA guns

Sources: K. Malin'in, 'Razvitie organizationnykh form sukhoputnykh voisk v Velikoi Otechestvennoi voine' [Development of the organizational forms of the ground forces during the Great Patriotic War], *Voenno-istoricheskii zhurnal* [Military-historical Journal], No. 9 (August 1967), 35–8; N. Popov, 'Razvitie samokhodnoi artillerii' [The development of self-propelled artillery], *Voenno-istoricheskii zhurnal* [Military-historical Journal], No. 1 (January 1977), 28–31; and *Sovetskaia voennaia entsiklopediia* [Soviet military encyclopedia] (Moscow: Voenizdat, 1976), Vol. 1:265, 269, 270.

immensely complex and diverse structure of field, antitank, and antiaircraft artillery to support both offensive and defensive operations, particularly to support penetration operations and to sustain deep advances. The artillery's only major limitations were its lack of mobility, which often prevented it from keeping up with rapidly advancing rifle and tank forces, and its voracious appetite for massive quantities of ammunition, which logistical support forces were hard-pressed to satisfy.

While the *Stavka* centralized control of the bulk of the Red Army's supporting artillery in its own strategic reserve, it parceled large amounts of this artillery out to operating *fronts* in accordance with their specific offensive and defensive requirements. The operating *fronts* then attached some of this artillery to subordinate armies, corps, and divisions, while maintaining a sizeable artillery reserve. Table 41 describes the nature and strength of the most significant types of artillery units in the Red Army force structure.

NOTES

1. *IVMV*, 195.
2. Ibid.
3. Ibid., 196
4. Eronin, *Strategicheskaia peregruppirovka*, 18, provides the most detailed and accurate breakdown of Soviet Far East Command strength. Three other Soviet sources, however, provide slightly differing figures.

	Vnotchenko, *Pobeda*, 66	*IVOVSS*, 551	*IVMV*, 197*
Men	1,577,725	1,577,725	1,747,465
Guns and mortars	26,137	26,137	29,835
Tanks	5,556	5,556	5,250
Aircraft	3,800	3,446	5,171

**IVMV* includes the fleet in its calculations.

5. *IVOVSS*, 1:444. See also P. A. Kurochkin, ed., *Obshchevoiskovaia armiia v nastuplenii* [The combined-arms army in the offensive] (Moscow: Voenizdat, 1966), 12, provides a higher theoretical figure of four to five rifle corps totaling 14 to 18 rifle divisions.
6. *Sovetskaya voyennaya entsiklopediya* [Soviet military encyclopedia] (Moscow: Voenizdat, 1979), 5:271. Hereafter cited as *SVE*.
7. *SVE*, 1:256; *IVOVSS*, 6:226; and Kurochkin, *Obshchevoiskovaia*, 192, cite a more comprehensive range of three to five rifle corps made up of nine to 14 rifle divisions augmented by one to two tank or mechanized corps, fielding 1,500 to 2,650 guns and mortars, 48 to 497 multiple rocket launchers, and 330 to 825 tanks and self-propelled guns.
8. A. Dunnin, 'Razvitie sukhoputnykh voisk v poslevoennym periode' [The development of ground forces in the postwar period], *VIZh*, No. 5 (May 1978), 34.
9. *SVE*, 7:571. The standard rifle corps included one artillery regiment, while a guards rifle corps included an artillery brigade of two artillery regiments.

10. Dunnin, 'Razvitie', 34.
11. A. I. Radzievsky, ed., *Taktika v boevykh primerakh (diviziia)* [Tactics by combat example (the division)] (Moscow: Voenizdat, 1976), scheme 1, and Kurochkin, *Obshchevoiskovaia*, 204.
12. Dunnin, 'Razvitie', 34; *SVE*, 7:568; and 'New Soviet Wartime Divisional TO&E'; *Intelligence Research Project No. 9520* (Washington, DC: Office, Assistant Chief of Staff, Intelligence, US Department of the Army, 1952), 1–6, with charts. Hereafter cited as *IRP 9520*.
13. *SVE*, 7:660–1; M. V. Zakharov *et al.*, eds., *50 let Vooruzhennykh sil SSSP* [50 years of the Soviet armed forces] (Moscow: Voenizdat, 1968), 334–5, 391; and I. Anan'ev, 'Sozdanie tankovykh armii i sovershenstvovanie ikh organizatsionnoi struktury' [The creation of tank armies and the perfection of their organizational structure], *VIZh*, No. 10 (October 1972), 38–47.
14. Vnotchenko, *Pobeda*, 87 and Zakharov, *Finale*, 83, which also contains a detailed order of battle.
15. Dunnin, 'Razvitie', 34–5; *IRP 9520*, 1–6.
16. Radzievsky, *Taktika (diviziia)*, scheme 3, and Kurochkin, *Obshchevoiskovaia*, 208
17. Radzievsky, *Taktika (diviziia)*, scheme 2.
18. Vnotchenko, *Pobeda*, 75; Zakharov, *Finale*, 402
19. Kurochkin, *Obshchevoiskovaia*, 206.
20. *IRP 9520*, 2.
21. *SVE*, 7:674; N. Popov, 'Razvitie samokhodnoi artillerii' [The development of self-propelled artillery], *VIZh*, No. 1 (January 1977), 27–31.
22. Dunnin, 'Razvitie', 34, and *Handbook of Foreign Military Forces, Vol. 2, USSR, pt. 1: The Soviet Army* (FATM-11-10) (Fort Monroe, VA: US Army Office, Chief of Army Field Forces, 1952), 74, 86, and 90. Regraded as unclassified.

5

Soviet Offensive Military Theory on the Eve of the Manchurian Offensive

THE EVOLUTION OF OFFENSIVE CONCEPTS

On the Eve of War

Just as the Red Army's force structure evolved during the war, so also did Soviet operational and tactics techniques. Born during the late 1920s and early 1930s under the tutelage of such imaginative military theorists as Marshal M. N. Tukhachevsky, V. K. Triandafillov, and many others, the spirit of the offensive pervaded Soviet military thought before and during the war years. The tactical concept of 'deep battle' and the operational concept of 'deep operations' formed the theoretical core of this fresh offensive theory. This spirit, the product of extensive and often open doctrinal debates, permeated Red Army field regulations during the 1930s, even though Stalin's ruthless purges of the late 1930s killed most of these theorists and, in the process, anesthetized the brain of the Red Army.[1]

Stalin and his cronies questioned the viability of Tukhachevsky's offensive concepts, ostensibly on the basis of the experiences of 'volunteers' the Soviet Union sent to fight in the Spanish Civil War, and, in the late 1930s, emasculated much of the Red Army's force structure designed to implement Tukhachevsky's concepts. Ironically, however, the spirit of the offensive predominated at least operationally prior to and during the initial period of the Soviet Union's Great Patriotic War, when Soviet military fortunes were at their lowest ebb. Despite the fact that Stalin demanded the Red Army adopt a defensive posture on the eve of the war, Soviet defense plans reflected a healthy dose of offensive theory, albeit in the form of counteroffensive action.

The Soviet fixation on the offensive and preoccupation with the conduct of deep operations at the operational level inhibited the development of sound defensive theory at both the strategic and operational levels and produced a congenital unwillingness to go on the defensive. Therefore, when the *Wehrmacht* overwhelmed the Red Army's defenses in the summer of 1941, the *Stavka* insisted that the Red Army apply the offensive principles of the 1930s by conducting incessant but ultimately futile counteroffensives and counterstrokes.

One of the Red Army's many problems was that, due to the military purges of the late 1930s, the Red Army lacked leadership capable of successfully implementing offensive techniques and stemming the German tide. In short, try as they did, the survivors of the purges proved unable to adapt Tukhachevsky's theories to the reality of a surprise attack employing massed panzer forces and audacious maneuver. The purges stifled battlefield innovation and prevented Red Army commanders from adjusting flexibly to the deadly, rapidly developing German threat. Worse still, Soviet industry, which was also hard hit by the purges, was unable to produce the weaponry needed to equip the massive new Red Army force structure.

The Initial Period of War

Despite the catastrophic setbacks the Red Army experienced early in the war, slowly but inexorably a new generation of confident and more capable commanders emerged. These commanders understood what Tukhachevsky's offensive theories required, but were too inexperienced to bring them to fruition. During the campaigns the Red Army conducted from 1941 through early 1943, these commanders often carried the spirit of the 'offensive' to the extreme, sometimes with disastrous consequences. The grasp of these commanders usually exceeded the Red Army's reach, their combat expectations surpassed battlefield realities, and, more often than not, the result was costly limited victory or outright defeat. The futile commitment of the Red Army's fledgling mechanized corps to battle during the border battles of 1941, the Red Army's massive counteroffensive around Moscow in the winter of 1941 and 1942, and the defeats the Red Army suffered at Khar'kov, in the Crimea, and at Voronezh in May and July 1942 characterized this reality.

Even during the Red Army's more successful counteroffensives at and west of Stalingrad from December 1942 through March 1943, when the *Stavka* was seeking to transform victory at Stalingrad into total German rout, the Red Army under its new audacious commanders frequently suffered battlefield reverses. This occurred along the Chir River and at Tatsinskaia in December 1942 and in the Donbas, at Khar'kov, and west of Kursk in February and March 1943. Despite suffering these tactical and operational reverses, the saving grace was that the Red Army was advancing inexorably westward.

Maturation of Offensive Techniques, 1943–45

By the summer of 1943, *Stavka* planners and Red Army commanders finally began exercising a more reasonable degree of restraint as they planned and conducted military operations. The result was ever more imposing offensive success. The *Stavka's* decision to begin its operations in the summer of 1943 by conducting a carefully prepared defense of the Kursk bulge (salient) bore witness to the increased maturity of Soviet military art. At Kursk, the *Stavka* employed a sophisticated defense against powerful German panzer forces to defeat 'Blitzkrieg' and pave the way for a powerful counteroffensive of its own.

This technique worked and produced spectacular results. The Red Army's offensives in July and August 1943 against German forces defending Orel, Belgorod, and Khar'kov marked a turning point in Soviet offensive fortunes and operational and tactical techniques. The *Stavka* launched its Orel offensive while the German assaults at Kursk were still under way and the Belgorod–Khar'kov offensive, in the shockingly brief period of only three weeks after the German offensive at Kursk, expired in complete defeat.

For the first time since the Battle of Stalingrad, during the Belgorod–Khar'kov offensive, Red Army forces advanced more than 60 miles (100 kilometers) deep into the German rear before *Wehrmacht* operational reserves were able to stem the Soviet tide. Worse still for the Germans, unlike the Battle of Stalingrad, at Belgorod–Khar'kov Red Army forces were contending with German panzer forces rather than Rumanian, Italian, and Hungarian infantry. During a furious five-day meeting engagement west of Khar'kov, Red Army mobile forces dueled German panzer divisions to a complete standstill, evidencing the degree to which Red Army commanders had learned the art of conducting modern maneuver warfare.

Thus, by the summer of 1943, the tactical and operational education that Red Army commanders had begun during the difficult days of 1941 as well as in 1942 and early 1943 was beginning to pay real dividends. And so also were the *Stavka's* experiments with reforming the Red Army's force structure. After August 1943 the Red Army's operational and tactical techniques matured as theory rooted in the 1930s and practice developed during wartime combat converged.

In late 1943, and, later, in 1944 and 1945, Red Army commanders and Soviet military theorists finally realized Tukhachevsky's hopes and expectations. Red Army operations were grander in intent, scope, complexity, and duration, combined-arms coordination became thorough, and operational results were more impressive. The Belorussian, L'vov–Sandomierz, and Iassy–Kishinev offensives in the summer of 1944 and the Vistula–Oder and East Prussian offensives in the winter of 1945 exemplified this increased maturity. These offensives ended only after Red Army forces and supply lines became overextended or when political considerations dictated the operations be halted.[2] The Red Army resumed its offensive operations once it had consolidated, reinforced, and resupplied its forces and replenished its logistical depots.

The Red Army's strategic offensive in the Far East proved to be a logical climax to these developments, a virtual post-graduate exercise in large-scale theater-offensive operations. The *Stavka* and major Red Army commands put to the test offensive theories and practices it had developed in the European war. It did so in a region where the geographical features challenged the most capable military planner and operator, under time constraints that called for the application of considerable imagination and individual initiative.

THE 1944 *FIELD REGULATIONS*

The Offensive

The Red Army's principal guiding document for the conduct of offensive operations in 1945 was the *Red Army Field Regulations* (*Polevoi ustav*) of 1944 and companion documents such as the *Regulations for the Penetration [Breakthrough] of Fortified Areas*.[3] These regulations, whose offensive content directly echoed the contents of the Red Army's 1936, 1939, and 1941 *Field Regulations*, were more detailed than their predecessors. The 1944 *Field Regulations* established the basic principles of offensive combat and delineated how the Red Army was to conduct operations within the context of a wide range of geographical conditions and operational and tactical situations.

The 1944 *Field Regulations* reaffirmed the preeminence of the offense as the sole source of military victory, declaring that contemporary tactical actions were mobile in nature, and asserting that only a force that relied completely on skillful maneuver could achieve success. In these circumstances, maneuver had to be simple in concept, secret in execution, rapid, and unexpected. The regulations rejected the concept of employing 'shock-and-holding groups', which had predominated in previous regulations. The former concept required 'shock groups' to conduct offensive operations, while 'holding groups' protected the adjacent sectors and the shock groups' flanks. This method of conducting offensive operations, the regulation argued, wasted precious combat power. In short, the 1944 *Regulations* required commands to employ all of their forces actively when conducting offensive operations.

Combined-Arms Combat

Noting the combined-arms nature of modern combat, the 1944 *Regulations* declared that contemporary combat required the coordinated mass participation of all types of forces. Accordingly, commanders had to achieve, 'the maximum and simultaneous participation of infantry and weaponry in combat from the very beginning of battle to the end'.[4] In order to bring all of their combat power to bear on the enemy, the regulations required Red Army commanders to echelon their forces in depth, normally in two echelons, and assign each echelon a distinct mission. The first echelon was to lead the offensive, but, rather than simply reinforcing the first echelon, the second echelon was to exploit (develop) success. Small reserves retained at each command level were to repel counterattacks and help to consolidate and exploit success.

The regulations declared that achieving surprise was the key to the attainment of victory. Commanders could achieve surprise by planning and executing their operations in total secrecy, by confusing the enemy with deceptive measures, by attacking unexpectedly, and by employing new combat formations and techniques. Since individual initiative by commanders was also an important element in achieving victory in fluid combat, the regulations directed commanders at every level to exercise initiative as long as it was in consonance with the overall plan of their senior commander.

Types of Forces

The regulations declared that, as the 'King of Battle', the *infantry* played the primary role in the achievement of victory in combat. While the effective application of infantry power was the basic means of defeating the enemy, the regulations also recognized artillery, armor, and air power as important basic elements of the combat team, whose purpose was to compensate for the use of and, hence, loss of manpower. It assigned to *tank forces* the specific function of combating enemy infantry rather than enemy armor. Instead, artillery and antitank forces and weapons were to engage, defeat, and destroy enemy tank forces and tanks. Red Army tanks were to engage enemy tanks only if they were clearly superior to the enemy force. The principal mission of Red Army tank forces was to support the rifle forces and exploit success.

The regulations then placed specific constraints on tank force operations. For example, army commanders were to attach their separate tank brigades and regiments to specific rifle divisions. At the rifle division level, the tank brigades and regiments were to coordinate closely with the infantry and help them destroy the opposing enemy infantry. Army commanders were also to employ their heavy tank forces to assault strongly fortified enemy defensive positions in conjunction with rifle forces, sappers, and engineers. When fulfilling their assigned missions, the commanders of Red Army tank forces were to avoid fragmenting their units for any purpose at any level of command. Specifically, the regulations directed tank force commanders at army level to avoid fragmenting their brigades or regiments.

The regulations specified that tank corps were 'strategic-tactical formations' subordinate directly to *front* or army commanders. The mission of the tank corps was to exploit success, attack the enemy's flanks, pursue the enemy, and conduct counterattacks against enemy mobile formations. Unlike the case with smaller tank units, the commanders of tank corps could employ their subordinate brigades separately in support of rifle forces should the need arise.

The regulation also termed mechanized corps as 'strategic tactical' formations subordinate to *front* or army command. Since they were 'heavier' in terms of motorized infantry than the tank corps, they were to perform an expanded array of missions. These missions included exploiting success, operating against the enemy flanks and rear, pursuing the enemy, retaining captured positions in the strategic depth, executing counterattacks, and conducting independent operations. The regulations specifically prohibited mechanized corps commanders from fragmenting their corps' brigades for employment in separate operations.

In the special circumstances of an offensive operation against a hasty enemy defense, a tank or mechanized corps could be assigned an independent mission, such as penetrating into the depths of the defense, but only if it was reinforced with requisite artillery and engineers. Under no circumstances, however, could a tank or mechanized corps participate in an assault against a fortified zone or heavily defended strong point. Although not specifically mentioned in the 1944 *Field Regulations*, the tank army was an 'operational' formation subordinate directly to a *front*, whose mission was to complete the penetration of the enemy defense and lead the exploitation of success into the depth of the enemy's rear area. By 1943 and thereafter, used singly or in combination, the tank army was the Red Army's principal exploitation force at *front* level. Prior to August 1945, Red Army commands seldom employed a tank army in the first echelon of an attacking *front* during the initial phases of an offensive operation.[5]

Operational and Tactical Formations (Echeloning)

Since the skillful employment of a variety of tactical combat formations was one way to achieve surprise and, hence, victory, the 1944 *Field Regulations* devoted considerable attention to that subject. Although the regulations described what it termed as 'typical' or standard combat formations, it directed commanders to employ variants to standard combat formations in accordance with the concrete conditions they faced or to deceive the enemy. The use of a typical combat formation was designed to facilitate the rapid concentration of forces along a decisive axis and, on the offensive, to permit the force to shift the weight of an attack. The standard combat formation promoted effective use of all types of forces and facilitated the exploitation of terrain and the defense of vulnerable flanks.

The 1944 *Regulations* indicated that the forces of a *front* could deploy in one or two echelons depending on the nature of the terrain, the strength of the enemy, and the desired rate of advance during the operation. In general, a successful assault against a strong enemy defense required the attacking *front* to deploy its forces in two echelons. The first echelon began the penetration operation, and the second echelon either reinforced the first echelon during the penetration or began the exploitation. Against a hasty defense, in which the defending forces were deployed across a broad front but in only limited depth, a single echelon *front* formation offered better chances for success, particularly if the attacking *front* wished to penetrate quickly and rapidly exploit its success.

Armies echeloned their forces generally in the same manner as *fronts* (see Figure 1). If the enemy's defense was particularly strong and its offensive sector was narrow, an attacking army could deploy in three echelons. Normally, however, an army deployed in two-echelon formation supported by a variety of artillery groups, each with a specific mission, and tank and antitank reserves. The attacking army's first echelon, which usually consisted of two rifle corps attacking abreast, included roughly 60 per cent of the army's force.

The army's second echelon, which was made up of one rifle corps and mechanized forces designated to function as the army's mobile group, retained about 40 per cent of the army's forces. By definition, the second echelon increased the power and sustainability of the attacking force, added depth to the combat formation, and performed specific missions such as exploiting the penetration, consolidating gains, and maintaining the continuity of the attack.

In general, an army attacking along a *front's* main offensive axis was stronger, more deeply echeloned, and concentrated in a narrower sector than an army advancing along a secondary axis of advance. Within the armies and rifle corps, rifle divisions normally deployed in two echelons of regiments, and a rifle brigade deployed in a single echelon of battalions formed in either a staggered or angled formation (see Figure 2).

A wide variety of artillery groups, tank reserve groups, and antitank reserve groups provided critical fire and maneuver support to rifle brigades, rifle divisions, rifle corps, and combined-arms armies. Commanders task-organized their armor and artillery forces and weapons at every level of command so that they could fulfill specific missions. Within the rifle division, regimental artillery groups (RAGs) made up of divisional artillery supported the division's subordinate rifle regiments. The division also formed a long-range artillery group from its own artillery to provide general fire support to its rifle divisions.

Above division level, rifle corps and combined-arms armies formed long-range artillery groups and destruction artillery groups from their

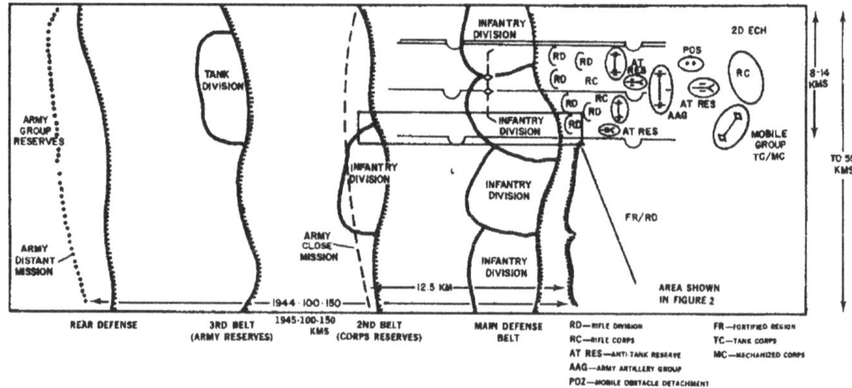

Figure 1. Typical Soviet Combined-Arms Army Offensive Formation

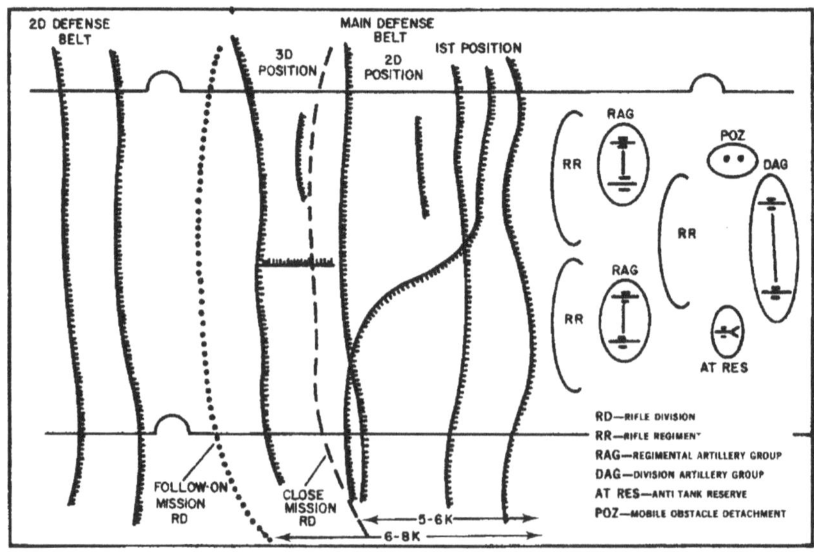

Figure 2. Typical Soviet Rifle Division Combat Formation

high-powered and heavy howitzer artillery. These groups provided long-range fire for rifle corps or armies or fire necessary to destroy or neutralize enemy fortified zones, strong points, or positions that disrupted the progress of the offensive. Tank and antitank reserve groups formed virtually at every command level from division to army were a source of extra offensive power necessary to halt or repel enemy attacks or counterattacks.

March-Column Formations

Just as a force's combat formation was critical to the achievement of its offensive mission, so also was the organization of its march-column formation, particularly during its commitment to combat or during the exploitation phase of any operation. As the Red Army's offensive successes mounted in 1944 and 1945, the exploitation and pursuit phases of combat operations became more prevalent and important. Successful exploitation and pursuit depended to a great degree on the manner in which a march-column formation was constructed and on the ability of the marching force to react quickly to changing conditions.

Ideally, an effective march-column formation permitted rapid concentration of forces, efficient force deployment, successful maneuver, and, when necessary, reliable defense of the march-column. Skillfully organized march-column formations improved a force's chances for victory in a meeting engagement or when advancing to attack a hastily prepared defense capable of being assaulted from the march. The most rudimentary consideration when forming a march-column formation was the number of routes the force used. Because of their large size, armies and rifle corps employed several different parallel march routes. Depending on the width of their advance sector, their sector of ultimate commitment into combat, and the nature of the terrain, rifle divisions marched along from one to three routes and rifle regiments along one.

March-column formations consisted of distinct functional groupings, each of which was assigned a specific mission. From front to rear, these groupings included a reconnaissance group, detachment, or patrol; an advanced party, a forward detachment; an advanced guard; the main body; and flank guards or march security outposts. The reconnaissance group, detachment, or patrol and the advanced party conducted reconnaissance and provided combat security for the march column.

By 1945 the most vital element in the marching formation was the forward detachment [*peredovoi otriad*]. Its mission was to disrupt enemy defenses, preempt enemy attacks, capture key terrain such as bridges, mountain passes and defiles, and river crossings, and to assist the deployment of the advanced guard. Only forces of brigade or larger size were required to form forward detachments.

Following in the tracks of the forward detachment, the advanced guard was to fix, attack, and crush the enemy. If unable to overcome the enemy's defenses, it would protect the deployment of the main force. The basic fighting force of the marching formation was the main force, which was supposed to employ fire and maneuver to engage and crush the enemy. Gun, antiaircraft, and antitank artillery units and weaponry were dispersed throughout the various subgroups of the marching column or formation. Tanks operated either in groups at the front or rear of the marching column or as separate columns, and commanders normally reinforced their forward detachments or advanced guards with tanks.

Forms of Offensive Action

After emphasizing the importance of offensive action in the achievement of military victory, the 1944 *Field Regulations* described in detail why and how to conduct offensive operations. By definition, offensive operations sought to smash the enemy's prepared defenses and project large forces into the depths of the enemy's rear area. Attacking forces could accomplish this feat attacking frontally or by enveloping enemy forces either deeply or shallowly. Although the most frequent method employed, the frontal attack to penetrate the enemy's defense was the most costly and, hence, least preferred method of offensive action.

Shallow envelopment involved turning or rolling up the flanks of an enemy defense either during or immediately after a successful penetration operation. This offensive method, which was preferable to a frontal attack since it resulted in fewer casualties, ultimately sought to encircle a portion of the enemy's forces. Deep envelopment, the most mobile form of offensive action, involved deep offensive operations against one or both of the enemy's flanks, usually in concert with a frontal attack, which sought to encircle and destroy part or all of the enemy's forces.

To conduct a successful frontal attack, it was absolutely essential for the commander to concentrate his forces in an extremely narrow attack sector, task-organize them carefully and effectively, and closely coordinate their actions during the assault. Since a force conducting a frontal attack had only limited space in which to maneuver, this form of attack was simpler to plan and far safer to conduct than an envelopment operation. Either type of envelopment, but particularly the deep form, required meticulous organization and crisp coordination of mobile forces both before and during the attack. It also required close mutual cooperation by all types of forces as they advanced into the depth of the enemy defense, a difficult feat to achieve. While a successful deep envelopment could produce a spectacular victory, a poorly executed one could result in disastrous defeat.

The 1944 *Field Regulations* described in detail the role various arms played during a frontal attack, the way a force developed a successful frontal attack, and the prerequisites that had to be satisfied for the attack's successful conduct. First and foremost, the force conducting the attack had to be numerically superior to the enemy, particularly on the main attack axis.[6] Infantry and tank forces jointly conducted the assault to penetrate the enemy's main defensive zone. Tank and self-propelled gun brigades and regiments supported the advancing infantry, sometimes placing tank and SP gun battalions and companies in direct support of rifle regiments and battalions. Artillery and aircraft also provided direct support to the attacking forces throughout the entire duration of the advance into the depth of the enemy's defense. Although not recommended by the regulations, on some occasions tank armies and tank and mechanized corps forming the mobile groups serving the attacking *front* or armies committed their lead tank brigades to help complete the penetration operation.

Once the penetration phase of the offensive was complete, tank armies, the tank and mechanized corps, and sometimes cavalry-mechanized groups serving as *front* or army mobile groups then broke out from the initial penetration to begin the exploitation phase of the offensive. During this phase, the mobile groups and follow-on rifle forces sought to break up the enemy's combat formation and destroy each element of it piecemeal. Throughout all phases of the frontal attack, other types of specialized forces such as airborne brigades, deep reconnaissance-diversionary detachments and groups, and partisan detachments conducted diversionary operations in the enemy rear to sow confusion, disrupt enemy command and control, and block the movement of enemy reserves.

The 1944 *Regulations* specified three different variants a commander could employ when conducting a frontal attack. The first and simplest variant was to attack in a single sector and subsequently develop his offensive in that sector. Alternatively, he could attack in several sectors and develop the offensive simultaneously in each. Finally, he could attack in several sectors consecutively in time-phased sequence. Obviously, the second and third form demanded increasingly detailed planning. When conducting a frontal attack, armies or rifle corps operating along the main attack axis normally deployed their rifle divisions in two echelons. The first echelon divisions attacked in sectors 1.8–2.5 miles (3–4 kilometers) wide, which were considerably narrower than in previous years. The second echelon divisions each received a specific combat mission and deployed 4.3–7.5 miles (7–12 kilometers) deep behind the first echelon divisions. The penetration battle was continuous throughout the entire depth of the enemy's forward defensive belt and required close coordination by the infantry, artillery, tanks, and engineers.

Assault on a Fortified Zone

The most difficult and costly form of frontal attack was an assault to penetrate a heavily fortified enemy defensive zone. This required extensive detailed preliminary planning to destroy or neutralize enemy strong points, to conduct the penetration, and to develop the exploitation. The regulations spelled out in detail how this should be accomplished. First, the attacking force had to reconnoiter the enemy's defense thoroughly right up to the moment of the assault so as to be able to plan an attack on each enemy defensive position and firing point throughout the entire depth of his defensive zone.

Prior to the infantry assault, the artillery fired an extensive time-phased artillery preparation (called an artillery offensive) to the depths of the defense to destroy or neutralize all of the enemy's firing positions. The artillery preparation, which usually consisted of extensive and heavy rolling barrages or concentrated fire against successive groups of targets, normally lasted for one to four hours. Either prior to or during the artillery preparation, aircraft struck the enemy's defenses, shifting their air strikes into the depths as the artillery fire marched forward.

While the artillery preparation was in progress, assault detachments formed from first echelon rifle regiments led the attack against the enemy's forward positions. Commanders normally used reserve rifle battalions from first echelon rifle regiments to form these assault detachments so that they could maintain the strength and structural integrity of their first echelon regiments' attacking battalions. When formed, assault detachments usually included infantry, machine gunners, sappers, regimental field guns (76 mm), antitank guns, one or two heavy tanks or self-propelled guns, and flame-throwers. These carefully tailored assault detachments ranged in strength from platoon to reinforced company, depending on the strength of the positions they were to assault. Several days prior to the actual assault, each assault detachment thoroughly rehearsed its mission by conducting mock attacks against a terrain model constructed on the basis of detailed preliminary reconnaissance of the specific enemy position it was to attack.

Armor consisting of tanks and self-propelled guns organized in two echelons followed and supported the assault groups. The first echelon of armor, which consisted of heavy tanks or heavy self-propelled guns provided by separate tank brigades or regiments, accompanied the assault groups, destroyed fortifications by direct fire, supported the advancing infantry with covering fire, and helped consolidate captured ground. The second echelon, made up of medium tanks, followed the assault groups (sometimes advancing with the lead rifle battalions of the first echelon rifle regiments), consolidated captured positions, and repulsed local enemy counterattacks. The first echelon rifle regiment's remaining three rifle battalions assaulted on the heels of the assault detachments with two rifle battalions abreast in first echelon and one battalion in second echelon. The first echelon rifle battalions attacked with three rifle companies abreast, and artillery and mortars continuously supported the attack.

Penetration of a Hasty Defense

The penetration of a hasty defense, which was the easiest and least costly form of frontal attack, was usually an integral part of the pursuit phase of an offensive operation. In all cases, successful penetration of a hasty defense required the skillful application of a variety of specific combat techniques. Above all, prior to the attack, the advancing force had to employ a correct and effective march-column formation so that it could react quickly enough when the enemy deployed into new defenses. Thereafter, the attacking force had to coordinate closely with neighboring units and exercise considerable initiative to preempt the enemy and successfully overcome his defense.

During a pursuit, an advancing army or rifle corps moved forward in march column, employing reconnaissance detachments to determine the exact dispositions of the enemy, forward detachments to preempt or disrupt enemy defenses, and advanced guards to protect its main body. When approaching expected enemy defensive positions, the army commander narrowed his front and the sectors of his advancing first echelon rifle divisions. At this time divisional artillery units accompanied the rifle regiments they were to support.

First, the army's or corps' forward detachment engaged and attempted to disrupt the enemy defense and capture favorable terrain to facilitate the deployment of the advanced guard. The advanced guard of each lead rifle division then engaged the enemy force either to defeat it or, in the event it failed to do so, to facilitate deployment and maneuver by the army's or corps' main body. Once fully deployed, the army's or corps' main body employed fire and maneuver to defeat and destroy the defending enemy.

Because of their heavy firepower and extreme mobility, tank and mechanized corps and brigades were especially well suited for employment in a frontal attack against a hasty defense. Usually, a tank brigade or battalion formed the nucleus of forward detachments serving armies or rifle corps. In addition, commanders normally attached some tank support to their advanced guards. At army level, commanders often committed their mobile groups (usually tank and mechanized corps) early against a hasty defense to complete the disruption begun by the forward detachments, advanced guards, and main forces. After penetrating the hasty defense, the mobile groups would then continue the exploitation and pursuit phase of the offensive.

Pursuit Operations

The pursuit phase of an offensive operation inevitably followed a successful penetration achieved either by a frontal attack or a shallow or deep envelopment. The 1944 *Field Regulations* stressed that the pursuit had to be relentless in order to prevent the enemy from regrouping his forces or establishing new defenses. The regulations required that commanders at every level thoroughly prepare for the pursuit phase before their forces actually penetrated the enemy's defenses so that the pursuit could begin immediately after the penetration was complete. Commanders used tank and motorized rifle forces, reinforced by engineers and supported by long-range artillery, to initiate the pursuit.

To be decisive, the pursuit had to be conducted along axes of advance parallel to the axis of enemy withdrawal on one or both of the enemy flanks. The regulations recommended that large tank and motorized rifle units lead the pursuit by advancing deep into the enemy's rear area to capture key road junctions and other vital terrain necessary to cut off and destroy the enemy's retreating forces in piecemeal fashion. In addition, rifle divisions and regiments could also perform similar deep missions while on the pursuit if they possessed the types of forces necessary to do so.

This had been a problem earlier in the war since tank and mechanized forces were not readily available. In addition, in 1942 and 1943, Red Army commanders experienced difficulty providing their exploiting tank and mechanized forces with necessary mobile infantry and artillery support and their rifle corps and divisions with mobile artillery. By 1944, however, they had solved this problem by fielding increased quantities of motorized infantry and mobile artillery. For example, by 1944 rifle divisions often led their pursuit with forward detachments formed from either their organic self-propelled artillery battalion or truck-mounted riflemen.

The Meeting Engagement

Another basic variation of offensive combat that the 1944 *Field Regulations* addressed was the meeting engagement or encounter battle. The meeting engagement, which normally occurred during the pursuit phase of an offensive or during the initial period of a war, was the most fluid form of combat and the form requiring the greatest degree of initiative on the part of commanders. Simply stated, a meeting engagement occurred when two forces advancing in march-column formation met one another. In this circumstance, the first force that was able to deploy and attack the other before it fully deployed would normally prevail. Therefore, the meeting engagement involved preemption, and the ability to preempt depended directly on the efficient march formation, rapid deployment, and skillful maneuver of the preempting force.

In anticipation of a meeting engagement, the regulation required the force commander to organize his march column into four distinct elements, specifically, a forward detachment, an advanced guard, a main body, and a mobile group, each with a precise composition and mission. At brigade, division, and higher level, the forward detachment consisting of tanks, artillery, and motorized rifle forces spearheaded the march column, with the mission of disrupting the enemy's dispositions, capturing key terrain, and assisting the deployment of the advanced guard.

Before the enemy could successfully deploy, the advanced guard, usually consisting of one battalion from a regiment, one regiment from a division, or one division from a corps with the next higher level commander in attendance, attacked and crushed the enemy and then protected the deployment of the main force. After deploying, the main force attacked the already disorganized enemy force and defeated it in detail, if possible by maneuver. If available, mobile groups then extended the depth of the operation, usually by conducting a deeper envelopment. Regulations stressed that the meeting engagement had to be followed by a vigorous pursuit. Like the pursuit operation, the meeting engagement took on far greater significance in 1944 and 1945.

Night Operations

After detailing the nature of offensive combat, the 1944 *Field Regulations* turned to the conduct of offensive battle under special circumstances, such as light, climatic, and specific geographical conditions. Derived from the experience of four years of warfare in a wide range of varying conditions, these sections had considerable applicability to operations in Manchuria's diverse terrain.

Night battle offered distinct advantages to forces that were able and willing to conduct it. The regulations admonished commanders to conduct night operations whenever possible to achieve surprise and deny any respite to a beleaguered enemy. In order for night battle to be successful, operational plans had to be simple, and forces had to attack along relatively straight and short attack axes to accomplish distinctly limited missions. Night utterly precluded resort to complicated maneuvers. Infantry played the main role in night attack, and, to guarantee surprise, commanders usually had to avoid firing elaborate artillery preparations. Although tank and self-propelled gun forces required suitable terrain to operate at night, they sometimes formed an integral part of the infantry formation. The main problem was to coordinate tanks and infantry safely without violating the requirements of mutual support.

Combat in Special Terrain Conditions

Throughout the war in Europe, Red Army forces had to operate in a wide variety of special terrain conditions, including urban areas, swamps, mountains, steppes, and deserts. By 1944 they had amassed enough experience to formulate specific techniques suited to operating successfully in these varied conditions. When assigning forces to the Far East Command, the *Stavka* was astute enough to select forces to conduct operations in specific regions of Manchuria based on their experience in conducting operations in similar regions in the west.

One of the most difficult challenges to military forces was to conduct operations successfully in populated areas. In this regard, the 1944 *Field Regulations* recommended that attacking forces avoid costly frontal attacks whenever possible by maneuvering around inhabited areas. If it was absolutely necessary to reduce defenses in and around an inhabited area, commanders were to overcome enemy defenses by using tailored assault groups made up of all types of forces well organized for mutual support. The assault groups consisted of infantry (primarily submachine gunners), sappers, light artillery and mortars, and sometimes a small number of tanks or self-propelled guns, organized into assault and covering groups and supported by intense artillery fire. Commanders at all levels were to retain strong reserves with which to reinforce and ensure the assault groups' effectiveness.

Successful offensive operations in forested or marshy regions also required the use of specific combat techniques. In such terrain, commanders usually attacked along separate axes with balanced combined-arms forces. To ensure a rapid advance and a degree of maneuver, forward detachments led the advance on each axis to preempt the enemy from deploying or erecting new defenses and to capture key terrain, in this case usually road junctions. Traffic control detachments performed the critical function of route and movement control to prevent confusion among the advancing units. In this instance, extensive engineer support was necessary to guarantee the continued trafficability of march routes and, in some cases, to construct roads from scratch.

To conduct successful offensive operations in mountainous regions, commanders had to task-organize their forces carefully and employ special tactical techniques to accord some degree of mobility to the advancing troops. Spearheaded by forward detachments, attacking forces advanced along valley floors and through mountain defiles. A rapid advance was essential to prevent the enemy from establishing strong defenses in bottlenecks such as defiles, passes, or rivers and streams traversing the valleys. Forward detachments, reinforced by sappers, and other types of engineer forces, routinely paved the way for the advance of larger tank and mechanized formations and units (corps and brigades). The tailored forward detachments contained enough combat power to overcome small enemy detachments, move rapidly, and operate deep in the enemy's rear areas.

Larger tank and mechanized formations and units followed the forward detachments to develop the exploitation and envelop extensive regions. All forces operating in valleys employed envelopment by enveloping detachments [*obkhodiaiushchye otriady*] as the basic form of maneuver to capture dominant key terrain such as ridges and mountain crests. In the wake of these mobile forces, follow-on main forces secured important road junctions and key terrain in the rear. Commanders whose forces were operating in mountainous terrain had to task-organize their forces with strong artillery, engineer, and tank support.

Desert (and steppe) conditions offered commanders the prospect of conducting deep operations to great depth with even greater freedom of maneuver and increased opportunities to conduct effective attacks against the enemy's flanks, strategically, operationally, and tactically. In these conditions, commanders tailored their forces and employed them along multiple axes to ensure greater independence of action and the survivability and sustainability of the attacking force.

Given their inherent maneuverability, tank and motorized units were instrumental in achieving success in desert operations. However, to do so they required extensive artillery, engineer, and logistical support. Since fuel, ammunition, water, and food were essential to ensure continuous sustained operations in the desert, the regulations stipulated that logistical planning be 'most detailed and accurate'. Because logistical requirements remained the central focus of all commanders during desert operations, sources of water became key terrain features governing the operation's mission and ultimate objectives.

The 1944 *Field Regulations* provided detailed operational and tactical guidance for all commanders of Red Army forces operating in Manchuria. The demanding nature of the Far East Command's operational plan insured that, collectively, these commanders would have to perform virtually every operational and tactical technique the regulation required. Furthermore, as the offensive developed, conditions would force many commanders to modify and adjust their combat techniques to meet the unique conditions prevalent in the Manchurian theater of military operations.

NOTES

1. Mikhail Tukhachevsky was a leading Soviet military leader and theoretician from 1918 to 1938, commander of the Red Army's Western Front during the Polish War of 1920–21, Chief of Staff of the Red Army from 1925 through 1928, Deputy People's Commissar of Defense after 1934, and commander of the Volga Military

District in 1937. He contributed to the modernization of the Red Army's force structure and weaponry in the 1920s and 1930s and was instrumental in the formation of aviation, mechanized, and airborne forces. As a theoretician, he was a driving force behind Soviet development of the twin theories of deep battle and deep operations. Accused of treason and shot during the military purges of 1937–41, Tukhachevsky's reputation was 'rehabilitated' in the 1960s. For a frank treatment of the Tukhachevsky affair, see Lev Nikulin, *Tukhachevsky: Biograficheskii ocherk* [Tukhachevsky: A biographical essay] (Moscow: Voenizdat, 1964), 189–97. The purges and their impact are covered by O. F. Suvenirov, *Tragediia RKKA 1937–1938* [The tragedy of the RKKA 1937–1938] (Moscow: 'TERRA,' 1998).

2. Contrary to official Soviet explanations, Stalin likely halted the Vistula–Oder offensive on the banks of the Oder River, 36 miles from Berlin, so that he could transfer forces and offensive operations to Hungary for an advance into Austria before the Germans surrendered.
3. This analysis of Soviet operational and tactics techniques is based on the Red Field's *Field Regulations (PU 1944)* and *Nastavlenie po proryvu pozitsionnoi oborony (proekt)* [Instructions on the penetration of a positional defense (draft)] (Moscow: Voenizdat, 1944), translated by the Directorate of Military Intelligence, Army Headquarters, Ottawa, Canada. Hereafter abbreviated as *PU 1944*.
4. *PU 1944*, Introduction and paragraph 1.
5. I. E. Krupchenko, 'Nekotorye osobennosti sovetskogo voennogo iskusstva' [Some characteristics of Soviet military art], *VIZh*, No. 8 (August 1975), 22. Notable exceptions to this generality were the Stalingrad counteroffensive and the Korsun–Shevchenkovskii and Iassy–Kishinev offensives. In the first instance, the 5th Tank Army, which deployed in first echelon, was a composite unit containing rifle and cavalry divisions. In the latter two operations, both tank armies had heavy rifle division reinforcements.
6. By 1945 Soviet offensive planners sought to achieve superiority over enemy forces in infantry and tanks of 3:1 strategically, 5:1 operationally, and 10:1 tactically. Artillery correlations were markedly higher.

Part II:

The Conduct of the Offensive

6

Stavka and Far East Command Planning

THE FORMATION OF THE FAR EAST COMMAND

As early as May 1945, the *Stavka* had decided to form a High Command in the Far East, complete with a Military Council and full staff necessary to coordinate the operations of ground, air, and naval forces in the region. Accordingly, on the night of 5 July, a group of generals and officers headed by Marshal of the Soviet Union A. M. Vasilevsky arrived in Chita, the headquarters of the Trans-Baikal Front, to begin work forming this command. Later, on 30 July, the *Stavka* officially ordered the formation of the Main Command of Forces in the Far East – the Far East Command – and on 1 August Stalin formally appointed Vasilevsky as commander of the Far East Command and provided him with a complete headquarters staff, which, in reality, had already been functioning as such since early June.

The new high command's military council (*voennyi sovet*) consisted of Vasilevsky as commander, Colonel General I. V. Shikin as member of the military council (commissar), and Colonel General S. P. Ivanov as Chief of Staff. Fleet Admiral N. G. Kuznetsov, the Chief of the Soviet Navy, was responsible for coordinating the operations of the Pacific Fleet and the Red Banner Amur Naval Flotilla with the other forces of the Far East Command. Chief Marshal of Aviation A. A. Novikov, the commander of the Red Army Air Force did the same for air operations.[1]

An operational group subordinate to the Far East Command under Colonel General V. I. Vinogradov, the deputy chief of the Red Army's Rear (Rear Services), worked on initial preparations for the offensive. It consisted on an officer group from Vinogradov's staff and representatives from the Central Directorate of Military Communications, the Main Automotive Directorate, the Main Road Directorate, the Fuel, Food, and Material Supply Directorate, the Main Medical Directorate, and the Main Trophy (captured material) Directorate.[2]

On 28 June the *Stavka* dispatched directives to the Trans-Baikal and Far Eastern Fronts and the Coastal Group of Forces concerning the preparation and conduct of an offensive with decisive aims leading to the rapid defeat and destruction of the Kwantung Army, which was to commence only upon the receipt of its special orders (see Appendix 6). Red Army ground and air forces were to be prepared to attack by 25 July and the Pacific Fleet by 1 August. These directives superseded previous directives, which had ordered the forces to be prepared to conduct a decisive offensive in the event 'of an attack by Japanese forces on the Soviet Union'.[3]

Shortly after assuming full command, on 3 August Vasilevsky presented a detailed report to the *Stavka* regarding the situation, the condition of his forces, and his assessment of ongoing planning. Reporting that the Japanese were reinforcing their defenses in Manchuria, he declared that, although his forces would be prepared to receive the order to attack by the morning of 5 August, it would take three to five more days to begin operations. Thus, according to Vasilevsky, the optimum period to cross the state borders would be 9–10 August. The *Stavka*, however, was to determine the exact hour and date.

Therefore, Vasilevsky's three *fronts* were to begin their offensive at 1800 hours on 10 August by Moscow time (or the morning of 11 August Far Eastern time). The *Stavka* made its final command adjustments on 5 August when it transformed the Coastal Operational Group of Forces into the 1st Far Eastern Front and the Far Eastern Front into the 2d Far Eastern Front. However, during the afternoon of 7 August, Vasilevsky received a new directive from the *Stavka* ordering him to accelerate his preparations by two days and attack at 1800 hours 8 August, Moscow time (on the night of 8–9 August Far East time) (see Appendix 6).[4]

Thus, the command made its final offensive preparations in a single day in accordance with brief orders which Vasilevsky sent out late on 7 August.[5] Although Russian sources claim that the *Stavka* accelerated its offensive by two days to maximize the element of surprise, it was not just coincidental that the United States dropped its first atomic bomb on the Japanese city of Hiroshima on 6 August.[6]

By 9 August the Trans-Baikal, 1st Far Eastern, and 2d Far Eastern Fronts and the 9th, 10th, and 12th Air Armies and Pacific Fleet and Amur Flotilla, which were to support them, were fully operational in the Far East. The Coastal, Amur, and Trans-Baikal PVO Armies were in place to provide necessary air defense, and the border guard forces of the Coastal, Khabarovsk, and Trans-Baikal Border Districts were prepared to participate in upcoming offensive operations.

THE *STAVKA'S* PLAN

The *Stavka's* plan for the conquest of Manchuria was simple in concept, but grand in scale and in its expectations. Subsequently described as a strategic 'Cannae' by Soviet historians, the plan called for the Far East Command's three *fronts* to conduct a massive strategic envelopment operation against the Japanese Kwantung Army by launching offensives along three strategic axes to chop up, encircle, and successively destroy the Japanese Kwantung Army piecemeal in northern and central Manchuria, and capture Manchuria's vital central valley, the Liaotung peninsula, and northern Korea.[7]

Once success was assured in the so-called Manchurian strategic offensive operation, the Far East Command's forces were to defeat Japanese forces on southern Sakhalin Island, the Kuril Islands, and later, if possible, on the northern portion of the Japanese home island of Hokkaido to hasten the defeat of Imperial Japan (see Map 25).

The most recent Russian official history describes the Soviet Union's offensive aims, which provided the context for the *Stavka's* plan:

> The Soviet Union's aims in entering the war were as follows: the provision of security for its own far eastern borders, which had been subjected to threat time and time again by Japan; the fulfillment of obligations to its allies; the aspiration to hasten the end of the Second World War, which was continuing to bring incalculable suffering to the people; the desire to provide assistance to the workers of eastern Asia in their liberation struggle; and the restoration of the USSR's historical rights in territory which Japan had earlier seized from Russia.[8]

Once formulated, the Far East Command's offensive plan required Malinovsky's Trans-Baikal Front to attack eastward into western Manchuria, bypass, isolate, and later destroy Japanese fortified regions at Hailar and Halung-Arshaan, fragment the Kwantung Army's 4th and 44th Armies, and advance to capture Changchun and Mukden (Shenyang) in central Manchuria. Malinovsky's shock groups were to traverse the waterless desert wastes of eastern Mongolia and Inner Mongolia and pierce the supposedly impenetrable Grand Khingan Mountains (see Map 26).[9]

Simultaneously, Meretskov's 1st Far Eastern Front was to attack into eastern Manchuria from the region north and south of Lake Khanka, smash the Japanese 3d and 5th Armies' defense along and west of the border, and advance toward Changchun and Kirin. The spearheads of Malinovsky's and Meretskov's forces were to converge and link up in the Mukden, Changchun, Harbin, and Kirin areas of central Manchuria.

To the north, Purkaev's 2d Far Eastern Front was to launch supporting attacks from the Amur and Sungari River regions into northern Manchuria, driving southward to Harbin and Tsitsihar, and a Mongolian–Soviet force

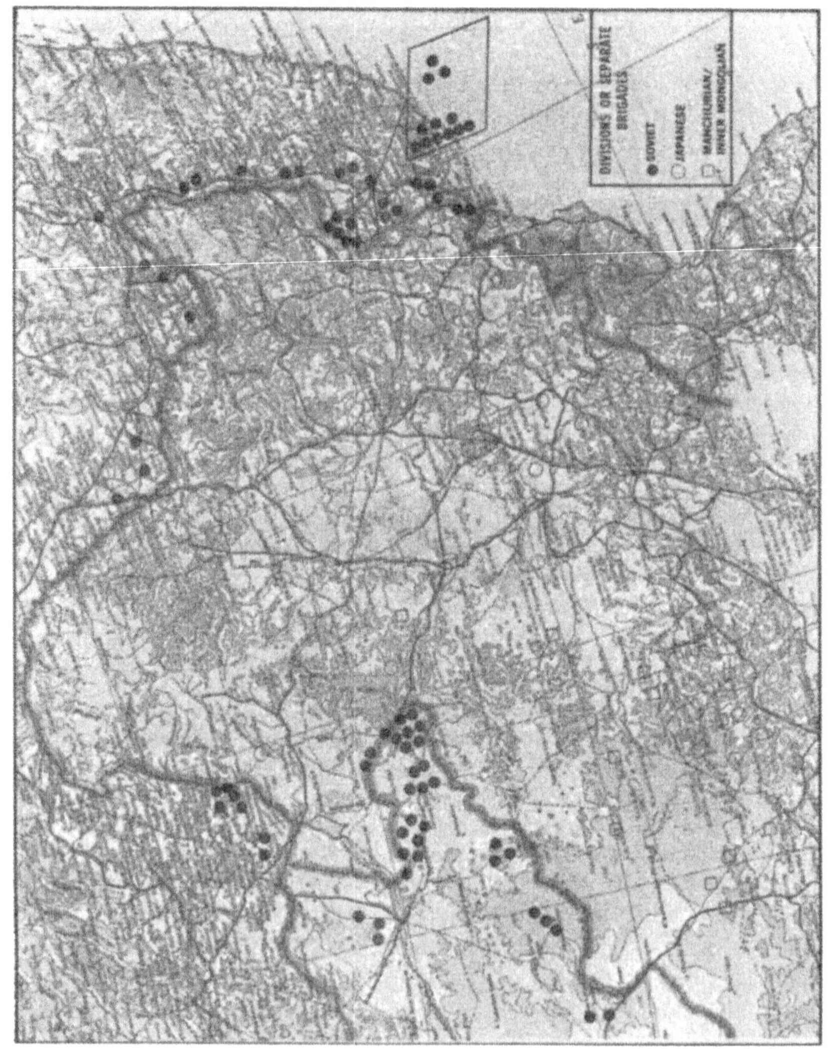

Map 25. Density and Distribution of Opposing Forces (Division Equivalents)

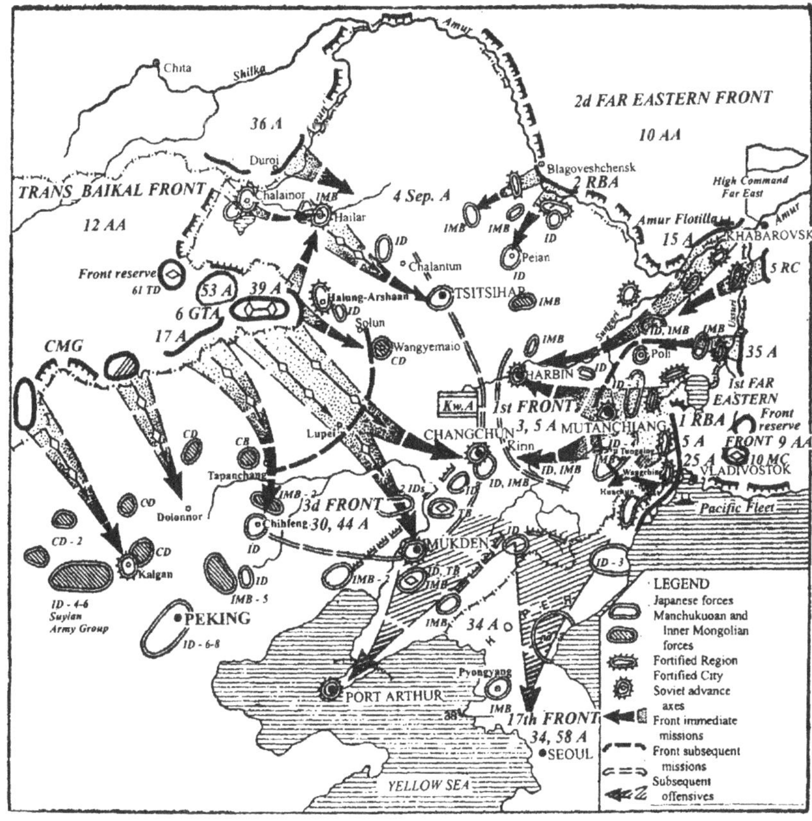

Map 26. Soviet Depiction of Far East Command Operational Plan

organized around the nucleus of a cavalry-mechanized group and commanded by Colonel General I. A. Pliev was to advance from southern Mongolia directly on Peking. The timing of on-order operations against southern Sakhalin Island, the Kuril Islands, and possibly, Hokkaido, would depend on the progress of the main attacks.

By resorting to this massive strategic envelopment, the *Stavka* strove, first of all, to destroy Japanese covering forces defending the border districts as rapidly as possible, overcome the forbidding terrain encasing the central portion of Manchuria, and seize favorable positions from which to launch decisive offensives by all three *fronts* into the central valley. Subsequently, the *Stavka* intended to engage and destroy Japanese reserves, occupy the central valley, and completely defeat the Kwantung Army before it could man its rear defenses, particularly the fabled redoubt region along the Manchurian–Korean border.

Virtually every aspect of the Far East Command's strategic and operational planning reflected the *Stavka's* insistence that the offensive be rapid so as to preempt Japanese defense plans, avoid a protracted war, and insure Soviet control over Manchuria before the Japanese surrendered to Allied powers in the Far East. As *Stavka* and Far East Command planners wrestled with how best to accomplish these goals, they developed several offensive variants. For example, one of the first variants they considered called for the Trans-Baikal Front to attack well before the 1st Far Eastern Front. However, since several *front* commanders objected to this scheme, instead, the Far East Command decided to commit the Trans-Baikal and the 1st Far Eastern Fronts in simultaneous offensives into Manchuria from west and east (see Maps 27 and 28).

Within the context of its 28 June directives, the *Stavka* assigned specific missions to its operating *fronts* and fleet prior to 25 July. Malinovsky's Trans-Baikal Front was to play the most important and most challenging role in the offensive by forming the western pincer of the massive envelopment operation. The *Stavka* ordered his *front* to conduct the Far East Command's main attack into western Manchuria with three combined-arms (the 39th, 17th, and 53d) and one tank army (the 6th Guards) to envelop the Halung-Arshaan fortified region from the south and advance in the general direction of Changchun. The *front's* immediate mission was to destroy opposing Japanese forces, cross the Grand Khingan Mountains, and reach the Solun, Lupei, and Palinyuchi (Tapanshang) region, 217 miles (350 kilometers) deep into Manchuria, by the fifteenth day of the operation.[10]

Deployed in the center of the *front's* first echelon, the 6th Guards Tank Army was to lead Malinovsky's main attack and force its way through the passes of the Grand Khingan Mountains by the tenth day of the operation. On the 6th Guards Tank Army's left flank, the 39th Army was to keep pace, cross the Grand Khingan Mountains to outflank the Halung–Arshaan fortified region from the south, and advance toward Changchun. On the 6th Guards

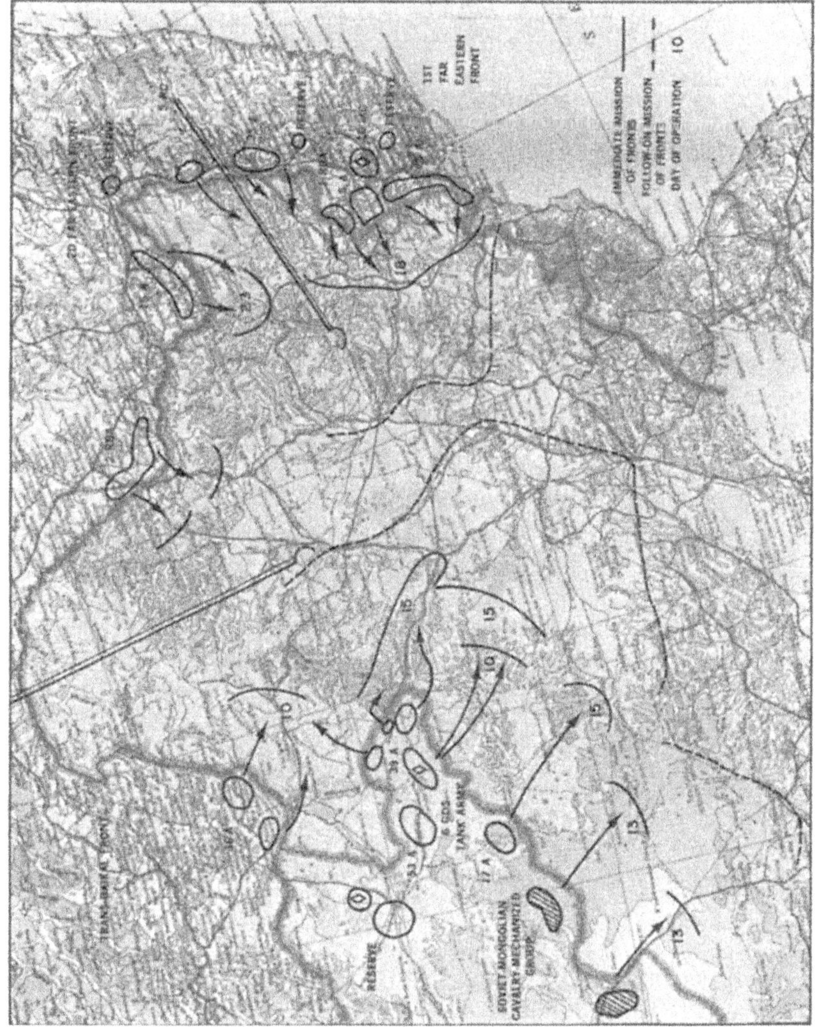

Map 27. Soviet Far East Command Plan

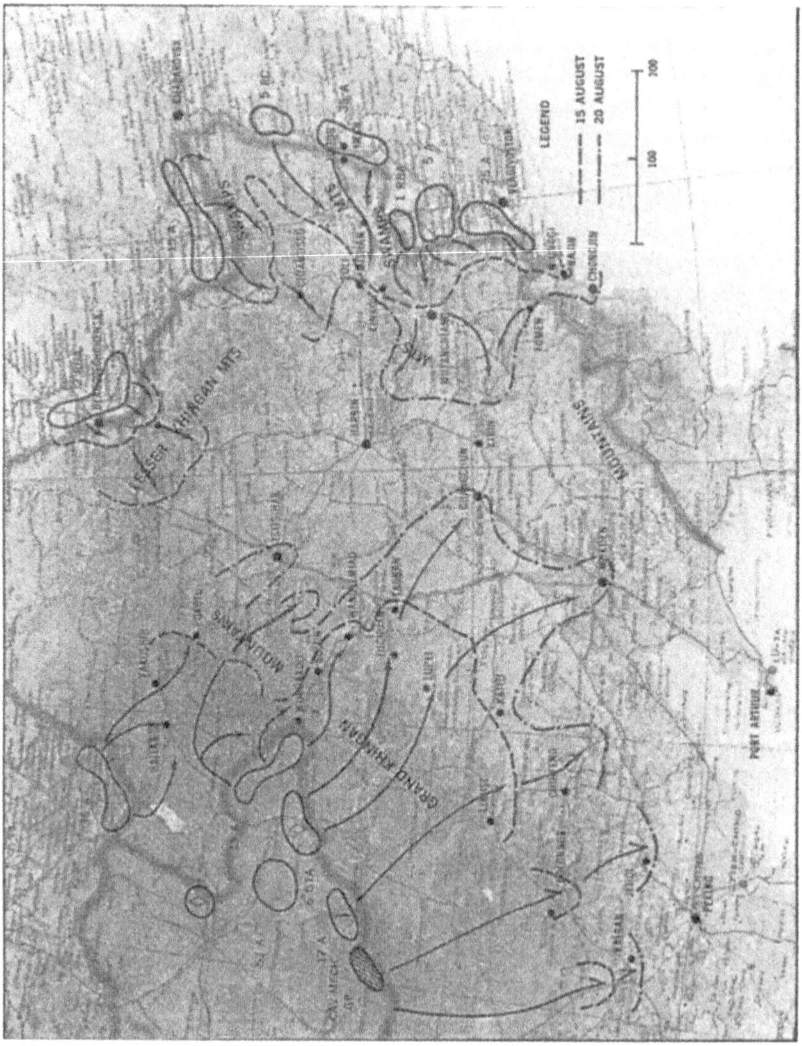

Map 28. Far East Command Operations, 9–20 August 1945

Army's right flank, the 17th Army was to cross the Grand Khingan Mountains, protect the 6th Guards Tank Army's right flanks, and advance toward Chihfeng in central Manchuria.

Once across the massive mountain barrier, the four armies of Malinovsky's main shock group were to regroup and advance to capture Chihfeng, Mukden, and Changchun. After they reached this line, they were to advance southward in tandem along the railroad line to occupy south-central Manchuria and the vital Liaotung peninsula. The *front* commander was to employ two artillery penetration divisions and the bulk of his RVGK artillery, tanks, and aircraft to support his main attack.

The *Stavka* also ordered Malinovsky to launch two secondary attacks, one by an army attacking on his left flank to the north and a second by a large force advancing on his right flank to the south. Specifically, on Malinovsky's left flank, the 36th Army was to attack into northwestern Manchuria, bypass the Japanese fortified region at Hailar, cross the Grand Khingan Mountains, and protect the Trans-Baikal Front's left flank. On Malinovsky's right flank, the Soviet–Mongolian Cavalry-Mechanized Group was to attack southeastward from southeastern Mongolia, traverse the Gobi Desert of Inner Mongolia, and advance into northern China to protect Malinovsky's right flank.

Malinovsky's forces were to advance in a sector demarcated by boundaries extending through Bayan-Somon in eastern Mongolia to Paotou west of Peking on the right (south) and Ksen'evka Station on the Trans-Siberian railroad southward across the Argun River past Mt. Kusushan in the Grand Khingan Mountains to Noho north of Tsitsihar on the left (north).

Meretskov's 1st Far Eastern Front formed the second pincer of the projected strategic envelopment. The *Stavka* ordered his *front* to penetrate or bypass Japanese frontier fortifications along the Mutanchiang axis with the 5th Army and 1st Red Banner Army, the 10th Mechanized Corps and one cavalry division, destroy opposing Japanese forces, and reach the Poli, Mutanchiang, and Wangching line by the 15th to 18th day of the operation.[11] Subsequently, when his main forces reached the western bank of the Mutanchiang River in the Wangching and Yenchi region, his forces were to develop the attack toward Kirin and Changchun with part of the force toward Harbin.

Two of Meretskov's armies were to launch attacks in support of the *front's* main effort. To the north, the 35th Army was to attack from the Lesozavodsk and Iman regions north of Lake Khanka in the general direction of Mishan to protect the main shock group's right wing. To the south, the 25th Army was to penetrate the Tumentzu Fortified Region, northwest of Ussurysk, and develop its attack toward the Tumen, Wangching, and Yenchi areas to cut off Japanese withdrawal routes into northern Korea.

If it became necessary, part of Meretskov's forces could be wheeled to the south from the Wangching and Yenchi region to strike Japanese forces in northern Korea. The boundaries of the 1st Far Eastern Front's sectors extended from Cape Sosunova through Guberovo to Poli on the right (north) and along the Korean state boundary on the left (south).

When the Trans-Baikal and 1st Far Eastern Front forces reached the Changchun and Kirin regions, the bulk of the Kwantung Army would be encircled in central and northern Manchuria. Subsequently, the forces of both *fronts* were to sharply alter the direction of their advance southward and exploit the offensive toward the Liaotung peninsula and into northern Korea to complete the destruction of Japanese forces.

The mission of Purkaev's 2d Far Eastern Front, which was deployed on a broad front across the Amur and Ussuri Rivers from the Blagoveshchensk region to south of Khabarovsk, was to attack in the general direction of Harbin and cooperate closely with the forces of the Trans-Baikal and 1st Far Eastern Fronts. It was to bring maximum pressure to bear on Japanese forces in northern Manchuria in order to destroy them or to prevent their orderly withdrawal south to assist Japanese forces resisting the main Soviet attacks.[12]

Initially, the 2d Far Eastern Front's 15th Army and 5th Separate Rifle Corps were to attack across the Amur and Ussuri Rivers along the Sungari and Jaoho axes, penetrate Japanese fortified regions, and destroy Japanese forces in the Tungchiang, Fuchin, and Chiamussu regions. The *front's* immediate mission was to capture the Fuchin Fortified Region and reach the Chiamussu region by the 23rd day of the operation. Subsequently, Purkaev's main force was to advance along the Sungari River to Harbin in close cooperation with the Amur River Flotilla. In addition, on order of the Far East Command, the *front's* 2d Red Banner Army was to attack across the Amur River south of Blagoveshchensk to smash Japanese defenses in the Aihun and Sunwu regions.

The mission of the 2d Far Eastern Front's 16th Army was to defend the western coast of the Tatar Strait, northern Sakhalin, and the Kamchatka peninsula jointly with the Kamchatka Defensive Region and the Petropavlovsk Naval Base and prevent any Japanese attacks on those regions. Simultaneously, the army's 56th Rifle Corps was to prepare to conduct an offensive against the southern portion of Sakhalin Island, and the forces of the Kamchatka Defensive Region and ships of the Petropavlovsk naval base were to prepare to launch amphibious assaults against Japanese forces defending the Kuril Islands.[13]

Since the *Stavka* required the Trans-Baikal and 1st Far Eastern Fronts to conduct the Far East Command's main attacks, they were far more powerful than the 2d Far Eastern Front, which was to play a supporting role in the offensive. Accordingly, the Trans-Baikal and 1st Far Eastern Fronts' shock groups comprised 60–70 per cent of all of the Far East Command's forces.

Prior to the commencement of the offensive, the Pacific Fleet was to lay defensive minefields and deploy its submarines into wartime positions. Once the offensive began, the fleet was to disrupt or destroy Japanese communications in the Sea of Japan, destroy Japanese ships in northern Korean ports, protect its sea communications in the Sea of Japan and the Tatar Strait, protect the ground forces' coastal flank, and prevent any amphibious landings on Soviet soil.[14] When it became feasible during the course of combat operations, the fleet was to capture the ports in northern Korea and support amphibious landings on southern Sakhalin Island and the Kuril Islands.

The *Stavka* assigned the Red Banner Amur Military Flotilla, which was operationally subordinate to the 2d Far Eastern Front, the mission of supporting the forced crossing of the Amur and Ussuri Rivers and cooperating with the forces attacking along the Sungari axis.

The air forces assigned to the Far East Command and Pacific Fleet were to perform several missions throughout the offensive. First, the air force was to achieve air superiority; second, protect the main force advance; third, disrupt the maneuver of enemy reserves by striking railroad lines, trains, and vehicular columns; fourth, support the ground force operations to penetrate the fortified regions and develop the offensive; fifth, destroy enemy command and control by striking his command posts, headquarters, and communications centers; and sixth, conduct continuous reconnaissance in the interest of the attacking forces.

The combined employment of ground and air forces in a surprise offensive of massive proportions was designed to preempt and paralyze the Japanese defenders and prevent them from escaping rapid destruction. The equally massive air strikes on Japanese communications were designed to prevent the Japanese from conducting any sort of operational or strategic maneuver or erecting subsequent defense lines once their border defenses were penetrated.

The *Stavka's* concept of operations for the Manchurian offensive involved employing decisive and imaginative combat techniques to achieve ambitious aims. The missions and associated directives and instructions it issued to its subordinate forces required those forces to conduct extensive maneuvers across terrain that most Japanese thought impenetrable. The resulting multi-*front* operational plan sought nothing short of the complete destruction of the Kwantung Army in Manchuria with maximum speed. The advancing Soviet forces would quickly end any Japanese hopes of receiving reinforcements from northern China or Korea. By attacking in virtually every combat sector, the Far East Command's forces would force the Japanese to defend in all sectors. The multiple and incessant mobile attacks across a broad front would prevent the Japanese from maneuvering their forces from one sector to another and would lead to the utter collapse and piecemeal defeat of defending Japanese forces.

The *Stavka's* planning assumptions proved to be correct. In the Trans-Baikal Front's sector opposite western Manchuria, the Japanese did not expect an attack across the entire length of the Grand Khingan Mountains. Therefore, their only defenses in the region were at Hailar and Chalainor and Manchouli in the north and Halung-Arshaan in the center. They left the rest of the mountain range utterly undefended. Worse still, the Japanese defended the border region with only small detachments, and the bulk of the Third Area Army was located 249–373 miles (400–600 kilometers) from where the Japanese defenses should have been to be effective.

From the Trans-Baikal Front's perspective, the wide expanse of empty desert and steppe and the absence of Japanese defenses permitted a rapid advance by tanks, motorized infantry, and cavalry across the Grand Khingans at breakneck speed. The rapid seizure of the passes and peaks of the Grand Khingans made it possible for the Trans-Baikal Front's massed rifle forces to enter Manchuria's central valley before the bulk of the Japanese Third Area Army could react. As Malinovsky's orders read, 'Success in the operation demands surprise and as much speed of operations as possible.'[15]

FRONT AND ARMY PLANS AND MISSIONS

The Trans-Baikal Front

In accordance with the *Stavka's* orders, Malinovsky, the commander of the Trans-Baikal Front, decided to make his main attack with his 17th, 39th, and 53d Armies and 6th Guards Tank Army. He ordered the four armies to envelop the Japanese Halung-Arshaan Fortified Region from the south and advance toward Changchun with the immediate mission of destroying Japanese covering forces, crossing the Grand Khingan Mountains, and reaching the Tapanshang, Lupei, and Solun regions by the fifteenth day of the operation, a depth of 217 miles (350 kilometers).

After crossing the Gobi Desert and the Grand Khingan Mountain passes, the 6th Guards Army, which was spearheading Malinovsky's advance, had to reach Lupei by the end of the fifth day of operations and Tuchuan by the 15th day of the operation. Subsequently, the *front's* forces were to capture Changchun and Mukden, where they were to establish contact with the 1st Far Eastern Front's forces, which were advancing toward Kirin. When Malinovsky's forces reached the Chihfeng, Mukden, Changchun, and Chalantun line, 490 miles (800 kilometers) deep into Manchuria, together with the 1st Far Eastern Front's forces, they were to have encircled the bulk of the Kwantung Army.[16]

Malinovsky organized his main *front* grouping (shock group) into two echelons, with the 17th Army, 6th Guards Tank Army, and 39th Army in first echelon and the 53d Army in second. His *front* reserve consisted of two rifle divisions (the 317th and 227th), one tank division (the 111th), one tank brigade (the 201st), and antitank and antiaircraft formations and units deployed in his main attack sector. Simultaneously, Malinovsky planned two secondary attacks aimed at supporting his main thrust. The first, conducted by a cavalry-mechanized group deployed in two echelons along a front of 217 miles (350 kilometers), was to advance from Mongolia southeastward toward Kalgan and Dolonnor. The second, made up of the 36th Army, also deployed in two echelons along a front of 155 miles (250 kilometers), was to attack toward Hailar and Chalantun.

The Trans-Baikal Front's main shock group, which was deployed along a 224-mile (360-kilometer) front in the center of its combat formation and was to advance toward Lupei and Changchun, contained 54 per cent of Malinovsky's rifle divisions, 73 per cent of his tanks and self-propelled artillery, and 62 per cent of his guns and mortars. Malinovsky planned to commence his offensive simultaneously in all axes across the entire breadth of his *front* and employ his tank army, cavalry-mechanized group, and three combined-arms armies in first echelon and only one army in second echelon. His plan called for his combined-arms formations to maintain a rapid advance tempo of 14 miles (23 kilometers) per day and his tank formations, 43 miles (70 kilometers.)[17]

The 6th Guards Tank Army, commanded by Colonel General of Tank Forces A. G. Kravchenko, was to launch a decisive attack from the region southeast of Tamsag-Bulag in the general direction of Lupei, cross the Grand Khingan Mountains and fortify the mountain passes, and reach Lupei with part of his forces. The army was to secure the mountain passes and capture Lupei in 'the shortest period and no later than the fifth day after the commencement of the offensive'.[18] Subsequently, Kravchenko's main forces were to reach the Mukden and Changchun line to secure the *front's* objectives.

Unlike the *front's* combined-arms armies, whose operations were planned to the depth of the *front's* immediate mission, Malinovsky's plan required Kravchenko's army to advance to the entire depth of the *front* operation and reach the *front* immediate objective (Lupei) ten days before the combined-arms armies. To do so, Kravchenko's force was equipped with 1,019 tanks and self-propelled guns, 188 armored vehicles, 1,150 guns and mortars, 43 multiple rocket launchers (*Katiushas*), and 6,489 vehicles.[19]

Kravchenko, Andrei Grigor'evich (1899–1963), commander, 6th Guards Tank Army

1918 – Joined the Red Army; corporal during the Civil War.

1921 – Commander, rifle company and rifle battalion; chief of staff, rifle regiment, and tactics instructor, Leningrad Armored Courses for the Improvement of Command Cadre.

1923 – Attended Poltava Infantry School.

1928 – Attended Frunze Academy.
1935 – Instructor, Saratov Armored School.
1939 (May) – Chief of staff, rifle division, motorized rifle division, and tank division (Finnish War).
1940 (June) – Chief of Staff, 16th Tank Division.
1941 (March) – Chief of Staff, 18th Mechanized Corps.
1941 (September) – Commander, 31st Tank Brigade (Battle of Moscow).
1942 (January) – Chief of the 61st Army's armored and mechanized forces.
1942 (March) – Chief of staff, 1st Tank Corps.
1942 (July) – Commander, 2d Tank Corps.
1942 (September) – Commander, 4th Tank Corps (5th Guards Tank Corps) (Battles of Stalingrad, Kursk, Dnepr River, Kirovograd, and Kiev).
1944 (January) – Commander, 6th Tank Army (Korsun'-Shevchenkovskii, Uman'-Botoshany, and Iassy-Kishinev offensives).
1944 – Commander, 6th Guards Tank Army (Debrecen, Budapest, Balaton, Vienna, and Manchurian offensives).
1946 – Commander, 6th Guards Tank Army.
1947 (June) – Commander of armored forces, Trans-Baikal and Baltic Military Districts.
1954 (January) – Deputy commander Far Eastern Military District for Tank Armaments, and deputy Supreme Soviet of the USSR.
1955 (October) – In the reserves.

Lieutenant General A. I. Danilov's 17th Army was to attack in the general direction of Tapanshang with the mission of protecting the 6th Guards Tank Army's right flank and communications against Japanese attacks from the south and southwest and capture the Lintung (Palintsochi), Linhsi, and Tapanshang region by the end of the fifteenth day of the operation. Danilov's army fielded 137 tanks and self-propelled guns, 830 guns and mortars, and 24 multiple rocket launchers.[20]

Danilov, Aleksei Il'ich (1897-1981), commander, 17th Army
1917 – Joined the Russian Army; attended the Alekseev Military School.
1918 – Joined the Red Army; platoon and company commander during the Civil War (Southwestern and Western Fronts).
1920 – Company commander and chief of regimental school.
1924 – Attended Vystrel' School and commander, rifle battalion.
1931 – Attended Frunze Academy.
1931 – Chief of operations, rifle division; chief of staff, 29th Rifle Division; and chief of staff, 5th Rifle Corps.
1937 – Chief of staff, 81st Rifle Division; and chief of staff and commander 49th Rifle Corps.
1939 – Attended Course for the Improvement of Senior Command Cadre.

1940 (July) – Deputy commander, Kiev Special Military District's PVO (Air defense) forces.
1941 (July) – Chief of PVO, Northwestern Front.
1941 (October) – Chief of staff, 21st Army (Khar'kov offensive).
1942 (June) – Commander, 21st Army.
1942 (November) – Chief of Staff, 5th Tank Army (Battle of Stalingrad).
1943 (April) – Chief of staff and commander, 12th Army (Donbas, Left Bank of the Ukraine, and Zaporozh'e offensives).
1943 (November) – Commander, 17th Army (Mongolia and Manchurian offensive).
1946 – Commander, army and rifle corps.
1948 – Attended Higher Academic Courses at the General Staff Academy; Chief of the Higher Academic Courses at the General Staff Academy.
1954 – Assistant commander, Trans-Baikal Military District.
1955 – Adviser to the North Korean People's Army.
1957 – Service in the General Staff.

The 39th Army, under the command of Colonel General I. I. Liudnikov and reinforced by the 61st Tank Division, was to launch its main attack from the region southeast of Halung-Arshaan in the general direction of Solun, bypassing the Halung-Arshaan Fortified Region from the south, with the immediate mission of reaching the Urlengui Gol (River), a depth of 37 miles (60 kilometers) into Manchuria. Subsequently, the army was to cut off the withdrawal of the Japanese Solun grouping to the southeast and capture Taonan and the region north of Changchun, 186–218 miles (300–350 kilometers) deep, by the fifteenth day of the operation.

In addition, Liudnikov's army was to conduct a secondary thrust toward Hailar from the south with two rifle divisions to isolate and destroy the Japanese Hailar grouping in conjunction with the 36th Army by seizing the Grand Khingan passes southeast of Hailar. This thrust was designed to thwart any cooperation between the Japanese Hailar and Solun groupings. Finally, one of Liudnikov's rifle divisions was to assault Halung-Arshaan from the north to tie down the fortified region's right flank. Liudnikov's army included 502 tanks and self-propelled guns, including 164 tanks in the 61st Tank Division.[21]

Liudnikov, Ivan Il'ich (1902–76), commander, 39th Army
1917 – Joined Red Guards and Red Army and fought in Civil War.
1925 – Attended Odessa Infantry School; platoon and company commander, 13th Dagestan Rifle Division; and battalion chief of staff, Vladivostok Infantry School.
1938 – Attended Frunze Academy.
1939 (November) – Chief of the Zhitomir Infantry School.

1941 (March) – Commander, 200th Rifle Division (Odessa defense).
1941 (November) – Commander, 16th Separate Student Officer Brigade and 390th Rifle Division (Battle of Moscow).
1942 (May) – Commander, 138th Rifle Division (Battle of Stalingrad).
1934 (February) – Commander, 70th Guards Rifle Division (Orel–Smolensk offensive).
1943 (June) – Commander, 15th Rifle Corps (Battle of Kursk).
1944 (May) – Commander, 39th Army (Belorussian, East Prussian offensives, Siege of Konigsberg, and Manchurian offensive).
1946 – Commander, 39th Army.
1949 (December) – Deputy commander, Group of Soviet Forces, Germany.
1952 – Attended Higher Military Academy.
1952 (November) – Assistant commander and first deputy commander, Odessa Military District.
1954 (September) – Commander, Tavrich Military District.
1956 (July) – Chief military adviser to the People's Republic of Bulgaria.
1959 (March) – Chief of the Vystrel' Courses.
1963 – Chief of Faculty, General Staff Academy and deputy Supreme Soviet of the USSR.
1968 – Retired.

Colonel General I. M. Managarov's 53d Army, which made up the *front's* second echelon, was to advance in the wake of the 6th Guards Tank Army and, after crossing the Grand Khingan Mountains, advance to the Lupei and Tuchuan region and be prepared to lead the final drive into central Manchuria.

Managarov, Ivan Mefod'evich (1898-1981), commander, 53d Army
1917 (April) – Joined the Red Guards; commander, Enakievsk Red Guards Detachment; commander, rifle regiment (Southern Front and Tsaritsyn).
1923 – Attended Cavalry School.
1923 – Commander, cavalry subunits (Leningrad Military District and Turkestan Front).
1926 – Secretary of the Party Bureau, cavalry regiment (Volga Military District).
1931 –Attended Political-Military Academy.
1931 – Commissar, mechanized regiment and cavalry regiment.
1936 – Special command inspector in China and Mongolia.
1939 – Commander, 8th Cavalry Division.
1941 (November) – Commander, 26th Rifle Corps (Far Eastern Front).
1942 (January) – Commander, 16th Cavalry Corps and (March) Commander, 7th Cavalry Corps (Briansk, Kalinin, and Northwestern Fronts).
1942 (December) – Commander, 41st Army (Rzhev–Viaz'ma offensive).
1943 (March) – Commander, 53d Army (Kursk, Belgorod–Khar'kov,

Uman'–Botoshany, Iassy-Kishinev, Budapest, Prague, and Manchurian offensives).
1946 – Commander, 4th Army (Trans-Baikal Military District).
1947 – Attended Courses at the Higher Military Academy.
1949 – Service in PVO forces.
1953 – Retired due to ill health.

Two forces, a cavalry-mechanized group and the 36th Army, were to launch secondary attacks along separate axes along the flanks of the Trans-Baikal Front sector to support the *front's* main shock group. The Soviet–Mongolian Cavalry-Mechanized Group under the command of Colonel General I. A. Pliev and his Mongolian deputy, General Zh. Lkhagvasuren, was to make its main attack from the Moltsok-Hid region in Mongolia across the Gobi Desert of Inner Mongolia and the southern Grand Khingan Mountains toward Dolonnor (Tolun). Its mission was to protect the right flank of the *front's* main shock group from the south. Further to the south, a smaller portion of Pliev's group was to conduct a secondary attack from the Dzamin-Uud region toward Kalgan (Changchiakou). The sector of advance of Pliev's group as a whole extended an extraordinary 217 miles (350 kilometers), and his main and secondary attacks were 112–124 miles (180–200 kilometers) apart. Pliev's force numbered more than 42,000 men, 23,000 horses, and 403 tanks and armored vehicles, mostly armored cars.[22]

Pliev, Issa Aleksandrovich (1903–79), Commander, Soviet–Mongolian Cavalry-Mechanized Group
1922 – Joined the Red Army.
1926 – Attended Leningrad Cavalry School.
1926 – Commander, Krasnodar Cavalry School.
1933 – Attended the Frunze Academy.
1933 – Chief of Operations, 5th Cavalry Division.
1936 – Adviser, Mongolian People's Army.
1939 – Commander, cavalry regiment, 6th Cavalry Division.
1941 – Attended General Staff Academy.
1941 (June) – Commander, 50th Cavalry (3d Guards Cavalry) Division (Battles of Smolensk and Moscow).
1941 (December) – Commander, 2d Guards Cavalry Corps (Battle of Moscow).
1942 (April) – Commander, 5th Guards Cavalry Corps, 3d Guards Cavalry Corps, and 4th Guards Cavalry Corps (Battle of Stalingrad, Melitopol', Bereznegovatoe-Snegerevka, Odessa, and Belorussian offensives).
1944 (November) – Commander, 1st Cavalry-Mechanized (1st Guards Cavalry-Mechanized) Group (Budapest, Balaton, and Vienna operations).
1945 – Commander, Soviet–Mongolian Cavalry-Mechanized Group.

1946 – Commander, various armies.
1955 – First Deputy commander, North Caucasus Military District.
1958 – Commander, North Caucasus Military District.
1960 – Commander, Soviet Strategic Rocket Forces in Cuba.
1968 (June) – Inspector-Adviser, General Inspector's Group, Ministry of Defense.

Finally, Lieutenant General A. A. Luchinsky's 36th Army was to conduct its main attack across the Argun River from Duroy and Staro-Tsurukhaitui northeast of Manchouli and a secondary attack from Zabaikal'sk (Otpor Station) region to capture the Hailar Fortified Region, a depth of 93 miles (150 kilometers), by the tenth day of the operation. Thereafter, Luchinsky's forces were to prevent Japanese forces from withdrawing intact across the Grand Khingan Mountains to Tsitsihar. Thus, the 36th Army was to conduct its advance in a 155-mile (250-kilometer) sector with 62 miles (100 kilometers) separating its two attacking forces. Because of rough terrain and lack of contact between the two *fronts*, the Far East Command drew no demarcation line to separate the Trans-Baikal Front from the 2d Far Eastern Front on its left.

Luchinsky, Aleksandr Aleksandrovich (1900–90), Commander, 36th Army
1919 – Joined the Red Army; commander, cavalry platoon and squadron on the Eastern Front and at Tsaritsyn.
1921 – Commander of platoon and squadron in the 50th Taman' Rifle Division and 14th Maikop Cavalry Division; chief of staff of a cavalry regiment (Turkestan Front).
1927 – Attended military school.
1930 – Attended the Cavalry Course for the Improvement of Command Cadre.
1936 (November) – Commander, cavalry regiment.
1937 – Military adviser in China.
1940 – Attended Frunze Academy.
1940 (November) – Chief of staff, 83d Mountain Rifle Division.
1941 (April) – Commander, 83d Mountain Rifle Division (Caucasus).
1943 (April) – Commander, 3d Mountain Rifle Corps (Taman' and Sevastopol' operations).
1944 (May) – Commander, 28th Army (Belorussian and East Prussian offensives and the siege of Konigsberg).
1945 – Commander, 36th Army (Manchurian offensive).
1946 – Commander, 4th and 28th Armies (Far East Military District).
1948 – Attended the Higher Military Academy (General Staff Academy).
1949 (April) – Deputy commander, Group of Soviet Forces, Germany.
1949 (September) – Commander, Leningrad Military District.
1953 (May) – Commander, Turkestan Military District.

1958 (April) – 1st Deputy Inspector of the Ministry of Defense.
1964 – Military inspector-adviser, Group of General Inspectors, Ministry of Defense.

The success of the Trans-Baikal Front operation depended on speed, surprise, and the skillful employment of mobile forces in virtually every sector in order to preempt effective Japanese defense. For swiftness and surprise, tank formations were to operate in the first echelon of units at every level of command. The operation also called for the employment of tank-heavy forward detachments at every level of command to serve as spearheads of the offensive. Accordingly, the 6th Guards Tank Army spearheaded the *front*'s advance, a tank division led the advance of the 39th Army, and tank brigades served as forward detachments for each first echelon rifle corps and individual divisions. The planned rates of advance for the operation were quite high, requiring an advance rate of 14.3 miles (23 kilometers) per day for combined arms units and 43.5 miles (70 kilometers) per day for tank units.

The operations planned by Malinovsky's *front* certainly involved taking considerable risks. For example, if Japanese units reacted quickly enough to the Soviet attack and managed to occupy positions in the Grand Khingan mountain passes, even with nominal forces, they could disrupt or severely slow the Trans-Baikal Front's advance. In addition, the operation relied heavily on the ability of logistical units to supply the fast-moving columns deep in Manchuria. Malinovsky confidently accepted both risks.

The 1st Far Eastern Front

The Japanese defenses opposite the 1st Far Eastern Front consisted of strong covering forces manning fragmented but well-prepared fortifications extending a depth of 92–110 miles (150–180 kilometers) westward to the Mulenho and Mutanchiang Rivers. The mountainous and heavily forested and brush-covered terrain restricted forward movement by attacking forces to several distinct but restrictive axes of advance.

Meretskov decided to conduct his 1st Far Eastern Front's main attack in the direction of Mutanchiang with the reinforced 1st Red Banner and 5th Armies.[23] The two armies' immediate mission was to penetrate the fortified region along the border and reach the Poli, Mutanchiang, Wangching regions by the end of the fifteenth to eighteenth days of the operation. Thereafter, Meretskov's main force was to advance toward Kirin and Changchun to link up with the Trans-Baikal Front's forces and help encircle and destroy the Kwantung Army's main forces in the central valley. The overall depth of Meretskov's operation was 310 miles (500 kilometers). Part of Meretskov's main shock group was then to advance on Harbin to link up with forces of the 2d Far Eastern Front.

Simultaneously, the *front's* 35th and 25th Armies were to conduct secondary assaults to protect the flanks of its main attack force. On the right flank, the 35th Army was to attack from the Lesozavodsk region north of Lake Khanka toward Mishan and Poli, and, on the left flank, the 25th Army was to attack toward Wangching to roll up Japanese defenses in eastern Manchuria from the south. Meretskov organized his armies in single echelon and ordered his mobile group (the 10th Mechanized Corps) and his *front* reserve (the 87th and 88th Rifle Corps and the 84th Cavalry Division) to exploit success along the main attack axis.

Meretskov's offensive plan included two possible variants depending on how the Japanese conducted their defense. If the *front's* mobile forces (forward detachments) quickly penetrated the Japanese defenses, the *front's* main forces would immediately follow without the support of an extensive artillery and air preparation. On the other hand, if Japanese resistance proved to be determined and slowed the forward detachments' advance, the main forces would attack only after a heavy and prolonged artillery preparation.

Meretskov ordered the 1st Red Banner Army, commanded by Colonel General A. P. Beloborodov, to conduct his main attack in the general direction of Pamientung (Muleng). His forces were to overcome the 19-mile (30-kilometer) deep mountainous and forested belt west of the border by the end of the third day of the operation and capture Pamientung no later than the end of the eighth day of the operation, while dispatching strong forward detachments westward to occupy Linkou. By the end of the eighteenth day, his main forces were to reach the Mutanchiang River north of the town of Mutanchiang. At the same time, Beloborodov was to employ strong covering forces to protect his forces against attack from the north and east and assist the 35th Army in defeating the Japanese Mishan grouping. To do so, Beloborodov had 410 tanks and self-propelled guns and 1,413 guns and mortars at his disposal.[24]

Beloborodov was to attack with his forces in march-column formation led by strong mobile forward detachments, which were prepared to deal quickly with the few Japanese outposts in the region. Intelligence informed him that the Japanese had failed to erect any credible defenses in the region because they thought it was impenetrable by military forces.

Beloborodov, Afanasii Pavlant'evich (1903–90), Commander, 1st Red Banner Army

1919 (November) – Commander, rifle platoon, Uvarov Partisan Detachment, Irkutsk.

1923 – Joined the Red Army and commander, rifle platoon.

1926 – Attended Nizhegorod Infantry School.

1929 – Attended Friedrich Engels Military-Political Course.

1929 – Political officer and commander, rifle company, 197th Rifle Regiment (Far East).
1936 – Attended the Frunze Academy.
1936 – Deputy commander, chief of operations, 66th Rifle Division, Separate Red Banner Army (Far East).
1939 (March) – Chief of operations, 31st Rifle Corps, Far Eastern Front.
1939 (June) – Chief of Staff, 43d Rifle Corps, Far Eastern Front.
1941 (January) – Chief, Training Department, Far Eastern Front.
1941 (July) – Commander, 78th (9th Guards) Rifle Division, Far Eastern and Western Fronts (Battle of Moscow).
1942 (September) – Commander, 5th Guards Rifle Corps (Velikie-Luki offensive).
1943 (August) – Commander, 2d Guards Rifle Corps (Nevel' and Vitebsk offensives).
1944 (May) – Commander, 43d Army (Belorussian and East Prussian offensives and Siege of Konigsberg).
1945 (June) – Commander, 1st Red Banner Army, Far Eastern Front.
1946 (April) – Chief of Rifle Forces Training, Central Group of Forces.
1946 (December) – Deputy commander of the Central Group of Forces.
1947 – Commander, 39th Army (Port Arthur).
1953 – Chief, Ground Forces Military Training Administration; chief of Vystrel' Courses.
1954 (May) – Military adviser to the Czech Ministry of Defense.
1955 (October) – Commander, Voronezh Military District.
1957 – Chief, Ministry of Defense's Main Cadres Directorate and member of the Ministry of Defense Collegium.
1963 – Commander, Moscow Military District.
1968 – Inspector and adviser, Group of Inspectors, Ministry of Defense and Deputy of the Supreme Soviet.

Colonel General N. I. Krylov's 5th Army was to play the key role in Meretskov's offensive by conducting its main attack in the general direction of Mutanchiang. Krylov's forces were to penetrate Japanese fortified defenses in a 7.5-mile (12-kilometer) sector near Suifenho, destroy the Suifenho Fortified Region, and capture positions extending from Suifenho to Mount Taipingling, to a depth of 25 miles (40 kilometers), by the end of the fourth day of operations. By the end of the eighth day of operations, Krylov's forces were supposed to reach the Mulenho River and the vital road junctions at Hsiachengtzu and Pamientung, a depth of 37–50 miles (60–80 kilometers).

Thereafter, the 5th Army was to force the Mutanchiang River and capture Mutanchiang, at an operational depth of 110 miles (180 kilometers). Simultaneously, the 17th Rifle Corps, deployed on Krylov's left flank, was to roll up the Japanese flank to the south by advancing on Tungning.

The 5th Army was to perform the most decisive role in the 1st Far Eastern Front's operation. After it reached the Mutanchiang region, the 10th Mechanized Corps, the *front's* mobile group, was to join the advance with the mission of advancing to Kirin where it was to link up with the forward elements of the Trans-Baikal Front. To perform its vital mission, Krylov's army fielded 607 tanks and self-propelled guns, 2,945 guns and mortars, and 432 multiple rocket launchers.[25] The *front's* mobile group, the 10th Mechanized Corps, with 249 tanks and self-propelled guns, and the *front* reserve, which consisted of the 335th and 355th Rifle Divisions and 150th and 162d Fortified Regions, were to reinforce Meretskov's main attack along the Mutanchiang axis.

Krylov, Nikolai Ivanovich (1903–72), Commander, 5th Army

1919 – Joined the Red Army; platoon and company commander (North Caucasus) and battalion commissar, 2d Trans-Baikal Rifle Division (Vladivostok).
1920 – Attended Infantry/Machine gun Course for Red Commanders.
1920 – Staff and command positions in the Siberian Military District and the Special Red Banner Far Eastern Army.
1928 – Attended Vystrel' Course.
1941 – Chief of staff, Danube Fortified Region; chief of operations and chief of staff, Maritime Army (Odessa and Sevastopol' defense).
1942 (September) – Chief of staff, 62d (8th Guards) Army (Battle of Stalingrad).
1943 (May) – Commander, 3d Reserve Army.
1943 (July) – Commander, 21st Army (Smolensk offensive).
1943 (October) – Commander, 5th Army (Vitebsk, Belorussian, and East Prussian offensives, the Siege of Konigsberg, and the Manchurian offensive).
1945 (September) – Commander, 15th Army.
1945 – Deputy commander, Maritime Military District.
1947 – Commander, Far Eastern Military District.
1956 – Commander, Ural Military District.
1957 – Leningrad Military District.
1960 – Commander, Moscow Military District.
1963 (March) – Commander, Strategic Rocket Forces and deputy Minister of Defense.

The 25th Army, commanded by Colonel General I. M. Chistiakov, had the mission of defending the 177-mile (285-kilometer) wide stretch of state border extending from south of Suifenho to the Korean border on the left flank of Meretskov's shock group. After the 5th Army had penetrated the Japanese fortified defenses and the 17th Rifle Corps (deployed on the 5th Army's left flank) had reached the region north of Tungning, Chistiakov's army was to take control of that corps, capture the Tungning Fortified Region, and develop an offensive in the general direction of Wangching. His army was to reach the Wangching–Hunchun line by the end of the twenty-fifth day of the operation.

Once it began its offensive, Chistiakov's army was to advance 112 miles (180 kilometers) in a period of 25 days at an average advance rate of five miles (eight kilometers) per day. Its principal role was to protect the 5th Army's left flank and develop the offensive to Wangching and Yenchi, widening the *front* penetration and threatening the Japanese fortified regions from the rear. Subsequently, its forces were to cooperate with the Pacific Fleet and conduct successive amphibious landings at the northern Korean ports of Unggi and Chongjin. Chistiakov's force fielded 121 tanks and self-propelled guns and 1,669 guns and mortars.[26]

Chistiakov, Ivan Mikhailovich (1900–79), Commander, 25th Army

1919 – Joined the Red Army; corporal and assistant platoon commander, 7th Tula Volunteer Regiment and 124th Rifle Regiment, 14th Stepin Rifle Division.

1920 – Attended Infantry/Machine gun School.

1921 – Commander, infantry platoon and battalion and assistant commander, 37th Rifle Regiment and commander, 3d Rifle Company, 3d Machine gun Command, and 3d Machine gun Command (North Caucasus).

1927 – Attended the Vystrel' Course.

1928 – Commander, machine gun command, 13th Rifle Division, 9th Rifle Corps (Belorussian Military District).

1932 – Deputy commander, rifle regiment, 13th Rifle Division.

1936 – Commander, 275th Rifle Regiment, 92d Rifle Division (Trans-Baikal Military District).

1936 – Chief, Operations Section, 92d Rifle Division.

1937 – Commander, 105th Rifle Division (Trans-Baikal Military District).

1939 – Deputy commander, 39th Rifle Corps (Trans-Baikal Military District).

1940 – Commander, Vladivostok Infantry School.

1941 – Commander, 56th Rifle Corps (Khar'kov Military District) and 39th Rifle Corps, 25th Army (Far Eastern Front).

1941 – Attended General Staff Academy.

1942 – Commander, 64th Separate Naval Rifle Brigade and 8th Guards Rifle Division (Battle of Moscow).

1942 (April) – Commander, 2d Guards Rifle Corps, 5th Tank Army (Voronezh defense and counterstrokes).

1942 (October) – Commander, 21st (6th Guards) Army (Battle of Stalingrad and Kursk, Belgorod-Khar'kov, Vitebsk, Belorussian, Memel', and Courland offensives).

1945 – Commander, 25th Army (Manchurian offensive).

1946 – Various command positions.
1954 – First deputy commander, Trans-Baikal Military District.
1957 – General Inspector, Inspectorate of Ground Forces.
1968 – Retired.

On the right flank of Meretskov's shock group, Lieutenant General M. D. Zakhvataev's 35th Army was to protect the railroad line and road in the Guberova and Spassk-Dal'nii sector east of the Ussuri River with part of his forces and, with his main force, attack westward north of Lake Khanka from the region southeast of Lesozavodsk against the southern flank of the Hutou Fortified Region and capture the important fortified point. Subsequently, Zakhvataev was to develop the attack toward Poli, protect the *front* shock group's right flank, and destroy the defending Japanese forces in conjunction with the 1st Red Banner Army, which was advancing south of Lake Khanka.

Considering the imposing strength of the Japanese Hutou Fortress, Meretskov ordered Zakhvataev to envelop it from the south and isolate it rather than assaulting it directly and, by so doing, also provide the requisite protection for the 1st Red Banner Army's right flank. The 35th Army fielded 166 tanks and self-propelled guns and 955 guns and mortars.[27]

Zakhvataev, Nikanor Dmitrievich (1898–1963), Commander, 35th Army
1916 – Joined the Russian Army.
1916 – Attended Warrant Officer's School; commander, machine gun command, rifle regiment.
1918 – Joined the Red Army with staff duties in artillery units.
1920 – Attended Artillery School; adjutant, artillery battalion.
1921 – Assistant chief of Malmyzh district Military Commissariat; Section chief, training section, military district; chief of staff, rifle regiment.
1930 – Attended Vystrel' Course.
1931 – RKKA Inspection Group (Military Training).
1935 – Attended Frunze Academy.
1936 – Commander, rifle regiment.
1935 – Member, Inspection Control Group, NKO.
1939 – (September) Student and Instructor, General Staff Academy.
1941 (June) – Deputy chief of operations, Southwestern Front.
1941 (November) – Chief of staff, 1st Shock Army (Battle of Moscow).
1942 (May) – Commander, 1st Guards Rifle Corps (Demiansk operation).
1942 (December) – Commander, 12th Guards Rifle Corps (Demiansk offensive, Operation 'Polar Star', and Leningrad–Novgorod operations).
1944 (May) – Commander, 1st Shock Army (Baltic, Tartu, and Riga offensives).
1945 (March) – Commander, 4th Guards Army (Budapest and Vienna offensives).

1945 (July) – Commander, 35th Army (Manchurian offensive).
1946 – Commander, 35th Army.
1947 (February) – Commander, Maritime Military District.
1950 (March) – Commander, Belorussian Military District.
1951 (December) – Commander, Don Military District.
1953 (November) – First deputy commander, Belorussian Military District.
1955 (April) – Deputy chief of the General Staff.
1957 (June) – Chief military adviser to the Hungarian People's Army.
1960 – Retired.

Finally, Meretskov, ordered the 1st Far Eastern Front's Chuguevka Operational Group, commanded by Major General F. A. Parusinov, to defend the coast of the Sea of Japan from Shkotovo to Vladimiro-Aleksandrovskoe and from Valentin to Tetiukhe against Japanese amphibious landings in cooperation with the Pacific Fleet.

After the 1st Far Eastern Front and the Trans-Baikal Front forces had linked up in the Changchun area, they were to advance side by side to crush final Japanese resistance on the Liaotung Peninsula and to secure Port Arthur, the key naval base at the southern tip of the peninsula.

Thus, Meretskov's plan envisioned a decisive advance through the fortified regions along the border, followed by an advance on Mutanchiang along the valley through which ran the main railroad and roads westward from the border into Manchuria's interior. On its left, the 1st Red Banner Army would advance through a mountainous and heavily wooded sector that the Japanese consciously chose not to defend, and on his right, the 25th Army was to traverse the separate valley axes leading to the Japanese rear area.

The 2d Far Eastern Front

Since Purkaev, the commander of the 2d Far Eastern Front, well understood that his forces would have to force the formidable Amur and Ussuri Rivers during their offensive, he closely coordinated his forces' operations with the Red Banner Amur Military Flotilla. Beyond the rivers, his troops would also have to penetrate heavy Japanese fortified defenses and traverse the difficult terrain of the Lesser Khingan Mountains. His plan required his forces to attack actively along a front of 323 miles (520 kilometers) out of his overall 1,324-mile- (2,130-kilometer) wide front.

Accordingly, Purkaev planned to make his main attack with the 15th Army from the Leninskoe region, located north of the Amur River, southward along the Sungari River through Chiamussu and Ilan to Harbin, supported by two brigades of river ships.[28] He also planned to deliver a supporting attack by the 5th Separate Rifle Corps and one brigade of river ships from the Bikin region north of Iman across the Ussuri River and along the Jaoho axis. During the first stage of the operation, his forces were to capture the Tungchiang Fortified Region, during the second stage, the Paoching Fortified Region, and, during the third stage, the major town of Chiamussu by the 23rd day of the operation. To accomplish these missions, Purkaev formed his forces in a single echelon with a rifle division and rifle brigade in reserve.

Initially, at least, Purkaev assigned almost half of his 2d Far Eastern Front only defensive missions. The 2d Red Banner and 16th Armies and the Kamchatka Defensive Region were to defend the Blagoveshchensk region, the coast of the Tatar Strait, northern Sakhalin Island, and the Kamchatka peninsula. When the Trans-Baikal and 1st Far Eastern Fronts began to exploit success along the Far East Command's main attack axes, Purkaev's defending forces were to launch several major supporting attacks. The 2d Red Banner Army was to attack from the Blagoveshchensk region toward Tsitsihar, and the 16th Army was to conquer southern Sakhalin and, together with forces of the Kamchatka Defensive Region, assault and capture the Kuril Islands.

Purkaev assigned the 15th Army, commanded by Lieutenant General S. K. Mamonov, the mission to assault across the Amur River near its junction with the Sungari River in cooperation with two brigades of river ships from the Amur Flotilla, destroy Japanese forces in the Tungchiang and Fuchin Fortified Regions, and capture Fuchin. By the end of the twenty-third day of operations, Mamonov's forces were to seize Chiamussu by advancing along the eastern bank of the Sungari River and subsequently advance southward to Harbin. His remaining forces were to defend along a front of 149 miles (240 kilometers). Mamonov's army fielded 240 tanks and self-propelled guns and 1,270 guns and mortars.[29]

Mamonov, Stepan Kirillovich (1901–74), Commander, 15th Army
1919 – Entered military service.
1924 – Commander, rifle platoon and rifle company and chief, regimental school.
1924 – Attended Infantry Command Course.
1927 – Completed command cadre course at Moscow Infantry School.
1932 – Chief of staff, rifle regiment.
1936 – Commander, rifle regiment.
1937 (October) – Chief of staff, 92d Rifle Division (Far East).
1938 (June) – Commander, 22d Rifle Division (Lake Khasan).
1939 (July) – Commander, 40th Rifle Division.
1942 (January) – Deputy commander, 25th Army (Far East).
1942 (August) – Commander, 39th Rifle Corps, 25th Army (Far East).
1942 (October) – Commander, 15th Army (Manchurian offensive).
1947 – Attended Higher Military Academy (General Staff Academy).
1947 (May) – Commander, rifle corps.
1950 (July) – Assistant commander, Ural Military District.

1. Trains moving east along the Trans-Siberian Railroad

2. Northern and central Grand Khingan Mountains

3. East slope of Grand Khingan Mountains near Pokotu

4. The Dolonnor region

5. Sand dunes and brush of the southern Barga Plateau

6. Marshy valley near Hailar on the Barga and Dalai plateaus

7. Grassy plains and bluffs on the Barga and Dalai plateaus near Hailar

8. Aihun on the Amur River

9. A cultivated river plain near Chiamussu

10. Eastern Manchurian Highlands

11. Suifenho

12. Railroad line through the Laoyeh Ling Mountains

13. Mutan River at Mutanchiang

14. Tunghua Mountains of southeastern Manchuria

15. Tunghua Mountains near the Korean border

16. Tailing Ho and Pei Piao Mountains of Southern Manchuria

17. Hills around Kirin

18. Highway from Changchun to Kirin in the central valley

19. Japanese forces on maneuvers in the central valley

20. Japanese convoy in the central valley

21. Marshal of the Soviet Union A. M. Vasilevsky, Commander, Far East Command

22. Marshal of the Soviet Union R. Ia. Malinovsky, Commander, Trans-Baikal Front

23. Marshal of the Soviet Union K. A. Meretskov, Commander, 1st Far Eastern Front

24. Army General M. A. Purkaev, Commander, 2d Far Eastern Front

25. Marshal A. M. Vasilevsky, Commander, Far East Command; Marshal R. Ia. Malinovsky, Commander, Trans-Baikal Front; and Marshal K. A. Meretskov, Commander, 1st Far Eastern Front

26. Marshal A. M. Vasilevsky, Commander, Far East Command; Lieutenant General S. P. Ivanov, Chief of Staff, Far East Command; and Colonel General I. I. Liudnikov, Commander, 39th Army

27. Army General I. I. Maslennikov, Deputy Commander, Far East Command, Marshal of Aviation A. A. Novikov, Commander, Red Army Air Forces; Marshal A. M. Vasilevsky, Commander, Far East Command; and Lieutenant General S. P. Ivanov, Chief of Staff, Far East Command

28. The Pacific Fleet's Military Council: Vice Admiral A. S. Frolov, Chief of Staff, Pacific Fleet; Admiral I. S. Iumashev, Commander, Pacific Fleet; and Lieutenant General of the Coastal Service S. E. Zakharov

29. Colonel General I. A. Pliev, Commander, Soviet–Mongolian Cavalry-Mechanized Group

30. Lieutenant General A. I. Danilov, Commander, 17th Army

31. Colonel General A. G. Kravchenko, Commander, 6th Guards Tank Army (center), accompanied by Marshal of Aviation S. A. Khudiakov, Commander, 8th Air Army (left), and Colonel General M. D. Solomatin, Commander, Far East Command's Armored and Mechanized Forces (right)

32. Colonel General I. I. Liudnikov, Commander, 39th Army

33. Lieutenant General A. A. Luchinsky, Commander, 36th Army

34. Colonel General I. M. Managarov, Commander, 53d Army

35. The 6th Guards Tank Army's reconnaissance units

36. The 6th Guards Tank Army approaching the Grand Khingan Mountains

37. Tank units at a rest halt

38. Lieutenant General M. P. Kovalev, Deputy Commander, Trans-Baikal Front (center), observes the forward movement of 6th Guards Tank Army

39. The 6th Guards Tank Army's tanks crossing the Grand Khingan Mountains

40. The 6th Guards Tank Army's 20th Tank Brigade enters the central Manchurian plain

41. The 6th Guards Tank Army's 5th Guards Tank Corps advances on Lupei

42. Tanks of the 9th Guards Mechanized Corps' 46th Guards Tank Brigade conduct a river crossing

43. 6th Guards Tank Army self-propelled guns in central Manchuria

44. Manchouli

45. Hailar

В боях под Хаиларом

46. Soviet artillery firing on Japanese positions at Hailar

47. Trans-Baikal Front air assault troops load onto aircraft

48. Air assault on Mukden

49. Soviet tanks entering Changchun

50. Colonel General N. I. Krylov, Commander, 5th Army

51. Lieutenant General N. D. Zakhvataev, Commander, 35th Army

52. Colonel General A. P. Beloborodov, Commander, 1st Red Banner Army, observes pre-offensive exercises

53. Colonel General I. M. Chistiakov, Commander, 25th Army

54. Lieutenant General I. D. Vasil'ev, Commander, 10th Mechanized Corps

55. Soviet bombers over Manchuria

56. ‘Katiushas’ firing on Japanese positions

57. Soviet heavy artillery pounds Japanese positions

58. Soviet artillery firing on Japanese positions

59. Soviet 5th Army infantry advance.

60. Soviet 25th Army assault forces storm 'Red' Hill

61. 5th Army tanks and troops on the road to Mutanchiang

62. Capitulation of Japanese forces

63. K. A. Meretskov, Commander, 1st Far Eastern Front, and A. M. Vasilevsky, Commander, Far East Command, give surrender instruction to General Hata, Commander, Kwantung Army

64. Discussion of Japanese capitulation (Changchun, August 1945)

65. The population of Harbin greet 1st Far Eastern Front forces

66. Soviet victory parade in Harbin (September 1945)

67. Lieutenant General S. K. Mamonov, Commander, 15th Army

68. Lieutenant General M. F. Terekhin, Commander, 2d Red Banner Army

69. Major General I. Z. Pashkov, Commander, 5th Separate Rifle Corps

70. 15th Army troops debark from Amur Flotilla ships along the Sungari River

71. Lieutenant General L. G. Cheremisov, Commander, 16th Army

72. Senior Lieutenant V. N. Leonov, Commander, Reconnaissance Detachment, 355th Naval Infantry Battalion

73. Soviet torpedo cutters attack Japanese ships in Chongjin port

74. Soviet frigate 'EK-9' fires on Japanese positions in Chongjin

75. Soviet amphibious assault forces land at Chongjin

76. Soviet naval infantry reconnoiter a Japanese position at Chongjin

77. 355th Separate Naval Infantry Battalion troops in street fighting at Chongjin

78. Soviet transport ships heading to southern Sakhalin

79. Army General M. A. Purkaev, Commander, 2d Far Eastern Front (right) and Lieutenant General D. S. Leonov, member of the front's Military Council, on Shumshir Island (October 1945)

1953 (November) – Senior Adviser to the Chinese People's Army.
1957 (September) – First deputy commander, Voronezh Military District.
1960 (December) – In the reserves.

Simultaneously, Major General I. Z. Pashkov's 5th Separate Rifle Corps, cooperating with a brigade of river ships and forces from the Khabarovsk Border Guards District, was to force the Ussuri River, destroy Japanese forces in the Jaoho Fortified Region, capture Jaoho, and advance through Paoching to Chiamussu. During the process, it was to destroy the Japanese Sungari grouping in cooperation with the 15th Army's forces. For support, Pashkov's corps contained 164 tanks and self-propelled guns and 1,433 guns and mortars, and 18 multiple rocket launchers.[30]

Initially, the 2d Red Banner Army, commanded by Lieutenant General of Tank Forces M. F. Terekhin, was to cooperate with the Zee-Bureisk Brigade and separate battalions of river ships of the Amur Flotilla in the defense of its sector along the northern bank of the Amur River and prevent any Japanese ships from penetrating into the Zeia and Bureia Rivers. Thereafter, Terekhin's army was to prepare to mount an on-order advance toward Tsitsihar. Initially, the 2d Red Banner Army occupied a sector of 612 miles (1,000 kilometers), with its main force (two rifle divisions) deployed on its left flank, and fielded 240 tanks and self-propelled guns and 1,270 guns and mortars.[31]

Terekhin, Makar Fomich (1896–1967), Commander, 2d Red Banner Army
1915 – Joined the Russian Army; commander, infantry platoon in the First World War.
1918 – Joined the Red Army; commander, rifle platoon in the Civil War.
1920 – Attended the Riazan' Infantry School.
1921 – Commander, rifle company and battalion.
1925 – Attended Vystrel' Course.
1935 – Attended Mechanization and Motorization Course.
1935 (October) – Commander, mechanized regiment.
1937 (July) – Commander, mechanized brigade.
1939 (March) – Commander, 20th Tank Corps (Khalkhin-Gol, Finnish War).
1940 (March) – Commander, 19th Rifle Corps.
1940 (June) – Commander, 5th Mechanized Corps.
1941 (April) – Commander, 2d Red Banner Army (Far East).
1946 – Commander, rifle corps.
1949 – Assistant commander, White Sea and Northern Military Districts.
1954 (August) – In the reserves.

Major General L. G. Cheremisov's 16th Army and Major General A. R. Gnechko's Kamchatka Defensive Region were to defend the western coast of the Tatar Strait, the northern portion of Sakhalin Island, and Kamchatka. At the same time, they were to prepare the 56th Rifle Corps to assault Japanese defenses on southern Sakhalin and forces from the Kamchatka Defensive Region and ships from the Kamchatka Naval Base to conduct amphibious assaults against the Japanese-occupied Kuril Islands, and later, the northern portion of Hokkaido Island.

Cheremisov, Leontii Georgievich (1893–1967), Commander, 16th Army
1919 – Joined the Red Army; commander, rifle regiment during the Civil War.
1938 – Attended the Frunze Academy.
1940 – Commander, army.
1941 (November) – Assistant commander, Far Eastern Front.
1943 (September) – Commander, 16th Army (Sakhalin offensive).

COMBAT AND COMBAT SERVICE SUPPORT

Armor and Mechanized Forces

Given the *Stavka's* desire for a quick resolution of the conflict, the Far East Command received, deployed, and employed an extremely large number of tank and mechanized forces in virtually every offensive sector.[32] Table 42 shows the distribution of these forces to each operating *front*.

TABLE 42: DISTRIBUTION OF TANK AND MECHANIZED FORCES, FAR EAST COMMAND, 9 AUGUST 1945

Forces	*Fronts*			
	Trans-Baikal	*1st Far Eastern*	*2d Far Eastern*	*Total*
Tank corps	1	–	–	1
Mechanized corps	2	1	–	3
Tank divisions	2	–	–	2
Tank brigades	10	12	8	30
Mechanized and motorized rifle brigades	8	2	–	10
Separate tank regiments	2	2	–	4
Self-propelled artillery regiments	6	12	–	18
Self-propelled artillery brigades	2	–	–	2
Separate tank battalions	8	–	2	10
Separate self-propelled artillery battalions	29	25	9	63

Source: A. N. Vnotchenko, *Pobeda na dal'nem vostoke* [Victory in the Far East] (Moscow: Voenizdat, 1971), 90.

The Far East Command employed the greatest density of tank and mechanized forces along the Trans-Baikal–Manchurian axis because this was the optimal place to use them. Otherwise, their employment within individual *fronts* and armies varied depending on the situation and the terrain. Thus, in order to guarantee as rapid an advance as possible, Malinovsky planned to employ the bulk of his armor (less the 111th Tank Division), particularly the 6th Guards Tank Army, in first echelon to lead his advance. This reflected his desire to cross the Grand Khingan Mountains and reach his objectives in the central valley before the Japanese could erect new defenses. After overcoming the mountains, the army's 9th Guards Mechanized and 5th Guards Tank Corps were to develop the attack on Mukden, and the 7th Mechanized Corps on Changchun. Furthermore, after seizing Mukden and Changchun, a portion of the army was to advance on and capture Port Arthur on the Liaotung peninsula.

The 6th Guards Tank Army was to penetrate through the Grand Khingans in two stages. During the first, which was to last for two days, the tank army's two lead corps (both mechanized) were to overcome any Japanese outposts along the border, cross the desert of Inner Mongolia, and reach the crest of the Grand Khingans, a distance of 124 miles (200 kilometers) at an advance rate of 62 miles (100 kilometers) per day. In the second stage, which was to last three days, the army was to secure the mountain passes, and enter the central Manchurian valley, a distance of 155 miles (250 kilometers), advancing at a rate of roughly 50 miles (80 kilometers) per day. Initially, the tank army was to advance along two separate march routes 47 miles (75 kilometers) apart with its 9th Guards and 7th Mechanized Corps in first echelon and the 5th Guards Tank Corps in second.

So as to reduce dispersion during the advance and preempt any enemy opposition, the tank army's lead mechanized corps advanced in two-echelon march formation led by strong forward detachments and movement support detachments. The forward detachments consisted of a motorized rifle regiment and single tank and artillery battalions, and the movement support detachment of two sapper companies and equipment to evacuate disabled tanks. Each column maintained its own tank reserve and was protected against air attack by antiaircraft artillery dispersed throughout the columns.

The 5th Guards Tank Corps, which was advancing in the tank army's second echelon, also deployed a forward detachment, whose function was to facilitate a rapid passage of lines into first echelon after the first echelon corps seized the crest of the Grand Khingans. All of the remaining tank brigades and regiments, which were assigned to rifle formations, served as the formations' forward detachments and, as such, had attached rifle forces, artillery, and sappers to accord them some freedom of action.

In the 1st Far Eastern Front's sector, all of the tanks and self-propelled guns were massed to support the infantry during penetration, achieving tank densities of 48–64 (30–40) vehicles per mile (kilometer) of penetration front in the 5th Army's sector. After the Japanese defenses had been penetrated, the tanks made up the nucleus of forward detachments designated to exploit into the depths of the Japanese defenses. The 10th Mechanized Corps was to operate as the *front* mobile group with orders to exploit the 5th Army's penetration and advance on Mutanchiang, more than 93 miles (150 kilometers) west of the state border.

The 2d Far Eastern Front grouped its armor along the few trafficable avenues of advance in its sector, allocating tank brigades to support the advance and lead the exploitation. The 2d Red Banner Army had three tank brigades and three self-propelled artillery battalions; the 15th Army, three tank brigades and four self-propelled artillery battalions; and the 5th Separate Rifle Corps, one tank brigade and two self-propelled artillery battalions. Purkaev chose to use seven tank brigades to support the assault crossing of the Amur and Ussuri Rivers and as forward detachments during the exploitation.

Artillery

The presence of heavily fortified Japanese defenses along the most trafficable axes of advance into Manchuria placed a high premium on effective and copious artillery support for the Far Eastern Command's ground offensive. The *Stavka*, Far East Command, and the three operating *fronts* did all in their power to provide that support where required. Ultimately, the type and quantity of artillery allocated to each force and the planned employment of artillery fire depended directly on the *front* commanders' maneuver plan, the missions that forces were assigned, and the nature of the terrain over which they would have to operate. Obviously then, the organization and employment of artillery differed widely between specific *fronts* and armies. In general, none of the *fronts* prepared a unified *front* artillery support plan since they were attacking along widely divergent offensive axes.

Thus, the presence of strong Japanese defensive fortifications in the 1st Far Eastern Front's sector required that *front* to create especially strong artillery groupings. On 9 August 1945, that *front* had more than 10,600 guns and mortars at its disposal, 8,000 of which were 76 mm or greater caliber. At the other extreme, since the 2d Far Eastern Front's offensive sector was three times larger than that of the 1st Far Eastern Front, the former fielded only 4,800 guns and mortars. Even so, the 2d Far Eastern Front had two and one half times more antiaircraft guns than the 1st Far Eastern Front in order to protect important objectives and force concentration regions. Despite its extremely wide operational sector, the Trans-Baikal Front fielded less than 9,000 guns and mortars because it faced a relative paucity of heavy Japanese defenses.[33]

Artillery within the operating *fronts* was also frequently concentrated on widely divergent axes. For example, most of the Trans-Baikal Front's artillery was concentrated opposite the Japanese Halung-Arshaan, Chalainor-Manchouli, and Hailar Fortified Regions. The 17th Army, which faced no prepared defenses whatsoever, and the 53d Army, which was in *front* second echelon, received little supporting artillery. On the other hand, the 1st Far Eastern Front concentrated more than 30 per cent of its artillery, 3,000 guns and mortars and 400 multiple rocket launchers, in the 5th Army's sector to support the penetration of the Suifenho Fortified Region. The 2d Far Eastern Front allocated the highest percentage of its artillery to the 15th Army, which was making the *front's* main attack.

Since the Trans-Baikal Front faced few organized Japanese defenses, it planned detailed fire plans only for the assault on the Hailar Fortified Region. Elsewhere, it anticipated firing no planned artillery preparations or coordinated fires to support major assaults. Therefore, it distributed its supporting artillery among its combined-arms formations and units with the sole mission of supporting them on their march. Thus, the artillery assigned to the 17th, 6th Guards Tank, and 39th Armies and the Cavalry-Mechanized Group only partially deployed along the state border with the missions of supporting the forward detachments in the destruction of Japanese border security forces. Most of the artillery remained integrated into the main forces' march-column formations. However, the 36th Army planned its artillery preparation for the assault on Hailar in more detail, preparing fire to support the crossing of the Argun River, fire to protect its bridgehead once across the river, and fire on individual enemy strong points prior to and during the assault on the fortified region itself.

The Trans-Baikal Front allocated the bulk of its artillery to the 36th and 39th Armies, which, in turn, deployed it in those sectors where the Japanese had heavily fortified defenses. For example, the 36th Army created artillery densities of up to 84 guns and mortars per kilometer of front to support its main attack, which was being delivered by the 2d and 86th Rifle Corps. On the secondary attack axis toward Chalainor and Manchouli, it concentrated 69 (43) guns and mortars per mile (kilometer) of front. During its assault crossing over the Argun River, the 36th Army planned to support each attacking rifle battalion with indirect fire from one artillery battalion and one mortar battalion. The rifle regiments' organic artillery and the army's anti-tank artillery battalions deployed opposite the penetration sectors with the mission of destroying enemy firing points by direct fire.

The 1st Far Eastern Front received comparatively greater amounts of artillery than its sister *fronts* because it faced the heaviest Japanese defenses. Its artillery fire plans were based directly on the necessity for penetrating these fortifications and then exploiting the attack along many separate axes. This meant that, initially, the armies employed highly centralized fire plans to deliver their artillery fire and, later, diverse plans tailored to meet local conditions.

The 1st Far Eastern Front's 5th Army, which fielded the largest quantity of artillery in the *front*, about 3,000 guns and mortars and more than 400 multiple rocket launchers, carefully prepared a detailed artillery fire plan in support of its assault on the Suifenho Fortified Region. The army created a density of no fewer than 290 (180) and as many as 402 (250) artillery and mortar tubes per mile (kilometer) of front on its main attack axis and no fewer than 90 (60) tubes per mile (kilometer) on secondary axes.[34] Its artillery preparation envisioned five distinct periods of artillery fire, including:

- advanced destructive fires against permanent fortifications on the day preceding the offensive;
- fire to support the advance of forward detachments for 1.5 hours during the night preceding the offensive;
- a four-hour artillery preparation;
- fire in support of the attack; and
- fire accompanying the ground force advance into the depths.[35]

This artillery fire plan paid particular attention to the destruction of permanent Japanese fortifications by creating special artillery destruction groups, which were to concentrate their fire against no fewer than 8–9.7 (5–6) targets per mile (kilometer) of front. The other armies of this *front*, which were attacking along separate and often restricted axes, planned their own artillery support plans, which were then checked and approved by Meretskov and his chief of artillery.

On the *front's* right flank, the 35th Army ordered its artillery to protect the forced crossing of the Ussuri River and the penetration of the Hutou Fortified Region. Along its main axis, the army planned to fire a 55-minute preparation in advance of its river crossing and an hour of fire to support the actual assault. It planned to support its subsequent advance into the depths with six to eight hours of artillery fired on successive concentrations. The 1st Red Banner and 25th Armies planned no artillery preparation since the former was advancing across difficult but undefended terrain, and the latter was assaulting at night. However, before the assault, the former positioned 50 per cent of its artillery to deliver on-call fire in support of its forces' march through the heavy taiga.

The 2d Far Eastern Front employed well-developed fire planning only in its 15th Army and 5th Separate Rifle Corps, which had to fight their way across the Amur and Ussuri Rivers. Both armies ordered their artillery to support the forced river crossings, the seizure and defense of bridgeheads on the rivers' far banks, the destruction of Japanese fortified regions, and the exploitation into the depths. With its existing artillery, these armies were able to achieve densities of up to 161–241 (100–150) guns and mortars per mile (kilometer) in main attack sectors. The artillery preparations lasted 30 minutes in the Jaoho sector (5th Rifle Corps) and 50 minutes in the Sungari sector (15th Army), and the artillery fire in support of the actual assault crossing lasted another 50 minutes. During the crossing phase, artillery fired five minutes of intense fire on preplanned targets in support of the forward detachments' assault landings, after which the fire shifted into the depths.

Aviation

Terrain considerations and vast differences in the nature and strength of Japanese defenses around the periphery of Manchuria also prompted the three *fronts* to create strikingly different air support plans.[36]

On the eve of the attack, the Trans-Baikal Front was supported by the 12th Air Army, which consisted of two bomber aviation corps (with four divisions), two separate bomber, two assault, three fighter, and two transport aviation divisions, and single reconnaissance and signal aviation regiments. According to the Trans-Baikal Front's air support plan, Marshal of Aviation S. A. Khudiakov's 12th Air Army was required to conduct reconnaissance to determine the dispositions and concentration areas of Japanese forces, protect the *front's* formations and units from enemy air attack, cooperate with the ground forces during the attack and exploitation, and block the approach of enemy reserves by railroad or road by striking hard at the Japanese communications network deep in Manchuria. Consequently, the 12th Air Army's aircraft had to cut off and isolate the Third Area Army's forces in central Manchuria from those defending along the border and prevent them from blocking the Soviet advance from western into central Manchuria.

Khudiakov's formal air support plan covered only the first five days of the operations. Initially, he concentrated the bulk of his aircraft in the offensive sector of the armies making the main attack. For example, he assigned two assault and one fighter aviation division to support the 6th Guards Tank Army's dash across the desert and passage of the Grand Khingan Mountains. In addition, he allocated two transport aviation divisions to carry fuel and ammunition to the tank army during its deep exploitation.[37] In addition, he allocated one bomber aviation division to support the 36th Army, one fighter aviation division (less one regiment) to the 39th Army, and one fighter aviation regiment to the Cavalry-Mechanized Group.

During the first five days of the offensive, the 12th Air Army was to conduct more than 6,000 air sorties, including two per day by every reconnaissance and fighter aircraft and one per day by bomber and assault aircraft. Almost 80 per cent of these sorties (4,980) were to support forces advancing on the *front's* main attack axes.

However, although the air army planned its support of the ground forces carefully and in detail, no such detailed plan governed the employment of the air army's bomber force. On the first day of the offensive, the 12th Air Army planned to inflict heavy bomber strikes on the railheads at Solun, Hailar, and Halung-Arshaan, staging areas, bridges, trains, and vehicular columns to destroy Japanese reserves and isolate Japanese forces in their forward positions. At the same time, other bombers were to strike Japanese airfields, while many other aircraft were conducting reconnaissance.

The only major deficiency noted in the Trans-Baikal Front's air support plan was the absence of a well-thought out plan to construct new bases for aircraft so that the aircraft could deploy forward to support operations to the depth of the *front's* ultimate advance. Fortunately, these new airfields proved to be irrelevant.

The 1st Far Eastern Front's 9th Air Army, under the command of Colonel General of Aviation I. M. Sokolov, was assigned special missions to assist in the penetration of the permanent Japanese fortifications along Manchuria's eastern border. Therefore, air support planning was far more thorough and detailed than in the other *fronts*, particularly regarding the assault on fortified Japanese positions and the subsequent exploitation toward Mutanchiang. Sokolov's air army consisted of one long-range bomber aviation corps (with two divisions), one separate bomber, two assault, and three fighter aviation divisions, single reconnaissance, corrective, signal, and transport aviation regiments, and six separate aviation squadrons totaling 1,196 aircraft.[38]

Initially, the 9th Air Army planned to conduct an air preparation by over 4,000 aircraft over a period of five to seven days. The intent of the air preparation was to detect enemy dispositions from the border to as far west as Mutanchiang and destroy enemy fortifications and personnel in the Suifenho (Volynsk) Fortified Region and in the shallow depths to the west. On the first day of the offensive, before the infantry assault, its aircraft were to deliver massive strikes against fortified positions, trenches, and firing points in the Suifenho Fortified Region. Thereafter, assault aircraft were to conduct continuous ground attacks to support the ground forces as they penetrated the Japanese defenses.

The 9th Air Army planned to concentrate 2,200 of its planned 3,514 air sorties on the first day of the offensive in the 5th Army's sector and another 4,330 sorties to support the ground forces' achievement of their immediate missions. Overall, the air army planned to fly 14,284 sorties in ten to twelve days of operations, including the five to seven days of preparation.[39] Given the fragmented nature of the subsequent advance, Khudiakov planned to designate specific aviation divisions to support specific ground forces, and to that end, the air staff closely coordinated with the corresponding ground force staff both throughout the planning process and during combat itself.

In the 2d Far Eastern Front, the combat operations of Colonel General of Aviation P. F. Zhigarev's 10th Air Army were planned only on the first day of the offensive, when the bulk (45 per cent) of its aircraft were concentrated in the 15th Army's offensive sector, the *front's* main attack axis. During this period, the air army's fighter aircraft were to protect the ground forces, the Amur Flotilla's ships, and vital railroad lines on the Soviet side of the border against Japanese air attack. Assault and bomber aircraft, which were initially left at their bases, were to be prepared to destroy Japanese reserves, defensive works, and Sungarian River Flotilla ships after reconnaissance aircraft detected their presence. Zhigarev's air army consisted of one mixed aviation corps (with two divisions and one regiment), one separate bomber, one assault, and two fighter aviation divisions in the mainland Far East, one mixed aviation division on Sakhalin Island, and one mixed aviation division in Kamchatka.

Finally, aircraft assigned to the Pacific Fleet had the mission of attacking Japanese ships in the ports of Unggi, Nanjin (Rasin), and Chongjin (Seisin) or at sea, destroying Japanese aircraft at airfields, protecting the fleet against air attack, and conducting reconnaissance.

Engineers

The extremely varied but always complex and difficult terrain conditions that the advancing Soviet forces had to contend with in Manchuria made extensive and effective engineer and sapper support essential. The Trans-Baikal Front had to overcome the vast expanse of desert terrain and the formidable Grand Khingan Mountains, and the 2d Far Eastern Front had to contend with wide rivers, extensive swamps, and the wooded and hilly terrain of the Lesser Khingan Mountains. The 1st Far Eastern Front's task was even more challenging given the heavy Japanese defenses and the forested and mountainous terrain in eastern Manchuria. Thus, the Far East Command reinforced the Trans-Baikal and 1st Far Eastern Fronts alone with 14 engineer-sapper and pontoon bridge brigades and all three *fronts* with 18 brigades of various types and 30 other engineer units. These forces performed the following missions:

- organizing and conducting engineer reconnaissance;
- preparing jumping-off positions for the offensive;
- constructing and repairing roads;
- camouflaging forces;
- arranging for water supply;
- preparing river crossing sites; and
- providing engineer support for the penetration of fortified regions.[40]

The degree of engineer support required varied from one *front* to another and within the *fronts* themselves based primarily on the nature of the

Japanese defenses and the terrain over which the forces had to operate. During the preparatory period for the offensive, engineers had to build or improve a road and track network necessary to deploy the forces forward into their jumping-off positions. During this period, engineers assigned to the three *fronts* constructed a total of 864 miles (1,390 kilometers) of new roads and repaired another 3,107 miles (5,000 kilometers).

Extraordinarily heavy engineer support was also required to prepare jumping-off positions for the forces assaulting Japanese positions in the rough terrain of eastern Manchuria. For example, in the 1st Far Eastern Front's 1st Red Banner Army alone, engineers built 335 miles (540 kilometers) of roads and column routes, 4,949 linear feet (1,509 meters) of bridges, 100 pillboxes, 182 bunkers, blindages, and dugouts, 3,859 artillery and mortar firing positions, and 209 command posts. During the same period, they repaired 339 miles (546 kilometers) of road, 6,143 feet (1,873 meters) of bridges, opened 517 miles (832 kilometers) of trenches and communications trenches, and laid 100 miles (161 kilometers) of barbed wire.[41]

The nature of engineer preparations in the Trans-Baikal Front was quite different. There, engineer forces and associated *ad hoc* water supply commands, which each formation and unit created, constructed 1,194 and repaired 322 wells and deployed 61 water supply points during the period from 10 July through 8 August. They dug these wells every 9.3–18.6 miles (15–30 kilometers) along the march routes of major forces and formed a water service detachment at each water point.[42] All army and formation commanders also established strict water rationing regimes within their forces.

Extensive engineer support was also required during the many river-crossing operations that the attacking forces had to conduct. The Amur, Argun, and Ussuri Rivers were not only wide and deep, but they also had wide and swampy valleys adjacent to their banks. For example, the Trans-Baikal Front's 36th Army had to construct 558 feet (170 meters) of bridges and corduroy (lay timber and fascines) along 8.7 miles (14 kilometers) of approach roads. Given the extensive widths of the rivers, the attacking forces planned to employ Amur River ferryboats and ships of the Amur River Flotilla to cross the rivers as well as organic river-crossing equipment. In addition, as they had done earlier in the war, the forces also used locally procured materials to construct barges, floats, and other improvised crossing means.

Communications

Command and *front* planning required massive forces to advance at an unusually rapid pace in excessively broad offensive sectors across difficult terrain that often lacked any decent roads.[43] These unique circumstances, plus the necessity of frequently relocating command and observation posts, placed immense pressure on the Far East Command's communications system, especially regarding wire communications. Therefore, the three *fronts* relied primarily on radio communications to command, control, and resupply their forces.

Only the 1st Far Eastern Front, whose rate of advance was appreciably slower than that of the other *fronts*, relied more heavily on wire communications. In the Trans-Baikal Front, the *front* and army headquarters used wire communications only during the first three to four days of the operation and thereafter employed only radio. For example, the 6th Guards Tank Army and Cavalry-mechanized Group created radio relay stations to maintain radio communications during their long marches. Only the 39th Army, which assaulted the Halung-Arshaan Fortified Region, used wire communications for a longer period.[44]

Despite the difficult communications situation within the theater, all three *fronts* maintained constant wire and radio communications with the General Staff and the Far East Command's headquarters. The *front* and army headquarters also extensively employed mobile means such as aircraft and highly mobile radio vehicles. To facilitate constant and reliable command and control of forces throughout the operations, the Far East Command directed that commanders at all levels from division through army position their command posts close to their operating forces. Thus, the mobile command post of the 6th Guards Tank Army was to remain no farther than 9.3–12.4 miles (15–20 kilometers) from its combat units.

Intelligence

Since the Far East Command sought to achieve surprise during its offensive, Soviet intelligence collection prior to the commencement of the operation was quite difficult. The maintenance of routine activities along the border made normal intelligence collection by such means as artillery instrumental reconnaissance, aerial photography, and, most important, combat reconnaissance impossible. In essence, the *fronts* relied primarily on intelligence collected by central military organs (the Main Intelligence Directorate – GRU) and their own visual reconnaissance. For example, the Far East Command established 576 observation posts, which could observe enemy territory to a depth of 3.7 miles (6 kilometers), in the sector of the 1st Far Eastern Front's 5th Army. In the 2d Far Eastern Front's 15th Army, it established 20 such posts in each front-line rifle regiment.[45]

After its arrival in Chita, the Far East Command organized an extensive network of radio intercept stations, and its subordinate *fronts* also conducted extensive radio reconnaissance.[46] Aircraft also photographed all Japanese defensive fortifications along the border and the Korean coast, but did so by employing oblique photography without flying across the border. Headquarters then prepared extensive mosaics and maps of Japanese defenses based on this aerial photography, which they distributed to commanders down to company level.

As well as providing combat support during the offensive itself, forces assigned to the many border guards detachments along the border participated actively in intelligence collection and, once the offensive began, formed and employed reconnaissance groups to determine Japanese defenses.

Rear Services

Given the scale and scope of the forthcoming offensive, the most difficult logistical missions assigned to the rear services in the Far East Command and operating *fronts* were the organization and preparation of *front* and army rear services and the accumulation of necessary equipment and supplies to conduct and sustain the offensive. This process began even before the defeat of Nazi Germany and continued right up to the very date the offensive began. The State Defense Committee (GKO) determined the scale of the reserves on 3 June 1945 and conducted the gathering effort continuously through 8 August.[47]

While the GKO and Far East Command assembled equipment and supplies for the main theater of operations by rail and road, it dispatched equipment and supplies to northern Sakhalin Island, Kamchatka, and Chukotka for the Pacific Fleet and ground forces in the coastal regions by sea transport. During the preparatory period for the operation, operational and supply transport traveled by way of the Seas of Japan and Okhotsk, the Bering Sea, and also the lower reaches of the Amur River through the Tatar Strait, which separates Sakhalin Island from the mainland. Before the offensive began, 267 transport ships with a carrying capacity of one million tons were located in these basins. While the tonnage capacity of these ships was sufficient to transport much of the required cargo, the inadequate number of ports and port facilities hindered the overall effort.

Front, army, and formation rear service organs faced a daunting task supplying their subordinate forces with requisite amounts of fuel, water, and firewood. In the Trans-Baikal Front alone, 35,200 tons of fuel was collected at fixed and mobile facilities by early July to supply the thirst of tank, aviation, and auto-transport formations and units. Particularly challenging was the task the Trans-Baikal Front faced in supplying its forces with solid fuel. Arriving formations and units brought with them field bakeries and field kitchens that operated on firewood and coal. However, since there were no forests in the forces' concentration areas, firewood had to be gathered in the taiga region of eastern Siberia and transported 372 or more miles (600 or more kilometers) by rail and road. Up to 50 railroad wagons and many vehicles had to be employed daily just to meet the daily requirements for firewood.

So large were these shipments that on some days they equaled the total volume of ammunition transported forward.

Rear service organs also strained every resource to provide the theater with necessary medical and veterinary services. In advance of the offensive, the NKO's Main Military Medical Directorate planned complex measures to organize and carry out medical support. The drastic increase in the number of personnel in the Far East region and the epidemic conditions prevailing in Inner Mongolia and Manchuria required considerable expansion of the number of medical personnel and facilities in the Far East, particularly the hospital network, which was clearly inadequate before July 1945.

Of the total of 80,000 hospital beds authorized in the region in April 1945, only 54,500 existed, including 30,000 in Chita and Irkutsk, which served wounded and sick evacuated from the Soviet–German front. Worse still, medical service units and facilities were woefully under strength. However, by the time the offensive began, the magnitude of the hospital network in all three *fronts* had grown to a total of 166,200 beds, including 72,700 in the Trans-Baikal Front, 68,900 in the 1st Far Eastern Front, and 24,600 in the 2d Far Eastern Front out of the planned quantity of 200,000–250,000 beds. Although this was considerably fewer than the 540,000 casualties, including 381,000 wounded, which the Operations Group of the Main Military Medical Directorate estimated the Red Army would suffer in the offensive, it proved more than adequate to satisfy the Far East Command's medical needs.[48]

Training

The Far East Command's three *fronts* and Pacific Fleet conducted an extraordinary amount of operational and tactical training for their troops and staffs during the preparatory period of the offensive. They paid special attention to the organization and conduct of penetration operations against fortified regions, decisive operations in desert, mountain, taiga, and swampy terrain, skillful conduct of long marches through roadless regions, river crossing operations, and overcoming mountain and forest barriers. For example, all commanders at division, corps, army, and *front* level and their principal staff officers participated in command and staff communications exercises, military war games, and maneuvers.

While the Trans-Baikal Front's veterans of the Soviet–German War studiously adapted themselves to the Manchurian terrain, the 1st and 2d Far Eastern Fronts' soldiers studied the experience of their counterparts in the veteran 5th Army.

CONCLUSIONS

The three *front* plans clearly satisfied the *Stavka* and Far East Commands' orders to smash the Kwantung Army rapidly and decisively and occupy much of Manchuria and adjacent regions as quickly as possible. Consequently, the shock groups of the three *fronts'* shock groups comprised 60–70 per cent of the three *fronts'* total force of rifle, armored, and mechanized forces, artillery, and aircraft. This accorded Soviet forces overwhelming, and sometimes absolute, superiority along all major axes of advance. Tables 43 and 44 show the official and actual correlation of forces in all three fronts.

TABLE 43: OFFICIAL SOVIET ASSESSMENT OF CORRELATION OF FORCES BETWEEN FAR EAST COMMAND AND KWANTUNG ARMY, 9 AUGUST 1945

Forces and Weapons	*Fronts*		
	Trans-Baikal	*1st Far Eastern*	*2d Far Eastern*
Infantry	1.7 × 1	1.5 × 1	1.4 × 1
Guns and mortars	8.6 × 1	4 × 1	2 × 1
Tanks and SP guns	5 × 1	8 × 1	8 × 1
Aircraft		Overall 3.6 × 1	

Source: A. N. Vnotchenko, *Pobeda na dal'nem vostoke* [Victory in the Far East] (Moscow: Voenizdat, 1971), 72.

TABLE 44: ESTIMATED ACTUAL CORRELATION OF FORCES BETWEEN FAR EAST COMMAND AND KWANTUNG ARMY, 9 AUGUST 1945

Forces and Weapons	*Fronts*		
	Trans-Baikal	*1st Far Eastern*	*2d Far Eastern*
Infantry	2.7 × 1	3.9 × 1	2.8 × 1
Guns and mortars	Greater than 15 × 1	Greater than 10 × 1	Greater than 5 × 1
Tanks and SP guns	Absolute	Absolute	Absolute

It is abundantly clear that the *Stavka* and, in particular, the Far East Command had to overcome many daunting problems when preparing the Manchurian strategic operation. Together with his staff, Marshal Vasilevsky constantly visited the *front* where he familiarized himself with the terrain, distributed forces and equipment, carefully helped determine appropriate forces' combat formations, and conducted map exercises on such critical operations as consecutive river crossings, the penetration of fortified defenses, surmounting desert, mountain, and forested sectors, and the employment of artillery and air support. He and his staff emphasized techniques for accelerating the tempo of the advance, supporting sustained deep operations, and working out coherent *front* operational plans. All of this was done to shorten the time necessary to fulfill combat missions, conduct a strategic offensive without any pauses, and destroy the Kwantung Army by means of a seamless multi-front operation.

Once planning was complete, the Manchurian strategic offensive operation consisted of three distinct *front* offensive operations and separate operations against southern Sakhalin Island, the Kuril Islands, and northern Hokkaido. The Trans-Baikal Front was to conduct the Khingan–Mukden offensive operation, the 1st Far Eastern Front, the Harbin–Kirin offensive operation, and the 2d Far Eastern Front, the Sungarian offensive operation. The ensuing operations developed in two distinct stages after the Far East Command launched its offensive on the morning of 9 August 1945, two days before planned. During the first phase of the offensive, which lasted from 9 to 14 August, the three *fronts'* first echelon armies penetrated Japanese defenses, destroyed first echelon Japanese units, and by 15 August had introduced forces into the central region of Manchuria. During the second phase of the operation, which began on 15 August and ended on 2 September, the Far East Command occupied the central region of Manchuria and northern Korea and accepted the Kwantung Army's surrender.

NOTES

1. *IVMV*, 11: 194.
2. Ibid.
3. V. A. Zolotarev, ed., *Russkii arkhiv: Sovetsko-iaponskaia voina 1945 goda: Istoriia voenno-politicheskogo protivoborstva dvukh dershav v 30–40-e gody. Dokumenty i materialy v. 2 t.*, T. 18 (7–1) [The Russian archives: The Soviet–Japanese war of 1945: A military-political history of the struggle between two powers in the 30s and 40s; Documents and materials in two vols, Vol. 18 (7–1)] (Moscow: 'Terra', 1997), 322.
4. See Vnotchenko, *Pobeda*, 69; Zakharov, *Finale*, 88–89; and Shtemenko, *The Soviet General Staff*, 348–9. The most definitive account is found in A. Vasilevsky, 'Pobeda na dal'nem vostoke' [Victory in the Far East], pt. 1, *VIZh*, No. 8 (August 1970), 8–10.
5. Ibid.
6. See Shtemenko, 'Iz istorii razgroma', 65–6; Shtemenko, *Soviet General Staff*, 338–49; and Zakharov, *Finale*, 83–6. According to Shtemenko, the original attack date was between 20 and 25 August.
7. Zakharov, *Finale*, 64. Cannae was a battle that took place on 2 August 216 BC between Hannibal of Carthage and Roman forces during which Hannibal orchestrated the perfect double envelopment operation, thereby destroying the Roman force. See also Vnotchenko, *Pobeda*, 48–9, and V. A. Zolotarev, ed., *Velikaia Otechestvennaia voina 1941–1945: Voenno-istoricheskie ocherki v chetyrekh knigakh, Kniga 3, Osvobozhdenie* [The Great Patriotic War 1941–1945: A military-historical survey in four books,

Book 3, Liberation] (Moscow: 'Nauka', 1999), 389, which states: 'The plan of combat operations of the USSR's armed forces envisioned the conduct of the Manchurian strategic offensive operation, the southern Sakhalin offensive operation, the Kurils amphibious operation and an amphibious operation for the capture of the northern part of Hokkaido Island up to a line extending from the town of Kushiro to the town of Rumoi.' Hereafter cited as *VOV*.

8. *VOV*, 389.
9. This section is based on Vnotchenko, *Pobeda*, 69–70, 85–90; *IVMV*, 11: 199; and Zakharov, *Finale*, 82–9.
10. Vnotchenko, *Pobeda*, 51–2; *IVMV*, 11: 199; and Zakharov, *Finale*, 86–9.
11. Vnotchenko, *Pobeda*, 52; *IVMV*, 11: 199; and Zakharov, *Finale*, 89–92.
12. Vnotchenko, *Pobeda*, 71–2; *IVMV*, 11: 200; and Zakharov, *Finale*, 93–4.
13. Vnotchenko, *Pobeda*, 53, and *IVMV*, 11: 201.
14. Vnotchenko, *Pobeda*, 53–4, and *IVMV*, 11: 200.
15. *IVMV*, 11: 201.
16. For further details on the Trans-Baikal Front's plan, see Vnotchenko, *Pobeda*, 60–4 and *IVMV*, 11: 201–2.
17. Vnotchenko, *Pobeda*, 61.
18. Ibid.
19. Ibid., 62.
20. Ibid., 63.
21. Ibid.
22. Ibid.
23. For further details on the 1st Far Eastern Front's plan, see Vnotchenko, *Pobeda*, 64–70, and *IVMV*, 11: 202–3.
24. Vnotchenko, *Pobeda*, 67.
25. Ibid., 68.
26. Ibid.
27. Ibid.
28. For further details on the 2d Far Eastern Front's plan, see Vnotchenko, *Pobeda*, 71–7, and *IVMV*, 11: 203–4.
29. Vnotchenko, *Pobeda*, 71.
30. Ibid.
31. Ibid.
32. For details on the planned employment of armored and mechanized forces in the campaign, see Vnotchenko, *Pobeda*, 89–92, and N. A. Antonov, *Nastuplenie 6-i gvardeiskoi tankovoi armii v Man'zhurskoi operatsii (avgust 1945 g.)* [The offensive of the 6th Guards Tank Army in the Manchurian operation (August 1945)] (Moscow: Voroshilov Academy of the General Staff, 1978).
33. For details on the employment of artillery, see *IVMV*, 204–6; M. Sidorov, 'Boevoe primenenie artillerii' [The combat employment of artillery], *VIZh*, No. 9 (September 1975), 13–21; V. M. Mikhalin, 'Boevoe primenenie artillerii v Man'chzhurskoi operatsii' [The combat employment of artillery in the Manchurian operation], *VIZh*, No. 8 (August 1958), 25–8; and S. Popov, 'Artilleristy v boiakh na Bol'shom Khingane' [Artillerymen in combat in the Grand Khingans], *VIZh*, No. 8 (August 1965), 88–92.
34. *IVMV*, 11: 205.
35. Vnotchenko, *Pobeda*, 80.
36. For details on the employment of aviation forces, see Vnotchenko, *Pobeda*, 84–9; I. Sukhomlin, 'Osobennosti vzaimodeistviia 6-i gvardeiskoi tankovoi armii s aviatsiei v Man'chzhurskoi operatsii' [Characteristics of the cooperation of the 6th

Guards Tank Army with aviation during the Manchurian operation], *VIZh*, No. 4 (April 1972), 85–91; O.K. Frantsev, 'Primenenie aviatsii v Man'chzhurskoi operatsii' [The employment of aviation in the Manchurian operation], *VIZh*, No. 8 (August 1985), 20–4; and 'Cherty primenenie aviatsii v Man'chzhurskoi operatsii' [The features of the employment of aviation in the Manchurian operation], *VIZh*, No. 8 (August 1979), 17–24.

37. *IVMV*, 11: 206.
38. Vnotchenko, *Pobeda*, 86.
39. Ibid., 88.
40. *IVMV*, 11: 206–7. For further details on engineer support, see Vnotchenko, *Pobeda*, 92–100; A. F. Khrenov, 'Inzhenernoe obespechenie nastupleniia v Man'chzhurskoi operatsii' [Engineer support of the offensive in the Manchurian operation], *VIZh*, No. 8 (August 1985), 29–32; and S. Kh. Aganov, *Inzhenernye voiska Sovetskoi armii 1918–1945* [Engineer forces of the Soviet Army 1918–1945] (Moscow: Voenizdat, 1985).
41. *IVMV*, 11: 207.
42. Ibid.
43. For further details on communications support, see V. I. Sokolov, 'Sviaz' v Man'chzhurskoi operatsii' [Communications in the Manchurian operation], *VIZh*, No. 8 (August 1985), 33–6; 'Upravlenie i sviaz' v boiakh na dal'nem vostoke (avgust–sentiabr' 1945 g)' [Command and control and communications in the Far East (August–September 1945)], *Voennyi vestnik* [Military Herald], No. 8 (December 1989), 79; and I. P. Grishin *et al.*, eds, *Voennye sviazisty v dni voiny i mira* [Military signalmen in wartime and peacetime] (Moscow: Voenizdat, 1968), 24–6.
44. *IVMV*, 11: 207–8.
45. Ibid., 11: 208.
46. The Far East Command headquarters moved to Khabarovsk on 19 August.
47. See also, V. S. Bichik, 'Nekotorye osobennosti tylovogo obespecheniia voisk 1-go Dal'nevostochnogo fronta v Man'chzhurskoi operatsii' [Some peculiarities of the 1st Far Eastern Front's rear service support in the Manchurian operation], *VIZh*, No. 8 (August 1985), 37–41; P. P. Butkov and V. V. Shmidt, 'Osobennosti tylovogo obespecheniia v gorno-pustynnoi mestnosti' [The peculiarities of rear service support in swampy desert terrain], *VIZh*, No. 9 (September 1988), 38–45; and V. S. Bichik and N. E. Medvedev, 'Tylobogo obespechenie 5-i armii v Kharbino–Girinskoi operatsii' [Rear service support of the 5th Army in the Harbin–Kirin Operation], *VIZh*, No. 8 (August 1987), 32–9.
48. *IVMV*, 11: 210, and O. S. Shevtsov, 'Meditsinskoe obespechenie Sovetskikh voisk v Man'zhurskoi strategicheskoi nastupatel'noi operatsii (9 avgusta–2 sentiabria 1945 g.)' [Medical support of Soviet forces in the Manchurian strategic offensive operation (9 August–2 September 1945)], *Voenno-meditsinskii zhurnal*, No. 9 (August 1990), 88–9. This article placed the number of medical support indices before the regrouping at 174 hospitals and 49,900 beds, including 129 hospitals and 38,000 beds in the Trans-Baikal Front and 45 hospitals and 11,900 beds in the Far Eastern Front and Coastal Group. According to this source, that figure rose to 423 hospitals and 164,500 beds by 9 August, 77.5 per cent of the total quantity planned.

7

The Trans-Baikal Front's Khingan–Mukden Offensive Operation

THE INITIAL ADVANCE, 9–11 AUGUST 1945

At 2300 hours on 8 August 1945, the Soviet government presented the Japanese Ambassador in Moscow with a declaration that read:

> After the destruction and capitulation of Nazi Germany, Japan remains the single great power that still stands for the continuation of the war. Japan rejected the demands made on 26 July of this year by the three powers – the United States of America, Great Britain, and China – concerning the unconditional capitulation of the Japanese Armed Forces. At the same time, the proposal of the Japanese government to the Soviet Union concerning mediation of war in the Far East has lost any foundation.[1]

After describing the agreements the Soviet Union had reached with its Western Allies at the Potsdam conference, the statement concluded:

> Such a policy is the sole means and method to hasten the approach of peace, liberate the peoples from further casualties and suffering, and provide the Japanese people with the possibility of escaping from the dangers and destruction that the Germans experienced after their rejection of unconditional surrender.
>
> In light of the above, the Soviet government declares that, from tomorrow, 9 August, the Soviet Union will consider itself to be in a state of war with Japan.[2]

9 August

Ten minutes after midnight on 9 August 1945 (Khabarovsk time), reconnaissance units, forward detachments, and advanced guards of the Trans-Baikal

Front's forces crossed the border into Inner Mongolia and Manchuria. No artillery or air preparation preceded the attack. Initially, the advancing units encountered resistance only in the 36th Army's sector, where the attack routes traversed fortified Japanese border installations. In other regions, the assault units moved forward virtually unopposed. At 0430 hours main force units advanced on the heels of the assault units (see Maps 29–31).[3]

On the extreme right flank of Malinovsky's *front*, Colonel General I. A. Pliev's Soviet–Mongolian Cavalry-Mechanized Group advanced in two march columns 124 miles (200 kilometers) apart. Forward detachments consisting of tanks and motorized riflemen from the 25th Mechanized Brigade and the 43d Separate Tank Brigade, reinforced by engineers, raced ahead of the two advancing columns.[4] By nightfall on 9 August, the forward elements of the two forward detachments had penetrated 34 miles (55 kilometers) deep into the arid wastes of Inner Mongolia along an axis extending southward toward Dolonnor and Kalgan, sweeping aside small detachments of Inner Mongolian cavalry.

To the east, Lieutenant General A. I. Danilov's 17th Army, which was advancing along the Chihfeng axis, kept pace, also entering Inner Mongolia virtually unopposed. Danilov's forces advanced in two columns, with the reinforced 70th and 82d Tank Battalions serving as their forward detachments. By nightfall the 17th Army's forward detachments had advanced 43 miles (70 kilometers) to Lake Tabun-Nur, while its main force trailed about 12 miles (20 kilometers) to the rear.[5]

On the Trans-Baikal Front's main attack axis on the 17th Army's left flank, Colonel General of Tank Forces A. G. Kravchenko's 6th Guards Tank Army formed the spearhead of the Trans-Baikal Front. Kravchenko's tank army advanced into Inner Mongolia in two columns of mobile corps. Lieutenant General of Tank Forces M. V. Volkov's 9th Guard Mechanized Corps marched on the right flank in march-column formation followed by Lieutenant General of Tank Forces M. I. Savel'ev's 5th Guards Tank Corps, which was in second echelon. Across the desert wastes 43–50 miles (70–80 kilometers) to the northeast marched Lieutenant General of Tank Forces F. G. Katkov's 7th Guards Mechanized Corps, also advancing in march-column formation.

Taken together, the march columns of the two advancing mobile corps, each of which was subdivided into four to six separate sub-columns, formed a massive and imposing array of armored forces stretching across a 9–12-mile (15–20-kilometer) wide belt. Forward detachments consisting of a rifle regiment, a tank brigade or regiment, and an artillery battalion preceded each of the corps.[6] Kravchenko's tank army encountered only limited opposition and, therefore, advanced rapidly. By nightfall on 9 August, his corps' forward detachments had traversed 93 miles (150 kilometers) of desert and steppe and halted in the foothills of the Grand Khingan Mountains west and north of Khorokhon Pass (see Map 32).

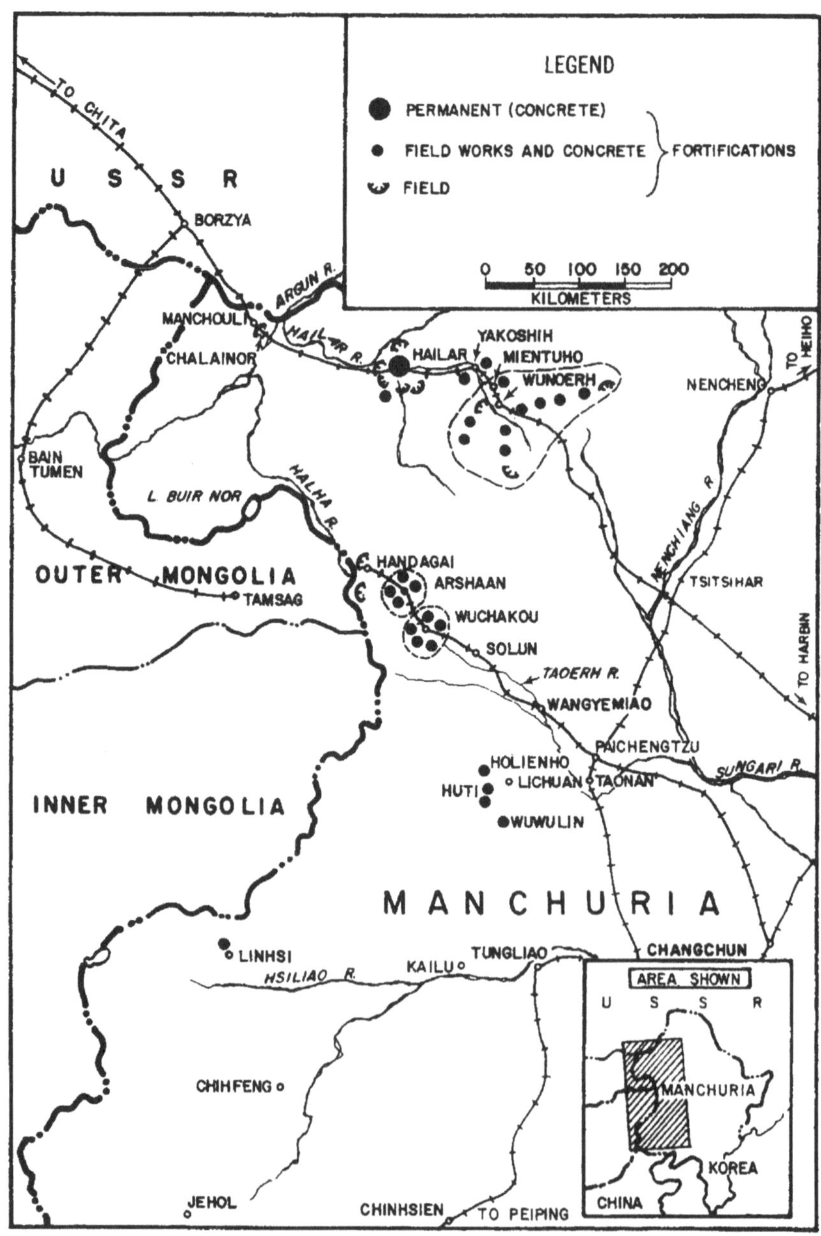

Map 29. Japanese Fortified Positions in Western Manchuria (Japanese View)

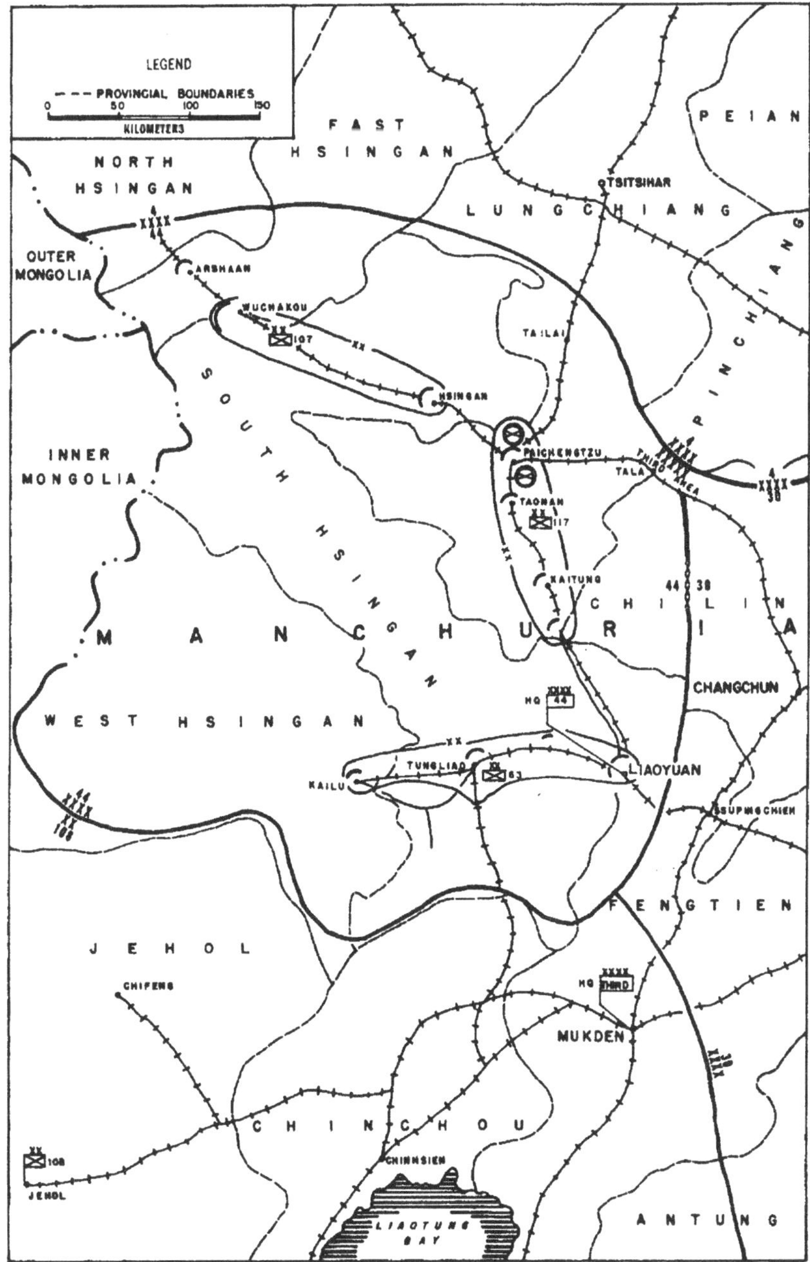

Map 30. Japanese 44th Army Defenses (Japanese View)

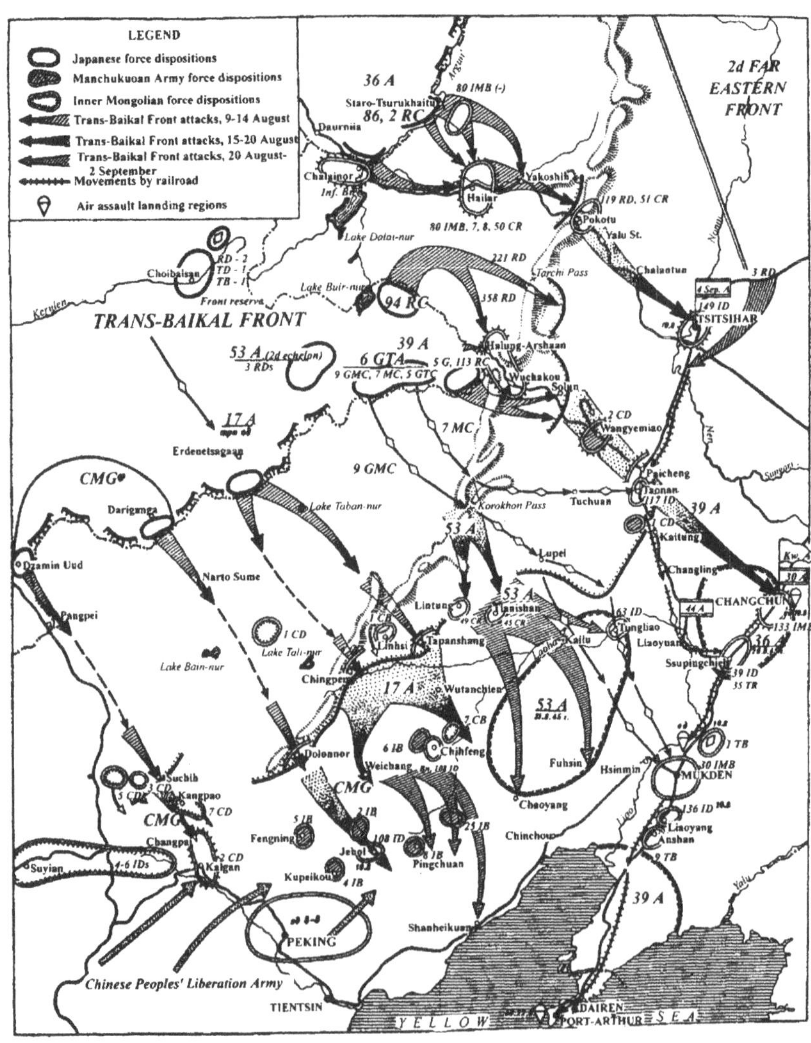

Map 31. Trans-Baikal Front Operations, 9 August–2 September 1945

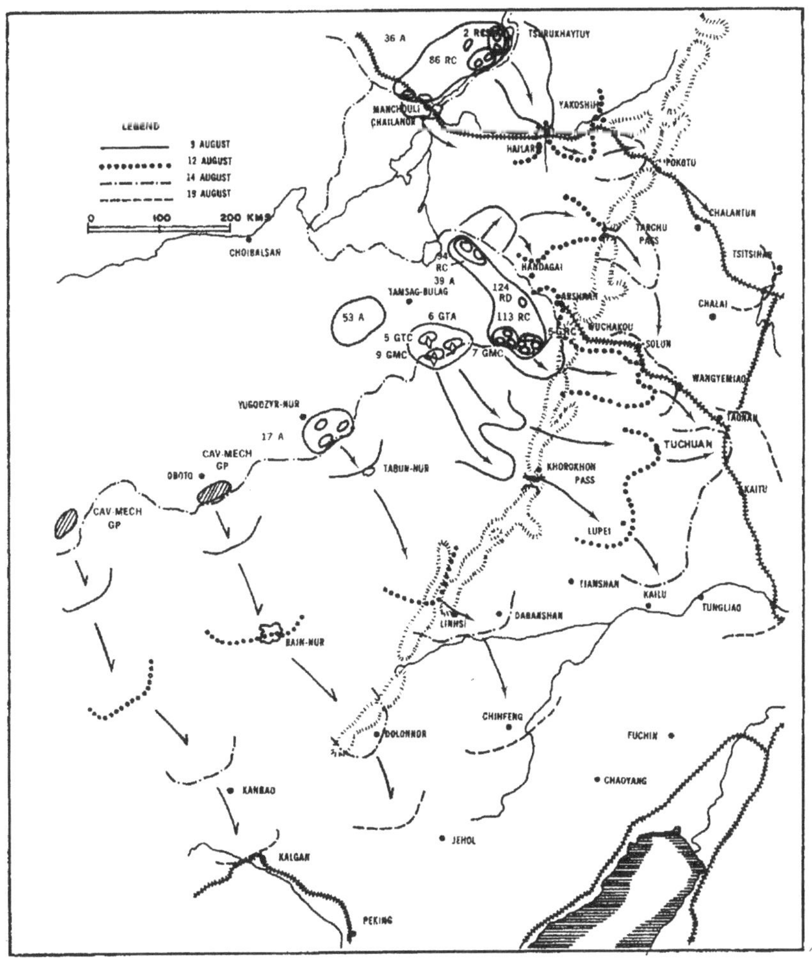

Map 32. Soviet Trans-Baikal Front Operations, 9–19 August 1945

On the 6th Guards Tank Army's left flank, two rifle corps of Colonel General I. N. Liudnikov's 39th Army, which was deployed in a single echelon of rifle corps, advanced southward and then southeastward along two main axes of advance in an attempt to bypass the Japanese Halung-Arshaan and Wuchakou Fortified Regions from the south (see Map 33).[7] A third rifle corps advanced northward to catch the Japanese fortified region at Hailar from the rear. North of the army's main axes, two regiments of the Japanese 107th Infantry Division defended the two fortified regions against attacks from all sides.

South of Halung-Arshaan, Lieutenant General I. S. Bezuglyi's 5th Guards and Lieutenant General N. N. Oleshev's 113th Rifle Corps advanced behind the 206th and 44th Tank Brigades, which were functioning as the corps' forward detachments. The army's forward detachment, Colonel G. I. Voronkov's 61st Tank Division, preceded the two corps and led the envelopment of the Japanese fortified regions from the south. In addition, the commanders of the two rifle corps' six divisions also formed forward detachments to lead their advance.

Farther to the north near the Khalkhin-Gol battlefield of 1939, Major General I. I. Popov's 94th Rifle Corps attacked northeastward from the eastern 'beak' of Mongolia with two rifle divisions abreast, driving toward the rear of the Hailar Fortified Region in support of elements of 36th Army, which was then advancing toward Hailar from the north. Popov's forces swept aside Japanese forces, which were defending in only platoon strength, and local Manchukuoan cavalry forces in the region.

Meanwhile, the 94th Rifle Corps' 124th Rifle Division manned the sizeable gap along the state border between the 94th Rifle Corps and the 5th Rifle Corps and prepared to assault Japanese defenses in the Halung-Arshaan Fortified Region directly once the 39th Army's advance had isolated them from reinforcements. Initially, on 9 August reconnaissance detachments and groups from the 124th Rifle Division probed Japanese defenses around the fortified region, while the division's main forces prepared to advance the next day.

The forward elements of Liudnikov's 39th Army, which were operating along the army's main axis of advance, successfully bypassed the Halung-Arshaan fortifications, moved forward 37 miles (60 kilometers) over very rough but generally treeless terrain on the first day of the operation. Because of terrain difficulties, however, the rifle divisions' forward detachments lagged far behind the tank brigades and tank division forming the advancing corps and army's forward detachments. As a result, the rifle corps commanders constituted new, more mobile forward detachments organized around the nuclei of the divisions' organic self-propelled artillery battalions.[8]

Confronted by the 39th Army's audacious advance, the Japanese 107th Infantry Division prepared to defend the Halung-Arshaan and Wuchakou Fortified Regions with two of its infantry regiments, but, since the commander was uncertain as to where the Soviets' main blow would fall, he

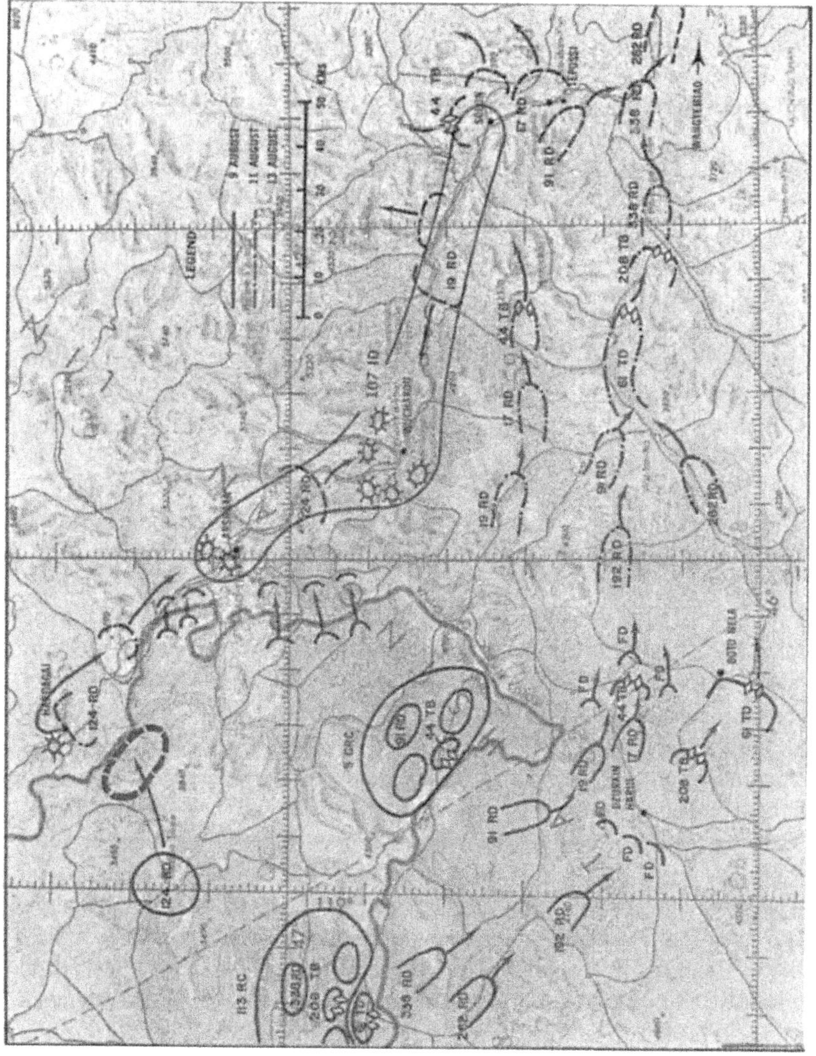

Map 33. Soviet 39th Army Advance, 9–19 August 1945

ordered his third regiment to concentrate along the rail line extending from Wuchakou to Solun to protect his lines of communications (see Map 34).[9] Meanwhile, the 39th Army's main forces continued their advance through the rugged central region of the Grand Khingan Mountains eastward and southeastward toward Solun and Wangyemiao in an attempt to cut the rail line to Taoan, thereby isolating the Japanese forces in their forward fortified regions.

Still farther to the north, on the Trans-Baikal Front's left flank, Lieutenant General A. A. Luchinsky's 36th Army advanced southward across the Argun River on two principal axes (see Maps 35 and 36).[10] Major General G. V. Revunenkov's 86th Rifle Corps and Major General D. E. Petrov's 2d Rifle Corps launched Luchinsky's main attack at 0020 hours on 9 August to secure crossing sites over the rain-swollen Argun River between Staro-Tsurukhaitui and Duroy. A single rifle battalion from each of the two corps' first-echelon rifle divisions served as the initial assault force. To accelerate the crossing process, Petrov ordered two rifle regiments to be transported across the river in 30 US Lend-Lease amphibious vehicles. By 0600 hours the 36th Army's main forces had begun to cross the river. These forces scattered the platoon- to company-size Japanese forces and auxiliaries defending the river.

Luchinsky then dispatched an army forward detachment organized around the nucleus of Lieutenant Colonel N. A. Kurnosov's 205th Tank Brigade toward Hailar, located 37 miles (60 kilometers) to the south, to preempt Japanese defense of the fortified region and cut the main railroad line running from Manchouli to central Manchuria. The Japanese 4th Separate Army's 80th Independent Mixed Brigade, which consisted of five infantry battalions and supporting units, and the 119th Infantry Division defended Hailar and manned the Hailar Fortified Region, assisted by Manchukuoan cavalry forces.

By late evening on 9 August, Kurnosov's forward detachment had secured key bridges north of Hailar. Hoping to preempt a complete Japanese defense of Hailar, Luchinsky then ordered the 205th Tank Brigade to conduct a night attack southward to envelop and capture the town. While Kurnosov's tank brigade attacked the Japanese defenses from the northeast, the 94th Rifle Division's 152d Rifle Regiment, which was trailing the forward detachment's advance, wheeled around the town to attack the Japanese defenses from the southeast. However, the initial assault proved only partially successful. Kurnosov's tank brigade managed to seize the railroad station in the northern part of the town, and, on the following morning (10 August), the 152d Rifle Regiment finally occupied the southern and eastern portions of the town after experiencing difficulty getting into position.[11]

Thus, the troops of the defending 80th Independent Mixed Brigade successfully delayed Luchinsky's advance and prevented the rapid fall of the town. While they busily prepared to defend the fortified areas northwest and southwest of the city, on 9 August the 119th Infantry Division withdrew eastward to establish new defenses that the 4th Separate Army command

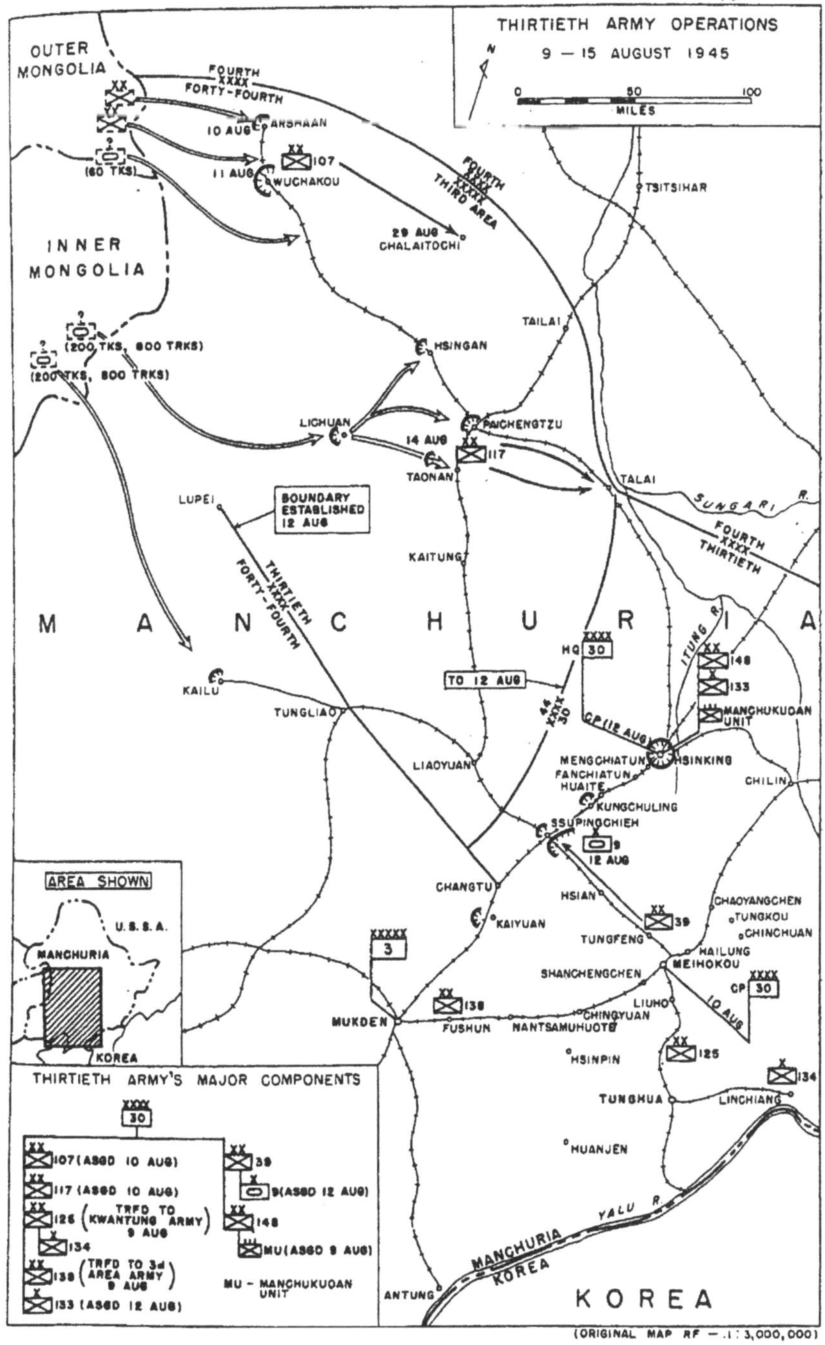

Map 34. Japanese 30th Army Defense, 9–15 August 1945 (Japanese View)

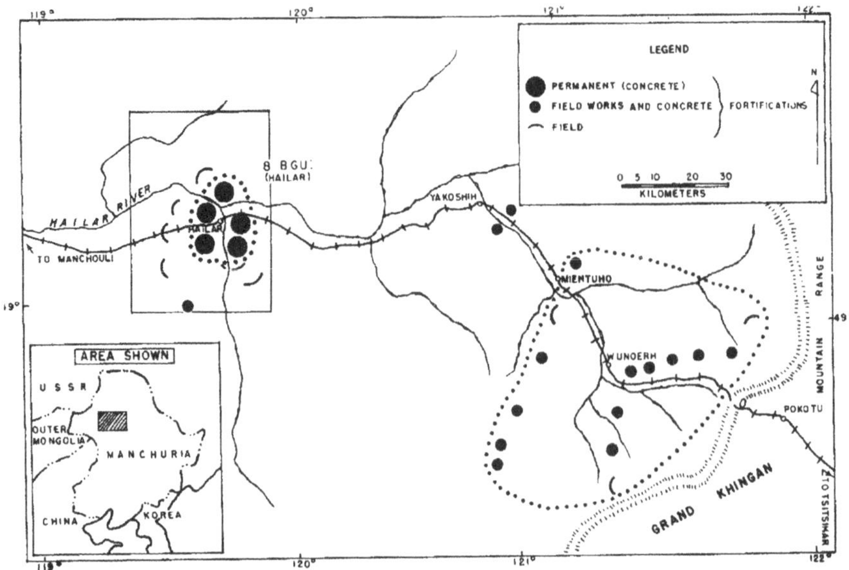

Map 35. Japanese 4th Army Defense in Northwestern Manchuria (Japanese View)

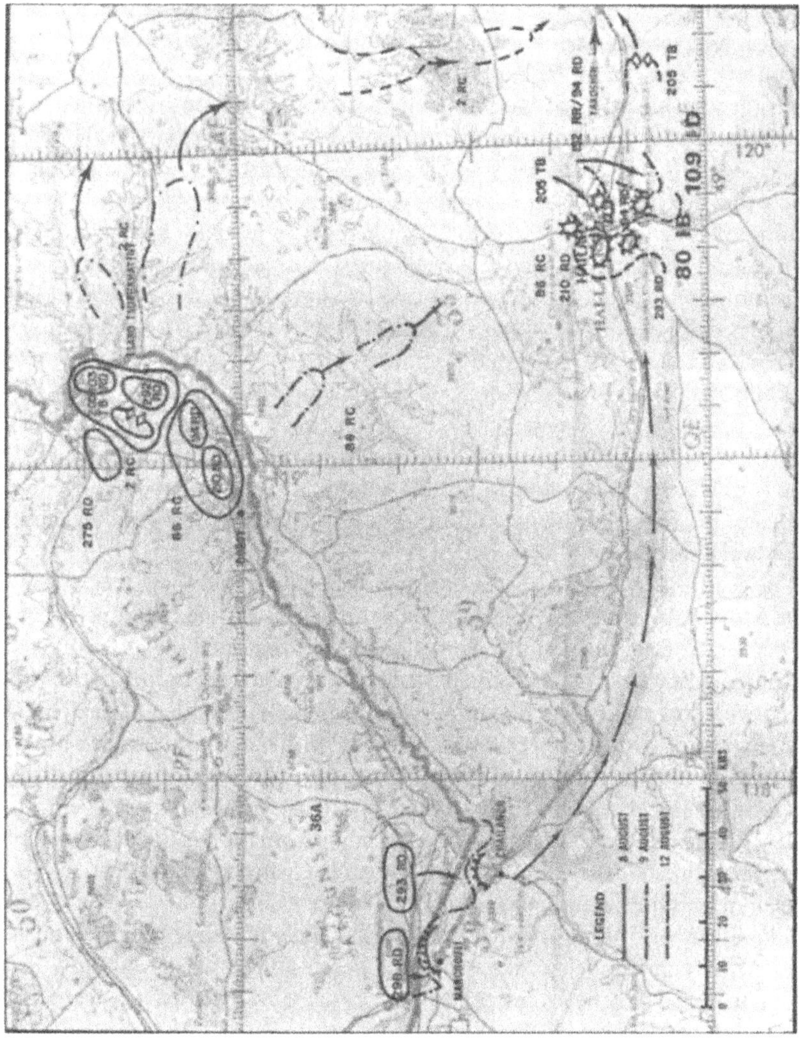

Map 36. Soviet 36th Army Advance to Hailar and Yakoshih, 9–12 August 1945

hoped would be able to block the Soviet advance in the passes through the Grand Khingan Mountains that ran from Yakoshih to Pokotu.[12]

On the extreme right flank of his 36th Army, Luchinsky formed an operational group consisting of the 293d and 298th Rifle Divisions reinforced by two artillery-machine gun battalions and ordered it to attack across the border and secure a foothold in the small Japanese fortified post at Manchouli, which was defended by several Japanese infantry companies. Thus, by the evening of 9 August, the forces of Luchinsky's 36th Army had advanced 37 miles (60 kilometers) deep into Manchuria and had partially secured its initial objective of Hailar. Intense fighting would occur, however, before the stubborn defenders of the 80th Independent Mixed Brigade relinquished their hold on the Hailar Fortified Region.

While the Trans-Baikal Front's first echelon armies savaged Japanese border defenses and plunged deep into Manchuria, Malinovsky's second echelon army, Colonel General I. M. Managarov's 53d Army, remained in its assembly areas in Mongolia until 10 August, when it began crossing the border in the tracks of the now distant 6th Guards Tank Army and headed east toward the Grand Khingans.

The Kwantung Army's operational plan had envisioned the forces of the 44th Army halting the Soviet advance in the belt of fortified regions along the border. Instead, the first few days of operations indicated the utter futility of that plan. Soviet forces had either crushed or bypassed the border defenses. Faced with this reality, the Kwantung Army command decided to delay the Soviet advance with whatever forces it had at its disposal in the west rather than dispatching fresh forces to the region, while it attempted to gain time to assemble forces required for a credible defense in Manchuria's central valley. This meant erecting defenses that could contain the Soviet advance along the railroad line extending from Tumen to Changchun and Changchun to Dairen on the Liaotung peninsula.

Therefore, on the morning of 9 August, General Ushiroku, the Third Area Army commander, ordered the Japanese 44th Army to withdraw its forces that had not been cut off by the initial Soviet thrust eastward to Changchun and Dalai. Ushiroku decided to concentrate the area army's forces and to defend north and south of Mukden in an effort to provide protection for the families of his soldiers. However, this unilateral decision by the area army commander directly conflicted with the plans of General Yamada, the Kwantung Army commander, who wished to construct a firm defense farther to the rear. Inevitably, this conflict produced serious confusion in Japanese ranks (see Map 37).[13]

Soon after, Ushiroku directed General Hongo, the 44th Army commander, to order the 107th and 117th Infantry Divisions, then defending at Halung-Arshaan, Wuchakou, and Taonan, to withdraw to Changchun. When they reached position between Dalai and Liaoyuan, they were to revert to control

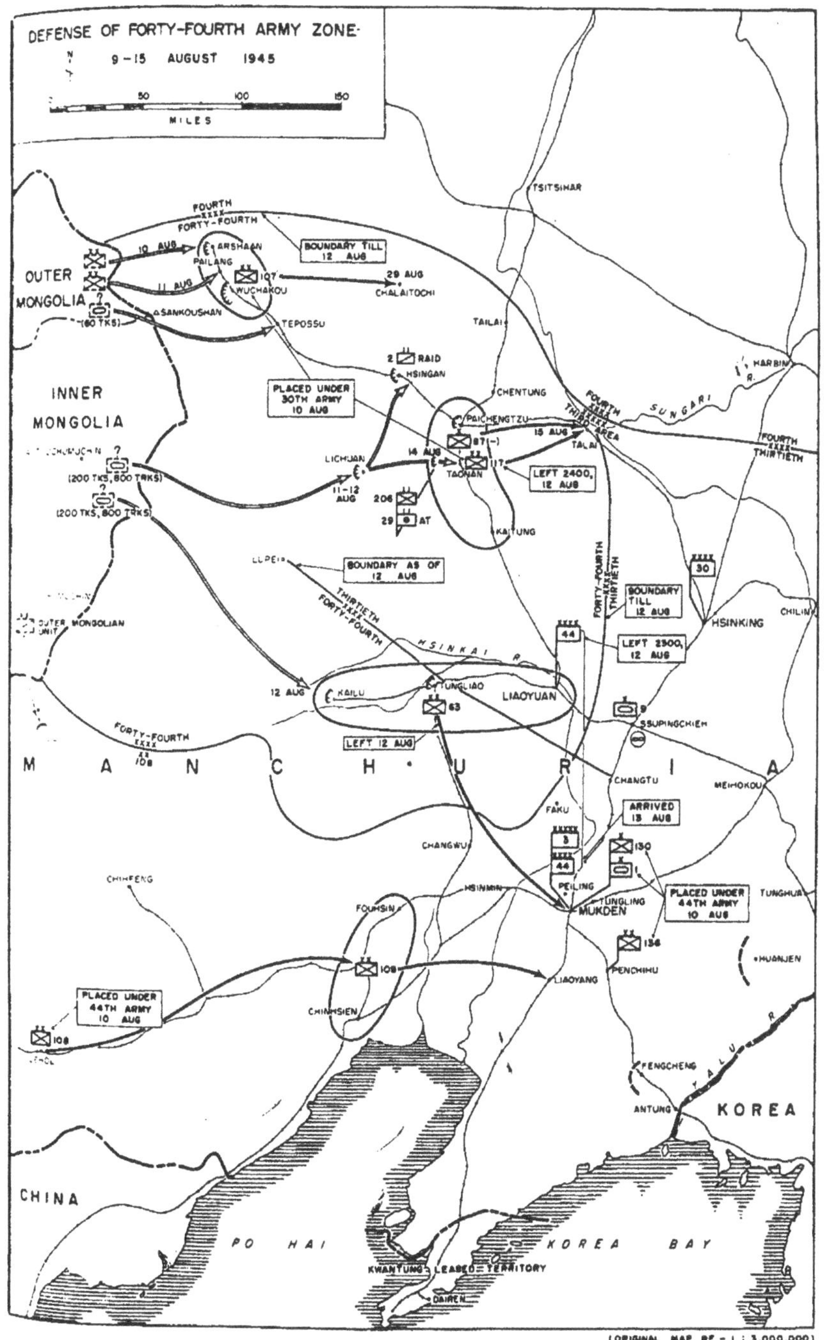

Map 37. Japanese 44th Army Defense, 9–15 August 1945 (Japanese View)

by the 30th Army. At the same time, the 149th Infantry Division at Tsitsihar and the 131st Infantry Brigade at Harbin were to begin withdrawing to Kirin, and the 63d Infantry Division at Tungliao and the 136th Infantry Division at Penchihu (near Fushun) were to concentrate at Mukden. When they arrived in the Mukden region, the 130th Infantry Division and 130th Mixed Brigade, previously in the Third Area Army's reserve, were to become subordinate to the 44th Army.

Despite the ensuing confusion, the 107th and 117th Infantry Divisions had become subordinate to the 30th Army by 12 August with the mission of defending positions from Ssupingchieh to Changchun, a mission which was utterly irrelevant since the two divisions were already decisively engaged and totally isolated in western Manchuria. As replacements for these two divisions, the 44th Army received the 108th Infantry Division, a garrison division from Jehol, north of Peking, and the 136th Infantry Division and 130th Mixed Brigade. Hongo's 44th Army was to occupy defenses southwest, west, and northwest of Mukden, halt the Soviet advance, and, supposedly, counterattack to destroy the Soviet forces. Meanwhile, the 4th Separate Army was to withdraw its forces back from the Hailar and Sunwu regions and man defenses north of Kirin.[14]

Thus, at a time when the Trans-Baikal Front's forces were racing toward and across the Grand Khingan Mountains and into Manchuria's vital central plain, the Japanese commands were reshuffling their forces in central Manchuria, leaving part of those reshuffled forces to contend with the Soviet juggernaut in the west, a juggernaut whose scale and menacing presence they barely understood. In reality, the massive Soviet assault totally disrupted the Kwantung Army's command and control system to the extent that the reshuffling produced nothing more than pure chaos. That would soon become abundantly clear.

In the midst of the deteriorating military situation, on 10 August the Japanese government agreed to accept the Allied ultimatum of 26 July based on the Potsdam Declaration. However, the Soviet government perceived the declaration as a mere propaganda measure and acted accordingly. The offensive continued at an accelerated pace.

10–11 August

The forces of Malinovsky's Trans-Baikal Front continued their precipitous advance on 10 August, whenever possible employing mobile forces as forward detachments to preempt any Japanese defense. Pliev's Cavalry-Mechanized Group lunged forward along the Kalgan and Dolonnor axes, brushing aside weak detachments of Inner Mongolian cavalry, and reached positions 12 miles (20 kilometers) north of the western base of the Grand Khingan Mountains by nightfall on 10 August. After a brief overnight pause to regroup, Pliev's forces traversed the remaining desert wastes and reached the foothills of the Grand Khingan Mountains, 124 miles (200 kilometers) from their start point by day's end on 11 August. Enemy resistance throughout the entire march was negligible.

The same situation prevailed in Danilov's 17th Army, which was advancing on Pliev's left flank toward Chihfeng. Still encountering weak opposition, Danilov's small army gained 25 miles (40 kilometers) on 10 August and, by the evening of 11 August, was also approaching the western foothills of the Grand Khingan Mountains, about 112 miles (180 kilometers) from where it had begun its advance.

The progress of Kravchenko's 6th Guards Tank Army was equally impressive, as his army pressed forward 62–75 miles (100–120 kilometers) across the desert on 10 August (see Maps 38–40). The evening before, while his forward detachments were approaching the western foothills of the Grand Khingan Mountains in the absence of any noticeable Japanese reaction, Kravchenko formulated his final plans for capturing and securing the mountain passes and conducting the difficult march through the rugged mountain chain. Because tracked vehicles offered better cross-country mobility on mountain tracks than his wheeled vehicles, and the 9th Guards Mechanized Corps was already running short of fuel, he decided to pull Volkov's 9th Guards Mechanized Corps from the first echelon of his right flank march column and replace it with Savel'ev's 5th Guards Tank Corps. He did so because the mechanized corps' Sherman tanks were less sure-footed in mountainous terrain and their fuel consumption was far greater than Soviet model tanks.

Kravchenko supervised the redeployment of the two corps on the afternoon of 10 August and then unleashed his reorganized march columns southeastward toward and into the mountains. For the actual mountain passage, Kravchenko ordered his two forward mobile corps to cross the Grand Khingan Mountains along the two axes that led through the most trafficable passes. On his left flank to the north, Katkov's 7th Guards Mechanized Corps was to cross the mountains using two roads (tracks) near Mokutin. On the tank army's right flank about 43 miles (70 kilometers) to the south, Savel'ev's 5th Guards Tank Corps with Volkov's 9th Mechanized Corps in second echelon was to traverse the mountains along one route east of Yukoto. Savel'ev's tank corps began winding its way through the mountains late on the afternoon of 10 August, and Katkov's mechanized corps began crossing the following morning.

The actual passage through the mountains was extremely difficult. The roads, which in reality were barely tracks, had surfaces of loose rock and pebbles and, in some places, were as narrow as ten feet (three meters) across. Mountain streams had gouged deep ruts into the surface, and the adjacent slopes and flanks of the roadbeds were covered with scattered boulders of various sizes. At times, the slope of the track reached 50 degrees. Drivers

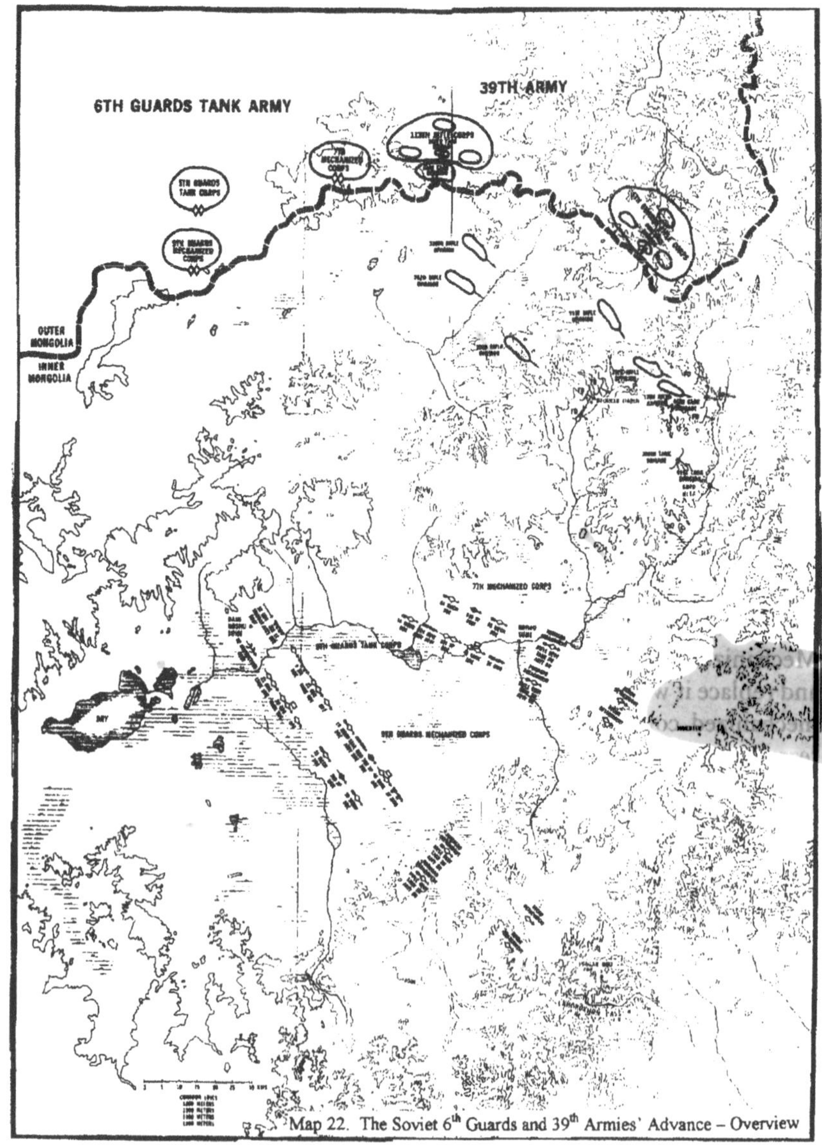

Map 38. Soviet 6th Guards Tank and 39th Armies' Advance – an Overview, 9–10 August 1945

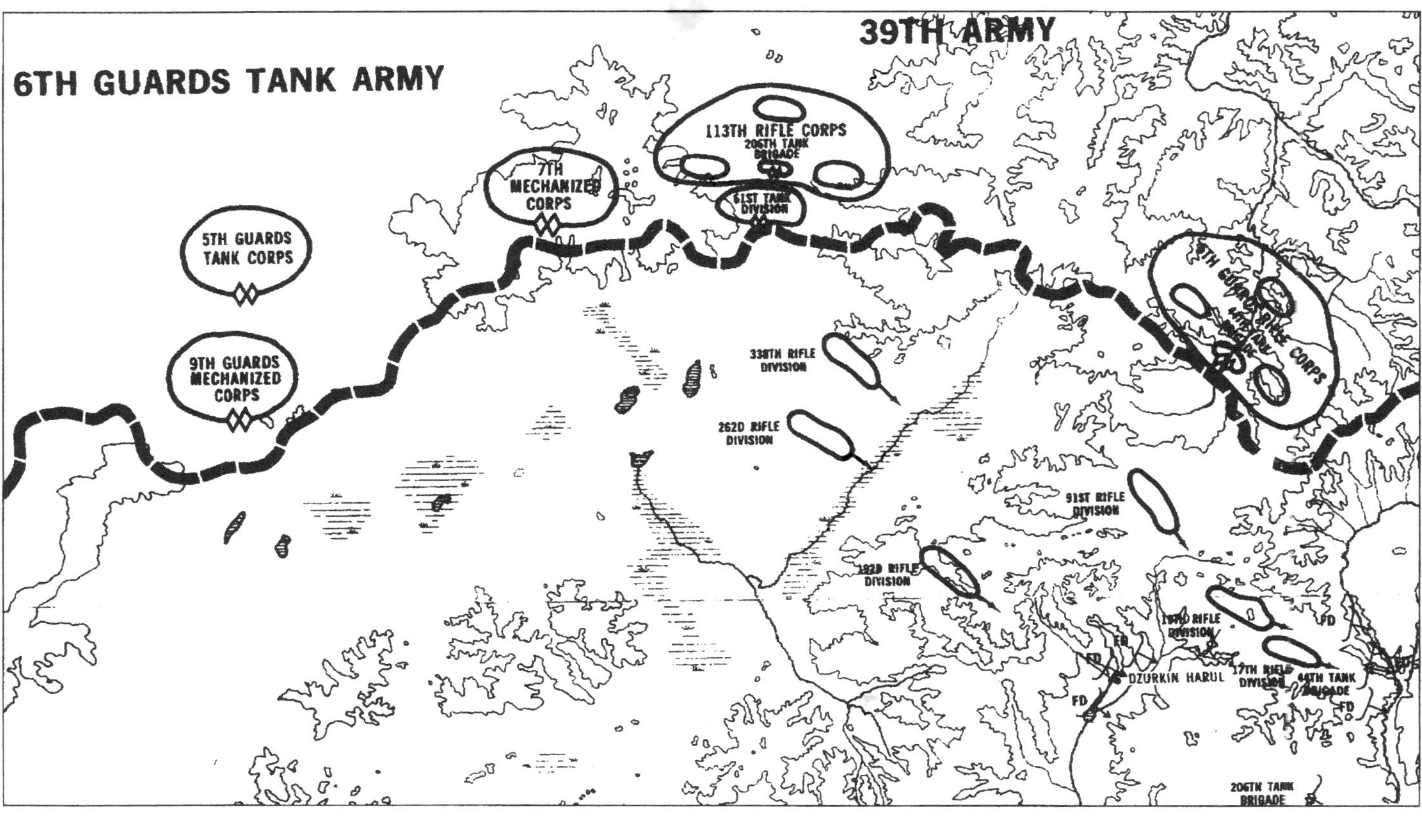

Map 39. 6th Guards Tank Army's Jumping-off Positions and 39th Army's Advance, 9–10 August 1945

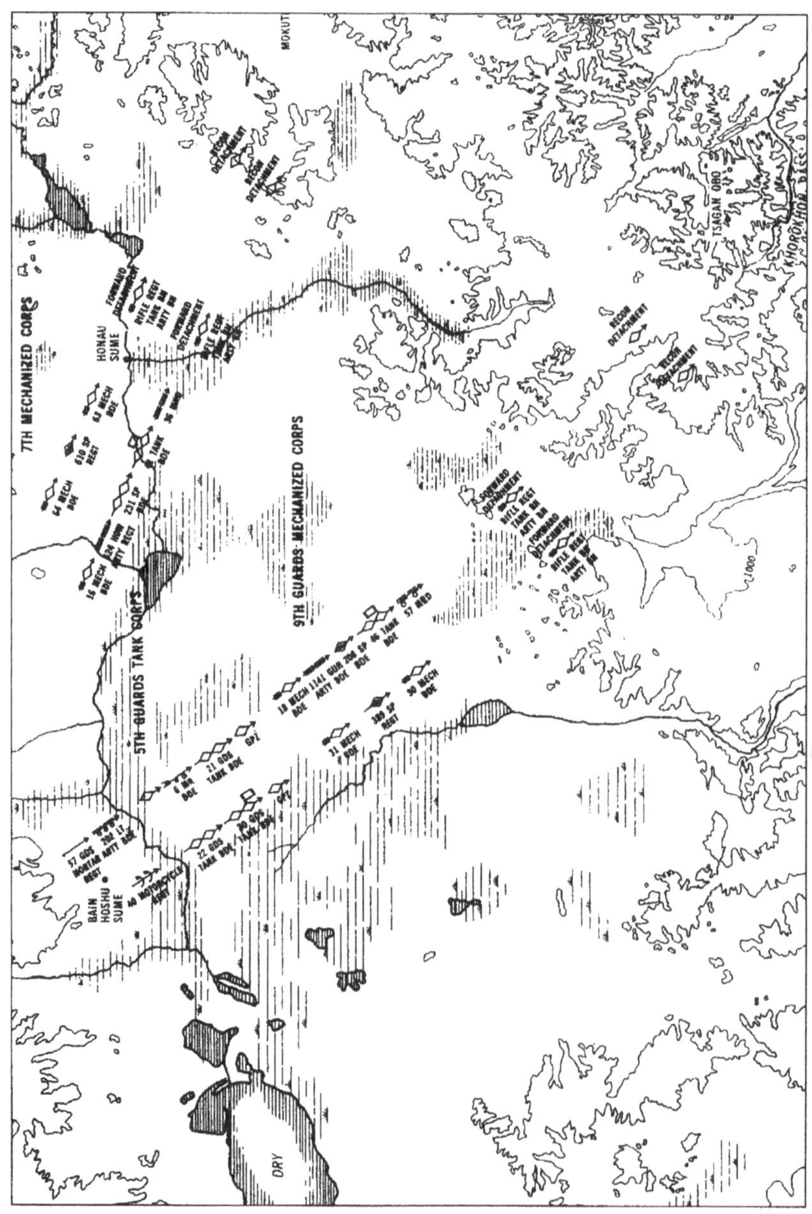

Map 40. 6th Guards Tank Army's March-column Formation, 9–10 August 1945

had to use all of their skills to negotiate the treacherous routes as sappers, engineers, and the tankers themselves used any material at hand to fill in the holes and ruts and make the roads more passable. Day and night, the columns moved on, often at an agonizingly slow rate of three to four miles (five to six kilometers) per hour.[15] Often one tank had to tow another just to keep the column moving forward.

At 2300 hours on 10 August, the lead tank brigade of Savel'ev's 5th Guards Tank Corps finally reached Tsagan Obo, the highest point during its passage through the Grand Khingans, and the 21st Tank Brigade approached Khorokhon. In darkness and intermittent rain, that made the march route even more challenging, Savel'ev's corps continued on to the eastern exits from the mountain pass. His tank corps managed to cover a distance of 25 miles (40 kilometers) through the winding pass in only seven hours, a feat made possible only by the fact that his column consisted primarily of tracked vehicles. To the north, Katkov's 7th Guards Mechanized Corps, impeded by its large number of wheeled vehicles, completed its passage of the mountains during the evening of 11 August.

Kravchenko's army suffered greatly from fuel shortages during the mountain crossing. The falling rain and difficult road conditions increased fuel consumption, and the army's vehicular columns, which included the fuel trucks, lagged as far behind as 186 miles (300 kilometers). Because of fuel shortages, by the time they crossed the mountains, the 46th Guards Tank Brigade consisted of only 18 tanks and the 30th Mechanized Brigade, seven tanks and two motorized infantry companies. Katkov's 7th Mechanized Corps had to remove the 36th Motorized Rifle Division from its first echelon and place it in second echelon because it ran out of fuel.[16] Both columns then entered the central Manchurian plain and continued their advance eastward as rapidly as possible. At 1800 hours on 11 August, the forward detachment of the 5th Guards Tank Corps reached Lupei.

Malinovsky attempted to assist Kravchenko in overcoming his logistical difficulties by supplying his marching columns with fuel and ammunition by air. To this end, the *front* commander ordered the 12th Air Army to employ its transport aviation in to support Kravchenko. Khudiakov assigned this mission to his 54th and 21st Guards Transport Aviation Divisions. In extremely difficult weather (rain, fog, and low ceilings) and without adequate landing sites, the transport aircraft flew 1,755 sorties, dropping 2,072 tons of fuel and 78 tons of ammunition to the advancing forces.[17]

On 12 August Japanese aircraft appeared for the first time above Kravchenko's advancing march columns. Although they were few in number, they attempted to bomb the columns, and when the bombs ran out, they conducted suicide attacks in futile efforts to halt Kravchenko's advance. For example, on 12 and 13 August, 12 aircraft launched suicide attacks directly against the 5th Guards Tank Corps but caused no damage in the process.[18]

Meanwhile, on 12 August Malinovsky ordered Kravchenko to turn his marching columns abruptly to the south to begin an advance on Mukden. By this time, because of the continuing fuel shortage and road difficulties, Katkov's 7th Mechanized Corp had fallen considerably behind Savel'ev's tank corps. Consequently, the forward detachment of Katkov's mechanized corps reached Tuchuan only on 13 August. Unlike the case with the 5th Guards Tank Corps, which encountered little resistance at Lupei, Katkov's corps faced far heavier resistance at Tuchuan, which was defended by a cavalry unit and at least one infantry battalion of the Japanese 117th Infantry Division, supported by artillery and aircraft. However, the 64th Mechanized Brigade repelled the surprise attack and secured the city by day's end.

Thus, against minimal resistance, Kravchenko's 6th Guards Tank Army reached and captured both of its objectives by the fourth day of an operation that had been planned to take five days.[19] Audacity had paid off. The speed of the advance surpassed Soviet expectations. The 6th Guards Tank Army covered 217 miles (350 kilometers) over difficult terrain in four days, preempting the ability of Japanese forces to react quickly enough to block the advance of the tank army. After 12 August, only logistical difficulties limited the Soviet advance. Pressure on other fronts and the collapse of the western sector would make it exceedingly difficult for the Japanese to restore a viable defensive line and to stave off total collapse.

Japanese resistance to Pliev's Mongolian Cavalry-Mechanized Group, Danilov's 17th Army, and Kravchenko's 6th Guards Tank Army was either extremely light or utterly nonexistent. Small groups of Inner Mongolian horse cavalry from the Inner Mongolian 1st Cavalry Division, which was stationed north of Kalgan, defended small outposts along the border. Offering little resistance to the strong and rapid advance by Soviet mechanized and horse cavalry, they fell steadily back to their base without offering anything other than token resistance.

The Japanese 108th Infantry Division, whose headquarters was located at Jehol, had an infantry battalion posted at Chihfeng and a company at Linhsi in the 17th Army's sector of advance. The Japanese 63d Infantry Division at Tunglaio also had an infantry battalion defending at Kailu but transferred none of its forces northwest to block 6th Guards Tank Army's advance (see Maps 41–43).

The Japanese 117th Infantry Division, which was stationed at Taonan, dispatched one infantry battalion and an antitank battalion 18.6 miles (30 kilometers) westward along the road running west from Tuchuan on 10 August with orders to intercept the advancing Soviet tank columns. On the same day, however, the Japanese 44th Army ordered both the 63d and the 117th Infantry Divisions to redeploy eastward to Mukden and Changchun (Hsinking), respectively. Thus, neither division was able to engage in any fighting with Soviet forces.

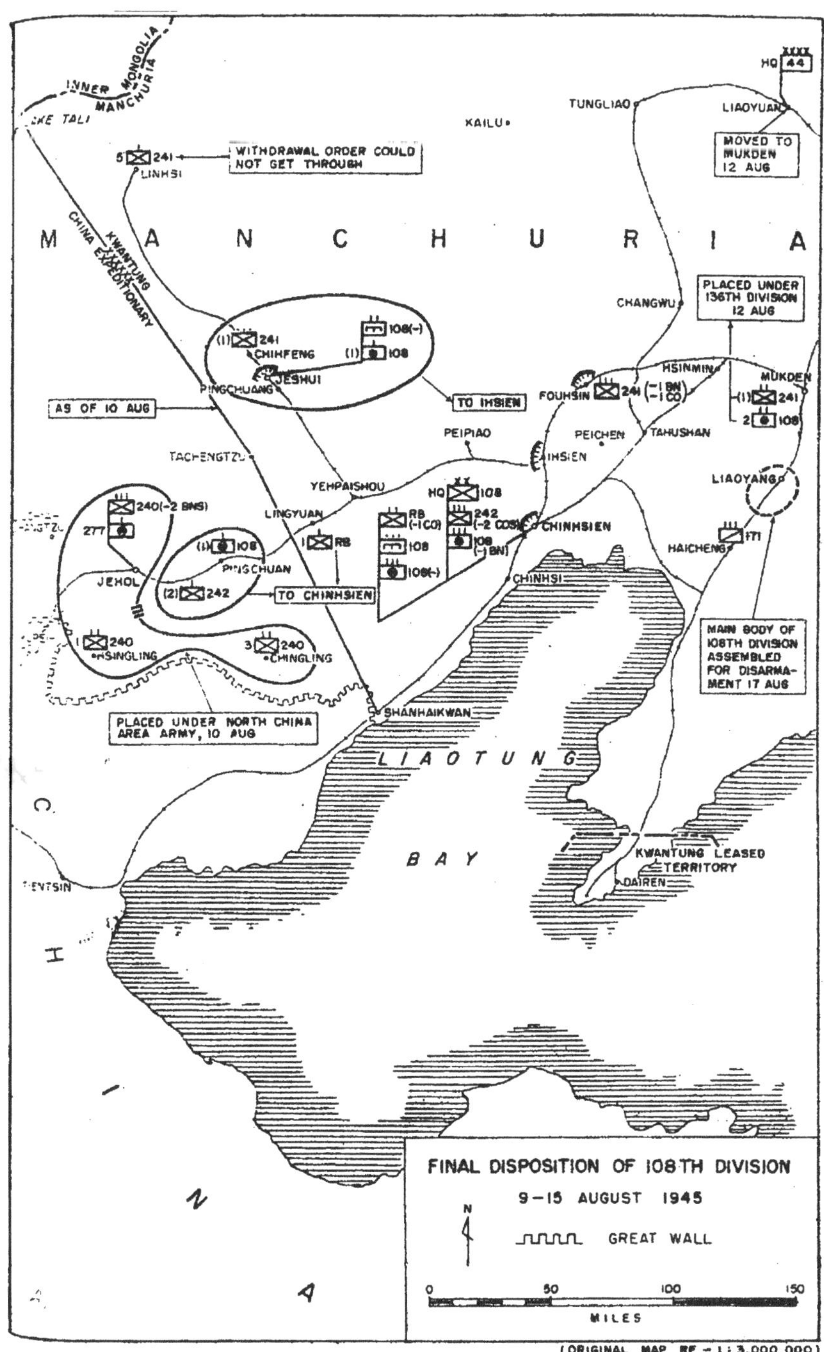

Map 41. Japanese 108th Infantry Division's Defense, 9–15 August 1945 (Japanese View)

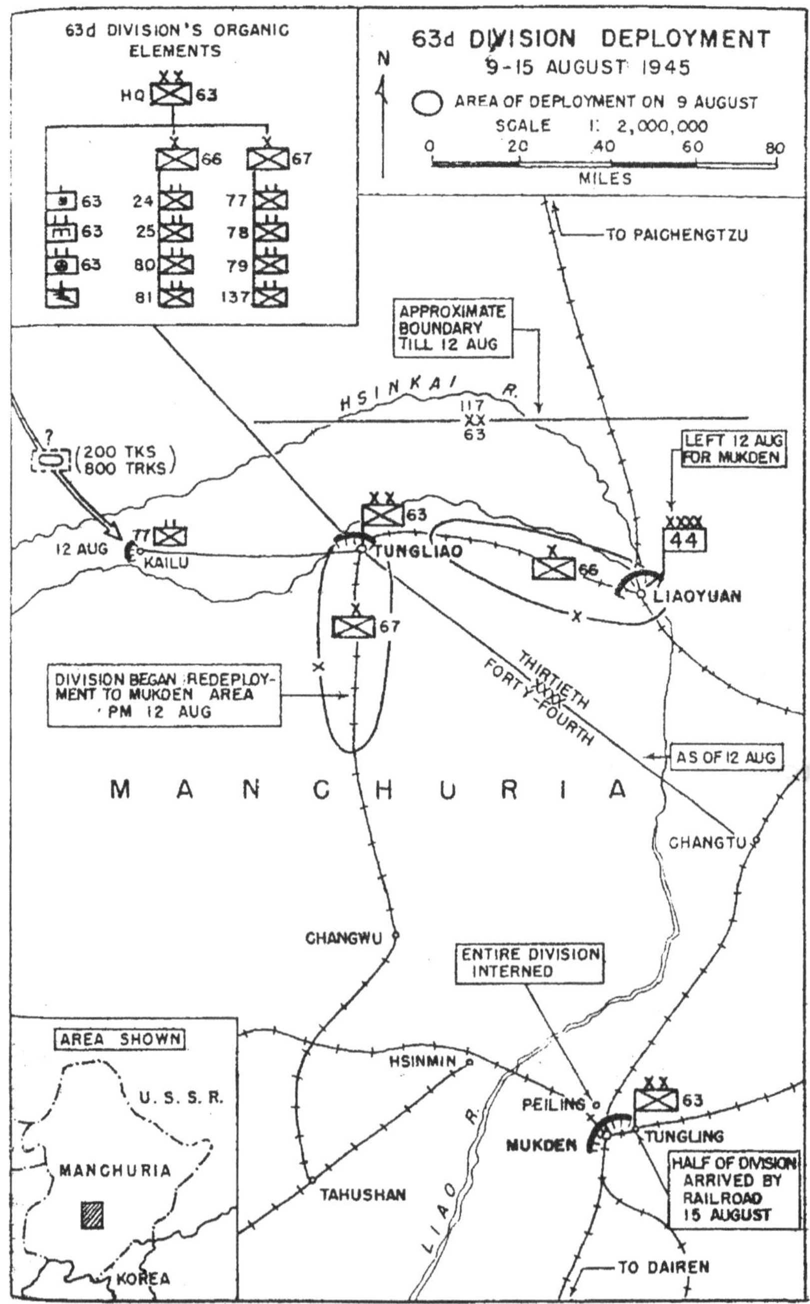

Map 42. Japanese 63d Infantry Division's Deployment, 9–15 August 1945 (Japanese View)

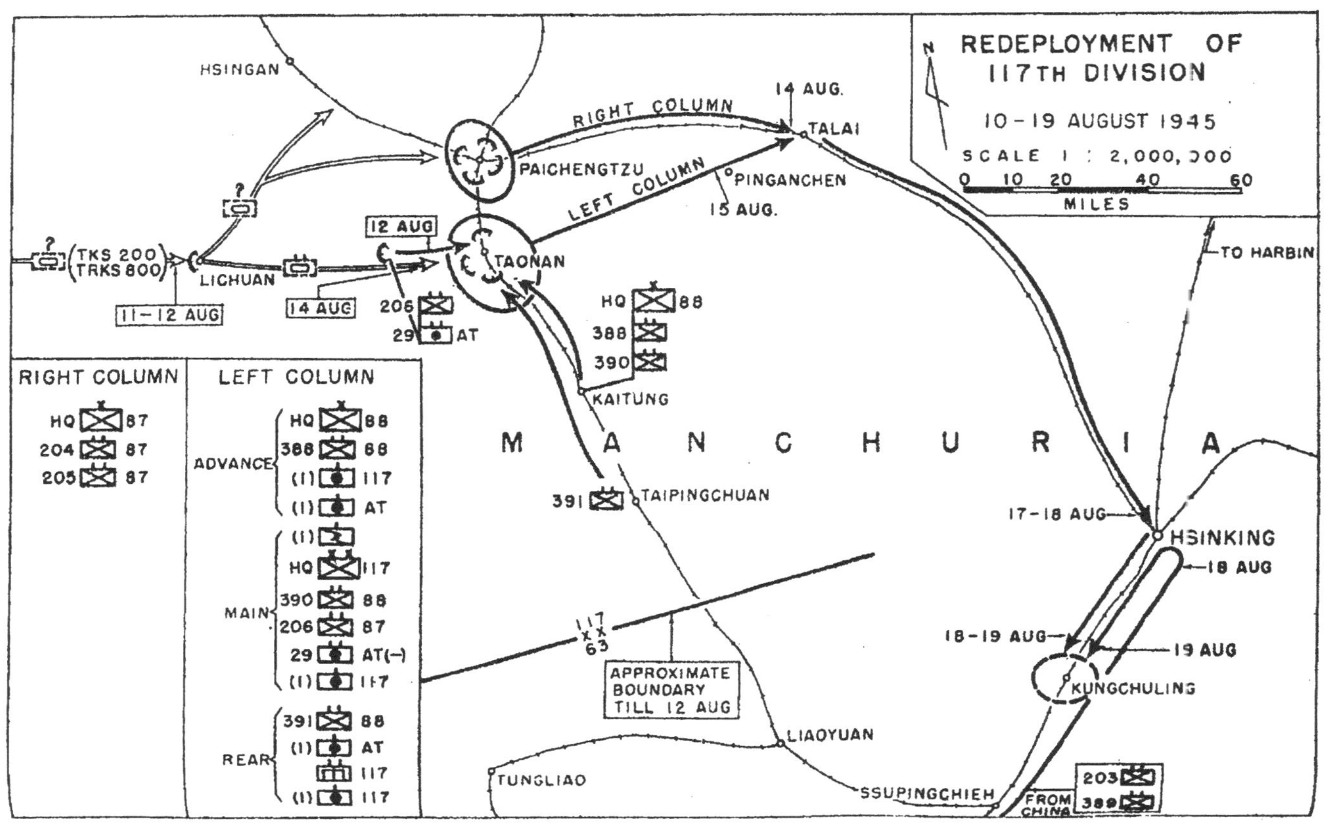

Map 43. Redeployment of Japanese 117th Infantry Division, 10–19 August 1945 (Japanese View)

The only forces capable of resisting the Soviet–Mongolian Cavalry-Mechanized Group's, the 17th Army's, and the 6th Guards Tank Army's advance were Inner Mongolian cavalry forces operating out of Kalgan and minor elements of the Japanese 108th Infantry Division. The other Japanese forces stationed in west central Manchuria withdrew eastward. In the 39th Army's sector, only the 107th Infantry Division, small elements of the 117th Infantry Division, and random unattached 44th Army units and local Manchurian forces offered any resistance.[20] However, the story was different in northwest Manchuria, where Japanese opposition severely hindered the advance of Luchinsky's 36th Army.

To the north, on the 6th Guards Tank Army's left flank, Liudnikov's 39th Army continued its rapid advance, as its main body bypassed portions of the Japanese 107th Infantry Division, which was besieged in the Halung-Arshaan and Wuchakou Fortified Regions. Bezuglyi's 5th Guards Rifle Corps marched eastward in a column of rifle divisions toward Solun and the railway station at Tepossi but encountered little Japanese resistance. Oleshev's 113th Rifle Corps, also advancing in a column of rifle divisions, advanced southeastward through the tortuously narrow, winding, and rain-swollen valley of the Wulan Ho River toward Wangyemiao. Lieutenant Colonel F. P. Solovei's 206th Tank Brigade and Lieutenant Colonel A. A. Smetanin's 44th Tank Brigade led the advance of the two rifle corps.

On the afternoon of 12 August, 39th Army forces encountered the first Japanese opposition. Elements of the Japanese 107th Infantry Division, which were hastily withdrawing southeast along the railroad from Wuchakou, ran into advanced elements of Bezuglyi's rifle corps. The advancing tank brigades destroyed several train cars, dispersed the Japanese, and opened the road to Solun. Only natural obstacles of swamps and rivers slowed their advance.[21]

On the 39th Army's left flank, Popov's 94th Rifle Corps advanced toward Hailar from the south. Because of the 36th Army's successful advance against Hailar from the north and the stiff resistance Japanese forces were offering against the 39th Army's 124th Rifle Division, which was attacking directly into the Halung-Arshaan Fortified Region, late on 10 August, Liudnikov ordered Popov's rifle corps to wheel its divisions to the south, help capture Halung-Arshaan, and, later, rejoin his main force.

Meanwhile, south of Hailar, Major General V. N. Kushnarenko's 221st Rifle Division of Popov's rifle corps surrounded 1,000 troops of the Manchukuoan 10th Military District and its commander General Houlin, forced Houlin's forces to surrender, and then marched rapidly eastward towards the pass through the Grand Khingan Mountains at Tarchu. Major General P. F. Zaretsky's 358th Rifle Division, also from Popov's corps, wheeled due south to join the 124th Rifle Division, which was then actively engaged in reducing Japanese forces in the Halung-Arshaan Fortified Region.[22]

In the attack sector of Luchinsky's 36th Army, Kurnosov's 205th Tank

Brigade, supported by the 152d Rifle Regiment, continued its struggle to overcome Japanese defenses in the central and southwest portion of Hailar town on 10 August. The Japanese continued to pour heavy fire against the attacking Soviet units from fortified firing positions on the high ground to the south and northwest. Luchinsky then regrouped his forces to restore momentum to his advance beyond Hailar toward the Grand Khingan Mountain passes to the east. He ordered Kurnosov's tank brigade to disengage from the fighting around Hailar and to support Petrov's 2d Rifle Corps, which was just beginning its advance east of Hailar. After Petrov's rifle corps completed bypassing the Hailar Fortified Region, it was to advance rapidly along the railroad to Yakoshih with the 205th Tank Brigade.

Forces of the Japanese 119th Infantry Division defended a series of fortified positions along the rail line from Yakoshih to Pokotu in company and battalion strength. Luchinsky also ordered Major General I. V. Zamakhaev's 94th Rifle Division of Revunenkov's 86th Rifle Corps to replace the 205th Tank Brigade and continue intense operations to capture Hailar. At 1400 hours on 11 August, Zamakhaev's rifle division, with strong air and artillery support, attacked and seized the southwestern portion of Hailar town. The defending Japanese units withdrew to the heavily fortified positions on the hills to the northwest and southwest. Luchinsky rushed the remainder of Revunenkov's rifle corps forward to become part of a special group assigned the mission of reducing the formidable Hailar fortifications.[23]

On the same day, Luchinsky's two-rifle division operational group, operating on his army's right flank, smashed Japanese resistance at Manchouli by a surprise assault and captured the fortified region in two days of fighting. After killing an estimated 450 Japanese soldiers and capturing another 100, the small Soviet force advanced eastward along the rail line to link up with the 36th Army's forces besieging Hailar.

THE EXPLOITATION, 12–14 AUGUST 1945

On the fourth day of the offensive (12 August), the Soviet offensive torrent swept forward, while Japanese forces defended in isolated outposts or withdrew to regroup and prepare to fight future battles. Soon the confusion of the chaotic withdrawal would be compounded by political confusion resulting from rumors of a Japanese call for a cease-fire.

On the right flank of Malinovsky's Trans-Baikal Front, on 12 and 13 August, the Soviet–Mongolian formations of Pliev's Cavalry-Mechanized Group raced across the barren wastes of the Gobi Desert of Inner Mongolia towards Dolonnor and Kalgan at an almost unprecedented rate of 56–62 miles (90–100 kilometers) per day, rudely shunting aside local cavalry forces. Pliev's principal concern was how to provide sufficient food, fuel, fodder, and water to his marching forces. Early on 14 August, the column marching on Pliev's left flank quickly overcame a small Manchukuoan cavalry force and entered the town of Dolonnor, which was located at the east end of the pass across the southern Grand Khingan Mountains. Pliev's force had traversed more than 186 miles (300 kilometers) of desert and mountains in five days and totally frustrated any Japanese hopes to defend the vital approaches to Peking from the west.

To the north, Danilov's 17th Army also successfully crossed the deserts and Grand Khingan Mountains, however, not without its own challenges. Rain storms also impeded the march of Danilov's forces, requiring his forces to take two days to pass through the mountains. Danilov's forces finally entered Tapanshang on 14 August, after dispersing its small Japanese garrison in a brief fight.[24]

Despite the problems with terrain and fuel and ammunition supplies, the forward progress of Kravchenko's 6th Guards Tank Army continued to be spectacular. After the 7th Guards Mechanized Corps had captured Tuchuan and the 5th Guards Tank Corps Lupei, both corps experienced severe fuel shortages. Katkov's 7th Mechanized Corps had 0.5 refills and Savel'ev's 5th Guards Tank Corps had only 0.4 refills. Because Volkov's 9th Guards Mechanized Corps was already short of fuel even before it began crossing the Grand Khingan Mountains, it had no fuel left whatsoever when it finally arrived at Lupei.[25]

By this time, the Trans-Baikal Front's transportation network, which stretched 435 miles (700 kilometers) to the rear, was badly overextended. When the campaign began, the 6th Guards Tank Army fielded 6,489 serviceable vehicles out of the 9,491 vehicles authorized by its tables of organization (TO&E). The tank army's automobile battalions had only 50–60 per cent of their assigned vehicles and were, thus, capable of carrying only 500 tons of supplies, far less than the army required. This heavy attrition in vehicles resulted primarily from the difficult march the tank army's corps had to make from its railheads along the Trans-Siberian railroad during the regrouping to its assembly and concentration areas in Mongolia.

To augment the truck transportation assets available to the 6th Guards Tank Army, the Trans-Baikal Front attached to it the 47th Automobile Regiment, which consisted of six battalions with a total of more than 1,000 trucks. To transport absolutely critical supplies of fuel, Vasilevsky also attached the 453d Aviation Battalion with 400 aircraft to Kravchenko's tank army.[26] However, the tank army's rapid advance strained even these resources to a breaking point. Thus, in order to increase fuel supplies to a level sufficient to maintain the tank army's offensive momentum, Kravchenko began airlifting fuel to his two forward corps on 11 August. Resort to this field expedient forced Kravchenko to halt his advancing mobile corps for a period of two days (12–13 August).

On 13 August, however, Kravchenko ordered his army to resume its offensive by pushing reconnaissance units forward towards Tungliao and Taonan. A reinforced tank or mechanized brigade from each of his forward corps followed the reconnaissance units to serve as forward detachments for the corps, and Kravchenko ordered his corps commanders to put all of the available fuel within each of their corps at the disposal of these forward detachments. The tank army's other forces remained in static positions awaiting fresh supplies of fuel. At nightfall on 14 August, after its march had been hindered by rainy weather, wet roads, and occasional Japanese *kamikaze* attacks, the forward detachment of Katkov's 7th Mechanized Corps defeated a Manchukuoan cavalry division and occupied Taonan, taking 1,320 Japanese soldiers prisoner. At the same time, Savel'ev's 9th Guards Mechanized Corps continued its thrust southeastward toward Tungliao and Kailu.[27]

To the north, on 13 August the forces of Liudnikov's 39th Army continued their attempts to overcome Japanese resistance at the Halung-Arshaan Fortified Region and capture the key railroad station at Solun. After a powerful artillery and air preparation, Solun fell to the assaulting forces of Major General A. P. Kvashnin's 17th Guards Rifle Division and Smetanin's 44th Tank Brigade during the afternoon. The next day, the victors had to repel several battalion-strength Japanese counterattacks.

Meanwhile, the 91st and 17th Rifle Divisions of Bezuglyi's 5th Guards Rifle Corps began to pursue Japanese forces southeastward from Solun along the railroad towards Wangyemiao. Smetanin's 44th Tank Brigade, which was serving as the forward detachment of Bezuglyi's rifle corps, spearheaded the attack in coordination with other forward detachments formed by the rifle corps' first echelon rifle divisions. However, persistent fuel shortages in the 44th Tank Brigade forced Bezuglyi to constitute yet another a forward detachment to replace Smetanin's tank brigade. When formed, the new forward detachment consisted of the 735th Self-propelled Artillery Regiment, one battalion of the 45th Artillery Regiment, the 74th Antitank Artillery Battalion, and the 508th Self-propelled Artillery Battalion.[28]

The southeastward march of Liudnikov's forces brought Bezuglyi's rifle corps into contact with Japanese artillery and infantry units of the 107th Infantry Division and the 2d Raiding (Suicide) Battalion at the village of Tepossi.[29] Bezuglyi's forces were able to scatter the Japanese defenders in a short but vicious battle that night and the following day. Thereafter, Colonel S. V. Salychev's 19th Rifle Division of Bezuglyi's 5th Guards Rifle Corps pursued Japanese forces retreating from the Wuchakou region along the railroad west of Solun. Ultimately, these Japanese forces found themselves trapped between Salychev's 19th Rifle Division and Major General M. D. Papchenko's 124th Rifle Division, which was advancing eastward from the Halung-Arshaan Fortified Region.

All the while, Oleshev's 113th Rifle Corps, which was led by Solovei's

206th Tank Brigade, continued its eastward march toward Wangyemiao. On 15 August, the soldiers of Oleshev's rifle corps and the Colonel G. I. Voronkov's 61st Tank Division occupied Wangyemiao. After launching several unsuccessful counterattacks to regain control of the town, Japanese forces retreated into the hills north of Wangyemiao, where they continued to harass Soviet forces.

On the Trans-Baikal Front's left flank, the forces of Luchinsky's 36th Army continued their siege of the Hailar fortifications and, at the same time, began an arduous advance through the Grand Khingan passes southeast of Yakoshih (see Maps 44 and 45). Revunenkov, the 86th Rifle Corps commander, employed 94th and 393d Rifle Divisions with heavy artillery support to pound away at the Japanese fortifications in and around Hailar.

Meanwhile, Petrov's 2d Rifle Corps, with Kurnosov's 205th Tank Brigade in the lead, battled for and captured Yakoshih, west of the Grand Khingans, on 12 August. Colonel K. F. Maiorov's 275th Rifle Division managed to advance beyond Yakoshih into the foothills of the mountains but was halted by Japanese forces entrenched near the railroad station at Wunuerh. Petrov's rifle corps battled with the Japanese 119th Infantry Division for possession of the Grand Khingan passes west of Pokotu on 13 and 14 August but was able to record only limited progress. Japanese fortified positions, which lined the roads and railroads through the Grand Khingan passes into the open plain around Pokotu, slowed Petrov's advance to a crawl. The fighting was intense, and the riflemens' gains were often measured in mere yards.[30]

THE COLLAPSE OF THE KWANTUNG ARMY, 15 AUGUST–2 SEPTEMBER 1945

While the precipitous Soviet advance was tearing gapping holes in the Kwantung Army's defenses, the Japanese government pondered a decision to surrender. The Soviet invasion of Manchuria and the US employment of the atomic bomb were but new disasters heaped upon earlier Japanese defeats. On 14 August representatives of the Japanese government contacted the Allied powers and offered to accept the terms the Allies had offered them at Potsdam. The Japanese camp, however, was confused as to the full meaning of the Allied offer.

Despite this confusion, on the evening of 14 August, the Japanese emperor issued a cease-fire order, which the High Command then passed on to its units in the field. General Yamada, however, contradicted the order, and the Soviets responded by ordering a continuation of hostilities, which in turn delayed transmission of the cease-fire order to Japanese forces in the field. Compounding the communications problem, many Japanese military commanders felt that the call for a cease-fire was in direct conflict with the

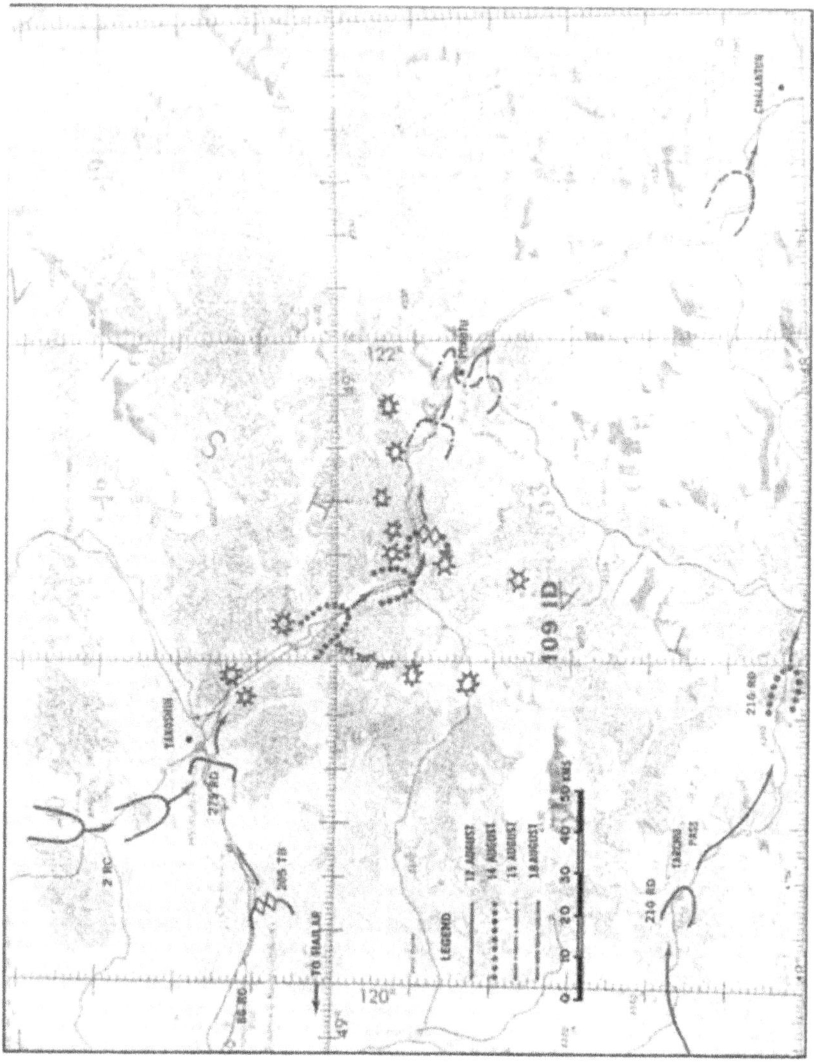

Map 44. Soviet 36th Army Advance from Yakoshih to Chalantun, 12–18 August 1945

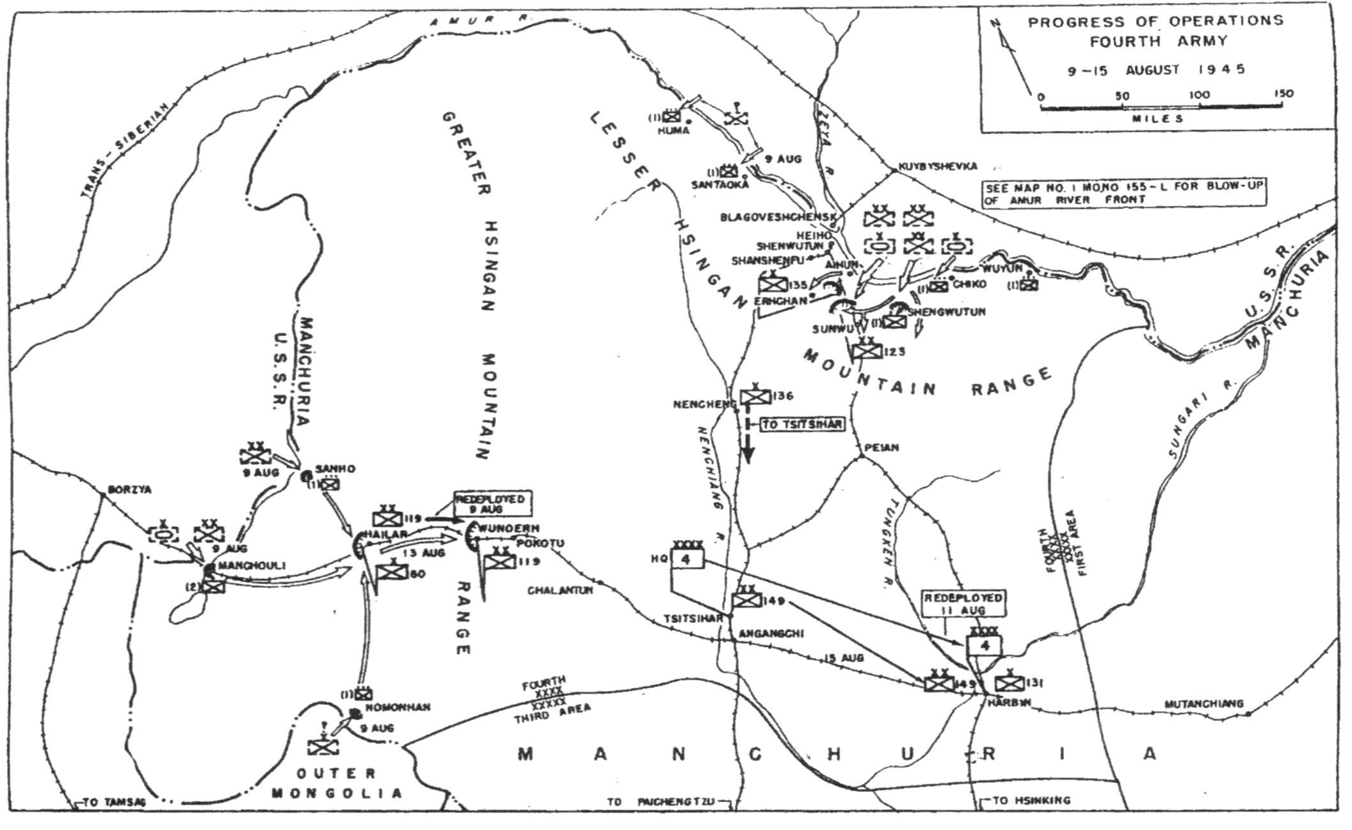

Map 45. Japanese 4th Army Defense, 9–15 August 1945 (Japanese View)

personal oath of fidelity they had made to the emperor. Genuine negotiations over a cease-fire between Soviet and Japanese forces began on 19 August, only after the Imperial High Command had settled the issue of personal oaths.[31]

Amidst the general confusion regarding the Japanese government's intentions, the *Stavka* ordered Vasilevsky's Far East Command to continue and even accelerate its offensive. The rationale was that individual Japanese units continued to resist actively, either in defiance of their government's orders or in ignorance of those orders.[32] While the partially implemented cease-fire order and the impact of the Soviet offensive paralyzed the Japanese Army, the Soviets moved to cement their control over all of Manchuria.

The forces of Malinovsky's Trans-Baikal Front had crossed the Grand Khingan Mountains in all sectors by 14 August. Having accomplished his immediate missions, the next day Malinovsky ordered his forces to advance to capture the ultimate objectives of the campaign, the cities of Mukden and Changchun, and, in addition, the towns of Kalgan, Chihfeng, and Tsitsihar, all by day's end on 23 August.[33]

The Trans-Baikal Front's offensive resumed on 15 August without a halt. That day, Pliev's Soviet–Mongolian Cavalry-Mechanized Group, which was still advancing in two columns along widely separated routes, encountered strong resistance at Changpei, 25 miles (40 kilometers) west of Kalgan, from the Inner Mongolian 3d, 5th, and 7th Cavalry Divisions. The forward detachment of Pliev's southernmost column, the 27th Motorized Rifle Brigade, attempted to dislodge the Mongolians with an assault from the march but failed to do so. Pliev then concentrated and reinforced his southern column, defeated the Inner Mongolian forces in two days of heavy fighting, captured 1,635 prisoners, and occupied the city. Among the prisoners, most of which were from the 3d and 7th Cavalry Divisions, was De Ban, the Inner Mongolian puppet ruler.[34]

On 18 August Pliev's group reached the outskirts of Kalgan. Although the Japanese High Command had announced the capitulation of the Kwantung Army only hours before, the defenders of the fortified region northwest of Kalgan did not end their resistance until 21 August. Pliev's victorious Mongolian and Soviet cavalrymen and tankers ceremoniously crossed the Great Wall of China and proceeded toward Peking, uniting on the march with units of the Communist Chinese 8th Route Army. The forces of Mao Tse Tung's Communist Chinese government had been operating in northern China both against Japanese forces and the forces of the Nationalist Chinese government of Chiang Kai-shek. Soon after the Soviet Army conquered Manchuria, they would turn the captured Japanese weaponry and equipment over to the Communist Chinese and provide the Communists an ideal base from which to operate against the Nationalists.

While Pliev's forces were nearing the western approaches to Peking, Danilov's 17th Army continued its advance toward Chihfeng, all the while hindered more by water shortages and the intense heat and sandy, dune-covered terrain conditions than by the virtually non-existent Japanese resistance. During the march, Danilov's soldiers sustained themselves on 7–10 ounces (200–300) grams of water per person and 1.32 gallons (5 liters) of water per horse. After a difficult march of 56 miles (90 kilometers), on 16 August Danilov's forces brushed aside light opposition by elements of the Japanese 108th Division and occupied Chihfeng the following day. Subsequently, Danilov's forces advanced toward the coast of the Yellow Sea, occupying Linguan, Pingchuan, and finally Shanhaikuan on the coast opposite the Liaotung Peninsula.

Managarov's 53d Army, previously in the Trans-Baikal Front's second echelon behind the 6th Guards Tank Army, advanced into the yawning gap between the 17th and 6th Guards Tank Armies on 15 August. Its mission was to capture the city of Kailu and move forward smartly to the coast of the Liaotung Gulf. Managarov's forces advanced almost totally unhindered and occupied Kailu, Chaoyang, Fuhsin, and Gushanbeitseifu on 1 September, long after the Japanese surrender. Within hours the army's forward detachments occupied the Chinchou area on the Gulf of Liaotung.

Kravchenko's 6th Guards Tank Army continued its march on 15 August along two axes opposed by decaying elements of the 63d and 117th Japanese Infantry Divisions and scattered Manchukuoan cavalry forces. While Katkov's 7th Mechanized Corps moved eastward toward Changchun, Volkov's 9th Guards Mechanized Corps and Savel'ev's 5th Guards Tank Corps advanced directly southeastward toward Mukden. A distance of up to 62 miles (100 kilometers) now separated the two forces from one another, and the corps' forward detachments operated an average of 62 miles (100 kilometers) in front of the corps' main forces. In the most extreme instance, the 9th Guards Mechanized Corps' 14th Separate Motorcycle Battalion ranged almost 124 miles (200 kilometers) in advance of its parent corps. Reconnaissance units (primarily motorcycle battalions), assisted by flights of PO-2 reconnaissance aircraft, filled the yawning gap between Kravchenko's two corps and their forward detachments.[35]

During this pursuit phase of the offensive, the forward detachments and reconnaissance units captured key objectives to facilitate the main forces' advance. For example, the 7th Mechanized Corps' reconnaissance detachment captured the town of Taoan by a surprise attack, and the 5th Guards Mechanized Corps' reconnaissance detachment seized the airfield and bridge at Tungliao, also virtually without a fight.

Hereafter, the march became nearly administrative in nature, as the defending Japanese forces simply melted away along their path. On 16 August the forward detachments of 5th Guards Tank Corps and 9th Guards Mechanized Corps secured Tungliao and Kailu, respectively. Three days later, the main body of the two mobile corps closed in on the two cities. After seizing Tungliao,

Savel'ev's tank corps and Volkov's mechanized corps marched southward in single corps columns along the railroad bed toward Mukden. The forward detachments from the two corps of Kravchenko's tank army occupied both Changchun and Mukden on 21 August, two days after Soviet air-landed assault detachments reached the airfields at both cities.

One air assault detachment consisting of 225 men had landed at Mukden airfield on 19 August, and the second, made up of 200 men, had landed on the same day at Changchun. Both greeted Japanese forces willing and eager to surrender. Upon its arrival at Mukden, the 6th Guards Tank Army accepted the surrender of Japanese forces and liberated American and British prisoners-of-war that the Japanese had kept imprisoned in camps near the city.[36]

Because of the continuing shortage of fuel, all of the 6th Guards Tank Army's subsequent movements to Port Arthur and the port of Darien took place only by rail.[37] Two tank brigades of the 5th Guards Tank Corps left the railroad station at Mukden on 22 August and headed for Port Arthur. Simultaneously, small assault detachments of about 250 men each air landed at airfields in Port Arthur and Darien (Dal'nyi), where they greeted Kravchenko's lead tank brigade when it arrived on 24 August.

The bulk of Liudnikov's 39th Army continued its advance along the railroad from Wangyemiao to Changchun on 16 August, leaving sizeable elements of the army in positions along the lines of communications to clean up bypassed Japanese and Manchukuoan forces. Late in the day, the main force forward detachment of the army reached and captured Taonan, while other army forces engaged fragmented Japanese units on both sides of the road and railroad from Halung-Arshaan to Wangyemiao, repelling repeated desperate Japanese counterattacks northwest of Solun.

By this time, both divisions of Popov's 94th Rifle Corps had rejoined the 39th Army in its main area of operations. Zaretsky's 358th Rifle Division of Popov's rifle corps played an instrumental role in the reduction of the last isolated Japanese positions at Halung-Arshaan, and after crossing the Grand Khingan Mountains at Tartu Pass, Kushnarenko's 221st Rifle Division turned south and engaged elements of the Japanese 107th Infantry Division north of Wangyemiao. The main body of Liudnikov's army (the 113th Rifle and 5th Guards Rifle Corps) concentrated at Taonan on 17 August and, the following day the army's forces entrained for movement to Changchun and, from there, southward to the Liaotung Peninsula.

Popov's 94th Rifle Corps, now responsible for mopping up Japanese resistance in the army rear area, reverted to *front* reserve, with its headquarters near Wangyemiao. The shattered remnants of the Japanese 107th Infantry Division continued to resist the 94th Rifle Corps through the remainder of August. However, on 30 August the Japanese division's thoroughly frustrated commander finally surrendered the remnants of his force, a total of 7,858 men, to Kushnarenko's 221st Rifle Division at Tailai, southwest of Tsitsihar.[38]

After 24 August, the 39th Army followed Kravchenko's tank army into the Liaotung peninsula. Liudnikov's forces ended the campaign by capturing Yingkou, on the northern shore of the Liaotung Gulf, Hsinpin, and Antung (Tantung) on the Yalu River.

Heavy Japanese resistance continued in the sector of Luchinsky's 36th Army, both in and around the Hailar Fortified Region and along the road and rail line southeastward through the Grand Khingan Mountains to Pokotu. Assisted by torrential August rains, the Japanese 119th Infantry Division vigorously defended Pokotu, delaying the advance of Petrov's 2d Rifle Corps from 15 to 17 August. However, Petrov's forces, assisted by Kurnosov's 205th Tank Brigade, finally overcame Japanese resistance in the town on 17 August and advanced rapidly southward and occupied the railroad station at Chalantun (Putehachi). The following day, Japanese forces in the entire region began laying down their arms. Reportedly, Luchinsky's army took 8,438 Japanese prisoners-of-war at Pokotu and another 985 at Chalantun.

The 36th Army's movement from Chalantun to Tsitsihar was unopposed and largely administrative in nature. The army occupied its ultimate objective of Tsitsihar on 19 August and accepted the surrender of 6,000 more Japanese troops.[39] However, deep in the 36th Army's rear, the Japanese forces surrounded at Hailar continued to resist fanatically. Using heavy artillery, the rifle divisions of Revunenkov's 86th Rifle Corps systematically reduced enemy strongholds in the hills northwest and southwest of the city. Position after position fell under heavy artillery, sapper, and infantry assault. Revunenkov's forces finally snuffed out the last Japanese resistance at Hailar on 18 August, when the remaining garrison of 3,827 men surrendered.[40]

CONCLUSIONS

The offensive by Malinovsky's Trans-Baikal Front managed to fulfill its assigned missions well ahead of Vasilevsky's schedule. For all practical purposes, organized Japanese resistance to the *front's* advance ceased after 18 August. From that time forward, the *front's* forces simply gathered up tens of thousands of prisoners-of-war, disarmed Japanese units, and conducted administrative movements to occupy the remaining areas of central and southern Manchuria.

The Trans-Baikal Front's success in the Khingan–Mukden offensive operation was due primarily to the audacious Soviet employment of maneuver and the lackluster passive Japanese response. The Japanese defenders were the least prepared to resist and hence most surprised in western Manchuria. Compounding their erroneous assumption that it was impossible for Soviet forces to attack massively in the west, the Japanese failed to plan any effective defense in the region.

Worse still from their perspective, the Japanese failed to place any force whatsoever in the passes through the Grand Khingan Mountains. Their failure to do so negated the mountains' value as a potentially formidable if not utterly insurmountable obstacle. Even after the Japanese detected Soviet forward movement in that region, the responsible Japanese commands deliberately chose to abandon any defense of the mountains and, instead, withdraw their units to central Manchuria, where they mistakenly thought they could contest the Soviet advance. By the time that Soviet armor was in the central valley, it was abundantly clear that further resistance was futile.

The Japanese forces left isolated in the border regions, such as the 107th Infantry Division at Halung-Arshaan and Wuchakou and the 80th Independent Mixed Brigade at Hailar, were overwhelmed, isolated, or bypassed, and ultimately destroyed. However, their heroic but futile resistance did tie down Soviet forces and slow the Soviet advance in northern Manchuria. Other Japanese units that withdrew into Manchuria, such as the 117th Infantry Division or those units already deployed in central Manchuria, never offered significant resistance to the Soviet advance. By the time the Trans-Baikal Front's forces reached Kalgan, Taonan, and Wangyemaio, tentative cease-fire proposals and the prospects for impending Japanese surrender preempted further credible Japanese defense.

Had the Japanese commands positioned their forces to defend the narrow Khingan Mountain passes, even minimally, their defense could have been far more effective. Even small forces deployed in the passes through the Grand Khingan Mountain west of Lupei and Tapanshang could have severely disrupted the Soviet advance. Given the Trans-Baikal Front's severe fuel shortages, Japanese forces deployed to defend Lupei and Tuchuan in any strength could have seriously disrupted the advance of Kravchenko's 6th Guards Tank Army at a critical juncture. The stout resistance Japanese units displayed at Hailar and Halung-Arshaan clearly demonstrated what credible resistance could accomplish. In addition, the tenacious defense by the 119th Infantry Division in the Grand Khingan passes between Yakoshih to Pokotu vividly illustrated how effective the defense of the mountain passes could be if conducted by a sizeable and determined enough force.

In time, however, despite where and how Japanese forces defended, the overwhelming power of the Trans-Baikal Front's advance was bound to prevail. The audacious offensive maneuver by Kravchenko, Pliev, and the Trans-Baikal Front army commanders and the wholly uncoordinated, indecisive, and often insubordinate actions of the Japanese Kwantung Army and Third Area Army commands predetermined the outcome and permitted Soviet forces to meet and exceed their most optimistic offensive timetable. The Trans-Baikal Front's offensive proved to be the 'stake in the Kwantung Army's heart'. Hence, the dramatic scope of Malinovsky's victory both conditioned and paralleled the Far East Command's strategic triumph in Manchuria as a whole.

NOTES

1. *IVMV*, 11: 212.
2. Ibid.
3. Vnotchenko, *Pobeda*, 174.
4. I. A. Pliev, *Konets kvantunskoi armii* [The end of the Kwantung Army] (Ordzhonikidze Izdatel'stvo: 'IN' Ordzhonikidze, 1969), 54.
5. Zakharov, *Finale*, 83–6.
6. I. E. Krupchenko, ed., *Sovetskie tankovie voiska 1941–45* [Soviet tank forces, 1941–45] (Moscow: Voenizdat, 1973), 312–13; Vnotchenko, *Pobeda*, 175–6; and Antonov, *Nastuplenie 6-i gvardeiskoi tankovoi armii*, 18–20.
7. I. I. Liudnikov, *Cherez Bol'shoi Khingan* [Across the Grand Khingan] (Moscow: Voenizdat, 1967), 50–3.
8. Ibid.
9. *JM 155*, 83, 86, 104.
10. A. A. Luchinsky, 'Zabaikal'tsy na sopkakh Man'chzhurii' [Trans-Baikal troops in the hills of Manchuria], *VIZh*, No. 8 (August 1971), 70–1, and Vnotchenko, *Pobeda*, 177–8.
11. Luchinsky, 'Zabaikal'tsy', 70.
12. *JM 155*, 185.
13. *JM 154*, 10–18.
14. Ibid., and Vnotchenko, *Pobeda*, 146–7.
15. For details on the crossing of the mountains, see Antonov, *Nastuplenie 6-i gvardeiskoi tankovoi armii*, 21–2.
16. Ibid., 22–3.
17. Vnotchenko, *Pobeda*, 151.
18. Antonov, *Nastuplenie 6-i gvardeiskoi tankovoi armii*, 25.
19. Vnotchenko, *Pobeda*, 184–7. Transportation and maintenance problems during the 6th Guards Tank Army's passage through the Grand Khingan Mountains are covered in N. Kireev and A. Syropiatov, 'Tekhnicheskoe obespechenie 6 i gvardeiskoi tankovoi armii v Khingano-Mukdenskoi operatsii' [Technical Support of the 6th Guards Tank Army in the Khingan-Mukden operation], *VIZh*, No. 3 (March 1977), 36–40. The most thorough accounts of the 6th Guards Tank Army's exploits are in I. E. Krupchenko, '6-ia gvardeiskaia tankovaia armiia v Khingano–Mukdenskoi operatsii' [The 6th Guards Tank Army in the Khingan–Mukden operation], *VIZh*, No. 12 (December 1962); and G. T. Zavizion and P. A. Kornyushin, *I na Tikham Okeane* [And to the Pacific Ocean] (Moscow: Voenizdat, 1967).
20. *JM 156* (Pt. A) map 1, (Pt. F) map 2, 102–9.
21. Liudnikov, *Cherez*, 59, and Vnotchenko, *Pobeda*, 176–7, 188.
22. Liudnikov, *Cherez*, 74.
23. Luchinsky, 'Zabaikal'tsy', 70–2; Vnotchenko, *Pobeda*, 190; *IVMV*, 11:224; and I. V. Shikin and B. G. Sapozhnikov, *Podvig na dal'nem-vostochnykh rubezhakh* [Victory on the far eastern borders] (Moscow: Voenizdat, 1975), 128–31.
24. Pliev, *Konets*, 91–100, and Vnotchenko, *Pobeda*, 192–4.
25. Vnotchenko, *Pobeda*, 194–5.
26. Ibid.
27. Ibid. Aviation support of 6th Guards Tank Army is covered in I. Sukhomlin, 'Osobennosti vzaimodeistviia 6-i gvardeiskoi tankovoi armii s aviatsiei v Man'chzhurskoi operatsii' [Characteristics of the cooperation of the 6th Guards Tank Army with aviation in the Manchurian operation], *VIZh*, No. 4 (April 1972), 86–91.

28. Liudnikov, *Cherez*, 63, and Vnotchenko, *Pobeda*, 196–7.
29. Liudnikov, *Cherez*, 63, and *JM 155*, 108.
30. Luchinsky, 'Zabaikal'tsy', 72; Vnotchenko, *Pobeda*, 197–8.
31. Shtemenko, 'Iz istorii razgroma', 56–60; Vnotchenko, *Pobeda*, 242–4, 277–8; Zakharov, *Finale*, 145–6, 163; *IVMV*, 11: 247–53; and cf. *JM 154*, 18–26.
32. Vnotchenko, *Pobeda*, 279.
33. Ibid., 245–6.
34. Ibid. and I. A. Pliev, *Cherez Gobi i Khingan* [Across the Gobi and Khingans] (Moscow: Voenizdat, 1965), 106–15.
35. Vnotchenko, *Pobeda*, 248.
36. Ibid., 281.
37. Ibid., 280–1.
38. Liudnikov, *Cherez*, 101.
39. Vnotchenko, *Pobeda*, 218; Luchinsky, 'Zabaikal'tsy'.
40. Vnotchenko, *Pobeda*, 281.

8

The 1st Far Eastern Front's Harbin–Kirin Offensive Operation

THE 5TH AND 1ST RED BANNER ARMIES' ADVANCE TO MUTANCHIANG

The forces of Marshal Meretskov's 1st Far Eastern Front confronted significantly different conditions from those faced by their counterparts in Malinovsky's Trans-Baikal Front. First, Meretskov's operational sector, which extended from the town of Iman on the Ussuri River north of Lake Khanka to the northern Korean border where the Tumen River flowed into the Sea of Japan, was shorter than Malinovsky's sector. Second, and even more important, the Japanese border districts in eastern Manchuria were more heavily fortified than those located in western Manchuria. Many of the fortified regions in eastern Manchuria were large defensive complexes made up of sophisticated reinforced concrete structures and firing positions. Although the Japanese manned these defenses with relatively light covering forces such as border guards and fortification units, the fortified regions were formidable obstacles that protected virtually every trafficable axis of advance and communications route from the Soviet border into eastern Manchuria.

The most important of these Japanese fortified regions were located at Jaoho and Hutou along the Ussuri River north of Lake Khanka and at Suifenho, Tungning, and Hunchun, along the heavily wooded border between Lake Khanka and the Yellow Sea. The Japanese First Area Army's 3d and 5th Armies defended the eastern Manchurian border with small covering units and planned to concentrate the bulk of their forces in strong successive defensive lines deployed in depth up to 50 miles (80 kilometers) west of the border (see Maps 46–51).

The Far East Command assigned Meretskov's forces a series of formidable offensive tasks. First, his armies had to penetrate Japanese border defenses rapidly along multiple axes. Second, they had to do so by traversing terrain that the Japanese believed was unsuited for the movement of large military forces, particularly mobile armored and mechanized forces. Third, once they had overcome, bypassed, or otherwise neutralized the Japanese fortified defenses, they had to advance quickly into the depths of eastern Manchuria, preempt Japanese establishment of viable defenses west of the border, reach the Mutan River line, and then exploit to Harbin and Kirin.

The timing of Meretskov's offensive required his forces to begin their assault during the hours of darkness and in the worst weather conditions, at a time when inundating thunderstorms caused by the August monsoon routinely soaked the forests and hills of eastern Manchuria. When Meretskov's forces attacked early on 9 August, heavy rains lasted from just after midnight until 0600 hours the next morning. While these rains provided some cover for the advancing Soviet troops and enabled them to take many of the Japanese defenders and border positions by surprise, it also rendered all of the planned air preparation and much of the artillery preparation superfluous because the aircraft could not fly, and the artillery fires could not be observed. Consequently, Meretskov's forces employed artillery preparations only against the Japanese fortified region at and around Hutou in the northern part of the 35th Army's sector.

At 0030 hours on 9 August, the reconnaissance parties and detachments of Meretskov's deployed armies advanced across the border in the heavy thunderstorms to reconnoiter and whenever possible overcome Japanese forward security and observation posts. Assault detachments and advanced battalions from army first echelon rifle divisions followed the reconnaissance forces at 0100 hours to perform the task of capturing specific Japanese fortified outposts and strong points and cutting lanes through minefields and defensive obstacles through which their parent main forces could safely advance. At 0830 hours, the lead rifle regiments of the attacking army's first echelon rifle divisions lunged forward to begin the main attack.

Colonel General N. I. Krylov's 5th Army led Meretskov's offensive by conducting the *front's* main attack directly into the center of Japanese defenses along the eastern Manchurian border.[1] With three rifle corps abreast (the 17th Rifle Corps on the left, the 72d Rifle Corps in the center, and the 65th Rifle Corps on the right), the attack struck the front and northern flank of the Japanese Volynsk (Kuanyuentai) Center of Resistance, which represented the northern portion of what the Japanese termed the Suifenho Fortified Region (see Map 52).

By Soviet definition, a fortified region consisted of several distinct centers of resistance, each of which was made up of fortified points, pillboxes, and an associated trench system. A single infantry battalion from the Japanese 124th Infantry Division's 273d Infantry Regiment defended the Volynsk Center of Resistance (see Map 53). On the left flank of Krylov's army, troops from the 105th Fortified Region and assault engineer units attacked the

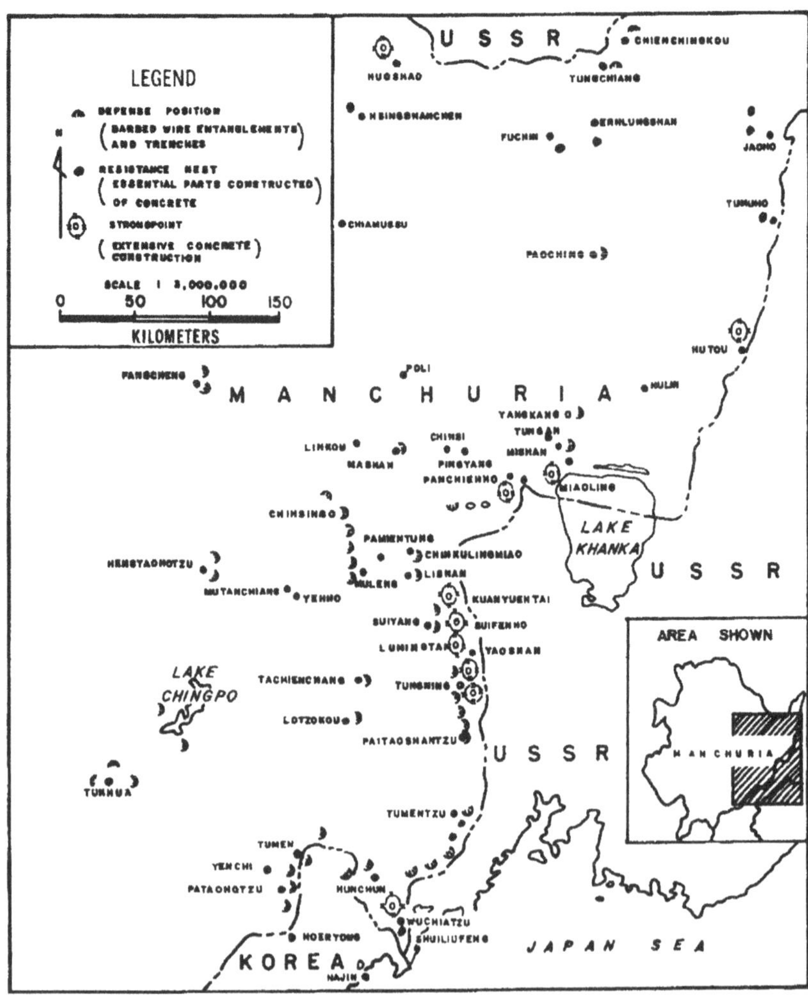

Map 46. Japanese Fortified Positions in Eastern Manchuria (Japanese View)

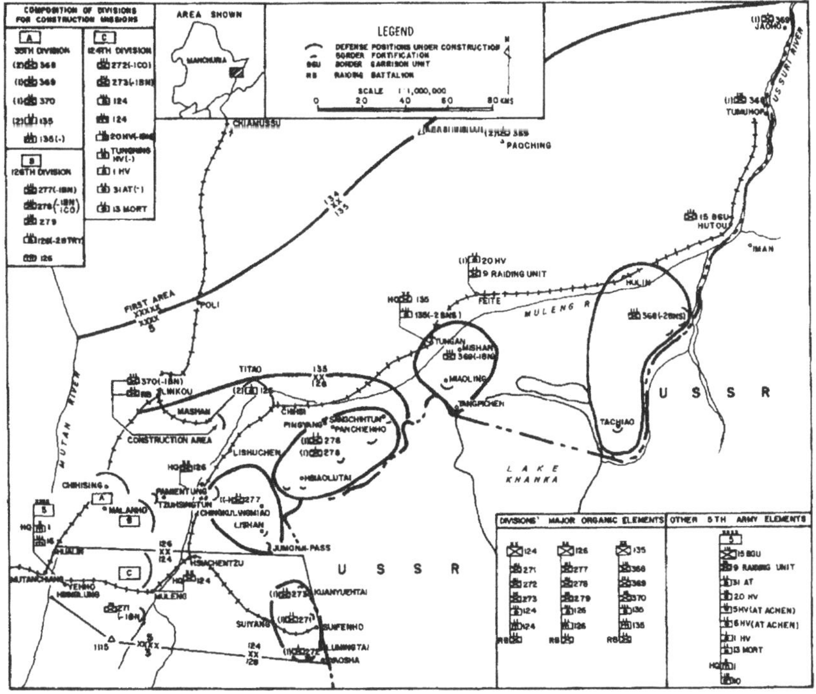

Map 47. Japanese 5th Army Defense (Japanese View)

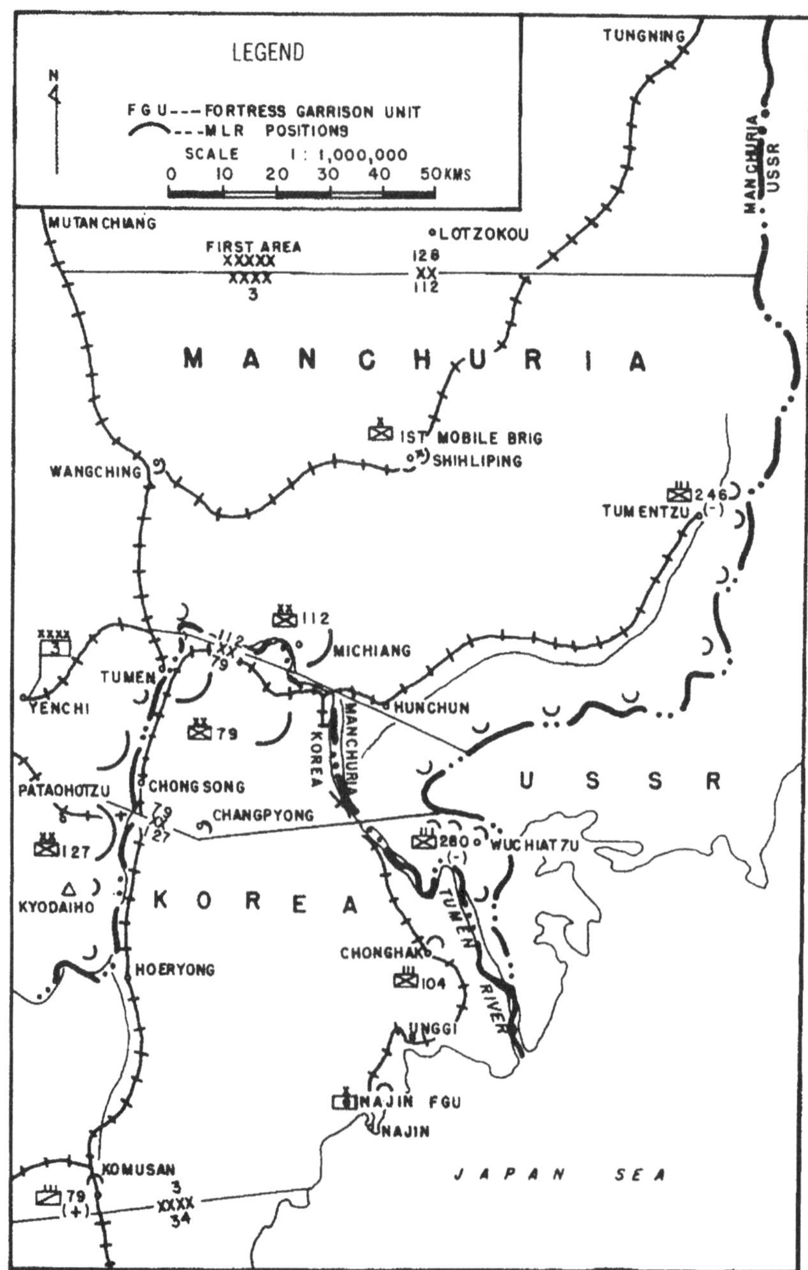

Map 48. Japanese 3d Army Defense (Japanese View)

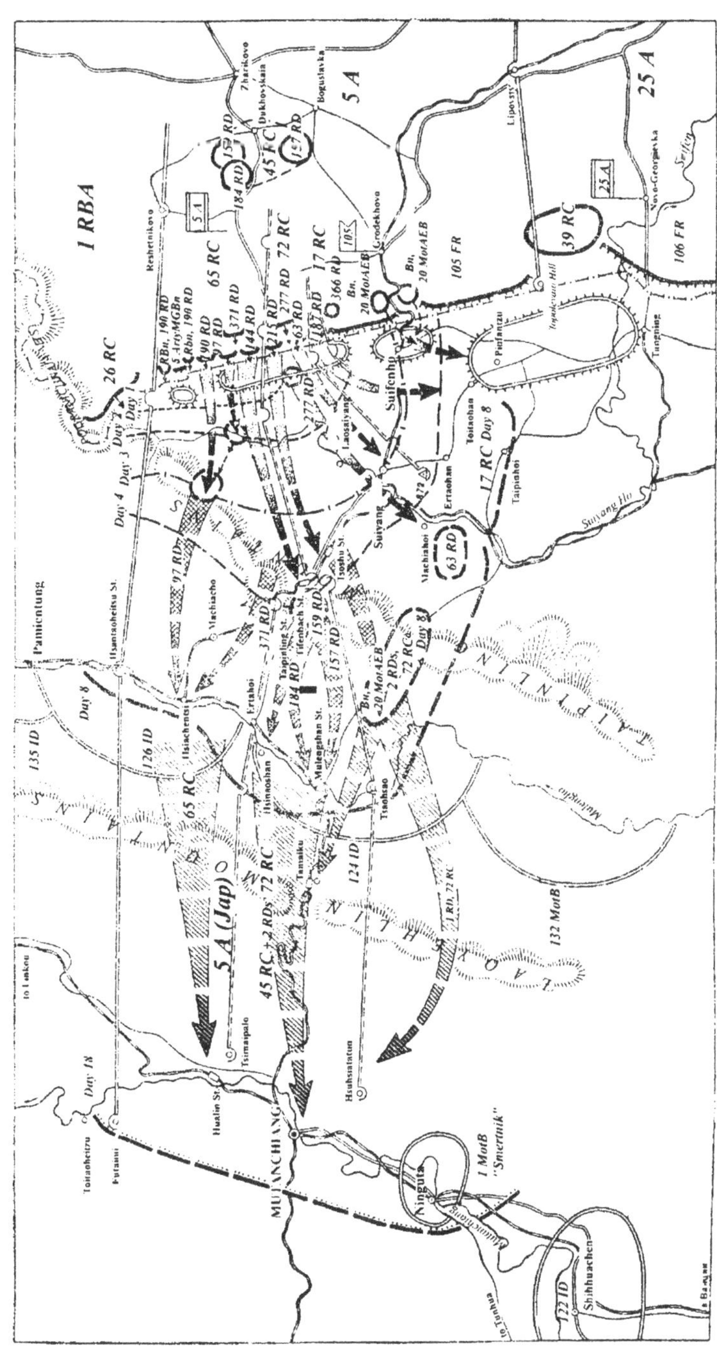

Map 49. Soviet 5th Army Offensive Plan

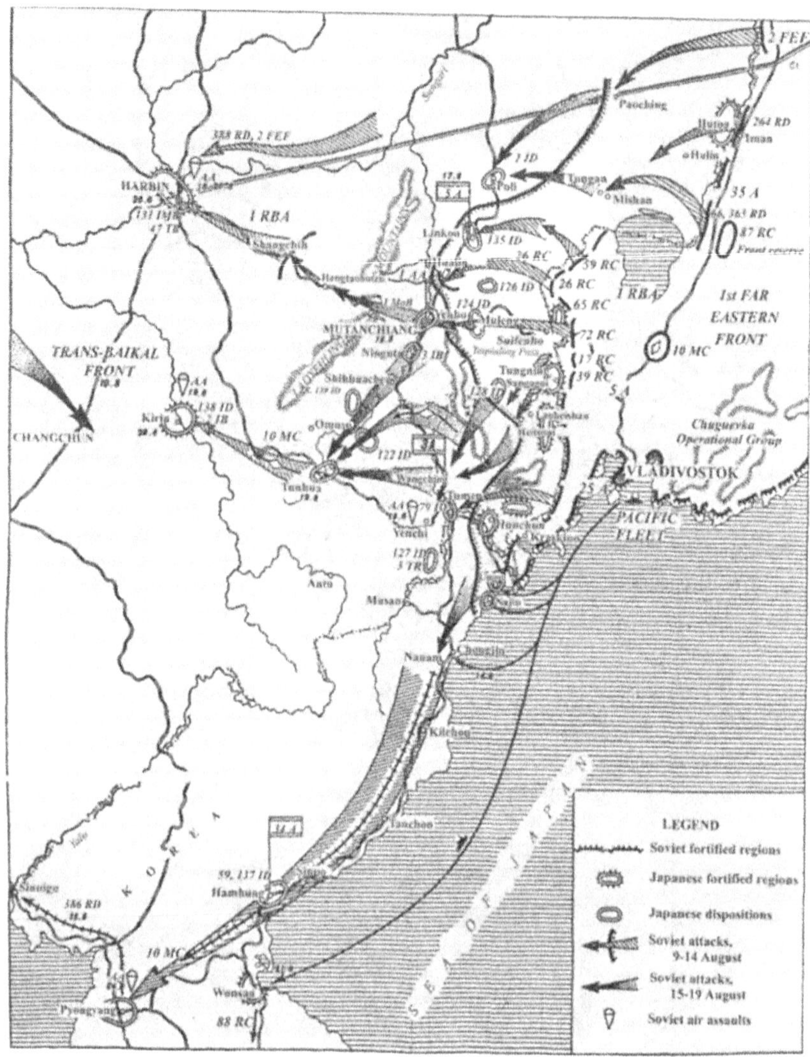

Map 50. Soviet 1st Far Eastern Front Operations, 9 August–2 September 1945

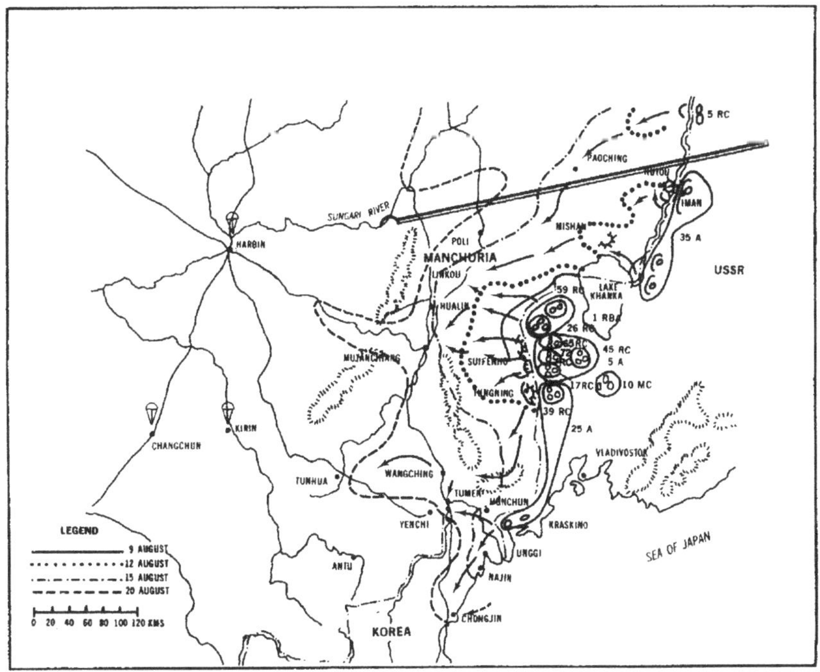

Map 51. Soviet 1st Far Eastern Front Operations, 9–20 August 1945

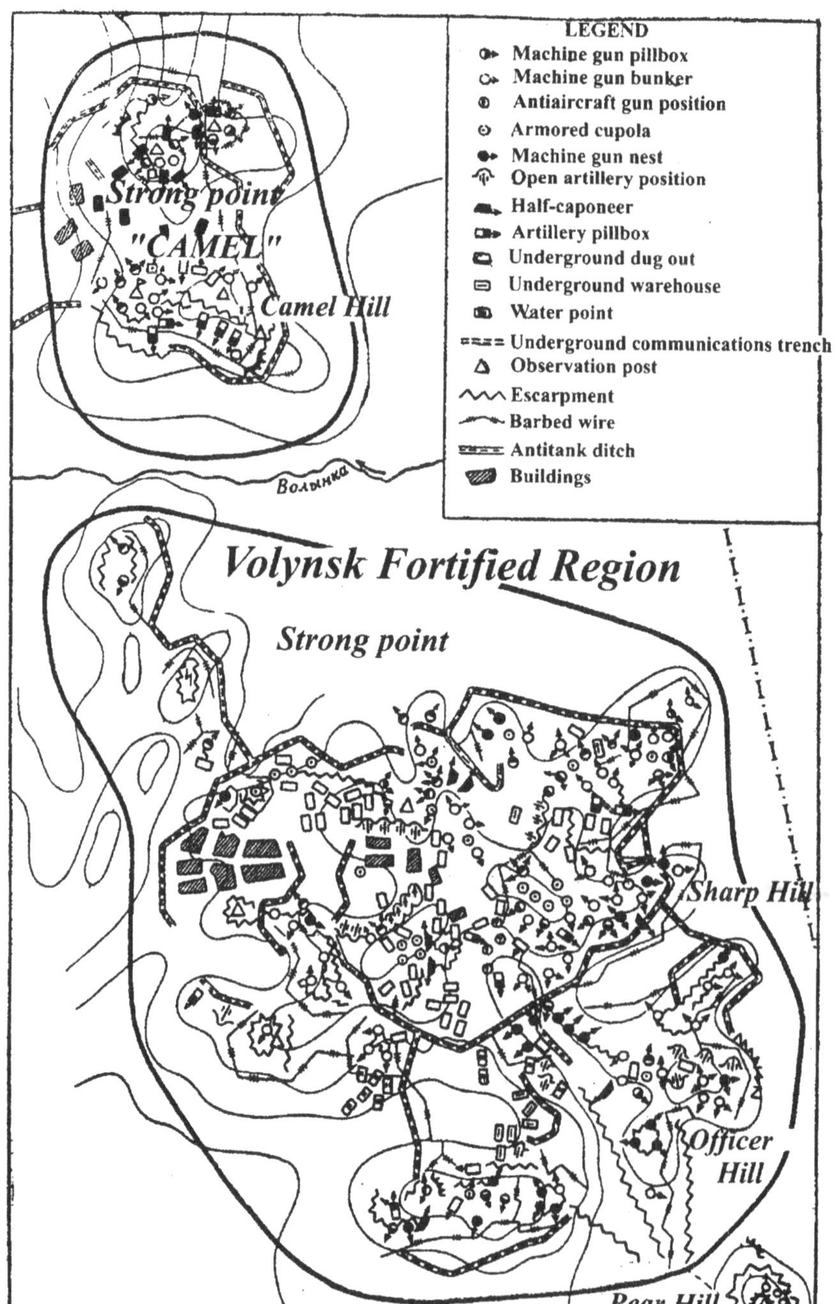

Map 52. Japanese Volynsk Center of Resistance of Suifenho Fortified Region

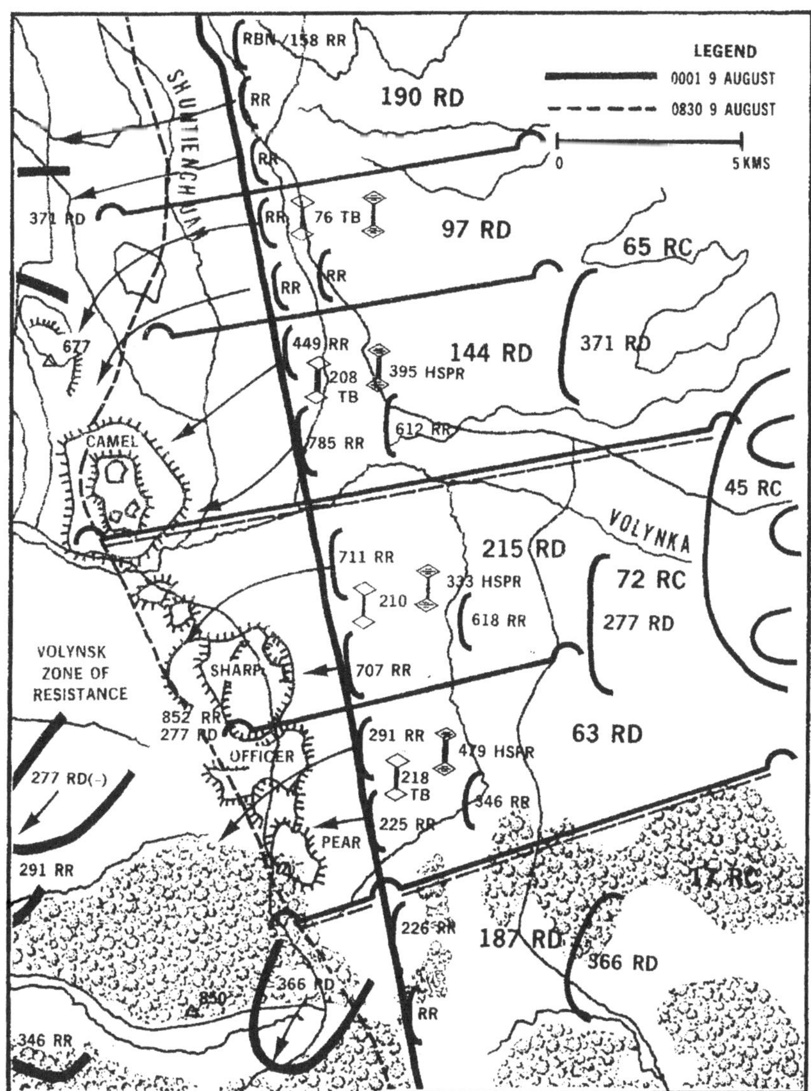

Map 53. Soviet 5th Army Main Attack Sector, 0100–0830 hours, 9 August 1945

Suifenho Center of Resistance, which was defended by an infantry battalion from the 124th Infantry Division's 371st Infantry Regiment.

The reconnaissance forces and assault detachments assigned to the lead rifle regiments' advanced battalions attacked at 0100 hours and, in four hours of complex fighting in heavy rain, thoroughly disrupted the Japanese forward defenses by capturing many of the forward outposts and observation points, often by surprise and without firing a shot. Promptly at 0830 hours, Krylov's first echelon rifle regiments went into action hard on the heels of the assault detachments with tanks and self-propelled guns from attached tank and self-propelled artillery brigades and regiments in support. On Krylov's main attack axis, one tank brigade and one heavy self-propelled artillery regiment supported each of his first echelon rifle divisions.

Once begun, the attack developed at breakneck speed. In the center sector of Krylov's army, the rifle divisions and supporting armor of Major General A. I. Kazartsev's 72d Rifle Corps assaulted and captured some key positions in the Volynsk Center of Resistance. After leaving forces from his second echelon to reduce the remaining positions, Kazartsev's rifle corps penetrated 2.5–3.1 miles (4–5 kilometers) deep into the rear of the Suifenho Fortified Region. At 1500 hours on 9 August, the forward rifle divisions of his rifle corps lunged westward into the Japanese rear area toward Laotsaiying, each with a tank brigade in the lead (see Map 54).

On the right flank of Krylov's 5th Army, Major General G. H. Perekrestov's 65th Rifle Corps enveloped the northern portion of the Volynsk Center of Resistance. Leaving second echelon forces to contend with isolated Japanese units in his rear, Perekrestov's rifle corps advanced rapidly northwestward toward Machiacho Station, led by a tank brigade that was serving as his forward detachment.

Meanwhile, Major General A. R. Kopychko's 17th Rifle Corps, deployed on the 5th Army's left flank, attacked through a weak sector of Japanese defenses north of Suifenho and swung southwestward around the Northeastern Center of Resistance of the Suifenho Fortified Region. At the same time, assault engineer forces and troops from the 105th Fortified Region assaulted and seized the critical railroad tunnels near Suifenho town along the main rail line into eastern Manchuria.[2]

By nightfall on 9 August, the three rifle corps of Krylov's 5th Army had torn a gaping 22-mile (35-kilometer) wide hole in the Japanese border defenses and had advanced 10–13 miles (16–22 kilometers) deep into the Japanese rear area. Major General N. I. Ivanov's 45th Rifle Corps, deployed in the second echelon of Krylov's 5th Army, followed the advancing forces through the breech. To the rear, the second echelon rifle regiments from each of Krylov's forward rifle divisions, which were reinforced by sappers and self-propelled artillery pieces, liquidated the remaining bypassed and encircled Japanese strong points in the Volynsk Center of Resistance and

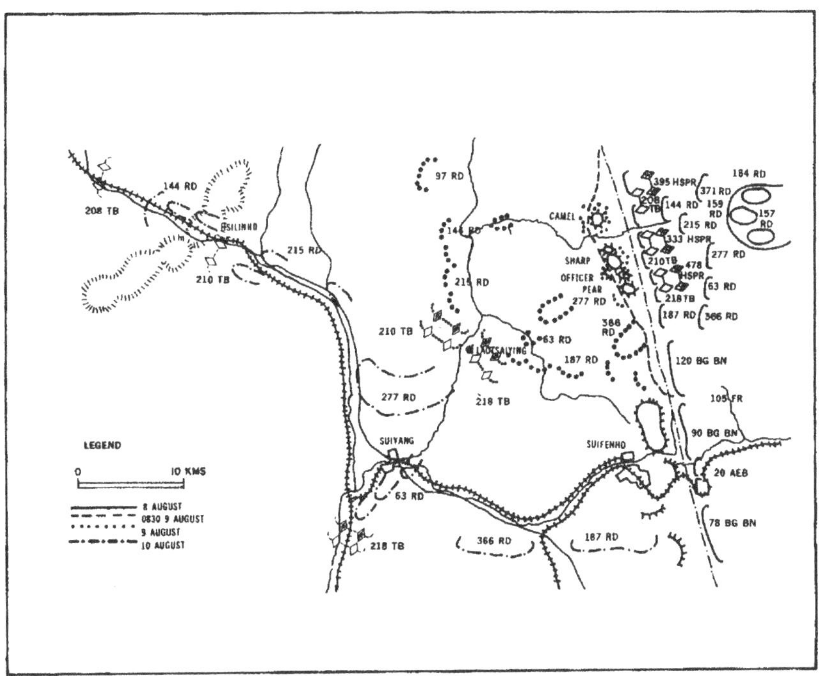

Map 54. Soviet 5th Army Advance, 9–10 August 1945

around Suifenho and Lumintai to the south, a process that they completed within three days. Japanese reserve forces deployed at Suiyang, located to the rear of the fortified regions along the border, withdrew quickly to the Muleng area where they hoped to reinforce the 124th Infantry Division's main defensive line.

Krylov's forces advanced rapidly westward and southward on 10 August, plunging deep into the rear areas of the other Japanese fortified regions in the region (see Map 55). In response, the Japanese 5th Army ordered its 124th Infantry Division to conduct a general withdrawal into preplanned prepared defensive positions along a line extending north and southwest of the town of Muleng, where it was to resist and contain the 5th Army's advance (see Map 56).[3]

Over the course of 10 August, Krylov's forces advanced to a depth of from 11–19 miles (18–30 kilometers) and widened the penetration sector to 47 miles (75 kilometers). Led by a tank brigade serving as its forward detachment, the main force of Perekrestov's 65th Rifle Corps marched in column formation northwestward toward Machiacho Station. To the south, also marching in a column formation of rifle regiments led by a tank brigade, Kazartsev's 72d Rifle Corps advanced along the railroad line northwestward toward Hsiachengtzu on the Muleng River. On Krylov's left flank, Kopichko's 17th Rifle Corps advanced southward into the rear of the Japanese center of resistance at Lumintai to link up with the forces of the 25th Army's 39th Rifle Corps, which were advancing into this region from the south.

Reinforced by a tank brigade, the 72d Rifle Corps' 63d Rifle Division, commanded by Colonel A. I. Gordienko, swung southward and then northwestward toward Muleng in an attempt to envelop the withdrawing Japanese forces. As previously planned, at 1700 hours on 10 August, Meretskov detached Kopychko's 17th Rifle Corps from Krylov's 5th Army and subordinated it to Chistiakov's 25th Army.[4]

Krylov's forces continued their spectacular forward progress on 11 August, when the reinforced forward detachments of the 65th and 72d Rifle Corps reached the Muleng River, an objective they had been ordered to capture by the eighth day of the operation. Impressed by the 5th Army's progress, Meretskov immediately ordered Krylov to accelerate his advance on Mutanchiang, which the 5th Army was originally supposed to capture by the seventeenth day of the offensive.[5]

In response to Meretskov's order, Krylov formed a strong army forward detachment made up of Lieutenant Colonel V. P. Chaplygin's 76th Tank Brigade, a heavy self-propelled artillery regiment, and two rifle battalions, and dispatched them on a rapid dash westward along the road from Muleng to Mutanchiang. Chaplygin's forward detachment began its thrust overnight on 11–12 August, with the 5th Army's rifle divisions following in march column. On the morning of 12 August, the Sasaki Detachment, consisting

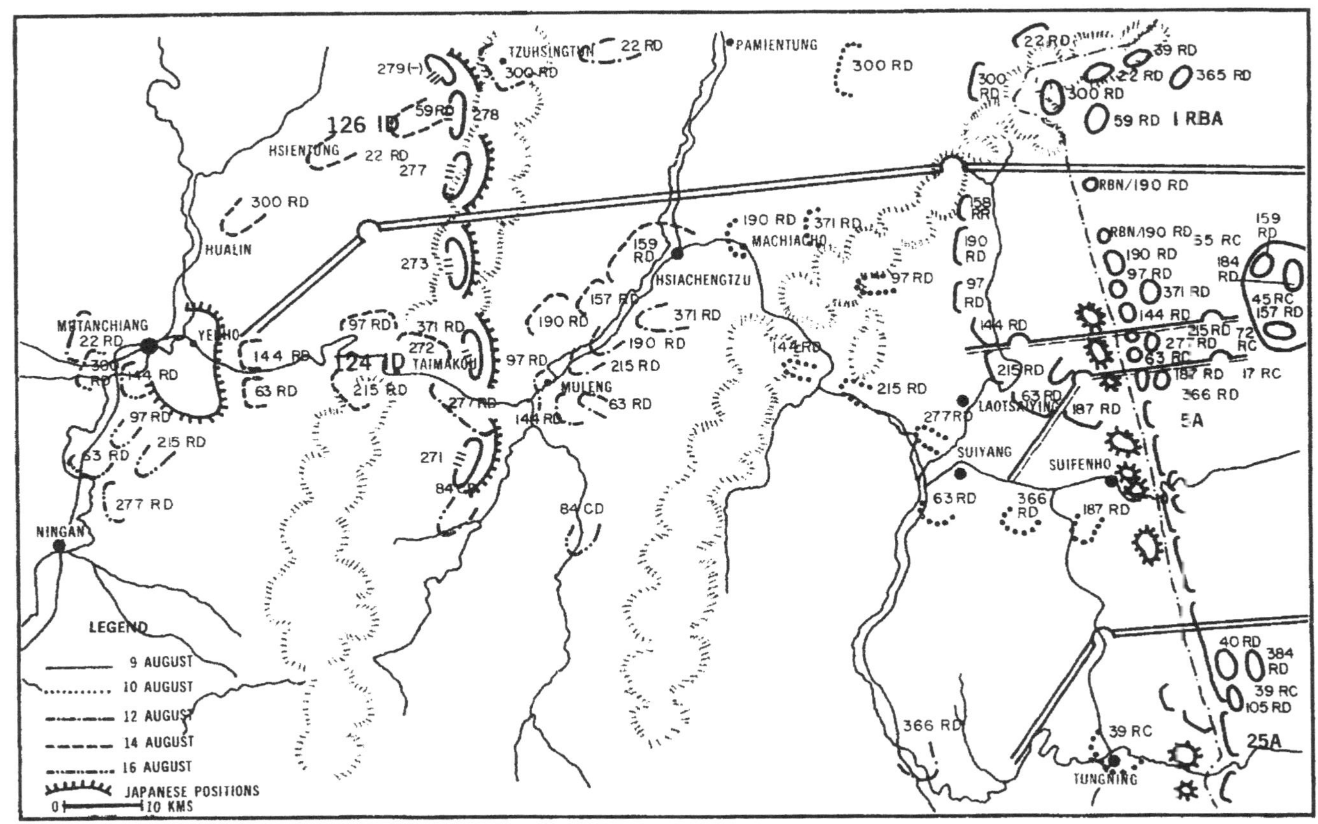

Map 55. Soviet 5th Army Advance to Mutanchiang, 9–12 August 1945

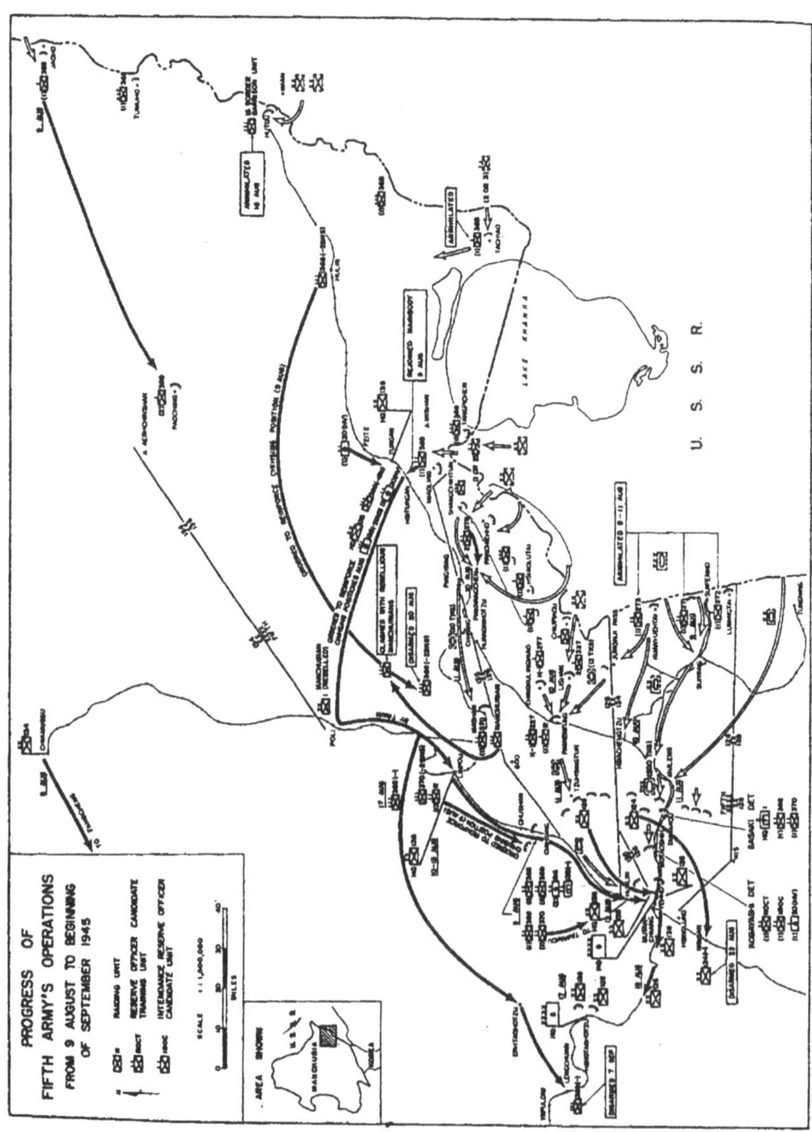

Map 56. Japanese 5th Army Defense, 9 August–2 September 1945 (Japanese View)

of two infantry battalions from the 135th Infantry Division, which were attached to the Japanese 124th Infantry Division, launched heavy counterattacks against Chaplygin's task force east of Tamakou, halting the small force and inflicting heavy casualties on it.[6] Krylov immediately dispatched reinforcements from Colonel N. T. Zorin's 144th and Major General A. K. Makar'ev's 97th Rifle Divisions, and, after a 30 minute artillery preparation, the 5th Army's forces carved a 2.5-mile (4-kilometer) swath through Japanese positions and continued their march toward Mutanchiang.

Krylov's forces continued their advance on 13 August, penetrating 18.6 miles (30 kilometers) deep in a 3–4.3-mile (5–7-kilometer) wide corridor along the road and rail line to Mutanchiang. Zorin's 144th and Gordienko's 63d Rifle Divisions, with tank brigades serving as forward detachments in the lead, spearheaded the advance. Krylov's remaining rifle divisions stretched out 37 miles (60 kilometers) to the east along the main road to the border and clearing the area north and south of the highway as they marched forward.

The battered, fragmented, and bypassed units of the Japanese 124th Infantry Division withdrew into the hills north of the highway in considerable confusion. These forces later infiltrated southwest through the hill country and surrendered to Soviet forces at Ningan, southwest of Mutanchiang, on 22 August.[7] Meanwhile, the Japanese 126th Infantry Division and part of the 135th Infantry Division, which were being pressured by the 1st Far Eastern Front's 1st Red Banner and 35th Armies, withdrew from their defensive positions north of 5th Army's advance sector and moved southwestward toward Mutanchiang, where they set up a defensive perimeter.

After repelling repeated Japanese harassing attacks by forces in platoon to battalion strength, at nightfall on 13 August, Krylov's forward forces approached the outer fortifications of Mutanchiang, having widened their advance corridor to 7.5–8.1 miles (12–13 kilometers).[8] The stage was now set for one of the few major set-piece battles to take place during the Soviet Manchurian offensive.

Colonel General A. P. Beloborodov's 1st Red Banner Army had the mission of supporting the 1st Far Eastern Front's main attack by advancing on the right (northern) flank of Krylov's 5th Army (see Map 55). The operational sector of Beloborodov's army extended from Krylov's right flank through the heavily forested mountainous region to the north and northwest and then eastward across the open country bordering the Tigra River valley to Lake Khanka. The Japanese defenses opposite the 1st Red Banner Army consisted of a string of security outposts manned in company and battalion strength by Japanese border guards units and elements of the 135th Infantry Division. In reality, the easternmost of these Japanese outposts were heavily fortified positions comprising the southern extension of the Japanese Mishan Fortified Region.[9]

Beloborodov concentrated the bulk of his forces in two rifle corps, Major General A. V. Skvortsov's 26th Rifle Corps, deployed on the army's left flank, and Major General V. A. Semenov's 59th Rifle Corps, positioned on the army's right flank, and ordered the two corps to deliver the army's main attack in a 10-mile (16-kilometer) sector on his army's left wing and center. In the remainder of his army's sector eastward to Lake Khanka, he deployed the reinforced 112th Fortified Region and the 6th Field Fortified Region.

The standard fortified region was a defensive formation consisting of a variable number of machine gun and artillery battalions, which normally performed economy-of-force defensive missions or fixed opposing forces during offensive operations. The field fortified region had the same general structure as a regular fortified region, with vehicles added to permit it to conduct limited mobile tactical operations.

The mission of Beloborodov's main attack force was to penetrate the 6–9.3 mile (10–15 kilometer) wide heavily forested, hilly region immediately in front of the army's sector and to develop the attack along two axes across relatively open country to capture Pamientung and Lishuchen on the Muleng River. Thereafter, the army was to advance southwestward toward Mutanchiang and northwestward toward Linkou. The two fortified regions on the army's right flank were to launch small-scale supporting attacks against Japanese fortifications and installations south of Mishan in concert with the forces of the 35th Army, which was to attack toward Mishan from the east. Eventually, the 1st Red Banner Army's forces were to link up with 5th Army forces at Mutanchiang and with 35th Army forces at Mishan and Linkou.[10]

The principal obstacle to the 1st Red Banner Army's advance was the heavily wooded and hilly terrain west of the border, which was now soaked from heavy rains. Japanese forces manned defenses just west of the border in scattered security outposts manned by platoons and companies and a few battalion-size defensive positions in the more open country 9.3–12.4 miles (15–20 kilometers) west of the border on the road to Pamientung. Since Beloborodov's advancing rifle divisions would have to construct corduroy roads through the forest as they advanced, they required heavy engineer support and had to advance in carefully organized march-column formation.

For example, in the sector of Skvortsov's 26th Rifle Corps, Major General A. P. Karnov's 300th and Major General N. K. Svirs' 22d Rifle Divisions led the advance, and in the sector of Semenov's 59th Rifle Corps, Colonel D. V. Makarov's 39th and Major General Ia. E. Timoshenko's 231st Rifle Divisions took the lead. Tank brigades followed each of the rifle corps' forward divisions with orders to take the lead as forward detachments after the two rifle corps completed their passage through the difficult terrain. Two more rifle divisions made up the advancing corps' second echelons.

Beloborodov's assault was timed to coincide with that of Krylov's 5th Army. Although heavy rains forced cancellation of the planned artillery preparation, reconnaissance detachments and assault groups led Beloborodov's attack at 0100 hours on 9 August, under illumination provided by massed searchlights.

The advanced battalions of the lead rifle divisions and the divisions' main forces followed closely behind advancing in multiple march column formations. The 300th Rifle Division advanced in three march-columns, the 22d Rifle Division in two columns, and the 39th Rifle Division in two.[11] The multiple march-columns constructed and widened the road as they advanced.[12]

By nightfall on 9 August, the forward elements of Beloborodov's lead rifle divisions had penetrated 3.1–3.7 miles (5–6 kilometers) deep into Manchuria and had crossed the first obstacle, the Shitou Ho (River) and half the forested region. Overnight on 9–10 August, the divisions' main forces closed on their advanced elements, and the tank brigades prepared to take the lead.

On the morning of 10 August, the arduous and intense road building continued. Late in the morning, the rifle divisions' main forces broke through to open country, and, taking the lead, the tank brigades pushed rapidly westward. In the sector of Skvortsov's 26th Rifle Corps, Colonel G. S. Anishchik's 257th Tank Brigade led the 300th Rifle Division's advance with Svirs' 22d Rifle Division following on its right flank. Lieutenant Colonel L. D. Krupetskoi's 75th Tank Brigade preceded the 59th Rifle Corps' 39th Rifle Division, followed by Colonel M. K. Gvozdikov's 365th Rifle Division.

After a short fight with elements of the Japanese 126th Infantry Division's 277th Infantry Regiment, Anishchik's tank brigade and Karnov's and Svirs' rifle divisions swept the resistance aside and captured portions of the town of Pamientung and the important bridge across the Muleng River at 2100 hours.[13] The 26th Rifle Corps' main body reached Pamientung on 11 August, after advancing 28 miles (45 kilometers) in three days. By the time Skvortsov's corps fully occupied the town, Anishchik's tank brigade and elements of Karnov's 300th Rifle Division were marching west and southwest in pursuit of withdrawing Japanese forces. To the north, Krupetskoi's 75th Tank Brigade duplicated Anishchik's feat by securing the bridge across the Muleng River at Lishuchen. The next morning, Makarov's 39th Rifle Division arrived in Lishuchen, and the general pursuit of Japanese forces toward Linkou began.

On the right flank of Beloborodov's 1st Red Banner Army, the forces of the 112th Fortified and 6th Field Fortified Regions, reinforced by a rifle regiment from the 59th Rifle Corps, stormed several Japanese border positions defended by elements of the Japanese 135th Infantry Division's 369th Infantry Regiment and slowly advanced northward toward Mishan. At nightfall on 11 August, these forces crossed the Muleng River south of Mishan and, in the ensuing days, cooperated with the 35th Army's forces in capturing the Mishan Fortified Region.

The Japanese 126th and 135th Infantry Divisions, which were responsible for defense of the Pamientung and Mishan sectors, withdrew rapidly after the initial Soviet attack. Their intent was to occupy preplanned defensive positions along a line running north and south of the 124th Infantry Division's defenses east of Mutanchiang. The 126th Infantry Division manned defenses near Tzuhsingtun, west of Pamientung, and the 135th Infantry Division defenses at Chihsing, protecting the road running from Linkou into Mutanchiang city from the north and northwest. Farther north, the Japanese offered only token opposition to Beloborodov's 59th Rifle Corps during its thrust towards Linkou.[14]

After capturing Lishuchen and Pamientung, Beloborodov's forces drove on relentlessly, virtually preempting Japanese defensive plans. Anishchik's 257th Tank Brigade and Svirs' 300th Rifle Division from Skvortsov's 26th Rifle Corps engaged, enveloped, and bypassed small detachments from the Japanese 126th Infantry Division at Tzuhsingtun and pushed on to Hsientung, 19 miles (30 kilometers) north of Mutanchiang, where they cut the Linkou–Mutanchiang railroad line on the afternoon of 12 August and enveloped and drove off another small defending Japanese force. By this time, Anishchik's tank brigade had only 19 serviceable tanks remaining, the rest having fallen victim to the rigors of the long march.[15]

In spite of the brigade's severely reduced strength, Anishchik relentlessly pushed his small task force on in an attempt to capture the rail bridge across the Mutan River at Hualin, 6 miles (10 kilometers) to the south. While still in march-column configuration, at 0500 hours on 13 August, Anishchik's tank brigade captured the railroad station at Hualin. The brigade then mounted a dash for the critical railroad bridge, which was just 1.2 miles (2 kilometers) to the south, but before the brigade could reach it, the bridge blew up with a resounding roar from explosives set off by Japanese sappers.

Anishchik's brigade tried all day to capture crossing sites over the Mutan River, only to be thwarted by heavy resistance by the Takikawa Infantry Battalion of the 135th Infantry Division's 370th Infantry Regiment.[16] During the intense battle, a train entered Hualin from the north carrying the commander of the 135th Infantry Division, his staff, and elements of one of his infantry regiments. Although Anishchik's tank brigade destroyed much of the train, the Japanese general managed to escape on foot to Japanese front lines to the south.[17]

By 1800 hours on 13 August, incessant heavy Japanese counterattacks forced Anishchik's tank brigade to withdraw northward to the outskirts of Hualin, followed by Japanese forces, who tried to encircle the beleaguered task force. After several anxious hours, the tank brigade broke out of a ring of Japanese troops overnight on 13–14 August, dug in on the hillside northeast of Hualin, and waited for reinforcements. Those reinforcements would come from the 1st Red Banner Army's 26th Rifle Corps, which was marching to the 257th Tank Brigade's assistance along two separate routes southwest from Pamientung and Tzuhsingtun. Karnov's 300th Rifle Division and Svirs' 22d Rifle Division of Skvortsov's rifle corps were advancing along the southern route, and Colonel I. F. Morozov's 77th Tank Brigade, followed by Major

General M. S. Batrakov's 59th Rifle Division, were trailing behind on the northern route.

On the far right (northern) flank of Beloborodov's army, Krupetskoi's 75th Tank Brigade and Makarov's 39th Rifle Division of Semenov's 59th Rifle Corps reached and captured the town of Linkou on 13 August. Elements of the Japanese 135th Infantry Division's 370th Infantry Regiment, which had been defending the town, together with the 135th Infantry Division's headquarters and staff, withdrew southward towards Chihsing and Mutanchiang. The division's 369th Infantry Regiment remained in defensive positions north of Linkou for several more days, only to begin retreating westward to Erhtaohotzu on 17 August. After the Japanese resistance in Linkou dissipated, Krupetskoi's tank brigade and Makarov's rifle division wheeled southward toward Mutanchiang, leaving Colonel M. K. Gvozdikov's 365th Rifle Division, which was in the 59th Rifle Corps' second echelon, to pursue the Japanese 369th Infantry Regiment from Linkou.

Thus, by 14 August the stage was set for battle to begin at Mutanchiang. The Japanese 126th Infantry Division and major elements from the 135th Infantry Division were now positioned to defend against any advance by the 1st Red Banner Army's forces against Mutanchiang from the north and to parry the advance of the 5th Army's forces, which were advancing on the city from the east. The priority mission of both Soviet forces was to seize the critical communications center at Mutanchiang, which also served as the headquarters and command posts of the Japanese First Area Army and 5th Army.

The battle for Mutanchiang raged on unabated for the next two days.[18] The 22d and 300th Rifle Divisions of the 1st Red Banner Army's 26th Rifle Corps, supported by the 77th and 257th Tank Brigades, attacked the northern and northeastern outskirts of the city and the railroad station at Yehho on the east bank of the Mutan River. The forces of Krylov's 5th Army did their part to smash Japanese defenses by striking the Japanese right flank at Ssutaoling and in the hills southeast of the city.

Ultimately, Beloborodov's forces cleared the city of Japanese defenders by the evening of 16 August, while Krylov's forces skirted the southern portion of the city and continued their advance southwestward toward Ningan. The Japanese 126th and 135th Infantry Divisions withdrew westward to Hengtaohotzu during the evening of 16 August. However, major portions of both divisions, in particular, the 126th Division's 278th Infantry Regiment and the 135th Division's Takikawa Battalion of the 135th Infantry Division, never received the orders to withdraw. The former perished almost to a man when the Soviet forces stormed the city and later disbanded and, in small groups, tried to infiltrate to the rear through Soviet lines.[19]

After capturing Mutanchiang, the forces of Beloborodov's 1st Red Banner Army began a rapid advance northwestward from Mutanchiang toward Harbin, while the forces of Krylov's 5th Army moved southwestward toward

Ningan, Tunghua, and Kirin in the central Manchurian plain. Beloborodov's forces covered almost 9 miles (14 kilometers) on 17 August, driving small enemy groups out of their path.

At the same time, Kazartsev's 72d Rifle Corps of Krylov's 5th Army marched southward along the eastern bank of the Mutan River and attempted to cross the river north of Ningan at midday on 17 August, but the first assault crossing failed. That night, however, Major General S. T. Gladyshev's 277th Rifle Division successfully fought its way across the river against heavy Japanese opposition. The following day, the remainder of Kazartsev's rifle corps crossed the Mutan River.

When the Japanese government announced its unconditional capitulation on 18 August, the forces of Beloborodov's 1st Red Banner and Krylov's 5th Armies deployed to receive and process the surrendering Japanese units. Two days later, on 20 August the forward detachments of Beloborodov's army reached Harbin, where they linked up with forces from the 1st Far Eastern Front's 20th Motorized Assault Engineer-Sapper Brigade, which had air-landed at Harbin airfield. Later in the day, the lead elements of the 2d Far Eastern Front's 15th Army, which had just completed their amphibious operations along the Sungari River, also reached Harbin.[20]

THE 35TH ARMY'S REDUCTION OF THE HUTOU AND MISHAN FORTIFIED REGIONS

Lieutenant General M. D. Zakhvataev's 35th Army deployed for action in the sector north of Lake Khanka, on the right (northern) flank of Meretskov's 1st Far Eastern Front, adjacent to the right flank of Beloborodov's 1st Red Banner Army. The 35th Army's mission was to assault across the Ussuri River, advance westward, reduce the formidable Japanese fortified regions at Hutou and Mishan, and capture the cities of Poli and Linkou. Zakhvataev's forces had to do so in a sector where the terrain differed markedly from the terrain Meretskov's other armies had to master (see Map 57). In short, to fulfill his mission, Zakhvataev's forces had to cross both the Ussuri River and its tributary, the Sungacha River, negotiate the extensive marshy regions between Lake Khanka and the Sungacha and Muleng Rivers, and overcome the strong permanent defenses of the Hutou and Mishan Fortified Regions.

The Japanese 15th Border Guard Unit and the 135th Infantry Division's 368th Infantry Regiment defended the Hutou Fortress complex, with infantry companies manning strong points scattered along the western bank of the Sungacha River and the border guards in the fortified region itself. The remainder of 135th Infantry Division was occupying defensive positions and garrisons near Tungan (Mishan) and Feite and company-size detachments manned defenses at Paoching and Jaoho to the north.[21]

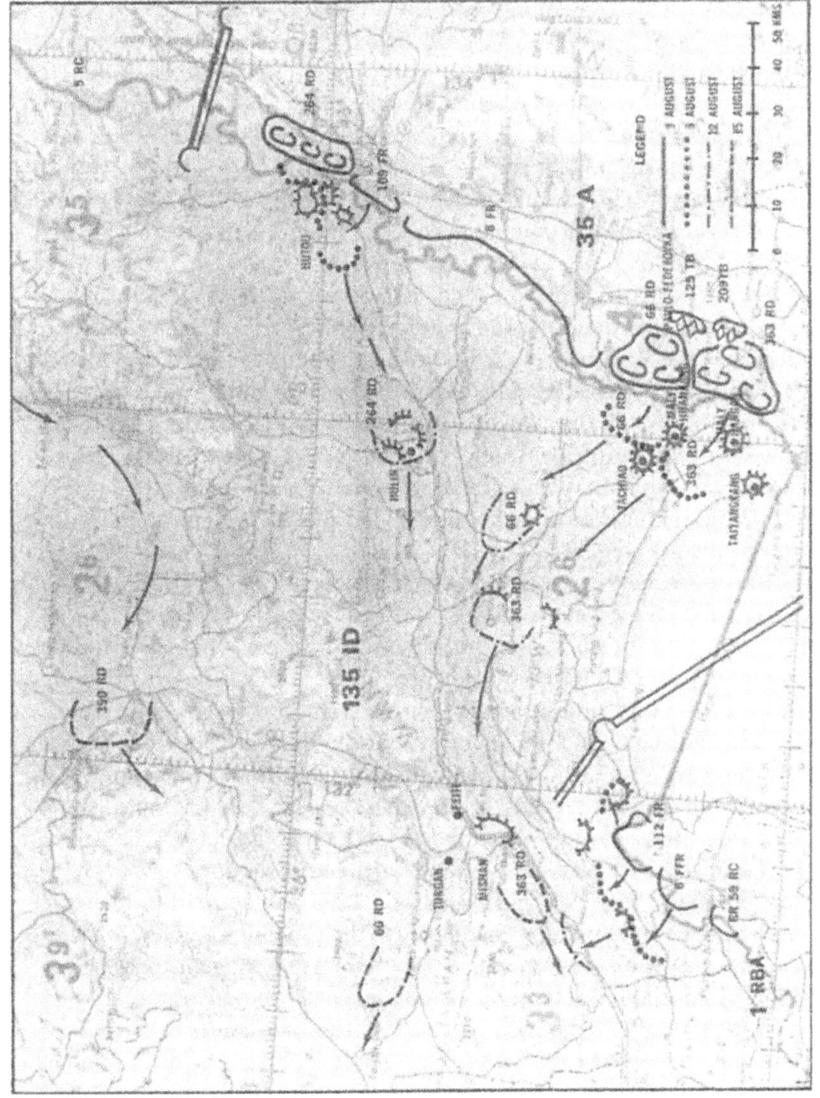

Map 57. Soviet 35th Army Advance to Mishan, 9–15 August 1945

Zakhvataev decided to conduct his main attack in the southern part of his army's sector, with Colonels S. D. Pechenenko's and F. K. Nesterov's 363d Rifle and 66th Rifle Divisions assaulting directly across the Sungacha River. Deployed from left to right, Pechenenko's and Nesterov's divisions were to cross the river west of Pavlo-Federovka, liquidate Japanese security outposts east of Lake Khanka, and, spearheaded by two tank brigades (the 125th and 209th), advance through the marshy region north of Lake Khanka to capture Tungan and sever Japanese communications routes to Hutou, thereby isolating the imposing fortress.

On the far northern flank of Zakhvataev's army, Major General B. L. Vinogradov's 264th Rifle Division and the 109th Fortified Region were to assault across the Ussuri River from Iman to south of Hutou, bypass and isolate the Hutou Fortified Region, advance to capture Hulin, and ultimately link up at Tungan with the rifle divisions operating on the army's left flank. Zakhvataev's reunited army would then advance along separate axes to capture Poli and Linkou. Finally, in the army's center sector, the 8th Fortified Region was to conduct local attacks across the Ussuri River from Lesozavodsk to south of Iman.[22]

At 0100 hours on 9 August, assault detachments from the NKVD's 57th Border Guards Detachment crossed the Ussuri and Sungacha Rivers on cutters, landed on the far shore, overcame small Japanese border outposts, and seized a small beachhead on the western bank of the Sungacha River by 0200 hours. After a 15-minute artillery preparation, two advanced battalions of the 363d and the 66th Rifle Divisions crossed the river but encountered virtually no enemy opposition. Flooding produced by heavy overnight rains, however, made the area virtually impassable even for infantry unless some sort of makeshift roads could hastily be constructed. To do so, Zakhvataev reinforced the two rifle divisions with extra engineer support.

After crossing the river, the troops of Nesterov's 66th Rifle Division advanced into the swamps, often wading up to their armpits in water. Advancing through the watery waste, which was punctuated by occasional grassy hummocks, somehow Nesterov's riflemen managed to penetrate 7.5 miles (12 kilometers) deep into the swamps, reaching a point 1.2 miles (2 kilometers) northwest of the village of Tachiao by about 2000 hours that evening. Meanwhile, the riflemen of Pechenenko's 363d Rifle Division completed crossing the Sungacha River at 0900 hours and advanced inland, only to encounter heavy fire from a company of Japanese troops defending five strong points near the small swamp settlement at Maly Huankang at 1100 hours. The stubborn Japanese defenders held out against repeated Soviet infantry assaults, which were supported by direct fire from 76mm regimental guns. Pechenenko's troops finally smashed the Japanese resistance at 1900 hours and continued their advance, reaching the southwest edge of Tachiao at 2300 hours.[23]

Pechenenko's and Nesterov's forces continued their advance northwestward on 10 August. Although fuel difficulties and poor terrain forced the tank brigades to withdraw to escape the swamps, both rifle divisions made excellent forward progress.[24] Pechenenko's troops captured Mishan late on 12 August, and Nesterov's forces occupied Tungan on 13 August, severing the highway and railroad between Linkou and Hutou. The already feeble Japanese resistance totally melted away as the 135th Infantry Division received orders to withdraw to Linkou and then to defensive positions at Mutanchiang.

On the right flank of Zakhvataev's army, Vinogradov's 264th Rifle Division and 109th Fortified Region prepared to assault Hutou. After a 30–50-minute artillery preparation, assault detachments crossed the Ussuri River south of Hutou town. Bombers from the 9th Air Army then pounded the entire Hutou region for two hours to destroy or neutralize the Japanese defenses. By nightfall on 9 August, Vinogradov's riflemen had outflanked Hutou to the south, captured the railroad depot near the town, and cut the highway to Hulin. The following day the city of Hutou fell, leaving the Japanese isolated in the strong fortifications north and northwest of the city.

Subsequently, the 264th Rifle Division's 1056th Rifle Regiment and the 109th Fortified Region prepared to reduce the fortress in methodical fashion, supported by extremely heavy artillery fire, a difficult process that was finally completed on 18 August. Officially, the Soviets claim that 3,000 Japanese perished in the bitter defense of Hutou.[25] Meanwhile, the two other regiments of Vinogradov's rifle division moved westward along the railroad toward Hulin, covering 22 miles (35 kilometers) and capturing the town on the afternoon of 12 August. The next day, Vinogradov's division joined the rest of Zakhvataev's 35th Army at Tungan and Mishan.

Urged on by Meretskov, Zakhvataev accelerated his army's advance on 14 August against only negligible opposition. While operating with the army's forward detachment along the Poli axis, the advanced guard of Nesterov's 66th Rifle Division dislodged light Japanese opposition and captured Poli on the evening of 15 August. The main body of Nesterov's division arrived in Poli on 17 August, followed on 19 August by elements of the 2d Far Eastern Front's 5th Separate Rifle Corps, which had crossed southward through the mountains from Paoching.

To the south, Pechenenko's 363d Rifle Division advanced westward from Tungan toward Linkou, employing Lieutenant Colonel A. V. Kuz'min's 125th Tank Brigade, which had been sent forward by rail from Pavlo-Federovka by way of Iman, as its forward detachment. Pechenenko's rifle division captured Chihsi on 17 August and arrived at Linkou on the night of 19–20 August, where it relieved the forces of Beloborodov's 1st Red Banner Army, which had arrived six days before. Zakhvataev's 35th Army completed its active operations by 19 August and began the more pleasant task of receiving the surrender of Japanese units.

THE 25TH ARMY'S ADVANCE TO WANGCHING

In the southern portion of the 1st Far Eastern Front's operational sector, Colonel General I. M. Chistiakov deployed his 25th Army to advance along two principal axes, separated from one another by over 62 miles (100 kilometers) (see Map 58). The northernmost of these advance axes crossed heavily wooded and brush-covered hilly terrain traversed by numerous river valleys that generally ran from east to west. The southern axis faced the broad Tumen River, beyond which stretched lightly forested plains extending westward 43 miles (70 kilometers) through the city of Tumen to Yenchi. Between these two axes were several other narrow but highly compartmented east–west corridors, the most important of which was defended by Japanese fortifications at Tumentsu.

Major General A. M. Morozov's 39th Rifle Corps was to attack along Chistiakov's northern axis of advance from positions near Novogeorgievka Station northwest of Pokrovka. The rifle corps consisted of Colonel Z. D. Sopel'tsev's 40th, Colonel M. E. Moskalik's 384th, and Colonel S. A. Tugolukov's 386th Rifle Divisions, supported initially by Lieutenant Colonel D. I. Korneev's 259th Tank Brigade and later by Colonel N. S. Grishin's 72d Tank Brigade, transferred just prior to the offensive from the 5th Army. Morozov's mission was to penetrate Japanese defenses, capture or isolate the Tungning Fortified Region by enveloping it from the north, capture the village of Tungning, and exploit southwestward to seize the city of Wangching, thus severing the Japanese First Area Army's communications with northern Korea.

On Chistiakov's extreme left flank, border guards units and forces from the 108th and 113th Fortified Regions, which were operating along the 25th Army's southern attack axis, were to force their way across the Hunchun and Tumen Rivers, attack the Japanese fortified regions at Hunyong and Tumen, and advance to capture Yenchi, smashing Japanese defenses on both sides of the border between Manchuria and northern Korea. In the broad sector between the 39th Rifle Corps' and the 108th Fortified Region's positions, the 106th, 109th, 110th, and 111th Fortified Regions were to assault local Japanese border installations, in particular at Paitoshantzu and Tumentzu, to tie down Japanese forces.

Finally, Lieutenant General P. E. Loviagin's 88th Rifle Corps, which consisted of Major General V. I. Seber's 105th and Colonel P. V. Dmitriev's 258th Rifle Divisions, initially in *front* reserve, was to prepare to exploit the 25th Army's attack by advancing southward along the eastern coast of northern Korea to capture the ports of Unggi, Najin, and Chongjin.

Chistiakov's army faced elements of the Japanese First Area Army and 3d Army deployed in scattered but strong fortified positions along the Manchurian-Far Eastern border. In the First Area Army's sector, the 132d

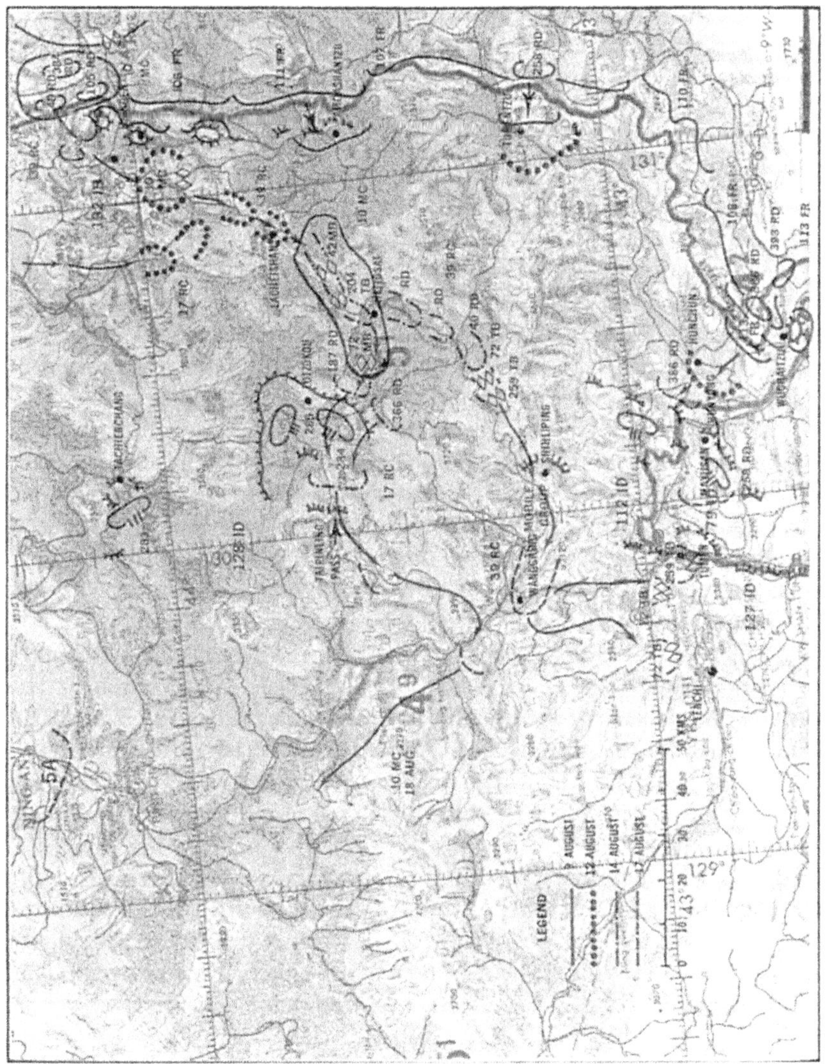

Map 58. Soviet 25th Army Advance to Wangching and Yenchi, 9–17 August 1945

Independent Mixed Brigade, which consisted of four infantry battalions and one raider battalion, was garrisoned at Tungning and manned the strong Tungning (Hsingen) Fortified Region, which stretched 18.6 miles (30 kilometers) from north to south along the border east of the village of Tungning (see Map 59). To the rear, 50 miles (80 kilometers) southwest of Tungning, the 128th Infantry Division had its headquarters and two infantry regiments in the immediate vicinity of Lotzokou, a key point dominating the most trafficable road network into southeastern Manchuria. The 128th Infantry Division's third regiment was stationed at Tachienchang, located 50 miles (80 kilometers) due west of Tungning, and small Japanese border outposts ran south along the border from Tungning to the Sea of Japan.

To the south, the Japanese 3d Army defended the Hunchun, Hunyong, Tumen, and Yenchi axis with three infantry divisions, a mobile brigade, and a separate infantry regiment. The 112th Infantry Division had the bulk of its forces deployed in the vicinity of Michiang, north of the Tumen River and northwest of Hunchun, but its forward outposts extended northeastward along the railroad to Tumentzu. The 79th Infantry Division defended the Hunyong Fortified Region and crossings over the Mutan River in the sector southeast of Tumen, and the 127th Infantry Division, which was deployed south of the 79th Infantry Division, defended the approaches to Yenchi west of the Tumen River. The 127th Infantry Division's 280th Infantry Regiment occupied a fortified region along the border near Wuchaitzu. In addition, the 101st Separate Infantry Regiment was stationed at Chongliak, situated north of the port of Unggi in northern Korea and the 1st Mobile Brigade was stationed on the main rail line at Shihliping, east of Wangching, with advanced elements occupying defensive positions farther east at Tumentzu.[26]

Chistiakov attempted to deceive the Japanese regarding his intent to attack by ordering his 39th Rifle Corps to occupy its final assault positions as late as possible on the evening of 8 August. After detailed consultations with Meretskov and his own subordinate commanders, Chistiakov decided to commence his attack by employing numerous small assault detachments made up of troops from his fortified regions and border guards units. He selected these forces to initiate the attack because they were acutely familiar with the terrain in their respective sectors and the Japanese forces that opposed them and also because they had already been well trained to assault these positions during special training exercises against mock-up objectives in the Soviet rear area.

After the assault detachments initiated the attack, one advanced battalion from each rifle regiment advancing in the first echelon of Morozov's attacking rifle divisions was to follow the assault detachments and complete the penetration of the forward Japanese defenses. The rifle divisions' main force regiments were to follow the advanced battalion and envelop the Tungning

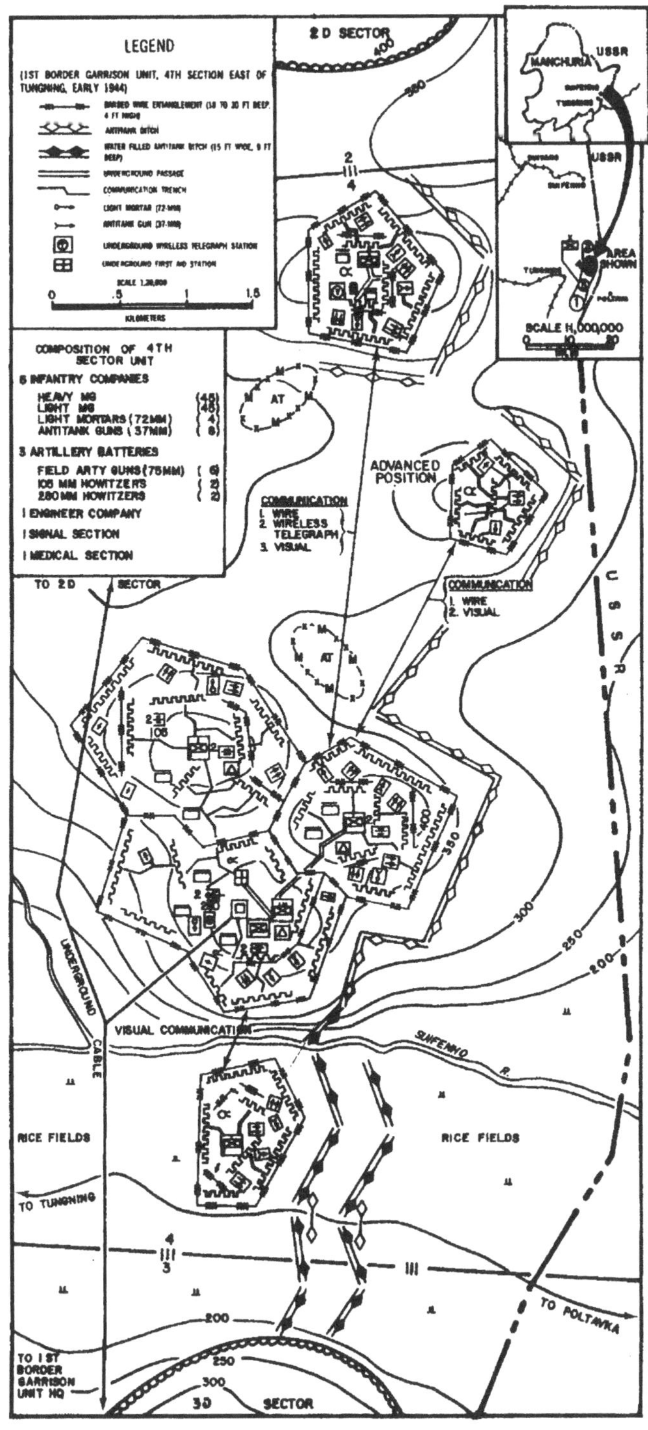

Map 59. Japanese Fortified Region at Tungning (Japanese View)

Fortified Region, while the two tank brigades were to support the infantry advance and begin the exploitation.[27] To ensure that his forces achieved surprise, Chistiakov planned to fire no artillery preparation prior to the 39th Rifle Corps' attack.

The assault detachments and advanced battalions of Morozov's 39th Rifle Corps occupied their jumping-off positions for the attack at 2330 hours on 8 August, just as light rain began to fall. At 2400 hours sappers began cutting through the barbed wire along the border as the rain intensified. Shortly after midnight on 9 August, despite the torrential rains, which continued falling until about 0600 hours the next morning, Marshal Meretskov gave Chistiakov permission to advance. Although the rain indeed hindered the forces as they advanced, it also accorded the advancing troops total surprise, since the Japanese utterly rejected the feasibility of an attack occurring in such appalling weather conditions.

Supported by sappers, at 0100 hours on 9 August, the assault detachments crossed the border and struck Japanese security outposts and forward defensive positions. Since the Japanese defenders had heard little else but pounding rainfall for almost an hour, the Soviet assaulting detachments surprised and quickly captured or destroyed most of the Japanese forward positions, often without a fight.[28] Beginning at 0300 hours, Morozov's advanced battalions pushed forward along the path blazed by the assault detachments, completing the destruction of the Japanese forward defenses. At 0830 hours the main bodies of the 40th and 386th Rifle Divisions advanced westward along the Pad Sennaia River to the north of the Tungning Fortified Region's main fortified positions with Korneev's 259th Tank Brigade in the lead.

By day's end on 9 August, the forces of Morozov's 39th Rifle Corps' forces had penetrated 6.2–7.5 miles (10–12 kilometers) deep into the Japanese rear area along the Pad Sennaia axis, and the lead elements of his rifle divisions, reinforced by Grishin's 72d Tank Brigade, were beginning the fight for possession of the village of Tungning and the vital railroad line from Tungning to Tumen. Further south, troops from Chistiakov's fortified regions struck and overcame Japanese defensive positions at Hsingen, Paitoshantzu, and Tumentzu.

Chistiakov's forces continued their advance on 10 August against stiffening Japanese resistance. General Onitake, the commander of the 132d Independent Mixed Brigade, left part of his forward battalions to defend the fortified region along the border but withdrew his remaining forces towards the west.[29] The forward elements of Korneev's tank brigade and Sopel'tsev's 40th Rifle Division captured Tungning village on the afternoon of 10 August, while Morozov employed Moskalik's 384th Rifle Division to reduce the Tungning Fortified Region.

To compound the dilemma Japanese forces faced, shortly after Chistiakov's initial assault, the 17th Rifle Corps of Krylov's 5th Army attacked southward from Suifenho into the rear of the southern portion of the Suifenho Fortified Region, an attack that ultimately also reached the rear area of Japanese forces defending north of Tungning. After the 17th Rifle Corps linked up with Morozov's 39th Rifle Corps west of Tungning, at 1700 hours on 9 August, Meretskov subordinated the 17th Rifle Corps and its two rifle divisions to Chistiakov's 25th Army.

Chistiakov's rapid capture of the Tungning Fortified Region prompted Meretskov to reassess the situation, in particular, the question as to when and where he could best commit his mobile group, the 10th Mechanized Corps, to begin the exploitation. Given Chistiakov's spectacular success, he decided that his best opportunity for a successful exploitation would be in the 25th Army's sector. Although Krylov's 5th Army had quickly overcome Japanese border defenses at Suifenho, his army still faced the main forces of the Japanese 124th, 126th, and 135th Infantry Divisions, which occupied strong defensive positions between Muleng and Mutanchiang. Therefore, the best chance for success seemed to be in Chistiakov's sector.

Consequently, Meretskov attached Loviagin's 88th Rifle Corps and its two rifle divisions to Chistiakov's 25th Army with orders to operate in the southern portion of his army's sector (the Hunchun–Yenchi axis) and issued warning orders to his mobile group, Lieutenant General of Tank Forces I. D. Vasil'ev's 10th Mechanized Corps, to prepare to commit to combat along the Tungning axis in the 25th Army's sector if the army continued to achieve success.[30]

Nor did the 25th Army's progress disappoint Meretskov. On 10 August Morozov's rifle corps completed clearing Japanese forces from the Tungning region and began coordinating with the 17th Rifle Corps for an advance west and southwest from Tungning in pursuit of the withdrawing Japanese. The 39th and 17th Rifle Corps began a coordinated advance on 11 August southwestward along the road from Tungning toward Wangching, Tumen, Tunhua, and Kirin. By noon on 12 August, the two corps had marched 18.6–25 miles (30–40 kilometers) to the southwest and were approaching Laoheishan. Pleased by their progress, Meretskov ordered the 10th Mechanized Corps to begin its exploitation to Wangching and beyond in the 25th Army's Tungning sector.

On 13 and 14 August, Kopichko's 17th and Morozov's 39th Rifle Corps and Vasil'ev's 10th Mechanized Corps advanced slowly to the southwest, sharing the single road alongside the military rail line that ran through the mountainous and heavily wooded region between Laoheishan and Heitosai. The combined force required considerable engineer support to clear the many minefields, repair the destroyed bridges, and improve the poor quality dirt roads as they advanced. Because the narrow road permitted only restricted movement in single column, only the corps' reconnaissance forces and forward detachments came into contact with Japanese forces. Fortunately, however, resistance was only minimal.

By nightfall on 14 August, although the combined march column had snaked forward up to 31 miles (50 kilometers), it extended 28 miles (45 kilometers) in length. Japanese resistance, however, remained only negligible. The 132d Independent Mixed Brigade completed withdrawing westward to Tachienchang, and the 128th Infantry Division was preparing to man defenses in the Lotzokou region and in the Taipingling Pass 18.6 miles (30 kilometers) to the west. The Japanese command, however, had failed to exploit an excellent opportunity to disrupt the Soviet advance as its forces maneuvered painfully through the bottleneck between Laoheishan and Heitosai.[31]

When Chistiakov's advancing forces reached Heitosai, he split them into two separate columns. Kopychko's 17th Rifle Corps, with elements of Vasil'ev's 10th Mechanized Corps, including the 72d Mechanized Brigade, which was operating as the corps' forward detachment, drove westward from Heitosai towards the Taipingling Pass. Morozov's 39th Rifle Corps, with Korneev's 259th Tank Brigade acting as its forward detachment, and other elements of the 10th Mechanized Corps, with Grishin's 72d Tank Brigade in the lead, marched southwestward from Heitosai toward Wangching.

On 15 August Kopychko's rifle corps struck defensive positions manned by elements of the Japanese 128th Infantry Division's 284th Infantry Regiment at Lotzokou. Major General I. M. Savin's 187th Rifle Division attacked the Japanese head on, while Colonel I. A. Manuilov's 366th Rifle Division enveloped the defenders from the south. The rifle corps' forward detachment, the 72d Mechanized Brigade, bypassed the Japanese defensive positions and drove straight westward to Taipingling Pass, where it encountered the 128th Infantry Division's 285th Infantry Regiment in dug-in positions. The defenses required the advancing Soviet force to halt and deploy for a hasty attack.[32]

Farther to the south, Grishin's 72d Tank Brigade, elements of the 10th Mechanized Corps, and Korneev's 259th Tank Brigade of Morozov's 39th Rifle Corps advanced relatively unimpeded toward Wangching. At Shihliping, Grishin's forward detachment and forces from the 40th Rifle Division engaged elements of the Japanese 1st Mobile Brigade and, after a brief bitter fight, drove off the Japanese defenders and continued their march.[33] Grishin's tank brigade and the lead elements of Morozov's rifle corps captured Wangching at 1700 hours on 15 August.

By this time, the remainder of the 10th Mechanized and 39th Rifle Corps stretched out along the road 130 miles (210 kilometers) to the rear. The lead elements of the 39th Rifle Corps' main body were 18.6 miles (30 kilometers) east of Wangching, with the corps' main force stretching eastward through Heitosai well to the rear. However, since Wangching had already fallen, this was utterly irrelevant.

The offensive by Chistiakov's 25th Army and Vasil'ev's 10th Mechanized Corps reached a climax the following day. Led by forward detachments from the 187th Rifle Division and 72d Mechanized Brigade, Kopychko's 17th

Rifle Corps continued its struggle for possession of Lotzokou and the Taipingling Pass. During the late evening of 16 August, the combined forces of the 187th and 366th Rifle Divisions and the 10th Mechanized Corps' 72d Mechanized Brigade finally overcame the Japanese defenses, drove the defenders from the region, and captured the pass.[34]

On the same day, while main forces of Morozov's 39th Rifle Corps were arriving in Wangching, the lead elements of Korneev's 259th Tank Brigade, together with small elements from Morozov's rifle corps, advanced 12 miles (20 kilometers) southwest from Wangching to the northern outskirts of Tumen, turning the left flank of the defending Japanese 127th Infantry Division. Simultaneously, Grishin's 72d Tank Brigade of the 10th Mechanized Corps' left Wangching and advanced 12 miles (20 kilometers) southwestward toward Yenchi. The combined thrusts by the two tank brigades totally unhinged Japanese defenses along the Manchurian–Northern Korean border.

In the southern portion of the 25th Army's operational sector, the Hunchun–Yenchi axis, the situation also developed favorably for Soviet forces. On the first day of their assault, the forces of the 108th and 113th Fortified Regions captured Japanese defensive positions on the western banks of the Hunchun and Tumen Rivers, secured a foothold in the Hunchun and Wuchaitzu Fortified Regions, and captured a sizeable bridgehead over the Tumen River at Kyonghung, just north of Lake Khasan, where the famous border incident had taken place between Red Army and Japanese forces in 1938.

The forces from the two fortified regions then bypassed and isolated the defensive positions manned by the Japanese 280th Infantry Regiment at Shangchiaoshen, northwest of Wuchaitzu.[35] The attack picked up momentum on 11 August when Chistiakov committed Loviagin's 88th Rifle Corps from his reserve to develop the attack along the southern axis. Loviagin's 195th and 258th Rifle Divisions advanced westward along the Hunchun–Tumen axis, while Colonel F. A. Isakov's 393d Rifle Division (minus the 541st Rifle Regiment), which Chistiakov also committed from his army reserve, reinforced the 113th Fortified Region, which, by this time, was fighting along the northeastern coast of Korea.

Early on the morning of 12 August, Isakov's rifle division launched a truck-mounted passage of lines and assault through the forward positions of the 113th Fortified Region against the Japanese 101st Separate Regiment, which was manning defenses south of Chonghak. The 101st Regiment withdrew westward to Hoeryong, where it became subordinate to the 127th Infantry Division. Three hours later, at 0900 hours, the lead elements of Isakov's rifle division advanced to the outskirts of the port of Unggi, which, together with a small naval task force from the Pacific Fleet, it captured after a short skirmish. Leaving a single rifle battalion to garrison the port, the main body of Isakov's division continued its march to the port of Najin, which it also captured on 14 August.

Active Soviet military operations in northern Korea ended on 16 August, when Isakov's 393d Rifle Division battled for and seized a mountain pass 7.5 miles (12 kilometers) north of the port of Chongjin. Thereafter, by 1500 hours Isakov's forces had advanced to the city, where it linked up with the Chuguevka Operational Group's 355th Rifle Division, which had conducted a successful amphibious assault on the port city.[36]

Farther north, Loviagin's 88th Rifle Corps joined the Soviet advance along the Hunchun–Tumen axis in support of the 113th Fortified Region, whose forces had captured Hunchun on 14 August and advanced toward the Tumen (Inan Ho) River, 6 miles (10 kilometers) to the northwest against heavy resistance by forces of the Japanese 112th Infantry Division. During the previous five days Chistiakov had reinforced the 88th Rifle Corps' and 113th Fortified Region's operational sector with Colonel S. A. Tugolukov's 386th Rifle Division, which he had detached from Morozov's 39th Rifle Corps, and with Lieutenant Colonel S. M. Iakovlev's 209th Tank Brigade, which had been detached from the 35th Army and assigned to Chistiakov's 25th Army on 10 August.

Loviagin's combined force advanced across the Tumen (Inan Ho) River on 15 August, but it ran into strongly entrenched Japanese forces from the 112th Infantry Division's 246th Infantry Regiment. Several attempts by Loviagin's force to dislodge the Japanese failed. Consequently, Loviagin committed Colonel P. V. Dmitriev's 258th Rifle Division from his corps' second echelon later in the day with orders to cross the Tumen River at Hunyong and attack to turn the right flank of Japanese forces defending west of Hunyong. Four infantry battalions from the Japanese 79th Infantry Division's 291st Infantry Regiment occupied prepared defensive positions along a ridge extending from Unmupi to Mayusan south and west of the bend in the Tumen River. The following day Dmitriev's rifle division began advancing westward, west and south of the Tumen River bend, against heavy opposition from Japanese forces defending the hills southwest of Mayusan.

At the same time, forces from the 113th Fortified Region extended their offensive operations eastward adjacent to the right flank of Tugolukov's 386th Rifle Division in an attempt to turn the Japanese 112th Infantry Division's left flank. This maneuver brought Tugolukov's force into contact with the 112th Infantry Division's 247th and 248th Regiments, which stoically defended their positions.[39] Thus, by the evening of 17 August, all of the Japanese forces defending the Tumen and Yenchi region were faced by potential envelopment by 25th Army from the north, east, and south, and were almost entirely cut off from other Japanese forces in northern Korea and Manchuria.

Japanese defenses farther north in the sector of Chistiakov's 25th Army continued to crumble at an alarming pace. Kopychko's 17th Rifle Corps, together with elements of Vasil'ev's 10th Mechanized Corps, advanced steadily westward, pursuing the remnants of the Japanese 128th Infantry Division from Lotzokou and the Taipingling Pass. The forward elements of Grishin's 72d Tank Brigade of the 10th Mechanized Corps approached Yenchi from the north, while Korneev's 259th Tank Brigade and the lead elements of Morozov's 39th Rifle Corps had passed though Wangching and were approaching the city of Tumen from the north. All the while, the main body of Morozov's rifle corps was still moving slowly westward along the road from Heitosai to Wangching. Last, but not least, Loviagin's 88th Rifle Corps was approaching Tumen city from the east.

The ring around the Japanese 112th and 79th Infantry Divisions tightened and finally closed on 17 August. The forward elements of Vasil'ev's 10th Mechanized Corps advanced 37 miles (60 kilometers) southwestward from Taipingling Pass and captured the important rail and road junction at Tahsingkou, 12 miles (20 kilometers) north of Wangching. South of Wangching, Grishin's 72d Tank Brigade and other forward elements of the 10th Mechanized Corps battled the Japanese 127th Infantry Division's forces for possession of the village of Nianyantsun, barely 8.7 miles (14 kilometers) north of Yenchi.

At the same time, Korneev's 259th Tank Brigade and forward elements of Morozov's 39th Rifle Corps, operating southeast of Wangching, captured the important city of Tumen, by doing so severing the escape routes of the Japanese 112th and 79th Infantry Divisions. The same day, Loviagin's 88th Rifle Corps brushed aside the defending 291st Infantry Regiment at Mayusan and occupied the town of Onsong, just 6 miles (10 kilometers) east of Tumen.[38] The surviving Japanese forces either surrendered or fled into the hill country south of the Tumen River.

With unconditional Japanese surrender imminent, pursuant to Meretskov's orders, on 18 August Chistiakov's forces consolidated their hold over northeastern Korea, while the army commander dispatched Vasil'ev's mechanized corps westward on an impetuous dash to capture the cities of Tunhua and Kirin in Manchuria's central valley. Led by a tank brigade serving as its forward detachment, the northern prong of the 10th Mechanized Corps, followed by Kopychko's 17th Rifle Corps, raced northwestward almost 18.6 miles (30 kilometers), where Vasil'ev's mobile corps linked up with the forward elements of Krylov's 5th Army at Tungchingcheng, where the main rail lines from Mutanchiang and Wangching met.

On 19 August Vasil'ev's corps continued its rapid westward advance, negotiated the passes through the Laoyeh Ling Mountains, and reached and captured Tunhua at nightfall on 16 August, the same day that Chongjin on the Korean coast fell to the 393d and 355th Rifle Divisions. All the while, Morozov's 39th and Loviagin's 88th Rifle Corps continued to clear Japanese forces from northeastern Korea south of the cities of Yenchi and Tumen.

The Kwantung Army's surrender, which the Japanese government had broadcast to Japanese forces by radio at 1700 hours on 17 August and the subsequent Kwantung Army's declaration to the Far East Command by radio at 0330 hours on 18 August that it accepted surrender terms, began to take effect as separate Japanese units surrendered to the advanced formations of the Soviet 1st Far Eastern Front.[39] Immediately after the Kwantung Army declared its surrender, Vasilevsky issued an order to all three of his operating *fronts* that required them to capture all major population centers as soon as possible with special mobile detachments formed in each major formation.[40]

> Given the fact that Japanese resistance has been smashed and the bad road conditions strongly prevent a rapid advance by the main bodies of our forces, it is necessary to make the transition to operations by specially formed, rapidly moving, and well-equipped detachments to quickly seize the cities of Changchun, Mukden, and Harbin.[41]

The 1st Far Eastern Front air-landed small detachments of troops at the airfields at Harbin and Kirin to arrange with Japanese authorities the surrender of Japanese garrisons.[42] By 20 August four forward detachments leading the advancing main forces formations of Meretskov's 1st Far Eastern Front had joined the air-landed forces at the two cities. Elements of the 2d Far Eastern Front's 15th Army also arrived in Harbin the same day on boats of the Amur River Flotilla. In the southern portion of the 25th Army's operational sector, after clearing Japanese forces from the Yenchi and Tumen regions, the forces of Loviagin's 88th Rifle Corps and Vasil'ev's 10th Mechanized Corps advanced southward into Korea, reaching the 38th parallel, the line agreed upon by Soviet and American authorities for separating their occupation forces by the end of August.

The 1st Far Eastern Front's forces finally snuffed out the last organized Japanese resistance in its sector on 26 August. The Japanese forces surrounded in the Tungning Fortified Region had held out since 9 August under constant assault by forces of the 106th Fortified Region and pounded unmercifully by artillery fire from the 223d Separate High-power Artillery Brigade, the 34th and 100th Separate Special-power Artillery Battalions, and Soviet aircraft. The attacking Soviet forces systematically reduced a total of 82 separate Japanese strong points, the last of which, the Shiminzas strong point, fell on 25 August. A total of 901 Japanese soldiers and auxiliaries fell captive to the Soviet forces at Tungning.[43] Other incidents occurred as Japanese units who did not receive, or who received but did not obey, the surrender order continued to engage Soviet troops.

The offensive by Meretskov's 1st Far Eastern Front more than adequately complemented the audacious advance by Malinovsky's Trans-Baikal Front. Meretskov's forces successfully tied down significant numbers of Japanese forces in eastern Manchuria and distracted Japanese attention from the disaster that was befalling them in the west. The twin offensives left Japanese forces no other recourse but to withdraw their shattered forces to interior defensive lines. Meretskov's forces applied unrelenting pressure against Japanese forces deployed along the entire extent of Manchuria's eastern front by conducting massive attacks in weather conditions considered unsuitable for the conduct of military operations, by capitalizing on surprise, and by attacking along multiple axes across supposedly impassable terrain. The unrelenting pressure overwhelmed forward-deployed Japanese forces and prevented the bulk of the Kwantung Army from consolidating its forces and erecting new defense lines to the rear.

Extensive Soviet employment of assault detachments, forward detachments, and advance guards and skillful reliance on complex maneuver utterly frustrated the 135th, 126th, and 124th Infantry Divisions' defense east of Mutanchiang, the 128th Infantry Division's and 1st Mobile Brigade's defense in the Lotzokou region, and the 112th and 79th Infantry Divisions' defense east of Tumen. Here, as elsewhere in Manchuria, the mobility and firepower of Soviet Army forces and their extensive and skillful use of armor and artillery decided the issue. The forward detachments made up of separate reinforced tank brigades swept through and around Japanese defensive lines, preempting any systematic defense. Follow-on rifle forces then crushed or bypassed any defenses the Japanese managed to establish. The capture of Mutanchiang and Wangching on 16 August signaled total Soviet success.

Throughout the entire operation, the almost total lack of armor and anti-tank weapons had an enormously negative impact on the First Area Army's combat performance, since it deprived it of any means by which it could counter the Soviet armored thrusts. Instead, and in vain, the Japanese relied on the rough terrain and its presumed adverse impact on Soviet logistics and suicidal expenditures of infantry to slow the Soviet advance. The defending troops in the Japanese fortified regions along the border put up a tenacious, brave, yet meaningless, defense. At Hutou, Mishan, Tungning, and, to a lesser extent, at Suifenho, the Japanese garrisons fought to the point of utter exhaustion or outright extermination.

Yet, even their gallant defense of these formidable obstacles, the Kwantung Army's 'Maginot Line', did little to stem the Soviet tide. Advancing Red Army forces simply bypassed the fortified positions and swept on to preempt Japanese defenses to the rear and capture key cities, towns, and communications centers deep in the Japanese rear area. In eastern Manchuria, as in the West, the Japanese High Command woefully underestimated the Red Army's offensive capabilities, and it showed. As a result, the Japanese paid dearly for their shortsightedness.

NOTES

1. Vnotchenko, *Pobeda*, 200–3, 207–11. For a detailed description of the first two days of the 5th Army's assault, see N. I. Krylov, N. I. Alekseev, and I. G. Dragan, *Navstrechu pobede: Boevoi put 5-i armii, oktiabr 1941g–avgust 1946 g.* [Toward victory: The combat path of the 5th Army, October 1941–August 1945] (Moscow: 'Nauka', 1970), 433–5, and P. Tsygankov, 'Nekotorye osobennosti boevykh deistvii 5-i armii v Kharbino-Girinskoi operatsii' [Some characteristics of the 5th Army's Combat Operations during the Harbin-Kirin operation], *VIZh*, No. 8 (August 1975), 83–9.
2. D. Khrenov, 'Wartime Operations: Engineer Operations in the Far East', *USSR Report: Military Affairs No. 1546* (20 November 1980): 81–97, JPRS 76847. Translated by the Foreign Broadcast Information Service from the Russian article in *Znamia* [Banner], August 1980.
3. *JM 154*, 184–5, 233–4.
4. Vnotchenko, *Pobeda*, 222.
5. Ibid., 220; Krylov *et al.*, *Navstrechu*, 442–3.
6. Vnotchenko, *Pobeda*, 220–1. Japanese sources concerning this fight are contradictory. The 124th Infantry Division's account credits the Sasaki Detachment with limited success (see *JM 154*, 236). The 5th Army's history claims that the Soviet tank forces 'easily broke through' the Sasaki Detachment, but were held up by the Kobayashi Detachment on the afternoon of 12 August (see *JM 154*, 197). Soviet accounts support the 124th Infantry Division's version of the action, although they also claim that the Japanese defenders continued to resist throughout the remainder of 12 August.
7. *JM 154*, 238-44.
8. Japanese forces delaying the 5th Army's advance included the Kobayashi Detachment, which was made up of officer candidates from two Kwantung Army schools.
9. *JM 154* (Pt. F) map 3, 250–3, 287.
10. A. Beloborodov, 'Na sopkakh Man'chzhurii' [In the hills of Manchuria], Pt. 1, *VIZh*, No. 12 (December 1980), 34–5.
11. No information available on the march-column configuration of the 231st Rifle Division.
12. Vnotchenko, *Pobeda*, 205–7, supplements 5, 6.
13. Ibid., 216–17. Japanese accounts in *JM 154*, 154, 186, 256–9, claim that the attack commenced at 1600 hours on 10 August and that the town fell at noon on 11 August. Beloborodov, 'Na sopkakh Man'chzhurii', Pt. 2, *VIZh*, No. 1 (January 1981), 45, states that the 257th Tank Brigade had secured the bridge and railroad yards at Pamientung by evening, but that the town itself was cleared of Japanese troops on 11 August. The Soviets estimated 400 Japanese dead, while the Japanese estimated 500.
14. *JM 154*, 187–90, 199–201, 260–2, and 289–92.
15. Beloborodov, 'Na sopkakh Man'chzhurii', Pt. 2, 45–6, and Vnotchenko, *Pobeda*, 218.
16. Beloborodov, 'Na sopkakh Man'chzhurii', Pt. 2, 46–7; Vnotchenko, *Pobeda*, 218–19; and *JM 154*, 207–8, 292–4.
17. Vnotchenko, *Pobeda*, 218-19; *JM 154*, 200–1, 297–8; V. Ezhakov, 'Boevoe primenenie tankov v gorno-taezhnoi mestnosti po opytu 1-go Dal'nevostochnogo fronta' [The combat use of tanks in mountainous-taiga regions based on the experience of the 1st Far Eastern Front], *VIZh*, No. 1 (January 1974), 80.
18. Vnotchenko, *Pobeda*, 253–60; Beloborodov, 'Na sopkakh Man'chzhurii', Pt. 2,

47–51; Krylov *et al.*, *Navstrechu*, 445–7; V. Timofeev, '300-ia strelkovaia diviziia v boiakh na Mudan'tsianskom napravlenii' [The 300th Rifle Division in combat along the Mutanchiang axis], *VIZh*, No. 8 (August 1978), 53–5; and *JM 164*, 202–8, 263–73, 292–7.

19. *JM 154*, 212, 272.
20. See D. S. Sukhorukov, ed., *Sovetskie vozdushno-desantnye* [Soviet air landing forces] (Moscow: Voenoizdat, 1980), 253–4, and Khrenov, 'Wartime Operations', 94–6.
21. *JM 154*, 274–6, 281, 287.
22. S. Pechenenko, 'Armeiskaia nastupatel'naia operatsiia v usloviiakh dal'nevostochnogo teatra voennykh deistvii' [An army offensive operation in the conditions of the Far Eastern theater of military operations], *VIZh*, No. 8 (August 1978), 44–5, and S. Pechenenko, '363-ia strelkovaia diviziia v boiakh na Mishan'skom napravlenii' [The 363d Rifle Division in combat along the Mishan axis], *VIZh*, No. 7 (July 1975), 38–40; and Vnotchenko, *Pobeda*, 203–4.
23. Pechenenko, 'Armeiskaia', 45, and Pechenenko, '363-ia strelkovaia diviziia', 42–4.
24. Pechenenko, 'Armeiskaia', 47.
25. Vnotchenko, *Pobeda*, 285–6.
26. *JM 154*, 85–6, 118–21, 140–3.
27. Chistiakov, *Sluzhim*, 280–2, and Khrenov, 'Wartime Operations', 92–3.
28. Chistiakov, *Sluzhim*, 286–91.
29. *JM 154*, 334–8.
30. Vnotchenko, *Pobeda*, 222.
31. Ibid., 225; Chistiakov, *Sluzhim*, 295.
32. Vnotchenko, *Pobeda*, 261–2; Chistiakov, *Sluzhim*, 295–6; and *JM 154*, 317–22.
33. M. Sidorov, 'Boevoe primenenie artillerii' [The combat use of artillery], *VIZh*, No. 9 (September 1975), 20.
34. Vnotchenko, *Pobeda*, 262, 263. *JM 154*, 320–2, 325–8, claims that the Japanese 128th Infantry Division stood firm throughout 16 August at Taipingling until surrender was negotiated.
35. Zakharov, *Finale*, 159; Chistiakov, *Sluzhim*, 300; and *JM 154*, 94–5, 145–6.
36. Vnotchenko, *Pobeda*, 223, 263, and *JM 154*, 97, 146.
47. Vnotchenko, *Pobeda*, 261–2, and *JM 154*, 98–100, 125–33.
38. Vnotchenko, *Pobeda*, 264, and *JM 154*, 131–2.
39. Vnotchenko, *Pobeda*, 278, claims that Soviet intelligence intercepted a Japanese radio transmission ordering surrender at 1700 hours on 17 August but few if any Japanese forces heeded the transmission.
40. Ibid., 279–80.
41. Ibid.
42. Sukhorukov, *Sovetskie*, 253–4; G. Shelakhov, 'S vozdushnym desantam v Kharbin' [With the air-landing at Harbin], *VIZh*, No. 8 (August 1970), 67–71.
43. M. Sidorov, 'Boevoe', 19; K. P. Kazakov, *Vsegda s pekhotoi, vsegda s tankami* [Always with the infantry, always with the tanks] (Moscow: Voenizdat, 1973), trans. Leo Kanner Associates for the US Army Foreign Science and Technology Center, 6 February 1975, 396–7; and Vnotchenko, *Pobeda*, 286.

9

The 2d Far Eastern Front's Offensive Operation

THE 2D FAR EASTERN FRONT'S PLAN

Although of secondary importance to the ultimate outcome of the Manchurian campaign, the 2d Far Eastern Front's operations contributed significantly to the Far East Command's success and, coincidently, left the legacy of a massive amount of military experience regarding how to conduct military operations in challenging terrain conditions. The *front's* forces conducted extremely complex military operations across an extremely broad front, often in concert with naval forces, and, while doing so, mastered some of the most difficult terrain in Manchuria. In addition, some of the heaviest and most costly fighting during the entire campaign occurred during the 2d Far Eastern Front's operations, in particular, when Japanese forces from the 134th and 123d Infantry Divisions and the 135th Independent Mixed Brigade resisted these secondary Soviet efforts (see Maps 60 and 61).

The operational sector of Army General M. A. Purkaev's 2d Far Eastern Front extended from the extreme northern tip of Manchuria southward along the Amur and Ussuri Rivers past Blagoveshchensk and Khabarovsk to Iman north of Lake Khanka. Across the broad rivers, which ran along most of his front, rose the broken terrain and wooded foothills of the Lesser Khingan Mountains, with the heavily wooded mountain peaks looming close behind. In many places, such as the confluence of the Sungari and Amur Rivers, swamps of various widths paralleled the rivers' banks, inhibiting ground movement of any sort. The only trafficable approaches into central Manchuria in Purkaev's sector were along the mountain roads south of Sunwu and through the Sungari River corridor at Chiamussu in the north, and along the dirt road from Jaoho on the Ussuri River across the Wanta Shan Mountains (highlands) to the railhead at Paoching.

In accordance with Vasilevsky's instructions, Purkaev concentrated his forces in three widely separate operational sectors, ordered them to conduct operations along three separate, diverging axes, and assigned each force its own specific objective (see Map 62).

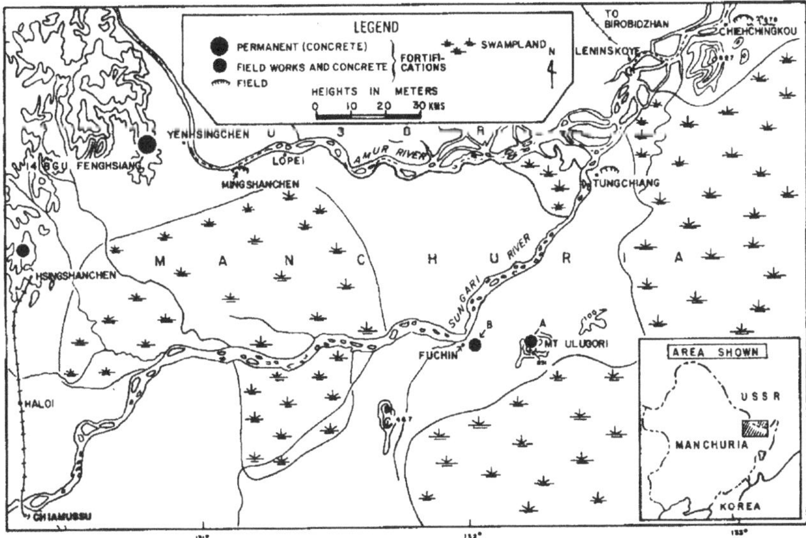

Map 60. Japanese 134th Infantry Division Defenses in the Chiamussu Region (Japanese View)

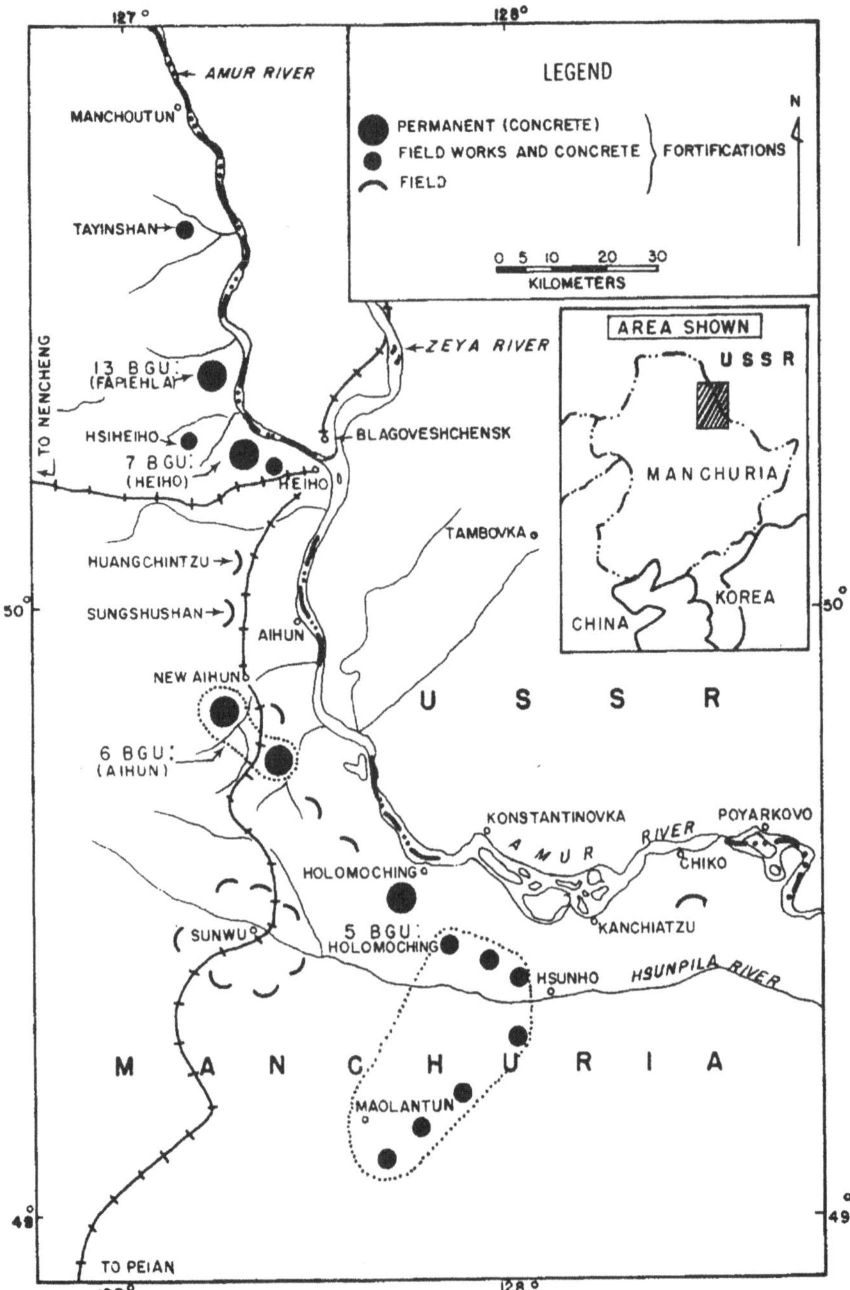

Map 61. Japanese 4th Separate Army Defenses in the Aihun-Sunwu Region (Japanese View)

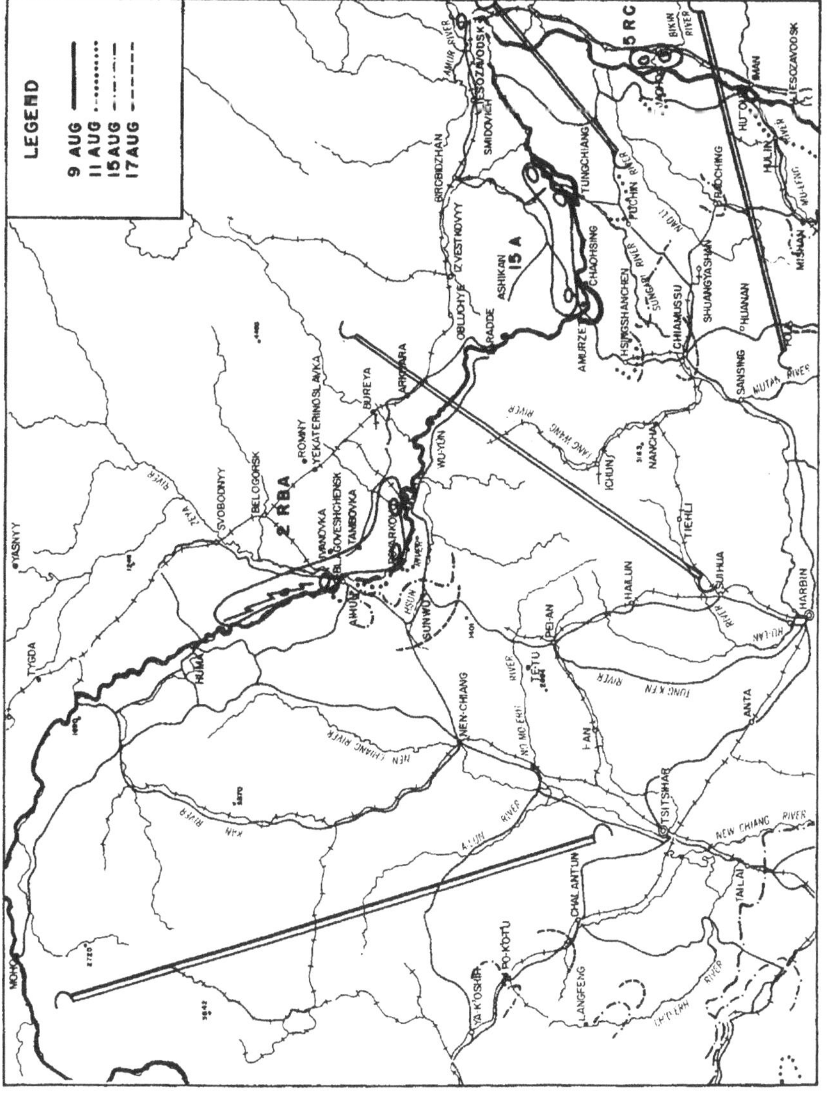

Map 62. Soviet 2d Far Eastern Front Operations, 9–19 August 1945

Purkaev ordered Lieutenant General S. K Mamonov's 15th Army, which consisted of three rifle divisions, to conduct the main attack in the *front's* central sector southwest of Khabarovsk. Mamonov planned his offensive in three phases. First, his forces were to assault across the Amur River at several points near Leninskoe, supported by elements of the Amur River Flotilla. After crossing the Amur River, they were to capture the Japanese fortified regions at Hsingshanchen, Fenghsiang, and Fuchin, near the confluence of the Amur and Sungari Rivers. Once the fortified regions were either isolated or in Soviet hands, his forces were to advance along the Sungari River to capture Chiamussu, Ilan (Sansing), and Harbin, where they were to link up with the forces of the 1st Far Eastern Front.

Lieutenant General M. F. Terekhin's 2d Red Banner Army, which consisted of three rifle divisions and a separate mountain rifle regiment concentrated far to the west of the 15th Army, were to conduct an on-order supporting attack well after 9 August against the Sakhalian (Heiho) region across the Amur River from Blagoveshchensk. Purkaev ordered Terekhin's forces to assault across the Amur River, reduce or isolate the Japanese fortified regions at Sakhalian, Aihun, and Holomoching and defenses around Sunwu, and advance southward through the Lesser Khingan Mountains to Tsitsihar and Harbin.

On the 2d Far Eastern Front's left flank, Major General I. Z. Pashkov's 5th Separate Rifle Corps, consisting of two rifle divisions, was to attack across the Ussuri River from the Bikin region, capture or isolate the Japanese fortified region at Jaoho, and subsequently, advance westward to capture the towns of Paoching and Poli, where Pashkov's rifle corps was to link up with the forces of the 1st Far Eastern Front's 35th Army, whose right wing was to be advancing from Linkou.

As was the case throughout all of Manchuria, all three of Purkaev's attacking armies planned to employ separate tank brigades as forward detachments to facilitate their advance, and they received more than ample artillery support. Purkaev also required each force to cooperate closely with Rear Admiral M. V. Antonov's Amur Naval Flotilla, which would enable their forces to conduct the amphibious assault crossing over the Amur and Ussuri Rivers. Once safely across these rivers, the flotilla was to support and transport the 15th Army's forces farther up the Sungari River to the army's final objective of Harbin.

The 2d Far Eastern Front also controlled Lieutenant General L. G. Cheremisov's 16th Army, which consisted of the 56th Rifle Corps, two rifle brigades, one tank brigade, two separate rifle regiments, one separate rifle and two separate tank battalions, and two fortified regions. The 16th Army's principal unit, Major General A. A. D'iakonov's 56th Rifle Corps, was to conduct on-order operations against Japanese forces on southern Sakhalin Island and, later, Hokkaido Island. D'iakonov's corps was made up of one rifle division, one rifle brigade, one separate rifle regiment, and one separate rifle battalion.[1]

The most formidable challenge Purkaev's 2d Far Eastern Front faced besides potential Japanese resistance was a series of imposing terrain barriers that had to be overcome. For example, about 93 miles (150 kilometers) of terrain containing spurs of the Lesser Khingan Mountains and the marshy lands on both sides of the Amur River separated the 15th Army from the 2d Red Banner Army. Further east, about 50 miles (80 kilometers) of swampy marshland stretching between the Sungari River and the Naioli (Haolino) River separated the 15th Army from the 5th Separate Rifle Corps. Before reaching their objectives, all three forces would have to cross the Lesser Khingan Mountains.

15TH ARMY'S SUNGARI OFFENSIVE OPERATION

Although the 15th Army operated along a front of more than 186 miles (300 kilometers), Mamonov concentrated his army's forces in three limited sectors (see Map 63). Lieutenant Colonel A. K. Oganezov's 361st Rifle Division, supported by Lieutenant Colonel S. G. Myslitsky's 165th and Lieutenant Colonel V. S. Potapov's 171st Tank Brigades, deployed near Leninskoe with orders to deliver the army's main attack across the Amur River and southward to Fuchin. Farther east, Colonel N. F. Mulin's 388th Rifle Division deployed near Voskresenskoe, about 19 miles (30 kilometers) east of Leninskoe, with orders to capture Japanese strong points at Chiehchingkou on the southern bank of the Amur River.

To the west, near Blagoslovennoe, 43 miles (70 kilometers) west of Leninskoe, Major General S. V. Kolomiets' 34th Rifle Division and Lieutenant Colonel R. A. Ushillo's 203d Tank Brigade prepared to attack across the Amur to capture Lopei and the Hsingshanchen Fortified Region. After capturing their designated objectives, the 34th, 361st, and 388th Rifle Divisions were to unite at Chiamussu on the Sungari River. In between the army's principal shock groups, the 102d Fortified Region defended the Amur River sector between Leninskoe and Blagoslovennoe.

Farther downriver, just west of Khabarovsk, the 630th Rifle Regiment was to assault across the Amur and capture the Japanese stronghold of Fuyuan. In the region due south of Khabarovsk, Major General M. A. Abilov's 255th Rifle Division, which was directly subordinate to the 2d Far Eastern Front, deployed to protect the city and, if necessary, serve as the 15th Army's reserve.[2]

The Japanese defended the southern bank of the Amur River in the 15th Army's sector with the 134th Infantry Division based at Chiamussu and the 14th Border Guards Unit, which manned the Hsingshanchen and Fenghsiang

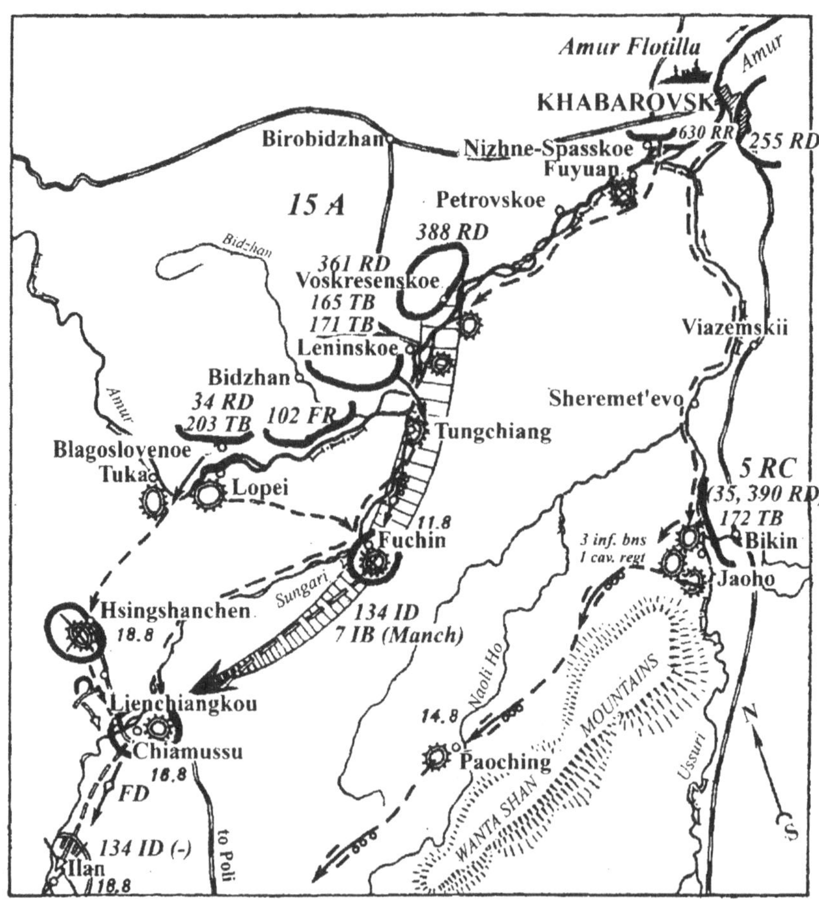

Map 63. Offensive of the 2d Far Eastern Front's 15th Army and 5th Separate Rifle Corps, 9–18 August 1945

Fortified Regions north of Chiamussu. Subordinate units in battalion and company strength garrisoned the various strong points and fortified points along the Sungari and Amur Rivers northeast east of Chiamussu.[3]

At 0100 hours on 9 August, reconnaissance detachments and advanced battalions from all of Mamonov's forward divisions attacked across the Amur River without firing an artillery preparation and captured the major islands in the Amur River. During a heavy rainstorm, the advanced battalions of Oganezov's 361st Rifle Division secured Tatar Island near the mouth of the Sungari River in coordination with the Amur Flotilla. The advanced battalions seized virtually all of the islands in the river, and, during the remainder of the night, the attacking rifle divisions dispatched reconnaissance parties across the river to its southern bank (see Map 64).

Farther down the river, west of Khabarovsk, at 0320 hours the 1st Battalion of the 630th Rifle Regiment, supported and transported by the 2d Brigade of the Amur Flotilla, assaulted Japanese positions at Fuyuan across the Amur from Nishne-Spasskoe and within one hour reached the northern outskirts of Fuyuan. Fire from the Amur River Flotilla's monitors, *Dal'nevostochnyi komsomolets* and *Sverdlov*, the gunboat *Proletarii*, and the 2d and 3d Detachment of River Cutters provided fire support for the final assault. The 630th Rifle Regiment's troops assaulted Japanese positions at Fuyuan at 0730 on 9 August and captured it after a brief fight. Throughout the remainder of the day, 15th Army reconnaissance units and advanced battalions consolidated their positions on the islands and the south bank of the river, while main forces concentrated to conduct a river crossing. All movement was difficult because of heavy rains, high water, and mud.[4]

Late in the evening of 9 August and on the morning 10 August, Mamonov's forces conducted reconnaissance-in-force against Japanese strong points south of the Amur River, particularly in the vicinity of the Tungchiang Fortified Region at the junction of the Amur and Sungari Rivers opposite Leninskoe and the Chiehchingkou Fortified Region across the Amur from Voskresenskoe. In addition, on the evening of 10 August, an advanced regiment from Kolomiets' 34th Rifle Division captured the village of Lopei on the river's southern bank west of Leninskoe and conducted reconnaissance of Japanese strong points to the south.

After completing the reconnaissance phase of the operation by the night of 9–10 August, forward detachments from each first echelon rifle division crossed the Amur River followed by the division's main force regiments. Amur Flotilla ships rafted tanks across the swollen river in a painfully slow process. Red Army engineers employed SP-19 ferryboat parks to transport tanks across the river. Each ferryboat, which consisted of three pontoon boats, had a carrying capacity of 60 tons and could transport one T-34 tank and two T-26 tanks, one T-34 tank and three cargo trucks, two T-34 tanks, or six T-26 tanks per single trip at a speed of 6 miles (10 kilometers) per hour with

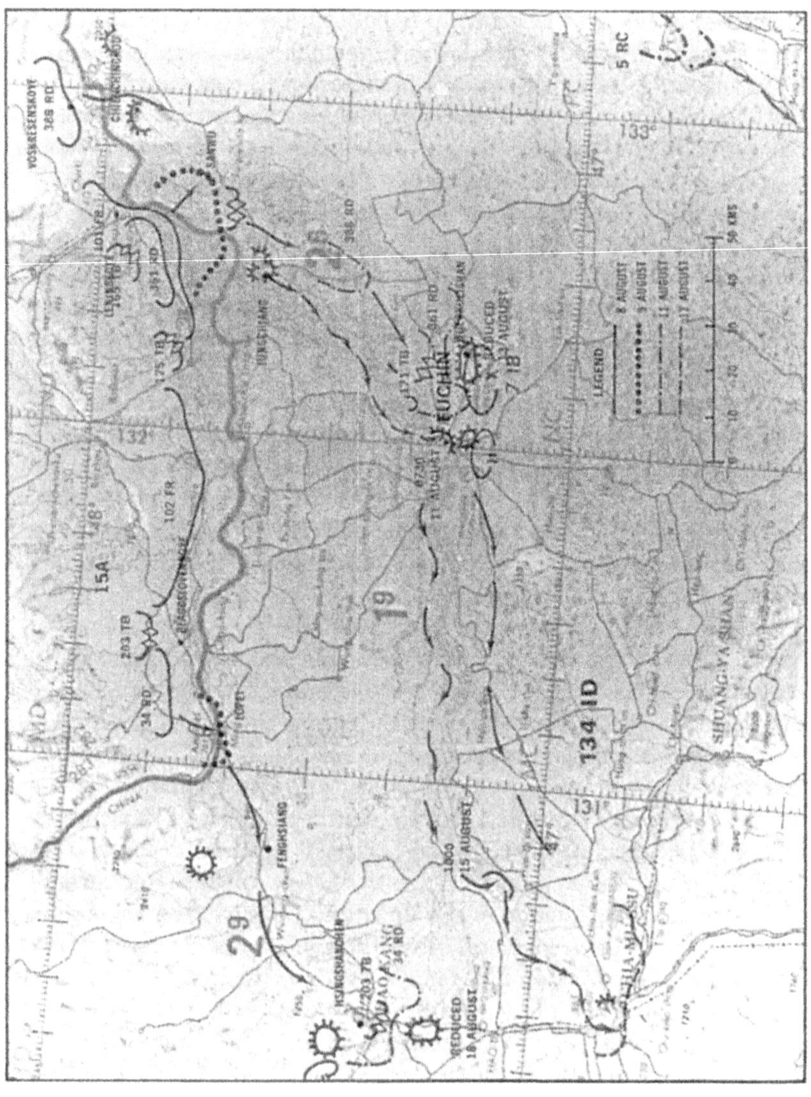

Map 64. Soviet 15th Army Advance to Chiamussu, 9–18 August 1945

the current or 3.7 miles (6 kilometers) per hour against the current.[5] Therefore, it took two to three days to transport one tank brigade across the river.

The tanks of Potapov's 171st Tank Brigade ferried across the Amur near Kuklevsky Channel using only four ferries instead of the planned 14; therefore the process of moving the brigade's tanks took 30 hours instead of the planned 14 hours. Potapov's entire brigade completed the crossing in four days. Thus, from the very beginning of the operation, the tank brigade's rear service units lagged far behind and by the third day were located 93–124 miles (150–200 kilometers) to the rear. Worse still, the flooded road and difficult swampy terrain prevented them from catching up with their parent force, which in turn made it very difficult to sustain the brigade's operations.[6]

The 15th Army employed the bulk (75 per cent) of its engineer forces to support the river crossings and reconstruct roads and only 25 per cent to support the reduction of the Japanese fortified region. For example, a total of eight engineer battalions built roads and constructed bridges during the advance south of the Amur River.

By day's end on 10 August, the 15th Army's forces had driven all Japanese forces from their defensive positions on the southern bank of the Amur in the area between the Sungari and the Ussuri Rivers. Kolomiets 34th Rifle Division and Ushillo's 203d Tank Brigade advanced southward after crossing the Amur River at Lopei, bypassed the Hsingshanchen Fortified Region to the east, and left a small force to reduce or isolate the fortified region. Heavy artillery and air attacks over a three-day period broke the spirit of the Japanese defenders, who retreated southward toward Chiamussu or into the mountains west of the fortified region.

Along the Sungari River, the advanced battalion of Oganezov's 361st Rifle Division, escorted by ships of the Amur Flotilla, landed on the south bank of the Sungari River near Tungchiang at first light on 10 August and captured the town and associated defensive positions after a two-hour battle with Japanese rear guards. Shortly after capturing Chiehchingkou, Mulin's 388th Rifle Division advanced southwestward and linked up with Oganezov's rifle division near Tungchiang. The two divisions, with Potapov's 171st Tank Brigade (reinforced by a rifle battalion) in the lead serving as the force's forward detachment, advanced slowly southward along the road to Fuchin. The Amur Flotilla provided fire support for the advance. Meanwhile, Mamonov ordered the 345th and 364th Rifle Regiments to load their 1st and 3d Rifle Battalions, respectively, on board the Amur Flotilla's ships for future employment in amphibious landings in support of the ground force's advance.

At this juncture, the Japanese 4th Army ordered its forces defending the lower Sungari River region to begin withdrawing southward into the depths of Manchuria, primarily because Soviet forces had reached the Mutanchiang region and were threatening the Fourth Army's right flank and rear.

The first of Mamonov's amphibious assault battalions, the 3d Battalion, 364th Rifle Regiment, reached the Fuchin region early on 11 August. Armored cutters from the 1st Brigade of the Amur Flotilla landed an assault company from the battalion north of Fuchin late on the night of 10 August. At 0730 hours the next day, while the 1st Brigade's ships bombarded Japanese positions at Fuchin, the flotilla assault landed another rifle company to secure a bridgehead near the town, and, at 0830 hours, the 3d Battalion, 364th Rifle Regiment landed to reinforce the bridgehead.

However, the rifle battalion made little headway against heavy Japanese artillery fire and incessant infantry counterattacks. Finally, at 0900 hours, tanks from Potapov's 171st Tank Brigade, advancing with the lead elements of Oganezov's 361st Rifle Division, reached the eastern outskirts of the town, which fell after a coordinated assault. Japanese forces from the 2d Battalion of the Sungari Flotilla and the 25th Security Battalion and Manchukuoan auxiliaries, which had been defending Fuchin, either surrendered or fled to the Fuchin Fortified Region, which was located south of the town, or to the Wuerhkulishan Fortified Region east of the town.[7]

The fortified regions south and east of Fuchin held out for two more days before surrendering on 13 August.[8] While the battle was raging at Fuchin, Potapov's 171st Tank Brigade led the forward elements of the 361st and 388th Rifle Divisions in an advance along the road running southwest from Fuchin towards Chiamussu. However, muddy and waterlogged roads and continuing rainy weather slowed the column's advance to a snail's pace.

Meanwhile, on the 15th Army's right flank, strong Japanese resistance south of the Hsingshanchen Fortified Region slowed the advance of Kolomiets' 34th Rifle Division, which was advancing along the Hsingshanchen–Chiamussu axis. The advancing forces finally broke through this bottleneck on 14 August, when ships from the Amur Naval Flotilla's 1st Brigade landed elements of the 349th and 83d Regiments from the 361st and 34th Rifle Divisions near Sustun (Huachuan) on the eastern bank of the Sungari River, 25 miles (40 kilometers) north of Chiamussu. Outflanked by the amphibious landing, the Japanese defenders fell back to Chiamussu.

Three days later, on 17 August the 632d Rifle Regiment conducted yet another amphibious assault at Chiamussu proper. This force, in coordination with the 1st and 2d Brigades of the Amur Flotilla, and with the 171st Tank Brigade and 361st and 388th Rifle Divisions, which were advancing into the eastern outskirts of Chiamussu along the road from the northeast, broke the Japanese resistance, forced the Manchukuoan 7th Infantry Brigade to surrender, and captured the city of Chiamussu.[9]

After capturing Chiamussu, the 15th Army's forces pushed southward along the Sungari River toward Sansing. Armored cutters of the Amur Flotilla conducted reconnaissance along the river to Sansing, while Amur Flotilla transport ships carried the 632d Rifle Regiment up the river as an assault force with the mission of capturing Sansing. On 19 August this force occupied Sansing against minimal resistance and began taking and processing prisoners from the many retreating Japanese units in the area.[10]

The 15th Army's forces continued their pursuit on and alongside the Sungari River until 21 August, when a forward detachment on board ships of the Amur Flotilla linked up with the 1st Far Eastern Front's forces in Harbin, the culmination of a 12-day offensive operation during which the 15th Army's forces advanced 435 miles (700 kilometers) in the most difficult of terrain conditions but accomplished all of their missions within the designated period of time.

THE 5TH SEPARATE RIFLE CORPS' JAOHO OFFENSIVE OPERATION

On the 2d Far Eastern Front's extreme left wing (and on the 15th Army's left flank), Pashkov's 5th Separate Rifle Corps concentrated its forces in the Bikin region with orders to cross the Ussuri River, capture the Japanese fortified defenses around Jaoho, and advance into the interior of Manchuria to seize Paoching and Poli. Pashkov ordered Colonel I. A. Tepliakov's 390th Rifle Division and Lieutenant Colonel S. F. Zamidchenko's 172d Tank Brigade to lead the assault across the Ussuri River, followed by Major General G. A. Vasilevich's 35th Rifle Division in the corps' second echelon.

The assaulting force faced the difficult task of conducting a river crossing operation, overcoming or bypassing the Japanese defenses at Jaoho, and traversing the hilly plateau region west of the river before marching westward along the poor quality dirt road running from Jaoho through Paoching to Poli.

At 0100 hours on 9 August, the corps' assault units and reconnaissance detachments crossed the Ussuri River, supported by ships from the Amur Flotilla's 3d Brigade. A single infantry company from the Japanese 135th Infantry Division's 369th Infantry Regiment defended the far shore of the Ussuri and the fortified positions around Jaoho with two battalions of Manchurian auxiliaries in support.[11] Preceded by an artillery preparation lasting 30 to 50 minutes, the advanced battalions of Tepliakov's 390th Rifle Division followed the assault units and, during the morning of 9 August, captured a bridgehead on the Ussuri River's western bank north of Jaoho. Main force units followed later in the day.

The Amur River Flotilla used rafts, barges, steamship ferries, and boats to transport forces across the Ussuri River. The transport of the 172d Tank Brigade's tanks across the river was especially difficult. Four 60-ton SP-19 ferries and two 30-ton SP-19 were employed for this purpose in a process that lasted a total of 15 hours. Since the approaches to the ferry loading sites lacked sufficient roads, and the sites themselves were muddy, the tank brigade left its rear services behind.[12]

By day's end on 10 August, the forces of Tepliakov's rifle division had cleared all Japanese forces from the Jaoho Fortified Region and the town of Jaoho, and the following day his riflemen began advancing southwestward toward Paoching in march-column formation with tanks from Zamidchenko's tank brigade in the lead. The march was a difficult one, primarily because the condition of the road was so poor.

Despite the poor roads, resistance was weak since the Japanese Fifth Army had already ordered its 135th Infantry Division to withdraw westward to join its main force. On 14 August, Zamidchenko's tank brigade and the lead elements of Tepliakov's rifle division reached and captured Paoching, driving off its garrison, and continued their march toward Poli. The 5th Separate Rifle Corps' main force followed in its wake.

In the face of virtually no Japanese resistance, on 19 August the lead elements of Pashkov's rifle corps linked up with the forces of the 1st Far Eastern Front's 35th Army at Poli. During its advance, the corps reported capturing 2,786 Japanese and Manchukuoan soldiers and officers.[13] For all practical purposes, the 5th Separate Rifle Corps ceased playing an active role in the Manchurian campaign after its arrival at Poli.

THE 2D RED BANNER ARMY'S SAKHALIAN (HEIHO) OFFENSIVE OPERATION

On the right (or west) wing of Purkaev's 2d Far Eastern Front, Terekhin concentrated the bulk of his 2d Red Banner Army's forces opposite the Japanese fortified regions at Sakhalian (Heiho), Aihun, and Holomoching and the Japanese defensive positions around Sunwu (see Map 65). In the center and on the left flank of his army's attack sector, General Terekhin deployed an operational group consisting of Major General P. P. Demin's 3d and Major General A. I. Kriuchkov's 12th Rifle Divisions, supported by Colonel M. F. Anisimov's 73d and Lieutenant Colonel A. S. Kuznetsov's 74th Tank Brigades. Terekhin ordered this operational group to attack southward across the Amur River from Konstantinovka to capture Sunwu and its associated fortified regions and subsequently march southward through Peian to Harbin.

A second operational group, consisting of Colonel S. M. Fochkin's 396th Rifle Division, the 368th Mountain Rifle Regiment, and Colonel F. S. Vinokurov's 258th Tank Brigade, was to launch a supporting attack from the Blagoveshchensk region across the Amur River to capture the Sakhalian and Aihun Fortified Regions and advance southward to Nencheng, Noho, and, eventually, Tsitsihar. Terekhin deployed the artillery and machine gun

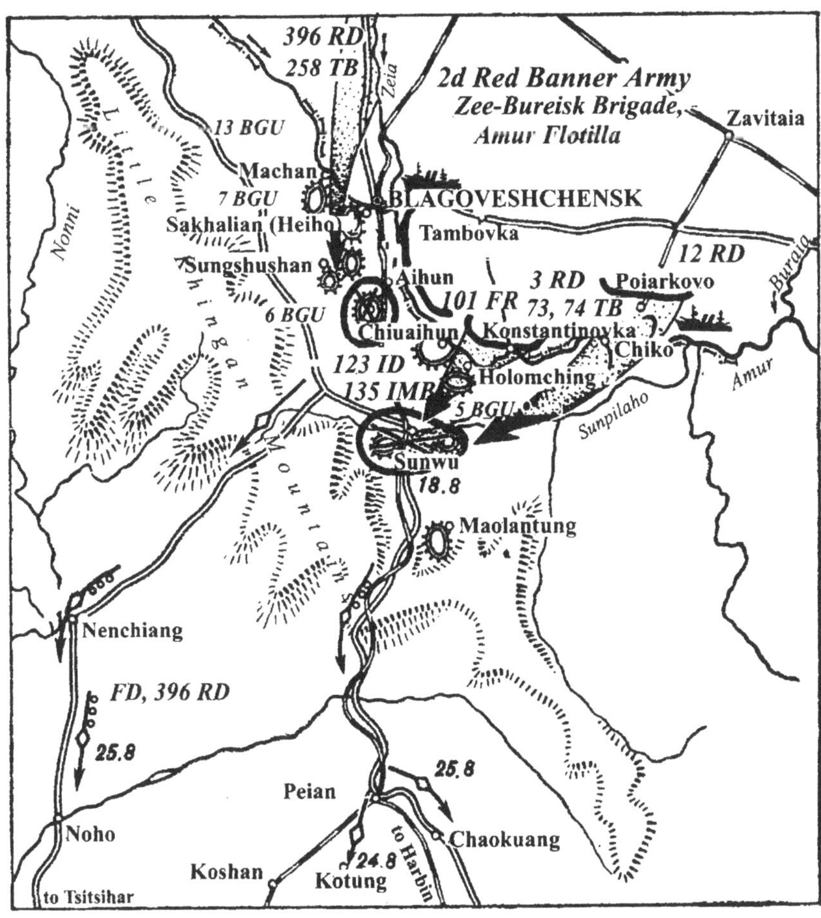

Map 65. Offensive of 2d Far Eastern Front's 2d Red Banner Army, 11–25 August 1945

battalions of the 101st Fortified Region in the sector between the two operational groups with orders to prepare to conduct local supporting attacks across the Amur River in support of his main and secondary attacks.[14]

The Japanese forces defending the southern bank of the Amur River and the numerous fortified regions opposite the 2d Red Banner Army's sector consisted of the 135th Independent Mixed Brigade, the 123d Infantry Division, and the 5th, 6th, 7th, and 13th Border Guards Units (see Maps 66 and 67). The 135th Independent Mixed Brigade, which consisted of five infantry battalions, was headquartered and had four infantry battalions in the main fortified region at Aihun, its fifth battalion at Shanshenfu, west of Sakhalian, and two companies at Chaoshi, just south of the Aihun Fortified Region. The 123d Infantry Division, whose headquarters was located at Sunwu, had the bulk of its three regiments deployed to defend defensive positions around Sunwu, a battalion of its 269th Infantry Regiment protecting the main roads running east from Sunwu and the Holomoching Fortified Region, and smaller elements covering potential crossing sites over the Amur River.

In addition to the two 4th Army formations, four border guards units manned the fortified regions from Sakhalian southward to east of Sunwu. From north to south, the 13th Border Guards Unit (BGU) defended the Fapiehla Fortified Region; the 7th BGU, the Heiho Fortified Region; the 6th BGU, the Aihun Fortified Region, and the 5th BGU, the Holomoching Fortified Region. Unlike the other Kwantung Army forces in Manchuria, both the 135th Independent Mixed Brigade and the 123d Infantry Division were at a high state of readiness in early August 1945 because their commanders had detected Soviet attack preparations and had acted accordingly.[15]

During the first two days of the Far East Command's Manchurian offensive, Terekhin's 2d Red Banner Army remained on the defensive, awaiting word of success from other *fronts*. Between 9 and 11 August, the army's forces limited their activity to conducting reconnaissance across the Amur River, capturing several of the islands in the river, and harassing the defending Japanese forces. The main bodies of Terekhin's designated operational groups remained in concentration areas 12–17 miles (20–28 kilometers) to the rear.

However, given the excellent progress recorded by Malinovsky's Trans-Baikal and Meretskov's 1st Far Eastern Fronts during the first two days of their offensive, late on 10 August, Purkaev ordered Terekhin's army to begin his planned offensive early the next morning. Specifically, Purkaev ordered Terekhin's forces to capture the towns of Aihun, Sunwu, and Hsunho by the end of the first day of operations, in concert with operations by the Amur River Flotilla's Zeya-Bureisk Brigade. The assault forces of Terekhin's operational groups moved forward into their jumping-off positions for the attack overnight on 10–11 August.

Early on the morning of 11 August, under the protection of an artillery

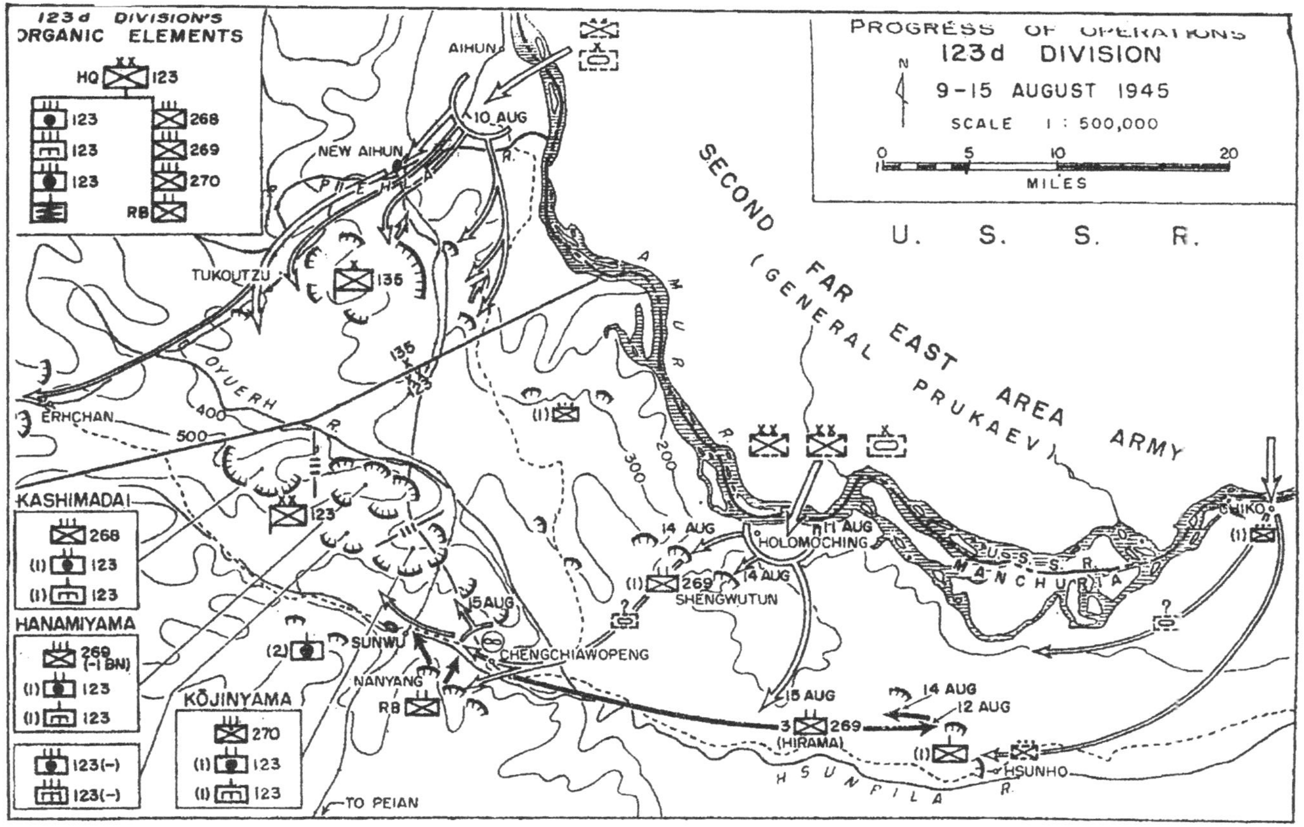

Map 66. Japanese 123d Infantry Division Dispositions and Operations, 9–15 August 1945 (Japanese View)

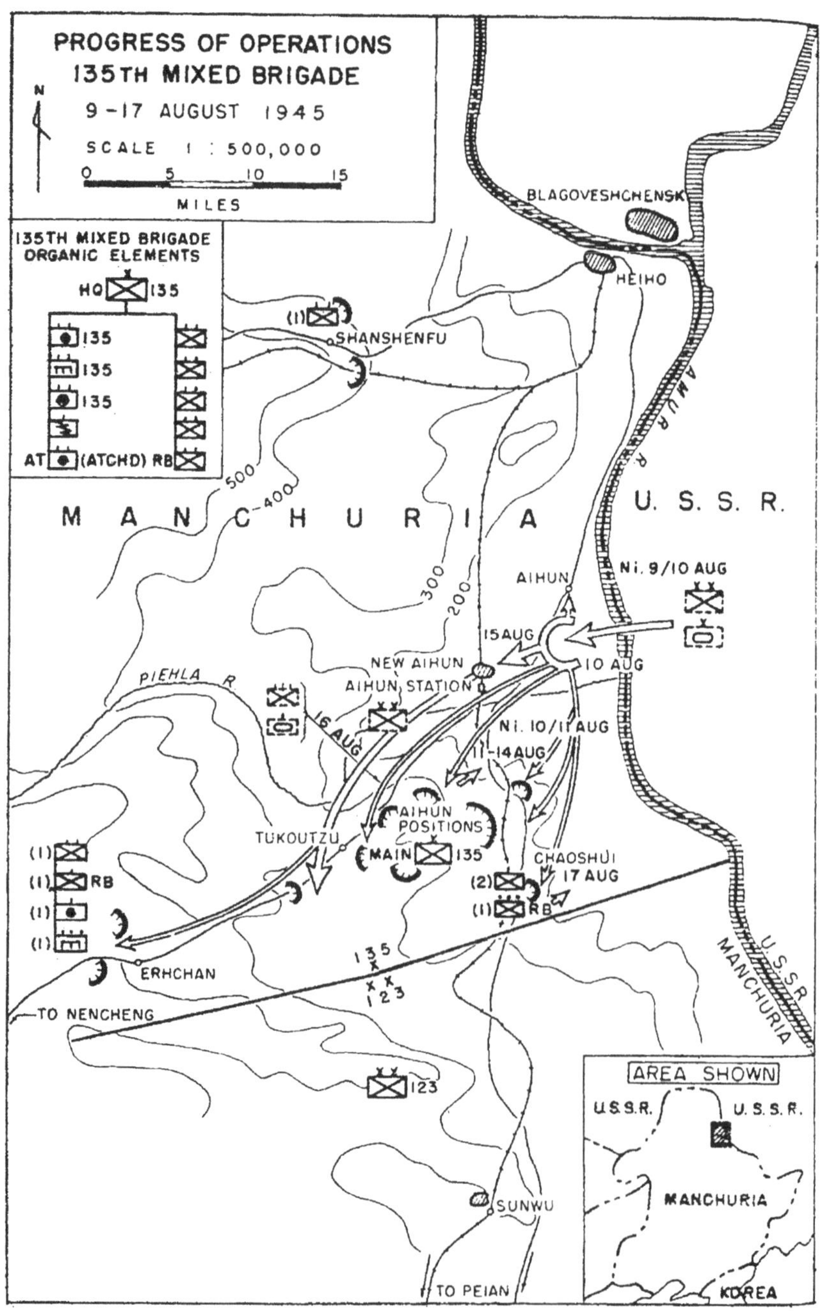

Map 67. Japanese 135th Mixed Brigade Dispositions and Operations, 9–17 August 1945 (Japanese View)

preparation, the reconnaissance parties and assault detachments from the operational groups' first echelons assaulted across the Amur River and seized footholds on the river's southern bank near Sakhalian (Heiho), Aihun, and Holomoching, where they engaged Japanese security outposts and covering forces. Shortly thereafter, the main forces of Terekhin's operational groups began crossing the Amur. Demin's and Kriuchkov's 3d and 12th Rifle Divisions (minus one regiment) crossed the Amur west and east of Konstantinovka, Fochkin's 396th Rifle Division and the 368th Mountain Rifle Regiment near Blagoveshchensk, and the 101st Fortified Region in the region south of Blagoveshchensk (see Map 68).[16]

Because of a scarcity of crossing equipment, it took five days (until 16 August) for the Amur Flotilla's ships to transport all of the 2d Red Banner Army's assault forces across the river.[17] The slow crossing pace forced Terekhin's subordinate commanders to commit their forces to combat in piecemeal fashion as they reached the river's southern bank. The operational groups' forward detachments and advanced battalions engaged the Japanese forward defensive positions south of Holomoching and north of Aihun on 12 August, while additional forces landed to reinforce those already engaged.

On 13 August, Terekhin had sufficient forces available to order his operational groups to press their offensive. Demin's 3d Rifle Division, with his 70th Rifle Regiment and tanks from Kuznetsov's 74th Tank Brigade in the lead, penetrated the defensive positions of the Japanese 269th Infantry Regiment's Murakami Battalion at Shenwutan on the heights northeast of Sunwu. East of Sunwu, the 214th Rifle Regiment of Kriuchkov's 12th Rifle Division crossed the Amur River at the small village of Chiko and advanced westward along the Sunwu road against the Japanese left flank, which was defended by Major Hirama's 3d Battalion of the 269th Infantry Regiment.

Meanwhile, Fochkin's 396th Rifle Division, Vinokurov's 258th Tank Brigade, and the 368th Mountain Rifle Regiment drove the defending forces of the 135th Independent Mixed Brigade back towards the main fortified region at Aihun.[18] Other small detachments from the 2d Red Banner Army crossed the Amur farther north at Huma and Santaoka, destroying small Japanese forces stationed near those towns.

On 14 and 15 August, fierce and heavy fighting raged for possession of the principal Japanese fortified regions east and north of Sunwu. The riflemen of Demin's and Kriuchkov's 3d and 12th Rifle Divisions, supported by tanks from Anisimov's 73d Tank Brigade, broke through Japanese defense at Shenwutan, scattered the Murakami detachment, forced the Hirami detachment back to Nanyang Hill, located just east of Sunwu, and attacked the main forces of the Japanese 123d Infantry Division in the Sunwu Fortified Region.

While the two divisions were struggling to overcome the heavy Japanese resistance east of Sunwu, Kuznetsov's 74th Tank Brigade, reinforced by a rifle company, artillery battalion, and full antitank regiment, drove southward,

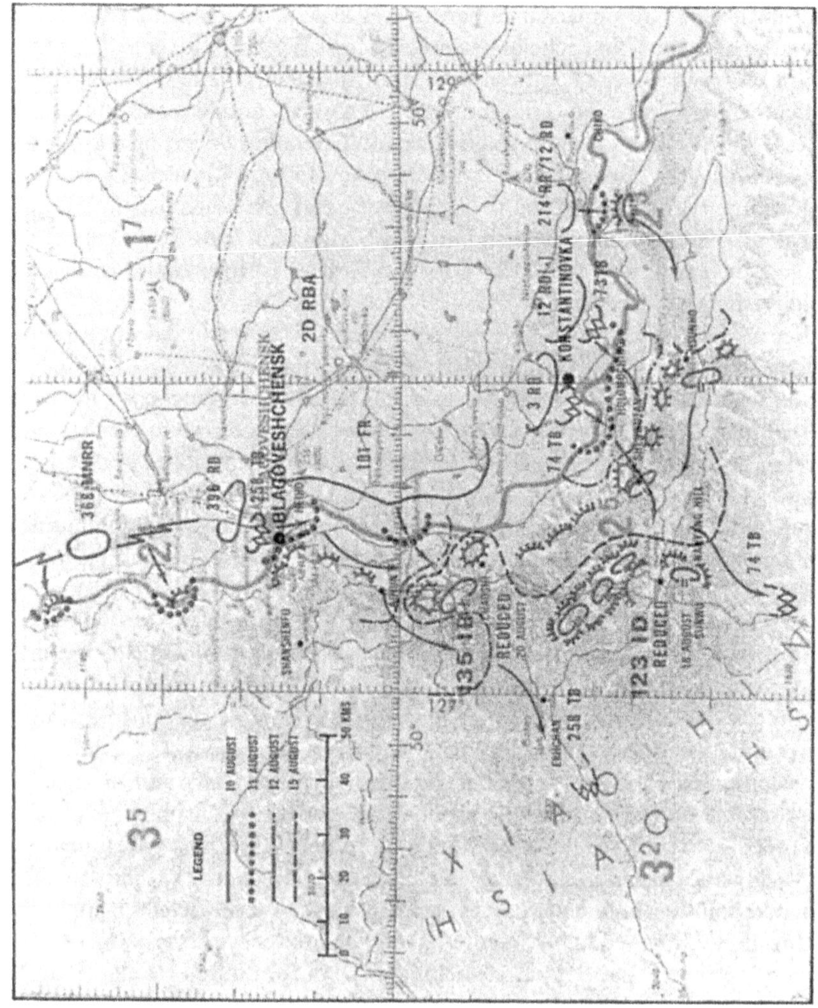

Map 68. Soviet 2d Red Banner Army's Operations, 9–15 August 1945

bypassing Sunwu, and advanced to sever the Sunwu–Peian road. Capitalizing on this success, Fochkin's 396th Rifle Division and the 368th Mountain Rifle Regiment advanced toward Sunwu from the north, surrounding the main body of the 135th Independent Mixed Brigade in the Aihun Fortified Region. The northern operational group also formed a forward detachment around the nucleus of Kuznetsov's tank brigade and ordered it to begin pursuing the remnants of the defeated Japanese force southwestward along the Nencheng road.[19]

After bypassing Aihun and Sunwu, both operational groups assigned the task of reducing the Japanese fortified regions to the 369th Rifle Division's 614th Rifle Regiment, the 101st Fortified Region, artillery, and border guards forces and followed their forward detachments southward along two march routes separated by more than 93 miles (150 kilometers) toward Nencheng and Peian. Forward progress, however, was exceedingly slow because of the bad weather and muddy and rutted roads. To facilitate the southward advance, Terekhin attached two engineer-sapper battalions to the forward detachments leading each of his operational groups' advance.

The remnants of Japanese forces continued to defend the fortified regions around Sakhalian, Aihun, and Sunwu for several days and launched frequent sorties against the Soviet forces that besieged them. Terekhin responded by committing additional heavy artillery to help smash the Japanese defenses, as well as a heavy aviation bombardment by the aircraft from the 10th Air Army's 18th Mixed Aviation Corps. Finally, on 17 and 18 August, the Japanese resistance began to flag, and many of the forces defending the fortified region surrendered or were destroyed. Overall, the 2d Red Banner Army recorded capturing 17,061 Japanese soldiers and officers at and around Sunwu. The Japanese defenders of the Aihun Fortified Region continued to resist until 20 August, when the 369th Rifle Division's 614th Rifle Regiment (the division's second echelon) and the 101st Fortified Region accepted the surrender of the remaining 4,520 Japanese troops.[20]

While Japanese resistance in the Sakhalian, Aihun, and Sunwu region was being overcome, the 2d Red Banner Army's forward detachments and two operational groups continued their slow march to the south, capturing Nencheng and Peian on 20 and 21 August. After the Japanese Kwantung Army formally surrendered on 18 August, Terekhin's two march columns continued their advance in administrative fashion toward Tsitsihar and Harbin.

The 2d Far Eastern Front's forces fulfilled their assigned missions, however, with considerable difficulty. In addition to being required to conduct its offensive in main attack sectors totaling 323 miles (520 kilometers) across an overall front of 808 miles (1,300 kilometers), the forces of Purkaev's *front* had to contend with constant bad weather and difficult terrain conditions as well as Japanese resistance that was more formidable than any other attacking Soviet force encountered during the Manchurian offensive.

In the 15th Army's sector, Mamonov mastered the daunting terrain problems his forces faced by fostering close and efficient cooperation between his ground, naval, and aviation forces. The joint amphibious assaults conducted by his forces and the Amur Flotilla played a significant role in his army's operational success.

In the 2d Red Banner Army's sector, Terekhin's forces faced Japanese resistance around Sunwu that was as fierce and fanatical as that faced by the Trans-Baikal Front's 36th Army at Hailar. At Sunwu, the Japanese 123d Infantry Division and 135th Independent Mixed Brigade resisted as fiercely as the 80th Independent Mixed Brigade and 119th Infantry Division at Hailar. The fighting was so severe in the Sunwu region that Terekhin's forward progress did not live up to Purkaev's expectations. At least in part, this was because the Japanese were forewarned of the Soviet offensive plus the difficulties Terekhin's forces experienced during their assault crossing of the Amur River during the first few days of his offensive.

Despite these difficulties, Purkaev's 2d Far Eastern Front clearly accomplished its assigned mission. His forces tied down most of the Japanese forces stationed in northern Manchuria and prevented them from uniting with the Kwantung Army's main force to the south. However, as is often the case with supporting attacks, the 2d Far Eastern Front's forces experienced some of the harshest fighting during the Manchurian campaign.

NOTES

1. Vnotchenko, *Pobeda*, 96–8; *IVMV*, 203–4; and V. N. Bagrov and N. F. Sungorkin, *Krasnoznamennaia amurskaia flotiliia* [The Red Banner Amur Flotilla] (Moscow: Voenizdat, 1976), 145–53.
2. Vnotchenko, *Pobeda*, 209.
3. *JM 154*, 61.
4. *IVMV*, 11: 234–36 and Vnotchenko, *Pobeda*, 230–1.
5. Vnotchenko, *Pobeda*, 231.
6. Ibid., 231–2.
7. Ibid., 233–4.
8. Shikin and Sapozhnikov, *Podvig*, 137–8 and Zakharov, *Finale*, 143–4.
9. Vnotchenko, *Pobeda*, 235.
10. Ibid., 266–7. Initially, the Soviets claim to have captured 3,900 Japanese soldiers at Sansing.
11. Ibid., 236; *JM 155*, 176–7.
12. Vnotchenko, *Pobeda*, 232.
13. Ibid., 232, 267, and *IVMV*, 11: 236.
14. Vnotchenko, *Pobeda*, 236–8, and *IVMV*, 11: 235, contain additional details about the river crossing operations.
15. *JM 155*, 199–205, 219–20.
16. Vnotchenko, *Pobeda*, 238.
17. Ibid.

18. Ibid.; Krupchenko, *Sovetskie*, 319; *JM 155*, 205–9, 221–2.
19. Vnotchenko, *Pobeda*, 238–39; *JM 155*, 210–12, 222–3; and Krupchenko, *Sovetskie*, 319.
20. Vnotchenko, *Pobeda*, 268.

10

Operations in Korea, Southern Sakhalin, and the Kuril Islands, and the Aborted Hokkaido Offensive

THE PACIFIC FLEET'S OPERATIONS AGAINST NORTHERN KOREAN PORTS (9–19 AUGUST 1945)

While the Far East Command was orchestrating its Manchurian offensive, the Pacific Fleet cooperated closely with the ground and air forces, principally regarding the defeat and destruction of Japanese forces deployed along the coast of the Sea of Japan on the Far East Command's right flank (see Map 69).

At 0330 hours on 8 August, the *Stavka* ordered Admiral I. S. Iumashev, the commander of the Pacific Fleet, to bring his forces up to operational readiness level No. 1, the highest state of readiness, to lay preplanned minefields, and to deploy his submarine force. Earlier, the *Stavka* had delineated Iumashev's area of operations, which encompassed the region bounded by a line extending along the eastern coast of the Kamchatka peninsula, by the northern part of the Kuril Island chain to the La Perouse Straits and the central portion of the Sea of Japan, and then turning south to Wonsan and the coast of the Korean peninsula.[1]

On the evening of 8 August, Iumashev ordered his 12 submarines to put to sea and occupy combat stations in the Tatar Strait and Sea of Japan and directed mines be laid on the approaches to Vladivostok and Petropavlovsk, in the Tatar Strait, and in other regions. Transports still at sea had to return to their designated ports, and the fleet organized air reconnaissance over its area of operations.

In accordance with the *Stavka's* 8 August directive, the Pacific Fleet began active military operations simultaneously with the Far East Command's ground and air forces. Overnight on 8–9 August and through the following

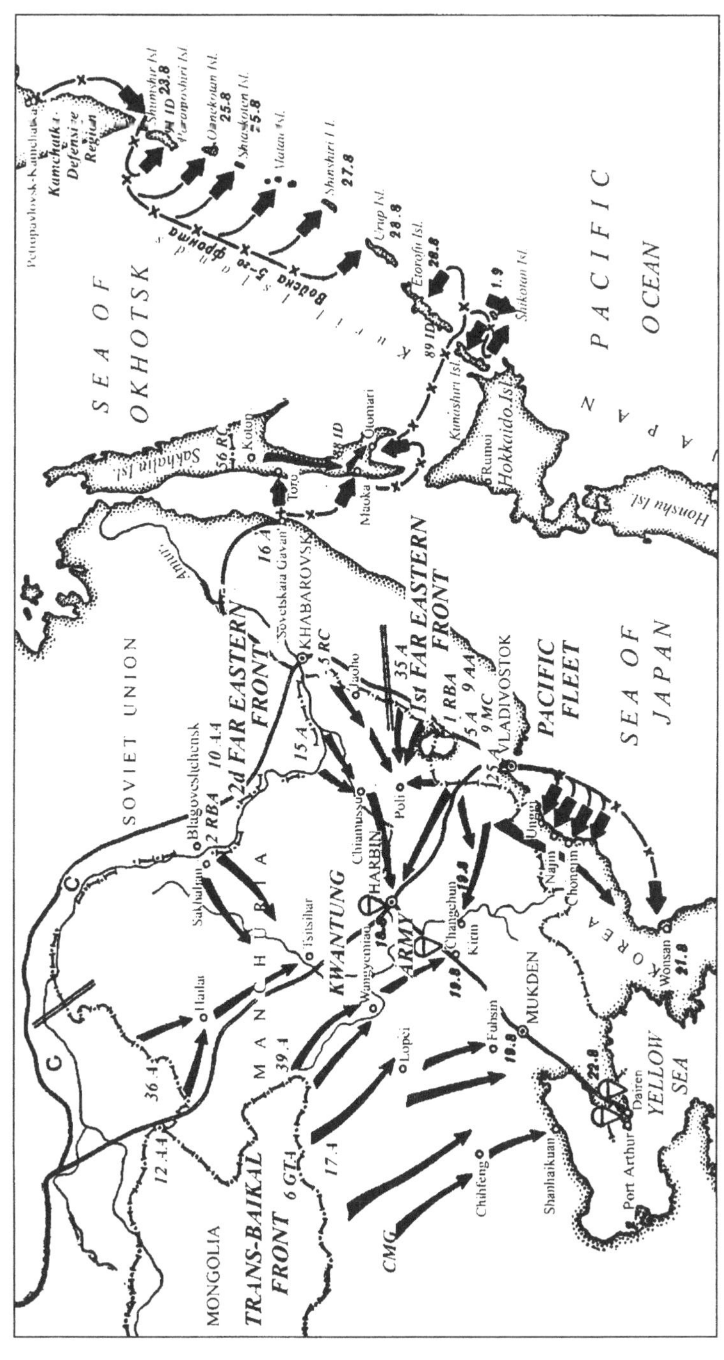

Map 69. Soviet Far East Command's Operations, 9 August–2 September 1945

day, fleet aircraft and torpedo cutters struck Japanese ships, coastal defenses, and other objectives in northern Korean ports. Throughout 9 and 10 August, naval aircraft flew 150 combat sorties against Japanese installations at the port of Unggi and more than 400 against the port of Najin, destroying or damaging a significant amount of Japanese shipping and demoralizing the Japanese coastal defenses. The air attacks created favorable conditions for subsequent amphibious assaults against the vital ports.

The first stage of the Pacific Fleet's operational plan required fleet amphibious and naval forces to capture the ports of Unggi and Najin and hold them until ground forces from the 1st Far Eastern Front arrived in the region. The amphibious assault force designated to capture the two ports consisted of several separate naval infantry battalions, the 13th Naval Infantry Brigade (with the 74th, 76th, 77th, and 78th Naval Infantry Battalions), and Colonel I. I. Malinovsky's 335th Rifle Division. The amphibious force designated to seize Unggi was made up of 922 men, two frigates, eight torpedo cutters, and two escort vessels.[2]

The landing at Unggi began at 1910 hours on 11 August from the torpedo cutters, when a reconnaissance group from the 140th Reconnaissance Detachment stormed ashore. The detachment commander was the famous scout, Senior Lieutenant V. N. Leonov, who had earned fame as the leader of a reconnaissance-diversionary group during the October 1944 Petsamo operation and later founded Soviet *Spetsnaz* (special designation – diversionary) forces. Leonov earned the title Hero of the Soviet Union for his performance in the Unggi landing.[3] The main amphibious force followed on 12 August, and the Japanese force successfully withdrew southward. After securing key points in the port, the naval infantry forces established communications with the 393d Rifle Division of Chistiakov's 25th Army, which was approaching Unggi from the north. Then both forces turned their attention southward to the port of Najin.

The joint Soviet amphibious and ground assault on Najin began on 12 August, preceded by bomber and assault aviation strikes against key targets, including antiaircraft batteries, the railroad station, and the port's docks. The amphibious assault force, which consisted of 973 naval infantrymen, began its landing with the 140th Reconnaissance Detachment, followed by the 354th Naval Infantry Battalion. The heavy air assaults so disorganized Japanese forces that the amphibious detachment's first echelon secured the port within one hour.[4]

After abandoning the port and town proper, Japanese forces took up defensive positions in the surrounding hills, from which they conducted a series of counterattacks against the amphibious force. Despite the counterattacks, the naval assault force tried to advance southward along the road from Najin to Chongjin but failed to make any headway. However, the force did manage to cut off the withdrawal routes west of the town along which

Japanese forces were attempting to flee southward from the advance by the 25th Army's 393d Rifle Division.

Simultaneously with the amphibious assaults on Unggi and Najin, the Pacific Fleet also prepared to conduct an assault against the Japanese port of Chongjin, located south of Najin, which was larger and more heavily defended than either Unggi or Najin (see Map 70). The Japanese had built about 120 semi-permanent defensive works in and around the city, complete with pillboxes and trenches, the strongest of which faced north along the Najin road. The Japanese garrison in Chongjin, which was brigade size overall, consisted of a student officer regiment, infantry and police battalions, and a two-company Korean cutter detachment. The 204th Infantry Regiment manned defenses on the hills around the city, the 202d Student Regiment was stationed in the suburb of Ranin with a force of roughly 1,000 men, and the Japanese command was sending the 4th Mixed Cavalry Regiment to Chongjin as reinforcements.[5]

Before launching the amphibious assault on Chongjin, fleet aircraft and torpedo cutters bombarded the city, destroying several Japanese transports and other ships. According to the fleet assault plan, the 140th Reconnaissance Detachment, led by Leonov, and the 390th Separate Naval Infantry Battalion's automatic weapons company, a total of 181 men, were to conduct a reconnaissance-in-force before the main force assault. The amphibious assault force itself consisted of three echelons: the first made up of the 355th Naval Infantry Battalion, the second of the 13th Naval Infantry Brigade, and the third of Malinovsky's 335th Rifle Division. The Pacific Fleet allocated one mine-laying squadron, one minesweeper, eight escort vessels, seven trawlers, 12 assault ships, six escort cutters, 18 torpedo cutters, and seven transports, totaling 60 ships, to land the assault force, secure the sea routes into the port, and provide fire support for the landing. Three aviation divisions and one aviation regiment with a total of 216 combat aircraft provided air support.[6]

The fleet's torpedo cutters landed the reconnaissance detachment at 0700 hours on 13 August under a screen of smoke from other ships that hid the small force from Japanese artillery fire. Once landed, the detachment broke up into two groups, one to strike the port and the other the city. The Japanese resisted with heavy artillery and small arms fire, forcing the detachment to withdraw to the village of Pohandong, where it occupied defensive positions on nearby hills. The machine gun company, which landed somewhat later, was itself pinned down and was unable to assist the beleaguered reconnaissance detachment.

Major M. P. Barabol'ko's 355th Naval Infantry Battalion, the amphibious assault's first echelon, landed at the port at 0500 hours on 14 August and immediately widened the bridgehead in both the port and the city (see Map 71). However, since the battalion lacked artillery and mortar support, it could make no further progress and was itself pinned down by Japanese fire

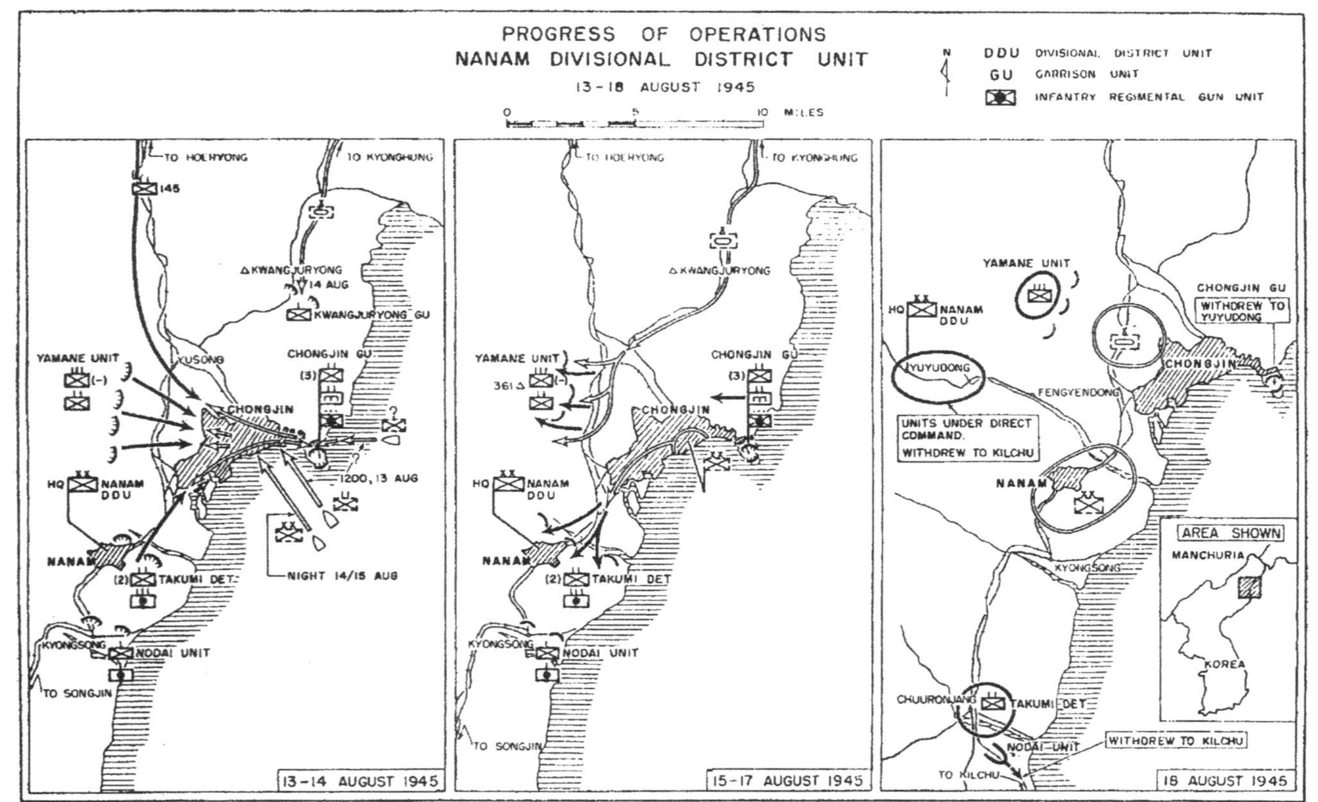

Map 70. Japanese Dispositions and Operations in the Nanam and Chongjin Sector, 13–18 August 1945 (Japanese View)

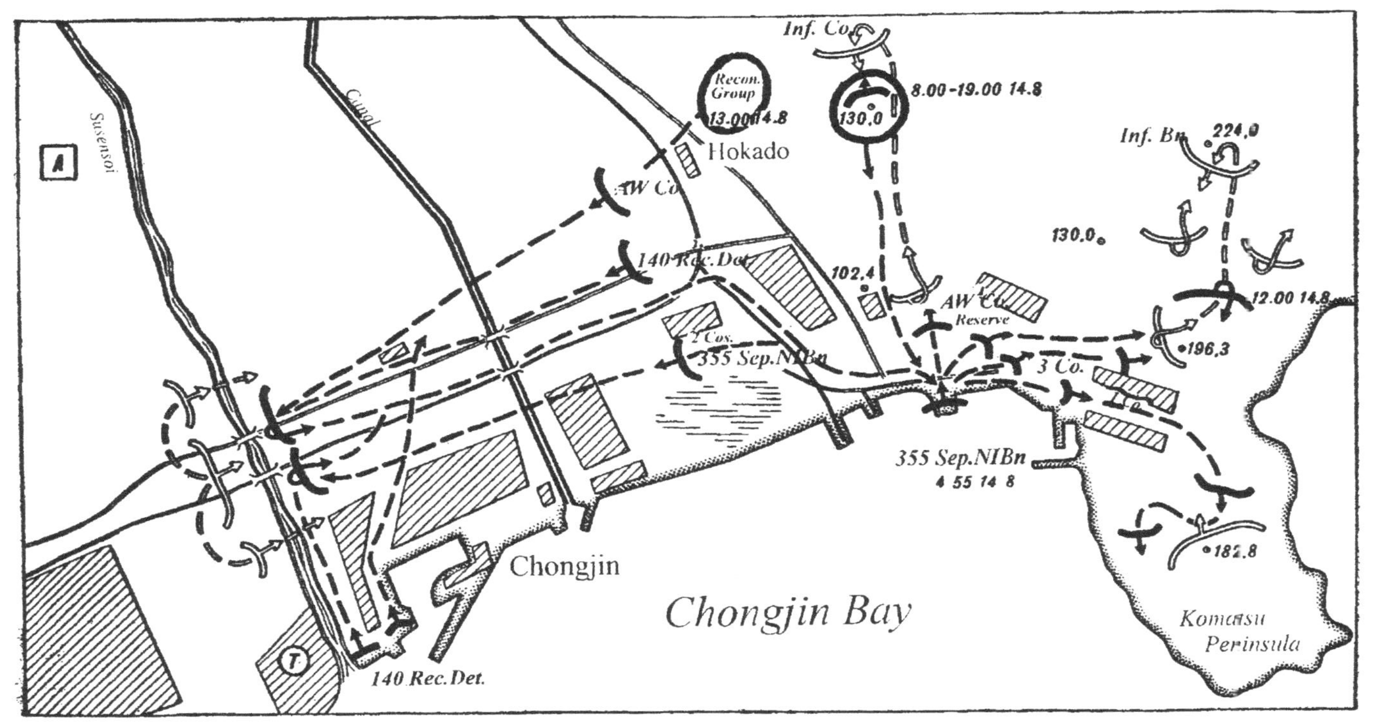

Map 71. Reconnaissance Detachment and 355th Separate Naval Infantry Battalion Operations, Chongjin, 14 August 1945

and almost encircled. At midday on 14 August, the Japanese assaulted two companies of Barabol'ko's battalion with two battalions of infantry supported by fire from artillery and an armored train. When the fleet's ships responded with naval gunfire directly from the ships in the harbor in support of the ground force, Japanese artillery and aircraft bombarded the ships, forcing the ships to put to sea.

The battle then intensified as the Japanese launched repeated attacks, even landing a small force against the naval infantrymen's defensive perimeter from the sea. The Japanese attacks isolated several companies of Soviet soldiers from their main force, forcing them to resort to hand-to-hand combat for their very survival. By day's end on 14 August, the bridgehead had shrunk considerably, and several companies were pressed back to the coast and the port's piers. At nightfall the fighting subsided, only to flare up several hours later as the Japanese assaulted the naval infantry's positions regardless of heavy casualties.

While Leonov's 140th Reconnaissance Detachment and Barabol'ko's 355th Battalion were fighting for their survival, the ships carrying Major General M. P. Trushin's 13th Naval Infantry Brigade, the amphibious assault force's second echelon, approached the port. Trushin's brigade began landing at 0330 hours on 14 August under a curtain of protective gunfire fired by the escort and support ships. All the while fires within the burning city illuminated the landing site. The battalion's assault groups immediately seized adjacent buildings and began driving into the city's center, forcing the defending Japanese to withdraw to the city's western outskirts.

By 0800 hours Trushin's forces and the rescued naval infantrymen of Barabol'ko's battalion had pursued the withdrawing Japanese and captured the bulk of the city and its port and were approaching new Japanese defenses on the hills around the city.[7] The Japanese resisted fanatically, supported by artillery and an armored train, and launched fresh counterattacks with a newly arrived cavalry regiment, but the naval infantrymen repelled the assault with the help of naval gunfire (see Map 72).

Early on 15 August, Lieutenant General S. I. Kabanov, the commander of the newly formed Southern Defensive Region, sent reinforcements in the form of four torpedo cutters to help reduce Japanese defenses on Komatsu peninsula, which was located north of Chongjin, and in the hills northwest and west of the city. Kabanov had just been appointed to command the defensive region, which extended from the Soviet border to Chongjin (and later southward to Wonsan).[8]

The most formidable Japanese defenses that impeded further Soviet operations were the defensive works on the Komatsu peninsula and the coastal batteries protecting the approaches to Chongjin harbor. The 78th Naval Infantry Battalion conducted the assault on the peninsula on 15 August, defeating Japanese defenders and killing an estimated 300 Japanese soldiers

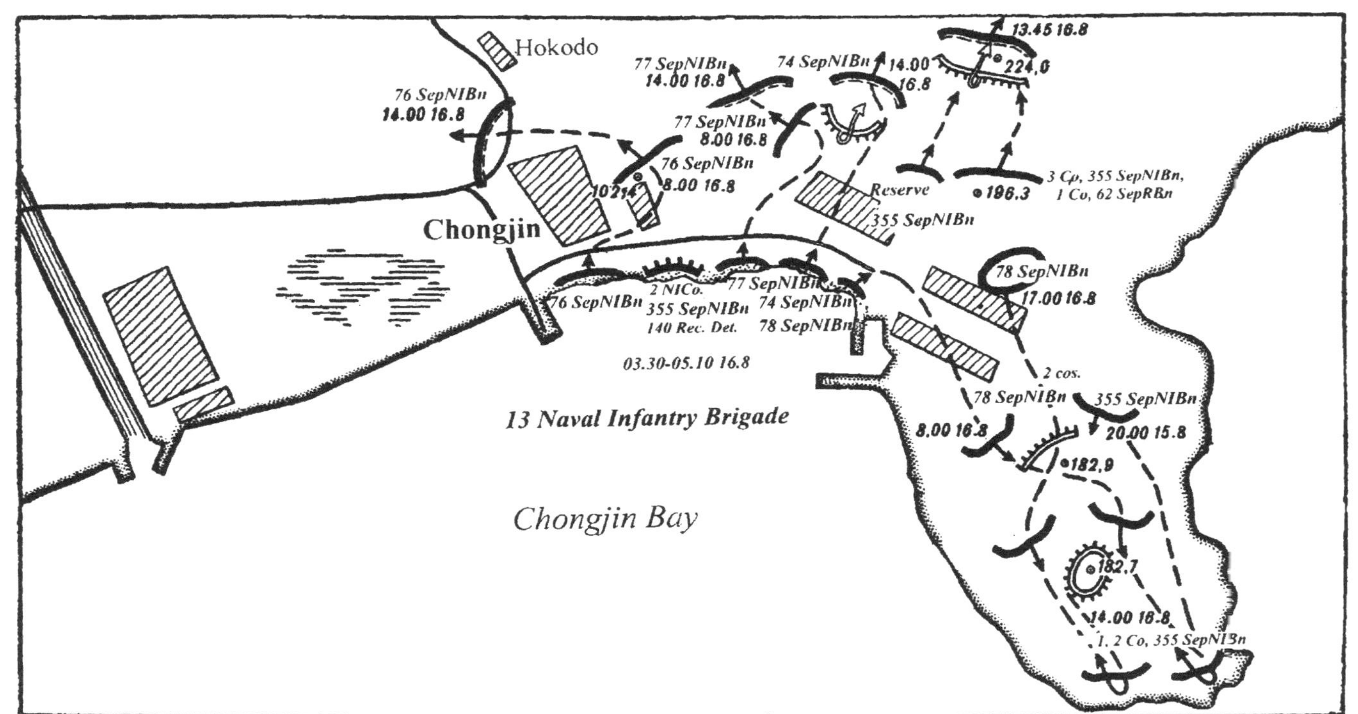

Map 72. 13th Naval Infantry Brigade operations at Chongjin, 15–16 August 1945

and destroying 15 pillboxes and bunkers. At the same time, the 76th, 77th, and 74th Naval Infantry Battalions attacked and captured the Japanese defenses on the hills west and northwest of the city, a process that took two days to complete. The lead elements of the 393d Rifle Division of Chistiakov's 25th Army finally reached the northern outskirts of Chongjin late on 16 August, catching the defending Japanese between his forces and the naval infantrymen and virtually ending the battle for the city.[9]

Three days later, on 19 August, the ships transporting the amphibious force's third echelon, Malinovsky's 355th Rifle Division, arrived at Chongjin after their short trip from the Soviet port of Nakhodka. Simultaneously, Iumashev, the Pacific Fleet commander, dispatched yet another smaller amphibious force to capture the Japanese port of Yededin, 31 miles (50 kilometers) south of Chongjin. Overall, the Pacific Fleet recorded capturing more than 7,000 Japanese troops during their amphibious operations against ports on the northern Korean coast.[10]

The Chongjin amphibious operation was the largest of its kind the Pacific Fleet conducted along the coast of northern Korea. The fall of Chongjin totally disrupted Japanese sea and ground communications between their mainland and the Kwantung Army in Manchuria and materially led to that army's decision to surrender, thus accelerating the end of the war in the Far East. Soviet sources credit their success in the operation to proper selection of the time and place to attack, the surprise they achieved, and the skillful and decisive ground operations by the amphibious assault forces. They single out, in particular, the actions of the 140th Reconnaissance Detachment, whose commander, Leonov, was awarded a second gold star to go with his title of Hero of the Soviet Union for his bravery and skill.

After the amphibious operations were complete, the Pacific Fleet actively supported the 1st Far Eastern Front's 25th Army and 10th Mechanized Corps as they drove southward to the 38th parallel, the dividing line between northern and southern Korea agreed upon by the Soviet Union and the United States, which they reached by the end of August.

THE SAKHALIN OFFENSIVE OPERATION (11–25 AUGUST 1945)

Simultaneously with the ground action in Manchuria proper and the amphibious operations against the northern Korean coast, the Far East Command conducted active offensive operations against Japanese forces on southern Sakhalin Island and the strategically important Kuril Islands (see Map 73).

Vasilevsky, the commander of the Far East Command, assigned the mission of reducing Japanese defenses on southern Sakhalin Island to Lieutenant General L. G. Cheremisov's 16th Army, which was subordinate to Purkaev's

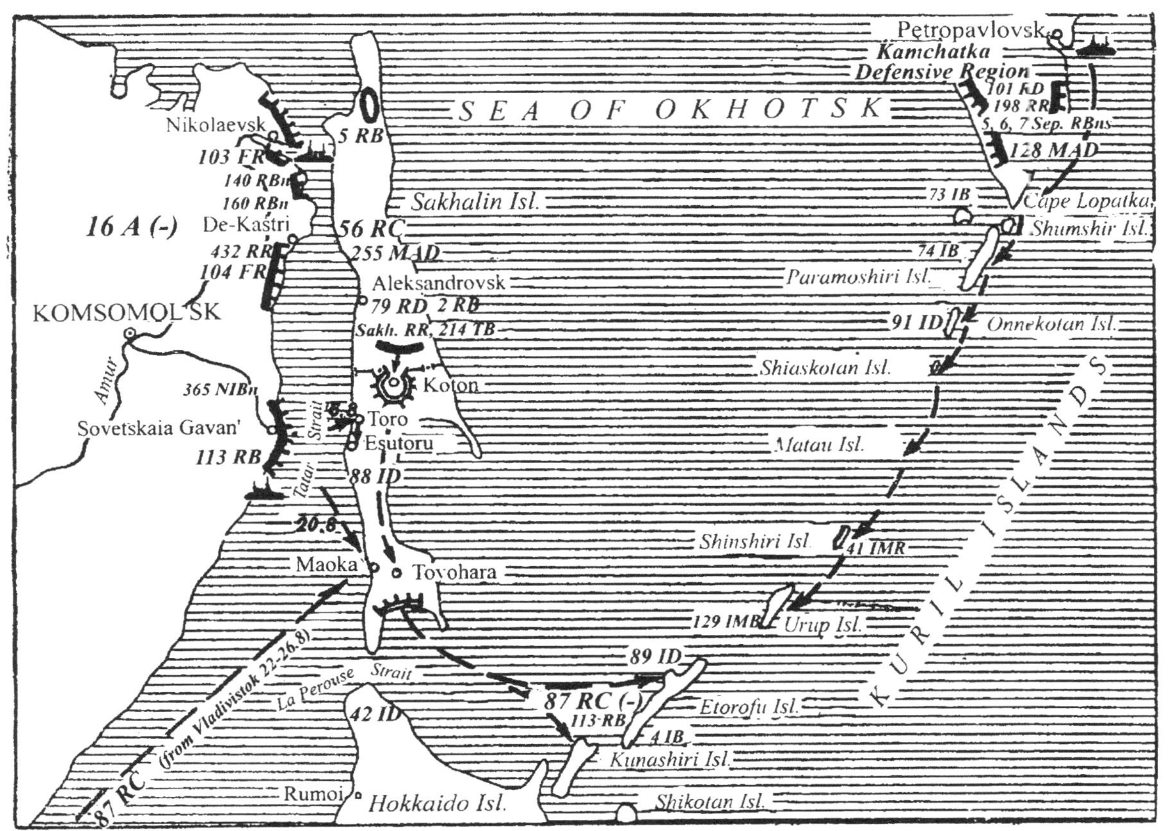

Map 73. Soviet Operations on Southern Sakhalin Island and the Kuril Islands, August 1945

2d Far Eastern Front, and the Pacific Fleet's Northern Pacific Flotilla, commanded by Vice Admiral V. A. Andreev. Cheremisov was to employ Major General A. A. D'iakov's 56th Rifle Corps to smash Japanese fortified defenses astride the island's center, while amphibious forces struck the western coast of southern Sakhalin Island.

The Japanese Fifth Area Army's 88th Infantry Division defended the southern half of Sakhalin Island. The division's 125th Infantry Regiment manned the Haramitog (Koton) Fortified Region, whose location near the Poronai River blocked any Soviet advance southward through the center of the island. Two battalions of the 88th Infantry Division's 25th Infantry Regiment protected the port of Maoka (Kholmsk) on the west coast of the southern half of the island, and one battalion the island's southwestern extremity. The division's 306th Infantry Regiment had its three infantry battalions stationed at Haihoro (Gastello), Sakahama (Dolinsk), and Odomari (Korsakov), respectively. The guns of the 88th Infantry Division's artillery regiment and other subordinate weaponry were attached to its regiments. In addition, border guards troops defended alongside the 88th Infantry Division, and the Fifth Area Army had several reserve units that could be mobilized to support the island's defense.

Overall, the Japanese force on the southern part of Sakhalin Island numbered 19,000 men and about 10,000 reservists, 5,400 of which were defending the Haramitog Fortified Region. However, supporting ships of the Japanese Navy had been transferred to Manchurian ports, thus were not available to assist in the defense.[11]

Because of its strategic location astride the principal potential Soviet invasion route, the Haramatog Fortified Region was the strongest and most important Japanese defensive position on the island; 7.5 miles (12 kilometers) wide and up to 10 miles (16 kilometers) deep, the fortified region contained a security belt and main and second defensive belts. The main belt included three centers of resistance immediately north of the village of Koton, several separate strong points on the flanks of the centers of resistance, 20–30 pillboxes and up to 100 bunkers, antitank ditches, and barbed wire entanglements. The second defensive belt passed through the village of Kiton. The fortified region's western flank was anchored on high hills, and a forested and swampy region in the Poronai valley protected its left flank. Dense forests covered the entire region. In short, any force attacking south had to do so through the very center of the fortified region.[12]

On 10 August through Purkaev, the 2d Far Eastern Front commander, Vasilevsky ordered Cheremisov to attack across the state border on Sakhalin Island the following morning and, in conjunction with the Pacific Fleet, capture the southern half of the island by day's end on 22 August.[13]

Cheremisov's hastily formulated operational plan required D'iakonov's 56th Rifle Corps to conduct the army's main attack on Sakhalin Island directly through the Haramitog Fortified Region to split the Japanese defensive front in two by reaching Kiton village. D'iakonov's rifle corps consisted of Major General I. P. Baturov's 79th Rifle Division, the 2d and 5th Separate Rifle Brigades, Lieutenant Colonel A. T. Timirgaleev's 214th Tank Brigade, the 678th and 178th Separate Tank Battalions, the Separate Sakhalin Machine gun Regiment (field fortified region), the 274th Artillery Regiment, the 487th Howitzer and 433d Gun Artillery Regiments, the 82d Separate Machine gun–Rifle Company, and one sapper company.[14]

So organized, D'iakonov's entire force numbered about 20,000 men, supported by 95 tanks, 282 guns and mortars, 634 machine guns, and 333 antitank rifles. The 255th Mixed Aviation Division with 106 aircraft was to provide air support for the ground forces. This accorded D'iakonov's force superiorities over the opposing Japanese 125th Regiment of 3.7 to 1 in infantry, 10.7 to 1 in artillery, and an absolute superiority in armor.[15]

In addition, an amphibious assault group made up of the 113th Rifle Brigade and 365th Naval Infantry Battalion, supported by ships of the Northern Pacific Flotilla, were to conduct an on-order amphibious assault against the ports of Toro and Maoka. This force was to sail from the port of Sovetskaia Gavan' on the western coast of the Tatar Strait (see Map 74).

D'iakonov decided to launch the 56th Rifle Corps' main attack along the Khanda–Koton axis, the road leading southward through the center of Sakhalin Island, and a supporting attack through Muika (6.2 miles (10 kilometers) northeast of Koton) to envelop the fortified region from the east. He organized his forces into two echelons and a small reserve. The first echelon consisted of the 79th Rifle Division's 157th, 165th, and 179th Rifle Regiments, reinforced by T-26 tanks of the 214th Tank Brigade and artillery, and the 2d Rifle Brigade was in second echelon. The 178th and 678th Separate Tank Battalions were in reserve, and the rest of the rifle corps' forces remained in defensive positions at Aleksandrovsk, along the coast of the Tatar Strait, and around the Okha oil refinery on the northern end of the island.[16]

Baturov also formed his rifle division into two attack echelons. The 165th Rifle Regiment was to attack southward along the Khanda–Koton road, followed by the 157th Rifle Regiment in second echelon, and the 179th Rifle Regiment was to attack from Muika to envelop the Koton Fortified Region from the east. On the right flank of the main force, a reconnaissance detachment made up of a rifle company, a squad of cavalry scouts, and a sapper squad were to advance along the axis toward the village of Nibu, 1.9 miles (3 kilometers) west of Koton.

D'iakonov's forces began their assault at 0730 hours on 11 August. The 2d Battalion, 165th Rifle Regiment, which was serving as the main force's forward detachment, crossed the state border and within two hours reached the Japanese strong point at Khanda, where it was halted by heavy Japanese fire from the right bank of the Kottonhai-Gava River. Heavy fighting broke

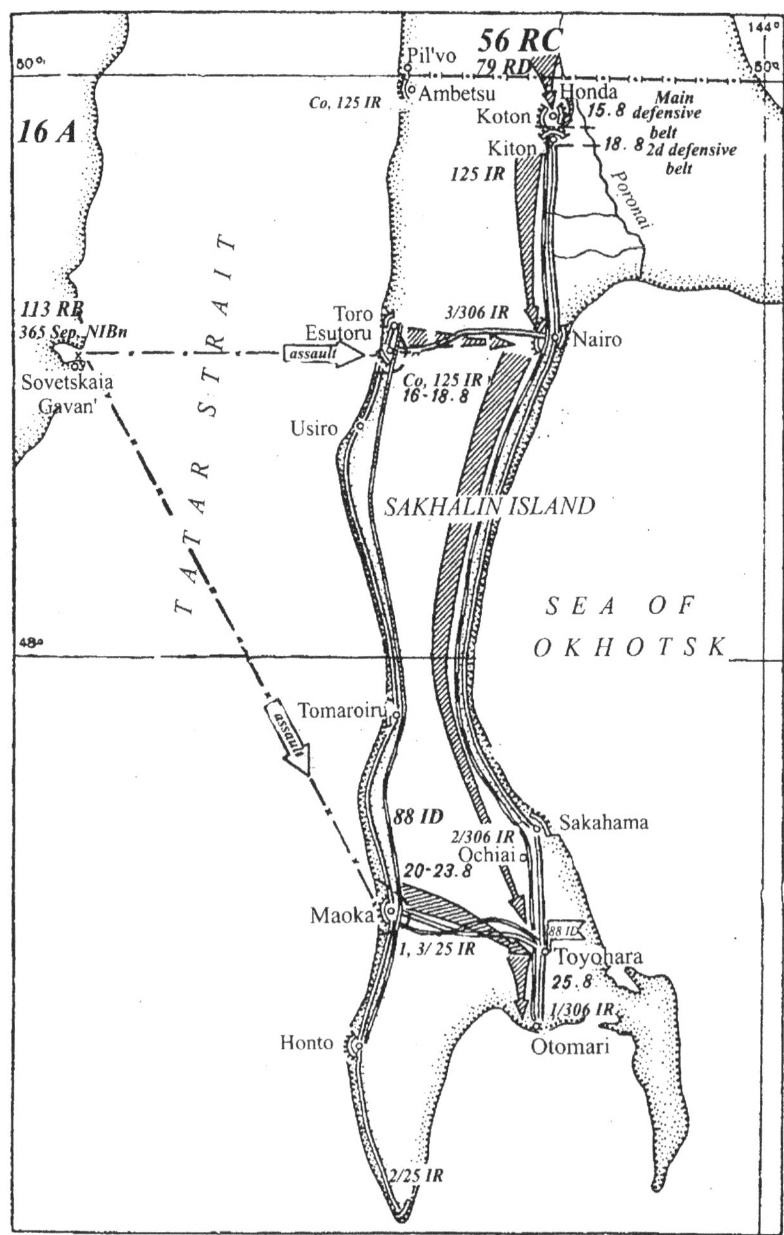

Map 74. Soviet Plan to Capture Southern Sakhalin Island

out, forcing the entire regiment to deploy for combat. However, the regiment's attacks also failed. It became clear that frontal attacks could not succeed since the Japanese defenses were strong and covered by interlocking small arms, machine gun and artillery fire. The only recourse was to attack the defenses by enveloping its flanks.

Consequently, the commander of the 165th Rifle Regiment left a small covering force along his front and led the remainder of his force on an enveloping maneuver through the forests about 1.9 miles (3 kilometers) east of Khanda. At the same time, the 157th Rifle Regiment marched forward from second echelon to envelop Khanda from the west. In spite of the lack of roads, the rifle regiment on the left flank and the reconnaissance force and rifle regiment on the right flank surprised and unhinged the Japanese strong point at Khanda, forcing the defenders to withdraw and opening the route along which the division's main force could advance.

Despite abandoning their strong point, the Japanese conducted a fighting withdrawal using small groups and even individuals to man ambushes along the road and in the forests and laying mines and booby traps to slow the Soviet advance. The tactics worked and significantly impeded D'iakonov's force from accomplishing its objectives within the designated period of time. By day's end on 15 August, the rifle division's lead elements reached the forward edge of the Japanese main Haramitog Fortified Region, where they began to deploy for a full assault.

At the same time, the 179th Rifle Regiment, which had been moving along the swampy banks of the Poronai River enveloping Japanese defenses from the east, emerged from the swamps and captured the village of Muika and the railroad bridge over the Poronai River by a surprise assault. The regiment then moved on southwestward through the swamps toward the eastern approaches to the Koton Fortified Region. However, it too then ran into blistering fire from Japanese strong points located along the road north of Koton village, which brought the advance to an abrupt halt. Without artillery support, it was abundantly clear that further assaults would be suicidal.

Given this problem, the regimental commander decided to blockade the strong point with two rifle companies, while the remainder of his regiment enveloped the Japanese position by a march through the swamp. After marching all night through waist-deep swamp water, early on 15 August the regiment's main body deployed, assaulted, and captured Koton Station, which the surprised Japanese abandoned after a short fight.

However, later in the day, the Japanese regrouped and launched several strong counterattacks, which pressed the 179th Rifle Regiment's soldiers back into defensive positions around the station. Realizing the precarious situation, D'iakonov reinforced the beleaguered defenders of Koton with a tank battalion and artillery regiment, with whose fires the regimental commander decimated the attacking Japanese forces. The same day, after capturing Nibu, the reconnaissance detachment, which had been reinforced by two rifle companies, established contact with the 179th Rifle Regiment.

By day's end on 15 August, five rifle battalions, one tank battalion, and the artillery regiment of D'iakonov's rifle division had reached the rear of the Koton Fortified Region. The next morning, D'iakonov's forces assaulted the fortified region simultaneously from three sides. After three days of additional heavy fighting, the bulk of the Japanese forces were destroyed, and roughly 3,000 troops surrendered to D'iakonov's forces.[17]

After capturing the Koton Fortified Region, the 56th Rifle Corps advanced southward toward Toyohara, the main city on southern Sakhalin Island, without meeting any further Japanese resistance and captured the city on 25 August, assisted by two air landings north of the city the day before.

At the same time that the 56th Rifle Corps was conducting its advance against the Koton Fortified Region, the ships and troops of the Northern Pacific Flotilla and the 16th Army began their operations against the west coast of Sakhalin Island. Initially, from 9 to 13 August, Soviet aircraft bombed Japanese forces and facilities on southern Sakhalin Island, including the ports of Toro and Esutoru and Japanese airfields, with more than 100 air sorties. The actual amphibious landings began on 16 August.

Andreev, the commander of the Northern Pacific Flotilla, received his specific mission concerning the assaults on Maoka and Toro and instructions regarding cooperation between ground and naval forces from the Pacific Fleet and 2d Far Eastern Front. Accordingly, he launched his first amphibious assault with 1,500 men from the 365th Naval Infantry Battalion and 2d Battalion, 113th Rifle Brigade, early on 16 August against the port of Toro. Seventeen combat ships and five transports supported the assault. The landing force drove the three companies of defending Japanese infantry from the port and from nearby Esutoru. A second amphibious force, made up of the 113th Rifle Brigade (minus one battalion) and a mixed battalion of sailors, numbering a total of 3,400 men, landed at Maoka on 20 August and quickly overcame Japanese resistance.[18]

Thereafter, from 22 through 26 August, the three divisions of Major General F. Z. Borisov's 87th Rifle Corps arrived in Maoka after being transported by ship from Vladivostok. The combined force completed clearing Japanese forces from southern Sakhalin on 25–26 August, capturing 18,320 Japanese soldiers.[19] Thus, Sakhalin was cleared of Japanese forces by 25 August rather than the 22 August date required by the original plan, a delay that may have had a decisive influence on the Soviet decision to cancel the Hokkaido operation.

Even though the 56th Rifle Corps played the most significant role in the operation, Soviet operations against Japanese defenses on southern Sakhalin Island were joint in nature, since they involved the close coordination of ground, naval, and air forces. The most compelling and instructive feature of the operation was the assault of the Koton Fortified Region, which involved the conduct of complex maneuvers in difficult restrictive swampy and forested terrain. Carefully tailored assault groups played a critical role in the reduction of the heavily fortified defenses. All the while, the amphibious assaults deprived the Japanese of the opportunity to maneuver their forces, paralyzed Japanese command and control, and paved the way for future operations on Hokkaido.

THE AMPHIBIOUS ASSAULT ON THE KURIL ISLANDS

No less significant from a strategic standpoint were the Far East Command's offensive operations against the Kuril Islands (Chishima in Japanese). By the second week of August 1945, the successes that Vasilevsky's three *fronts* had recorded in Manchuria and the 56th Rifle Corps' apparent victory on Sakhalin Island had created favorable conditions for operations against the Kuril Islands. Consequently, on 15 August Purkaev ordered Major General A. R. Gnechko, the commander of the Kamchatka Defensive Region, to prepare an amphibious operation to seize Shumshir (Shumshu), Paramoshiri (Paramushir), and Onnekotan (Onekotan) islands, the northernmost islands in the Kuril chain.

Forces from the Kamchatka Defensive Region and ships and units of the Petropavlovsk Naval Base were to conduct the amphibious operation under Gnechko's direction. Captain 1st Rank D. G. Ponomarev, the commander of the Petropavlovsk Naval Base, was to supervise the transport and landing of the amphibious landing forces, and Major General P. I. D'iakov, the commander of the 101st Rifle Division, was to command the actual landing force.

D'iakov's force consisted of his 101st Rifle Division (less its 302d Rifle Regiment), one battalion of naval infantry, a company of border guard troops, one battalion of the 428th Howitzer Artillery Regiment, and ships from the Petropavlovsk Naval Base. The 42 aircraft of the 128th Mixed Aviation Division provided air support. Gnechko's reserve, which remained at the naval base in readiness to reinforce the assault, consisted of the 198th Separate Rifle Regiment, the 7th Separate Rifle Battalion, and two artillery battalions. So configured, D'iakov's assault force numbered seven infantry battalions with 8,824 men, supported by 126 guns and 79 mortars (45 mm or greater caliber), 120 heavy and 370 light machine guns, but no tanks.[20]

The Japanese garrison on Shumshir Island consisted of the 92d Infantry Division's 73d Infantry Brigade, one battalion of the 31st Antiaircraft Regiment, the Kuril Fortress Artillery Detachment, one engineer regiment, and portions of the 11th Tank Regiment with 60 light tanks. These forces, which totaled six infantry battalions, fielded 98 guns and mortars and 200 light and 75 heavy machine guns and was supported by only seven aircraft. The garrison on Paramoshiri consisted of the 92d Infantry Division's 74th Infantry Brigade (less two battalions), an artillery detachment, and two battalions of the 31st Antiaircraft Regiment for a total of four infantry battalions, 70 guns and mortars, and 112 light and 40 heavy machine guns. The 129th Infantry Brigade was scattered about the remaining islands of the Kuril chain.[21]

The Japanese force on Shumshir numbered 8,480 men. Another 14,500 troops were available as reinforcements from other islands, in particular, Paramushir Island.[22] In addition, Shumshir's 75 miles (120 kilometers) of fairly trafficable roads made it possible for the Japanese defenders to deploy and maneuver reserves and reinforcements rapidly.

As far as the geography and terrain is concerned, the Kuril Islands stretch for a distance of 621 miles (1,000 kilometers) from the southern tip of the Kamchatka peninsula to the northern coast of Hokkaido Island. The northernmost island, Shumshir, which is less than 12.4 miles (20 kilometers) from the southern tip of Kamchatka and 180 miles (290 kilometers) by sea from the port of Petropavlovsk, measures 18.6 miles (30 kilometers) from northeast to southwest and a maximum of 6.2 miles (20 kilometers) wide, for an area of 193 square miles (500 square kilometers). Its terrain, which rises from sea level in the northeast to Height Marker 189.9 meters in the southwest, is flat and treeless but cut by numerous hollows and ravines through which run small streams.

Paramoshiri Island is larger, encompassing 1,003 square miles (2,600 square kilometers), but Onnekotan is also 193 square miles (500 square kilometers). The most suitable landing site on Shumshir was located on Cape Kataoka and on Paramoshiri, near Cape Kasivabara, where the Japanese maintained two small naval bases.[23]

Purkaev's directive to Gnechko read:

> The immediate mission of the amphibious operation is to capture the islands of Shumshir, Paramoshiri, and Onnekotan. The forces will be ready to embark on the ships with their weapons and equipment at 1800 hours 15 August 1945. Submit your operational decision [plan] and associated orders on sea movement to Purkaev, Leonov, and Shevchenko by 1600 hours 15 August 1945.[24]

Gnechko issued orders to his subordinate forces concerning the amphibious operation at 1500 hours on 15 August. His plan called for a surprise amphibious landing on the northeastern coast of Shumshir Island to capture that island, followed by assaults on Paramoshiri and Onnekotan islands. If conditions were favorable, the landings on Shumshir and Paramoshiri were to be simultaneous.

Gnechko organized his amphibious force into a forward detachment, two main force echelons, and a demonstrative assault (feint). The forward detachment consisted of a naval infantry battalion (less one company), a company from the 60th Naval Border Guards Detachment, an automatic weapons company, reconnaissance and chemical defense platoons from the 302d Rifle Regiment, and a sapper company from the 119th Separate Sapper Battalion. The forward detachment's mission was to land on the coast of Shumshir near Cape Kokutan-Saki, seize a bridgehead, and protect the landing of the main amphibious force.[25]

The first echelon of the main force was made up of the 138th Rifle Regiment, a battalion of the 428th Howitzer Artillery Regiment, the 2d Battalion, 279th Artillery Regiment, the 169th Separate Antitank Artillery Battalion, and a company of antitank rifles. This force was to follow immediately behind the forward detachment, attack toward Cape Murokami-Saki, capture Kataoka, and prepare to conduct a follow-on amphibious assault on Paramoshiri Island.

The second echelon, consisting of the 373d Rifle Regiment, the 1st and 2d Battalions of the 279th Artillery Regiment, and a naval infantry company, was to either reinforce the first echelon if Japanese resistance proved strong or, if the first echelon made significant progress, land near Lake Bettobu on the island's western shore and attack toward Kataoka in support of the first echelon's advance. If Japanese resistance on Shumshir was feeble, Gnechko's plan required the second echelon to land on Paramoshiri Island to capture, first, the base at Kasivabara and, then, the entire island.

To deceive the Japanese regarding his actual objectives, Gnechko planned a demonstrative amphibious assault with two rifle companies, an automatic weapons company, an antitank rifle company, and other small subunits from his second echelon. After landing, the diversionary force was to operate in the Japanese rear area to conceal the actual landing sites.

The Petropavlovsk Naval Base provided 14 transport ships, 16 assault boats, two self-propelled barges, four *Kawasaki* cutters, eight coastal cutters, four trawlers, two cutter-trawlers, the minelayer *Okhotsk*, and the coastal escort ships *Dzerzhinsk* and *Kirov* to transport, land, and support the amphibious force. These were formed into separate fire support, minesweeping, assault boat, landing boat, security, and covering detachments. Seventy-eight aircraft from the 128th Mixed Aviation Division and a naval aviation regiment were to provide air cover and support for the amphibious landing, which was to commence overnight on 18 August.[26]

Before the operation began, Soviet intelligence assessed that Japanese forces defending Shumshir manned 34 pillboxes and 24 bunkers and dugouts protected by up to 25 miles (40 kilometers) of antitank ditches. Unfortunately, the intelligence services of the Kamchatka Defensive Region had a poor understanding of the strength and dispositions of Japanese defenses on the island.

The ships carrying the amphibious assault force sailed from the port of Petropavlovsk and adjacent Avachinsk Bay at 0400 hours on 17 August and set course for Shumshir Island. While they were under way, Soviet aircraft bombed Japanese positions on Shumshir and Paramoshiri Island. At 0430 hours on 18 August, in a dense fog, the forward detachment landed in the region between Capes Kokutan and Kotomari-Saki on the island's north-eastern coast (see Map 75). Although the few Japanese troops who defended this shore quickly retreated in surprise, the detachment encountered heavy machine gun, mortar, and artillery fire as it advanced inland toward Hill complex 170.7 (which consisted of the twin hills 171 and 165) and Cape Kotomari-Saki.

The dense Japanese defenses inland and the heavy machine gun and artillery fire from well-dug-in Japanese forces halted the forward detachment in its tracks. Worse still for the attackers, the Japanese began counterattacking with tanks and infantry, but were driven back after losing many of the tanks to Soviet naval gunfire. With the foothold on the shore secure, the main force's first echelon began landing at 0630 hours along with the forces of the diversionary assault, which altered its course due to the heavy fog and dangerous shoals near its original landing site near Nakagava-Van Bay. At this time, Japanese shore batteries opened intense fire on the Soviet landing and support ships. Soviet fire in response proved ineffective because the Japanese batteries were fortified and well camouflaged.[27]

Compounding the landing difficulties, a loss of communications disrupted command and control of the landing force since, during the landing operation, the radios assigned to the forward detachment and the accompanying artillery correction posts were dropped into the seawater and would not operate. The headquarters of the Kamchatka Defensive Region, 101st Rifle Division, and 138th Rifle Regiment were still on board the ships and lacked any communications with their subunits that had already landed. Consequently Gnechko received the first radio messages relating to the forward detachment's operations five to six hours later, when the detachment was still locked in heavy fighting for possession of Hills 165 and 171.

The main force's first echelon finally completed its landing operation at 0900 hours, but was unable to land much of its supporting artillery because it lacked sufficient means to move the artillery from the ships to the shore. Immediately thereafter, the troops from the second echelon also began landing but also without their supporting artillery. All the while, heavy Japanese artillery fire pounded the landing sites and ships offshore. To overcome the problem of transporting the artillery and supporting tanks, the sailors constructed special berths out of excess logs and rafts while under heavy enemy fire. The second echelon's forces finally completed their landing operations at 1300 hours.[28]

Heavy fighting raged on for possession of the heavily fortified Japanese positions on Hills 165 and 171 as the second echelon reinforced the forward detachment and first echelon already fighting in the region and the Japanese

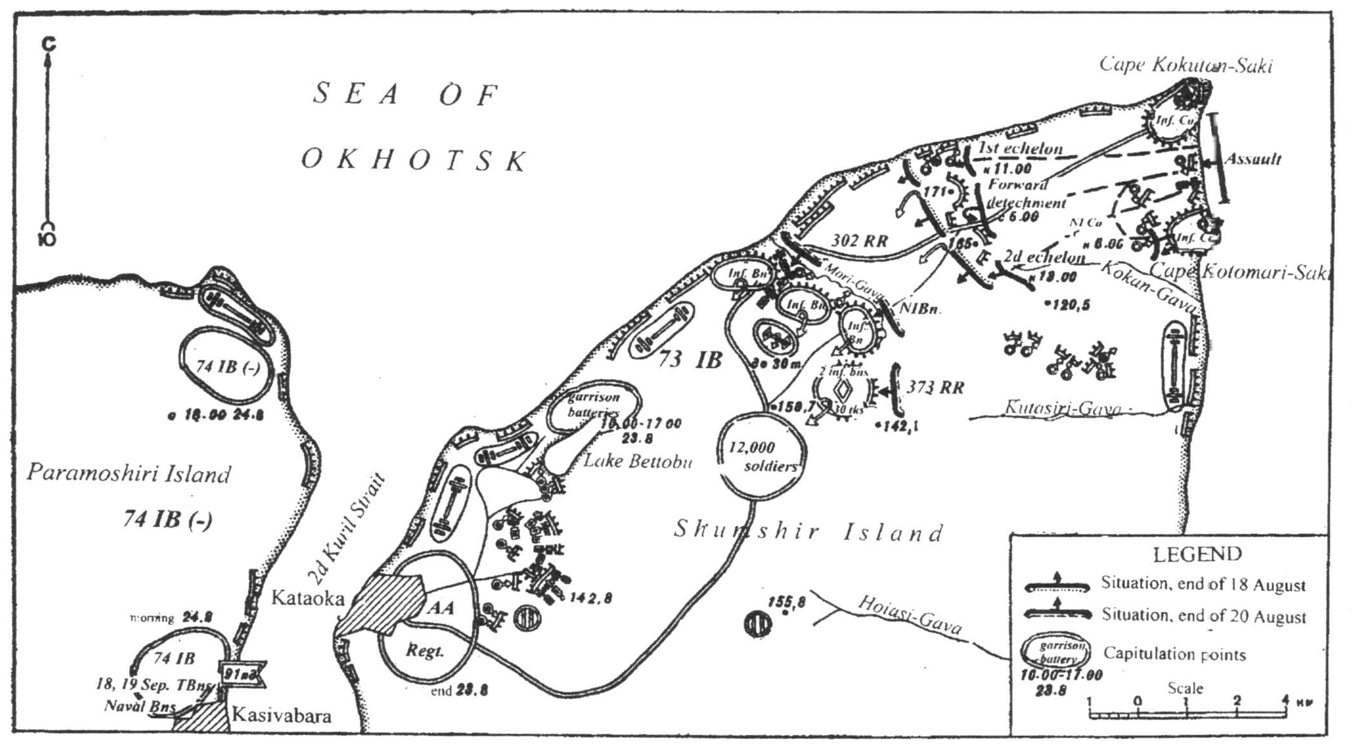

Map 75. The Soviet Amphibious Assault on Shumshir Island, 18–20 August 1945

reinforced their defenses with elements of the 73d Infantry Brigade. At 1400 hours two battalions of Japanese infantry counterattacked with 18 light tanks, trying to force the Soviet troops back into the sea, but were once again answered by naval gunfire, reportedly losing 17 of their 18 tanks. After five hours of heavy assaults, during which the heights changed hands three times, the amphibious force finally captured the Japanese defensive positions on Hills 165 and 171.[29]

Thereafter, the battled tilted decisively in the Soviet favor. During the night of 18–19 August, specially formed assault groups attacked and seized the Japanese coastal artillery batteries on Cape Kokutan-Saki and Kotomari-Saki, and, on the morning of 19 August, boats landed 11 more Soviet artillery pieces on shore, providing the assault force with enough firepower to develop its offensive further.

Even though the Japanese Fifth Area Army command issued its declaration of surrender on 18 August, Japanese forces continued their fanatical resistance, opening fire on Soviet ships that were attempting to traverse the Kuril Straits to bring naval gunfire to bear on Japanese port facilities at Kataoka and coastal batteries at Kasivabara. Nevertheless, on 20 August the amphibious force resumed its advance, throwing Japanese forces back beyond the Mari-Gava River, while aircraft from the 128th Aviation Division bombed the Kataoka and Kasivabara regions. As a result of the renewed fighting, the Japanese forces in those regions surrendered on 21 August.

Between 22 and 28 August, the forces of the Kamchatka Defensive Region landed on and occupied all of the islands in the northern part of the Kuril Island chain southward to Urup Island. By the time the operation against the northern Kuril Islands ended, the amphibious forces captured 30,442 Japanese soldiers, 20,108 rifles, 932 machine guns, 303 guns and mortars, and 60 tanks. In the ensuing five days, Soviet forces captured another 24,000 Japanese.[30]

The Far East Command assigned the task of occupying the southern islands in the Kuril chain to General Borisov's 87th Rifle Corps of the 1st Far Eastern Front immediately after it captured the Japanese towns on southern Sakhalin Island. An amphibious assault by Borisov's forces secured Kunashiri (Kunasiri) Island and the larger islands in the Lesser Kuril Islands chain on 1 September, and on 4 September small amphibious forces from the same rifle corps captured the smaller Habomai group of islands south of Kunashiri, completing the Kuril operation.

The amphibious operations against the Kuril Islands involved transporting a force of more than 8,000 men more than 497 miles (800 kilometers) by sea with only an extremely limited number of ships. This required stringent security measures to ensure the secrecy of the preparations and subsequent sea movement. The force designated to conduct the landing had performed only defensive missions during the war and was ill prepared to launch a complex amphibious operation. This necessitated extensive training before the operation could be conducted. Furthermore, the designated landing site lacked any port facilities, therefore making it difficult to land heavy weaponry and tanks. Finally, the vital naval base at Kataoka had to be captured by a ground assault from inland rather than by a direct assault from the sea.

Although the force ultimately fulfilled its mission, it experienced considerable difficulty doing so. During the assault landing itself, these included poor or non-existent reconnaissance of Japanese defenses, inadequate fire support for the forward detachment and main force's first echelon, and serious disruption of command and control due to a lack of radio communications. After landing, the main force failed to form and employ assault groups with which to attack the Japanese fortified positions on Hills 165 and 171, permitting the Japanese to reinforce the positions and inflict heavier than expected casualties on Soviet forces. Throughout the operation, logistical support was poor, particularly regarding ammunition, because of poor prior planning and the absence of requisite ships and boats.[31] Despite these problems, however, the Soviet forces were able to overcome Japanese defenses and capture the entire Kuril Islands chain.

TARGET HOKKAIDO

Until very recently, most aspects of Soviet planning for the Far Eastern Campaign were well known and well documented, including the Soviet objectives agreed upon by the Allies at Potsdam. Newly released Soviet documentary materials, however, now clearly indicate that Hokkaido was also among the targets of the Soviet Far East Command in August 1945. This, and the fact that the Soviet Hokkaido invasion ultimately did not occur, should prompt further speculation over why the Soviets aborted the invasion and its consequences if it had occurred.

Soviet planning for the Far Eastern Campaign, which began in early 1945, called for Vasilevsky's Far East Command to conduct four distinct operations beginning in and after mid-August 1945. These operations included the Manchurian strategic offensive operation against the Japanese Kwantung Army, the southern Sakhalin offensive operation, the Kuril Islands amphibious operation, and finally, an amphibious operation to capture the southern half of Hokkaido Island. Initially, the *Stavka*, Communist Party Central Committee, and State Defense Committee approved the General Staff's concept for the four operations on 27 June but left the question of the Hokkaido offensive open. In the original plan, the 2d Far Eastern Front was to conduct the Hokkaido operation on order, in conjunction with the Pacific Fleet, once it had completed its operations against Sakhalin Island, that is, after 22 August 1945.

As originally prepared by the 1st Far Eastern Front, the plan for the conquest of Hokkaido called for Soviet forces to conduct an amphibious assault on the northwestern coast of Hokkaido, possibly in concert with an air-landing operation, and subsequently develop the offensive to occupy all of the island north of a line extending from Kushiro to Rumoi on its western and eastern shores, in essence the northern half of the island (see Map 76).[32] In the event Japanese forces resisted, Soviet forces would then conquer the southern half of the island by mounting an even larger effort. The Far East Command timed the commencement of the operation to coincide with the defeat of Japanese forces on southern Sakhalin and the Soviet occupation of northern Korea.

The Far East Command earmarked Borisov's 87th Rifle Corps from the 1st Far Eastern Front's reserve and, subsequently, D'iakonov's 56th Rifle Corps of the 2d Far Eastern Front's 16th Army to conduct the Hokkaido operation in cooperation with amphibious elements of the Pacific Fleet. The two rifle corps were to be available to do so by 23 August, after they had completed their offensive operations on southern Sakhalin Island.

On the evening of August 18, after D'iakonov's forces had finally completed penetrating the forward Japanese defenses in the Koton Fortified Region on Sakhalin Island and while preparations for the Hokkaido amphibious assault were nearing completion, Vasilevsky requested *Stavka* approval to proceed with the operation (see Appendix 7).[33] At the same time, he assigned Meretskov, the 1st Far Eastern Front commander, with the mission, 'to occupy the half of Hokkaido island north of a line running from Kushiro to Rumoi' and 'the southern half of the Kuril Islands to Simushir Island ... during the period from 19 August 1945 through 1 September 1945', and to base one fighter and one bomber aviation division from the 1st Far Eastern Front's 9th Air Army on the island.[34]

The following day Marshal of Aviation A. A. Novikov, the commander of the Soviet Air Forces, and Admiral Iumashev, the commander of the Pacific Fleet, presented Vasilevsky with their revised detailed plans for supporting the Hokkaido operation (see Appendices).[35] Their plans called for ships from the civil transport fleet to transport the assault force.

Having received no reply from the *Stavka*, at 0800 hours on 20 August Vasilevsky sent another message reviewing the progress of all ongoing Far East Command operations and the detailing his preparations for the Hokkaido landings. In part it read:

> At the present time, the 1st Far Eastern Front and I are seriously engaged in preparations for the amphibious operations on Hokkaido. We are now conducting naval reconnaissance and preparing aviation, artillery, infantry, and transport means. With your approval, the amphibious operation will begin shortly after the occupation of the southern portion of Sakhalin, on approximately 22 August 1945.[36]

Map 76. Soviet Plan for the Assault on Hokkaido Island

A return message from Stalin to Vasilevsky late the same day approved continued preparations for the offensive.[37] Early the next morning, Vasilevsky ordered his subordinate forces to complete their preparations, report their readiness to attack by no later than 2300 hours on 22 August, and be ready to launch the assault on his personal order, no later than the end of 23 August. He also ordered Borisov's 87th Rifle Corps, whose forces had not yet occupied all of southern Sakhalin, to complete his operations, concentrate at the Sakhalin port of Maoka, and to commit initially against Hokkaido a force of no fewer than two rifle divisions, each formed into two to three assault echelons (see Appendices).[38]

Then, at midday on 22 August, Stalin suddenly ordered Vasilevsky to hold off on his attack.[39] Shortly before 1500 hours that day, Vasilevsky dutifully ordered that the Hokkaido operation begin only 'on the special orders of the *Stavka*'. At the same time, he ordered Borisov to accelerate the movement of his 87th Rifle Corps to its designated assembly areas at Maoka on southern Sakhalin Island (see Appendices).[40]

In all likelihood, even if Stalin had not intervened to halt the operation, it could not have been launched any earlier than 24 or 25 August . As a report Vasilevsky sent to the *Stavka* at 1640 hours on 23 August indicated, Soviet operations on Sakhalin had proved more difficult than anticipated. D'iakonov's 56th Rifle Corps did not overcome Japanese resistance in the central portion of the island until 20 August, and the 113th Rifle Brigade did not capture Maoka until 20 August. This delayed the arrival of Borisov's 87th Rifle Corps in Maoka until 22 August, and Borisov's rifle corps failed to capture Odomari and Toyohara on the eastern side of the island until 25 and 26 August.[41]

These unforeseen delays also prevented Borisov's corps from fully satisfying Vasilevsky's ambitious timetable for operations against Hokkaido. Nevertheless, the operation could have begun late on 24 August or on the following day had Vasilevsky been willing to begin it without the full 87th Rifle Corps. Given the Japanese decision to surrender, even a weak naval force could have gained Stalin his desired foothold on the strategically vital island.

After Soviet forces finally crushed Japanese resistance on southern Sakhalin, on 27 August Colonel General S. P. Ivanov, the chief of staff of the Far Eastern Command, sent out an order that, in part, explained why the operation was canceled: 'To avoid the creation of conflicts and misunderstandings in relation to the Allies, I categorically forbid the dispatch of any ship or aircraft near Hokkaido.'[42]

No doubt diplomatic factors as much as military realities influenced Stalin's fateful decision to abort the invasion of Hokkaido. Partial review of fragmentary diplomatic correspondence permits certain judgments to be made about the cancellation.[43] Clearly Stalin considered operations against Hokkaido, where the Japanese Fifth Area Army was headquartered, to have both military and political significance and to be an integral part of operations against southern Sakhalin. Despite the Potsdam demarcation line that ran north of Hokkaido, Stalin approved planning for the operation; Potsdam did, after all, permit contingency planning, which Allied commands could later approve.

On 15 August President Harry S. Truman had sent Stalin his General Order No. 1, which suggested appropriate procedures for the Japanese surrender. The next day Stalin boldly proposed that the Soviets receive the surrender of Japanese forces on northern Hokkaido, regarding it as appropriate considering Japanese occupation of the Far East in 1919–21, as well as the legitimate demands of Soviet public opinion. However, on 18 August Truman responded with a terse message rejecting any changes to the Potsdam agreement.[44]

Stalin's 20 August message to Vasilevsky to continue offensive preparations probably responded to existing military conditions and the real possibility for further Soviet gains. Despite the Japanese Emperor's 15 August surrender declaration, Stalin obviously felt that continued heavy Japanese resistance in many regions justified further Soviet belligerence. Even after 20 August, when it became clear that the official surrender would occur no later than 2 September, Japanese forces on southern Sakhalin and in the Kurils continued to resist, and they would do so until 29 August. Until the cancellation of the Hokkaido operation, the Soviets could and did rationalize it as a means of outflanking the strong resistance in the Kurils.

In light of this resistance, the Soviet dilemma was whether to ignore Allied wishes concerning the Hokkaido operation. Russian historians have recently claimed that Stalin's motives for aborting the invasion were to prevent further loss of life and avoid further dispute with the Allies. In reality, it was probably a combination of intense Allied pressure, the impending and by now certain Japanese surrender, and operational difficulties on Sakhalin and with amphibious transport that prompted Stalin to give in on Hokkaido. Only full revelation of the diplomatic exchanges between Stalin and Truman and release of all of Stalin's internal private correspondence will answer this question with finality.

What is certain is that the Soviets planned for a Hokkaido invasion, and, up to 22 August, they were intent on carrying it out. Moreover, they timed it to occur long before planned Allied landings on the home islands farther south. If successful, it would have given the Soviets an even more advantageous position for subsequent military operations in Japan had they become necessary, and an even greater role in surrender negotiations. The Soviets would have certainly occupied all of the island and probably, had resistance continued, participated in the invasion of the main island of Honshu.

In light of what subsequently occurred in Korea and China, the implications for future regional and international tension, if not open conflict, were immense. Soviet control of all or part of Hokkaido would have created a situation in the Far East analogous to that which came to exist in postwar central Europe. A two- (or even three-) power division of Japan would have forestalled postwar Japanese reconstruction, prolonged the military occupation of Japan, compounded future difficulties in Korea, and placed Japan at the focal point of a more intense Cold War in northeastern Asia for decades to come.

NOTES

1. Vnotchenko, *Pobeda*, 270–1.
2. Ibid., 271.
3. I. N. Shkadov *et al.*, ed., *Geroi Sovetskogo Soiuza, T. 1* [Heroes of the Soviet Union, Vol. 1] (Moscow: Voenizdat, 1987), 862.
4. Vnotchenko, *Pobeda*, 271.
5. Ibid., 272.
6. Ibid.
7. Ibid., 273–4.
8. S. E. Zakharov, M. N. Zakharov, V. N. Badrov, and M. P. Kotukhov, *Tikhookeanskii flot* [The Pacific Fleet] (Moscow: Voenizdat, 1966), 185.
9. Ibid., 183–5, and Vnotchenko, *Pobeda*, 275.
10. Vnotchenko, *Pobeda*, 285.
11. S. E. Zakharov, V. N. Bagrov, S. S. Bevz, M. N. Zakharov, and M. P. Kotukhov, *Krasnoznamennyi tikhookeanskii flot* [The Red Banner Pacific Fleet] (Moscow: Voenizdat, 1973), 220.
12. Vnotchenko, *Pobeda*, 290. More details on the Japanese defenses and the ensuing battle are found in 'Proryv Kotonskogo (Kharamitogskogo) ukreplennogo raiona iapontsev na o. Sakhalin' [The Penetration of the Japanese Koton (Haramitog) fortified region on Sakhalin Island based on materials of the Far Eastern Military District] in *Sbornik takticheskikh primerov po opytu Otechestvennoi voiny, No. 21 (iiul'–avgust 1946 g.)* [Collection of tactical examples based on the experiences of the Patriotic War, No. 21 (July–August 1946)] (Moscow: Voenizdat, 1947), 71–84. Prepared by the Directorate for the study of war experience of the General Staff of the Soviet Union's Armed Forces and classified secret.
13. Zakharov *et al.*, *Krasnoznamennyi*, 219, states that the operation was to be completed by 25 August. Zolotarev, ed., *Velikaia Otechestvenaia voina 1941–1945*, K. 3, 397, admits that the operation was to have been completed by 22 August. For details on the planning and conduct of the operation, see also V. N. Bagrov, *Iuzhno-sakhalinskaia i Kuril'skaia operatsii (avgust 1945 goda)* [The southern Sakhalin and Kuril Operations (August 1945)] (Moscow: Voenizdat, 1959).
14. Vnotchenko, *Pobeda*, 290.
15. 'Proryv Kotonskogo', 75.
16. Vnotchenko, *Pobeda*, 290–1.
17. Ibid., 293–4.
18. Ibid.
19. Ibid.
20. Bagrov, *Iuzhno-sakhalinskaia i kuril'skaia operatsii*, 43.
21. 'Kuril'skaia desantnaia operatsiia (po materialam Kamchatckogo oboronitel'nogo raiona)' [The Kuril amphibious operation (based on materials of the Kamchatka

defensive region)] in *Sbornik takticheskikh primerov po opytu Otechestvennoi voiny, No. 22* [Collection of tactical examples based on the experience of the Patriotic War, No. 22] (Moscow: Voenizdat, 1947), 67. Prepared by the Directorate for the study of war experience of the General Staff of the Soviet Union's Armed Forces and classified secret.

22. Zakharov *et al.*, *Krasnoznamennyi*, 233.
23. 'Kuril'skaia desantnaia operatsiia,' 67–8.
24. Vnotchenko, *Pobeda*, 297.
25. Ibid.
26. Ibid., 298.
27. Ibid., 299.
28. Ibid., 300.
29. See ibid., 300–1, for further details on the fighting.
30. Ibid., 301.
31. For details, see 'Kuril'skaia desantnaia operatsiia', 83.
32. For details on planning for the Hokkaido operation, see V. P. Galitsky and V. P. Zimonin, 'Desant na Khokkaido Otmenit!' [Cancel the amphibious assault against Hokkaido], *VIZh*, No. 3 (March 1994), 5–10.
33. Ibid., 7.
34. Full text of the message in *Shifrovka* [Cipher Message] No. 1723 of the Far Eastern Command, dated 18.8.45 2220. Classified *sovershenno sekretno* [Top Secret]. Copy of the original.
35. For full texts, see *Shifrtelegramma* [Enciphered telegram] No. 302/K of the Far Eastern Command, dated 19.8.45 1445, classified *osobo vazhnoe* [specially important] and *Shifrovka* No. 20094 of the Far Eastern Command, dated 19.8.45 1730, classified *sovershenno sekretno* [top secret]. Copies of the originals.
36. Full message text in Galitsky and Zimonin, 'Desant', 7–8.
37. Ibid., 8.
38. Ibid., 8. Copy of the original also available.
39. Galitsky and Zimonin, 8.
40. Ibid., 9, and copy of the original.
41. Ibid., 9, and copy of the original.
42. Ibid., 9.
43. Cited diplomatic correspondence from Galitsky and Zimonin, 9–10.
44. Zolotarev, *Velikaia Otechestvenaia voina*, 398.

Part III:

Analysis and Conclusions

11
Analysis of the Offensive

GENERAL

When conducting their Manchurian offensive, Soviet commanders at all levels adhered closely to operational and tactical concepts and techniques prescribed by the 1944 *Field Regulations* modified to reflect the Red Army's most recent combat experience and the peculiar conditions in Manchuria. The necessity for a rapid advance, the vast expanse of diverse terrain in the Manchurian theater of military operations, and the nature of Japanese defenses ultimately determined how specific Soviet forces would operate. To achieve the high rates of advance demanded by the *Stavka* and Far East Command, *front*, army, and corps commanders often modified these concepts and techniques to reflect their assigned missions and the unique conditions in their designated operational or tactical sectors and axes of advance.

This was entirely permissible, since, by their very nature, the field regulations were simply 'guides' based on distilled combat experience, which indicated how commanders should operate in a given set of circumstances. Commanders were expected to display imagination and initiative by adjusting their combat techniques to suit the concrete conditions they faced. For example, the regulations advised commanders to deploy their forces in original and diverse operational and tactical formations to surprise the enemy and stressed that individual initiative was the key to achieving surprise and maintaining offensive momentum.

In every combat sector in Manchuria and at every level of command, Soviet commanders planned bold and often risky operations involving extensive maneuver to great depths, and most executed their plans vigorously, imaginatively, and successfully. They were able to do so, because, unlike their counterparts of 1941 and 1942, they had survived over four years of intense combat and had matured in the process. Only the fittest survived the war in the west. Consequently, experienced and thoroughly competent *front*, army, corps, division, brigade, and regimental commanders, whose mettle had been tested and expertise had been forged in the most prolonged and fierce struggle in modern military history, led Soviet forces in Manchuria.

This generation of officers and most of the men they led understood that the Manchurian offensive was the last campaign in a long and costly war. They also realized that only quick victory would produce the peace they so ardently desired and guarantee their survival. This will for peace and survival provided impetus for this last brief but violent spasm of war. Within just 11 days, the violence of war was over.

COMMAND AND CONTROL

Considered within the context of four years of war in Europe, the Manchurian offensive was characterized by several unique features distinguishing it from previous offensive operations. The most obvious was the geography of the theater of military operations, the size and diversity of which forced Soviet commanders to alter their command and control procedures and employ a wide range of fresh operational and tactical techniques. The geographical diversity of Manchuria prevented a concerted, well-coordinated, and contiguous advance by multiple *fronts* along parallel axes, the offensive procedure employed by the Red Army during most of its operations in the West.

In Manchuria, the Far East Command's three *fronts* operated along a 2,734 mile (4,400 kilometer) front toward objectives 249–560 miles (400–900 kilometers) deep in the Japanese rear area. Major and minor mountain ranges, extensive hilly and forested regions, major and minor rivers, lakes, marshes, and deserts, and sometimes simply space separated one *front* sector from another. Only a full-fledged theater command with a complete staff could control operations in so vast and varied a theater. The *Stavka* met this challenge by forming the Far East Command, its first theater of military operations headquarters.

The same mountains, rivers, and deserts that fragmented the theater of military operations as a whole and forced the Far East Command to assign its *fronts* widely separate sectors also fragmented the sectors of each individual *front*. Just as the diverse terrain required the *fronts* to operate along separate axes without direct contact with one another, the broken terrain also forced the armies, corps, and divisions within each *front* to operate in the same manner. While successful operations in these circumstances required detailed and careful planning and crisp and effective execution of missions, it also required commanders at every level to display initiative and react quickly and independently to changing combat conditions. Higher commanders simply could not be everywhere at once, and the limitations of radio were obvious.[1]

TAILORING OF FORCES

The diverse terrain in Manchuria also required commanders to 'tailor' their forces so that they could operate effectively in various types of terrain. 'Tailoring' meant selecting forces and force-mixes whose composition, capability, and previous combat experience best suited them to accomplish their assigned mission in a given terrain sector. The Far East Command applied this principal at every level from *front* down to division and separate brigade. Thus, Malinovsky's 2d Ukrainian Front, whose forces had successfully mastered warfare in the Carpathian Mountains of southeastern Europe, became the Trans-Baikal Front, whose mission was to penetrate the deserts and Grand Khingan Mountains of western Manchuria. Similarly, Meretskov's Karelian Front, which had operated successfully in the forests of Karelia, became the 1st Far Eastern Front, whose mission was to traverse the hilly taiga terrain of eastern Manchuria.

Within the *fronts*, Kravchenko's 6th Guards Tank Army, whose tanks had crossed the Carpathians and had often acted independently on deep exploitation missions, was called upon to lead the bold advance across the Grand Khingan Mountains. Likewise, Krylov's 5th Army and Liudnikov's 39th Armies, which had overcome the heavily fortified German defenses at Konigsberg, were assigned the missions of cracking the Japanese fortified defenses in eastern and western Manchuria.

The same principal applied as well to lower level forces. For example, border guard detachments and fortified regions all along the Manchurian border conducted assault operations against an enemy and across terrain they had studied for years. Often Soviet commands assigned experienced Far Eastern divisions missions over familiar terrain and carefully reinforced these forces with the means necessary for them to accomplish their assigned missions. For example, the 1st Far Eastern Front attached sufficient engineer and sapper forces to the 1st Red Banner Army's 300th Rifle Division so that it could master Japanese defenses in the familiar heavily forested and hilly region to its front.

Likewise, the Trans-Baikal and 1st Far Eastern Fronts reinforced their 5th, 39th, and 25th Armies with the additional sapper and heavy artillery support they required to assault and destroy fortified regions and with requisite mobile forces necessary to exploit once they had completed their penetration operations. In the same manner, the Far East Command provided additional bridging forces and equipment to the 2d Far Eastern Front's armies and separate rifle corps so that they could cross the formidable Amur and Ussuri Rivers.[2] Finally, in western Manchuria, the Trans-Baikal Front assigned to 6th Guards Tank Army extra aviation assets to assist in reconnoitering regions the army could not cover on the ground and to establish communications between units operating on widely separate axes of advance.[3]

OPERATIONAL SECURITY AND SURPRISE

The *Stavka* and Far East Command achieved strategic and operational surprise in the Manchurian offensive by means of a variety of carefully planned measures. First and foremost, it did so by planning and conducting a massive regrouping of forces to and within the Far East region, while keeping the bulk of the regrouping secret from the Japanese. Draconian security measures masked the scale of movements and the transfer of key command personnel to the area. Thereafter, Soviet forces moved from their assembly areas to jumping-off positions at the last possible moment, reinforcing the strategic surprise and surprising Japanese forces operationally and tactically as well.

Force after Soviet force deployed forward from jumping-off positions 12.4–50 miles (20–80) kilometers from the state borders and began the invasion literally from the march. For example, the Trans-Baikal Front's 6th Guards Tank Army conducted its final march from its assembly areas and crossed the border without halting in final jumping-off positions.[4] Even when its forces attacked two days after its neighboring *fronts* commenced their operations, the 2d Red Banner Army's forces moved into their jumping-off positions from areas far to the rear.[5]

All of the attacking *fronts* and armies cloaked their operational planning in an impenetrable veil of secrecy and limited active planning to a restricted and finite number of senior officers. The *Stavka* directive that ordered planning to begin ended with this warning:

> The *front* commander, the member of the Military Council [commissar], *front* chiefs of staff, and the chiefs of the *front's* operational department are to be permitted to take full part in working out the plan of operations. The chiefs of branches and services may be allowed to take part in working out their special sections of the plan without being informed of the *front's* general objectives. The army commanders are to be told their objectives orally without passing on written *front* directives. The plan for working out an army's operational plan is to be the same as for the *front*. All documents regarding troop plans and actions shall be kept in the personal safes of the *front* commander and the army commanders.[6]

The timing of the offensive also contributed to the achievement of surprise. The *Stavka* did not assign new *front* designations to the Far East Command's assigned force groupings until 2 August and instructed all of the Far East Command's forces to achieve full combat readiness by 9 August. The *Stavka* and Far East Command reached their final decision on the offensive's timing at 1630 hours on 7 August, less than two days before the attack was to begin.

Japanese sources provide more than ample evidence that the Soviets indeed achieved strategic surprise. Most Kwantung Army intelligence organizations assessed that the Soviets would not conduct major offensive operations against Japanese forces in Manchuria until the mid-fall of 1945, after the rainy season had ended, at the earliest, and most insisted that such operations could not occur until the spring of 1946. The most pessimistic Japanese estimates insisted that the Soviets could not mount a large-scale offensive before September 1945.[7]

General Uemura, the Japanese 4th Army commander, made the only relatively accurate assessment of Soviet intentions when he warned that a Soviet attack could occur as early as August 1945 and had his subordinate units prepare for that eventuality.[8] Japanese complacency, however, smothered his and all other warnings. Certainly, the Japanese reasoned, the Soviets were building up forces, but they were doing so at a rate that prohibited any impending attack.

The defensive measures taken by the Japanese command demonstrated the faith they placed on their assessments. When the Soviet offensive materialized, the Japanese had only partially completed the redeployments mandated by their new defense plan. They had not yet completed reequipping and fully supplying their forward units and, in some instances, had not even begun to do so. On the very night of the Soviet attack, senior commanders of the Japanese 5th Army were attending a planning conference at Yehho and were unable to return to their posts on the morning of the attack. General Yamado, the Kwantung Army commander, was also absent from his headquarters on a trip to Darien.[9]

The marked degree of casualness, if not haughtiness, that prevailed in the Japanese camp reflected their abiding faith in their own predictions and their firm belief that they could resist any attack successfully. This also reflected the tendency on the part of senior Japanese commanders, perhaps born of their appreciation of the Red Army's poor performance in 1941 and 1942, to denigrate Soviet military capabilities. At the other end of the spectrum, the argument that the dismal performance of Japanese forces during the ensuing offensive reflected the low quality and poor *esprit de corps* of Japanese troops is refuted by the performance of those forces that saw combat during the offensive. While many Japanese units never entered combat, those that did so acquitted themselves valiantly. The failures of the Japanese Kwantung Army and other higher commands in the summer of 1945 was a product of overconfidence, indifference, or simple lethargy on the part of senior Japanese commanders and the ability of the Soviets to mask effectively their military preparations and offensive intentions.

The form and location of the Soviet offensive at the strategic, operational, and even tactical levels also contributed to the achievement of surprise. At the highest level, the *Stavka* and Far East Commands' decision to conduct a two-*front* envelopment of Japanese forces from both the east and the west confounded Japanese expectations and redeployments. Although Japanese military planners expected the Soviet to attack in the west, they expected only limited-scale attacks along well-defined axes of advance against Japanese fortified regions in that region. Thus, they totally discounted the feasibility of a major Soviet thrust through the Grand Khingan Mountains, which they considered utterly impenetrable.

The Japanese command also believed that transport and other logistical difficulties ruled out any large-scale Soviet redeployment of forces from the West to the Far East, and the forbidding terrain in eastern Mongolia categorically prevented the deployment of any large forces into that region. If, thought the Japanese, by some stretch of the imagination, the Soviets managed to master these logistical problems, then the problem associated with traversing the wide desert expanses of Outer and Inner Mongolia, obtaining water to sustain so large a force, and surmounting the imposing barrier of the Grand Khingan Mountains certainly ruled out any attack from that region.

The Kwantung Army deployed its forces in concert with these assessments, concentrating the bulk of its forces in central and eastern Manchuria and leaving the west virtually undefended. Nor did the army have any plan for defending that region in an emergency. Having forgotten the lessons they learned along the Khalkhin-Gol in August 1939, they painfully relearned them in August 1945.[10]

Other Soviet operational techniques surprised, confused, and demoralized Japanese forces. First, the Soviet penchant for bypassing Japanese fortified regions by exploiting terrain the Japanese thought to be impassible routinely perplexed Japanese commanders and preempted their defensive plans. Second, Soviet forces attacked along virtually every potential axis of advance, many of which the Japanese thought unsuited for the conduct of military operations because of the poor terrain. Even had they wished to defend this terrain, however, the Japanese lacked sufficient forces to do so.

Finally, sometimes initially and always subsequently, the Soviets led their attacks with mobile forces, usually armor, at every level of command. The use of armor in forward detachments and first echelons caught the Japanese off guard. Since they had discounted the armored threat in such difficult terrain, they were woefully unprepared to deal with it. Without adequate antitank guns, the Japanese resorted to their only means for defeating tanks, *kamikaze* tactics by soldiers with explosives strapped to their backs, who hurled themselves bodily at the Soviet tanks. It was an enormously costly but, sometimes, effective field expedient.

Soviet forces also employed tactical techniques the Japanese had not anticipated. The most productive was their use of small, task-oriented assault groups with heavy fire and engineer support to reduce Japanese fortified defensive positions. This practice clashed with the stereotypical Japanese view that Russians always attacked with massed human waves of infantry, an impression that prevented the Japanese from effectively countering the assault groups before they wrought havoc in Japanese prepared defenses. Soon, but too late, the Japanese understood that the Soviet Army now relied on machines and explosives rather than wholesale expenditure of manpower to accomplish their missions.

Because they remained transfixed by accounts (primarily Finnish and German) of the human wave tactics the Red Army employed in 1939, 1941, and 1942, the Japanese were unaware that Soviet manpower shortages and the increased skill of Soviet commanders led to increased Red Army reliance on firepower and maneuver by tanks and assault guns to overcome enemy defenses. In short, they fell victim to a stereotype, which was invalid by 1945. Even more distressing to Japanese commanders were the pesky Soviet forward detachments, which were constantly probing and bypassing Japanese forward defenses and advancing deep into their rear along unanticipated axes. While these prevented the Japanese from either establishing or maintaining coherent defenses, when halted or damaged they simply grouped or were reconstituted.

Most surprising of all to the Japanese was the high degree of initiative and flexibility Soviet commanders displayed. This clashed sharply with their perception of Soviet commanders stolidly insisting on fighting rigid set-piece battles. In fact, the entire Japanese defense plan was based on the premise that, if they attacked, Soviet forces would engage in successive set-piece combat from the beginning of their offensive. Given the expected attrition to Soviet forces, the Japanese planned to fight the climactic battle against a worn-down Soviet force in southern Manchuria. Partly due to the flexibility and resourcefulness of Soviet commanders, the Kwantung Army did not survive to wage this climactic battle.

MANEUVER

Extensive Soviet reliance on strategic, operational, and tactical maneuver throughout the offensive also surprised the Japanese. In accordance with the 1944 *Field Regulations*, Soviet forces incorporated maneuver in their offensive plans at every level of command and in every phase of the offensive. The rewards were immense. The Far East Command's overall strategic plan required its three *fronts* to envelop a large portion of the Kwantung Army and paralyze the remainder of its forces.

Nowhere did it employ maneuver to greater effect than in Malinovsky's Trans-Baikal Front. Malinovsky's employment of Kravchenko's tank army and Pliev's cavalry-mechanized group in the first echelon of his *front* with the mission of conducting a rapid dash across the Gobi desert and Grand Khingan mountains underscored the audacity of Malinovsky's plan and his confidence that successful maneuver would produce victory. The ensuing deep advance by Pliev's cavalry-mechanized group, Kravchenko's tank army, and Danilov's and Liudnikov's 17th and 39th Armies embodied audacious maneuver and were instrumental in the Trans-Baikal Front's ultimate victory. To a lesser extent, the forces of Meretskov's 1st Far Eastern Front relied on maneuver to achieve victory in eastern Manchuria, although on a smaller scale.

Within the Far East Command's *fronts*, Soviet forces exploited maneuver to compensate for the exceptional spatial separation between operating units. The inability of Japanese commanders to respond effectively reinforced the deleterious effect maneuvering Soviet forces had on Japanese defenses. Luchinsky's 36th Army relied heavily on skillful maneuver to isolate and bypass the Japanese Fortified Region at Hailar and cross the Grand Khingan Mountains, as did Liudnikov's 39th Army when it bypassed the Halung-Arshaan Fortified Region and subsequently advanced rapidly southeast toward Solun.

Even in the restrictive terrain of eastern Manchuria, the 1st Far Eastern Front's 1st Red Banner and 5th Armies managed to envelop and bypass the Japanese 124th Infantry Division, rendering that division utterly irrelevant to subsequent combat. Finally, the joint operations of Mamonov's 15th Army with the Amur Flotilla and the leapfrog assaults on the northern Korean coast, the Sakhalin assaults, and the advance down the Kuril Islands supported by the Pacific Fleet added the new dimension of amphibious envelopment to maneuver.

At the tactical level, the 205th Tank Brigade's bold advance to Hailar, the 257th Tank Brigade's dash from Pamientung to Mutanchiang, and forward detachment operations by the 39th Rifle and 10th Mechanized Corps vividly illustrated the imaginative employment of maneuver within armies and corps. The constant Soviet use of forward detachments to complete the penetration of defenses, to exploit, and to pursue to the depths of the defense was a virtual model for the conduct of successful tactical maneuver. In the final analysis, the paralytic effect of this tactical maneuver on Japanese commands was the single most important reason for Japanese defeat.

Soviet commands relied on maneuver even when conducting penetration operations against prepared Japanese defenses. During the 1st Far Eastern Front's assaults against Japanese fortified regions at Suifenho, Tungning, and Volynsk in eastern Manchuria, Krylov and Chistiakov's 5th and 25th Armies used maneuver by small assault groups to infiltrate, bypass, and isolate fortified positions and maneuver by forward detachments to begin exploitations. Whenever possible, the assault groups enveloped Japanese defenses from the flanks and rear, leaving the isolated defenses to be crushed by concentrated artillery fire. This enveloping maneuver at the small unit level served as a microcosm of Soviet maneuvers at the operational and strategic levels.

RATES OF ADVANCE AND FORWARD DETACHMENTS

Soviet insistence on achieving and maintaining high rates of advance placed a premium on effective operational and tactical maneuver and increased Japanese surprise. Speed was necessary to prevent Japanese forces from establishing credible defenses inside Manchuria and to ensure Soviet occupation of Manchuria, northern Korea, southern Sakhalin Island, the Kuril Islands, and Hokkaido before the Japanese capitulated.

The Soviets generally generated their rapid rate of advance by employing a disproportionate number of tank forces in first echelon to lead their main attacks and to serve as forward detachments. The Trans-Baikal Front led its advance with the 6th Guards Tank Army to preempt Japanese defenses and ensure the *front's* speedy passage of the Grand Khingan Mountains. The 6th Guards Tank Army received a large number of speedy, but older, BT tanks [*bystrokhodnyi-tanki* – fast-moving tanks] to achieve speed in its advance. The 61st Tank Division performed a similar role in the sector of 39th Army.

The Soviets' extensive employment of forward detachments at every level of command demonstrated their intent to record high rates of advance during the offensive (see Table 45). Usually operating 12.5–50 miles (20–80 kilometers) apart, forward detachments led the advance in virtually every operational and tactical sector at a distance of from 6.2 to 31 miles (10 to 50 kilometers) in front of their parent forces. Main force commanders also permitted the forward detachment commanders to exercise far greater freedom of action than in earlier campaigns. The forward detachments' missions included seizing key terrain such as river crossing sites, vital road junctions, and key terrain features such as mountain passes and defiles to facilitate the main force's advance and preventing the Japanese from establishing new defenses in the depths.

For the first time in the war, an entire tank army (the 6th Guards Tank Army) served as a virtual forward detachment for the whole Trans-Baikal Front. As had been the case during the Red Army's offensive operations in the European theater in 1945, army commanders employed forward detachments to generate a rapid advance. For example, Liudnikov's 39th Army spearheaded its advance south of the Halung-Arshaan Fortified Region with the 61st Tank Division, and Krylov's 5th Army led his army's dash from Muleng to Mutanchiang with the reinforced 76th Tank Brigade, although not without experiencing some difficulties.

Likewise, Luchinsky's 36th Army used the reinforced 205th Tank Brigade to blaze a path to Hailar and the Grand Khingan Mountains, Mamonov's 15th Army used the 171st Tank Brigade to lead the ground advance on Fuchin and Chiamussu, and Vasil'ev's 10th Mechanized Corps used two forward detachments to lead the 25th Army's advance to Wangching and Yenchi. In the case of the 10th Mechanized Corps, its forward detachments

TABLE 45: SOVIET EMPLOYMENT OF FORWARD DETACHMENTS IN MANCHURIA COMMAND LEVEL AT WHICH THE FORWARD DETACHMENTS OPERATE

Force	*Level of forward detachment*		
	Army	*Corps*	*Division*
36th Army	205th Tank Brigade 152d Mot. Rifle Regiment 97th Artillery Regiment 491st SP Artillery Battalion 465th Antiaircraft Artillery Regiment 32d Guards-Mortar Regiment (1 battalion) 1 sapper company 1 mortar battalion 158th Antitank Battalion		
39th Army	61st Tank Division 53d Antitank Brigade 1st Howitzer Brigade 11th Guards-Mortar Brigade 203d Engineer-Sapper Brigade	44th Tank Brigade (+) 206th Tank Brigade (+)	1 rifle battalion 1 SP battalion 1–2 artillery battalions 1 antitank battalion 1 guards-mortar battalion
25th Army	259th Tank Brigade (+)		
15th Army	171st Tank Brigade 1 rifle battalion		
2d Red Banner Army	74th Tank Brigade 1 rifle company 1 artillery battalion 1 antitank regiment 258th Tank Brigade 1 rifle battalion 1 mortar regiment		
5th Separate Rifle Corps		172d Tank Brigade 1 rifle battalion 1 antitank regiment 1 sapper company/battalion	
17th Army	70th Tank Battalion 56th Antitank Brigade Training Battalion, 209th Rifle Division 82d Tank Battalion 482d SP Battalion		

Cavalry-Mechanized Group	25th Mechanized Brigade 43d Tank Brigade 267th Tank Regiment	27th Motorized Rifle Brigade 7th Armored Car Brigade 30th Motorcycle Brigade			
6th Guards Tank Army	1 tank battalion 1 rifle regiment 1 artillery battalion 1 tank battalion 1 rifle regiment 1 SP battalion	1 tank regiment 1 rifle regiment 1 artillery battalion			
1st Red Banner Army			1 tank brigade 1 SP battery 1 sapper platoon		1 rifle battalion with 5 T-34 tanks 2 automatic weapons companies 1 sapper platoon
5th Army	76th Tank Brigade 478th Heavy SP Regiment 2 rifle battalions				1 tank brigade 1 heavy SP regiment 1 rifle regiment or battalion 1 antitank battery 1 sapper company
10th Mechanized Corps			72d Mechanized Brigade 1419th SP Regiment 2d Guards-Mortar Battalion	72d Tank Brigade 2d Motorcycle Regiment	

were the only army and corps forces in constant contact with the enemy throughout the advance. Finally, Terekhin's 2d Red Banner Army used two forward detachments to spearhead its advance from Aihun through Sunwu and southwards towards Nencheng and Peian.

A similar pattern existed at the corps level, where corps commanders usually employed a reinforced tank brigade as a forward detachment. This was the case in the 39th Army's 5th Guards and 113th Rifle Corps, in the 1st Red Banner Army's 26th and 59th Rifle Corps, in 5th Separate Rifle Corps, in both march columns of the 10th Mechanized Corps, and in the 6th Guards Tank Army, where both first-echelon corps formed forward detachments consisting of reinforced tank regiments or battalions. Rifle divisions too formed forward detachments, particularly when conducting an exploitation or pursuit. For example, a tank brigade and a heavy self-propelled artillery regiment supported each 5th Army rifle division operating along a main attack axis during the penetration phase. After this phase was complete, these units became the nuclei of forward detachments and immediately led the pursuit deeper into the rear of the Japanese defenses.

Forward detachments operated in great numbers and to greater depths than ever before at every level of command and did so with crippling effect on Japanese defenses. Their often bold and audacious maneuver and relentless advance operations perpetuated the momentum of initial assaults, created a momentum of their own, and imparted that momentum to army and *front* operations as a whole.

EXPLOITATION OF TERRAIN AND WEATHER

During the Manchurian offensive, Soviet commanders exploited geographical and climatic conditions unique to Manchuria to achieve surprise to a far greater extent than during previous offensive operations and with devastating effect. Initially and throughout the offensive, commanders deliberately conducted operations in adverse weather and in darkness. For example, in the 1st Far Eastern Front, Meretskov unleashed his initial reconnaissance and initial assault during heavy thunderstorms and in the dark of night. While the terrible weather prevented his forces from firing an artillery preparation and using searchlights to illuminate Japanese defenses (in the 300th Rifle Division's sector), the bad weather masked the attack and helped Soviet forces capture the Japanese forward defenses by surprise.[11]

The Trans-Baikal and 2d Far Eastern Fronts' forces also conducted their operations in bad weather. For example, Kravchenko's 6th Guards Tank Army drove across the Grand Khingan Mountains in the dark and under rain-laden skies. The 5th Guards Rifle Corps and 113th Rifle Corps of Liudnikov's 39th Army advanced in miserable weather conditions, particularly after 15 August, and the assault battalions of Mamonov's 15th Army captured the islands in the Amur River at night during heavy rains.

Although the poor weather often impeded the Soviet advance, particularly near large and small rivers and in the mountains, it also had the beneficial effect of lulling the Japanese into a deeper false sense of security. While being debriefed after their surrender, several Japanese commanders registered their profound disbelief that the offensive had begun during such miserable weather.[12] The conscious Soviet decision to launch their initial assaults in total darkness and bad weather proved successful precisely because they achieved complete surprise.

Even during clear weather, Soviet forces often exploited darkness to conceal movement and attacks. For example, throughout the Far East Command, virtually all of the regrouping and deployment from assembly areas into jumping-off positions took place at night, as did all of the initial assaults. The 36th Army's 205th Tank Brigade and 152d Rifle Regiment attacked and attempted to envelop Japanese defenses at Hailar during the night. The 5th Army's 76th Tank Brigade conducted its costly march down the road toward Mutanchiang on the night of 11–12 August. While the Soviet's willingness to conduct night operations and disregard bad weather did cause some problems for Soviet commanders, it paid immense dividends in terms of the surprise it produced and the immense, unexpected, and relentless pressure it placed on the defending Japanese.

OPERATIONAL AND TACTICAL FORMATIONS (ECHELONMENT)

The 1944 *Field Regulations* exhorted Soviet commanders to employ imaginative tactical combat formations to surprise and confuse the enemy. In practice, this meant that commanders were to tailor how they echeloned their force in response to such concrete factors as the nature of the enemy defense, terrain conditions, and the specific mission they were assigned. As has been the case with other armies in other periods, the Japanese made the mistake of oversimplifying or stereotyping how Soviet forces echeloned for combat by assuming that they would always and everywhere attack in two-echelon formation. They were, however, badly mistaken.

By 1945 the Red Army employed a wide variety of flexible combat formations. As the regulations stated, the primary factors determining what formation a commander would employ were the specific conditions the force faced. The most valid rule applied to how forces were echeloned was the stronger the defense, the deeper the echeloning (see Figure 3).

Malinovsky deployed the forces of his Trans-Baikal Front in two echelons of armies weighted heavily forward to bring maximum pressure across his

LEVEL		UNIT		
THEATER	1ST ECHELON	TRANS-BAIKAL FRONT	2D FAR EASTERN FRONT	1ST FAR EASTERN FRONT
	2D ECHELON			
	RESERVE			

LEVEL		CAV-MECH GROUP	17A	6GTA	39A	36A	2RBA	15A	5RC	35A	1RBA	5A	25A
FRONT	1ST ECHELON	CAV-MECH GROUP	17A	6GTA	39A	36A	2RBA	15A	5RC	35A	1RBA	5A	25A
	2D ECHELON			53A									
	RESERVE			227 RD 317 RD 111 TD				255 RD				10 MC (MOBILE GROUP) 87 RC 84 CD	88 RC

LEVEL	Army	1ST ECHELON	2D ECHELON	RESERVE
ARMY	CAV-MECH GROUP	OPN GP; OPN GP		
	17A	RD-; RD-		
	6GTA	9 GMC; 7 GMC	5 GTC	
	39A	113 RC; 5 GRC; 94 RC		124 RD
	36A	OPN GP; 86 RC; 2 RC		275 RD
	2RBA	396 RD; 3 RD; 12 RD		
	15A	34 RD; 361 RD; 388 RD		
	5RC	RD	RD	
	35A	264 RD; 66 RD; 363 RD		
	1RBA	26 RC; 59 RC		
	5A	65 RC; 72 RC; 17 RC	45 RC	
	25A	39 RC; ROS & FRS		

CORPS: IN TWO ECHELONS OF DIVISIONS

Figure 3. Soviet Far East Command's Echelonment

entire front and help project power rapidly forward to great depths. His first echelon consisted of four combined-arms armies and one tank army, he kept only one combined-arms army in second echelon, and his *front* reserve consisted of two rifle divisions, one tank division, and one tank brigade.

Within Malinovsky's *front*, his army commanders tailored their combat formations to suit the conditions they faced. Liudnikov and Luchinsky deployed their 36th and 39th Armies in a single echelon of three rifle corps (or operational groups) advancing abreast. Danilov formed his 17th Army's forces in a single echelon of three rifle divisions attacking abreast, while Kravchenko, whose mission was to conduct sustained operations to great depths, deployed his 6th Guards Tank Army in two echelons of tank and mechanized corps.

Within the Trans-Baikal Front's 36th and 39th Armies, the rifle corps designated to attack fortified regions deployed in two echelons of divisions, while the 39th Army's 94th Rifle Corps and the 36th Army's operational group, which faced only limited resistance, deployed in a single echelon of divisions. Malinovsky deployed virtually all of his *front's* tank forces, specifically, the tank army, tank divisions, and separate tank brigades, in first echelon in order to increase the speed of his advance.

On the other hand, Meretskov deployed the four armies in his 1st Far Eastern Front in single echelon so as to bring maximum pressure to bear on the Japanese defenses across his entire operational sector. Meretskov retained the 10th Mechanized Corps to serve as his *front's* mobile group for exploitation and kept the 88th Rifle Corps and the 84th Cavalry Division in reserve. Most of the army commanders in Meretskov's *front* formed their armies in single echelon consistent with Meretskov's plan to advance along as many axes as possible.

Chistiakov formed the forces of his 25th Army in a single echelon of one rifle corps, one rifle division, and several fortified regions advancing abreast, Zakhvataev deployed the forces of his 35th Army in a single echelon of three rifle divisions, and Beloborodov deployed his 1st Red Banner Army's forces in a single echelon of two rifle corps.

Finally, Krylov, whose 5th Army forces faced the extensive Japanese fortifications at Volynsk and Suifenho, deployed his forces in two echelons of rifle corps. Within these armies, the 5th Army's two first-echelon rifle corps and the 25th Army's 39th Rifle Corps, all of which faced heavy fortified sectors, were deployed in two echelons of rifle divisions. The only exception was the 5th Army's 17th Rifle Corps, which formed its two rifle divisions in a single echelon, since its mission was to attack through a relatively lightly defended sector against the northern flank and rear of the Suifenho center of resistance.

The forces of Purkaev's 2d Far Eastern Front, which were operating across an extremely broad front in support of the theater's main efforts, deployed in a single echelon of two armies and one rifle corps operating along widely separate axes. Mamonov's deployed his 15th Army in a single echelon of three rifle divisions to make his main attack and retained only an extremely small reserve. Terekhin's 2d Red Banner Army also deployed its three rifle divisions in single echelon, while Pashkov's 5th Separate Rifle Corps, which consisted of two rifle divisions operating on a narrow and lightly defended front, employed a single echelon formation. Throughout the entire Far East Command, rifle divisions routinely formed in two echelons of rifle regiments. This varied echeloning was tailored to specific terrain and anticipated Japanese resistance contributed to the Japanese's surprise.

ASSAULT GROUPS

Soviet commanders in the Far East Command's three *fronts* employed imaginative tactical techniques to defeat the Japanese other than conducting extensive maneuver in all weather conditions and forming flexible operational and tactical formations. The most important of these was the use of assault groups to overcome Japanese fortified regions, primarily during the initial phase of the offensive. While doing so, they also closely followed the 1944 *Field Regulations* admonition that, if possible, attacking forces were to bypass these regions and neutralize them by artillery fire and air strikes.

If assault proved unavoidable, however, commanders formed assault groups, which they carefully tailored to suit the mission and terrain, to attack and destroy these fortifications. In addition, they committed these assault groups to combat in a carefully time-phased fashion to build up combat power in a given sector and accomplish their missions with as little loss of manpower as possible.

The penetration operations conducted by Krylov's 5th Army and the 39th Rifle Corps of Chistiakov's 25th Army illustrated the tactical skills the Red Army had developed by 1945. Both forces deployed to conduct the penetration in narrower than usual attack sectors, with rifle corps concentrating on 2.8–3.1 mile-wide (4.5–5 kilometer) fronts and rifle divisions on 1.6–1.9 mile-wide (2.5–3 kilometer) fronts.

The actual assault groups operated along even narrower fronts, supported by extremely high densities of artillery fire. Normally 322 (200) guns and mortars, and 48 to 64 (30–40) tanks and self-propelled guns per mile (kilometer) of front supported the assault groups, and many of the tanks and self-propelled guns accompanied the assault groups as part of their combat formation.[13] Even when mounting these frontal attacks, whenever possible, Soviet commanders attempted to envelop the fortified position rather than assault it frontally, and the massed artillery and armor permitted commanders to economize on precious manpower.

As far as the assault itself was concerned, each assault group consisted of about 100 men formed from the advanced rifle battalion of the lead rifle division's first echelon rifle regiment. Each assault group was normally subdivided into maneuver elements such as reconnaissance, attack, and blocking subgroups and support elements, such as fire subgroups, and contained sappers, flamethrowers, antitank guns, submachine guns, light and heavy machine guns, mortars, and two or three tanks or heavy self-propelled guns (see Figure 4).

In addition to being formed in regular rifle divisions (as was the case of 5th Army), border guards units and fortified regions also formed and employed assault groups (as in the cases of the 39th Rifle Corps and the 25th Army).[14]

After the assault groups initiated the attack, their parent rifle divisions followed with two rifle regiments in first echelon and one in second. Advanced rifle battalions, formed from the rifle division's second echelon rifle regiments, followed the assault detachments, and, soon after, the main force of the rifle division's first echelon rifle regiments also advanced (see Table 46).

TABLE 46: TIME-PHASED COMMITMENT OF FORCES TO COMBAT IN 1ST FAR EASTERN FRONT

Units	*Time of Attack*
Assault groups (platoon or company, with 100 men from the rifle division or border guards units)	0010–0100 hours
Advanced battalions (1 per rifle regiment) reinforced with a tank company from the first echelon tank brigade	0300–0830 hours
The division's main force (2 rifle regiments) and attached tank brigade	0830 hours
The division's second echelon (1 rifle regiment)	0930–1100 hours
The rifle corps second echelon (1 division)	1600+ hours

The rifle division's first echelon rifle regiments formed with two rifle battalions in first echelon, each deployed with three rifle companies on line, and one battalion in second echelon. The forward regiments' first echelon rifle battalions had tanks and self-propelled artillery from tank brigades and self-propelled artillery regiments integrated into their combat formation to provide direct fire support.

For example, in Krylov's 5th Army, one tank brigade and one heavy self-propelled artillery regiment, totaling 86 tanks and self-propelled guns, supported each first echelon rifle division. If the Japanese fortified position resisted too strongly to be overcome by the assault groups, the rifle division's main force maneuvered around their flanks to bypass them and left its second echelon rifle regiment to reduce the fortified point.

While reducing the fortified position, the stay-behind rifle regiment normally cooperated closely with follow-on forces from an adjacent fortified or field fortified region. Normally, army and corps commanders attached a

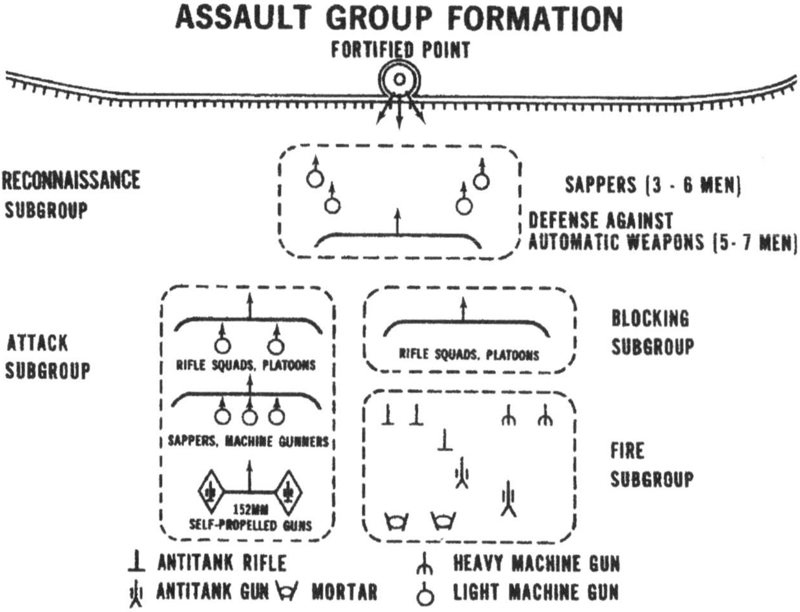

ASSAULT GROUP FORMATION

FORTIFIED POINT

RECONNAISSANCE SUBGROUP

SAPPERS (3 - 6 MEN)

DEFENSE AGAINST AUTOMATIC WEAPONS (5- 7 MEN)

ATTACK SUBGROUP

RIFLE SQUADS, PLATOONS

SAPPERS, MACHINE GUNNERS

152MM SELF-PROPELLED GUNS

BLOCKING SUBGROUP

RIFLE SQUADS, PLATOONS

FIRE SUBGROUP

ANTITANK RIFLE

ANTITANK GUN

MORTAR

HEAVY MACHINE GUN

LIGHT MACHINE GUN

Figure 4. Soviet Assault Group Formation

self-propelled artillery battalion, a sapper battalion, and a heavy artillery battery or battalion to the stay-behind rifle regiment and supported it with direct fire from heavy and light artillery and an air bombardment, if available. This pattern occurred at Hutou, Suifenho, Volynsk, Tungning, Sunwu, Fuchin, Hailar, and Halung-Arshaan. In a few instances, when Japanese resistance or fortifications were too strong for the second echelon to overcome, the army commander assigned a complete second echelon rifle division to accomplish the task.

While the lead rifle divisions' second echelon rifle regiments destroyed Japanese strong points, the divisions' main forces initiated the pursuit, led by forward detachments consisting of separate tank brigades, reinforced by a rifle battalion and sapper and artillery battalions allocated on the basis of one forward detachment for each rifle division or rifle corps. Soviet army and corps commanders designated the makeup of the forward detachment before conducting the penetration operation. All of the armies that attacked Japanese fortified regions throughout Manchuria followed this same general pattern of time-phased commitment of forces with only minor variations.

However, in sectors where Soviet forces anticipated or encountered lighter resistance during their penetration operations, the army and corps commanders led their attack with reconnaissance groups followed by advanced rifle battalions formed on the basis of one per rifle regiment, usually with considerable engineer, tank, and artillery support. During the actual assault phase of the operation, in this instance, the advanced battalions served as the forward detachments of the lead rifle regiments. Soviet forces not designated to deliver frontal attacks against heavily fortified regions or not already advancing to contact in march-column formation employed advanced battalions with notable success. The best examples were the advance of the 1st Red Banner Army's 300th Rifle Division toward Pamientung, the forced crossing of the 35th Army's 363d Rifle Division over the Sungacha River, and the crossing of the 36th Army's lead rifle divisions over the Argun River.

PURSUIT OPERATIONS AND MARCH FORMATIONS

Soviet army and corps commanders routinely began pursuit operations after their forces completed their penetration operations. During the first two years of the war, Red Army forces had experienced considerable difficulties in sustaining pursuit operations. However, the army's positive experiences in 1944 and 1945 prepared them well to conduct an effective pursuit against Japanese forces into the depths of Manchuria. Given the size of the theater of operations and the immense logistical demands on a successful pursuit, at times the process proved to be quite difficult, primarily due to limited logistical support.

Pursuit operations in Manchuria required the advancing forces to cover immense distances in extremely limited periods of time. In all operational sectors, the pursuit involved numerous forward detachments followed by a vast number of rifle divisions advancing in march-column formation. The size and number of the pursuing formations, units, and subunits placed immense strain on command and control and logistical systems, and the initiative displayed by Soviet commanders only added to this pressure.

In general, because of the ambitious missions assigned to them and the difficult terrain, army and corps commanders devoted greater than usual attention to providing their pursuit force with requisite engineer support, including additional sapper, engineer, and bridging units necessary to surmount the frequent terrain obstacles. Despite this support, forces often had to resort to a variety of field expedients to keep the advance moving forward. For example, in the 35th Army, Zakhvataev assigned extra engineer bridging forces and equipment to his 66th Rifle Division so that it could cross the Ussuri River. Nevertheless, once across the river, the army's 175th Tank Brigade had to resort to the use of inverted pontoons to transport fuel across the flooded open country to facilitate the army's advance.[15] In western Manchuria, the aerial reconnaissance provided by Malinovsky to Kravchenko's 6th Guards Tank Army materially assisted the tank army's rapid pursuit in that sector.

Paralleling the heavy Soviet reliance on pursuit operations was the extraordinary degree to which Soviet commanders relied on the use of march-column formations throughout the operation. In fact, most Soviet force spent the bulk of their time during the offensive in march-column formation. Therefore, the survivability and success of Soviet forces in combat depended in large measure on how well their commanders organized their marching columns for mutual support, defense, and rapid deployment into combat formation (see Figures 5–7).

In the Trans-Baikal Front, the bulk of Malinovsky's forces advanced in march-column formation throughout most of the offensive. For example, the 6th Guards Tank and 17th Armies and the Soviet–Mongolian Cavalry-Mechanized Group crossed the Gobi desert on the march and passed through the Grand Khingan Mountains in constricted march formation. Aside from its assault on Japanese defenses at the Wuchakou and Halung-Arshaan Fortified Regions and its attacks against Japanese defensive positions around Solun and Wangyemiao, the 39th Army also advanced, for the most part, in march-column formation, as did the 36th Army in its advance to Hailar and the Grand Khingan passes at Yakoshih.

Even in the more restrictive terrain of eastern Manchuria, often the armies of Meretskov's 1st Far Eastern Front advanced in march-column formation, both initially and during the pursuit phase of the operation. For example, the 1st Red Banner Army's forces conducted its initial advance through the heavily forested region between the border and Pamientung in

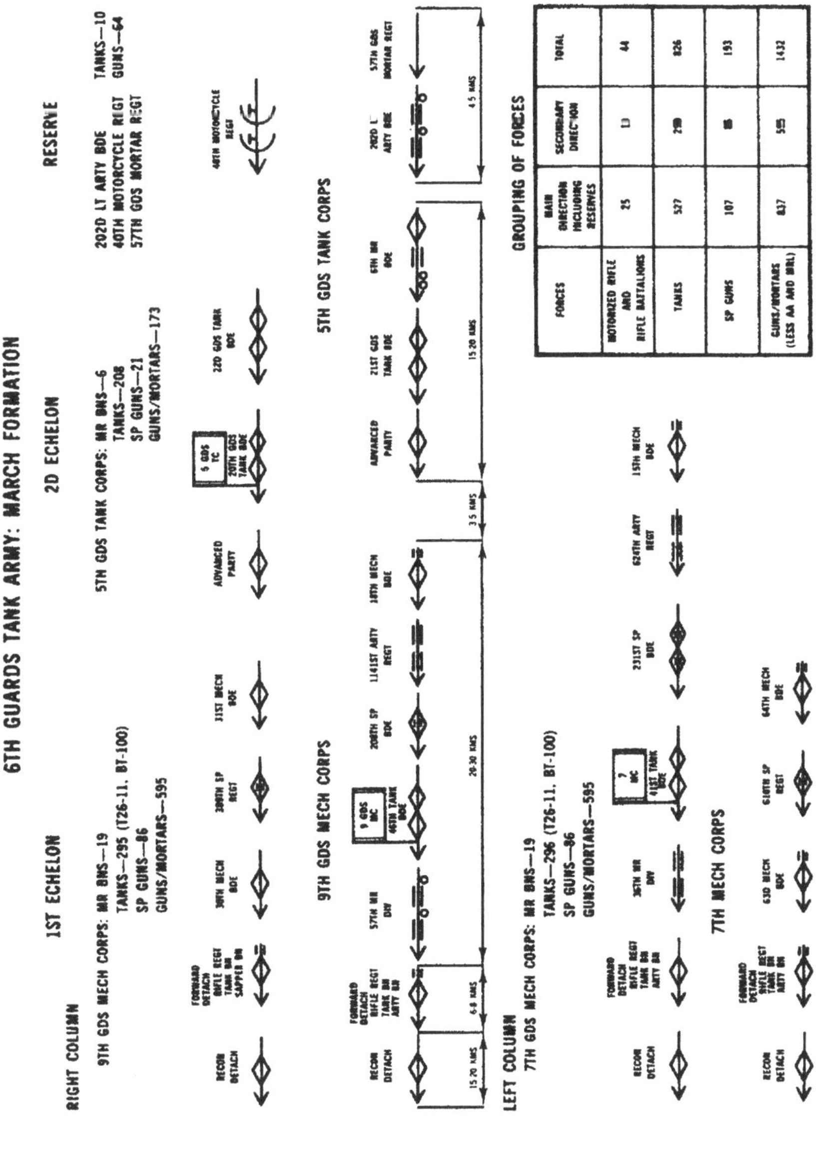

6TH GUARDS TANK ARMY: MARCH FORMATION

1ST ECHELON

RIGHT COLUMN

9TH GDS MECH CORPS: MR BNS—19
TANKS—295 (T26-11, BT-100)
SP GUNS—86
GUNS/MORTARS—595

RECON DETACH — FORWARD DETACH RIFLE REGT TANK BN SAPPER BN — 30TH MECH BDE — 380TH SP REGT — 31ST MECH BDE

2D ECHELON

5TH GDS TANK CORPS: MR BNS—6
TANKS—208
SP GUNS—21
GUNS/MORTARS—173

ADVANCED PARTY — 5 GDS TC / 20TH GDS TANK BDE — 22D GDS TANK BDE

RESERVE

202D LT ARTY BDE
40TH MOTORCYCLE REGT
57TH GDS MORTAR REGT

TANKS—10
GUNS—64

40TH MOTORCYCLE REGT

9TH GDS MECH CORPS

RECON DETACH — FORWARD DETACH RIFLE REGT TANK BN ARTY BN — 57TH MR DIV — 9 GDS MC / 46TH TANK BDE — 208TH SP BDE — 1141ST ARTY REGT — 18TH MECH BDE

15-20 KMS — 6-8 KMS — 20-30 KMS — 3-5 KMS

5TH GDS TANK CORPS

ADVANCED PARTY — 21ST GDS TANK BDE — 6TH MR BDE — 202D LT ARTY BDE — 57TH GDS MORTAR REGT

15-20 KMS — 4-5 KMS

LEFT COLUMN

7TH GDS MECH CORPS: MR BNS—19
TANKS—296 (T26-11, BT-100)
SP GUNS—86
GUNS/MORTARS—595

RECON DETACH — FORWARD DETACH RIFLE REGT TANK BN ARTY BN — 36TH MR DIV — 7 MC / 41ST TANK BDE — 231ST SP BDE — 624TH ARTY REGT — 15TH MECH BDE

7TH MECH CORPS

RECON DETACH — FORWARD DETACH RIFLE REGT TANK BN ARTY BN — 63D MECH BDE — 610TH SP REGT — 64TH MECH BDE

GROUPING OF FORCES

FORCES	MAIN DIRECTION INCLUDING RESERVES	SECONDARY DIRECTION	TOTAL
MOTORIZED RIFLE AND RIFLE BATTALIONS	25	1[illegible]	44
TANKS	527	2[illegible]	826
SP GUNS	107	[illegible]	193
GUNS/MORTARS (LESS AA AND MRL)	837	5[illegible]5	1432

Figure 5. March Formation, Trans-Baikal Front 6th Guards Tank Army

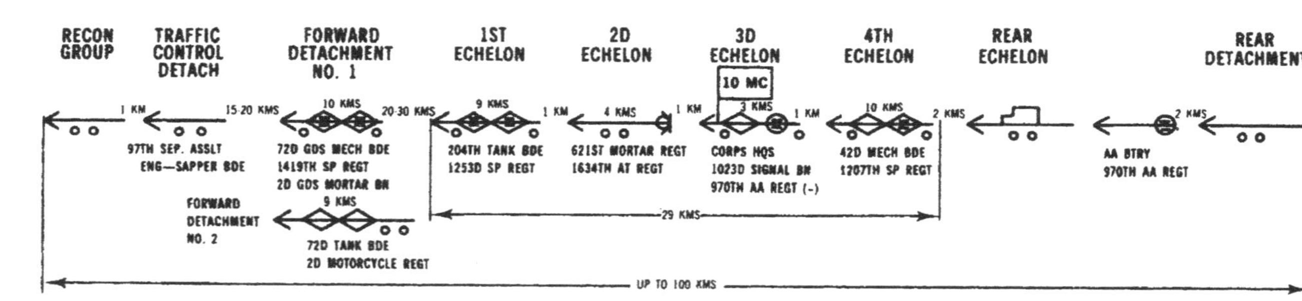

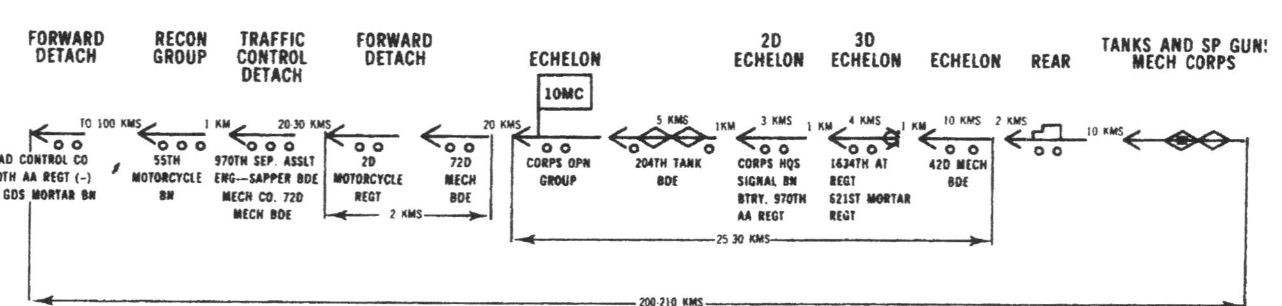

Figure 6. March Formation, 1st Eastern Front 10th Mechanized Corps

MARCH ORDER 22D RIFLE DIVISION, 26TH RIFLE CORPS, 1ST RBA

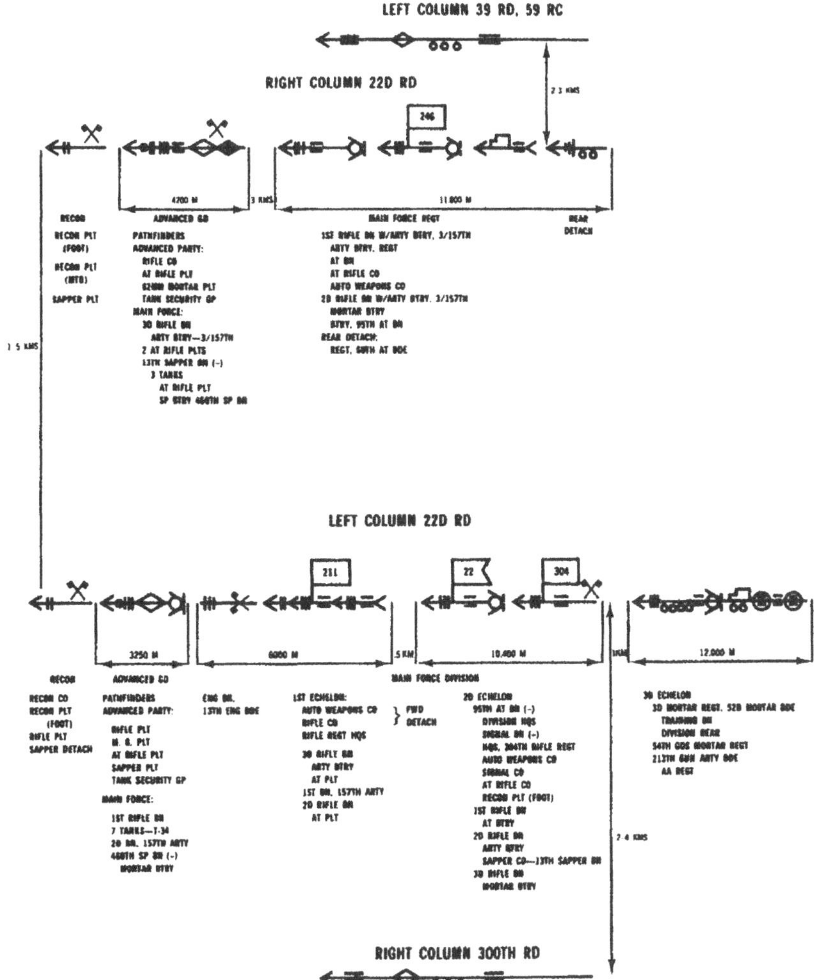

Figure 7. March Order, 1st Far Eastern Front's 22d Rifle Division

similar formation, albeit at a slow rate of advance, and, subsequently, the bulk of the army advanced from Pamientung to Mutanchiang in column formation. The 5th Army also advanced in march-column formation from the time it completed its penetration operation until it deployed for combat on the eastern outskirts of Mutanchiang.

Other than the brief periods when a portion of their forces deployed to fight briefly at Heitosai and Taipingling, the same applied to the 25th Army and 10th Mechanized Corps' advance from Tungning to Wangching. Likewise, the 35th Army advanced from Hutou to Mishan and Linkou on the march, leaving only a small portion of its force to assault Japanese defenses in the Hutou Fortified Region. Technically at least, the 2d Far Eastern Front's forces also advanced in march-column formation during most of their offensive, although a sizeable portion of the 15th Army's forces moved south in amphibious convoys along the Sungari River.

Admittedly, the ill-prepared and porous Japanese defenses and weak Japanese resistance were the principal reasons why Soviet forces could advance in such a manner. However, skillful Soviet organization and employment of march-columns also explains why this formation proved so effective. Simply stated, Soviet forces demonstrated that they could fight and win using such a formation without deploying for combat. With a few notable exception, the ubiquitous forward detachments and advanced guards proved more than capable of dealing with what little Japanese resistance materialized. Therefore, few Soviet main forces had to waste time deploying for set-piece combat and, a lightning fast Soviet advance resulted.

Soviet army, corps, and division commanders carefully tailored their march-column formations so that they could fight effectively on the march and sustain offensive momentum. They task-organized their marching columns so that they contained a balanced mixture of combined-arms elements such as infantry, armor, artillery, and engineers essential for providing mutual support, conducting high-speed maneuvers, and, if required, erecting all-around defense. They were also careful to lead their advance with tanks and interspersed tanks and field, antiaircraft, antitank, and self-propelled artillery throughout the marching columns. This enabled any portion of the column to function as a semi-independent, balanced, and survivable force.

Commanders also provided heavier than usual engineer support for the columns to enable them to cope with the difficult Manchurian terrain. For example, the *front* commanders attached heavy engineer reinforcements to 6th Guards Tank Army so that it could traverse the deserts and mountains of western Manchuria, to the 25th and 1st Red Banner Armies so that they could traverse the mountainous taiga terrain in eastern Manchuria, and to the 35th Army so that it could cross the Ussuri River and operate effectively in the swampy and marshy region north of Lake Khanka. The army commanders then artfully wove the additional engineer units and equipment into the fabric of their marching columns. The additional engineer support helps explain why Soviet commanders were able to achieve rapid rates of advance throughout the entire offensive.

JOINT OPERATIONS

The Manchurian offensive was also characterized by extensive and close cooperation between ground, air, and naval forces. In many operational sectors, effective joint operations between the three force branches proved essential to achieving victory. At the highest level, the *Stavka* decision to create the Far East Command, the first true theater of military operations headquarters, was the most critical factor in assuring the ground, air, and naval forces cooperated effectively. Subsequently, air and naval forces played a decisive role in many component operations.

While air forces performed their traditional reconnaissance, bombing, ground support, and interdiction missions, they also provided vital logistical support to the Trans-Baikal Front's 6th Guards Tank Army and Cavalry-Mechanized Group, primarily by dropping fuel and ammunition to sustain the forces during their advance. Late in the offensive, the air forces conducted numerous small air assault landings in Manchuria's major cities to receive the surrender of important Japanese commands.[16]

Naval forces of the Pacific Fleet and Amur Military Flotilla played a vital and effective role in many operations, particularly along the rivers of northern and eastern Manchuria, along the northern Korean coast, and in the Pacific basin. For example, the Amur Flotilla provided river crossing means and ferrying capacity, transportation, and fire support for the 1st Far Eastern Front's 35th Army north of Lake Khanka and for the 2d Far Eastern Front's 2d Red Banner and 15th Armies and the 5th Separate Rifle Corps in their operations along the Amur, Sungari, and Ussuri Rivers. Likewise the Pacific Fleet conducted strategically vital amphibious operations against Japanese ports in northern Korea and against southern Sakhalin and the Kuril Islands.

PROBLEMS

Although the Far East Command's Manchurian offensive proved spectacularly successful, as is the case with any major successful military operation, the advancing forces did experience some difficulties. Generally speaking, however, these difficulties resulted primarily from the ambitious nature of the campaign plan and the audacious manner in which Soviet commanders carried it out. In particular, the attempts by Soviet commanders to overcome every terrain obstacle and achieve high rates of advance simultaneously in every operational sector sometimes resulted in local and limited failures. These occurred primarily when forces became overextended and vulnerable to enemy attack or when the terrain simply turned out to be insurmountable.

For example, in the sector of the 1st Far Eastern Front's 25th Army, Meretskov committed his mobile group, the 10th Mechanized Corps, along an advance axis that lacked a sufficient road network to accommodate the corps. This reality, combined with the rough and heavily wooded terrain in the region, restricted the mobile corps' movement. As a result of the ensuing congestion, the 10th Mechanized Corps' march-column ultimately extended a distance of 124 miles (200 kilometers) westward from Wangching toward the eastern border of Manchuria.[17] The mechanized corps' march-column was so overextended and its deployment space so restricted that only its forward detachments maintained contact with the withdrawing Japanese. Worse still, when the corps encountered Japanese resistance, it could deploy only its forward detachments into combat formation, a fact that delayed its advance westward in Manchuria.

On a lesser scale, the same problem delayed the advance by the 2d Far Eastern Front's 15th Army to Chiamussu. Here, the poor weather and swampy terrain combined to hinder the army's advance. Often the excessive length of the army's march-columns and the overextension of its advancing forces caused its artillery to lag far behind and denied the lead elements necessary artillery support. A similar case occurred in the sector of the Trans-Baikal Front's 39th Army, where the army's heavy artillery lagged significantly behind its advancing rifle and tank forces.

In some instances forward detachments advanced too audaciously and, as a result, became overextended and had to fight in isolation from their supporting parent formations. For example, the 5th Army's 76th Tank Brigade outran its support during its frenetic westward advance on the road to Mutanchiang. As a result, the Japanese 124th Infantry Division was able to halt the isolated tank brigade until additional Soviet units came to its rescue. The same phenomenon occurred in the 1st Red Banner Army's sector when the 257th Tank Brigade, which was leading the 300th Rifle Division's march west of Pamientung toward Mutanchiang, outran its support and attempted to capture the railroad bridge at Hualin on its own. The Japanese were able to repulse the tank brigade's unsupported attacks repeatedly, and counterattacking Japanese forces drove the brigade back into defensive positions north of Hualin, where it remained until reinforced by follow-on Soviet infantry.

On several notable occasions, poor terrain itself disrupted Soviet advances. For example, in the southern sector of the 1st Far Eastern Front's 35th Army, the 209th and 125th Tank Brigades, which were to lead the 66th and 363d Rifle Divisions' advance toward Mishan, could not operate as planned in the swampy marshlands west of the Ussuri River. Even though the army employed such field expedience as using inverted pontoons to transport fuel through the swamps, it had no other recourse but to withdraw both brigades and transfer them to other sectors of the front.[18] Even though this problem did not delay the army's advance, it might have done, had Japanese resistance proved more formidable.

On at least one occasion during the offensive, a Soviet force crossing barren terrain simply got lost. On 11 August in the sector of the Trans-Baikal Front's 39th Army, the 113th Rifle Corps' 192d Rifle Division lost its way while marching across the Grand Khingan Mountains south of Halung-Arshaan. The division floundered about on mountain tracks for two days before army reconnaissance aircraft sent to retrieve it found the force and directed it to its correct march route. In this case, the general lack of decent maps of the region led to the force's total disorientation. This and numerous other instances when forces had to change direction, often more than once, drastically increased fuel consumption and contributed to the overall strain on logistical systems.[19]

Providing adequate logistical support to their far-flung and often over-extended forces was the most serious problem Soviet commanders faced during the Manchurian offensive. Even though the Far East Command and its subordinate *fronts* had anticipated this problem prior to the offensive and had done everything in their power to remedy it, they well understood that achieving success in military operations requires taking risks. They did so, and, therefore, the resulting logistical problems were predictable and inevitable.

Fuel shortages headed the list of logistical problems, particularly among forces operating in the vast empty spaces of western Manchuria. For example, the 6th Guards Tank Army, whose tanks guzzled fuel at an enormous rate, ran low on fuel even before it began crossing the Grand Khingan Mountains. After the crossing was complete, the army faced chronic fuel problems up to the day its corps reached Mukden. In the face of these problems, any resolute or even token Japanese resistance would have compounded the 6th Guards Tank Army's logistical difficulties and perhaps even brought its advance to an abrupt halt. Other forces, including the Trans-Baikal Front's 39th Army and the 1st Far Eastern Front's 35th Army, experienced similar problems albeit on a lesser scale.

The second most serious logistical problem related to shortages of ferrying and bridging equipment within the Far East Command. This problem surfaced primarily during the river crossing and ferrying operations in the 2d Red Banner and 15th Armies and 5th Separate Rifle Corps, where the shortages led to lengthy crossing times and subsequent piecemeal commitment of forces to battle.

Yet, when all was said and done, all of these problems resulted from Soviet action rather than inaction. In the end, an army's vulnerabilities count for little unless the opposing army takes advantage of them. In this case, however, the Japanese did little or nothing to capitalize on them. This Japanese negligence only magnified the scope of the ensuing Soviet victory.

NOTES

1. Vnotchenko, *Pobeda*, 360-4.
2. Ibid., 344–58; Khrenov, 'Wartime Operations', 81–97.
3. Sukhomlin, 'Osobennosti', 87–91.
4. Zakharov, 'Nekotorye voprosy voennogo iskusstva v sovetsko-iaponskoi voine 1945-goda' [Some questions concerning military art in the Soviet–Japanese War of 1945], *VIZh*, No. 9 (September 1969), 17.
5. Vnotchenko, *Pobeda*, 237
6. Shtemenko, *Soviet General Staff*, 343.
7. *JM 154* and *JM 155*.
8. *Senshi sosho: Kantogun (2)* [Military History Series: The Kwantung Army, Vol. 2], prepared by Boeicho Boei Kenshujo Senchishitsu [Japan Self Defense Forces, National Defense College Military History Department] (Tokyo: Asagumio Shinbunsha, 1974), 440.
9. *JM 154*, 3, 179–80.
10. At Khalkhin-Gol in August 1939, future Marshal of the Soviet Union G. K. Zhukov and a force of more than 50,000 men thoroughly outmaneuvered and destroyed two Japanese divisions in a remote area of Eastern Mongolia. Here also, Japanese commanders underestimated Soviet capabilities. Later the French and Americans also made similar errors and fell victim to the curse of an enemy operating over 'inhibiting terrain' in the Ardennes in 1940 and 1944, respectively.
11. Khrenov, 'Wartime Operations', 90; K. A. Meretskov, 'Dorogami srazhenii' [Along combat roads], *Voprosy istorii* [Questions of History], No. 2 (February 1965), 107. Vnotchenko, *Pobeda*, 107, and Zakharov, *Finale*, 96, claim that no artillery preparation was planned.
12. Chistiakov, *Sluzhim*, 288.
13. A. A. Strokov, ed., *Istoriia voennogo iskusstva* [A history of military art] (Moscow: Voenizdat, 1966), 516, and Vnotchenko, *Pobeda*, 101, 108, 125.
14. Khrenov, 'Wartime Operations', 91–2, and Vnotchenko, *Pobeda*, 131–3. See also Chistiakov, *Sluzhim*, 280–1, for the 25th Army's use of border guards in assault detachments. Border guards operations are surveyed in V. Platonov and A. Bulatov, 'Pogranichnie voiska perekhodiat v nastuplenie' [Border troops go over to the offensive], *VIZh*, No. 10 (October 1965), 16.
15. Vnotchenko, *Pobeda*, 214, and Pechenenko, '*Armeiskaia*', 47.
16. Vnotchenko, *Pobeda*, 338–44.
17. Ibid., 386.
18. The 125th Tank Brigade redeployed within the army area. The 1st Far Eastern Front transferred the 209th Tank Brigade to 25th Army control. See Krupchenko, *Sovetskie*, 321; Pechenenko, 'Armeiskaia', 47.
19. Liudnikov, *Cherez*, 80–2.

12

Conclusions and Lessons

CONCLUSIONS

The *Stavka* and Far East Command anticipated that its strategic offensive against the Kwantung Army in Manchuria would last for about 30 days and prepared accordingly. Achieving victory in so brief a campaign involved redeploying massive quantities of forces, weaponry, and supplies to the new theater of military operations secretly and within an extremely short period of time. To control these forces effectively, the *Stavka* created a unified theater command structure and manned it with commanders and staffs whose experience suited them to control massive forces operating across a broad front in the challenging and diverse terrain and weather conditions of Manchuria.

At all levels of command, strategic, operational, and tactical, Soviet commanders formulated sound missions and designated appropriate, and often imaginative, axes of advance and objectives and tailored their forces so that they could fulfill their missions and achieve their objective within the shortest possible time. To exploit terrain most effectively, all commands reinforced their attacking infantry with an imposing array of all types of supporting forces, especially armor and engineers. Contrary to Japanese stereotypes, the Far East Command's military leaders generally conducted their operations with unanticipated flexibility, audacity, and individual initiative and, as a result, won a signal victory.

Time, terrain, and Japanese resistance posed the greatest challenges to the successful conduct of the offensive. While the Soviet Army overcame the first two challenges itself, faulty Japanese defensive planning and a clumsy Japanese defense helped the Soviet Army overcome the third. Consequently, the Soviet Army essentially achieved victory in seven days (by 16 August). The subsequent Soviet advance was essentially pro forma. The three Soviet *fronts* overwhelmed the Kwantung Army exceeding the Far East Command's offensive timetable by three weeks, while suffering surprisingly light casualties.

According to their respective accounts, the Soviet Army killed, wounded, or captured over 674,000 Japanese troops at a cost of 12,031 killed, mortally wounded, or missing, and 24,425 wounded or sick Soviet soldiers (see Tables 47 and 48).[1]

TABLE 47: SOVIET AND JAPANESE LOSSES IN THE MANCHURIAN STRATEGIC OFFENSIVE, 9 AUGUST–2 SEPTEMBER 1945

	Japanese losses			*Soviet losses*		
Source	*Killed*	*Wounded*	*Prisoners*	*Irrecoverable*	*Wounded*	*Total*
Soviet	84,000		590,000	12,031	24,425	36,456
Japanese	21,000*			–	–	10,000

*These figures are from the 1st Demobilization Bureau. Force combat accounts record heavier casualties. This figure also ignores the large number of missing Japanese soldiers and does not include Manchukuoan and Inner Mongolian casualties, mobilized Japanese reservists, or Japanese civilians caught up in the fighting.

TABLE 48: SOVIET LOSSES IN MANCHURIAN STRATEGIC OFFENSIVE, 9 AUGUST–2 SEPTEMBER 1945

		Losses		
Force	*Initial Strength*	*Irrecoverable*	*Medical*	*Total*
Trans-Baikal Front	638,300	2,228	6,155	8,383
2d Far Eastern Front	334,700	2,449	3,134	5,583
1st Far Eastern Front	586,500	6,324	14,745	21,069
Pacific Fleet	97,500	998	300	1,298
Amur Military Flotilla	12,500	32	91	123
Total	1,669,500	12,031	24,425	36,456
Mongolian Army	16,000	72	125	197

Source: G. F. Krivosheev, ed., *Rossiia i SSSR v voinakh XX veka: Statisticheskoe issledovanie* [Russia and the USSR in twentieth century wars: A statistical survey] (Moscow: 'Olma-press', 2001), 309.

Why did the Far East Command achieve so spectacular a victory at so minimal a cost? The simple answer is that the Soviet victory was inevitable given the Soviet Army's preponderance of forces, the crumbling Japanese strategic posture in the western Pacific, the United States' devastating bombing offensive against Japan (including the atomic bomb), and the weakened state of the Kwantung Army. The only remaining question then is why the Soviet Army achieved victory so quickly. Although the reasons listed above seem adequate to answer this question, they mask other cogent reasons for the Kwantung Army's quick collapse.

The Far East Command's offensive plan was a bold one both because the *Stavka* required it to be and because, based on their experiences in 1938 and 1939, Soviet military planners respected the Kwantung Army's reputation and recognized the prowess, skill, and bravery of the individual Japanese soldier. Nor did the command's clear knowledge that the Kwantung Army of 1945 was but a pale reflection of its former self measurably lessen that respect. The Far East Command understood Japanese defensive plans quite well and planned accordingly. In so doing, it probably overestimated the strength of Japanese defenses along the border and planned assaults that were more massive than actually required.

Soviet planners also anticipated far greater resistance on the part of Japanese forces in central Manchuria and the redoubt area of southern Manchuria than actually materialized. Because they overestimated Japanese strength, Soviet planners decided to structure the offensive so as to reach the central Manchurian plain from several directions, fragment Japanese forces, and destroy them piecemeal before they could consolidate in fresh defensive positions. Thus, the Far East Command's forces advanced along virtually every possible axis, including into northern Korea. Even the Soviet commanders themselves were surprised by the scale and speed of their victory.

Although the Kwantung Army of 1945 was no longer as effective as its predecessor in terms of leadership, equipment, and manpower, it was not as utterly ineffective as the outcome of the offensive indicated. In many instances, its new replacements performed as well as its veterans, but only when and where their commanders permitted them to fight. Even in their reduced state of 1945, the Japanese infantry divisions and brigades were larger than their Soviet counterparts, at least in manpower, and, where they fought, they fought well.

In particular, the Japanese 80th Independent Mixed Brigade and the 119th Infantry Division did a remarkably effective job resisting the 36th Army's advance to Hailar and on the road through the Grand Khingan Mountains to Pokotu. The 135th Independent Mixed Brigade and the 123d Infantry Division acquitted themselves well in their defenses of the Aihun and Sunwu Fortified Regions against the 2d Red Banner Army. Many Japanese border garrisons, which defended their fortified positions against overwhelming numbers, performed heroically and earned the grudging respect of their adversaries, who perhaps thought of similar Red Army sacrifices at Brest and Sevastopol'.

The Soviets observed the suicidal attacks by Japanese *kamikaze* units, the raiding battalions whose soldiers (whom the Soviets termed *smertniks*) hurled their explosive-laden bodies at Soviet tanks, with a mixture of awe and incredulity.[2] In fact, where Japanese forces stood and fought under competent leadership, they did a credible job and offered the Soviets the opposition they had expected. In reality, it was the Kwantung Army's senior leadership that engineered the army's overall mediocre performance.

Unquestionably, the incessant rumors of an impending cease-fire and the off-and-on-again decisions to surrender produced havoc in Japanese ranks, disrupted Japanese defensive operations, and forestalled possibly greater Japanese resistance in southern Manchuria. Yet, by this time, much of the damage had already been done and could not be undone. Soviet actions aside, the Japanese High Command reacted to the Soviet invasion sloppily and indecisively because of its overconfidence, complacency, confusion, or pessimism, depending on the command. Where it existed, this overconfidence and complacency had persisted for years prior to 1945 despite the Red Army's victory in 1939 at Khalkhin-Gol, from which, surprisingly, the Japanese had learned so little. Instead, the Japanese preferred to remember only the Red Army's dismal performance against the Finns in 1939 and 1940 and against the Germans in 1941 and 1942.

Consequently, by 1945 the Japanese had done precious little to modernize their infantry divisions to make them capable of engaging a modern Soviet rifle division, much less a tank or mechanized force. The Japanese infantry division lacked antitank weapons entirely, and although it was heavier in manpower than its Soviet equivalent, it was far lighter in firepower. Japanese tanks were light varieties scarcely justifying the term 'tank' and could not compete with the light Soviet BT tank, much less the renowned T-34. In short, the Kwantung Army was no better equipped to conduct modern mobile war in 1945 than it had been in 1939.

Japanese military planners also forgot or ignored another lesson from their 1939 war, namely the Soviets' penchant for doing the seemingly impossible, such as exploiting the arid wastes of eastern Mongolia as a launching pad for a major invasion of Manchuria. Whether through complacency or overconfidence, congenital Japanese underestimation of Soviet military capabilities spelled doom for the Kwantung Army. Japanese commanders failed their army, confusion reigned throughout higher levels of command, and area army and army commanders issued conflicting orders prompting many units to withdraw from combat, while others were engulfed by the Soviet offensive tide. The unexpected form of the Soviet offensive only compounded the many problems the Japanese faced.

Japanese defensive plans might have achieved greater success against a less experienced foe. Unfortunately, the Kwantung Army faced a highly professional force led by the cream of the Soviet officer corps, men who had been blooded and educated in four years of warfare in the West. For the most part, the Far East Command's formations and units were among the best in the Soviet Army, and their equipment had been tested against the best weaponry European arsenals could produce. For the Soviet Army, the Manchurian offensive was the last campaign in a long and difficult war, quite literally a postgraduate exercise for the Soviet Army and the culmination of a rigorous education in combat on the battlefield that had begun in western Russia in June 1941. Given one last opportunity to excel, the Soviet Army did so in dramatic fashion.

LESSONS LEARNED

True to their long tradition of intensely studying their war experiences and those of other countries in the service of improving their armed force's performance in future war, Russian military theorists and historians have treated the Manchurian offensive as an ideal case study in the conduct of modern war at theater level. Considered against the backdrop of ever-changing military technology and weaponry, the Manchurian offensive seemed to represent the first valid case study regarding how to conduct a theater strategic offensive operation. This study produced a host of important lessons, many of which seemed applicable to warfare in a relatively large but isolated theater of military operations in the future.

The most important lesson was how a modern army could win quick victory in an initial period of war [*nachal'nyi period voiny*], that is, during that brief period after the beginning of hostilities when an army's performance dictated whether the war would be long or short. This was a particularly vital issue to the Soviet Union given its bitter experiences during the initial period of the Soviet–Finnish War (1939–40) and its Great Patriotic War against Germany (1941–45), as well as the equally sobering experiences of Russian (Tsarist) armies in the Russo-Japanese War (1903–4) and the First World War (1914–18).

Within this dreadful historical context, the circumstances the Soviet Armed Forces faced in Manchuria and the techniques Soviet military planners and leaders developed and implemented to win so rapid a victory seemed to offer clear answers to the lasting strategic dilemma of prevailing in an initial period of war. In short, the Far East Command was able to mount an offensive whose scale, form, and intent quickly overcame Japanese initial defenses, preempted subsequent Japanese resistance, defeated and destroyed the Kwantung Army, and captured the strategically critical heartland of Manchuria and adjacent regions before the Japanese surrendered.

The Far East Command accomplished this feat by secretly regrouping to the Far East sufficient forces to create decisive superiority over the Japanese in all major operational sectors, by surprising the Japanese regarding the form and timing of the offensive, and by employing operational and tactical techniques that preempted Japanese resistance and produced rapid victory. By attacking along every conceivable axis of advance with the bulk of its forces deployed in first echelon and by employing maneuver at every opportunity, the Far East Command applied unbearable pressure against an already overextended foe, utterly collapsed Japanese defenses, and generated offensive momentum that propelled its forces into the depths of Manchuria. In each and every operational sector, Soviet commanders massed their forces at the most critical points and artfully maneuvered their forces over seemingly impassable terrain to objectives most Japanese considered unattainable.

The Far East Command and its component *fronts* achieved initial success and generated requisite offensive momentum by applying combat power incrementally through the time-phased commitment to combat of forward detachments or assault groups, advanced battalions, and the first and second echelons of main force divisions and corps. From the very beginning of the offensive, this application of power threw the Japanese defenders off balance, and they remained off balance throughout the entire duration of the short campaign. The confusion that the form and location of the Soviet offensive sowed in Japanese ranks utterly negated subsequent effective Japanese response.

To exploit its initial success and preempt subsequent Japanese reaction, the Far East Command ordered all of its subordinate forces to employ tank-heavy, and combat-capable forward detachments, which were tailored to master the terrain over which they were to operate, to lead and sustain the advance into the operational and strategic depths. The quantity and effectiveness of these forward detachments permitted Soviet forces to continue their advance with only limited forces deployed forward, and the forward detachments' success allowed the Soviet main forces to follow almost totally unhindered by serious Japanese resistance.

Each forward detachment functioned like a carpenter's awl by boring a hole into hard wood to prepare it for the subsequent penetration by a screw. Punctured in numerous sectors, the Japanese defenses lost all of their coherence and never regained it. The forward detachments tore into the disrupted defense, leaving it fragmented and paralyzed, and raced on to seize their next objectives.

Soviet (Russian) study of the Manchurian strategic offensive operation produced many other clear lessons, the most important of which include:

- *Echelon forces for combat flexibly and imaginatively, especially against unprepared or only partially prepared defenses.* In the Manchurian offensive, Soviet analysts concluded that the single echelon operational formation at theater, *front*, and army level, which involved forces operating along multiple axes across a broad front, collapsed and fragmented the Japanese defense before the defense could gel.
- *Commit combat forces to battle incrementally in time-phased sequence.* In Manchuria, the successive application of combat power in time-phased sequence using maneuver to a maximum produced unbearable pressure against Japanese defenses. The relentless strengthening of the attack destroyed the coherence and equilibrium of Japanese defenses and led to utter and irreparable Japanese collapse. In a contemporary context, these multiple penetrations and the inevitable intermingling of forces that results also makes it exceedingly difficult or impossible for the defender to employ high-precision weaponry or weapons of mass destruction such as tactical nuclear weapons.

- *Lead any offensive with operational maneuver (mobile) groups, forward detachments, or other forces configured to conduct ground or vertical maneuver at every command level.* During the Manchurian offensive, the Far East Command relied on operational maneuver groups (in this case, the 6th Guards Tank Army and 10th Mechanized Corps) and numerous forward detachments to fragment and confuse Japanese tactical defenses, to preempt subsequent defenses, and to sustain operations into the operational and strategic depths. Analysts agree that the careful conduct of tactical and operational maneuver, either on the ground or from the air, provides the key to achieving success in any future military operation.

The Far East Command's violent but brief offensive in Manchuria represented a fitting end to the Soviet Union's (and Russia's) longest and most costly war. By fulfilling commitments it made to its Allies at the Yalta and Potsdam Conferences, the Soviet Union materially assisted in the defeat of Imperial Japan. While doing so, the Soviet Army was able to apply all of the most important lessons it had learned during four years of war with Nazi Germany and, in the process, learn many new lessons that helped shape the postwar Soviet Army.

The most important political legacy of the Soviets' Manchurian venture was that, by virtue of the war, the Soviet Union emerged as a dominant power in eastern Asia and the Pacific basin. Furthermore, the Soviet Union's enhanced stature in the region contributed significantly to the ultimate emergence of Communist China as a key regional and later global power and the subsequent division of Korea into Communist North Korea, and democratic South Korea, which still endures today.

Militarily, while helping shape the form of the modern Soviet Army, the Manchurian 'strategic model' fundamentally shaped Soviet military strategy, operational art, and tactics for generations to come, particularly regarding strategic regrouping, the nature of initial periods of war, the nature and form of potential theater strategic offensives, and the conduct of modern operational and tactical maneuver.

NOTES

1. For Soviet casualties, see I. D. Sergeev, ed., *Voennaia entsiklopediia v vos'mi tomakh, T. 4* [Military encyclopedia in 8 vols, vol. 4] (Moscow: Voenizdat, 1999), 562, and G. F. Krivosheev, ed., *Rossiia i SSSR v voinakh XX veka: Statisticheskoe issledovanie* [Russia and the USSR in twentieth century wars: A statistical survey] (Moscow: 'Olma-press', 2001), 309. The marked difference between Soviet and Japanese sources regarding combat losses in the campaign is understandable considering the fragmented nature of the fighting, the wide variety of participants, and Japan's loss of all of the Kwantung Army's records. The Soviet estimates of total Japanese losses in Manchuria fall well short of the strength of the forces that Japanese sources claimed were

stationed in Manchuria and northern Korea (713,000). This is compounded by the fact that the Soviet calculation of Japanese losses also includes Manchukuoan casualties, which accounted for a significant portion of the losses in some regions (at Tuchuan, Chiamussu, and Solun). The Soviet figures also include an indeterminate number of Japanese reservists and civilians who joined the garrisons of fortified regions to fight alongside Japanese soldiers, as well as missing Japanese who continued to resist long after Japan's formal surrender. Clearly, therefore, many Japanese soldiers escaped the Soviet juggernaut or were simply not counted after they perished.

The strength and casualty figures recorded in Japanese official accounts are limited to regular soldiers and do not include the large numbers of Japanese missing or casualties among the Manchukuoan and Inner Mongolian auxiliaries. Even at that, those who wrote battle accounts of individual Japanese divisions tended to describe higher casualties. In light of this, the Soviet figures are probably valid and may even be conservative. Although the Soviet estimates of their own casualties are quite low, the Japanese estimates of Soviet losses are even lower.

2. Meretskov, *Serving the People*, 353, and Beloborodov, 'Na sopkakh Man'chzhurii', Pt. 2, 46, 48–9.

Appendix 1: Kwantung Army's Order of Battle, 30 July 1945

KWANTUNG ARMY HEADQUARTERS: COMMANDER-IN-CHIEF, GENERAL YAMADA OTOZO

1st Mobile Brigade
  1st Independent Balloon Company
1st Armored Train Unit
2d Armored Train Unit
Kwantung Army 1st Noncommissioned Officer Candidate Infantry Unit
Kwantung Army 2d Noncommissioned Officer Candidate Infantry Unit
Kwantung Army 1st Cadre's Infantry Training Unit
Kwantung Army 2d Cadre's Infantry Training Unit
Kwantung Army Noncommissioned Officer Candidate Cavalry Unit
Kwantung Army Noncommissioned Officer Candidate Artillery Unit
Kwantung Army Noncommissioned Officer Candidate Antiaircraft Artillery Unit
Kwantung Army Noncommissioned Officer Candidate Engineer Unit
Kwantung Army Noncommissioned Officer Candidate Transport Unit

FIRST AREA ARMY: GENERAL KITA SEIICHI

First Area Army Headquarters
  122d Infantry Division: Lieutenant General Akashika Tadashi
  134th Infantry Division: Lieutenant General Izeki Jin
  603d Special Guard Battalion
  627th Special Guard Company
  139th Infantry Division: Lieutenant General Tominaga Kyoji
  Kwantung Army 2d Special Garrison Unit
  12th Independent Engineer Regiment
  17th Signal Regiment

620th Special Guard Company
621st Special Guard Company
622d Special Guard Company
624th Special Guard Company
636th Special Guard Company
613th Special Guard Engineer Unit

3d Army: Lieutenant General Murakami Keisaku
3d Army Headquarters
132d Independent Mixed Brigade
101st Mixed Regiment
2d Heavy Artillery Regiment
3d Heavy Artillery Regiment
Tungning Heavy Artillery Regiment
2d Independent Heavy Artillery Company
1st Independent Heavy Mortar Company
55th Signal Regiment
Najin Fortress Garrison
Najin Fortress Artillery Unit
460th Special Guard Battalion
623d Special Guard Company
651st Special Guard Company
79th Infantry Division: Lieutenant General Ota Teisho
112th Infantry Division: Lieutenant General Nakamura Jikizo
127th Infantry Division: Lieutenant General Koga Ryutaro
128th Infantry Division: Lieutenant General Mizuhara Yoshishige

5th Army: Lieutenant General Shimizu Noritsune
5th Army Headquarters
15th Border Garrison Unit
9th Raiding Unit
31st Independent Antitank Battalion
20th Heavy Field Artillery Regiment
5th Independent Heavy Artillery Battalion
8th Independent Heavy Artillery Battalion
1st Independent Heavy Artillery Battalion
13th Mortar Battalion
1st Engineer Unit Headquarters
18th Independent Engineer Regiment (road bridge construction)
3d Field Fortification Unit
46th Signal Regiment
628th Special Guard Company
629th Special Guard Company

630th Special Guard Company
641st Special Guard Company
124th Infantry Division: Lieutenant General Shiina Masatake
126th Infantry Division: Lieutenant General Nomizo Kazuhiko
135th Infantry Division: Lieutenant General Hitomi Yoichi

THIRD AREA ARMY: GENERAL USHIROKU JUN

Third Area Army Headquarters
108th Infantry Division: Lieutenant General Iwai Torajiro
171st Cavalry Regiment
610th Special Guard Battalion
606th Special Guard Company
616th Special Guard Company
617th Special Guard Company
618th Special Guard Company
649th Special Guard Company
650th Special Guard Company
611th Special Guard Engineer Unit
612th Special Guard Engineer Unit
136th Infantry Division: Lieutenant General Makamura Toru
Fushun Guard Unit
602d Special Guard Company
603d Special Guard Engineer Unit
Penchihu Guard Unit
603d Special Guard Company
604th Special Guard Engineer Unit
Anshan Guard Unit
601st Special Guard Company
605th Special Guard Company
79th Independent Mixed Brigade
130th Independent Mixed Brigade
134th Independent Mixed Brigade
1st Independent Tank Brigade, Kwantung Army
1st Special Garrison Unit
11th Raiding Unit
Kwantung Territory Garrison Unit
61st Independent Heavy Fortress Artillery Battery
171st Antiaircraft Artillery Regiment
651st Special Guard Battalion
607th Special Guard Engineer Unit
611th Special Guard Battalion

612th Special Guard Battalion
613th Special Guard Battalion
614th Special Guard Battalion
615th Special Guard Battalion
616th Special Guard Battalion
608th Special Guard Company
609th Special Guard Company
610th Special Guard Company
22d Field Antiaircraft Artillery Unit
26th Antiaircraft Artillery Regiment
85th Field Antiaircraft Artillery Battalion
88th Field Antiaircraft Artillery Battalion
90th Field Antiaircraft Artillery Battalion
91st Field Antiaircraft Artillery Battalion
92d Field Antiaircraft Artillery Battalion
100th Field Antiaircraft Artillery Battalion
65th Independent Field Antiaircraft Artillery Battery
1st Field Searchlight Battalion
6th Field Searchlight Battalion
7th Field Searchlight Battalion
14th Independent Field Searchlight Company
68th Field Machine gun Company
69th Field Machine gun Company
70th Field Machine gun Company
71st Field Machine gun Company
72d Field Machine gun Company
73d Field Machine gun Company
74th Field Machine gun Company
75th Field Machine gun Company
76th Field Machine gun Company
77th Field Machine gun Company
85th Field Machine gun Company
54th Signal Regiment
656th Special Guard Battalion
653d Special Guard Battalion
602d Special Guard Engineer Unit
606th Special Guard Engineer Unit
607th Special Guard Battalion
608th Special Guard Battalion
611th Special Guard Company
612th Special Guard Company
613th Special Guard Company
609th Special Guard Engineer Unit

610th Special Guard Engineer Unit

30th Army: Lieutenant General Iida Shojiro
30th Army Headquarters
21st Independent Heavy Field Artillery Battalion
27th Independent Heavy Mortar Battalion
1st Heavy Artillery Regiment
19th Heavy Artillery Regiment
7th Independent Heavy Artillery Battalion
2d Engineer Unit Headquarters
40th Independent Engineer Regiment
601st Special Guard Battalion
604th Special Guard Battalion
609th Special Guard Battalion
614th Special Guard Company
638th Special Guard Company
639th Special Guard Company
640th Special Guard Company
642d Special Guard Company
601st Special Guard Engineer Unit
39th Infantry Division: Lieutenant General Sasa Shinnosuke
125th Infantry Division: Lieutenant General Imari Tatsuo
138th Infantry Division: Lieutenant General Yamamoto Tsutomu
148th Infantry Division: Lieutenant General Suemitsu Motohiro

44th Army: Lieutenant General Hongo Yoshio
44th Army Headquarters
9th Independent Tank Brigade
2d Raiding Unit
29th Independent Antitank Battalion
17th Heavy Field Artillery Regiment
30th Heavy Field Artillery Regiment
6th Independent Heavy Artillery Battery
31st Signal Regiment
605th Special Guard Company
607th Special Guard Company
112th Independent Motor Transport Battalion
73d Independent Transport Company
40th Construction Duty Company
619th Special Guard Company
643d Special Guard Company
644th Special Guard Company
648th Special Guard Company

63d Division: Lieutenant General Kishikawa Kenichi
107th Infantry Division: Lieutenant General Abe Koichi
117th Infantry Division: Lieutenant General Suzuki Hiraku

4th Separate Army: Lieutenant General Uemura Mikio
4th Separate Army Headquarters
131st Independent Mixed Brigade
135th Independent Mixed Brigade
136th Independent Mixed Brigade
57th Reconnaissance Regiment
Kwantung Army 3d Special Garrison Unit
12th Raiding Unit
30th Antitank Battalion
10th Independent Field Artillery Battalion
17th Mortar Battalion
29th Independent Engineer Regiment (road-bridge construction)
42d Signal Regiment
102d Guard Unit Headquarters
654th Special Guard Battalion
625th Special Guard Company
626th Special Guard Company
631st Special Guard Company
632d Special Guard Company
633d Special Guard Company
634th Special Guard Company
635th Special Guard Company
637th Special Guard Company
645th Special Guard Company
646th Special Guard Company
647th Special Guard Company
608th Special Guard Engineer Unit
614th Special Guard Engineer Unit
119th Infantry Division: Lieutenant General Shiozawa Kiyonobu
80th Independent Mixed Brigade
606th Special Guard Battalion
123d Infantry Division: Lieutenant General Kitazawa Teijiro
149th Infantry Division: Lieutenant General Sasaki Toichi

34th Army: Lieutenant General Kushibuchi Senichi (attached to the Kwantung Army on 10 August)
34th Army Headquarters
11th Independent Field Artillery Battalion
Mutanchiang Heavy Artillery Regiment

15th Mortar Battalion
Nanam Divisional District Unit (DDU) (Chongjin)
Nanam Headquarters
3d Antiaircraft Company
131st Special Guard Engineer Unit
Kwangjuryong Guard Unit
Chongjin Guard Unit
144th Special Guard Battalion
451st Special Guard Battalion
410th Special Guard Engineer Unit
Yamane Unit
1st Special Guard Regiment (-)
14th Special Guard Battalion
Takumi Detachment
142d Special Guard Unit
143d Special Guard Unit
Nodai Unit
Hungnam Detachment
402d Special Guard Battalion
403d Special Guard Battalion
401st Special Guard Engineer Unit
Yonghung Bay Fortress Garrison
Yonghung Bay Fortress Artillery Unit
462d Special Guard Battalion
Songjin Detachment
2d Special Guard Regiment
461st Special Guard Battalion
56th Signal Regiment
133th Independent Mixed Brigade (attached to the Kwantung Army on 9 August)
59th Infantry Division: Lieutenant General Fujita Shigeru
137th Infantry Division: Lieutenant General Akiyama Yoshisuke

SEVENTEENTH AREA ARMY: LIEUTENANT GENERAL KOZUKI YOSHIO

(assigned to the Kwantung Army Effective 0600 Hours 10 August – major subordinate forces only)

Seventeenth Area Army Headquarters
120th Infantry Division: Lieutenant General Shinichi Yanagawa
150th Infantry Division: Giichiro Mishima
160th Infantry Division: Masao Yamawaki

320th Infantry Division: Kinzaburo Yasumi
39th Independent Mixed Brigade
40th Independent Mixed Brigade
127th Independent Mixed Regiment

58th Army
58th Army Headquarters
96th Infantry Division: Mamoru Iinuma
111th Infantry Division: Tamio Iwasaki
121st Infantry Division: Yoshito Masai
108th Independent Mixed Regiment

FIFTH AREA ARMY: GENERAL HIGUCHI KIICHIRO

(responsible for the defense of southern Sakhalin Island, the Kuril Islands, and Hokkaido – Fifth Area Army Headquarters: Sapporo)

The Kurils
91st Infantry Division – Shumshir, Paramoshiri, Onekotan, Shiaskotan
11th Tank Regiment – Shumshir
129th Independent Mixed Brigade – Urup
41st Separate Mixed Regiment – Matau
Kuril Fortress Artillery Regiment – All islands
31st Antiaircraft Regiment – Shumshir
89th Infantry Division – Etorofu, Kunashiri, and the lesser Kurils

Hokkaido
42d Infantry Division – Wakkanai
7th Infantry Division – Kushiro
101st Independent Mixed Regiment – Tomakomai

Southern Sakhalin
88th Infantry Division

Sources: 'Record of Operations Against Soviet Russia – On Northern and Western Fronts of Manchuria and in Northern Korea (August 1945)', in *Japanese Monograph No. 155* (Tokyo: Military History Section, US Army Forces Far East, 1954) and 'File of Messages Exchanged with US Military Mission to Moscow', *SRH-198, Record Group 457* (Washington, DC: Military Branch, MIS, 25 October 1945), 011, 026. Classified Top Secret Ultra.

Appendix 2:

Actual Strength of Kwantung Army Components at Outbreak of Hostilities (August 1945) and Killed-in-Action Estimates

Actual Strength of Kwantung Army Components at
Outbreak of Hostilities (August 1945) and KIA Estimates*

Units	Actual Strength	KIA (%)
Kwantung Army		
GHQ	3,308	-
125th Div	11,450	-
Kwantung Army Supply Department	73,093	185
Directly assigned units	77,182	527
Total:	165,033	712 (0.4%)
First Area Army		
HQ	741	1
122d Div	16,027	49
128th Div	12,634	1,095
134th Div	14,056	471
139th Div	9,793	20
132d IMB	5,545	725
Directly assigned units	24,650	320
Total:	83,446	2,681 (3.2%)
Third Army		
HQ	968	-
79th Div	15,633	142
112d Div	15,068	930
127th Div	12,839	853
Najin FGU	1,280	136
Directly assigned units	17,152	375
Total:	62,940	2,436 (3.9%)
Fifth Army		
HQ	800	10
124th Div	14,824	2,297
126th Div	16,613	1,857
135th Div	14,228	1,631
15th BGU	1,700	1,400
Directly assigned units	27,606	2,196
Total:	75,771	9,391 (12.4%)
First Area Army Total:	222,157	14,508 (6.5%)
Third Area Army		
HQ	1,660	-
138th Div	8,810	-
79th IMB	6,772	-
134th IMB	4,448	-
Directly assigned units	20,788	157
Total:	42,478	157 (0.4%)
Thirtieth Army		
HQ	610	-
39th Div	16,274	1
107th Div	14,070	1,380

117th Div	13,694	150
148th Div	9,828	16
133d IMB	4,898	-
9th Tk Brig	2,281	-
Directly assigned units	7,748	-
Total:	69,403	1,547 (2.2%)
Forty-fourth Army		
HQ	400	-
63d Div	10,499	-
108th Div	18,141	110
136th Div	13,559	-
130th Div	7,400	-
1st Tk Brig	5,371	-
Directly assigned units	13,720	170
Total:	69,090	280 (0.4%)
Third Area Army Total:	180,971	1,984 (1.1%)
Fourth Army		
HQ	928	-
119th Div	18,721	1,253
123d Div	17,764	879
149th Div	12,100	-
80th IMB	7,068	1,077
131st IMB	4,797	3
135th IMB	4,138	228
136th IMB	4,318	-
Directly assigned units	25,630	-
Total:	95,464	3,440 (3.6%)
Thirty-fourth Army		
HQ	650	-
59th Div	14,916	-
137th Div	9,806	-
Nanam DDU	19,267	745
Directly assigned units	5,465	-
Total:	50,104	745 (1.5%)
Grand Total:	713,729	21,389 (2.9%)

These data were furnished by the 1st Demobilization Bureau and in some instance differ from the figures given by authors of sub-monographs.

LEGEND

Div ...... Infantry Division
IMB ...... Independent Mixed Brigade
FGU ...... Fortress Garrison Unit
BGU ...... Border Garrison Unit
DDU ...... Divisional District Unit

Appendix 3: The Operational Strength of Kwantung Army Forces, 9 August 1945

1. STRENGTH OF KWANTUNG ARMY FORCES DEPLOYED AGAINST TRANS-BAIKAL FRONT

Division/Brigade	*Date Organized*	*Strength Relative to the 12th Infantry Division in 1937 (%)*
119th Infantry Division	11 October 1944	70
80th Independent Mixed Brigade	January 1945	15
107th Infantry Division	16 May 1944	60
108th Infantry Division*	12 September 1944	65
117th Infantry Division**	July 1944	15
63d Infantry Division**	30 June 1943	15
133d Independent Mixed Brigade	July 1945	15
148th Infantry Division***	10 July 1945	15
9th Armored Brigade	–	–
125th Infantry Division	16 January 1945	20
138th Infantry Division****	10 July 1945	15
39th Infantry Division*****	30 June 1939	80
1st Armored Brigade	–	–
130th Independent Mixed Brigade	July 1945	15
136th Infantry Division	10 July 1945	15
79th Independent Mixed Brigade	January 1945	15

* The 108th Infantry Division was part of the China Expeditionary Army.
** The 117th and 63d Infantry Divisions were garrison divisions with two brigades of four battalions each. Neither division had more than 18 mountain artillery pieces as opposed to 24 as required by their tables of organization.
*** The 148th Infantry Division lacked small arms for its regiments.
**** The 138th Infantry Division was in the midst of mobilization and did not exceed 2,000 effectives.
***** The 39th Infantry Division was newly arrived from central China and lacked its artillery.

2. STRENGTH OF KWANTUNG ARMY FORCES DEPLOYED AGAINST 2D FAR EASTERN FRONT

Division/Brigade	*Date Organized*	*Strength Relative to the 12th Infantry Division in 1937 (%)*
135th Independent Mixed Brigade	July 1945	15
123d Infantry Division*	16 January 1945	35
136th Independent Mixed Brigade	July 1945	15
134th Independent Mixed Brigade	July 1945	15
134th Infantry Division	10 July 1945	15
149th Infantry Division**	10 July 1945	15

* The 123d Infantry Division's artillery lacked any mobility.
** The 149th Infantry Division had no artillery.

3. STRENGTH OF KWANTUNG ARMY FORCES DEPLOYED AGAINST 1ST FAR EASTERN FRONT

Division/Brigade	*Date Organized*	*Strength Relative to the 12th Infantry Division in 1937 (%)*
15th Border Guards Unit*	20 July 1945	–
135th Infantry Division	10 July 1945	15
26th Infantry Division	16 January 1945	20
124th Infantry Division	16 January 1945	35
132d Independent Mixed Brigade	July 1945	15
128th Infantry Division**	16 January 1945	20
112th Infantry Division	10 July 1944	35
1st Mobile Brigade	–	–
79th Infantry Division	6 February 1945	15
127th Infantry Division	20 March 1945	20
122d Infantry Division	16 January 1945	35
139th Infantry Division	10 July 1945	15
134th Independent Mixed Brigade	July 1945	15
59th Infantry Division	2 February 1942	–
137th Infantry Division	10 July 1945	15

* The 15th BGU was authorized 12 infantry companies and three artillery batteries but had only four infantry companies and one artillery battery.
** Of the 128th Infantry Division's authorized strength of 23,000 men, only 14,000 were available for duty and these lacked training.

Appendix 4: The Soviet Far East Command's Order of Battle, 9 August 1945

THE FAR EAST COMMAND HEADQUARTERS

Commander in Chief, Marshal of the Soviet Union A. M. Vasilevsky
Chief of Staff, Colonel General S. P. Ivanov
Member of Military Council (Commissar), Lieutenant General I. V. Shikin

TRANS-BAIKAL FRONT

Commander in Chief, Marshal of the Soviet Union R. Ia. Malinovsky
Chief of Staff, Army General M. V. Zakharov
Member of the Military Council, Lieutenant General A. N. Tevchenkov

17th Army: Lieutenant General A. I. Danilov
- 209th Rifle Division
- 278th Rifle Division
- 284th Rifle Division
- 70th Separate Tank Battalion
- 82d Separate Tank Battalion
- 185th Gun Artillery Regiment
- 413th Howitzer Artillery Regiment
- 1910th Antitank (Tank Destroyer) Artillery Brigade
- 178th Mortar Regiment
- 809th Separate Reconnaissance Artillery Battalion
- 56th Antitank (Tank Destroyer) Artillery Brigade
- 39th Guards-Mortar Regiment
- 1916th Antiaircraft Artillery Regiment
- 66th Separate Antiaircraft Artillery Battalion

382d Separate Antiaircraft Artillery Battalion
67th Motorized Engineer Brigade

36th Army: Lieutenant General A. A. Luchinsky
2d Rifle Corps: Lieutenant General A. I. Lopatin
103d Rifle Division
275th Rifle Division
292d Rifle Division
86th Rifle Corps: Major General G. V. Revunenkov
94th Rifle Division
210th Rifle Division
Operational Group
293d Rifle Division
298th Rifle Division
31st Fortified Region
32d Fortified Region
205th Tank Brigade
33d Separate Tank Battalion
35th Separate Tank Battalion
68th Separate Armored Train
69th Separate Armored Train
6th Machine gun-Artillery Brigade
15th Machine gun-Artillery Brigade
267th Gun Artillery Regiment
1233d Gun Artillery Regiment
259th Howitzer Artillery Regiment
1146th High-Power Howitzer Artillery Regiment
1912th Antitank (Tank Destroyer) Artillery Regiment
176th Mortar Regiment
177th Mortar Regiment
190th Mountain Mortar Regiment
32d Guards-Mortar Regiment
7th Antiaircraft Artillery Division
465th Antiaircraft Artillery Regiment
474th Antiaircraft Artillery Regiment
602d Antiaircraft Artillery Regiment
632d Antiaircraft Artillery Regiment
120th Separate Antiaircraft Artillery Battalion
405th Separate Antiaircraft Artillery Battalion
68th Engineer-Sapper Brigade

- 39th Army: Colonel General I. I. Liudnikov
  - 5th Guards Rifle Corps: Lieutenant General I. S. Bezuglyi
    - 17th Guards Rifle Division
    - 19th Guards Rifle Division
    - 91st Guards Rifle Division
  - 94th Rifle Corps: Major General I. I. Popov
    - 124th Rifle Division
    - 221st Rifle Division
    - 358th Rifle Division
  - 113th Rifle Corps: Lieutenant General N. N. Oleshev
    - 192d Rifle Division
    - 262d Rifle Division
    - 338th Rifle Division
  - 61st Tank Division
  - 44th Tank Brigade
  - 206th Tank Brigade
  - 735th Self-propelled Artillery Regiment
  - 927th Self-propelled Artillery Regiment
  - 1197th Self-propelled Artillery Regiment
  - 5th Artillery Penetration Corps: Major General L. N. Alekseev
    - 3d Guards Artillery Penetration Division
      - 8th Guards Howitzer Artillery Brigade
      - 22d Guards Gun Artillery Brigade
      - 99th Heavy Howitzer Artillery Brigade
      - 43d Mortar Brigade
      - 50th Heavy Mortar Brigade
      - 14th Guards-Mortar Brigade
    - 6th Guards Artillery Penetration Division
      - 29th Guards Gun Artillery Brigade
      - 69th Light Artillery Brigade
      - 134th Howitzer Artillery Brigade
      - 87th Heavy Howitzer Brigade
      - 4th Mortar Brigade
      - 10th Guards-Mortar Brigade
  - 139th Gun Artillery Brigade
  - 390th Gun Artillery Regiment
  - 629th Gun Artillery Regiment
  - 1142d Gun Artillery Regiment
  - 1143d Gun Artillery Regiment
  - 55th Antitank (Tank Destroyer) Artillery Brigade
  - 610th Antitank (Tank Destroyer) Regiment
  - 555th Mortar Regiment
  - 24th Guards-Mortar Brigade

34th Guards-Mortar Regiment
46th Guards-Mortar Regiment
64th Guards-Mortar Regiment
14th Antiaircraft Artillery Division
715th Antiaircraft Artillery Regiment
718th Antiaircraft Artillery Regiment
721st Antiaircraft Artillery Regiment
2013th Antiaircraft Artillery Regiment
621st Antiaircraft Artillery Regiment
63d Separate Antiaircraft Artillery Battalion
32d Engineer-Sapper Brigade

53d Army: Colonel General I. M. Managarov
18th Guards Rifle Corps: Lieutenant General I. M. Afonin
1st Guards Airborne Division
109th Guards Rifle Division
110th Guards Rifle Division
49th Rifle Corps: Lieutenant General G. N. Terent'ev
6th Rifle Division
243d Rifle Division
57th Rifle Corps: Lieutenant General G. B. Safiulin
52d Rifle Division
203d Rifle Division
152d Gun Artillery Brigade
1316th Antitank (Tank Destroyer) Artillery Regiment
461st Mortar Regiment
52d Guards-Mortar Regiment
53d Guards-Mortar Regiment
17th Antiaircraft Artillery Division
1267th Antiaircraft Artillery Regiment
1276th Antiaircraft Artillery Regiment
1279th Antiaircraft Artillery Regiment
2014th Antiaircraft Artillery Regiment
239th Separate Antiaircraft Artillery Battalion
376th Separate Antiaircraft Artillery Battalion
54th Engineer-Sapper Brigade

6th Guards Tank Army: Colonel General A. G. Kravchenko
5th Guards Tank Corps: Lieutenant General M. I. Savel'ev
20th Guards Tank Brigade
21st Guards Tank Brigade
22d Guards Tank Brigade

6th Guards Motorized Rifle Brigade
390th Self-propelled Artillery Regiment
15th Guards Motorcycle Battalion
301st Light Artillery Regiment
454th Guards-Mortar Regiment
127th Guards-Mortar Battalion
392d Guards Antiaircraft Artillery Regiment
9th Guards Mechanized Corps: Lieutenant General M. V. Volkov
18th Guards Mechanized Brigade
30th Guards Mechanized Brigade
31st Guards Mechanized Brigade
46th Guards Tank Brigade
389th Guards Self-propelled Artillery Regiment
14th Guards Motorcycle Battalion
458th Guards-Mortar Regiment
35th Guards-Mortar Battalion
388th Guards Antiaircraft Artillery Regiment
7th Guards Mechanized Corps: Lieutenant General F. G. Katkov
16th Mechanized Brigade
63d Mechanized Brigade
64th Mechanized Brigade
41st Guards Tank Brigade
1289th Self-propelled Artillery Regiment
94th Motorcycle Battalion
614th Mortar Regiment
40th Guards-Mortar Battalion
1713th Antiaircraft Artillery Regiment
36th Motorized Rifle Division
57th Motorized Rifle Division
208th Self-propelled Artillery Brigade
231st Self-propelled Artillery Brigade
4th Guards Motorcycle Regiment
1st Separate Tank Battalion
2d Separate Tank Battalion
3d Separate Tank Battalion
4th Separate Tank Battalion
275th Separate Special-designation (Spetsnaz) Battalion
202d Light Artillery Brigade
870th Gun Artillery Regiment
1324th Light Artillery Regiment
1426th Light Artillery Regiment
624th Howitzer Artillery Regiment
1141st Gun Artillery Regiment

57th Guards-Mortar Regiment
30th Antiaircraft Artillery Division
1361st Antiaircraft Artillery Regiment
1367th Antiaircraft Artillery Regiment
1373d Antiaircraft Artillery Regiment
1375th Antiaircraft Artillery Regiment
8th Motorized Engineer Brigade
22d Motorized Engineer Brigade

Cavalry-Mechanized Group: Colonel General I. A. Pliev
85th Rifle Corps Headquarters
59th Cavalry Division
25th Mechanized Brigade
27th Motorized Rifle Brigade
43d Tank Brigade
25th Mechanized Brigade
30th Motorcycle Regiment
5th Mongolian Cavalry Division
6th Mongolian Cavalry Division
7th Mongolian Cavalry Division
8th Mongolian Cavalry Division
7th Motorized Armored Brigade (Mongolian)
3d Heavy Tank Regiment
Armored Car Brigade (Mongolian)
35th Antitank (Tank Destroyer) Artillery Brigade
1914th Antiaircraft Artillery Regiment
1917th Antiaircraft Artillery Regiment
60th Guards-Mortar Regiment
3d Artillery Regiment (Mongolian)

12th Air Army: Marshal of the Soviet Union S. A. Khudiakov
6th Bomber Aviation Corps: Major General I. P. Skok
326th Bomber Aviation Division
334th Bomber Aviation Division
7th Bomber Aviation Corps: Lieutenant General. V. A. Ushakov
113th Bomber Aviation Division
179th Bomber Aviation Division
30th Bomber Aviation Division
247th Bomber Aviation Division
248th Assault Aviation Division
316th Assault Aviation Division
190th Fighter Aviation Division
245th Fighter Aviation Division
246th Fighter Aviation Division

21st Guards Transport Aviation Division
54th Transport Aviation Division
12th Reconnaissance Aviation Regiment
368th Fighter Aviation Regiment
541st Bomber Aviation Regiment
257th Transport Aviation Regiment
23d Separate Heavy Bomber Aviation Squadron

Front Units
227th Rifle Division
317th Rifle Division
1st Parachute Battalion
2d Parachute Battalion
111th Tank Division
201st Tank Brigade
67th Separate Armored Train
70th Separate Armored Train
79th Separate Armored Train
46th Antitank (Tank Destroyer) Artillery Brigade
47th Antitank (Tank Destroyer) Artillery Brigade
1913th Antitank (Tank Destroyer) Artillery Regiment
11th Guards-Mortar Brigade
63d Guards-Mortar Regiment
1915th Antiaircraft Artillery Regiment
32d Separate Antiaircraft Artillery Battalion
92d Separate Antiaircraft Artillery Battalion
242d Separate Antiaircraft Artillery Battalion
401st Separate Antiaircraft Artillery Battalion
410th Separate Antiaircraft Artillery Battalion
414th Separate Antiaircraft Artillery Battalion
467th Separate Antiaircraft Artillery Battalion
40th Corrective-Aviation Squadron
41st Corrective-Aviation Squadron
115th Reconnaissance Aviation Squadron
116th Reconnaissance Aviation Squadron
131st Reconnaissance Aviation Squadron
132d Reconnaissance Aviation Squadron
133d Reconnaissance Aviation Squadron
5th Assault Engineer-Sapper Brigade
9th Assault Engineer-Sapper Brigade
13th Assault Engineer-Sapper Brigade
9th Pontoon-Bridge Brigade
653d Armored Amphibious Vehicle Battalion

Forces Added to the *Front* on 16 August
- 3d Guards Mechanized Corps: Lieutenant General V. T. Obukhov
  - 7th Guards Mechanized Brigade
  - 8th Guards Mechanized Brigade
  - 9th Guards Mechanized Brigade
  - 35th Guards Tank Brigade
  - 1st Guards Motorcycle Battalion
  - 129th Mortar Regiment
  - 1705th Antiaircraft Artillery Regiment
  - 743d Separate Antitank (Tank Destroyer) Artillery Battalion
  - 334th Separate Guards-Mortar Battalion

2D FAR EASTERN FRONT

Commander in Chief, Army General M. A. Purkaev
Chief of Staff, Lieutenant General F. I. Shevchenko
Member of Military Council, Lieutenant General D. S. Leonov

2d Red Banner Army: Lieutenant General M. F. Terekhin
- 3d Rifle Division
- 12th Rifle Division
- 396th Rifle Division
- 368th Separate Mountain Rifle Regiment
- 101st Fortified Region
- 135th Separate Machine gun Artillery Battalion
- 73d Tank Brigade
- 74th Tank Brigade
- 258th Tank Brigade
- 1st Separate Armored Train
- 2d Separate Armored Train
- 3d Separate Armored Train
- 40th Separate Armored Train
- 66th Separate Armored Train
- 77th Separate Armored Train
- 5th Separate Armored Trolley Battalion
- 42d Gun Artillery Regiment
- 388th Gun Artillery Regiment
- 1140th Gun Artillery Regiment
- 147th Howitzer Artillery Regiment
- 1129th Howitzer Artillery Regiment
- 1628th Antitank (Tank Destroyer) Artillery Regiment
- 181st Mortar Regiment

465th Mortar Regiment
310th Guards-Mortar Regiment
1589th Antiaircraft Artillery Regiment
9th Separate Antiaircraft Artillery Battalion
42d Separate Antiaircraft Artillery Battalion
10th Separate Pontoon Bridge Battalion
277th Separate Engineer Battalion

15th Army: Lieutenant General S. K. Mamonov
34th Rifle Division
255th Rifle Division (initially in *front* reserve)
361st Rifle Division
388th Rifle Division
4th Fortified Region
102d Fortified Region
165th Tank Brigade
171st Tank Brigade
203d Tank Brigade
21st Antitank (Tank Destroyer) Artillery Brigade
52d Gun Artillery Regiment
145th Gun Artillery Regiment
1120th Gun Artillery Regiment
1121st Gun Artillery Regiment
1637th Gun Artillery Regiment
424th Howitzer Artillery Regiment
1632d Antitank (Tank Destroyer) Artillery Regiment
1633d Antitank (Tank Destroyer) Artillery Regiment
183d Mortar Regiment
470th Mortar Regiment
85th Guards-Mortar Regiment
99th Guards-Mortar Regiment
73d Antiaircraft Artillery Division
205th Antiaircraft Artillery Regiment
402d Antiaircraft Artillery Regiment
430th Antiaircraft Artillery Regiment
442d Antiaircraft Artillery Regiment
1648th Antiaircraft Artillery Regiment
29th Separate Antiaircraft Artillery Battalion
46th Separate Antiaircraft Artillery Battalion
302d Separate Antiaircraft Artillery Battalion
505th Separate Antiaircraft Artillery Battalion
10th Pontoon-Bridge Brigade
21st Motorized Assault Engineer-Sapper Brigade

101st Separate Engineer Battalion
129th Separate Engineer Battalion

16th Army: Major General. L.G. Cheremisov
56th Rifle Corps: Major General A. A. D'iakonov
79th Rifle Division
2d Rifle Brigade
Separate Sakhalin Rifle Regiment
6th Separate Rifle Battalion
103d Fortified Region
104th Fortified Region
5th Rifle Brigade
113th Rifle Brigade
432d Separate Rifle Regiment
540th Separate Rifle Regiment
206th Separate Rifle Battalion
214th Tank Brigade
178th Separate Tank Battalion
678th Separate Tank Battalion
433d Gun Artillery Battalion
487th Artillery Regiment
82d Separate Artillery Battalion
428th Separate Artillery Battalion
221st Separate Antiaircraft Battalion

10th Air Army: Colonel General P. F. Zhigarev
18th Mixed Aviation Corps: Lieutenant General V. F. Niukhtilin
296th Fighter Aviation Division
96th Assault Aviation Division
777th Fighter Aviation Regiment
140th Reconnaissance Aviation Squadron
28th Corrective-Aviation Squadron
83d Bomber Aviation Division
128th Mixed Aviation Division
255th Mixed Aviation Division
253d Assault Aviation Division
29th Fighter Aviation Division
254th Fighter Aviation Division
7th Reconnaissance Aviation Regiment
411th Reconnaissance Corrective-Aviation Regiment
344th Transport Aviation Regiment
1604th Antiaircraft Artillery Regiment
1681st Antiaircraft Artillery Regiment
1685th Antiaircraft Artillery Regiment

Front Units
5th Rifle Corps: Major General I. Z. Pashkov
35th Rifle Division
390th Rifle Division
Kamchatka Defense Region: Major General A. P. Gnechko
101st Rifle Division
198th Separate Rifle Regiment
5th Separate Rifle Battalion
7th Separate Rifle Battalion
428th Howitzer Artillery Regiment
123d Separate Artillery Battalion
362d Separate Artillery Battalion
367th Separate Artillery Battalion
726th Separate Antiaircraft Artillery Battalion
88th Rifle Brigade
172d Tank Brigade
32d Guards Tank Brigade
26th Separate Armored Train
76th Separate Armored Train
14th Antitank (Tank Destroyer) Artillery Brigade
76th Gun Artillery Regiment
177th Howitzer Artillery Regiment
1604th Antiaircraft Artillery Regiment
1649th Antiaircraft Artillery Regiment
1685th Antiaircraft Artillery Regiment
183d Separate Antiaircraft Artillery Battalion
622d Separate Antiaircraft Artillery Battalion
47th Motorized Engineer Brigade
3d Heavy Pontoon-Bridge Regiment

1ST FAR EASTERN FRONT

Commander in Chief, Marshal of the Soviet Union K. A. Meretskov
Chief of Staff, Lieutenant General A. N. Krutikov
Member of Military Council, Colonel General T. F. Shtykov

1st Red Banner Army: Colonel General A. P. Beloborodov
26th Rifle Corps: Major General A. V. Skvortsov
22d Rifle Division
59th Rifle Division
300th Rifle Division

59th Rifle Corps: Major General V. A. Semenov (Lieutenant General G. I. Khetagurov after 12 August 1945)
- 39th Rifle Division
- 231st Rifle Division
- 365th Rifle Division

6th Fortified Region
112th Fortified Region
75th Tank Brigade
77th Tank Brigade
257th Tank Brigade
48th Separate Heavy Tank Regiment
335th Guards Heavy Self-propelled Artillery Regiment
338th Guards Heavy Self-propelled Artillery Regiment
339th Guards Heavy Self-propelled Artillery Regiment
213th Gun Artillery Brigade
216th Corps Artillery Brigade
217th Corps Artillery Brigade
60th Antitank (Tank Destroyer) Artillery Brigade
52d Mortar Brigade
33d Guards-Mortar Regiment
54th Guards-Mortar Regiment
33d Antiaircraft Artillery Division
- 1378th Antiaircraft Artillery Regiment
- 1710th Antiaircraft Artillery Regiment
- 1715th Antiaircraft Artillery Regiment
- 1718th Antiaircraft Artillery Regiment
- 115th Separate Antiaircraft Artillery Battalion
- 455th Separate Antiaircraft Artillery Battalion
- 721st Separate Antiaircraft Artillery Battalion
- 12th Engineer-Sapper Brigade
- 27th Engineer-Sapper Brigade

5th Army: Colonel General N. I. Krylov
- 17th Rifle Corps: Lieutenant General N. A. Nikitin
  - 187th Rifle Division
  - 366th Rifle Division
- 45th Rifle Corps: Major General N. I. Ivanov
  - 157th Rifle Division
  - 159th Rifle Division
  - 184th Rifle Division
- 65th Rifle Corps: Major General G. H. Perekrestov
  - 97th Rifle Division
  - 144th Rifle Division

190th Rifle Division
371st Rifle Division
72d Rifle Corps: Major General A. I. Kazartsev
63d Rifle Division
215th Rifle Division
277th Rifle Division
105th Fortified Region
72d Tank Brigade
76th Tank Brigade
208th Tank Brigade
210th Tank Brigade
218th Tank Brigade
333d Guards Heavy Self-propelled Artillery Regiment
378th Guards Heavy Self-propelled Artillery Regiment
395th Guards Heavy Self-propelled Artillery Regiment
478th Guards Heavy Self-propelled Artillery Regiment
479th Guards Heavy Self-propelled Artillery Regiment
480th Guards Heavy Self-propelled Artillery Regiment
78th Separate Armored Train
15th Guards Gun Artillery Brigade
225th Gun Artillery Brigade
226th Gun Artillery Brigade
227th Gun Artillery Brigade
236th Gun Artillery Brigade
107th High-Power Howitzer Artillery Brigade
119th High-Power Howitzer Artillery Brigade
223d High-Power Howitzer Artillery Brigade
218th Corps Artillery Brigade
219th Corps Artillery Brigade
220th Corps Artillery Brigade
222d Corps Artillery Brigade
237th Howitzer Artillery Brigade
238th Howitzer Artillery Brigade
61st Antitank (Tank Destroyer) Artillery Brigade
20th Special-power Gun Artillery Regiment
32d Separate Special-power Artillery Battalion
34th Separate Special-power Artillery Battalion
696th Antitank (Tank Destroyer) Artillery Regiment
53d Mortar Brigade
55th Mortar Brigade
56th Mortar Brigade
57th Mortar Brigade
283d Mortar Regiment

17th Guards-Mortar Brigade
20th Guards-Mortar Brigade
26th Guards-Mortar Brigade
2d Guards Mortar Regiment
26th Guards-Mortar Regiment
42d Guards-Mortar Regiment
72d Guards-Mortar Regiment
74th Guards-Mortar Regiment
307th Guards-Mortar Regiment
48th Antiaircraft Artillery Division
231st Guards Antiaircraft Artillery Regiment
1277th Antiaircraft Artillery Regiment
1278th Antiaircraft Artillery Regiment
2011th Antiaircraft Artillery Regiment
726th Antiaircraft Artillery Regiment
129th Separate Antiaircraft Artillery Battalion
300th Separate Antiaircraft Artillery Battalion
461st Separate Antiaircraft Artillery Battalion
20th Motorized Assault Engineer-Sapper Brigade
23d Engineer-Sapper Brigade
63d Engineer-Sapper Brigade
46th Motorized Engineer Brigade
55th Separate Pontoon-Bridge Battalion

25th Army: Colonel General I. M. Chistiakov
39th Rifle Corps: Major General A. M. Morozov
40th Rifle Division
384th Rifle Division
386th Rifle Division
393d Rifle Division
7th Fortified Region
106th Fortified Region
107th Fortified Region
108th Fortified Region
110th Fortified Region
111th Fortified Region
113th Fortified Region
259th Tank Brigade
28th Separate Armored Train
214th Gun Artillery Brigade
221st Corps Artillery Brigade
100th Separate Special-power Artillery Battalion
1631st Antitank (Tank Destroyer) Artillery Regiment

1590th Antiaircraft Artillery Regiment
22d Separate Antiaircraft Artillery Battalion
24th Separate Antiaircraft Artillery Battalion
100th Separate Engineer Battalion
222d Separate Engineer Battalion
143d Separate Sapper Battalion

35th Army: Lieutenant General N. D. Zakhvataev
66th Rifle Division
264th Rifle Division
363d Rifle Division
8th Fortified Region
109th Fortified Region
125th Tank Brigade
209th Tank Brigade
9th Separate Armored Train
13th Separate Armored Train
215th Gun Artillery Brigade
224th High-Power Howitzer Artillery Brigade
62d Antitank (Tank Destroyer) Artillery Brigade
64th Mortar Brigade
67th Guards-Mortar Regiment
1647th Antiaircraft Artillery Regiment
43d Separate Antiaircraft Artillery Battalion
110th Separate Antiaircraft Artillery Battalion
355th Separate Antiaircraft Artillery Battalion
280th Separate Engineer Battalion

9th Air Army: Colonel General I. M. Sokolov
19th Bomber Aviation Corps: Lieutenant General N. A. Volkov
33d Bomber Aviation Division
55th Bomber Aviation Division
34th Bomber Aviation Division
251st Assault Aviation Division
252d Assault Aviation Division
32d Fighter Aviation Division
249th Fighter Aviation Division
250th Fighter Aviation Division
6th Reconnaissance Aviation Regiment
799th Reconnaissance Aviation Regiment
464th Reconnaissance Corrective-Aviation Regiment
81st Medical Aviation Regiment
281st Transport Aviation Regiment

Front Units
- 87th Rifle Corps: Major General F. Z. Borisov
  - 342d Rifle Division
  - 345th Rifle Division
- 88th Rifle Corps: Lieutenant General P. E. Loviagin
  - 105th Rifle Division
  - 258th Rifle Division
- Chuguevka Operational Group: Major General V. A. Zaitsev
  - 335th Rifle Division
  - 355th Rifle Division
  - 150th Fortified Region
  - 162d Fortified Region
- 84th Cavalry Division
- 10th Mechanized Corps: Lieutenant General I. D. Vasil'ev
  - 42d Mechanized Brigade
  - 72d Mechanized Brigade
  - 204th Tank Brigade
  - 1207th Self-propelled Artillery Regiment
  - 1253d Self-propelled Artillery Regiment
  - 1419th Self-propelled Artillery Regiment
  - 55th Motorcycle Battalion
  - 621st Mortar Regiment
  - 2d Guards-Mortar Battalion
  - 970th Antiaircraft Artillery Regiment
- 2d Guards Motorcycle Regiment
- 1634th Antitank (Tank Destroyer) Artillery Regiment
- 1588th Antiaircraft Artillery Regiment
- 28th Separate Antiaircraft Artillery Battalion
- 613th Separate Antiaircraft Artillery Battalion
- 758th Separate Antiaircraft Artillery Battalion
- 11th Pontoon-Bridge Brigade
- 5th Separate Pontoon-Bridge Battalion
- 30th Separate Pontoon-Bridge Battalion
- 193d Separate Backpack Flamethrower Company

AMUR FLOTILLA

Commander, Rear Admiral N. V. Antonov
Chief of Staff, Captain lst Rank A. M. Gushchin
Member of the Military Council, Rear Admiral M. G. Iakovenko

1st Brigade (River Ships)
2d Brigade (River Ships)

3d Brigade (River Ships)
4th Zee-Bureisk Brigade (River Ships)
Sretensk Separate Battalion (River Ships)
1st Separate Battalion of Gunboats
2d Separate Battalion of Gunboats
3d Separate Battalion of Gunboats
1st Separate Battalion of Armored Cutters
2d Separate Battalion of Armored Cutters
3d Separate Battalion of Armored Cutters
Ussuri Separate Detachment of Armored Cutters
Khanka Separate Detachment of Armored Cutters
5th Separate Special Reconnaissance Naval Detachment
71st Separate Special Reconnaissance Naval Detachment
45th Separate Fighter Aviation Regiment
67th Separate Antiaircraft Artillery Battalion
94th Separate Antiaircraft Artillery Battalion
115th Separate Antiaircraft Artillery Battalion

NATIONAL AIR DEFENSE (PVO) FORCES (*PVO-STRANY*)

TRANS-BAIKAL PVO ARMY
(protects Trans-Baikal Front)

92d PVO Division
- 1863d Antiaircraft Artillery Regiment
- 1868th Antiaircraft Artillery Regiment
- 150th Separate Antiaircraft Artillery Battalion
- 387th Separate Antiaircraft Artillery Battalion
- 17th Antiaircraft Projector (Searchlight) Battalion
- 25th Separate VNOS (Early Detection and Warning) Battalion
- 79th Separate VNOS (Early Detection and Warning) Battalion
- 80th Separate VNOS (Early Detection and Warning) Battalion
- 81st Separate Antiaircraft Armored Train
- 182d Separate Antiaircraft Armored Train

93d PVO Division
- 187th Separate Antiaircraft Artillery Battalion
- 232d Separate Antiaircraft Artillery Battalion
- 262d Separate Antiaircraft Artillery Battalion
- 264th Separate Antiaircraft Artillery Battalion
- 404th Separate Antiaircraft Artillery Battalion
- 408th Separate Antiaircraft Artillery Battalion

86th Antiaircraft Artillery Battery
30th Antiaircraft Machine gun Battery
58th Separate Antiaircraft Armored Train
210th Separate Antiaircraft Armored Train

94th PVO Division
750th Antiaircraft Artillery Regiment
1878th Antiaircraft Artillery Regiment
10th Separate Antiaircraft Artillery Battalion
20th Separate Antiaircraft Artillery Battalion
107th Separate Antiaircraft Artillery Battalion
162d Separate Antiaircraft Artillery Battalion
166th Separate Antiaircraft Artillery Battalion
207th Separate Antiaircraft Artillery Battalion
390th Separate Antiaircraft Artillery Battalion
411th Separate Antiaircraft Artillery Battalion
71st Antiaircraft Battery
65th Antiaircraft Machine gun Company
78th Antiaircraft Machine gun Company
94th Antiaircraft Machine gun Company
96th Antiaircraft Machine gun Company
102d Antiaircraft Machine gun Company
55th Separate VNOS (Early Detection and Warning) Battalion
55th Separate Antiaircraft Armored Train
83d Separate Antiaircraft Armored Train
124th Separate Antiaircraft Armored Train
131st Separate Antiaircraft Armored Train
171st Separate Antiaircraft Armored Train
231st Separate Antiaircraft Armored Train

297th Fighter Aviation Division
401st Fighter Aviation Regiment
938th Fighter Aviation Regiment
939th Fighter Aviation Regiment

AMUR PVO ARMY
(protects 2d Far Eastern Front)

3d PVO Corps
111th Antiaircraft Artillery Brigade
524th Antiaircraft Artillery Regiment
749th Antiaircraft Artillery Regiment
138th Separate Antiaircraft Artillery Battalion
147th Separate Antiaircraft Artillery Battalion

163d Separate Antiaircraft Artillery Battalion
190th Separate Antiaircraft Artillery Battalion
217th Separate Antiaircraft Artillery Battalion
393d Separate Antiaircraft Artillery Battalion
543d Separate Antiaircraft Artillery Battalion
102d Antiaircraft Battery
117th Antiaircraft Battery
122d Antiaircraft Battery
8th Antiaircraft Machine gun Battalion
24th Antiaircraft Projector (Searchlight) Battalion
12th Aerostatic Balloon Battalion
12th Separate VNOS (Early Detection and Warning) Battalion
20th Separate VNOS (Early Detection and Warning) Battalion
53d Separate VNOS (Early Detection and Warning) Battalion
53d Separate Antiaircraft Armored Train
59th Separate Antiaircraft Armored Train
61st Separate Antiaircraft Armored Train
68th Separate Antiaircraft Armored Train
69th Separate Antiaircraft Armored Train
215th Separate Antiaircraft Armored Train
217th Separate Antiaircraft Armored Train
227th Separate Antiaircraft Armored Train

15th PVO Corps

29th Antiaircraft Artillery Brigade
757th Antiaircraft Artillery Regiment
1134th Antiaircraft Artillery Regiment
132d Separate Antiaircraft Artillery Battalion
167th Separate Antiaircraft Artillery Battalion
175th Separate Antiaircraft Artillery Battalion
195th Separate Antiaircraft Artillery Battalion
66th Separate Antiaircraft Artillery Battalion
104th Separate Antiaircraft Artillery Battalion
105th Separate Antiaircraft Artillery Battalion
28th Antiaircraft Machine gun Battalion
109th Antiaircraft Machine gun Company
118th Antiaircraft Machine gun Company
259th Antiaircraft Machine gun Company
19th Antiaircraft Projector (Searchlight) Battalion
38th Separate VNOS (Early Detection and Warning) Battalion
24th Separate Antiaircraft Armored Train
57th Separate Antiaircraft Armored Train
122d Separate Antiaircraft Armored Train
224th Separate Antiaircraft Armored Train

97th PVO Division
- 752d Antiaircraft Artillery Regiment
- 1887th Antiaircraft Artillery Regiment
- 305th Separate Antiaircraft Artillery Battalion
- 407th Separate Antiaircraft Artillery Battalion
- 465th Separate Antiaircraft Artillery Battalion
- 571st Separate Antiaircraft Artillery Battalion
- 9th Antiaircraft Machine gun Battalion
- 75th Separate VNOS (Early Detection and Warning) Battalion
- 173d Separate Antiaircraft Armored Train
- 229th Separate Antiaircraft Armored Train

98th PVO Division
- 742d Antiaircraft Artillery Regiment
- 1919th Antiaircraft Artillery Regiment
- 102d Separate Antiaircraft Artillery Battalion
- 456th Separate Antiaircraft Artillery Battalion
- 457th Separate Antiaircraft Artillery Battalion
- 736th Antiaircraft Machine gun Company
- 61st Separate VNOS (Early Detection and Warning) Battalion

149th Fighter Aviation Division
- 3d Fighter Aviation Regiment
- 18th Fighter Aviation Regiment
- 60th Fighter Aviation Regiment
- 400th Fighter Aviation Regiment

COASTAL PVO ARMY
(protects 1st Far Eastern Front)

11th PVO Corps
- 755th Antiaircraft Artillery Regiment
- 1880th Antiaircraft Artillery Regiment
- 78th Separate Antiaircraft Artillery Battalion
- 186th Separate Antiaircraft Artillery Battalion
- 126th Antiaircraft Battery
- 132d Antiaircraft Battery
- 20th Antiaircraft Machine gun Battalion
- 3d Antiaircraft Projector (Searchlight) Regiment
- 37th Separate VNOS (Early Detection and Warning) Battalion
- 33d Separate Antiaircraft Armored Train
- 60th Antiaircraft Artillery Division
  - 1775th Antiaircraft Artillery Regiment
  - 1777th Antiaircraft Artillery Regiment

1779th Antiaircraft Artillery Regiment
1781st Antiaircraft Artillery Regiment
1783d Antiaircraft Artillery Regiment
346th Separate Antiaircraft Artillery Battalion

95th PVO Division
133d Antiaircraft Artillery Brigade
155th Separate Antiaircraft Artillery Battalion
398th Separate Antiaircraft Artillery Battalion
97th Antiaircraft Machine gun Company
23d Separate Antiaircraft Armored Train
62d Separate Antiaircraft Armored Train
88th Separate Antiaircraft Armored Train
168th Separate Antiaircraft Armored Train
169th Separate Antiaircraft Armored Train
179th Separate Antiaircraft Armored Train
185th Separate Antiaircraft Armored Train
190th Separate Antiaircraft Armored Train
200th Separate Antiaircraft Armored Train
201st Separate Antiaircraft Armored Train

96th PVO Division
352d Antiaircraft Artillery Regiment
639th Antiaircraft Artillery Regiment
4th Separate Antiaircraft Artillery Battalion
392d Separate Antiaircraft Artillery Battalion
129th Antiaircraft Battery
54th Separate VNOS (Early Detection and Warning) Battalion
125th Separate Antiaircraft Armored Train
20th Separate Antiaircraft Armored Train

147th Fighter Aviation Division
34th Fighter Aviation Regiment
404th Fighter Aviation Regiment
429th Fighter Aviation Regiment
564th Fighter Aviation Regiment

Sources: Boevoi sostav Sovetskoi armii, chast' 5 (ianvar'–sentiabr' 1945 g.) [The combat composition of the Soviet Army, Part 5 (January–September 1945)] (Voenizdat, 1990), 199–202, and M. V. Zakharov, ed., *Final: istoriko-memuarny ocherk o razgrome imperialisticheskoi iapony v 1945 godu* [Finale: A historical memoir-survey about the rout of imperialistic Japan in 1945] (Moscow: 'Nauka', 1969), 382–404.

Appendix 5:

Operational Indices of the Manchurian Offensive

1. SECTOR FRONTAGES, WIDTHS, DEPTHS, AND RATES OF ADVANCE, FAR EAST COMMAND

Force	*Width of Attack Frontage (km)*	*Depth of Advance (kms)*	*Rate of Advance (kms per day)*
Trans-Baikal Front (2,300 km front, 1,500 km active sector)			
6th Guards Tank Army	100	820	82
39th Army	120	380	38
17th Army	90	450	45
36th Army	20	450	45
Cavalry-Mechanized Group	250	420–550	42–55
1st Far Eastern Front (700 km front)			
1st Red Banner Army	135	300	30
5th Army	65	300	30
35th Army	215	250	25
25th Army	285	200	20
2d Far Eastern Front (1,610 km front, 500 km active sector)*			
15th Army	330	300	30
2d Red Banner Army	150	200	20

*Other sources cite a frontage of 2,300 km.
Source: 'Kampaniia sovetskikh vooruzhennikh sil na dal'nem vostoke v 1945g (facti i tsifry)' [The campaign of the Soviet armed forces in the Far East in 1945: Facts and figures], *Voenno-istoricheskii zhurnal* [Military-historical journal], No. 8 (August 1965), Table 6.

2. LOGISTICAL STOCKS IN THE FAR EAST COMMAND'S *FRONTS*, 9 AUGUST 1945

Fronts	*Trans-Baikal*	*1st Far Eastern*	*2d Far Eastern*	*Far East Command*
Ammunition (combat loads)				
Rifle	4.0	4.6	4.0	4.2
AA (45–76 mm)	6.5	7.9	6.5	7.2
122–152 mm	17.0	7.9	18.0	14.3
Mortar	11.0	8.4	10.0	9.8
Aviation bombs	60.0	76.0	60.0	65.0
Fuel (refills)				
High quality benzine	4.7	1.9	2.0	
Benzine KB 70	6.9	2.0	0.7	
Autobenzine	4.3	1.7	2.0	
Diesel oil	4.0	1.5	2.6	
Weight of one refill (in tons)	8,100	7,800	3,250	19,150
Food and fodder (days of supply)				
Flour and groats	33.4	65.4	122	
Meat products	35.7	64.9	73	
Sugar	72	67.4	237	
Fodder	6.3	7	25	
Weight of one day's supply (in tons)	1,273	903	553	2,729

Source: 'Kampaniia sovetskikh vooruzhennikh sil na dal'nem vostoke v 1945g (facti i tsifry)' [The campaign of the Soviet armed forces in the Far East in 1945: Facts and figures], *Voenno-istoricheskii zhurnal* [Military-historical Journal], No. 8 (August 1965), Table 6.

Appendix 6:
Soviet Documents on Operations in Manchuria

Stavka VKG Directive to the Far Eastern Front Commander on the Preparation and Conduct of an Offensive Operation

No. 11112 **28 June 1945**

As an addendum to directive No. 11048 dated 26 March 1945, the *Stavka* of the Supreme High Command ORDERS:

1. Conduct and complete all preparatory measures within the *front's* forces concerning the grouping of forces, their combat and material-technical support, and command and control of forces by 1 August for the purpose of conducting an offensive operation on a special order of the *Stavka* of the Supreme High Command.

2. Be guided by the following when preparing the operation:

(a) The purpose of the operation is to defeat the Japanese Kwantung Army and capture the Harbin region in cooperation with the forces of the Trans-Baikal Front and Coastal Group; and

(b) Conduct an offensive operation along the Sungarian axis with the forces of the 15th Army in cooperation with the Amur Military Flotilla.

Employ no fewer than three rifle divisions, the main mass of RGK artillery, tanks, aviation, and crossing equipment to conduct the operation with the immediate missions of forcing the Amur River, capturing the Tungchiang Fortified Region, and reaching the Chiamussu region by the 23d day of the operation.

Subsequently, anticipate operations along the Sungari River to Harbin.

3. The forces of the 2d Red Banner Army and the 5th Rifle Corps will reliably defend the state border in accordance with *Stavka* directive No. 11048 dated 26 March 1945.

Envision offensive operations by the 5th Rifle Corps along the Jaoho axis with the aim of assisting the 15th Army along the Fuchin and Chiamussu axis or the right flank of the Coastal Group in the direction of Paoching.

4. The principal mission of the 16th Army is to reliably defend Sakhalin

Island, prevent a Japanese intrusion into our territory of the island, and also the landing of Japanese amphibious forces on the coast of Sakhalin Island.

5. Transfer three rifle divisions from the *front* to the Coastal Group no later than 15 July.

6. Conduct all preparatory measures within strict secrecy.

Permit the commander, the member of the military council, the *front's* chief of staff, and the *chief* of the *front's* operational directorate to work on the plan in full measure.

Permit the chiefs of force branches and services to work on specific sections of the plan without becoming familiar with the overall missions of the *front*.

Assign missions to army commanders personally by mouth without handing out written *front* directives.

Establish the same order of admittance for working out the armies' operational plans as for the *front*.

Secure all documents concerning the forces' operational plans in the personal safes of the *front* and army commanders.

7. Conduct all transmissions and conversations on matter related to the operational plan personally only through the chief of the Red Army General Staff.

The *Stavka* of the Supreme High Command
I. Stalin
Antonov

Source: Zolotarev, V. A., ed., *Russkii arkhiv: Sovetsko-iaponskaia voina 1945 goda: Istoriia voenno-politicheskogo protivoborstva dvukh derzhav v 30-40-e gody: Dokumenty i materially v 2 t.*, T. 18 (7-1) [The Russian archives: The Soviet–Japanese War of 1945: A military-political history of the struggle between two powers in the 30s and 40s: Documents and materials in two volumes, Vol. 18 (7-1)] (Moscow: 'Terra', 1997), 332–3.

Stavka VKG Directive to the Coastal Group of Forces Commander on the Preparation and Conduct of an Offensive Operation

No. 11113 **28 June 1945**

As an addendum to directive No. 11047 dated 26 March 1945, the *Stavka* of the Supreme High Command ORDERS:

1. Conduct and complete all preparatory measures within the Coastal Group of Forces concerning the grouping of forces, their combat and material-technical support, and command and control of the forces by 25 July for the purpose of conducing an offensive operation with the Coastal Group's forces on a special order of the *Stavka* of the Supreme High Command.

2. Be guided by the following when preparing the operation:

(a) The purpose of the operation is to invade central Manchuria together with the forces of the Trans-Baikal and Far Eastern Fronts, defeat the Japanese

Kwantung Army, and capture the Harbin, Changchun, and Seisin (Chongjin) regions.

(b) Launch the main attack with the forces of two combined-arms armies (the 1st Red Banner Army with six rifle divisions and the 5th Army with 12 rifle divisions), one mechanized corps, and one cavalry division to penetrate the enemy defense on a 12-kilometer front north of Grodekovo and advance in the general direction of Muleng and Mutanchiang with the immediate mission of reaching the Poli, Ninguta [Ningan], Tuntsinchen [Shihhuanchen], and Sanchogou Station front by the 23d day of the operation.

Subsequently, operate in the direction of Harbin and Changchun to project the main forces to the Harbin, Changchun, Antu, and Ranan [Nanam] front.

3. Employ the main mass of RGK artillery, tanks, and aviation on the main attack axis.

4. To protect the right flank of the Coastal Group's forces and the uninterrupted operations of the Khabarovsk–Vladivostok railroad, conduct a secondary attack with the forces of the 35th Army (three rifle divisions) along the Lesozavodsk axis toward Mishan with the mission of capturing the Hutou Fortified Region, and, in cooperation with part of the 1st Red Banner Army's forces, capture the Mishan region and, subsequently, the Mishan Fortified Region.

5. To protect the left flank of the main grouping and prevent the subsequent approach of enemy reserves through the northern Korean ports of Ranan [Nanam], Seisin [Chongjin], and Racin [Najin], make provisions for earmarking part of your forces to exhaust the enemy's defense in front of the 5th Army's left flank and in front of the 25th Army's right flank and launching a secondary attack from the Barabash, Kraskino, and Slavianka region toward Hsinchun [Shihhsien] and Antu with part of the 25th Army's forces (four rifle divisions) with the aim of subsequently capturing the northern Korean ports of Ranan [Nanam], Seisin [Chongjin], and Rasin [Najin].

6. Accept in the Coastal Group's forces three rifle divisions from the Far Eastern Front by 15 July 1945.

Station two of the rifle divisions you have received on the Lesozavodsk axis and one in the Chuguevka region, keeping both of them in your reserve.

7. Conduct all preparatory measures within strict secrecy.

Permit the commander, the member of the military council, the *front's* chief of staff, and the *chief* of the *front's* operational directorate to work on the plan in full measure.

Permit the chiefs of force branches and services to work on specific sections of the plan without becoming familiar with the overall missions of the *front*.

Assign missions to army commanders personally by mouth without handing out written *front* directives.

Establish the same order of admittance for working out the armies' operational plans as for the *front*.

Secure all documents concerning the forces' operational plans in the personal safes of the *front* and army commanders.

8. Conduct all transmissions and conversations on matter related to the operational plan personally only through the chief of the Red Army General Staff.

The *Stavka* of the Supreme High Command
I. Stalin
Antonov

Source: Zolotarev, V. A., ed., *Russkii arkhiv: Sovetsko–iaponskaia voina 1945 goda: Istoriia voenno-politicheskogo protivoborstva dvukh derzhav v 30-40-e gody: Dokumenty i materially v 2 t.*, T. 18 (7-1) [The Russian archives: The Soviet–Japanese War of 1945: A military-political history of the struggle between two powers in the 30s and 40s: Documents and materials in two volumes, Vol. 18 (7-1)] (Moscow: 'Terra', 1997), 333–4.

Stavka VKG Directive to the Trans-Baikal Front Commander on the Preparation and Conducting of an Offensive Operation

No. 11114 **28 June 1945**

The *Stavka* of the Supreme High Command ORDERS:

1. In the event of an attack by the Japanese armed forces on the Soviet Union the forces of the Trans-Baikal Front will prevent an enemy incursion into territory of the Soviet Union and the Mongolian People's Republic by a reliable defense and will protect the concentration of new forces on the *front's* territory.

2. While organizing the defense, pay special attention to the protection of uninterrupted railroad operations within the *front's* boundaries and protect the Tamsag [Tamsag–Bulag] salient from the south, east, and north most reliably and also the Solov'evskoe and Bain–Tumen' railroad sector.

3. Without waiting for the complete concentration of the 53d Army, conduct and complete in the *front's* forces all preparatory measures concerning the grouping of forces, their combat and material-technical support, and command and control of the forces for the purpose of conducting an offensive operation of the *front* and the Mongolian People's Revolutionary Army on a special order of the *Stavka* of the Supreme High Command.

4. Be guided by the following when preparing the operation:

(a) The purpose of the operation is to invade central Manchuria swiftly together with the forces of the Coastal Group and Far Eastern Fronts, defeat the Japanese Kwantung Army, and capture the Chihfeng, Mukden, Changchun, and Chalantun (Putehachi) regions.

(b) Formulate the operation [on the basis] of a surprise blow and the employment of the *front's* mobile formations, in the first instance the 6th Guards Tank Army, for a rapid forward advance.

(c) Make the main attack with the forces of three combined-arms armies (the 39th Army with nine rifle divisions, the 53d Army with nine rifle divisions, and the 17th Army with three rifle divisions) and one tank army (the 6th Guards Tank Army with two mechanized corps and one tank corps) in the general direction of Changchun to envelop the Halung-Arshaan Fortified Region from the south.

The armies will conduct [the attack] on a broad front with the immediate missions to smash the enemy, force the Grand Khingan Mountains, and reach the Tapanshang, Lopei, and Solun front with the main forces by the 15th day of the operation.

The 39th Army will attack from the Khamar-Daba region in the direction of Hailar with one rifle corps to meet the 36th Army with the missions, together with the 36th Army, to prevent the enemy from withdrawing to the Grand Khingans, destroy the Japanese Hailar grouping of forces, and capture the Hailar region.

(d) Operating in the main attack sector in the general direction toward Changchun, the 6th Guards Tank Army will force the Grand Khingans by the 10th day of the operations, fortify the passes through the mountains, and, until the approach of the main infantry forces, admit no enemy reserves from central and eastern Manchuria.

(e) Subsequently, anticipate projecting the *front's* main forces to the Chihfeng, Mukden, Changchun, and Chalantun line.

5. Allocate two artillery penetration divisions and the main mass of artillery, tanks, and aviation to the axis of the main attack.

6. Anticipate protecting the main grouping against enemy counterattacks from the Ganchur region to the south and from the Dolonnor and Chihfeng region to the north.

7. Conduct [the following] secondary attacks:

(a) With the forces of the Mongolian People's Revolutionary Army, reinforced with two motorized brigades and the 59th Cavalry Division from the *front*, from the Hongor-Ula-Somon, Hudugyin-Khid, and Shine-Dariganga-Somin regions toward Kalgan and Dolonnor with the missions of distracting enemy forces from this axis and reaching the Kn. Tsun Sunitvan Station, Kn. Barun Sunitvan Station, and Huate regions.

Subsequently capture Dolonnor and Kalgan.

The offensive by the Mongolian People's Revolutionary Army is permitted to begin 2-3 days after the beginning of the offensive by the *front's* main forces.

(b) With the main forces of the 36th Army (four to five rifle divisions) to force the Argun River in the Duroi, Staro-Tsurukhaitui, and Novo-Tsurukhaitui regions and advance on Hailar with the immediate missions to prevent an enemy withdrawal to the Grand Khingans, destroy the Japanese Hailar group of forces, and capture the Hailar region and the Hailar Fortified Region, together with part of the 39th Army's forces.

Reliably defend the state border with the remaining forces in readiness to attack to envelop the Manchouli-Chalainor Fortified Region from the south along the Dashimak and Hailar axis, and link up with the army's main forces at Hailar.

Subsequently, the army will force the Grand Khingans and capture the Chalantun (Putehachi) region with its main forces.

8. Conduct all preparatory measures within strict secrecy.

Permit the commander, the member of the military council, the *front's* chief of staff, and the *chief* of the *front's* operational directorate to work on the plan in full measure.

Permit the chiefs of force branches and services to work on specific sections of the plan without becoming familiar with the overall missions of the *front*.

Assign missions to army commanders personally by mouth without handing out written *front* directives.

Establish the same order of admittance for working out the armies' operational plans as for the *front*.

Secure all documents concerning the forces' operational plans in the personal safes of the *front* and army commanders.

9. Conduct all transmissions and conversations on matter related to the operational plan personally only through the chief of the Red Army General Staff.

The *Stavka* of the Supreme High Command
I. Stalin
Antonov

Source: Zolotarev, V. A., ed., *Russkii arkhiv: Sovetsko–iaponskaia voina 1945 goda: Istoriia voenno-politicheskogo protivoborstva dvukh derzhav v 30–40-e gody: Dokumenty i materially v 2 t.*, T. 18 (7-1) [The Russian archives: The Soviet–Japanese War of 1945: A military-political history of the struggle between two powers in the 30s and 40s: Documents and materials in two volumes, Vol. 18 (7-1)] (Moscow: 'Terra', 1997), 334–6.

Stavka VGK Order Concerning the Appointment of Marshal of the Soviet Union A. M. Vasilevsky as Supreme Commander of Soviet Forces in the Far East

No. 11120 **30 July 1945**

Marshal of the Soviet Union A. M. Vasilevsky is appointed Supreme High Commander of Soviet Forces in the Far East with the Trans-Baikal and Far Eastern Fronts, the Coastal Group of Forces, and the Pacific Fleet subordinate to him effective 1 August 1945.

The *Stavka* of the Supreme High Command
I. Stalin
Antonov

Source: Zolotarev, V. A., ed., *Russkii arkhiv: Sovetsko–iaponskaia voina 1945 goda: Istoriia voenno-politicheskogo protivoborstva dvukh derzhav v 30-40-e gody: Dokumenty i materially v 2 t.*, T. 18 (7-1) [The Russian archives: The Soviet–Japanese War of 1945: A military-political history of the struggle between two powers in the 30s and 40s: Documents and materials in two volumes, Vol. 18 (7-1)] (Moscow: 'Terra', 1997), 336.

Stavka VGK Order About the Formation of the 1st and 2d Far Eastern Fronts and the Headquarters of the High Command of Soviet Forces in the Far East

No. 11121 **2 August 1945**

The *Stavka* of the Supreme High Command ORDERS:

Effective 5 August, rename:

1. The Coastal Group of Forces (commander, Marshal of the Soviet Union K. A. Meretskov) as the First Far Eastern Front.
2. The Far Eastern Front (commander, Army General M. A. Purkaev) as the Second Far Eastern Front.
3. The Operational Group of Colonel General Vasil'ev [Vasilevsky] as the headquarters of the High Command of Soviet Forces in the Far East.
4. Appoint Colonel General S. P. Ivanov as chief of staff of the High Command of Soviet Forces in the Far East.

The *Stavka* of the Supreme High Command
I. Stalin
Antonov

Source: Zolotarev, V. A., ed., *Russkii arkhiv: Sovetsko–iaponskaia voina 1945 goda: Istoriia voenno-politicheskogo protivoborstva dvukh derzhav v 30-40-e gody: Dokumenty i materially v 2 t.*, T. 18 (7-1) [The Russian archives: The Soviet–Japanese War of 1945: A military-political history of the struggle between two powers in the 30s and 40s: Documents and materials in two volumes, Vol. 18 (7-1)] (Moscow: 'Terra', 1997), 337.

Stavka VGK Directive to the High Commander of Soviet Forces in the Far East Concerning the Commencement of Combat Operations

No. 11122 **1630 hours 7 August 1945**

The *Stavka* of the Supreme High Command ORDERS:

1. The forces of the Trans-Baikal and 1st and 2d Far Eastern Fronts will begin combat operations on 9 August to fulfill the missions set forth in *Stavka* directives No. 11112 (for the 2d Far Eastern Front), No. 11113 (for the 1st Far Eastern Front), and No. 11114 (for the Trans-Baikal Front).

The combat operations of all of the *fronts*' aviation will begin on the morning of 9 August, first and foremost to bomb Harbin and Changchun.

The ground forces will cross the Manchurian borders [as follows]:

The Trans-Baikal and 1st Far Eastern Fronts on the morning of 9 August; and

The 2d Far Eastern Front on the order of Marshal Vasilevsky.

2. On receipt of this order, the Pacific Fleet will:

(a) Move up to readiness [level] number 1;

(b) Begin to emplace mine obstacles in accordance with the approved plan, with exception to the mouth of the Amur River and Tauiskaia Bay;

(c) Cease individual shipping and direct transports to their concentration points.

Subsequently, organize shipping on convoys under escort by military ships; and

(d) Deploy the submarines. Begin fleet combat operations on the morning of 9 August.

3. Consider all times to be according to Trans-Baikal time.

4. Report receipt and fulfillment.

The *Stavka* of the Supreme High Command
I. Stalin
Antonov

Source: Zolotarev, V. A., ed., *Russkii arkhiv: Sovetsko–iaponskaia voina 1945 goda: Istoriia voenno-politicheskogo protivoborstva dvukh derzhav v 30–40-e gody: Dokumenty i materially v 2 t.*, T. 18 (7-1) [The Russian archives: The Soviet–Japanese War of 1945: A military-political history of the struggle between two powers in the 30s and 40s: Documents and materials in two volumes, Vol. 18 (7-1)] (Moscow: 'Terra', 1997), 341.

The High Command of Soviet Forces in the Far East's Directive to the Commander of the Trans-Baikal Front Concerning the Commencement of Combat Operations

No. 80/nsh **2300 hours (Trans-Baikal time)**
7 August 1945

In accordance with additional directives of the *Stavka* of the Supreme High Command I order:

The timing of the beginning of combat operations by forward units, designated as 1800 hours 10 August 1945 Moscow time, is changed to 1800 hours 8 August 1945 Moscow time or 2400 hours 8 August 1945 Trans-Baikal time.

Therefore, it is necessary:

1. For the main forces of Comrade Kravchenko and the group of Comrade Pliev to reach their jumping-off regions no later than the evening of 8 August 1945 so that, having begun operations along these axes with strong forward detachments at 2400 hours 8 August 1945 (Trans-Baikal time), the main forces can be committed into battle no later than 0430 hours on 9 August 1945 (Trans-Baikal time).

2. The operations by strong forward detachments and reconnaissance units along the axes of Comrades Danilov and Liudnikov, whose pre-determined missions have already been assigned to them, will also begin approximately at 2100 hours 8 August 1945. Undertake all measures so that the main forces of Comrades Liudnikov's and Danilov's main forces will be in their designated jumping-off regions no later than the morning of 9 August 1945 so that, beginning at 0430 hours on 9 August 1945 (Trans-Baikal time) with the tank and mechanized forces, the main infantry forces of these armies are committed along these axes without fail no later than 1200 hours on 9 August 1945.

3. The forces of the main grouping of Comrade Luchinsky's army will set about forcing the Argun River along its designated axis at 2400 hours 8 August 1945 (Trans-Baikal time).

4. Include all frontal aviation in combat operations, effective on the morning of 9 August 1945, to fulfill missions envisioned for them in your plan. Bear in mind that, in connection with the decisive offensive by the 1st Far Eastern Front, which is simultaneous with yours, the 19th Long-range Bomber Aviation Corps will be employed initially in the interests of the latter.

5. Immediately report receipt of the directive and issued orders.

Vasilevsky
Ivanov

Source: Zolotarev, V. A., ed., *Russkii arkhiv: Sovetsko–iaponskaia voina 1945 goda: Istoriia voenno-politicheskogo protivoborstva dvukh derzhav v 30–40-e gody: Dokumenty i materially v 2 t.*, T. 18 (7-1) [The Russian archives: The Soviet–Japanese War of 1945: A military-political history of the struggle between two powers in the 30s and 40s: Documents and materials in two volumes, Vol. 18 (7-1)] (Moscow: 'Terra', 1997), 341.

The High Command of Soviet Forces in the Far East's Directive to the Commander of the 1st Far Eastern Front Concerning the Commencement of Combat Operations

No. 81/nsh **2235 hours (Trans-Baikal time) 7 August 1945**

In accordance with additional directives of the *Stavka* of the Supreme High Command I order:

To fulfill the plan envisioned for 0100 hours 10 August 1945 Khabarovsk time, postpone to 0100 hours 9 August 1945 Khabarovsk time (1800 hours 8 August 1945 Moscow time), to which end:

1. Conduct all preparatory measures for it on the night of 7–8 August 1945 and during 8 August 1945.

2. Commit all frontal aviation into action no later than first light on 9 August 1945.

3. Immediately exploit the success, which you have received from the operations of the strong forward units on 9 August 1945, for the introduction

of main forces into the battle. Thus, you are left with the right, if favorable conditions are present, to set about fulfilling the main *front* plan with an advanced report to me about it.

4. In a change of previously issued instructions, employ the 19th Aviation Corps in the interests of your *front* both during the night of 8–9 August 1945 and henceforth until further orders from me. Report concerning the missions assigned to it on 9 August 1945 to me no later than 1200 hours on 8 August 1945.

5. Immediately report about the receipt of this directive and all issued orders.

Vasilevsky
Ivanov

Source: Zolotarev, V. A., ed., *Russkii arkhiv: Sovetsko–iaponskaia voina 1945 goda: Istoriia voenno-politicheskogo protivoborstva dvukh derzhav v 30–40-e gody: Dokumenty i materially v 2 t.*, T. 18 (7-1) [The Russian archives: The Soviet–Japanese War of 1945: A military-political history of the struggle between two powers in the 30s and 40s: Documents and materials in two volumes, Vol. 18 (7-1)] (Moscow: 'Terra', 1997), 342.

The High Command of Soviet Forces in the Far East's Directive to the Commander of the Pacific Fleet Concerning the Commencement of Combat Operations

No. 82/nsh **2240 hours (Trans-Baikal time)**
7 August 1945

In accordance with additional directives of the *Stavka* of the Supreme High Command, the beginning of combat operations on the land, in the air, and at sea is designated for 1800 hours on 8 August 1945 Moscow time or 0100 hours 9 August 1945 Khabarovsk time. In this regard, you are given the right to conduct all necessary preparatory measures during 8 August 1945.

The *Stavka* of the Supreme High Command's order for the subsequent dispatch of commercial ships through the La Perouse Strait remains in force. Report the receipt of this directive and all issued orders.

Vasilevsky
Ivanov

Source: Zolotarev, V. A., ed., *Russkii arkhiv: Sovetsko–iaponskaia voina 1945 goda: Istoriia voenno-politicheskogo protivoborstva dvukh derzhav v 30–40-e gody: Dokumenty i materially v 2 t.*, T. 18 (7-1) [The Russian archives: The Soviet–Japanese War of 1945: A military-political history of the struggle between two powers in the 30s and 40s: Documents and materials in two volumes, Vol. 18 (7-1)] (Moscow: 'Terra', 1997), 342.

The High Command of Soviet Forces in the Far East's Directive to the Commander of the 2d Far Eastern Front Concerning the Commencement of Combat Operations

No. 83/nsh **2310 hours (Trans-Baikal time)**
7 August 1945

In accordance with additional directives of the *Stavka* of the Supreme High Command, the period for the beginning of combat operations for forces in the Far East is changed to 1800 hours on 8 August 1945 Moscow time or 0100 hours 9 August 1945 Khabarovsk time.

The missions of the 2d Far Eastern Front's forces remain as before, and the principal of these is the protection of the uninterrupted operation of the railroad in the *front's* sector.

Commit all frontal aviation into battle to fulfill the missions set forth in the plan from the morning of 9 August 1945.

I will determine later the time the *front's* main forces will go over to the offensive

Report the receipt of this directive and all issued orders.

Vasilevsky
Ivanov

Source: Zolotarev, V. A., ed., *Russkii arkhiv: Sovetsko–iaponskaia voina 1945 goda: Istoriia voenno-politicheskogo protivoborstva dvukh derzhav v 30–40-e gody: Dokumenty i materially v 2 t.*, T. 18 (7-1) [The Russian archives: The Soviet–Japanese War of 1945: A military-political history of the struggle between two powers in the 30s and 40s: Documents and materials in two volumes, Vol. 18 (7-1)] (Moscow: 'Terra', 1997), 343.

The High Command of Soviet Forces in the Far East's Report to the Supreme High Commander Concerning the Beginning of Operations Against Japanese Forces

0940 hours (Trans-Baikal time)
9 August 1945

I am reporting: In accordance with YOUR orders, beginning at 1800 hours 8 August 1945 Moscow time, our forces in the Far East are in a state of war with Japan. During the period from 1800 hours through 2230 hours on 8 August 1945 (Moscow time), the operations of our forces along the axes have been limited to operations of only reconnaissance and forward units in the spirit of the plan approved by YOU.

By 2230 hours 8 August 1945 (Moscow time) or 0430 9 August 1945 by Trans-Baikal time, the main forces of the Trans-Baikal Front crossed the border along all of their main axes.

During the night the forces of the 19th Long-range Bomber Aviation Corps delivered bombing strikes against the cities of Changchun and Harbin, the results of which I will report later.

By 0700 hours 9 August 1945 (Trans-Baikal time), 0100 hours 9 August 1945 (Moscow time), the situation of Soviet forces in the Far East is as follows:

Trans-Baikal Front:

While advancing behind their forward detachments, the 7th and 9th Mechanized Corps, reinforced by the 36th and 57th Motorized Rifle Divisions of Kravchenko's army, reached the Ikhe-Sume, Lake Tsagan-Nur line.

By this time the 5th Guards Rifle Corps and 113th Rifle Corps of Comrade Liudnikov's army had reached the Saburutei-gora, Hill 1036 line, advancing up to 20 kilometers [12.4 miles] from the border.

The 14th Rifle Corps, which is operating along the Hailar axis, advanced from 5 to 12 kilometers [3.1 to 7.5 miles].

The main forces of Comrade Pliev's group and Danilov's army have advanced from 15 to 25 kilometers [9.3 to 15.5 miles] from the border.

On the right flank of Luchinsky's army, after capturing bridgeheads and constructing four pontoon bridges across the Argun River in the Staro-Tsurukhaitui and Duroi sector, the 2d and 86th Rifle Corps have occupied crossings on the northeastern bank, and, on the left flank, part of the reinforced 298th Rifle Division was fighting for Manchouli on 7 August 1945 (Trans-Baikal time).

The 2d Far Eastern Front (Purkaev):

There is occasional firing along the entire front and operations by forward reconnaissance units. Two rifle battalions of the 361st Rifle Division captured Tatar Island. The enemy is not showing any activity. We have captured 32 men along the Bikin axis

The 1st Far Eastern Front:

At 0100 hours 9 August 1945 Khabarovsk time, the forward units of Beloborodov's and Krylov's armies crossed the state borders. Operating in total darkness, thunder, and in heavy rain, the units of Beloborodov's 1st Red Banner Army advanced up to 5 kilometers (3.1 miles) along separate axes, and the units of Krylov's 5th Army from 2 to 3 kilometers (1.2 to 1.9 miles), The Pacific Fleet began reconnaissance actions and aviation operations against the ports of Rasin (Najin) and Seisin (Chongjin).

Conclusions: The attack on the enemy caught him by surprise. By morning, other than the outskirts of Manchouli, the enemy has been confused by the surprise and is offering no organized resistance.

The operations of our forces are developing in accordance with the plan YOU approved.

Vasilevsky
Ivanov

Source: Zolotarev, V. A., ed., *Russkii arkhiv: Sovetsko–iaponskaia voina 1945 goda: Istoriia voenno-politicheskogo protivoborstva dvukh derzhav v 30-40-e gody: Dokumenty i materially v 2 t.*, T. 18 (7-1) [The Russian archives: The Soviet–Japanese War of 1945: A military-political history of the struggle between two powers in the 30s and 40s: Documents and materials in two volumes, Vol. 18 (7-1)] (Moscow: 'Terra', 1997), 348.

Summary Combat Report by the 1st Far Eastern Front Commander To the High Commander of Soviet Forces in the Far East Concerning the Initial Days of Combat Operations

0300 10 August 1945

First. Fulfilling the *Stavka* of the Supreme High Command's order, the forces of the 1st Far Eastern Front launched their offensive at 0100 hours on 9 August 1945 and, after overcoming the resistance of enemy border forces, reinforced by his field forces, which were defending strongly prepared fortified defensive lines and fortified regions in impassable taiga, mountainous-forested, and swampy terrain and in unfavorable weather (thunderous rain), penetrated the enemy's border defense sector along the main axis on a front of up to 60 kilometers (37 miles) and to a depth of up to 20 kilometers (12.4 miles).

Along the remaining axes from Hutou to Lake Khasan, the 1st Far Eastern Front's forces penetrated up to 10 kilometers (6.2 miles) into enemy territory. We destroyed 2,322 enemy soldiers and officers and seized 58 prisoners, including 2 officers.

By preliminary calculating, we destroyed 120 pillboxes and bunkers and captured four 300mm mortars, eight heavy railroad guns, four large warehouses with ammunition, foodstuffs, and engineer equipment, three large railroad tunnels in the Pogranichnaia region, and one railroad train (seven railroad cars with a locomotive) with ammunition as trophies. During this period, the *front* lost 153 killed and 1,020 wounded.

Second. The 35th Army forced the Ussuri and Sungacha Rivers and, after overcoming the swampy region on the western bank of the Sungacha River, in several days, the main forces widened the penetration to a front of 40 kilometers (25 miles) and a depth of 20 kilometers (12.4 miles). Along the Iman axis in the Hutou region, the army captured Krepost' (6 kilometers (3.7 miles) southwest of Hutou) with part of the 264th Rifle Division's forces and cut the Hutou–Mishan road and railroad line in the vicinity of Iueia and Eiuia Stations, having captured both stations. To the east of Lake Khanka, the 35th Army reached a line extending from Sydaoho, through Lavrentia, Tacho, the separate building 4 kilometers (2.5 miles) west of Mal. Khingangan, to a separate building 2 kilometers (1.2 miles) west of Marker 96.8 with the forces of the 66th and 363d Rifle Divisions.

Third. The 1st Red Banner Army reached the line from Marker 729.6 through Zol. Pr. Nan'tsin'chan, and Marker 568.6, to the Shitouho (Sysaoho) River with its main forces (the 59th and 26th Rifle Corps), cutting the Changchun (Shinhulinmiao)–Matsiaoho road in the region 13 kilometers (8 miles) northwest of the village of Metla (Height Marker 769.8).

Fourth. The 5th Army reached a line from the eastern slopes and main passes of the Huanvotszilin (Tsingolin) peak, through Fanzi (Kit.Bazar),

Laotsin (inclusive), to Guanfyntan (border post) with the forces of its first echelon (two rifle regiments from its first echelon rifle divisions). The army captured the strongly fortified Volynsk center of resistance of the Pogranichnaia [Border] Fortified Region and seized trophies (guns, ammunition, warehouses, and prisoners).

In the Pogranichnaia region, the 5th Army's 105th Fortified Region captured three railroad tunnels and at 2000 hours penetrated into Pogranichnaia from the east and southeast, capturing Pogranichnaia Station and fighting for the center of Pogranichnaia.

Fifth. The 25th Army penetrated to a depth of 10–12 kilometers (6.2–7.5 miles) into enemy territory with strong forward detachments, captured the Taipinling [Pass] and Height Marker 631.0 region (north of Dunnin), cut the Dunnin–Tumentzu road in the Haolon, Mainza, Wanbabostsi, Taipinchuan, Sibaigoi, Madida, and Waganzai region, having captured all designated population points, forced the Hunchunho River in the Madida region, captured Iantunleitszy and Mal. Chertova, forced the Tumyntszian (Tumen-ula) River, and captured Keiko (Ekhyn) in northern Korea and cleared the enemy from the territory to the west and southwest from Lake Khasan to the Tumyntszian (Tumen-ula) River, capturing Siuiua (Homuku) and Siuidin.

Sixth. During the night of 9 August, the 9th Air Army bombed Harbin, Changchun, and Kirin and the enemy fortified center at Hutou and supported the operations of the main forces on the battlefield with ground attacks.

[The air army] conducted 660 aircraft sorties on 9 August in difficult meteorological conditions. The air army's units destroyed or blew up nine locomotives, three railroad trains, and six enemy warehouses, and shot down one enemy aircraft (long-range reconnaissance).

Seventh. All of the forces are continuing their offensive on 10 August.

The commander of the 1st Far Eastern Front,
Marshal of the Soviet Union Meretskov
Member of the Military Council, 1st Far Eastern Front,
Colonel General Shtykov
Front chief of staff,
Lieutenant General Krutikov

Source: Zolotarev, V. A., ed., *Russkii arkhiv: Sovetsko–iaponskaia voina 1945 goda: Istoriia voenno-politicheskogo protivoborstva dvukh derzhav v 30-40-e gody: Dokumenty i materially v 2 t.*, T. 18 (7-1) [The Russian archives: The Soviet–Japanese War of 1945: A military-political history of the struggle between two powers in the 30s and 40s: Documents and materials in two volumes, Vol. 18 (7-1)] (Moscow: 'Terra', 1997), 348–9.

Combat Order of the Commander of the 2d Far Eastern Front to the Commander of the 16th Army on an Offensive with the Mission to Capture the Southern Part of Sakhalin Island

0030 hours 10 August 1945

I ORDER:

1. The 56th Rifle Corps will launch an offensive on the morning of 11 August 1945 with the overall missions to clear southern Sakhalin of Japanese forces; the immediate mission of the 56tn Rifle Corps is to capture the towns of Sikiga, Sikuka, and Nairo no later than 12 August with mobile (tank) units.
2. I permit you to transfer two separate tank battalions from the Aleksandrovsk region to the Anor axis.
3. Submit copies of all orders given to me.

Purkaev
Leonov
Shevchenko

Source: Zolotarev, V. A., ed., *Russkii arkhiv: Velikaia Otechestvennaia. Sovetsko–iaponskaia voina 1945 goda: Istoriia voenno-politicheskogo protivoborstva dvukh derzhav v 30-40-e gody: Dokumenty i materially v 2 t.*, T. 18 (7-2) [The Russian archives: The Great Patriotic: The Soviet–Japanese War of 1945: A military-political history of the struggle between two powers in the 30s and 40s: Documents and materials in two volumes, Vol. 18 (7-1)] (Moscow: 'Terra', 2000), 7.

Combat Report of the Commander of the 56th Rifle Corps to the Commander of the 16th Army Concerning the Capture of Koton

1816 hours 16 August 1945

After launching an offensive in difficult conditions of mountainous-forested and taiga terrain on 11 August, and having overcome the security belt, while doing so, destroying three strongly fortified company strong points, units of the 56th Rifle Corps, in cooperation with aviation, penetrated the enemy's strongly fortified position north of Koton (the Haramitog Fortified Region) on 16 August by an enveloping maneuver on the flank and rear with a simultaneous attack from the front, and, after destroying the broken-up enemy strong point piecemeal, captured the town of Koton Station. As a result of fierce combat in roadless conditions and impassable mountainous and forested-swampy terrain, the corps' forces defeated the enemy 125th Infantry Regiment, seized and destroyed 66 permanent railroad works, and several warehouses. We captured prisoners and trophies about which we will elaborate. I am continuing the attack in the direction of Koton.

I am presenting for governmental award Major General V. A. Baturov, Lieutenant Colonel Timirgaleev, Lieutenant Colonel Kudriavtsev, Lieutenant

Colonel Kurmanov, Captian Kuchevetsky, Captain Zaitsev, and Major Tregubenko. I request permission to present the remaining list.

D'iakonov

Source: Zolotarev, V. A., ed., *Russkii arkhiv: Velikaia Otechestvennaia. Sovetsko–iaponskaia voina 1945 goda: Istoriia voenno-politicheskogo protivoborstva dvukh derzhav v 30-40-e gody: Dokumenty i materially v 2 t.*, T. 18 (7-2) [The Russian archives: The Great Patriotic: The Soviet–Japanese War of 1945: A military-political history of the struggle between two powers in the 30s and 40s: Documents and materials in two volumes, Vol. 18 (7-2)] (Moscow: 'Terra', 2000), 8.

Stavka VGK Directive No. 11125 to the Representative of the High Commander of Soviet Forces in the Far East at the High Command of American Forces in the Pacific TVD [Theater of Military Operations] Concerning Additional Occupation Regions and the Disposition of Soviet Forces in Manchuria and Japan

Copy to the High Commander of Soviet Forces in the Far East **1615 hours 17 August 1945**

In addition to the instructions transmitted to you on 15 August 1945 in directive No. 11124, deliver the following instructions to the leadership

1. The American government has proposed to the Soviet government the following regions, in which all ground, naval, aviation, and auxiliary Japanese forces must be taken prisoner by Soviet forces – Manchuria, Sakhalin (Karafuto), and Korea north of the 38th parallel of northern latitude.

2. The Soviet government accepts the above proposal with the proviso that it considers the Liaotung Peninsula with the ports of Darien and Port Arthur to be within the limits of Manchuria, and, in addition, demands the following regions in which all ground, sea, air, and auxiliary Japanese forces must be taken prisoner by Soviet forces – the Kuril Islands and the northern half of Hokkaido Island north of a line running from the city of Kushiro to the city of Rumai, while including both indicated cities in the Soviet region. You are obliged to insist on the fulfillment of this demand of the Soviet government before General MacArthur.

3. In addition to the above, present to General MacArthur the question of the Soviet Union's government concerning any sort of stationing zone for Soviet forces in Tokyo.

4. You are required to fly quickly to MacArthur in Manila with your group. Report on the time of your flight and arrival.

I. Stalin
A. Antonov

Source: Zolotarev, V. A., ed., *Russkii arkhiv: Velikaia Otechestvannaia. Stavka VGK: Dokumenty i materially 1944–1945*, T. 16 (4-5) [The Russian archives: The Great

Patriotic: Stavka VGK: Documents and materials 1944–1945, Vol. 16 (4-5)] (Moscow: 'Terra', 1999), 251–2.

The High Command of Soviet Forces in the Far East's Report to the Supreme High Commander Concerning the Situation in the *Fronts* as of 17 August and the Further Plans of Soviet Forces in the Far East

18 August 1945

On 17 August the forces of the Far Eastern *fronts* are continuing to carry out their assigned missions in the face of sharply decreasing enemy resistance. Along separate axes during the day, there were instances when separate enemy units and subunits capitulated and also parliamentarians were dispatched to us. Both the Kwantung Army Command's appeal to the Soviet Command in the Far East and the reports of the parliamentarians speak about an order issued to Kwantung Army forces concerning the cessation of the Japanese Army's combat operations and about its capitulation. During the day up to 25,000 Japanese–Manchukuoan soldiers and officers were disarmed. The capitulation is continuing, although there are often skirmishes in some sectors of the front.

Given the mission assigned to the forces of the Far East and Pacific Fleet, and namely, the occupation of the territory of all of Manchuria, Inner Mongolia, the Liaotung Peninsula with the ports of Darien and Port Arthur, Korea to the 38th parallel, the southern half of Sakhalin Island, the southern half of Hokkaido Island north of the line running from the city of Kushiro to the city of Rumai, including both above-mentioned cities in the Soviet region, and completely all of the Kuril Islands, the *front's* forces have been assigned the following missions in the near future:

The **Trans-Baikal Front**, together with the MPA's [Mongolian People's Army] forces, will occupy the territory of Manchuria and Inner Mongolia within the limits of a line from Tsitsihar to Changchun and further along the Yalu River to the Korean peninsula, the Liaotung and Kwantung Peninsulas in full, and further to the southern border of former Manchuria and Inner Mongolia.

While doing so, the *front's* forces must occupy the city of Changchun with ground forces no later than 20 August, and the city of Mukden by 21 August, and the Liaotung and Kwantung Peninsulas no later than 28 August.

To hasten the occupation of the cities of Changchun and Mukden, the *front* commanders have been ordered to send their representative to the indicated cities on 18 August and provide the Kwantung Army command with advanced warning [of this action.].

The **1st Far Eastern Front** will occupy Manchuria to the south of the Poli line, including Harbin, to the east of the Changchun, Tunhua, Yalu River line, and the territory of Korea north of the 38th Parallel.

The period for occupying the city of Harbin is no later than the morning of 21 August and northern Korea, no later than 1 September.

To speed up the occupation of the cities of Kirin and Harbin, the *front* commanders will send their representatives by aircraft on 18 August 1945.

Simultaneously, the *front's* forces are entrusted with occupying the half of Hokkaido Island north of a line running from Kushiro to Rumai and the southern part of the Kuril Islands to Simusiru-To (Shinshiri) Island inclusively.

To this end, assisted by ships of the Pacific Fleet and the naval cargo fleet, the *front* commander will transfer three rifle divisions from the 87th Rifle Corps, under the command of corps commander Ksenefontov, successively, stationing two of them on Hokkaido Island, and one on the Kuril Islands.

Together with the 87th Rifle Corps, during this period, one fighter and one bomber aviation division from the 9th Air army will be re-based.

The 2d Far Eastern Front will occupy the territory of northern Manchuria within the limits of the Poli, Harbin (inclusive), and Tsitsihar (inclusive) line.

Simultaneously, the *front* is assigned the mission to occupy the southern half of Sakhalin Island, and the northern part of the Kuril Islands to Simusiru-To Island inclusively.

Employ your presently assigned forces for the occupation of the southern half of Sakhalin Island and an additional rifle division will subsequently be transferred to you.

Set about the occupation on the morning of 18 August 1945.

Two rifle regiments of the 101st Rifle Division, which is deployed on Kamchatka, will be transferred to the island on 18 August for the occupation of the northern part of the Kuril Islands.

Subsequently, reinforce the capes in the Kamchatka region and the northern part of the Kuril Islands with one more rifle division, entrusting the command and control of all forces there to the chief of the Kamchatka Defensive Region.

To reinforce the defenses of Kamchatka, the Kuril Islands, Sakhalin, and Hokkaido Island, in accordance with your orders, I request your permission to re-base part of the Pacific Fleet's forces in Petropavlovsk-on-Kamchatka and its main forces in the port of Otomari (in the southern part of Sakhalin) during the period from 20 August through 15 September, calculating to have [the following]:

In Petropavlovsk-on-Kamchatka – a brigade of escort ships, a brigade of submarines, a minelayer division, a torpedo cutter division, a division of trawlers, and one aviation regiment of bomber aviation;

In the region of port Otomari – a division of escort ships, a division of submarines, a division of torpedo cutters, a division of trawlers, and a mixed aviation division from naval aviation;

In the region of port Seisin (Chongjin) – create a naval defensive region to reinforce the defense of Korea, including a division of minelayers, a division of torpedo cutters, a division of trawlers, and the 113th Naval Infantry Brigade.

The priority focus of the [defensive] region will be the defense of the ports of Rasin (Najin), Seisin (Chongjin), and Genzan (Wonsan).

With regard to the allocation of naval forces in the region of the ports of Darien and Port Arthur, it is necessary to receive YOUR further instructions.

It is also necessary to have YOUR permission on the employment of the naval cargo fleet for the sea transport of forces during the period up to 15 September.

All warning orders regarding this plan have been given to the *front* commanders. I presented orders to the commander of the Pacific Fleet personally in Vladivostok on 18 August.

Simultaneous with the fulfillment of the missions envisioned in this plan, I categorically demanded that the forces of all of the *fronts* immediately organize the accounting and collection of captured arms, foodstuffs, and equipment from industrial enterprises in their territories.

I request YOUR approval or instructions on the given plan.

Vasilevsky

Source: Zolotarev, V. A., ed., *Russkii arkhiv: Sovetsko–iaponskaia voina 1945 goda: Istoriia voenno-politicheskogo protivoborstva dvukh derzhav v 30–40-e gody: Dokumenty i materially v 2 t.*, T. 18 (7-1) [The Russian archives: The Soviet–Japanese War of 1945: A military-political history of the struggle between two powers in the 30s and 40s: Documents and materials in two volumes, Vol. 18 (7-1)] (Moscow: 'Terra', 1997), 355–6.

The High Command of Soviet Forces in the Far East's Combat Order to the Commanders of the Trans-Baikal and 1st Far Eastern Fronts Concerning a Transition to the Operations by Forward Detachments

0500 hours (Trans-Baikal time)
18 August 1945

Given that Japanese resistance has been broken and the difficult state of the road hinders the rapid advance of our forces' main forces while fulfilling their assigned missions, it is necessary to make a transition to operations by specially formed, highly mobile, and well-equipped detachments for the immediate capture of the cities of Changchun, Mukden, Kirin, and Harbin. Employ these detachments or one similar to them for the resolution of missions without fear of sharply separating them from the main forces.

Vasilevsky
Trotsenko

Source: Zolotarev, V. A., ed., *Russkii arkhiv: Sovetsko–iaponskaia voina 1945 goda: Istoriia voenno-politicheskogo protivoborstva dvukh derzhav v 30–40-e gody: Dokumenty i materially v 2 t.*, T. 18 (7-1) [The Russian archives: The Soviet–Japanese War of 1945: A military-political history of the struggle between two powers in the 30s and 40s: Documents and materials in two volumes, Vol. 18 (7-1)] (Moscow: 'Terra', 1997), 355.

Summary Report by the High Commander of Soviet Forces in the Far East to the Supreme High Commander Concerning the Completion of the Far Eastern Campaign

3 September 1945

I am reporting:

1. Having begun the offensive on 9 August, Soviet forces in the Far East, consisting of the Trans-Baikal and 1st and 2d Far Eastern Fronts, fulfilled the combat mission YOU assigned to them by 1 September and occupied Manchuria in full, the Liaotung and Kwantung peninsulas, northern Korea to the 38th Parallel, the southern part of Sakhalin Island, and all of the Kuril Islands. In general, the disarming and imprisonment of the Kwantung Army is already complete. By 1 September 1945, 573,984 soldiers and officers of the Japanese Army, including 110 generals, have laid down their weapons, 861 aircraft, 372 tanks, 1,434 guns, 379 locomotives, 9,129 wagons and many warehouses with food, military supplies, and matériel have been seized.

Our forces have fully restored the KVZhD (Chinese Eastern Railroad) and restored rail movement along a series of other railroads of Manchuria.

2. At present, the command and *fronts'* forces are occupied with the formation of NKVD convoy regiments and divisions and, after their formation, beginning on 10 September 1945 the NKVD forces will carry out the transfer of prisoners for export to the territory of the USSR.

This work of transferring prisoners will be completed no later than 10 October 1945.

3. The beginning of the export of his troops from the territory of Manchuria is intended on the first days of October so that the territory of Manchuria will be fully liberated by 3 December 1945.

4. I request to establish the following order for transferring the territory of Manchuria liberated by our forces to the authority and forces of Chang Kai Shek.

To turnover the territory successively as forces leaver to the north in accordance with a schedule of withdrawal from the south and, in no circumstances, permit the arrival of Chang Kai Shek's forces and authorities into the territory where our forces are located; otherwise the work of commissar Comrade Saburov on the removal of equipment from Manchuria will be extremely difficult.

Vasilevsky
Shikin
Ivanov

Source: Zolotarev, V. A., ed., *Russkii arkhiv: Sovetsko–iaponskaia voina 1945 goda: Istoriia voenno-politicheskogo protivoborstva dvukh derzhav v 30–40-e gody: Dokumenty i materially v 2 t.*, T. 18 (7-1) [The Russian archives: The Soviet–Japanese War of 1945: A military-political history of the struggle between two powers in the 30s and 40s: Documents and materials in two volumes, Vol. 18 (7-1)] (Moscow: 'Terra', 1997), 371–2.

Appendix 7: Soviet Documents on Operations on Southern Sakhalin, the Kuril Islands, and Hokkaido

The High Commander of Soviet Forces in the Far East's Order to the Commander of the 1st Far Eastern Front on the Occupation of the Projected Regions of Manchuria, Korea, the Northern Portion of Hokkaido Island, and the Southern Part of the Kuril Islands

2220 hours 18 August 1945

While developing the offensive in the Far East, on 17 August 1945, the *front's* forces are continuing to carry out the mission assigned to them in the face of sharply decreasing enemy resistance. Along separate axes during the day, there were instances when separate enemy units and sub-units capitulated, and also parliamentarians were dispatched to us. During the day on 17 August 1945, up to 25,000 Japanese–Manchukuoan soldiers and officers were disarmed. The capitulation is continuing although there are often skirmishes in some sectors of the front.

Given the mission assigned to the forces of the Far East, I order:

1. The 1st Far Eastern Front to occupy the territory of Manchuria to the south of the Poli line, including Harbin, to the east of the Changchun, Tunhua, Yalu River line, and the territory of Korea north of the 38th Parallel in the period from 20 August to 1 September.

While occupying the indicated territory take all measures to accelerate the disarmament of Japanese–Manchurian forces and complete the occupation of the cities of Harbin and Kirin no later than the morning of 21 August.

In all sectors of the front where the enemy has ceased combat operations, immediately cease combat operations on the Soviet side.

To speed up the occupation of Manchuria and Korea, create mobile detachments for the rapid seizure of the most important cities, points, bases, and road junctions.

Besides the establishment of disarmament points of Japanese–Manchurian forces by *front* and army commands, allow division and brigade commands to establish communications with Japanese–Manchurian commands and independently determine the order of receiving and disarming enemy forces in their sectors.

Once again confirm with the forces the necessity of displaying good relations with Japanese–Manchurian soldiers and officers who voluntarily surrender.

2. Simultaneously with carrying out the missions indicated in point 1 of this order, during the period from 19 August 1945 through 1 September 1945, occupy the half of Hokkaido Island to the north of a line extending from the town of Kushiro to the town of Rumoi and the southern part of the Kuril Islands to Simushir (Shinshiri] inclusively.

To that end, during the period from 19 August 1945 through 1 September 1945, transfer two rifle divisions from the 87th Rifle Corps with the help of ships of the Pacific Fleet and partially the naval cargo fleet.

During the same period, re-base one fighter aviation and one bomber aviation division of the 9th Air Army on Hokkaido and the Kuril Islands.

3. Simultaneously with the fulfillment of the missions indicated above, I categorically demand the *front's* forces organize speedy accounting and removal from its territory of captured weapons, foodstuffs, and the equipment of industrial enterprises.

4. Confirm the receipt of this order and send all orders given and copies of instruction to me and the chief of the Red Army General Staff.

Submit daily periodic reports according to table of operational reports regarding the course of the occupation.

Vasilevsky
Trotsenko

Source: Zolotarev, V. A., ed., *Russkii arkhiv: Velikaia Otechestvennaia. Sovetsko–iaponskaia voina 1945 goda: Istoriia voenno-politicheskogo protivoborstva dvukh derzhav v 30–40-e gody: Dokumenty i materially v 2 t.*, T. 18 (7-2) [The Russian archives: The Great Patriotic: The Soviet–Japanese War of 1945: A military-political history of the struggle between two powers in the 30s and 40s: Documents and materials in two volumes, Vol. 18 (7-2)] (Moscow: 'Terra', 2000), 35–6.

Combat Report of the Commander of the Pacific Fleet on the Conduct of an Amphibious Operation against the Northern Portion of Hokkaido Island and the Southern Part of the Kuril Islands

1300 hours 19 August 1945

1. The enemy's naval forces are not conducting active operations. In a series of sectors of the front, the Kwantung Army's formations and units have begun an organized surrender. However, the enemy is continuing to offer stubborn resistance on the islands of Sakhalin, Shumshu (Shumshir), and Paramushir

(Paramoshiri), while trying to evacuate materials of value to the Mother country.

According to existing intelligence, American aircraft have mined the approaches and roadstead of the port of Rumoi.

2. The forces of the 2d Far Eastern Front are conducting offensive operations on Sakhalin Island with the mission of occupying the southern part of Sakhalin Island.

Two submarines of the 1st Brigade of Submarines have deployed to positions 'A' and 'B' with the mission of reconnoitering and destroying enemy ships.

Aircraft are conducting reconnaissance over the western part of Hokkaido Island.

3. The forces of the 1st Far Eastern Front have the mission of occupying the northern part of Hokkaido Island with two rifle divisions and the southern part of the Kuril Islands to Simushir Island inclusively with one rifle division. The fleet has the mission to land three rifle divisions of the 87th Rifle Corps on Hokkaido Island and the southern part of the Kuril Islands during the period from 20 August 1945 through 1 September 1945.

Decision: The landing of the three rifle divisions will be in three echelons. Carry the first echelon, consisting of one rifle division, across on transports with the first wave on combat ships and fast amphibious assault boats.

The following echelons will be on transports

I ORDER:

A. The commander of the landing is Vice Admiral Sviatov.

Land the amphibious assault force, consisting of three rifle divisions of the 87th Rifle Corps and the 354th Separate Naval Infantry Battalion, in the port of Rumoi:

(a) The first echelon – one rifle division on transports from the first wave consisting of one rifle regiment and the 354th Separate Naval Infantry Battalion on combat ships and fast amphibious landing boats.

Land at first light on 24 August 1945.

The 354th Separate Naval Infantry Battalion has the mission of seizing the port and town of Rumoi while preparing it for basing the fleet.

(b) The second and third echelons will be on transports protected by combat ships on my special command.

B. The commander of the amphibious assault force is the commander of the 87th Rifle Corps.

Land in the port of Rumoi and subsequently operate according to the orders of the commander of the 1st Far Eastern Front.

C. The commander of the air forces is Lieutenant General of Aviation Lemeshko.

(a) Determine the presence of enemy ships in the southern part of Sakhalin Island, Hokkaido Island, the Sakhalin Straits, and the defense of the port of Rumoi.

(b) Protect the amphibious assault force on the sea crossing and in the landing region.

(c) Have assault aviation consisting of one regiment of bombers in the region of the amphibious assault landing by 0800 hours 25 August 1945 and, simultaneously, have two regiments of bomber aviation in immediate readiness to fly into the airfield.

The attack will take place only on the signal of the landing commander, Vice Admiral Sviatov.

4. My location is the fleet command post on board the *Skala*, and my second deputy is the commander of the VMOR [unknown abbreviation].

Fleet commander,
Admiral Iumashev
Member of the Fleet Council
Lieutenant General of the Coastal Service,
Zakharov
Fleet Chief of Staff,
Frolov

Source: Zolotarev, V. A., ed., *Russkii arkhiv: Velikaia Otechestvennaia. Sovetsko–iaponskaia voina 1945 goda: Istoriia voenno-politicheskogo protivoborstva dvukh derzhav v 30–40-e gody: Dokumenty i materially v 2 t.,* T. 18 (7-2) [The Russian archives: The Great Patriotic: The Soviet–Japanese War of 1945: A military-political history of the struggle between two powers in the 30s and 40s: Documents and materials in two volumes, Vol. 18 (7-2)] (Moscow: 'Terra', 2000), 36–7.

Organizational Order of the Commander of the Pacific Fleet on the Conduct of an Amphibious Assault Operation on Hokkaido Island

1400 hours 19 August 1945

I am establishing the following composition of forces and command organization for the conduct of an amphibious assault operation to land occupation forces on the island of Hokkaido:

1. Ship composition of the assault.

Security and support ships:

Leader [LD] *Tbilisi*; destroyers [EM] *Razvyi*, *Raziashchii*, and *Ryianyi*; four escort ships [CKR] EK Nos. 1, 2, 8, and 9; four trawlers [TShCh] *AM* Nos. 331, 332; four cutters *BO* Nos. 303, 305, 316, and 318; and six torpedo cutters [TKA] type *A-1*.

Assault boats:

Six assault boats [DC] Nos. 31, 34, 37, 38, 39, and 42 and six transports: *Nevastroi*, *Dal'stroi*, *Mendeleev*, *Sevzaples*, *Plekhanov*, and *Ural*.

2. I am appointing Rear Admiral Sviatov as the commander of the Detachment of Light Forces (OLC) with his flag on the destroyer *Tbilisi*.

The headquarters of the Detachment of Light Forces is the headquarters of the amphibious assault force.

Major Chumichev is the representative of the Pacific Fleet.

I am appointing Captain 3d Rank Bespalov, the commander of the Detachment of Escort Ships (DSKR), as the commander of the amphibious assault's 1st echelon with his flag on the escort ship *EK-9*. The commanders of the following two echelons of the amphibious assault force [will be appointed] by special order of the fleet headquarters.

3. I am appointing Captain 3d Rank Koshkarev, the commander of the Detachment of Light Force's 2d Detachment of Destroyers as the commander of the first wave.

4. The composition of the amphibious assault – the 1st Far Eastern Front's 87th Rifle Corps consisting of three rifle divisions and the fleet's 354th Separate Naval Infantry Battalion.

One rifle division and the 254th Separate Naval Infantry Battalion will move in the first echelon of the amphibious assault.

One rifle division each will move in the second and third echelons.

The commander of the 1st Far Eastern Front's 87th Rifle Corps is the amphibious assault commander.

The commanders of the 87th Rifle Corps' rifle divisions are the commanders of the assault echelons.

5. The commander of the Detachment of Light Forces will re-base the destroyers *Retivyi* and *Reshutel'nyi* from the operational attachments in Vladimir Bay and keep them in his reserve. I am appointing Captain 2d Rank Iakov, the commander of the 1st Detachment of Destroyers, as commander of the group of reserve ships with his flag on the destroyer *Retivyi*.

6. Lieutenant General Lemeshko, the commander of the fleet's air force will determine the composition of aviation participating in the operation and re-base them at airfields of the Vladimir-Ol'ginskaia Naval Base while envisioning a reserve consisting of two DB-3 aviation regiments.

Submit your decision to me for approval by 1200 hours on 20 August 1945.

7. I am appointing Captain 2d Rank Shcherbatov as the commander of the detachment of transports of the amphibious assault forces' main force.

8. I will keep for myself the overall direction of the amphibious assault force.

9. The commander of the Naval Defensive Region [VMOR] will transfer four trawlers [TShCh] type *AM* Nos. 331, 332, and 354; the commander of the 1st Brigade of Escort Ships, four escort ships [SKR] *EK* Nos. 1, 2, 8, and 9; the commander of the 1st Brigade of Large Hunters [*BO*], four large hunters Nos. 303, 305, 316, and 318; and the commander of the 1st Brigade of Torpedo Cutters, twelve torpedo cutter type *A-1* by 1200 hours on 20 August 1945, and the commander of the landing will accept the forces indicated in operational subordination.

10. The ships and amphibious assault forces designated in this order will be prepared for operations by 1800 hours on 20 August 1945.

11. The embarkation of the amphibious assault force will occur on Zolotoi Rog Bay. Form the convoy in Bosfor Vostochnyi Strait.

12. Upon completion of the amphibious assault force's landing, the commander of the landing ships will return the assault boats and transports to Vladivostok, while keeping one escort ship *EK* and one destroyer in the port of Rumoi at the disposal of the commander of the Rumoi Naval Base to maintain communications with the fleet commander.

13. At the request of the commander of the Detachment of Light Forces, I am entrusting the material-technical support of the amphibious assault operation to the chief of the fleet rear services.

14. Rear Admiral Sviatov, the commander of the Detachment of Light Forces, will work out the operational plan and submit it for approval by 1800 hours on 20 August 1945.

15. My location is at the Fleet Command Post on the *Skala*. My second deputy is the commander of the Naval Defensive Region.

The commander of the Fleet,
Admiral Iumashev
The Member of the Fleet's Military Council,
Lieutenant General of the Coastal Service,
Zakharov
The Chief of Staff of the Fleet,
Vice Admiral Frolov

Source: Zolotarev, V. A., ed., *Russkii arkhiv: Velikaia Otechestvennaia. Sovetsko–iaponskaia voina 1945 goda: Istoriia voenno-politicheskogo protivoborstva dvukh derzhav v 30–40-e gody: Dokumenty i materially v 2 t.*, T. 18 (7-2) [The Russian archives: The Great Patriotic: The Soviet–Japanese War of 1945: A military-political history of the struggle between two powers in the 30s and 40s: Documents and materials in two volumes, Vol. 18 (7-2)] (Moscow: 'Terra', 2000), 37–8.

Report of the Commander of the Pacific Fleet to the High Commander of Soviet Forces in the Far East with an Account of the Operational Plan for the Transportation of the 87th Rifle Corps to Hokkaido Island and the Southern Islands of the Kuril Chain

19 August 1945

I am reporting an operational plan for the transportation of the 87th Rifle Corps to Hokkaido Island and the southern part of the Kuril Islands.

1. The operation will be conducted in three stages:

(a) The first stage – The transportation of one rifle division to the port of Rumoi.

(b) The second stage – The transportation of one rifle division to the port of Rumoi.

(c) The third stage – The transportation of one rifle division to the Kuril Island chain through Hokkaido Island

2. The fulfillment of the operation:

(a) Concentrate two regiments of DB-3, a regiment of Iak-9, and 20 Iak-9iu at the airfields of the Vladimir-Ol'ginskaia Naval Base;

(b) Deploy four submarine positions from the sides of the Sangarskaia and La Perouse Straits with the missions of reconnaissance and destroying enemy combat ships. A total of four submarines; and

(c) Conduct reconnaissance of the ports and naval bases on southern Sakhalin, Hokkaido Island, the Sangarskaia Strait, and the approaches to the western shore of Hokkaido beginning on 19 August 1945 with the aim of clarifying the presence of combat ships.

3. Carry out the transport of forces [as follows]:

The first wave – consisting of one naval infantry battalion and one rifle regiment on six assault boats with four destroyers and six torpedo cutters as security. In the event of resistance, the destroyers will be employed as artillery support ships and, in favorable conditions, the cutters will be used as landing means for the first wave.

The rifle division's main force will be transported on six transports with four frigates, four trawlers, and four large hunters as security.

The first wave will arrive in the landing region, the port of Rumoi, calculated to be 2 hours before the approach of the rifle division's main force.

4. Support. Two destroyers and six *Vladimir* torpedo cutters. Fighter aviation will cover everything on the passage and bomber and torpedo aviation will occupy a watch zone over the port at the moment the ships approach the port of Rumoi.

Conduct a strike on the port only on the signal of the landing commander.

Rear Admiral Sviatov will command the landing. I will keep overall direction of the operation.

The ships will be prepared to embark the first division at 1200 hours on 19 August 1945. The departure will be at 2000 hours on 21 August 1945.

The landing will be at 0500 hours on 24 August 1945 and the embarkation of the remainder will occur as transports become available.

I request your approval.

Commander, Pacific Fleet, Iumashev
Member of the Fleet Military Council, Zakharov

Source: Zolotarev, V. A., ed., *Russkii arkhiv: Velikaia Otechestvennaia. Sovetsko–iaponskaia voina 1945 goda: Istoriia voenno-politicheskogo protivoborstva dvukh derzhav v 30–40-e gody: Dokumenty i materially v 2 t.*, T. 18 (7-2) [The Russian archives: The Great Patriotic: The Soviet–Japanese War of 1945: A military-political history of the struggle between two powers in the 30s and 40s: Documents and materials in two volumes, Vol. 18 (7-2)] (Moscow: 'Terra', 2000), 39.

Order of the Commander of Air Forces of the Main Command of Soviet Forces in the Far East to the Commander of the 9th Air Army Concerning the Protection of the Amphibious Assault Operation against Hokkaido Island and the Southern Islands of the Kuril Chain

19 August 1945

In fulfilling the decision of the main commander, I order:

1. To protect the landing of amphibious assault ground forces on Hokkaido Island and the southern group of the Kuril Islands from the air in every way possible, employ the 9th Air Army's aircraft in cooperation with the Pacific Fleet's naval aviation.

Work out a plan for the aviation support of the amphibious assault operation and report it to me no later than 2400 hours on 19 August 1945.

2. Prepare the 32d and 34th Aviation Divisions for their transport in full composition to the northern part of Hokkaido Island and the islands of Kunashir and Iturup.

To support the named divisions allocate one aviation basing region consisting of four airfield support battalions, a region headquarters, and an advanced warehouse. Envision the transport of five refills of fuel and three combat loads of ammunition for the Bombers and ten refills of fuel and five combat loads of ammunition for the fighters.

Fully support the re-basing of the aviation divisions with radio communications means and attach one Si-47 aircraft each, which will come to you from the 12th Air Army, to each aviation division (32d and 34th Aviation Divisions).

3. Organize the movement of the flying echelon along the march route through Khabarovsk, Komsomol'sk, and Sakhalin to Hokkaido Island.

Move the land echelon, the communications means, and the ammunition by sea transport.

4. Envision the dispatch to Hokkaido Island of an operational group from the region headquarters and one airfield support battalion with the first dispatched rifle division, and one more airfield support battalion and the entire region headquarters with the second re-based rifle division.

5. Receive the time for moving the divisions and the period for conducting the operation from the *front* commander.

6. Report to me daily at 2400 hours concerning the fulfillment of this order.

Chief Marshal of Aviation Novikov

Source: Zolotarev, V. A., ed., *Russkii arkhiv: Velikaia Otechestvennaia. Sovetsko–iaponskaia voina 1945 goda: Istoriia voenno-politicheskogo protivoborstva dvukh derzhav v 30–40-e gody: Dokumenty i materially v 2 t.*, T. 18 (7-2) [The Russian archives: The Great Patriotic: The Soviet–Japanese War of 1945: A military-political history of the struggle between two powers in the 30s and 40s: Documents and materials in two volumes, Vol. 18 (7-2)] (Moscow: 'Terra', 2000), 40.

The High Command of Soviet Forces in the Far East's Report to the Supreme High Commander Concerning the Situation in the Fronts, the Meeting with the Kwantung Army Chief of Staff, and the Preparation of the Amphibious Operation against Hokkaido Island.

0800 hours 20 August 1945

I am reporting on the situation in the Far Eastern Fronts at day's end on 19 August 1945.

On 19 August 1945 the resistance of Japanese forces ceased on all of our *fronts* in Manchuria, and our forces are setting about the planned disarming of enemy forces. During 19 August around 65,000 Japanese–Manchukuoan troops were disarmed.

During the day, the Trans-Baikal Front landed air assault forces with responsible representatives of the *front* command in Changchun and Mukden, totaling 250–300 men per each city.

The Japanese command and representatives of the Japanese authorities greeted our forces in the above mentioned cities cordially. They completely agreed to fulfill all of the demands of our representatives in these cities.

Our forward mobile units are approaching these cities on the night of 20 August.

We will fully secure the cities of Changchun and Mukden by 20 August 1945.

Throughout the day, the forces of the 1st Far Eastern Front are continuing to disarm forces in the units of the Japanese 3d and 5th Armies.

During the day, the *front's* forces landed air-landing assaults and, with their assistance, liberated the city of Kirin. The mobile ground forces will reach the city no later than 20 August 1945.

After capturing Sansin (Chiamussu), the forces of the 2d Far Eastern Front are continuing movement along both banks of the Sungari River without encountering enemy resistance.

As before, the city of Harbin is firmly occupied by our forces, which were landed by the 1st Far Eastern Front on 18 August 1945.

On Sakhalin Island, the Japanese set about surrendering their forces, which were located immediately in front of our *front*, on the morning of 19 August. During the day on 19 August 1945, more than 3,000 Japanese soldiers and officers from the 88th Infantry Division capitulated here, and by day's end on 19 August 1945, our forces advanced southward up to 25 kilometers. On the evening of 19 August 1945, we sent an assault consisting of 4,240 men with artillery and transports from Sovgavan (Sovetskaia Gavan') to land in the region of Maoka (the southern part of Sakhalin) at first light on 20 August to hasten the complete occupation of the island.

By our calculations, Sakhalin Island should be fully occupied no later than the evening of 21 August 1945.

Heavy fighting continued on the Kuril Islands, and they were repelling enemy counterattacks on Simushir Island until 1900 hours on 19 August 1945. Combat on that island ceased at 1900 hours 19 August 1945, and the enemy surrendered totally through their parliamentarians.

We will launch an amphibious assault on Paramushir-To Island on the morning of 20 August 1945.

I had a meeting with General Hata, the chief of staff of the Kwantung Army, on 19 August 1945. In accordance with YOUR instructions, I created the most favorable conditions for his reception in all respects.

General Hata asked to hasten with the matters of occupying all of the territory in Manchuria so that Soviet forces could rapidly take the Japanese Army as well as the Japanese population in Manchuria under their protection. At the same time, General Hata asked that the disarming of Japanese units in separate regions of Manchuria and Korea be delayed until our forces arrived so as to maintain required order and protect installations and their equipment.

Hata declared that, during recent days, the aggravation in the relationship between the Japanese and Manchurians and also the Koreans has reached its limit.

Speaking of the accelerated introduction of our forces into Manchuria and, further, about the capitulation of his army, at the same time, General Hata asked about the appropriate relationship of both generals and officers and soldiers of the Japanese Army to our side and also about their necessary feeding and medical support. I have given the necessary orders to our forces in this regard.

General Hata finished his conversations with me by assuring me that all of my demands regarding the order of carrying out the capitulation will be carried out immediately and in full and also expressed his hope that this meeting will be a token of firm friendship between Japan and the Soviet Union in the future.

On my request to notify the command of Japanese forces, which is defending the Kuril Islands, about the futility of their struggle against Soviet forces that are trying to occupy these islands, General Hata promised to turn his attention to that question with the Japanese High Command immediately.

With my instructions, General Hata flew back to the city of Changchun at 1700 hours on 19 August 1945, where he landed in poor weather conditions at 2100 hours.

At present, I and the 1st Far Eastern Front command are seriously occupied with preparing the amphibious assault on Hokkaido Island. We are now seriously conducting naval reconnaissance, and preparing aviation, artillery, infantry, and transport means.

With YOUR permission, we can begin the naval operation here immediately after the seizure of southern Sakhalin Island, on approximately 22 August 1945.

The Emperor of Manchukuo, Ho Pi, and his retinue were conveyed from

Mukden to the headquarters of Kravchenko's army on 19 August 1945. In accordance with YOUR instructions I will intern him, and I think accommodate him in the Chita region.

In accordance with YOUR orders, I have given the Trans-Baikal Front command instructions concerning the preparation of an air assault to capture the ports of Darien and Port Arthur.

Vasilevsky

Source: Zolotarev, V. A., ed., *Russkii arkhiv: Sovetsko–iaponskaia voina 1945 goda: Istoriia voenno-politicheskogo protivoborstva dvukh derzhav v 30–40-e gody: Dokumenty i materially v 2 t.*, T. 18 (7-1) [The Russian archives: The Soviet–Japanese War of 1945: A military-political history of the struggle between two powers in the 30s and 40s: Documents and materials in two volumes, Vol. 18 (7-1)] (Moscow: 'Terra', 1997), 364–5.

Operational Directive of the High Commander of Soviet Forces in the Far East on the Preparation of an Amphibious Assault Operation against Hokkaido Island and the Southern Islands of the Kuril Chain

0115 hours 21 August 1945

The *Stavka* of the Supreme High Command will point out the time for the beginning of the landing of our forces in the northern part of Hokkaido Island and the southern part of the Kuril Islands additionally.

The landing of our forces on the islands indicated will occur from the southern part of Sakhalin Island. To this end:

1. Exploiting the favorable situation in the region of the port of Maoka, immediately set about loading the 87th Rifle Corps, on no account no later than the morning of 21 August 1945, so that you can concentrate it within minimum time limits in the regions of the ports of Otomari and the city of Toyohara in the southern part of Sakhalin Island.

2. Comrade Iumashev, the commander of the Pacific Fleet, will consider as his main mission the transport of the 87th Rifle Corps with the necessary means of the Naval cargo fleet attached. Report the transport plan to me by enciphered means no later than 1200 hours on 21 August 1945.

3. Without waiting for the landing of the advanced units of the 1st Far Eastern Front's 87th Rifle Corps, the commander of the 2d Far Eastern Front will continue operations to clear enemy forces from the southern part of Sakhalin Island so as to occupy the port of Otomari and the region of the city of Toyohara no later than the morning of 22 August 1945. After the arrival of the 87th Rifle Corps, the freed up forces of the 2d Far Eastern Front will be employed for the defense of Sakhalin Island or, depending on the situation, for the reinforcement of its forces operating on the Kuril Islands.

4. After the occupation of the southern part of Sakhalin by our forces, Chief Marshal of Aviation Comrade Novikov, the commander of Red Army

aviation, and Admiral Comrade Iumashev, the commander of the Pacific Fleet, will set about re-basing the main mass of the 9th Air Army's aviation and the Pacific Fleet on Sakhalin Island and, no later than 23 August 1945, will have them prepared to take part in an operation for the seizure of the northern part of Hokkaido Island. I am entrusting Chief Marshal of Aviation Comrade Novikov with the overall direction, both in the matters of re-basing and in the matter of planning the combat operations of the 9th Air Army and the Pacific Fleet in the forthcoming operation. Report the plan for re-basing and employing aviation to me no later than 1400 hours on 22 August 1945.

5. After the seizure of the southern part of Sakhalin Island and the port of Otomari by our ground forces, Admiral Comrade Iumashev, the commander of the Pacific Fleet, will re-base there the necessary quantity of combat ships and transport means in order to immediately begin an amphibious assault operation from the southern part of Sakhalin Island on Hokkaido upon receipt of an order of the Supreme High Command. When planning the amphibious assault operation, consider a simultaneous transport to Hokkaido Island of no fewer than two infantry division, each in two-three echelons.

6. The commanders of the 1st Far Eastern Front and the Pacific Fleet will report their views on the forthcoming operation to me no later than 2300 hours on 22 August 1945.

7. I once again emphasize that it is necessary to begin the operation for the transport of the 87th Rifle Corps to the port of Maoka on Sakhalin Island immediately. I will indicate the time for beginning the amphibious operation against Hokkaido Island additionally. The main base in this operation, both for the ground forces and for the aviation and Pacific Fleet must be the southern part of Sakhalin Island. The readiness time for this operation is day's end on 23 August 1945.

Vasilevsky
Trotsenko

Source: Zolotarev, V. A., ed., *Russkii arkhiv: Velikaia Otechestvennaia. Sovetsko–iaponskaia voina 1945 goda: Istoriia voenno-politicheskogo protivoborstva dvukh derzhav v 30–40-e gody: Dokumenty i materially v 2 t.*, T. 18 (7-2) [The Russian archives: The Great Patriotic: The Soviet–Japanese War of 1945: A military-political history of the struggle between two powers in the 30s and 40s: Documents and materials in two volumes, Vol. 18 (7-2)] (Moscow: 'Terra', 2000), 42.

Directive Order of the High Commander of Soviet Forces in the Far East to the High Commander of the Naval Fleet and the Commander of the Pacific Fleet Concerning the Postponement of the Amphibious Operation against Hokkaido Island and the Transfer of Forces to the Islands of the Southern Kuril Chain

1445 hours 22 August 1945

The Supreme High Commander has ordered:

1. Undertake no sort of naval operations to seize the ports of Port Arthur and Dal'nii (Darien) and dispatch no ships there without his permission. Our forces will occupy the indicated ports from the air and from the ground on 23 August 1945.

2. Devote maximum attention to seriously reinforcing both combat ships and fleet aviation in the Kamchatka region so as to clear the Japanese from the islands of Shumshu (Shumshir), Paramushir (Paramoshiri), and Araito, and subsequently firmly fortify them, since the Kuril Straits are our primary exit to the ocean.

Undertake serious measures to reinforce that sector of the front with ground forces and aircraft.

I request you report your views on this question for inclusion in a report to the Supreme High Commander no later than 2400 hours on 22 August.

3. It is necessary to refrain from an operation for the amphibious landing of our forces from Sakhalin Island to Hokkaido Island until special orders of the *Stavka*. Continue the transfer of the 87th Rifle Corps to Sakhalin Island.

4. In connection with the declaration of the Japanese concerning their readiness to capitulate on the Kuril Islands, I request you think through the question of the possible transfer of the 87th Rifle Corps' lead division from Sakhalin Island to the southern Kuril Islands (Kunashir [Kunashiri] and Iturup [Torofu]), omitting Hokkaido. I request you report your views on this matter to me no later than the morning of 23 August 1945.

Glavkom [High Commander] Vasilevsky Ivanov

Source: Zolotarev, V. A., ed., *Russkii arkhiv: Velikaia Otechestvennaia. Sovetsko–iaponskaia voina 1945 goda: Istoriia voenno-politicheskogo protivoborstva dvukh derzhav v 30–40-e gody: Dokumenty i materially v 2 t.*, T. 18 (7-2) [The Russian archives: The Great Patriotic: The Soviet-Japanese War of 1945: A military-political history of the struggle between two powers in the 30s and 40s: Documents and materials in two volumes, Vol. 18 (7-2)] (Moscow: 'Terra', 2000), 43.

Appendix 8:

Japanese Maps Showing the Daily Development of Operations in Manchuria

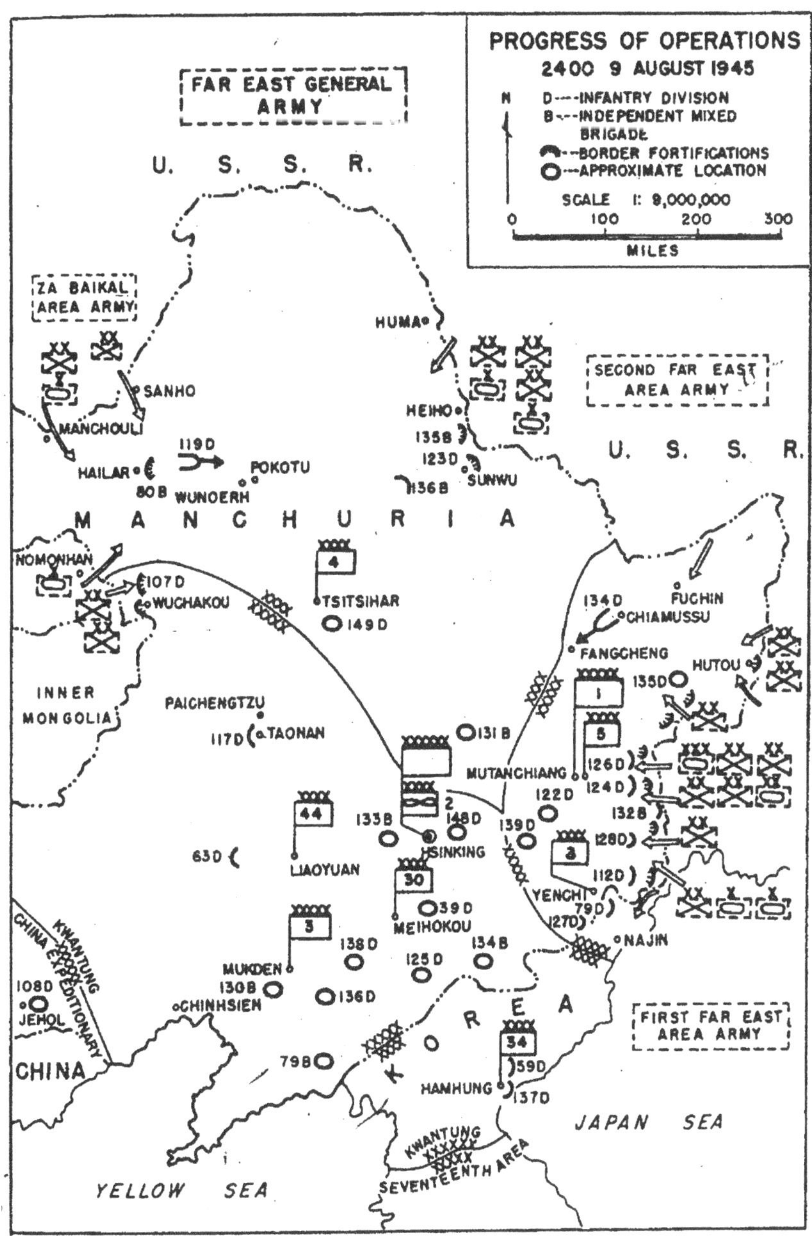

Map 77. Progress of Operations, 2400 hours 9 August 1945 (Japanese View)

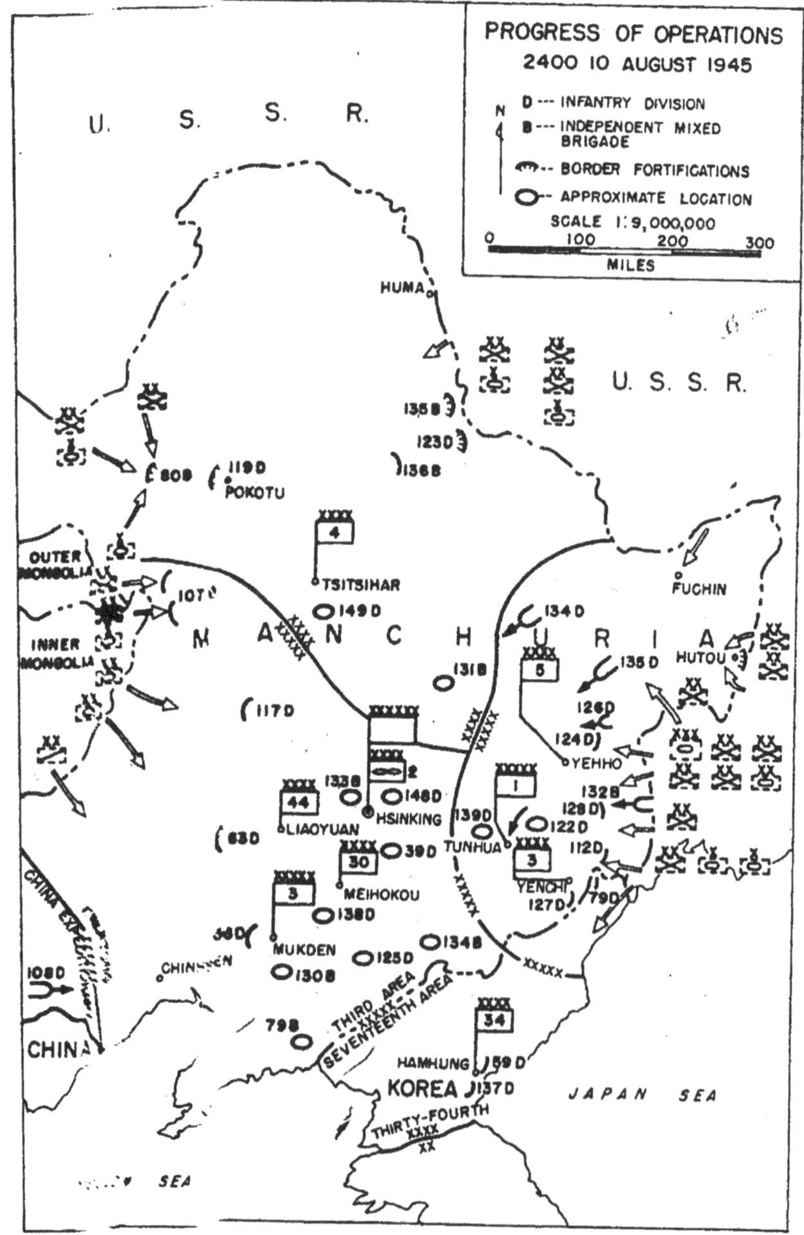

Map 78. Progress of Operations, 2400 hours 10 August 1945 (Japanese View)

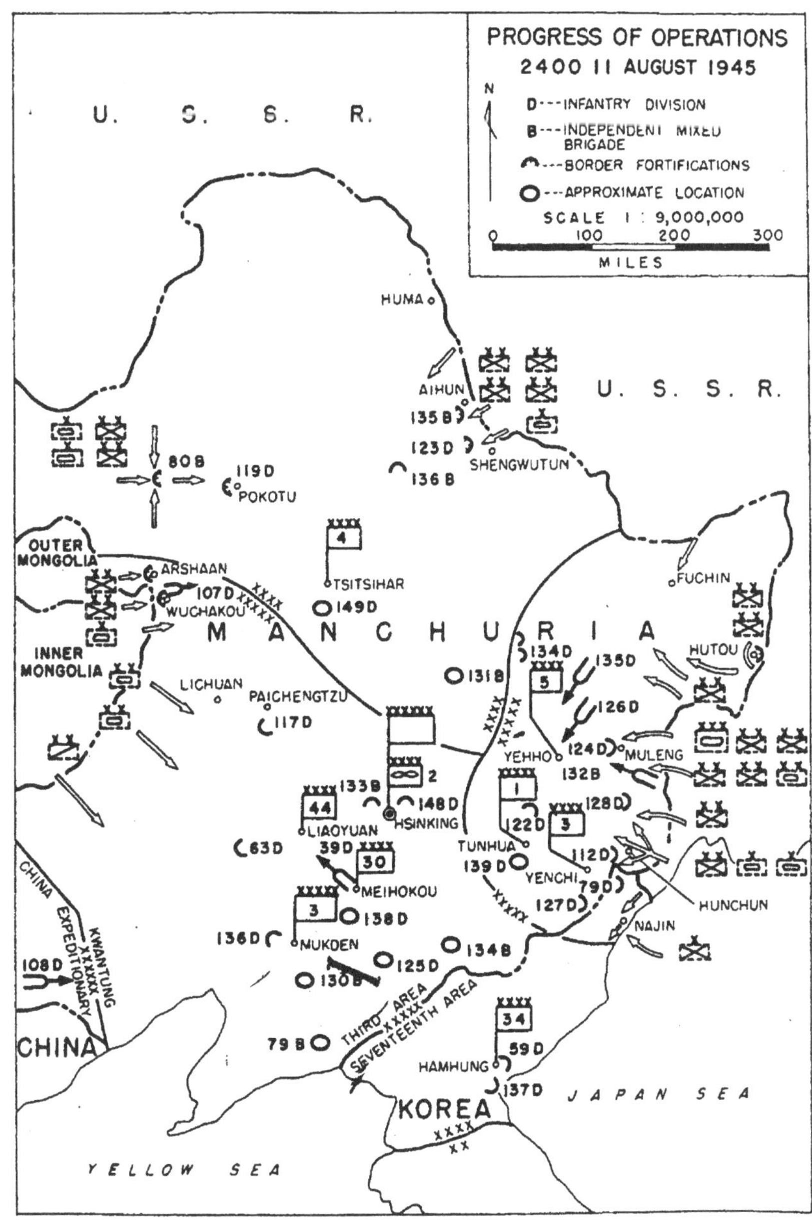

Map 79. Progress of Operations, 2400 hours 11 August 1945 (Japanese View)

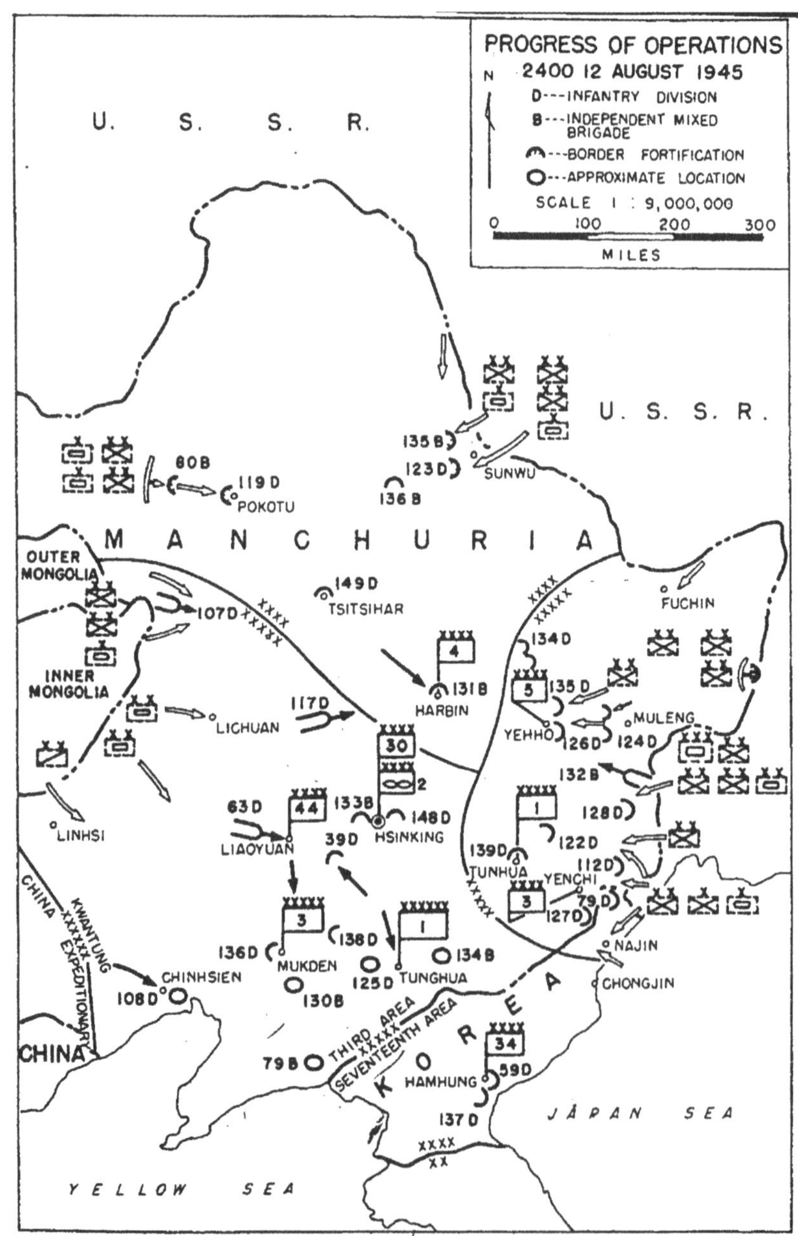

Map 80. Progress of Operations, 2400 hours 12 August 1945 (Japanese View)

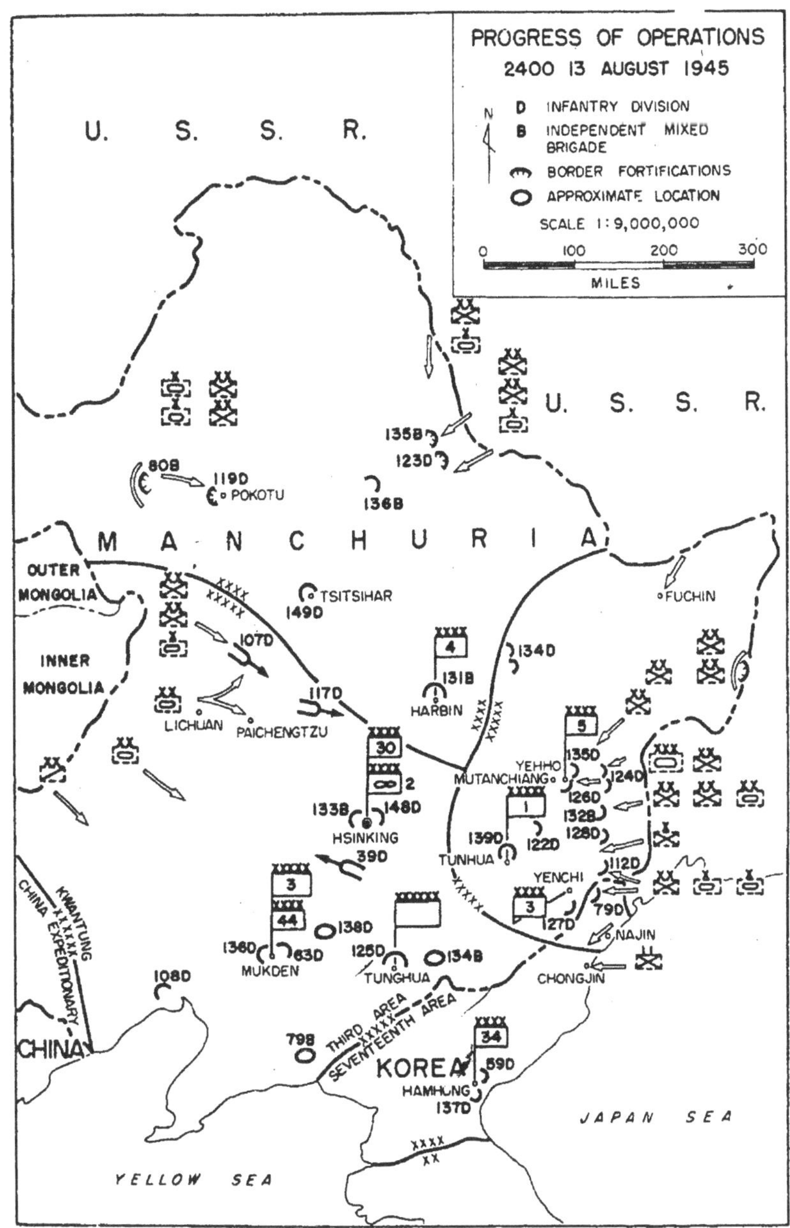

Map 81. Progress of Operations, 2400 hours 13 August 1945 (Japanese View)

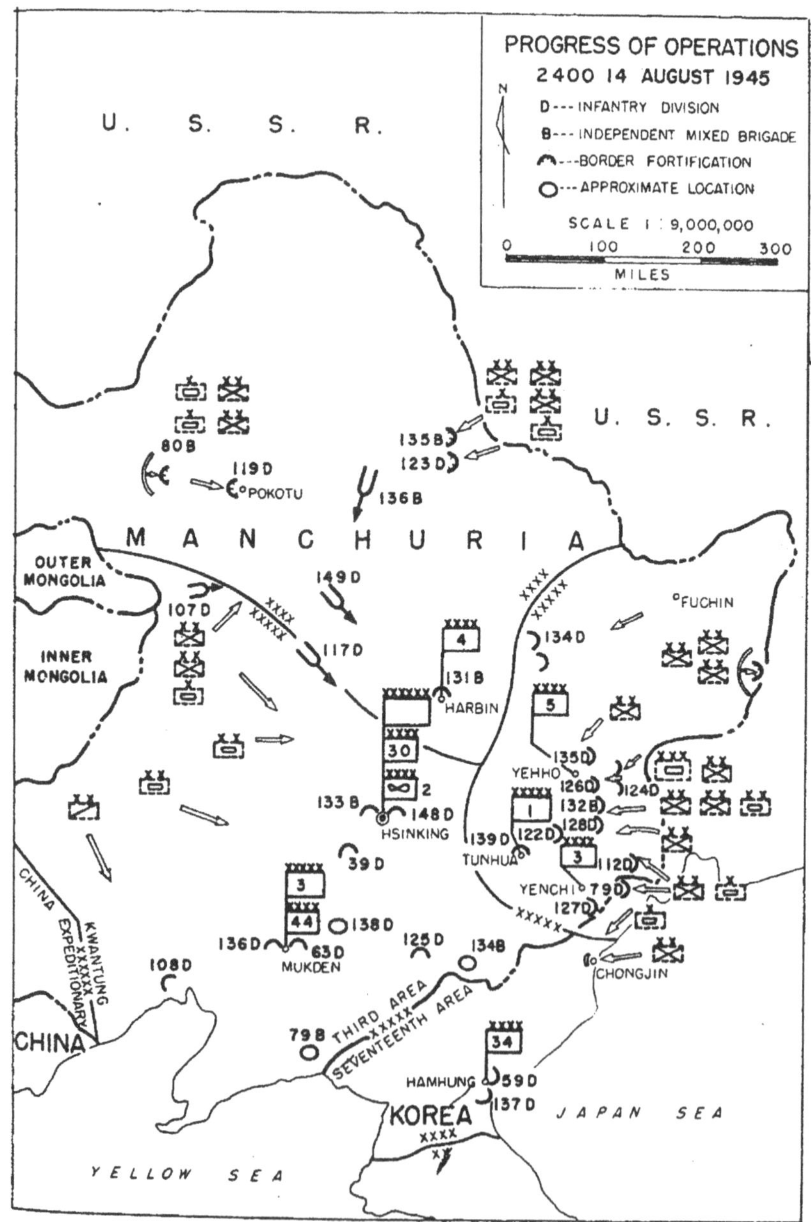

Map 82. Progress of Operations, 2400 hours 14 August 1945 (Japanese View)

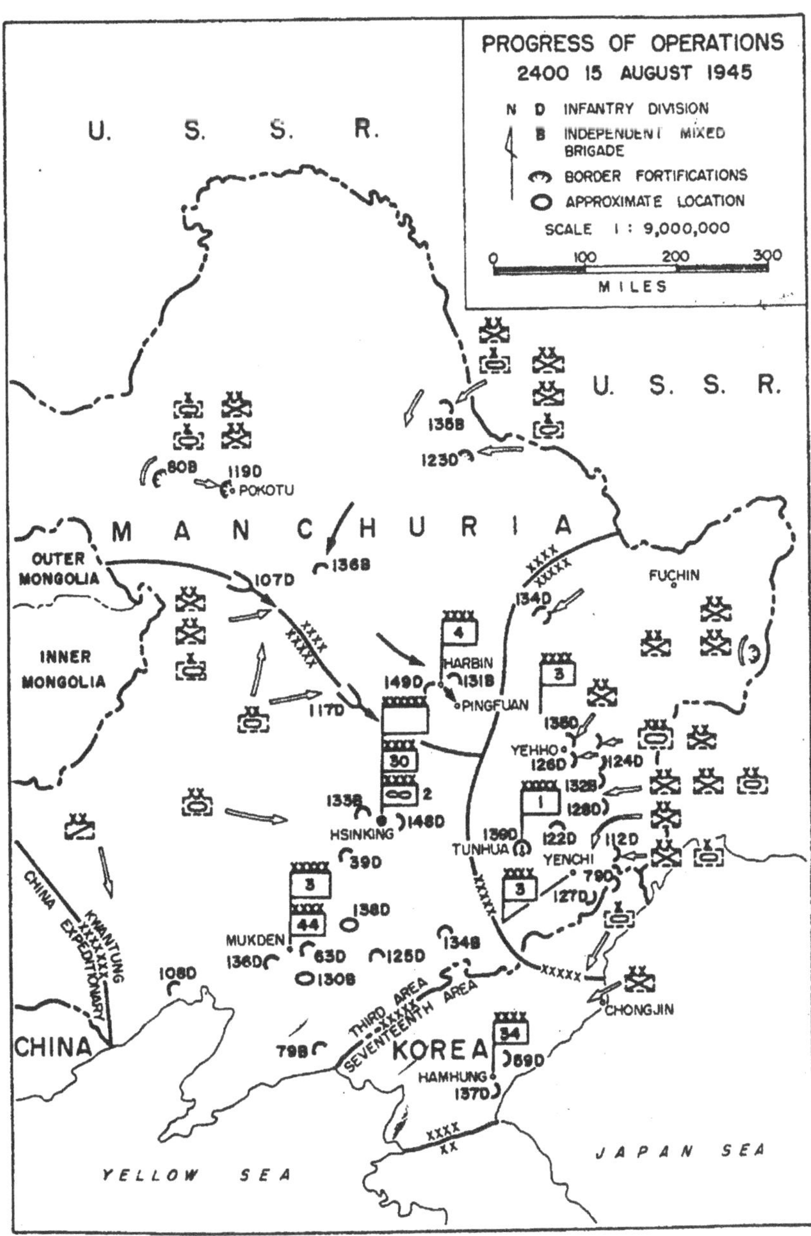

Map 83. Progress of Operations, 2400 hours 15 August 1945 (Japanese View)

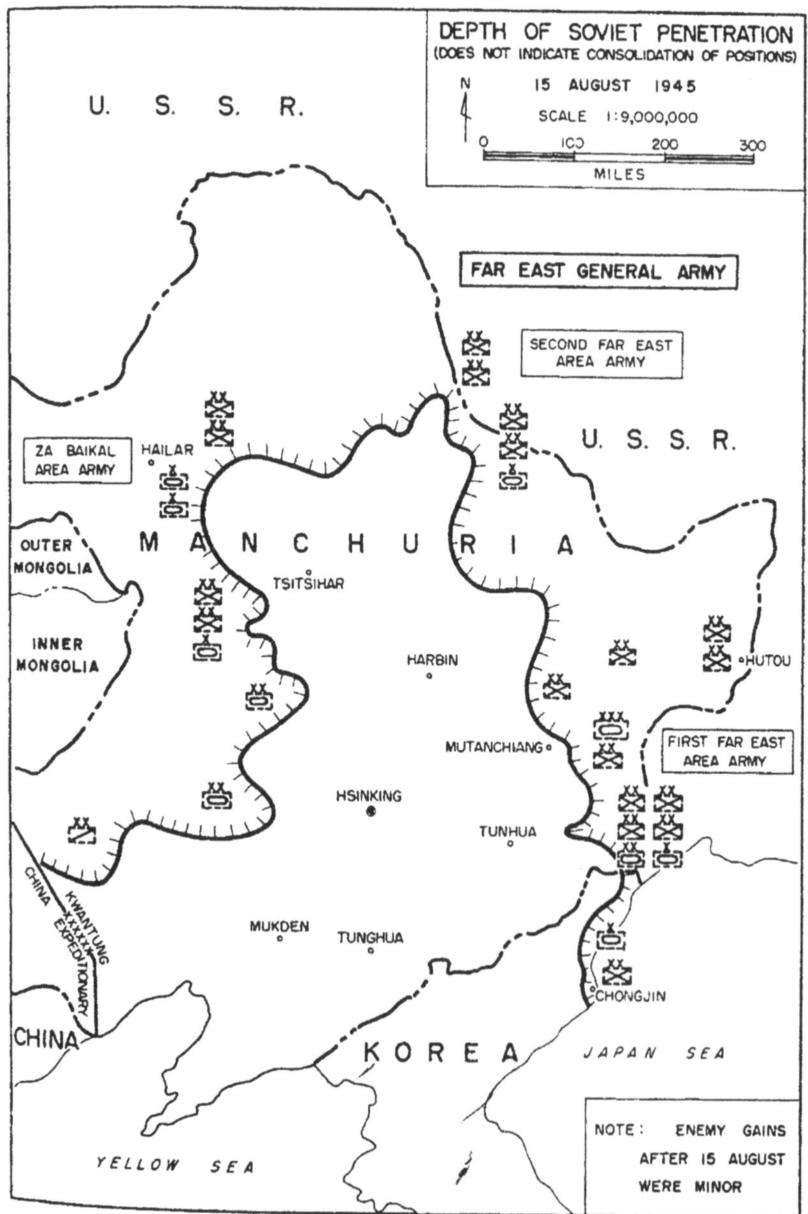

Map 84. Depth of Soviet Penetration by 15 August 1945 (Japanese View)

Bibliography

Note: In bibliographical entries, *VIZh* is used to denote articles from *Voenno-istoricheskii zhurnal* [Military-historical journal].

PRIMARY SOURCES

Antonov, N. A. *Nastuplenie 6-i gvardeiskoi armii v Man'chzhurskoi operatsii (avgust 1945g.)* [The 6th Guards Tank Army's offensive in the Manchurian operation (August 1945)]. Moscow: Voroshilov Academy of the General Staff, 1978.

—— *Sovetskoe voennoe iskusstvo v kampanii na Dal'nem vostoke (9 avgusta–2 sentiabria 1945 g.)* [Soviet military art in the Far East campaign (9 August–2 September 1945)]. Moscow: Voroshilov Academy of the General Staff, 1981.

Boevoi sostav Sovetskoi armii, chast' 5 (ianvar'–sentiabr' 1945 g.) [The combat composition of the Soviet Army, Part 5 (January–September 1945). Moscow: Voenizdat, 1990.

Eronin, N. V. *Strategicheskaia peregruppirovka Sovetskikh vooruzhennykh sil (pri podgotovka Dal'nevostochnoi kampanii 1945 goda* [The strategic regrouping of the Soviet armed forces (during the preparations for the 1945 Far Eastern campaign of 1945]. Moscow: Voroshilov General Staff Academy, 1980. Classified secret.

Khrenov, A. F. *Inzhenernoe obespechenie nastupatel'nykh operatsii (po opytu Volkhovskogo, Karel'skogo, 1-go i 2-go Dal'nevostochnykh i Zabaikal'skogo frontov)* [Engineer support of offensive operations (based on the experiences of the Volkhov, Karelian, 1st and 2d Far Eastern, and Trans-Baikal Fronts)]. Moscow: Voenizdat, 1952. Classified secret.

Komandovanie korpusnogo i divizionnogo zvena Sovetskikh vooruzhennykh sil perioda Velikoi Otechestvennoi voiny 1941–1945 gg. [The commanders of the Soviet Armed Forces at the corps and division level during the Great Patriotic War 1941–1945]. Moscow: Frunze Academy, 1964. Classified secret.

'Kuril'skaia desantnaia operatsiia (po materialam Kamchatskogo oboronitel'nogo raiona)' [The Kuril amphibious operation (based on materials of the Kamchatka defensive region)] in *Sbornik takticheskikh primerov po opytu Otechestvennoi voiny, No. 22* [Collection of tactical materials based on the experiences of the Patriotic War, No. 22]. Moscow: Voenizdat, 1947. Prepared by the Directorate for the Study of War Experience of the General Staff and classified secret.

Nastavlenie po proryvu pozitsionnoi oborony (proekt) [Instructions on the penetration of a positional defense (draft)]. Moscow: Voenizdat, 1944. Trans. Directorate of Military Intelligence, Army Headquarters, Ottawa, Canada.

Polevoi ustav Krasnoi armii 1944 [Field regulations of the Red Army 1944]. Moscow: Voenizdat, 1944. Trans. Office, Assistant Chief of Staff, G-2, General Staff, US Army, 1951.

'Proryv Kotonskogo (Kharamitogskogo) ukreplennogo raiona iapontsev na o. Sakhalin (po materialam shtaba Dal'nevostochnogo voennogo okruga)' [The penetration of the Japanese Koton (Haramitog) fortified region on Sakhalin Island (based on materials of the Far Eastern Military District)] in *Sbornik takticheskikh primerov po opytu Otechestvennoi voiny,* No. 21 *(iiul'–avgust 1946 g.)* [Collection of tactical examples based on the experiences of the Patriotic War, No. 21 (July–August 1946)]. Moscow: Voenizdat, 1947. Prepared by the Directorate for the Study of War Experience of the General Staff and classified secret.

'Proryv Volynskogo ukreplennogo raiona 72-m strelkovym korpusom (po materialam 1-go Dal'nevostochnogo fronta)' [The penetration of the Volynsk fortified region by the 72d Rifle Corps (based on materials from the 1st Far Eastern Front)] in *Sbornik takticheskikh primerov po opytu Otechestvennoi voiny,* No. 21 *(iiul'–avgust 1946 g.)* [Collection of tactical examples based on the experiences of the Patriotic War, No. 21 (July–August 1946)]. Moscow: Voenizdat, 1947. Prepared by Directorate for the Study of War Experience of the General Staff and classified secret.

Shevchenko, V. N. *Problema podgotovki i vedeniia nastupatel'noi operatsii na Dal'nevostochnom TVD po opytu Man'chzhurskoi operatsii* [The problems of regrouping and the conduct of offensive operations in the Far Eastern theater of military operations based on the experiences of the Manchurian operation]. Moscow: Voroshilov Academy of the General Staff, 1988.

Tsygankov, P. Ia. *Osobennosti voennogo iskusstva Sovetskikh voisk v voine protiv militaristskoi iaponii* [The features of the military art of Soviet forces in the war against militaristic Japan]. Moscow: Frunze Academy, 1980.

Zolotarev, V. A., ed. *Russkii arkhiv: Velikaia Otechestvennaia: General'nyi shtab v gody Velikoi Otechestvennoi voiny: Dokumenty i materially, 1944–1945 gg.*, T. 23 (12–4) [The Russian archives: The Great Patriotic: The General Staff in the Great Patriotic War: Documents and materials, 1944–1945), Vol. 23 (12–4)]. Moscow: 'Terra', 2001.

——*Russkii arkhiv: Velikaia Otechestvennaia: Prikazy Narodnogo komissara oborony SSSR (1943–1945 gg,),* T. 13 (2–3) [The Russian archives: The Great Patriotic: Orders of the USSR People's Commissariat of Defense (1943–1945), Vol. 13 (2–3)]. Moscow: 'Terra', 1997.

——*Russkii arkhiv: Sovetsko–iaponskaia voina 1945 goda: Istoriia voenno-politicheskogo protivoborstva dvukh derzhav v 30–40-e gody: Dokumenty i materialy v 2 t.*, T. 18 (7–1) [The Russian archives: The Soviet–Japanese War of 1945: A military-political history of the struggle between two powers in the 30s and 40s: Documents and materials in two volumes, Vol. 18 (7–1)]. Moscow: 'Terra', 1997.

—— *Russkii arkhiv: Velikaia Otechestvennaia. Sovetsko–iaponskaia voina 1945 goda: Istoriia voenno-politicheskogo protivoborstva dvukh derzhav v 30–40-e gody: Dokumenty i materially v 2 t.*, T. 18 (7–2) [The Russian archives. The Great Patriotic: The Soviet–Japanese War of 1945: A military-political history of the struggle between two powers in the 30s and 40s: Documents and materials in two volumes, Vol. 18 (7–2)]. Moscow: 'Terra', 2000.

—— *Russkii arkhiv: Velikaia Otechestvennaia: Stavka VKG: Dokumenty i materially 1944–1945,* T. 16 (4–5) [The Russian archives: The Great Patriotic: The Stavka VKG: Documents and materials 1944–1945, Vol. 16 (4–5)]. Moscow: 'Terra', 1999.

BOOKS

Akshinsky, V. *Kuril'skii desant* [The Kuril amphibious assault]. Petropavlovsk, Kamchatka: Dal'nevostochnoe knizhnoe izdat'elstvo, 1984.

Bagramian, I. Kh., ed. *Istoriia voin i voennogo iskusstva* [History of war and military art]. Moscow: Voenizdat, 1970.

—— *Voennaia istoriia* [Military history]. Moscow: Voenizdat, 1971.

Bagrov, V. N. *Iuzhno-sakhalinskaia i Kuril'skaia operatsii (avgust 1945 goda)* [The southern Sakhalin and Kuril operations (August 1945)]. Moscow: Voenizdat, 1959.

Bagrov, V. N., and N. F. Sungorkin. *Krasnoznamennaia amurskaia flotiliia* [The Red Banner Amur Flotilla]. Moscow: Voenizdat, 1976.

Beloborodov, A. *Skvoz ogon i taigu* [Through the fire and taiga]. Moscow: Voenizdat, 1969.

'Boeicho Bo-ei Kenshujo Senshishitsu' [Japan Self Defense Forces, National Defense College Military History Department]. *Senshi sosho: Kantogun (2)* [Military history series: The Kwantung Army, Vol. 2]. Tokyo: Asagumo Shinbunsha, 1974.

Boiko, V. R. *Bol'shoi Khingan–Port Artur* [The Grand Khingans–Port Arthur]. Moscow: Voenizdat, 1990.

Chistiakov, I. M. *Sluzhim otchizne* [In the service of the fatherland]. Moscow: Voenizdat, 1975.

Coox, A. D. *Soviet Armor in Action Against the Japanese Kwantung Army*. Baltimore, MD: Operations Research Office, Johns Hopkins University Press, 1952.

Despres, J., L. Dzirkals, and B. Whaley. *Timely Lessons of History: The Manchurian Model for Soviet Strategy*. Santa Monica, CA: Rand, 1976.

D'iakonov, A. A. *General Purkaev*. Saransk, USSR: Mordovskoe Knizhnoe Izdatel'stvo, 1971.

Feis, Herbert. *The Atomic Bomb and the End of World War II*. Princeton, NJ: Princeton University Press, 1966.

Gel'fond, G. M. *Sovetskii flot v voine s iaponiei* [The Soviet fleet in the war with Japan]. Moscow: Voenizdat, 1958.

Griaznov, B. *Marshal Zakharov*. Moscow: Voenizdat, 1979.

Grishin, I. P., *et al. Voennye sviazisty v dni voiny i mira* [Military signalmen in wartime and peacetime]. Moscow: Voenizdat, 1968.

Gusarevich, S. D., and V.B. Seoev. *Na strazhe Dal'nevostochnykh rubezhei* [At the limits of the Far Eastern borders]. Moscow: Voenizdat, 1982.

Handbook of Foreign Military Forces, Vol. 2, USSR, Pt. 1: The Soviet Army (FATM-11-10). Fort Monroe, VA: US Army Office, Chief of Army Field Forces, 1952. Restricted but re-graded to unclassified.

Hayashi, Saburo, and Alvin Coox. *Kogun: The Japanese Army in the Pacific War*. Quantico, VA: Marine Corps Association, 1959.

Istoriia Ural'skogo voennogo okruga [A history of the Ural Military District]. Moscow: Voenizdat, 1970.

Istoriia vtoroi mirovoi voiny 1939–1945 [A history of the Second World War 1939–1945]. Moscow: Voenizdat, 1980.

Ivanov, S. P., ed. *Nachal'nyi period voiny* [The initial period of war]. Moscow: Voenizdat, 1974.

'Japanese Preparations for Operations in Manchuria, January 1943–August 1945', *Japanese Monograph No. 138*. Tokyo: Military History Section, US Army Forces Far East, 1953.

Kabanov, S. I. *Pole boia-bereg* [The field of battle, the coast]. Moscow: Voenizdat, 1977.

Kamalov, Kh. *Morskaia pekhota v boiakh za rodinu (1941–1946 gg.)* [Naval infantry in combat for the Homeland, 1941–1945]. Moscow: Voenizdat, 1966.

Kazakov, K. P. *Vsegda s pekhotoi, vsegda s tankami* [Always with the infantry, always with the tanks]. Moscow: Voenizdat, 1973. Trans. Leo Kanner Associates for the US Army Foreign Science and Technology Center, 6 February 1975.

Khetagurov, G. I. *Ispolnenie dolga* [Performance of duty]. Moscow: Voenizdat, 1977.

Khrenov, A. F. *Mosty k pobede* [Bridges to victory]. Moscow: Voenizdat, 1982.

Kir'ian, M. M., ed. *Fronty nastupali: Po opytu Velikoi Otechestvennoi voiny* [The *fronts* are attacking: Based on the experiences of the Great Patriotic War]. Moscow: 'Nauka', 1987.

Kovalev, I. V. *Transport v Velikoi Otechestvennoi voine (1941–1945 gg.)* [Transport in the Great Patriotic War, 1941–1945]. Moscow: 'Nauka', 1981.

Kozhevnikov, M. N. *Komandovanie i shtab VVS Sovetskoi Armii v Velikoi Otechestvennoi voine 1941–1945 gg* [The command and staff of the air force of the Soviet Army in the Great Patriotic War 1941–1945]. Moscow: 'Nauka', 1977.

Krivel', A. M. *Eto bylo na Khingane* [It was in the Khingans]. Moscow: Politizdat, 1985.

Krivosheev, G. F., ed. *Rossiia i SSSR v voinakh XX veka: Statisticheskoe issledovanie* [Russia and the USSR in Twentieth Century Wars: A statistical survey]. Moscow: 'Olma-press', 2001.

Krupchenko, I. E., ed. *Sovetskie tankovie voiska 1941–45* [Soviet tank forces, 1941–45]. Moscow: Voenizdat, 1973.

Krylov, N. I., N. I. Alekseev and I. G. Dragan. *Navstrechu pobede: Boevoi put 5-i armii, oktiabr 1941g–avgust 1945g* [Toward victory: The combat path of the 5th Army, October 1941–August 1945]. Moscow: 'Nauka', 1970.

Kumanev, G. A. *Na sluzhbe fronta i tyla: Zheleznodorozhnyi transport SSSP nakanune i v gody Velikoi Otechestvennoi voiny 1938–1945* [In the service of front and rear: The rail transport of the USSR on the eve of and during the Great Patriotic War]. Moscow: 'Nauka', 1976.

Kurochkin, P. A., ed. *Obshchevoiskovaia armiia v nastuplenii* [The combined–arms army in the offensive]. Moscow: Voenizdat, 1966.

Kusachi Teigo. *Sonohi, Kantogun wa* [That day, the Kwantung Army]. Tokyo: Miyakawa shobo, 1967.

Lisov, I. I. *Desantniki: Vozdushnye desanty* [Airlanded troops: Airlandings] Moscow: Voenizdat, 1968.

Liudnikov, I. I. *Cherez Bol'shoi Khingan* [Across the Grand Khingans]. Moscow: Voenizdat, 1967.

—— *Doroga dlinoiu v zhizn* [The long road in life]. Moscow: Voenizdat, 1969.

Losik, O. A. *Stroitel'stvo i boevoe primenenie sovetskikh tankovykh voisk v gody Velikoi Otechestvennoi voiny* [The formation and combat use of Soviet tank forces in the Great Patriotic War]. Moscow: Voenizdat, 1979.

Manosov, V. F., ed. *Razgrom Kvantungskoi armii iaponi* [The destruction of the Japanese Kwantung Army]. Moscow: Voenizdat, 1958.

Mee, Charles L. *Meeting at Potsdam*. New York: M. Evans, 1975.

Meretskov, K. A. *Serving the People*. Moscow: Progress Publishers, 1971.

Milovsky, M. P., ed. *Tyl Sovetskoi armii* [The rear services of the Soviet Army]. Moscow: Voenizdat, 1968.

Nedosekin, R. *Bol'shoi Khingan* [The Grand Khingans]. Moscow: Izdatel'stvo DOSAAF, 1973.

'New Soviet Wartime Divisional TO&E', *Intelligence Research Project No. 9520*. Washington, DC: Office, Assistant Chief of Staff, Intelligence, US Department of the Army, 15 February 1956. Secret but regraded to unclassified in 1981.

Nikulin, Lev. *Tukhachevsky: Biograficheskii ocherk* [Tukhachevsky: A biographical essay]. Moscow: Voenizdat, 1964.

Organization of a Combat Command for Operations in Manchuria. Fort Knox, KY: The Armor School US Army, May 1952. Regraded as unclassified on 12 April 1974.

Osvobozhdenie Korei [The liberation of Korea]. Moscow: 'Nauka', 1976.

Ota Hisao. *Dai 107 shidan shi: Saigo made tatakatta Kantogun* [A history of the 107th Division: The Kwantung Army that resisted to the last]. Tokyo: Taiseido Shoten Shuppanbu, 1979.

Ovechkin, K. *Cherez Khingan* [Across the Khingans]. Moscow: DOSAAF, 1982.

Pitersky, N. A. *Boevoi put' Sovetskogo Voenno-morskogo Flota* [The combat path of the Soviet fleet]. Moscow: Voenizdat, 1967.

Platonov, S. P., ed. *Vtoraia mirovaia voina 1939–1945 gg.* [The Second World War 1939–1945]. Moscow: Voenizdat, 1958.

Pliev, I. A. *Cherez Gobi i Khingan* [Across the Gobi and Khingans]. Moscow: Voenizdat, 1965.

—— *Konets Kvantunskoi armii* [The end of the Kwantung Army]. Ordzhonikidze: Izdatel'stvo 'IN' Ordzhonikidze, 1969.

Pospelov, P. N., ed. *Istoriia Velikoi Otechestvennoi voiny Sovetskogo Soiuza 1941–45 v shesti tomakh*, T 5 [A history of the Great Patriotic War of the Soviet Union 1941–45 in six volumes, Vol. 5]. Moscow: Voenizdat, 1963.

Radzievsky, A. I. *Tankovyi udar* [Tank blow]. Moscow: Voenizdat, 1977.

—— ed. *Armeiskie operatsii: primery iz opyta Velikoi Otechestvennoi voiny* [Army operations: examples from the experience of the Great Patriotic War]. Moscow: Voenizdat, 1977.

—— ed. *Proryv (Po opytu Velikoi Otechestvennoi voiny 1941–1945 gg.)* [Penetration (Based on the experiences of the Great Patriotic War 1941–1945)]. Moscow: Voenizdat, 1979.

—— ed. *Taktika v boevykh primerakh (diviziia)* [Tactics by combat example (the division)]. Moscow: Voenizdat, 1976.

—— ed. *Taktika v boevykh primerakh (polk)* [Tactics by combat example (the regiment)]. Moscow: Voenizdat, 1974.

Ranseikai, ed. *Manshukokugunshi* [History of the Manchukuoan Army] Tokyo: Manshukokugun kankokai, 1970.

'Record of Operations Against Soviet Army on Eastern Front (August 1945)', *Japanese Monograph No. 154*. Tokyo: Military History Section, US Army Forces Far East, 1954.

'Record of Operations Against Soviet Russia on Northern and Western Fronts of Manchuria and in Northern Korea (August 1945)', *Japanese Monograph No. 155*. Tokyo: Military History Section, US Army Forces Far East, 1954.

Rudenko, S. N., ed. *Sovetskie voenno-vozduzhnye sily v Velikoi Otechestvennoi voine 1941–1945 gg.* [The Soviet air force in the Great Patriotic War 1941–1945]. Moscow: Voenizdat, 1968.

Salmanov, G. I., ed. *Ordena Lenina Zabaikal'skii* [The order of Lenin Trans-Baikal]. Moscow: Voenizdat, 1980.

Samsonov, A. M., ed. *Sovetskii soiuz v gody Velikoi Otechestvennoi voiny 1941–1945* [The Soviet Union in the Great Patriotic War 1941–1945]. Moscow: 'Nauka', 1976.

Seaton, Albert. *Stalin as Military Commander*. New York: Praeger, 1976.

Sergeev, I. D., ed. *Voennaia entsiklopediia v vos'mi tomakh,* T. 4 [Military encyclopedia in eight volumes, Vol. 4]. Moscow: Voenizdat, 1999.

Shashlo, T. *Dorozhe zhizni* [The paths of life]. Moscow: Voenizdat, 1960.

Shchen'kov, Iu. M. 'Man'chzhuro–Chzhalainorskaiia operatsiia 1929' [Manchurian–Chalainor Operation of 1929]. *Sovetskaia voennaia entsiklopediia* [Soviet military encyclopedia]. Moscow: Voenizdatel'stvo, 1978, 5:127–8.

Shikin, I. V., and B. G. Sapozhnikov. *Podvig na Dal'nem-vostochnykh rubezhakh* [Victory on the far eastern borders]. Moscow: Voenizdat, 1975.

Shtemenko, S. M. *The Soviet General Staff at War, 1941–1945*. Moscow: Progress Publishers, 1974.

'Small Wars and Border Problems', *Japanese Studies on Manchuria*, Vol. 11, Pt. 2. Tokyo, Military History Section, US Army Forces Far East, 1956.

Sovetskaia voennaia entsiklopediia [The Soviet military encyclopedia]. 9 Vols. Moscow: Voenizdat, 1976–80.

Stephan, John. *The Kuril Islands*. New York: Oxford University Press, 1976.

'Strategic Study of Manchuria Military Topography and Geography: Regional Terrain Analysis', *Japanese Studies on Manchuria*, Vol. 3, Pts. 1-4. Tokyo: Military History Section, US Army Forces Far East, 1956.

Strokov, A. A., ed. *Istoriia voennogo iskusstva* [A history of military art]. Moscow: Voenizdat, 1966.

'Study of Strategical and Tactical Peculiarities of Far Eastern Russia and Soviet Far East Forces', *Japanese Studies on Manchuria*, Vol. 13. Tokyo: Military History Section, US Army Forces Far East, 1955.

Sukhorukov, D. S., ed. *Sovetskie vozdushno-desantnye* [Soviet air landing forces]. Moscow: Voenizdat, 1980.

Tsirlin, A. D., P. I. Buriukov, V. P. Istomin and E. N. Fedoseev. *Inzhenernye voiska v boiakh za Sovetskuiu rodiny* [Engineer forces in combat for the Soviet fatherland]. Moscow: Voenizdat, 1970.

Ustinov, D. F., ed. *Istoriia vtoroi mirovoi voiny 1939–1945 v dvenadtsati tomakh,* T. 11 [A history of the Second World War 1939–45 in 12 vols, Vol. 11]. Moscow: Voenizdat, 1980.

Vasilevsky, A. M. *Delo vsei zhizni* [Life's work]. Moscow: Politizdat, 1975.

Vnotchenko, L. N. *Pobeda na dal'nem vostoke: Voenno-istoricheskii ocherk o boevykh deistviiakh Sovetskikh voisk v avguste–sentiabre 1945 g.* [Victory in the Far East: A military-historical survey about the operations of Soviet forces in August–September 1945]. Moscow: Voenizdat, 1996 and 1971.

Vorob'ev, F. D., and V. M. Kravtsov. *Pobedy Sovetskikh vooruzhennykh sil v Velikoi Otechestvennoi voine 1941–1945: Kratkii ocherk* [The victory of the Soviet armed forces in the Great Patriotic War 1941–45: A short survey]. Moscow: Voenizdat, 1953.

Werth, Alexander. *Russia at War 1941–1945*. New York: Dutton, 1964.

Zabaikal'skii voennyi okrug [The Trans-Baikal Military District]. Irkutsk: Vostochno-Sibirskoe Knizhnoe Izdatel'stvo, 1972.

Zakharov, M. V, ed. *Final: istoriko-memuarny ocherk o razgrome imperialisticheskoi iapony v 1945 godu* [Finale: A historical memoir-survey about the rout of imperialistic Japan in 1945]. Moscow: 'Nauka', 1969.

—— *et al.*, ed., *50 let Vooruzhennykh sil SSSP* [50 years of the Soviet armed forces]. Moscow: Voenizdat, 1968.

—— *et al.*, ed. *Final: istoriko-memuarny ocherk o razgrome imperialisticheskoy iapony v 1945 godu* [Finale: A historical memoir-survey about the rout of imperialistic Japan in 1945]. Moscow: Progress Publishers, 1972.

Zakharov, S. E., V. N. Bagrov, S. S. Bevz, M. N. Zakharov, and M. P. Kotukhov, *Krasnoznamennyi tikhookeanskii flot* [The Red Banner Pacific Fleet]. Moscow: Voenizdat, 1973.

Zavizion, G. T., and P. A. Kornyushin. *I na Tikhom Okeane* [And to the Pacific Ocean]. Moscow: Voenizdat, 1967.

Zenkoku Kotokai [National Hutou Society], ed. *So Man kokkyo Koto yosai no senki* [The Soviet Manchurian border: The battle record of the Hutou Fortress]. Tokyo: Zenkoku Kotokai jimukyo-ku, 1977.

Zolotarev, V. A. *Velikaia Otechestvennaia voina 1941–1945: Voenno-istoricheskie ocherki v chetyrekh knigakh,* K. 3, *Osvobozhdvenie* [The Great Patriotic War 1941–1945: A military-historical survey in four books, Book 3, Liberation] Moscow: 'Nauka', 1999.

ARTICLES

Anan'ev, I. 'Sozdanie tankovykh armii i sovershenstvovanie ikh organizatsionnoi struktury' [The creation of tank armies and the perfecting of their organizational structure]. *VIZh*, No. 10 (October 1972), 38–47.

Bagramian, I. and I. Vyrodov. 'Rol' predstavitelei Stavki VGK v gody voiny: Organizatsiia i metody ikh raboty' [The role of the *Stavka* of the Supreme High Command representatives in the war years: The organization and method of their work]. *VIZh*, No. 8 (August 1980), 25–33

Beloborodov, A. 'Besslavnyi konets Kvantunskoi armii' [The inglorious end of the Kwantung Army'. *Voennii vestnik* [Military herald], No. 9 (September 1970), 97–101.

—— 'Na sopkakh Man'chzhurii' [In the hills of Manchuria]. Pts. 1, 2. *VIZh*, No. 12 (December 1980), 30–6, and No. 1 (January 1981), 45–51.

Bichik, V. S. 'Nekotorye osobennosti tylovogo obespecheniia voisk 1-go Dal'nevostochnogo fronta v Man'chzhurskoi operatsii' [Some peculiarities of the 1st Far Eastern Front's rear service support in the Manchurian operation], *VIZh*, No. 8 (August 1985), 38–41.

Butkov, P. P., and V. V. Shmidt. 'Osobennosti tylovogo obespecheniia v gorno-pustynnoi mestnosti' [The peculiarities of rear service support in swampy desert terrain]. *VIZh*, No. 9 (September 1988), 38–45.

Dragon, I. G. 'Cherez sopki, taigu i bolota Man'chzhurii' [Across the hills, taiga, and swamps of Manchuria]. *VIZh*, No. 8 (August 1988), 62–86.

Dunnin, A. 'Razvitie sukhoputnykh voisk v poslevoennym periode' [The development of ground forces in the postwar period]. *VIZh*, No. 5 (May 1978), 33–40.

Ezhakov, V. 'Boevoe primenenie tankov v gorno-taezhnoi mestnosti po opytu 1-go Dal'nevostochnogo fronta' [The combat use of tanks in mountainous-taiga regions based on the experience of the 1st Far Eastern Front]. *VIZh*, No. 1 (January 1974), 77–81.

Frantsev, O. K. 'Primenenie aviatsii v Man'chzhurskoi operatsii' [The employment of aviation in the Manchurian operation]. *VIZh*, No. 8 (August 1985), 20–4.

Galitsky, V. P., and V. P. Zimonin. 'Desant na Khokkaido Otmenit'! (Razmyshleniia po povodu odnoi nesostoiasheisia operatsii)' [Cancel the amphibious assault against Hokkaido! (Reflections concerning one operation that did not take place)]. *VIZh*, No. 3 (March 1994), 5–10.

Galitson, A. 'Podvig na dal'nevostochnykh rubezhakh' [Victory on the far eastern borders]. *VIZh*, No. 1 (January 1976), 110–13.

Garkusha, I. 'Osobennosti boevykh deistvii bronetankovykh i mekhanizirovannykh voisk' [The characteristics of combat operations of armored and mechanized forces]. *VIZh*, No. 9 (September 1975), 22–9.

Garthoff, Raymond L. 'Soviet Operations in the War with Japan, August 1945'. *US Naval Institute Proceedings*, No. 92 (May 1966), 50–63.

—— 'The Soviet Manchurian Campaign, August 1945'. *Military Affairs*, No. 33 (October 1969), 31–6.

Germanov, G. P. 'Rabota zheleznodorozhnogo transporta pri podgotovke i provedenii Man'chzhurskoi operatsii [The work of railroad transport during the preparation and conduct of the Manchurian operation]. *VIZh*, No. 8 (August 1985), 42–6.

Ivanov, S. P. 'Victory in the Far East'. *Voennyi vestnik* [Military herald], No. 8 (August 1975), 17–22. Trans. Office, Assistant Chief of Staff, Intelligence, US Department of the Army.

—— 'Sokrushitel'ny udar [A shattering blow]. *Voennyi vestnik*, No. 8 (August 1980), 15–17.

Ivanov, S. P., and N. Shekhavtsov. 'Opyt raboty glavnykh komandovanii na teatrakh voennykh deistvii' [The experience of the work of high commands in theaters of military action]. *VIZh*, No. 9 (September 1981), 18.

Kalashnikov, K. 'Na dal'nevostochnykh rubezhakh' [On the far eastern borders]. *VIZh*, No. 8 (August 1980), 55–61.

'Kampaniia sovetskikh vooruzhennikh sil na dal'nem vostoke v 1945g (facti i tsifry)' [The campaign of the Soviet armed forces in the Far East in 1945: Facts and figures]. *VIZh*, No. 8 (August 1965), 64–74.

Khrenov, A. F. 'Wartime Operations: Engineer Operations in the Far East'. *USSR Report: Military Affairs No. 1545* (20 November 1980), 81–97. In JPRS 76847. Trans. Foreign Broadcast Information Service from the Russian article in *Znamia* [Banner], August 1980.

—— 'Inzhernernoe obespechenie nastupleniia v Man'chzhurskoi operatsii' [Engineer support of the offensive in the Manchurian operation]. *VIZh*, No. 8 (August 1985), 29–32.

Kireev, N., and A. Syropiatov. 'Tekhnicheskoe obespechenie 6-i gvardeiskoi tankovoi armii v Khingano-Mukdenskoi operatsii' [Technical support of the 6th Guards Tank Army in the Khingan–Mukden operation]. *VIZh*, No. 3 (March 1977), 36-40.

Kireev, N., and P. Tsigankov. 'Osobennosti podgorovka v gorno-pustynnoi mestnosti po opytu Zabaikal'skogo fronta v 1945 godu' [The peculiarities of preparing and conducting operations in mountainous-desert terrain based on the experiences of the Trans-Baikal Front in 1945]. *VIZh*, No. 8 (August 1978), 13–20.

Kovtun-Stankevich, A. 'Zapiski voennogo komendanta Mukdena' [The notes of the military commandant of Mukden], *VIZh*, No. 1 (January 1960), 51–71.

Krupchenko, I. E. 'Nekotorye osobennosti Sovetskogo voennogo iskusstva' [Some characteristics of Soviet military art]. *VIZh*, No. 8 (August 1975), 17–27.

—— 'Pobeda na dal'nem vostoke' [Victory in the Far East]. *VIZh*, No. 9 (August 1970), 8–10.

—— '6-ia gvardeiskaia tankovaia armiia v Khingano-Mukdenskoi operatsii' [The 6th Guards Tank Army in the Khingan–Mukden Operation]. *VIZh*, No. 12 (December 1962), 15–30.

Kumin, L. G. 'Partiino-politicheskaia rabota v Man'chzhurskoi operatsii'

[Party-political work in the Manchurian operation]. *VIZh*, No. 8 (August 1985), 47–51.

Kurochkin, P. A. 'V shtabe glavkoma na dal'nem vostoke' [In the staff of the high command in the Far East]. *VIZh*, No. 11 (November 1967), 74–82.

Kurov, M. 'Togda, v avguste 1945-go' [Then, in August 1945]. *Vestnik protivovozdushnoi oborony* [Herald of air defense], No. 8 (August 1990), 89–91.

Larchenkov, V. 'Banzai to the Soviet Union'. *Soviet Soldier*, No. 7 (July 1991), 66–8.

Liudnikov, I. '39-ia armiia v Khingano-Mukdenskoi operatsii' [The 39th Army in the Khingan–Mukden Operation]. *VIZh*, No. 10 (October 1965), 68–78.

Loskutov, Iu. 'Iz opyta peregruppirovki 292-i strelkovoi divizii v period podgotovki Man'chzhurskoi operatsii' [From the experience of 292d Rifle Division's regrouping during the preparatory period for the Manchurian operation]. *VIZh*, No. 2 (February 1980), 22–8.

Luchinsky, A. A. 'Zabaikal'tsy na sopkakh Man'chzhurii' [Trans-Baikal troops in the hills of Manchuria]. *VIZh*, No. 8 (August 1971), 67–74.

Malin'in, K. 'Razvitie organizatsionnykh form sukhoputnykh voisk v Velikoi Otechestvennoi voine' [The development of ground forces' organizational structure in the Great Patriotic War]. *VIZh*, No. 8 (August 1967), 35–8.

Maliugin, N. 'Nekotorye voprosy ispol'zovaniia avtomobil'nogo transporta v voennoi kampanii na dal'nem vostoke' [Some questions on the use of automobile transport in the military campaign in the Far East]. *VIZh*, No. 1 (January 1969), 103–11.

Maslov, V. 'Boevye deistvia tikhookeanskogo flota' [The combat operations of the Pacific Fleet]. *VIZh*, No. 9 (August 1975), 28–37.

Medvedev, N. E. 'Tylovoe obespechenie 5-i armii v Kharbino-Girinskoi operatsii [The rear service support of the 5th Army during the Harbin–Kirin operation]. *VIZh*, No. 8 (August 1987), 32–9.

Meretskov, K. A. 'Dorogami srazhenii' [Along combat roads]. *Voprosy istorii* [Questions of history], No. 2 (February 1965), 101–9.

Mikhalkin, V. M. 'Boevoe primenenie artillerii v Man'chzhurskoi operatsii' [The combat employment of artillery in the Manchurian operation]. *VIZh*, No. 8 (August 1985), 25–8.

Novikov, A. 'Voenno-vozdushnye sily v Man'chzhurskoi operatsii' [The air force in the Manchurian operation]. *VIZh*, No. 9 (August 1975), 66–71.

Pavlov, B. 'In the Hills of Manchuria'. *Voennyi vestnik* [Military herald], No. 8 (August 1975), 30–2. Trans. Office of the Assistant Chief of Staff, Intelligence, US Department of the Army.

Pechenenko, S. 'Armeiskaia nastupatel'naia operatsiia v usloviiakh dal'nevostochnogo teatra voennykh deistvii' [An army offensive operation in the conditions of the Far Eastern theater of military operations]. *VIZh*, No. 8 (August 1978), 42–9.

—— '363-ia strelkovaia diviziia v boiakh na Mishan'skom napravlenii' [The 363d Rifle Division in combat along the Mishan axis]. *VIZh*, No. 7 (July 1975), 39–46.

Platonov, V., and A. Bulatov. 'Pogranichnie voiska perekhodiat v nastuplenie' [Border troops go over to the offensive]. *VIZh*, No. 10 (October 1965), 11–16.

Pliev, I. A. 'Across the Gobi Desert'. *Voennyi vestnik* [Military herald], No. 8 (August 1975), 14–17. Trans. Office of the Assistant Chief of Staff, Intelligence, US Department of the Army.

Popov, N. 'Razvitie samokhodnoi artillerii' [The development of self-propelled artillery]. *VIZh*, No. 1 (January 1977), 27–31.

Popov, S. 'Artilleristy v boiakh na Bol'shom Khingane' [Artillerymen in combat in the Grand Khingans]. *VIZh*, No. 8 (August 1985), 88–93.

'Razgrom Kvantunskoi armii: 30-letie pobedy nad militaristskoi iaponiei' [The rout of the Kwantung Army: The 30th anniversary of the victory over militarist Japan]. *VIZh*, No. 8 (August 1975), 3–16.

Savin, A. S. 'Spravedlivyi i gumannyi akt SSSR' [The just and humanitarian act of the USSR]. *VIZh*, No. 8 (August 1985), 56–62.

Sekistiv, V. A. 'Kritika burzhuaznykh fal'sifikatsii roli SSSR v razgrome militaristskoi Iaponii' [Criticism of bourgeois falsifiers of the USSR's role in the defeat of militaristic Japan]. *VIZh*, No. 8 (August 1985), 63–6.

Shelakhov, G. 'S vozdushnym desantam v Kharbin' [With the air landing at Harbin]. *VIZh*, No. 8 (August 1970), 67–71.

—— 'Voiny-dal'nevostochniki v Velikoi Otechestvennoi voine' [Far easterners in the Great Patriotic War]. *VIZh*, No. 3 (March 1969), 55–62.

Shtemenko, S. M. 'Iz istorii razgroma Kvantunskoi armii' [From the history of the rout of the Kwantung Army]. Pts 1, 2. *VIZh*, No. 4 (April 1967), 54–66, and No. 5 (May 1967), 49–61.

Sidorov, A. 'Razgrom iaponskogo militarizma' [The rout of Japanese militarism]. *VIZh*, No. 8 (August 1980), 11–16.

Sidorov, M. 'Boevoe primenenie artillerii' [The combat use of artillery]. *VIZh*, No. 9 (September 1975), 13–21.

Sidorov, V. 'Inzhenernoe obespechenie nastupleniia 36-i armii v Man' chzhurskoi operatsii' [Engineer support of the 36th Army's offensive in the Manchurian operation]. *VIZh*, No. 4 (April 1978), 97–101.

Sokolov, V. I. 'Sviaz' v Man'chzhurskoi operatsii' [Communications in the Manchurian operation]. *VIZh*, No. 8 (August 1985), 33–6.

Sologub, V. 'Partpolitrabota v 12 ShAD VVSTOF v voine s imperialisticheskoi iaponiei' [Political work in the 12th Assault Aviation Division of the Pacific Fleet Air Force in the war with imperialist Japan]. *VIZh*, No. 8 (August 1982), 80–3.

Sukhomlin, I. 'Osobennosti vzaimodeistviia 6-i gvardeiskoi tankovoi armii s aviatsiei v Man'chzhurskoi operatsii' [Characteristics of the cooperation of the 6th Guards Tank Army with aviation in the Manchurian operation]. *VIZh*, No. 4 (April 1972), 85–91.

Timofeev, V. '300-ia strelkovaia diviziia v boyakh na Mudan'tsianskom napravlenii' [The 300th Rifle Division in combat along the Mutanchiang axis]. *VIZh*, No. 8 (August 1978), 50–5.

Tret'iak, I. 'Ob operativnoi obespechenii peregruppirovki voisk v period podgotovki Man'chzhurskoi operatsii' [Concerning the operational security of regrouping forces during the preparatory period of the Manchurian operation]. *VIZh*, No. 11 (November 1979), 10–15.

—— 'Organizatsiia i vedenie nastupatel'nogo boia' [The organization and conduct of offensive battle]. *VIZh*, No. 7 (July 1980), 42–9.

—— 'Razgrom Kvantunskoi armii na Dal'nem vostoke' [The destruction of the Kwantung Army in the Far East]. *VIZh*, No. 8 (August 1985), 9–19.

Tsirlin, A. D. 'Organizatsiia vodosnabzheniia voisk Zabaikal'shogo fronta v Khingano-Mukdenskoi operatsii' [The organization of water supply of the Trans-Baikal Front's forces during the Khingan–Mukden operation]. *VIZh*, No. 5 (May 1963), 36–48.

Tsygankov, P. 'Nekotorye osobennosti boevykh deistvii 5-i armii v Kharbino-Girinskoi operatsii' [Some characteristics of the 5th Army's combat operations during the Harbin–Kirin operation]. *VIZh*, No. 8 (August 1975), 83–9.

Vasilevsky, A. 'Kampaniia na dal'nem vostoke' [The campaign in the Far East]. *VIZh*, No. 10 (October 1980), 60–73.

—— 'Pobeda na dal'nem vostoke' [Victory in the Far East]. Pts 1, 2. *VIZh*, No. 8 (August 1970), 3–10, and No. 9 (September 1970), 11–18.

—— 'The Second World War: The Rout of Kwantung Army'. *Soviet Military Review*, No. 8 (August 1980), 2–14.

Vigor, Peter W., and Christopher Donnelly. 'The Manchurian Campaign and Its Relevance to Modern Strategy'. *Comparative Strategy*, No. 2 (February 1980), 159–78.

Yamanishi Sakae. 'ToManshu Koto yosai no gekito' [Eastern Manchuria: The fierce battle of the Hutou Fortress]. *Rekishi to Jinbutsu* (August 1979), 98–107.

Zakharov, M. V. 'Kampaniia Sovetskikh Vooruzhennykh Sil na Dal'nem Vostoke (9 avgusta–2 sentiabria 1945 goda)' [The Soviet Armed Forces' campaign in the Far East, 9 August–2 September 1945]. *VIZh*, No. 9 (September 1960), 3–16.

—— 'Nekotorye voprosy voennogo iskusstva v Sovetsko-iaponskoi voine 1945-goda' [Some questions concerning military art in the Soviet–Japanese War of 1945]. *VIZh*, No. 9 (September 1969), 14–25.

Index